2/04

Biology of Aging

Biology of Aging

Observations and Principles

Second Edition

Robert Arking

*Department of Biological Sciences
and Institute of Gerontology
Wayne State University*

Sinauer Associates, Inc • *Publishers*
Sunderland, Massachusetts USA

The Cover

Self-portrait in red chalk by Leonardo da Vinci, ca. 1512. Reproduced by permission and courtesy of the Royal Library, Turin, Italy.

BIOLOGY OF AGING: OBSERVATIONS AND PRINCIPLES, Second Edition
Copyright © 1998 by Sinauer Associates Inc. All rights reserved. This book may not be reproduced in whole or in part without permission from the publisher. For information address Sinauer Associates, Inc., 23 Plumtree Road, Sunderland, MA 01375-0407 U.S.A.

FAX: 413-549-1118
Internet: publish@sinauer.com
http://www.sinauer.com

Library of Congress Cataloging-in-Publication Data

Arking, Robert.
      Biology of aging : observations and principles / Robert Arking —
2nd ed.
          p.   cm.
      Includes bibliographical references and index.
      ISBN 0-87893-043-4
      1. Aging. 2. Physiology, Comparative. I. Title.
QP86.A75 1998   98-4247
612.6´7—dc21   CIP

Printed in U.S.A.

5 4 3 2

To Lucy, who encouraged
and
For Benjamin, Jared, and Joshua, who will know

Contents

Preface to the Second Edition

Writing a textbook is a presumptuous task, involving as it does the compression of a broad slice of human endeavor into a thin sliver of a book, hopefully done in a manner that provides a framework that is coherent to novice and professional alike. One of my excuses for presuming once again is that I was encouraged to do so by the kind words of both reviewers and students, as well as by the lack of harsh words from my colleagues, following the publication of the first edition of this book some 6 years ago. But, while such kindness is a much-appreciated necessity, it is not a sufficient motive to justify taking up the pen again. The startling advances being made in the field of biogerontology in the past few years have brought us to places that were undreamed of when I first put pen to paper. Delaying the onset of aging is no longer a pipe dream. The inevitability of biological aging is yielding here and there to the increasingly focused knowledge of the factors modulating biological mechanisms. The game is becoming more exciting. Static words need updating if they are to accurately reflect the changing dynamics of modern biogerontology. And so the urge to tell a more complete version of the emerging story is the real justification for my presumption.

But the changing facts alter not only our theories, but also our conceptual framework. For example, I originally used the CUPID definition of aging to draw a line in the sand between "normal" and "abnormal" (or "pathological") aging. Age-related diseases, in other words, were viewed as being an "abnormal" way to age, and thus beyond our purview. But because most older humans (and many older animals) exhibit symptoms consistent with the presence of some age-related disease, using CUPID meant that much of the aging actually taking place in this world was excluded from our analysis; our definition excluded much of the data. My recognition of this paradox was catalyzed by the writings of Robin Holliday, among others.

The solution to this paradox did not reside in converting biogerontology into human geriatrics, but rather in viewing diseases as *systemic failures that highlight the weak points of the evolved anatomical and physiological design of the organism and thereby allow us to identify and investigate them.* This conceptual change, as described in Chapters 3, 5, and elsewhere, allows us to unify the biology of aging at a functional level instead of arbitrarily continuing the division between "normal" and "pathological" aging. Other changes are scattered throughout the book. Some involved only simple updates of facts; others involved comparable changes in viewpoint, and are pointed out to the reader. The main lesson to be captured here is the increasing subtlety and sophistication of the field, and (one hopes) of its practitioners as well. Such practitioners and such readers deserve a co-evolving text.

In a recent essay, Richard Miller (1997: *J. Am. Ger. Soc.* v. 45, p. 1258) asked a provocative question: "When will the biology of aging become useful?" When will our knowledge of the topic allow us to do something useful that could not be done before? A legitimate query, especially to researchers asking for more money. I think that our increasing knowledge of the control mechanisms regulating the expression of a variety of genetic, molecular, cellular, tissue, and organismal activities essential to continued good health suggests that the time is soon. The transition from a fanciful science to a "verge" science is a major step forward.

The organization of the book has changed only slightly, for I believe the strategy outlined in the original preface is still valid. But experience teaches the teacher. I have broken the original "Observations" into two sections—"Defining and Measuring Aging" and "The Evolution and Description of Aging"—in recognition of the different focus of each. I have retained the "Principles" section more or less as before, as "Theories of Aging." A new "Conclusions and Prospects" section includes two chapters that sum up my views on the biological and social aspects of aging. It has not escaped my notice (nor that of my long-suffering students) that this organization lends itself admirably to the testing schedule of the university. However, I am aware that many colleagues prefer a different but equally effective approach, and the following suggested chapter sequence might prove useful: 1–5, 8–9, 6, 11–12, 7, and 13–14. Other arrangements are certainly possible; the point is to tell a coherent and realistic story.

● *Acknowledgments*

I have been fortunate in the acuity of my critics. Their sharp eyes have saved me once again from an embarrassment of errors, some of commission and some of omission. I accepted willingly and gratefully most of their suggestions and criticisms, for they were made in a spirit of collegiality. These colleagues were generous of their time and knowledge in critiquing the draft of this new edition. I must particularly thank T. M. Witten (University of Michigan), Don Ingram (Gerontology Research Center, National Institute on Aging), George Martin (University of Washington), Richard Miller (University of Michigan), Steven Austad (University of Idaho), Michael Rose (University of California, Irvine), and Richard Weindruch (University of Wisconsin). But stubbornness dies hard; I did not accept every suggestion, and so I must accept full responsibility for any errors or inaccuracies in the work. And of course I must acknowledge the sometimes vocal assistance of the students in my Biology of Aging classes at Wayne State University, who pointed out to me the strengths and weaknesses of the revised text as I was preparing it. The text is now more readable because of their efforts. I apologize to those of my colleagues whose work I have overlooked or not cited accurately; my only excuse is that the field is expanding rapidly and my desk is overflowing.

I am grateful to Andy Sinauer and his colleagues at Sinauer Associates for having the faith to help me develop this textbook into what we hope will be a fitting companion for this increasingly sophisticated field. They have done wonders in transforming a manuscript into a book. Their reputation for patient professionalism is well deserved. In particular, Stephanie Hiebert did a marvelous copyediting job in which she taught me something about writing with style and coherence. And Carol Wigg and her colleagues worked hard to put together a good-looking book that invites your eyes.

I have not written this book by myself, but with the support of many other people. I must acknowledge the people who have kept my laboratory going while I spent time in the library and at the keyboard: Steven Buck (who has been my colleague since 1981), Vasanti Burde, Elliot Feldman, John Vettraino, Kevin Graves, and Ibrahim Kadura. They all have ably carried the load during this past year, and I owe them much.

And, of course, there was the invisible support of several friends and mentors. In particular, the enthusiasm of George T. Baker III will not be forgotten though his voice is stilled. He was indeed a happy warrior. As a friend and as a colleague, he is missed. I think he would have liked this book.

Robert Arking
The Cottage on Long Lake
Harrison, Michigan
March 1998

Preface to the First Edition

If we are truly fortunate, we will age. Each of us will struggle with this fate in our own way. There has been much attention focused on the biomedical, economic, social and psychological aspects of human aging; but until recently serious biological attention was given to this topic by only a few farsighted innovators. In part, this was because our attention was mostly focused elsewhere, perhaps on the triumphs of molecular genetics in deciphering the genetic code and in unraveling the molecular mechanisms that regulate gene action. These biological insights are traditionally viewed in the context of embryological development. The reasons for the neglect of the rest of the life cycle are not clear but they probably had a lot to do with the scientific and cultural prejudice that aging is not a fundamentally interesting or attractive biological process. But our concepts have now changed, in part due to the demographic changes taking place in society and in part because we are now beginning to understand that our present biological views will not fully explain aging. Perhaps it was necessary to attain our present level of understanding of embryological development before we could appreciate the complexities inherent in the biological problem of aging.

I view aging as a fundamental biological process that can be defined, measured, described and manipulated. My researches and readings have led me to suggest that aging is a genetically determined, environmentally modulated, event-dependent process. I have tried to construct this book so as to serve the reader as a guided tour through the literature which has led me (and others) to this conclusion. While I have taken care to present the conflicting data and opposing points of view that characterize this unsettled field, the book is not intended as a monograph addressed to other specialists. I have written this book for students of aging (be they formally enrolled or not) who have a level of biological knowledge no more sophisticated than that provided by any good introductory biology textbook. I believe it is important for people conversant with the sociological and psychological aspects of gerontology to also be knowledgeable about the biological aspects of aging and the implications of the current research for their own fields. I have tried to explain in a clear manner the logical bases of the arguments and have veered away from overwhelming the reader with too much unnecessary jargon and details. But interpretations cannot be made without data, nor without thought, so I selected what I believe to be pertinent facts and observations. I hope the reader will think about them and not just accept them uncritically.

Let me explain the organization of the book. I believe it is important to first be sure of what it is we think we know. Accordingly, we begin the journey with a rigorous definition and exposition of exactly what does—and does not—constitute an aging change. The CUPID definition developed here guides us through the thickets of facts, interpretations and complexities that beset the path. We then discuss the several ways of measuring aging. It is a difficult task and one which is often skipped, particularly by those of us bearing childhood fears of mathematical thoughts, but it is important to master the concepts involved (if not the numbers) simply because of the old axiom: "If you cannot measure what you are studying, then you do not know what you are talking about." I do not propose to weigh the human spirit, but there is no reason not to assay our bodies or measure our molecules. I have deliberately adopted a comparative approach to the study of aging. If aging is a fundamental biological process, then we can learn much from the study of diverse and even exotic laboratory animals, some of which will, if we are fortunate, age in such a way as to illuminate some particular aspect of the aging process. I have surveyed comparative aging research by using those examples which illustrate particularly well some special aspect of aging that might otherwise have been overlooked or not appreciated. An anthropomorphic approach is an illogical process to use when trying to attain an understanding of basic biology. Nevertheless, I have not ignored ourselves. I have used humans as the examples of vertebrate aging and so a comprehensive (but far from definitive) chapter on the normal and abnormal aspects of human aging has been included. Instructors, students, and other readers may choose to go over this in detail, amplifying it as necessary; or else choose to read the highlights at the beginning and end of the chapter, depending on their background and goals. We then round out our survey of the known facts by examining the proven genetic and physiological predictors of longevity as well as the various tested methods of modulating the life span.

Once we know what it is that we know, then we are finally equipped to discuss and critically evaluate the several different theories of aging. This task fills up the second half of the text. All the theories are plausible; what I hope the reader will come away with is a sense as to which theories have been critically disproved, which are still untested and which appear to be both plausible and probable. The proper assignment of the probable mechanisms of aging now will have much to do with our eventual success in better understanding it later. The facts presented in the first half of the book play an integral role in this analysis. We conclude the investigation by examining whether or not there exists a fundamental aging mechanism.

At one level, of course, it is obvious that there are a multiplicity of aging processes. Yet this cannot be taken to foreclose the existence of common processes any more than the existence of the multiple ways in which different species progress from an egg to an adult be used to obscure the fact that there are probably only a small number of fundamental developmental mechanisms, mechanisms common to broad groups of organisms. The existence of common fundamental aging mechanisms might make it easier for us to more fully understand and perhaps even manipulate the aging process in the future. Of course, such a proposal is only a target at which future researchers may take aim to disprove.

If aging as a process baffles all of us, then how presumptuous is the ordinary professor who believes that he can write something of value about it? Especially since the Sage has lamented that "Of the making of books, there is no end." Well, yes but . . . My motivation in writing this text grew out of my own need to understand the field of biological gerontology, an area towards which my research was leading me, and to organize it within a conceptual framework that made sense to me. I enjoy teaching and sharing with students whatever it is that I know. The text evolved and grew out of the lectures I wrote for such a course, a course I volunteered to teach since it struck me as an efficient and easy way in which to learn and understand and organize the literature. With the wisdom of hindsight, I can say that it was mostly enjoyable, it may even have been efficient, but it was certainly far from easy! It was only because of the efforts of many other people that I was able to complete the task I had so presumptuously set for myself and it is to them that much credit is due.

Part I
Defining and Measuring Aging

1

Perspectives on Aging

Introduction

Through the centuries, sages have pointed out that many of the more profound aspects of human culture, the sometimes tragic struggle of humans against fate, originate in the fact that we all must die. Great art and major religions flow from the contrast between our boundless dreams and ambitions and the realities of our temporal prison. It is unclear when this concept appeared; indeed, it is unclear whether any other species shares with us a recognition of the inevitability of death, although some primate cousins share our sensation of an individual consciousness. Our Neolithic ancestors almost certainly were aware of our common fate and felt the same tension, for 50,000 years ago at Shanidar in what is now Iran they buried their dead on a bed of wildflowers.

Then, as now, senescence and death were likely to have been accepted by most people as given conditions of existence. The few dissenters searched for a magic potion or fountain of youth in attempts to escape their fate. Most people just searched for an explanation to justify their fate and were satisfied with a supernatural or religious interpretation. All were aware that humans age. Our preference for the new is not due solely to the efforts of the advertising industry to sell us the latest consumer item. Each of us absorbs as we grow up the undeniable truth that old things tend to wear out and break down: old toys, old cars, old machines—and old people.

Our reaction to this reality takes at least four forms, three of which have been best expressed by the artists among us. First is the acceptance and celebration of our mature years, freed of lingering diseases, as penned by Robert Browning:

Grow old along with me. The best is yet to be,
the last of life, for which the first was made . . .

"Rabbi Ben Ezra," 1864

3

Second is a refusal to accept aging. Many have fought senescence and death, knowing it to be a struggle they must lose but nevertheless fighting because they could do nothing else. Dylan Thomas (1953) perhaps best echoes their feelings in these lines:

> Do not go gentle into that good night,
> old age should burn and rave at close of day;
> rage, rage against the dying of the light.
>
>   *"Do Not Go Gentle Into That Good Night,"* 1953

The difference between these two views is due, in part, to how one sees life. Perhaps Browning's proponent celebrates mature love and companionship, secure in the belief that mortality makes life and the enjoyment of it precious; that the sense of not having world enough and time is the spur to our achievements, not the least of which should be to master the art of living well. To these arguments the advocate of Dylan Thomas might reply that he rages precisely because there is neither world enough nor time for a short-lived human to know what can be known or to explore what is not yet known.

A vital and vigorous life is precious to us; that is why we both celebrate and rage at its finite length. A cooler, more intellectual reaction is to describe life's events; this approach constitutes the third form of response. An important advance was the explicit recognition that each human follows the same path of growth, development, maturity, and senescence—a process that has never been described better than by Shakespeare:

> All the world's a stage,
> and all the men and women merely players:
> They have their exits and their entrances;
> and one man in his time plays many parts,
> his acts being seven ages. At first the infant,
> mewling and puking in the nurse's arms.
> And then the whining school-boy, with his satchel
> and shining morning face, creeping like snail
> unwillingly to school. And then the lover,
> sighing like furnace, with a woeful ballad
> made to his mistress' eyebrow. Then a soldier,
> full of strange oaths and bearded like the pard,
> jealous in honour, sudden and quick in quarrel,
> seeking the bubble reputation
> even in the cannon's mouth. And then the justice,
> in fair round belly with good capon lined,
> with eyes severe and beard of formal cut,
> full of wise saws and modern instances;
> and so he plays his part. The sixth age shifts
> into the lean and slipper'd pantaloon,
> with spectacles on nose and pouch on side,

his youthful hose, well saved, a world too wide
for his shrunk shank; and his big manly voice,
turning again toward childish treble, pipes
and whistles in his sound. Last scene of all,
that ends this strange eventful history,
is second childishness and mere oblivion,
sans teeth, sans eyes, sans taste, sans everything.

"As You Like It," 1600 (act 2, scene 7)

The regularity is what catches our eye, for it suggests an underlying and predictable mechanism. The fourth form of our reaction to the reality of aging is
then the scientific investigation of the biological mechanisms responsible for the
predictability of our aging.

It took the three centuries following Shakespeare, during which classical biology was established, before August Weismann (1891) could even begin to formulate the first mechanistic questions relating aging and evolution. These questions
were reformulated through the experimental efforts of various investigators, such
as Élie Metchnikoff in Russia and Raymond Pearl in the United States. Together,
Metchnikoff and Pearl demonstrated that a characteristic similarity of aging and
senescence transcends species boundaries, and they postulated mechanistic theories to explain and predict the aging process. But the complexity of the topic
defeated these initial attempts at understanding, and the attention of biologists
was otherwise captured by the more promising ideas being developed by Thomas
Hunt Morgan in genetics, by Hans Spemann in embryology, by J. B. S. Haldane in
physiology, and by Otto Warburg in biochemistry.

Shortly after the molecular biologists had begun unraveling the mysteries of
the gene, the publication and widespread acceptance of Alex Comfort's book *The
Biology of Senescence* (1956), led to an affirmation of research on aging as an
important aspect of basic biological inquiry. Comfort achieved this affirmation by
summarizing the available data with a critical eye and well-turned phrase and by
being succinct (Comfort 1979, p. 16):

> The primary assignment of gerontology—that of finding an accessible
> mechanism that times the human life-span as we observe it—remains
> undischarged. But it is nonetheless far closer to that objective today then
> when we last reviewed the subject—partly because, through the growth of
> experimental evidence which the theories of the past have generated, the
> possibility of a hierarchy of aging processes integrated by a life-span
> "clock" has come to be reorganized and the nature of that clock is becom-
> ing clearer.

This statement very specifically defines the problem and how to face it. But the
increase in knowledge that Comfort was instrumental in effecting has altered our
concepts and redirected the problem. Many biogerontologists would today dispute
the idea of a "life-span clock" that measures our time and would instead advocate
in both fact and metaphor a more multifaceted and diffuse type of mechanism.

For example, Finch (1990, p. 6) has pointed out that biological time is functionally equivalent to cascades of specific physical or chemical events and thus is fundamentally independent of absolute sidereal or calendar time. Time does not directly measure the changes we each undergo.

The fact that we continuously modify our concepts is not surprising, given the variety of disciplines from which the knowledge required to solve this problem must be drawn. It should be evident on reflection that gerontology is a field of inquiry, not an autonomous academic discipline. Gerontologists, then, are people from a variety of backgrounds who share an avid interest in aging. To understand the biology of aging requires the posing of testable and reasonable questions: Why do two species so closely related as mouse and man have such very different life spans? What causes the deteriorative changes during the life span of each of these species? Are the causes the same in both species? Can the deteriorative changes be postponed? Reversed? Is it possible to reliably predict the life span of an individual? Is it possible to prolong the life span? Is it worth it?

It is the task and the goal of gerontologists to find the answers to these and similar questions. Although we still know very little about the nature and causes of aging and senescence, the knowledge is accumulating increasingly rapidly. In the last decade the rigor of gerontological thinking has increased remarkably, as evidenced by its shift from a purely descriptive to an increasingly analytical approach, as well as by its correspondingly more detailed quantitative examination of various cellular and physiological mechanisms. We do not yet know the answers, but the fog that obscures them is lifting. It is not unreasonable to hope that in the next decade we will decipher at least the outlines of the answers.

One question—whether prolonging the maximum human life span would benefit society—has already been answered. The answer to this question has guided modern gerontology research: Given our present state of knowledge, it is more beneficial to opt for a healthy and vigorous, albeit finite, life than to search in vain for the elixir of immortality. Thus, gerontology is committed not to a search for immortality but to the elimination of premature disability and death and to the deciphering of the mechanisms that regulate our longevity and our aging. The contentedness of Robert Browning has prevailed over the rage of Dylan Thomas.

• On the Nature of the Puzzle: The Difficulties in Studying Aging

Apart from the historical and philosophical blinders that make it difficult to visualize the topic of gerontology as a whole, a fundamental problem of causality impedes our progress toward an understanding of the mechanisms of aging and senescence. A normative scientific inquiry such as gerontology usually begins by a more or less systematic description of the functional and structural changes that accompany aging. These descriptions initially may be based on human studies and later involve animal models. They are usually qualitative at first, as Shakespeare's description was; later they become quantitative, as the longitudinal studies reported by Shock demonstrate (1985).

Because aging is a complex process that affects a wide variety of functions, even the most casual investigator is soon overwhelmed by the large number of statistically significant correlations between the aging process and various phenomena. In most cases, these correlations furnish few direct clues regarding the nature and identity of the underlying causal mechanisms, despite the high degree of statistical significance. For example, graying hair in humans has a very high coefficient of correlation with chronological age, yet no one would seriously propose that gray hair is a cause of aging.

Most of the theories that result from this correlative approach appear to be more plausible than this extreme example, usually because they involve important changes and postulate a physiologically reasonable mechanism that could bring about the desired effect. Gerontologists are ingenious, and consequently the field has never suffered from a lack of theories. For example, consider the large differences in rate and timing of the age-dependent decrements of different physiological functions in humans, as shown in Figure 1.1. These longitudinal and cross-sectional data clearly illustrate that different functions decay at different rates, even within a single individual. The heterogeneity of these age decrements has been used as an argument against the idea that the rate of aging is controlled by any single basic process. It is only reasonable to suppose that the difference in

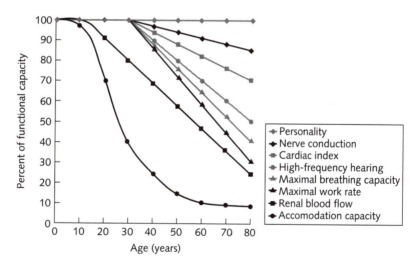

Figure 1.1   Age-dependent changes in some anatomical and physiological factors in humans, as reported in various reports of cross-sectional and/or longitudinal studies from the Baltimore Longitudinal Study on Aging. For most factors, the level at age 30 was taken to represent the optimal response and assigned a value of 100 percent; the other age-specific data are expressed relative to this base value. Younger baseline ages are used for measures of high-frequency hearing and of personality. The data are presented here as schematic linear projections that omit the inter- and intrapopulation variability inherent in the original data; however, the overall trend is not obscured. (Data assembled by G. T. Baker III and J. Frozard on the basis of Gerontology Research Center studies.)

the rate of aging of each organ reflects the fact that different processes are at work in each one. Conversely, the same data have been used to buttress the idea that there is one central pacemaker process, for the heterogeneity is exactly what would be expected if different systems were responding at different rates to the same stimulus.

With enough ingenuity, descriptive data can be argued both ways. Persuasive arguments are available; solid evidence is needed. The problem now confronting gerontology is to apply critical tests capable of disproving specific hypotheses. Only by this method can events that are merely correlated with aging (and thus are not fundamentally interesting) be distinguished from events that might bear a causal relationship to the aging process (and thus are worthy of further study). As should be expected, opinions in the scientific community differ as to the most efficient manner of pursuing this goal. My opinion is that the most efficient way to unambiguously apply such a critical test is to adopt the approach advocated by Weismann in 1891 and to develop long-lived animal strains by artificial selection. Having clearly and unambiguously affected the processes that govern aging and longevity, we can then examine the theories of interest and determine whether their predictions are upheld by comparing the long-lived strains to strains with a normal life span.

These selection experiments are very expensive in terms of both money and time. Richard Miller and his colleagues have developed an interesting modification in which they blend such experiments with the candidate gene approach. First, they identified a specific control system, such as the immune system, known to be essential for health and longevity. Then they created a genetically heterogenous population (of mice, in this case) and used modern genotyping techniques to identify alleles that enhanced the performance of different aspects of immune function. The genes so identified can then be tested for their effect on longevity.

These two approaches are not that different conceptually, for each allows for a stringent test of one's theory in the whole animal. Such critical theory testing has only recently become feasible in gerontology research and thus did not play a major role in the development of many current gerontological theories. However, we should keep this type of theory testing in mind when assessing the concepts and theories of aging and senescence that are popular now.

People have been aging since our evolutionary history began. What, then, accounts for the recent interest in aging and senescence? Certainly the interest in the social, psychological, and medical aspects of gerontology had a dual genesis: first, in the demographers' realization that the elderly would soon become a significant aspect of the population; second, in the federal training, service, and research programs established in the mid-1960s in response to this awareness. The biological interest came a little later and a little differently. It is a commonplace observation that scientists appear to possess a collective awareness that causes many of them to ask the same sorts of questions more or less simultaneously. The cause is not a metaphysical process; it is simply the summation of numerous individual assessments of recent advances, measured against the kinds of questions to which the new knowledge might be most appropriately applied.

Traditionally, biologists usually attempted to explain the aging process in terms of general biological phenomena that were under intensive study or that seemed most important at the time. Much of the recent progress in fields such as genetics, evolution, developmental biology, and ecology has been integrative, in part because many phenomena are now seen to have multiple causes. Thus there is a need to formulate a synthesis of ideas that will extend our understanding to processes that are simultaneously and importantly rooted in each of these diverse disciplines. These integrative approaches have necessarily made many people more receptive to a study of the interactions involved in aging. The process has been facilitated by the enormous accumulation of empirical data concerning aging, as well as the organization of those data into meaningful and accessible review articles and symposia. As a consequence, the divisions between gerontology and the rest of biology are gradually being blurred by the realization that all parts of the life cycle are continuous with one another in process and mechanism, if not in detail.

As the interest in the biology of aging spreads outward, attracting scientists from other disciplines, it also spreads downward, engaging the interest of people other than practicing research biologists and gerontologists. Numerous best-selling how-to books, by combining an incomplete description of human aging with a favorite set of putative interventions, have made their authors wealthy and their readers believers. This book will do neither. But it may contribute to an increased understanding of the questions we face and an appreciation of what we know and what we don't know. This book is written both for the biology student who, early in his or her career, wishes to learn the essentials of the subject, and for the clinically or social science-oriented gerontologist who wishes to learn about the mechanisms that count our days.

• *Defining Aging and Senescence*

The fact that we have used the terms "aging" and "senescence" thus far without defining them suggests that these familiar words have a universal definition. They are familiar, but they are also imprecise in that there is no single formal definition. Different authorities use different words. Costa and McCrae (1995, p. 25) take the broad view and define aging as "what happens to an organism over time." Their reason for adopting such an all-inclusive definition is to draw our attention as much to functions that are preserved as to those that change. Understanding the mechanisms that underlie stability may provide insight into the processes that promote loss of function. This is a good point, and we should not lose sight of it. But this broad view does not allow us to distinguish aging from anything else that happens to the organism, so it is not useful for our purposes.

Comfort (1960, p. 8) proposed that aging is "an increased liability to die, or an increasing loss of vigour, with increasing chronological age, or with the passage of the life cycle." In a similar vein, John Maynard Smith (1962, p. 115) defined aging processes as "those which render individuals more susceptible as they grow older to the various factors, intrinsic or extrinsic, which may cause death." Frolkis (1982, p. 4) said, "Aging is a naturally developing biological process which limits the adaptive possibilities of an organism, increases the likelihood of death, reduces the life span and promotes age pathology." And Rothstein (1982, p. 2) stated that "the changes from maturity through senescence constitute the 'aging' process."

These different definitions give the initial impression that they each describe the same phenomenon, albeit in different words. Does the similarity of words imply that the underlying concept is accurate? Strehler (1982) tried to formulate an answer to this question. He pointed out that aging is not simply the sum total of the aggregate pathologies and of disease-induced damage, and that, conversely, not all the changes in structure and function that are correlated with age may be appropriately considered as fundamental age-related changes per se. These two concepts, unlike the preceding definitions, impose limits on what we may regard as the fundamental aging processes. In an effort to incorporate this rigor into an operational definition, Strehler (1982) suggested that fundamental age-related changes must meet the following four conditions:

1. They must be deleterious; that is, they must reduce function.

2. They must be progressive; that is, they must take place gradually.

3. They must be intrinsic; that is, they must not be the result of a modifiable environmental agent.

4. They must be universal; that is, all members of a species should show such gradual deficit with advancing age.

For a long time these criteria were thought to define aging processes adequately and to allow us to distinguish them operationally from nonaging phenomena such as diseases and accidents. As new data have developed, however, it has become clear that the concept of universality is the Achilles' heel of this definition. Chapter 3 will present these data; for now, it will suffice to say that there is so much individual variation in aging that it is impossible to talk of universal or even specieswide aging processes. However, Strehler's concept of deleterious, progressive, and intrinsic changes is still useful today.

More recently, Masoro (1995a, p. 3) proposed that aging refers to the "deteriorative changes with time during postmaturational life that underlie an increasing vulnerability to challenge, thereby decreasing the ability of the organism to survive." This definition is similar to Strehler's, but not all would agree with the inclusion of time in a definition of aging. The role of time in aging is worth discussing, particularly since Chapter 3 will present evidence suggesting that physiological biomarkers are a much more useful index of aging than is the simple passage of time. Finch (1991, p. 5) points out that "aging" is generally used to describe a host of time-related alterations that biological entities from molecules to ecosystems undergo.

Is there a theoretical or empirical reason to assume that time itself plays a causal role in the progression of an organism from birth to death? Biological time is measured by interlocking cascades of specific physical or chemical events, and the underlying mechanisms are just now being worked out. For example, the biological clock in the fruit fly *Drosophila*, the mold *Neurospora*, and presumably other organisms depends on the cyclic interaction between at least two specific gene products, which then unstably repress their own transcription on exposure to light and thus provide the rhythmic circadian output that is characteristic of a biological clock (Gekakis et al. 1995; Kay and Millar 1995; Sehgal et al. 1995). The fundamental units of the biological "clock" are transcription cycles. The fundamental units of the sidereal "clock" are day and night, which are based on the relationship of Earth to the sun. The involvement of light connects these two otherwise disparate clocks and connects time to aging.

Thus, although it is theoretically permissible to view aging as a time-based process, this approach is not useful, because the translation of time into biological rhythms subjects it to myriad biological controls, which act to interpret it differently for each organism. We each know individuals who are the same chronological age but appear to be very different physiological ages. Something is missing. As Arking and Dudas (1989) noted, one indication that we had attained a more sophisticated understanding of aging would be our ability to remove time from the analysis of aging, since time is only an imperfect correlate of the presently unknown physiological processes involved in aging. Only when we can substitute the operation of the actual physiological mechanisms for time will we have a firm idea of what we're talking about.

In other words, we need to make time an independent rather than a dependent variable in our analyses. Instead of using the calendar to measure aging, we need to be able to use the changes in important physiological variables to measure aging. This goal has been accomplished in a few experimental systems, including humans (see Manton, Woodbury, and Stallard 1995 and the related discussion in Chapters 2 and 4). For these reasons, Finch (1991) has rejected use of the word "aging" itself because of its strong and "illicit" connections to the idea of time as an independent variable. He has written an excellent book on the topic without once using the word! Instead he favors the word "senescence," which he defines as follows:

> the age-related changes in an organism that adversely affect its vitality and function, but most importantly, increase the mortality rate as a function of time (such that) senility represents the end stage of senescence, when mortality risk is approaching 100%.

There is an obvious similarity between this definiton and that of Masoro cited earlier. However, some of the data presented in Chapter 2 will require the modification of the implication in this definition that mortality rates must always increase with time.

Although "senescence" is often used interchangeably with "aging," Lamb (1977, p. 2) suggests that "senescence" and "senescent" should be reserved for instances "when talking about the changes which occur during the period of obvious functional decline in the later years of an animal's life-span."

This usage is in agreement with the earlier suggestion of Strehler (1982), who defined "senescence" as "the changes which occur generally in the postreproductive period and which results in a decreased survival capacity on the part of the individual organisms." Thus, senescent changes are those that most noticeably occur during the latter part of the life cycle and that are somehow associated with the increased mortality characteristic of the last stage of life. The terms "aging" and "senescence" seem to overlap considerably, and the difference between them may be one of emphasis rather than of fundamentals. Finally, it is worth taking note of Kohn's (1978) distinction between developmental changes and age-related changes:

> By teleological criteria, development can be viewed as consisting of early processes that enhance the functional capacities of a system, whereas aging consists of later processes that diminish or have no effects on ability to function.

We will return to this distinction in our discussion of mortality kinetics in Chapter 2.

Some of the concepts contained in the definitions presented here are worth emphasizing:

1. Not all time-dependent changes should automatically be considered fundamental age-related changes. Time should be a dependent variable.

2. Age-related changes usually manifest themselves beginning at reproductive maturity, although their genesis may have taken place earlier.

3. Age-related changes are deleterious, progressive, and cumulative. The death of the organism is the ultimate end point of aging. It is a sudden and acute transformation from one state to another; yet the process of aging involves a progressive increase in the probability of dying.

4. Aging and senescence are fundamental and intrinsic properties of most living organisms.

As a result of this survey, we may define aging as the time-independent series of *cumulative, progressive, intrinsic, and deleterious functional and structural changes* that usually begin to manifest themselves at reproductive maturity and eventually culminate in death. A simple mnemonic for this definition is CPID (*cumulative, progressive, intrinsic, deleterious*). We will henceforth use this CPID definition as our operational method for identifying age-related changes.

Using the points emphasized above as a working definition of aging has the advantage of allowing us to be precise in categorizing a particular process as a normal age-related change. For example, we can easily distinguish deleterioius changes due to aging from changes due to infectious disease (the latter is the result of a parasite and is not intrinsic), or from changes that have no obvious deleterious effect (for example, gray hair). However, this precision does not come without a price. Rigid adherence to typological thinking might cause us to reject any age-dependent change that does not occur in all individuals. This would be a serious error, since the underlying assumption is contradicted by the data (see

Chapter 3). Age-related changes are not universal within a species; different individuals may age differently. Probably the best approach is to use the CPID criteria as a general guide, and to resolve questionable cases on the basis of the evidence available. Some internal contradictions may result, but consistency is not the highest virtue.

Is Aging a Universal Trait?

Is there such a thing as a nonaging system? In a fundamental sense, such a system cannot exist, for the cosmologists seem generally agreed on the idea that our universe (probably) and our solar system (certainly) have a finite life span. At the other end of the scale, the physicists have agreed that most subatomic particles—perhaps even the proton—decay. If both the universe and its component particles age, then so must all the intermediate organizational levels. Nothing is forever, for there is no forever. Despite this exercise in logic, it is reasonable to ask if, on a more familiar time scale, nonaging systems do exist.

Nonaging systems would be systems that, when periodically examined, exhibited no changes. Are there any? Kohn (1979) claimed that nonaging systems do exist, and that they are always composed of dynamic processes. The simplest type, a chemical system at equilibrium, can be depicted as follows:

$$A + B \rightleftharpoons C + D$$

The chemicals A and B interact to yield products C and D; similarly, the products C and D may interact to yield A and B. The reaction will proceed until predictable amounts of the four chemicals are present. The amounts depend only on the initial concentrations and the amount of free energy available. Once the reaction reaches this equilibrium point, it will stay there forever, provided that no work is done on the system and that environmental conditions remain constant. Given the stringency of the conditions, it is understandable that such systems are not found in nature, remaining only laboratory curiosities.

One type of nonaging process that is common in nature is a steady-state process, such as the one depicted in Figure 1.2. In this case we have a series of several different sequential reactions, each of which may be reversible. The reaction as a whole is driven in one direction by the continuous addition of compo-

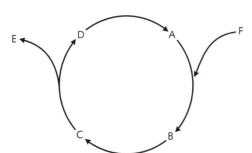

Figure 1.2   A steady-state process in which the concentration of components A, B, C, and D will not change as long as the inflow of F and the outflow of E are balanced. In the absence of change, this constitutes a nonaging system. (From Kohn 1978. © Prentice-Hall, Inc.)

nent F and the compensating continuous removal of component E. When the net flows of E and F are balanced and the rates of the various reactions are steady, the amounts of components A, B, C, and D will not change with time. This is a nonaging system. It could be converted to an aging system by a progressive and irreversible change in the rates of the utilization of F and/or the production of E.

It may not appear sensible to talk about age-related or non-age-related changes in a steady-state system, because the system contains different populations of molecules at different times. Since the system is continually being renewed, what is there to age or not age? The answer is that the identity of the system is independent of the turnover of its components; rather it depends on the interactions of the components. A more familiar physiological counterpart of the steady state is illustrated by the generalized homeostatic process depicted in Figure 1.3. Here various processes counteract each other to maintain a particular factor or activity at a steady, optimal level. Figure 1.4 shows data from an actual homeostatic process. The fasting blood glucose levels in human males did not change during the 2-hour period of examination, although the number of both glucose molecules and insulin molecules in the systems increased substantially. This is a nonaging system in which the identity and the numbers of the insulin and glucose molecules change from one moment to the next, but changes in one component evoke changes in the other such that the variable affected—in this case the blood glucose level—remains constant.

The measured levels usually do not remain identical from one measurement to the next even in this nonaging system. The regulatory components of the system consistently undershoot or overshoot the optimal value, leading to a long-term fluctuation about the optimal level. Statistics represents this situation by showing the mean and variance, as in all three curves of Figure 1.4. However, if the interactions of the regulatory subcomponents change, the system might be transformed into a non-steady-state system characterized by a progressive alteration in the mean level and/or in the variance. This phenomenon is nicely illustrated by the data contained in many of the figures found throughout this book.

Now let's answer the question we posed at the start of this section: Is aging a universal biological trait? The answer is simple: It is widespread but not universal. No evidence suggests, for example, that aging as we have defined it occurs in prokaryote species. Aging is found only among eukaryotes (see Chapter 4), but not in all of them, and not in the same manner among those that do age. A bewil-

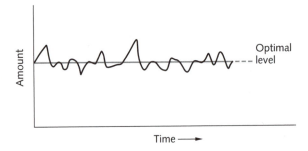

Figure 1.3 A homeostatic steady-state process being maintained at an optimal level by means of periodic fluctuations above and below this value. The optimal value is represented by the mean; the periodic fluctuations constitute the variance, which is usually expressed either as the standard error of the mean or as the standard deviation. (From Kohn 1978. © Prentice-Hall, Inc.)

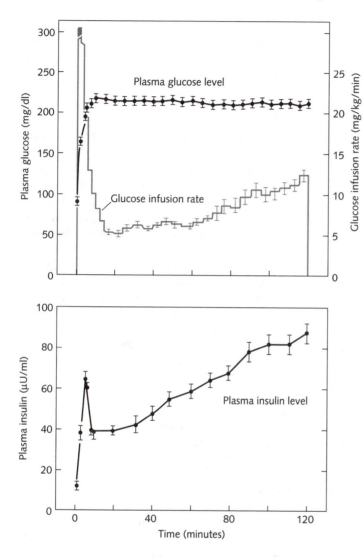

Figure 1.4 Measurements from an actual homeostatic process—the maintenance of glucose levels in the blood. Plasma glucose levels stay almost constant for 2 hours in healthy volunteers during the hyperglycemic glucose clamp technique (a method for quantifying insulin secretion and resistance), despite large alterations in the glucose infusion rate, which causes corresponding alterations in the plasma insulin levels. (From DeFronzo, Tobin, and Andres 1979.)

dering array of lifestyles and life spans confronts the investigator who seeks broad generalizations, from mayflies that live 1 day to bushes that live 11,000 years or more. Finch (1991) has sorted this cacophony into three classes: (1) organisms that show no or negligible signs of aging, (2) organisms that display a gradual progression of aging, and (3) organisms that exhibit a rapid onset of aging. We will deal with these classes in more detail in our discussion of plasticity later in this chapter, as well as in Chapter 4 and at other points throughout our tour of the topic. However, as we discuss this material we should keep in mind the nature of the mechanism(s) that distinguish these three groups, and we should consider whether the differences between them are qualitative or quantitative. These three categories crosscut and otherwise disregard the common phylogenetic and evolutionary relationships, a phenomenon that a complete explanation of aging must encompass. If evolution is the fundamental theorem of biology, what enables a trait as fundamental as aging to escape being phylogenetically constrained? We will answer this question in Chapter 4.

● *Measuring Age-Related Changes*

Aging is a deteriorative process that shows itself in two distinctly different manners. First, aging increases the probability with time that the individual will die. Second, it decreases the ability of an individual to withstand extrinsic stresses. The latter is commonly referred to as a loss of vigor or of vitality, although we don't usually bother to define these terms rigorously, other than that they mean the ability to survive. It follows then that either the timing of death or the age-related decrease in functional properties may be used to measure the occurrence of age-related changes.

Death is a singular and acute event in an individual's life span. Simply knowing its chronological time for one individual gives us no useful information with which to determine the rate of aging of that individual. Knowing the times of death (or the lengths of the life spans) for numerous individuals raised under similar conditions will allow us to determine whether the probability of any single individual's dying is constant. A constant probability throughout the time period studied, as in Figure 1.5a, implies that the chance an animal will die in any given period is not related to the age of the animal. Given this observation, we must conclude that age-related changes are not taking place and that the deaths are probably a result of accidental, stochastic causes. On the other hand, an increase in the probability of dying as the animal grows older, as depicted in Figure 1.5b and c, is empirical evidence that age-related changes are taking place. Note, however, that the determination of the presence or absence of age-related changes within individual animals is based on an assessment of population data. Such data are often presented in the form of two-dimensional survival curves, as in Figure 1.5.

We will deal with the measurement of senescence in more detail in Chapter 3. For now, keep in mind that these two-dimensional plots abstract the actual information and in the process both highlight and obscure various kinds of information. The information that is obscured in the plots of Figure 1.5 has to do with the individuality of the rates of aging. It is all too easy to assume that every member of the population loses its vigor in a constant manner, as in Figure 1.6a. The real situation is much more complex; Figure 1.6b attempts to identify some of these complexities.

First, different individuals age at different rates. We are all aware that different people of the same chronological age often have very different levels of vim and vigor. The different slopes of the individual lives in Figure 1.6b are an attempt to indicate this heterogeneity. Second, the death threshold is not constant; rather it fluctuates as a result of various environmental factors. Third, there may be more than one death threshold (Figure 1.6c). For example, one individual may have an intrinsically greater lung capacity than another person,; the other person, however, may be blessed with a highly efficient set of kidneys. Different envi-

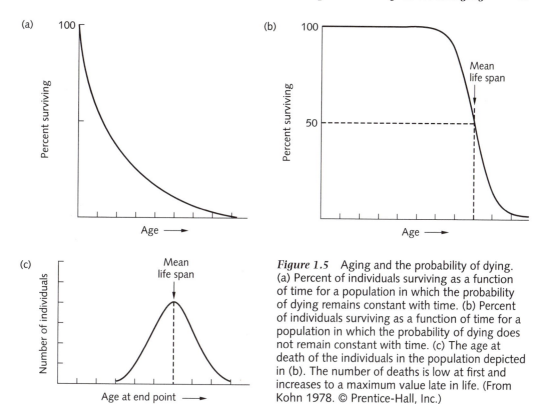

Figure 1.5 Aging and the probability of dying. (a) Percent of individuals surviving as a function of time for a population in which the probability of dying remains constant with time. (b) Percent of individuals surviving as a function of time for a population in which the probability of dying does not remain constant with time. (c) The age at death of the individuals in the population depicted in (b). The number of deaths is low at first and increases to a maximum value late in life. (From Kohn 1978. © Prentice-Hall, Inc.)

ronmental stresses, such as pneumonia or kidney infections, will affect these different individuals in different ways. Hence the existence of multiple thresholds. Fourth, some deaths are accidental, caused by random environmental reasons and not due to our operationally defined age-related changes. All of these complexities are subsumed within the simple survival curve. The longevity of any particular individual, as well as the mean life span of a population of individuals, is determined both by the individual's rate of aging and by the environment in which that individual lives.

Would it be more beneficial, then, to study the age-related decrements that take place within the life span of one individual and to determine their importance by comparing them with the mean population values? This has been the goal of the longitudinal studies undertaken by Nathan Shock and his colleagues (1984). This type of study design is very powerful and has contributed much valuable information that otherwise could not have been obtained.

There are two problems here. First is the obvious one of determining beforehand which physiological or biochemical parameters are adequate and predictive measures of aging. This task is difficult but not insurmountable. The second point is more germane. These longitudinal studies have led to the conclusion that many individuals do not follow the pattern of age-related changes that is predicted from

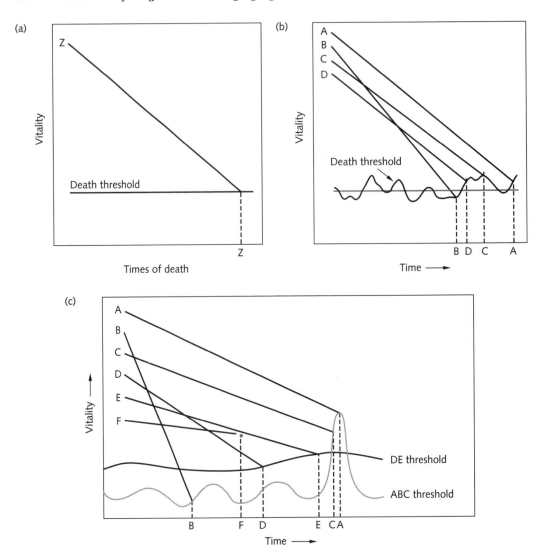

Figure 1.6   Diagrammatic representations of aging, based on different assumptions: (a) that all members of the population lose their vigor in a constant manner and that there is a single and consistent death threshold; (b) that individuals age at different rates and there is a single but variable death threshold; (c) that individuals age at different rates and there are multiple and variable death thresholds. All values are arbitrary. (a and b from Lamb 1977. © John Wiley and Sons.)

the averages based on the summed measurements made on different subjects (see Figure 1.5). The differences between individuals become even more pronounced as the individuals age. Aging is so highly individual that average curves give only a rough approximation of the pattern of aging followed by individuals. Thus, knowing that a certain individual has a measurable decrement in a particular physiological function may or may not be a sufficient basis for saying anything reliable about that individual's rate of aging, much less predicting his or her longevity. Nonetheless, the widespread dissatisfaction with the idea of using time to measure aging has given impetus to the development of biological markers of aging. Such biomarkers, as they have been termed, have shown some promise of being able to measure individual rates of aging. We will discuss biomarkers in some detail in Chapter 3.

● *Models for Studying Aging*

The Choice of an Organizational Level

As the preceding discussion showed, age-related changes may be measured either on a population level, in which the life spans of various similar individuals are measured, or on an individual basis, in which the change in performance of various physiological functions is measured. Regardless of the measurement device employed, it is possible to describe age-related changes and search for their causes on some level other than that of the whole individual. We know that diverse organizational levels ranging from subcellular organelles to entire organ systems often exhibit what appear to be intrinsic age-related changes. If an organism dies because its weakest component fails, then it is only logical to examine these sub-organismal organizational levels for clues to the biology of aging. However, the result of such investigations must be carefully considered, lest we misinterpret them and start down a false path.

Information that may be correct and valuable at one organizational level may be meaningless at another level of complexity. For example, one school of thought views organismal aging as due to autonomous changes taking place in individual cells. Consequently, much effort has focused on deciphering the age-related changes taking place in individual cells in both *in vitro* and *in vivo* situations. Changes have been found in the number and kinds of molecules present in the cell, in the activity of various enzymatic and repair systems operating in the cell, in the ability of the cell to divide mitotically in particular environments, and so forth. One can describe and catalogue these age-related changes that take place in a short-lived cell, such as a fibroblast or an intestinal cell. Does this knowledge then assist us in understanding the biology of a long-lived cell, such as a neuron? What is the relationship between the longevity and senescence of any component level, such as molecules, organelles, cells, tissues, or organs, and the longevity and senescence of the whole organism? Will the knowledge obtained from any single organizational level be sufficient to provide us with a model for aging in the whole animal? Is there a better way to proceed? These are important questions that are not easy to answer. Yet our perception of the form that the answers might take will inevitably guide the course of future research in gerontology. These answers, which we will struggle with in later chapters, will probably be constrained by the following three observations.

First, mere turnover of a component, whether molecules or cells, does not necessarily constitute an age-related change as defined here. Second, transferring a term from one organizational level to another often results in semantic confusion. For example, we talk of the life span of cells. At the organismal level, "life span" is an unambiguous term because it has a well-defined end point—death. Yet not all cells are destined to die before the organism does. Many cells (such as neurons) exist as viable functioning entities throughout the life span of the organism. Other cells end their individual existence by dividing mitotically into two daughter cells, which will themselves undergo mitosis later. Does the term "life span" refer to the individual cells or to the whole clonal line of cells? If, for example, we choose the former alternative, then we are equating organismal death with mitotic reproduction. If we choose the latter definition, then what does this definition mean when the organism dies even though the clonal lines of cells of which it was composed are still alive at the point of death? Forcing the identity appears to lead us to equate very different processes.

And finally, are the age-related changes observed in one organizational level intrinsic and autonomous, or are they a secondary consequence of deteriorative changes occurring elsewhere in the body? Does neuronal death imply a programmed life span in which the cell dies because its clock has reached midnight? Has the cell died because of a specific neurotoxin, or has the neuron died simply because a failure in respiratory and/or cardiovascular functions has resulted in a lethal lowering of the oxygen supply?

Despite these cautions, it must be said that the senescence of the whole animal ultimately must be caused by changes in the lower levels of organization. We will pragmatically adopt a reductionist approach, believing that only by studying aging at the lower levels of organization will we ever be able to understand the nature and causes of the age-dependent declines in the survivability of the whole organism. But we must not be too enthusiastic in this approach, lest we become too simplistic in our interpretations.

Choosing an Experimental Organism

The choice of an experimental organism is dictated both by pragmatic considerations and by one's perception of the goal of gerontology. If one perceives the goal to be the study and understanding of human aging only, then the value of any proposed experimental organism will be in direct proportion to its biological similarity to humans. The more distant the evolutionary relatedness between "us" and "them," the less useful are the lessons to be learned and thus the less desirable they are as models with which to study aging. The use of such less desirable organisms might be justified on the basis of pragmatic considerations of cost or time or because of their special utility in answering a particular question, but they are a poor substitute for humans in such studies.

Another approach views the study of aging as leading to the eventual understanding of a fundamental biological phenomenon, one that is an intrinsic evolutionary part of the life history of most organisms. In this viewpoint, aging is as worthy of study in its own right as is developmental biology. In fact, one definition of developmental biology describes it as "the progress of an organism through its life cycle" (Ham and Veomett 1980, p. 5). This definition clearly includes aging as a major (although somewhat neglected) component of the overall development of the organism. Nature has evolved an overwhelming diversity of life cycles. It is my perception that developmental biologists choose an experimental organism on the basis of the particular insights provided by that system into how a particular fundamental biological process is expressed in a group of related life cycles, and not solely on the basis of its perceived utility to human beings. Accordingly, although insights and application of these studies to human biology would be anticipated and even welcomed, they are not the sole justification of these endeavors. As Moment (1982, p. 4) wrote:

> The deepest unity of life is undeniable. Consequently there is no animal and, in theory at least, no plant from which information might not be gained which would be applicable to human aging. All the cytochromes are much the same throughout the plant and animal kingdoms. . . . The DNA spiral is the same everywhere and its behavior is the same whether in spore formation between the gills of a mushroom or in gamete formation within the gonads of a mouse.

This approach has been extraordinarily effective in deciphering the mechanisms regulating embryonic development. Nonetheless, there is no more reason to believe that the underlying mechanisms of aging must be the same in all organisms than there is reason to believe that all organisms develop in exactly the same way. On both the anatomical and the biochemical level, the same functional requirements may be met in very different ways. Thus the information obtained from invertebrates may not be directly applicable to vertebrates in general or to humans in particular. However, fundamental biological processes are usually quite similar to one another in different organisms, once one makes allowances for the structural and/or functional differences in the different systems. Thus the study of different organisms wisely chosen is likely to be of great value in allowing us to identify the diversity of mechanisms that underlie aging and senescence in our own species.

No single animal or plant model is the best one in which to study aging processes. An investigator's choice of an animal model depends on various criteria, not the least of which is the nature of the question being asked. For example, a genetic analysis of the mechanisms of aging almost by necessity focuses the choice on organisms, such as *Drosophila melanogaster* (the fruit fly), *Caenorhabditis elegans* (the nematode worm), or *Mus musculus* (the lab mouse), that are well suited by virtue of the genetic tools and knowledge that has been deliberately accumulated about them over the years. Other experimental goals might be (1) describing the changes with normal aging within one species, (2) describing and analyzing the causes of longevity within or between species, or (3) describing and analyzing models of accelerated or decelerated aging (Weindruch 1995a). Each of these goals would impose its own constraints on the choice of the organism to study. Birds, for example, live much longer than mammals of comparable size (Holmes and Austad 1995a,b); hence they might serve as one component of the comparisons referred to in the second or third options outlined here.

An analysis by Weindruch (1995a) of animal usage patterns in gerontology studies during the two decades from 1972 to 1992 reveals that most of the 2,476 reports sampled studied either rats (48 percent) or mice (28 percent). *Drosophila*, the third most popular organism, accounted for only 5.3 percent of the studies.

Another large gap separates this number from the percentage of studies done on all other organisms (a total of 18.7 percent)—which include nematodes, houseflies, rabbits, hamsters, fish, protozoans, birds, dogs, nonhuman primates, other insects, lizards, cows, and a herd of other rarely studied beasts—at frequencies ranging from 0.2 to 2.0 percent.

There is an obvious risk that our knowledge will be overly dependent on aging processes easily studied in rodents and that consequently we will miss an important insight that might be best obtained in another, rarely studied animal model. The situation is even worse than one might imagine, since half the rat studies are based on the use of only the male Fisher 344 (F344) rat strain. The dangers of this overreliance on one strain are well illustrated by the fact that the older F344 rat develops nephropathy (a kidney defect) when fed a diet containing casein as the protein source but not when fed a soy protein diet or a calorie-restricted casein diet. In the absence of the latter two facts, it would have been—and was—easy to conclude erroneously that kidney failure is a normal component of aging in rats. Only by comparison of that conclusion with data taken from other strains was the error recognized and corrected. Fortunately, the National Institute on Aging quickly recognized the need to develop and support rat and mouse strains well suited for again research, along with developing sophisticated genetic techniques to best probe their aging mechanisms (Harrison and Roderick, 1997; Sprott, 1997).

Similar traps await those who wish to base their knowledge of aging solely on human geriatric studies. A comparative biological approach to the study of aging and senescence is the most prudent and conservative course available to us. Approaching this field of inquiry with a less anthropomorphic point of view may not tell us directly how to manipulate the human life span, but it does promise to be the most efficient approach that will tell us which physiological systems and which organizational levels we should investigate.

Problems Peculiar to Gerontology

Regardless of the species chosen for study, many animals of good quality are needed for studies on aging. "Good quality" is a nebulous term that may mean different things to different investigators. Certainly, investigators should comply with all applicable regulations, not merely because of legal implications but because any investigator worth his or her salt would want to use healthy animals so as not to confound aging with disease. The details of animal husbandry will depend on whether the animals must be germ-free, or free of a specified pathogen, or the like. Once these criteria are decided, the next decision involves numbers.

Aged animals are, by definition, survivors. If an investigator devises an experiment that will require the use of ten very old rats, he or she must be prepared to set up a large starting population of young animals and/or be prepared to pay the cost of rearing the colony for 3 years. For example, Sprague-Dawley nonbreeding male rats have a mean life span of about 27 months and a maximum of about 37 months (National Research Council 1981). Ninety percent of the animals are dead by 32 months. The ability to determine these numbers depends on the availability of good life span data for the strains and species being used. In the absence of such basic quantitative data, what one investigator calls an old animal will likely be considered middle-aged or even young by another investigator. This has been a major source of confusion in the past. Thus, if ten 32-month-old rats were required for an experiment, the full cost of these old rats to our investigator would have to reflect the entire cost of raising 100 animals in order to harvest the surviving ten. The prices could easily reach several hundred dollars per animal. Old rats and mice of defined strains can be bought at reasonable prices only because of the collections developed and subsidized by the National Institute on Aging (Sprott 1991). The same problems arise regardless of the species being examined; old flies are proportionately expensive as well. The age of the animals illustrates two of the major problems confronting gerontology research: the need to plan experiments months or years ahead, and the extraordinarily high cost of aged animals.

For any animal model, then, the life span should be short, as a matter of convenience and expense. Yet it would not do if the life span were short because the animals were dying prematurely of an infectious disease or other preventable pathology. And it would not do if we let the convenience of a short life span cause us not to investigate the mechanisms promoting a long life span. In addition, the environmental conditions necessary for an optimal life span should be known and defined over the entire life span. Failure to control these conditions, as in the case of the F344 rats fed casein, may lead to incorrect conclusions.

Incidentally, there is no substitute for animal experimentation in biogerontology. Since we do not know the biological mechanisms that underlie the aging process, clearly we cannot use "substitutes" such as computers, which cannot synthesize knowledge but can only reflect our own ignorance. Computer simulations are proving to be very valuable, but as an adjunct and companion to animal studies.

• *The Plasticity of Aging*

Intraspecific Plasticity

The longevity of an organism is a phenotype. That is, it is one of the observable properties of an organism that are produced by the interaction between the organism's genetic potential (its genotype) and its environment. The life span can be affected not only by changes in the genotype alone or in the environment alone, but also by changes in the manner in which these two variables interact. This change in the expressed phenotype of a genotype as a function of the environment is termed phenotypic plasticity (Scheiner 1993). Mice provide an example of this phenomenon. One might expect inbred mice—which are so genetically similar that they can accept skin grafts from one another—raised in a constant and defined environment to exhibit identical life spans. They don't; there is always a significant variance about the mean (Witten 1994; Ghirardi et al. 1995). In this case we can only conclude that we have fully defined neither the genetic nor the environmental factors, nor the interactions between them.

An example of phenotypic plasticity in which we have at least partly defined one of the environmental parameters and its interaction with a particular genotype is the case of the F344 rat and its diet, as described earlier. Clearly the presence of casein rather than soy protein in the diet has an effect on renal tissue such that almost all the rats will develop nephropathy by 27 months of age. This premature mortality, and its concomitant effect on the life span of the population, is due to the interaction between the F344 genome and this specific dietary component. If it were a simple interaction, all the rats would show the phenotype of renal neuropathy at the same age. The fact that there is some variability in the incidence and age of onset suggests that the interactions between the genetic and environmental factors are complex and that we are far from precisely defining each of them.

Two methods of dealing effectively with a multitude of complex and ill-defined interactions are to employ statistical analyses (Scheiner 1993) or to use computer modeling or simulation studies (Witten 1992; Kowald and Kirkwood 1996). Both caloric restriction and ambient temperature are examples of stringent and defined environmental variables that bring about widespread and partly defined changes in the patterns of gene expression within the organism and in all levels of the longevity phenotype expressed by the affected organism (see Chapter 7 for a more detailed discussion). Different genomes often respond in uniquely different ways to each of these variables. Chapter 3 offers a more detailed description of particular environmental effects.

The life span phenotype of an organism, or of a population, is modulated—often quite significantly—by environmental factors. The phenotypic plasticity, as defined here, arises from that common observation. Such plasticity rests, at least in part, on two different types of genetic effects (Via et al. 1995): First, some alleles may be expressed differentially in particular environments, with varying effects on the phenotype. Second, regulatory loci, sensitive to environmental perturbations, may cause other genes to be turned on or off in particular environments. The major result of this interaction between genotype and environment for biogerontology is that we can, even in principle, speak of a particular longevity as being characteristic of the organism only in a defined but limited set of environments. There is no single life span for all seasons.

Interspecific Plasticity

We tend to judge what we do not yet know by an extension of what is already familiar to us. This method often helps us grasp the unfamiliar, but it can lead us into difficulties. Humans and the various domesticated animals with which we are familiar age in a similar manner. After a developmental period that culminates in sexual maturity, adults maintain physical vigor for a relatively long period of time before beginning to manifest progressive dysfunctions in various physiological systems over a relatively extended period of time. Despite the substantial differences in absolute life span, the pattern of aging in humans, dogs, cats, horses, mice, and other placental mammals follows this progression. Life spans range from the 1 year of the shrew to the 120 years of the human. But not all organisms age in this familiar manner. What are we to make of the mayfly, which lives but 1 day? Or the Pacific salmon or octopus, each of which spawn once and die? And how are we to understand the senescence of an organism such as the bristlecone pine, which can live as long as 5,000 years? Between the mayfly and the bristlecone pine lies an almost incomprehensible millionfold difference in life span. We need to impose some order on nature's exuberant and untidy range of longevities and thus begin the abstraction necessary to understanding.

Finch (1990) has proposed that we characterize senescence by viewing it as a continuum with three general subdivisions according to the observed rate of degenerative change: rapid, gradual, or negligible. This approach has proven to be a most useful organizing principle, and the description that follows is drawn from Finch's description (1990, pp. 9–10). The first point is that these patterns of senescence are not intended to represent discrete and absolute categories arising from the operation of three different mechanisms. Environmental effects such as temperature or nutrition can shift the rate of senescence of certain species from rapid to gradual, or vice versa. The categories are rather plastic and depend on the interplay of environmental and developmental factors with the organism's genome.

Rapid senescence is characterized by the rapid onset of major pathophysiological changes at a particular common time after maturation in most or all members of a birth cohort. These changes quickly cause exponential increases in mortality rates (see Chapter 2), as well as the death of most members of the cohort within a relatively short period of time, usually a year or less. Thus senescence and death occur almost synchronously throughout the population. Mayflies and other short-lived invertebrates are considered to exhibit rapid senescence. But rapid senescence is evident also in other species, some of which are quite long lived but are characterized by a long developmental or juvenile phase that culminates in a short but intense period of reproduction, after which the organism dies. Examples of such semelparous species (see Chapter 4), as organisms that reproduce only once in their life span are called, include the Pacific salmon, the octopus, the marsupial mice, and most species of bamboo. The reproductive fitness (a measure of physiological functioning; see Chapter 4) of such species reaches a maximum value but once and then vanishes.

Gradual senescence, which characterizes almost all placental mammals, is the familiar pattern of aging sketched out earlier. One important and diagnostic difference between rapid and gradual senescence patterns is that the latter does not display synchronous senescence and death. Another difference is that the reproductive fitness of organisms displaying gradual senescence generally reaches an early peak or plateau and then gradually decays to zero. Here again, human reproductive patterns can serve as a familiar guide (but see Chapter 5).

Negligible senescence is assumed to operate in long-lived species for which it has not yet been possible to describe dysfunctional changes. Since no individual is immortal, such senescent changes must take place in all organisms. But given the fact that many of these long-lived species live in habitats that are inconvenient for scientists (for example, underwater) or substantially outlive the scientists studying them (such as sequoias, bristlecones, and other trees), it is not surprising that our knowledge of such species increases only very slowly. However, one indication that we have correctly categorized these species as showing negligible senescence is that many of them show an increase in reproductive fitness as they grow older. This would not happen if they were senescing.

Finch (1990) has speculated that the tetrapod ancestors had a slow rate of senescence as a primitive trait and that the other patterns represent derived or secondary traits. These three patterns of senescence are not evolutionarily distinct in the sense of being restricted to only certain related phylogenetic groups; rather they are scattered among a variety of different such groups. The life history characteristics of any particular species appear to play a deciding role as to the type of senescence pattern the population will display (see Chapter 4).

• *Summary*

It is difficult, yet essential, to define aging—difficult because aging is a complex phenomenon affecting many different systems in an individualistic manner; essential because it would be nice to agree on exactly what constitutes the topic of our investigations. After reviewing others' definitions, we have defined aging as the time-independent series of cumulative, progressive, intrinsic, and deleterious (CPID) functional and structural changes that usually begin to manifest themselves at reproductive maturity and eventually culminate in death. However, aging is a mosaic process at both the population and the individual levels. Not all members of a population age in exactly the same way; not all the organs and tissues of one individual age at the same rate. Life span is a plastic phenotype, as evidenced by the organization of the data into three organismal patterns of senescence (rapid, gradual, and negligible). Finally, there is no reason to doubt that aging is a widespread and fundamental biological process. Although the real differences among species must be duly considered, a comparative approach to the biology of aging will best tell us which physiological systems and which organizational level may reveal insights into human aging.

2

Measuring Age-Related Changes in Populations

Introduction

Senescence is a deteriorative process. It is very difficult to predict the increasing probability of dying of any given individual. The estimates we do have and use are based on the statistical analysis of a population of like organisms. When constructed in the form of a survival curve in which we use death as the measure of the end point, this procedure is informative, although subject to all the simplifying assumptions mentioned in the previous chapter. However, the mere fact that a cohort of organisms eventually dies does not necessarily mean that the population underwent aging and senescence. Death does not require aging. All the organisms in a population may have died of accidental causes before any of them had the chance to display senescent changes.

Very clearly, then, aging and death are not the same thing. All populations die, but not all of them die of age-related causes. We must have a method of reliably distinguishing aging from nonaging populations, if for no other reason than to keep us from wasting our time examining populations that cannot serve us in our search to understand the biological bases of aging. The analysis of survival curves will accomplish that task, and in the bargain it will give us some additional useful information about the dynamics of the aging process.

Life Tables and Survival Curves

Let's begin with an example in which we assume that we have a population of 1,000 mature individuals who do not deteriorate in any way as chronological time passes. They are potentially immortal. Let's assume further that the only causes of death are predation and accidents, and that these random events have an equal chance of happening to a young organism as to an older one. Finally, let's assume that the predation rate is 20 percent per year. What would the survival curve for such an odd population look like? What would be the values of the various statistical parameters?

Constructing a life table is one way to answer these queries. A life table is a concise and standardized summary of the survival statistics in relation to age and was originally developed to meet the needs of the insurance industry. The tabular format has no theoretical basis, but reflects an empirical approach to the measurement of mortality. A survival curve is a graphical representation of the data in a life table. A good but brief discussion of life tables may be found in Chapter 2 of Rustagi 1985. As Table 2.1 shows, seven different kinds of numerical relationships are found in most life tables, as follows:

x = the age interval, with the time units specified by the person constructing the table. The initial age is represented by x, the following ages by $x + t$, $x + 2t$, $x + 3t$, and so forth, where t is the time interval (days, weeks, months, years) used in the particular case.

l_x = the number of organisms alive at the beginning of each interval. In most but not all cases, this number must be obtained by counting the population. As such, it represents the raw data. All other values in the table are derived from this number.

d_x = the number of animals dying during each age interval; that is, the number of deaths between age x and age $x + t$. This number is obtained either by counting or by subtraction of the second census number from the first. If it is obtained by counting, in some cases it could represent the raw data from which the other values are derived.

q_x = the age-specific death rate, or the proportion of the animals alive at the beginning of the age interval that die during that interval. This number is obtained as shown by the following equation: $q_x = d_x/l_x$.

L_x = the average number of animals alive during the age interval x. An approximate value of this number is obtained by taking the average of the two succeeding time intervals (t), as shown by the equation

$$L_x = \frac{l_x + \left(l_x + t\right)}{2}$$

T_x = the total number of organism age units to be lived by the total number of organisms alive at the beginning of the age interval. This number may be obtained by summing the values of L_x, as shown by the equation

$$T_x = L(x) + L(x + t) + L(x + 2t) + \ldots$$

e_x = the mean further expectation of life at the beginning of the age interval x. A close approximation of this value may be obtained by using the value of T_x, as shown in the equation

Table 2.1 **A Life Table for a Hypothetical Population of Organisms with a Constant Mortality Rate**[a]

x	l_x	d_x	q_x	L_x	T_x	e_x
0–1	1000	200	0.2	900	5000	5
1–2	800	160	0.2	720	4000	5
2–3	640	128	0.2	576	3200	5
3–4	512	102	0.2	461	2560	5
4–5	410	82	0.2	369	2050	5
5–6	328	66	0.2	295	1640	5
6–7	262	52	0.2	236	1310	5
7–8	210	42	0.2	189	1050	5
8–9	168	34	0.2	151	840	5
9–10	134	27	0.2	121	670	5
10–11	107	21	0.2	96.5	535	5
11–12	86	17	0.2	77.5	430	5
12–13	69	14	0.2	62	345	5
13–14	55	11	0.2	49.5	275	5
14–15	44	9	0.2	39.5	220	5
15–16	35	7	0.2	31.5	175	5
16–17	28	6	0.2	25	140	5
17–18	22	4	0.2	20	110	5
18–19	18	4	0.2	16	90	5
19–20	14	3	0.2	12.5	70	5
20–21	11	2	0.2	10	55	5
21–22	9	2	0.2	8	45	5
22–23	7	1	0.2	6.5	35	5
23–24	6	1	0.2	5.5	30	5
24–25	5	1	0.2	4.5	25	5
25–26	4	1	0.2	3.5	20	5
26–27	3	1	0.2	2.5	15	5
27–28	2	1	0.2	1.5	10	5
28–29	1	1	0.2	0.5	5	5
29–30	0	—	—	—	—	—

Source: From Lamb 1977. © John Wiley and Sons.
[a]See text for explanation of variables.

$$e_x \cong \frac{T_x}{l_x}$$

Note that the accuracy of this estimate depends on the values of x (column 1 of Table 2.1) and of q_x (column 4), and increases as these values decrease. In cases where the age interval, x, may be a value other than 1 unit (1 day, 1 year, and so on), then

$$e_x \cong \frac{\left(T_x\right)\left(\text{length of age interval}\right)}{l_x}$$

One convention of note is that the number of organisms involved is always adjusted so that the value of l_x in a life table is 1,000 (or 100,000 for human populations). In most cases the data on which the life table is based represent only a fraction of this nominal number. Remember that the values in all the columns can be derived from the given values of x and l_x.

Having briefly described the tabular arrangement of a life table, let's construct one for our hypothetical population of potentially immortal organisms. Plotting the survival data, l_x, of Table 2.1 yields the survival curve shown in Figure 2.1. The curve shows an exponential decrease of mortality with time. A distribution plot of the absolute numerical value of d_x also decreases with time, simply because in each succeeding age interval there are fewer survivors left to die (Figure 2.2). As specified in our initial assumption, the value of q_x is a constant (in this case set equal to 0.2) and therefore plots as a straight line with time (Figure 2.3). The values of L_x and of T_x do not give rise to graphical plots; rather they are used to calculate the value of e_x, the further expectation of life at the beginning of age interval x. Since q_x has been defined as a constant in this population, it follows that the average expectation of further life at any age for our hypothetical organism is 5 years.

Therefore, a population that dies as result of random predation rather than of senescence generally displays the following characteristics:

1. The number surviving is a decreasing exponential function of time.

2. The age-specific death rate is constant at all ages.

3. The further expectation of life is constant at all ages.

As a result of these three characteristics, the probability of any individual living long enough to age is almost zero. Thus, unless the original population were quite

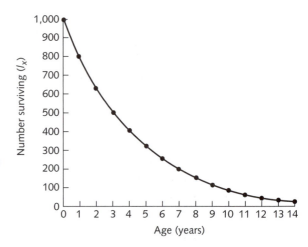

Figure 2.1   A survival curve, based on the l_x data of Table 2.1, for the population of individuals that do not senesce, but die as a result of accidental events that affect 20 percent of the survivors each year. See text for further explanation. (From Lamb 1977. © John Wiley and Sons.)

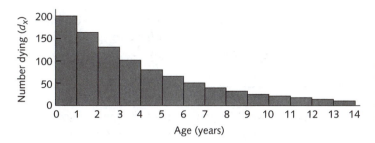

Figure 2.2 Distribution of the ages at death in a population of individuals that do not senesce, based on the d_x data of Table 2.1. (From Lamb 1977. © John Wiley and Sons.)

large, it is highly improbable that there would be any individual aging survivors. Even if there were one or two such survivors, their presence could not alter the fact that the population as a whole died from non-age-related phenomena. (See Witten 1994 for a more detailed description.)

Suppose we alter the assumptions underlying this life table such that a constant number—not a constant proportion—of our hypothetical population would die in each time period. The life table for this altered population is shown in Table 2.2. The graphs corresponding to the values of l_x, d_x, and q_x are shown in Figure 2.4a, b, and c, respectively. The survival curve (Figure 2.4a) describes a linear decrease with time, since the constant number of deaths represents a larger and larger proportion of the dwindling number of survivors. The value of d_x (Figure 2.4b) is constant by definition. Note particularly the very large difference in the values of e_x, the expectation of further life at birth, between the two populations of Tables 2.1 and 2.2.

These are interesting theoretical distributions. Do any real populations have life table characteristics similar to those of either of these two hypothetical populations? Inanimate yet breakable objects might be a good real-world substitute for our hypothesized nonaging and supposedly immortal organisms. A life table for cafeteria tumblers was constructed from empirical data; the corresponding survival curves are shown in Figure 2.5. The survival curve for ordinary (annealed) tumblers approximates the exponentially decaying curve that is characteristic of a constant age-specific death rate (as in Figure 2.1). The survival curve for toughened tumblers approximates the linear decay that is characteristic of a constant, age-independent number of deaths (as in Figure 2.4). In this case, the toughened

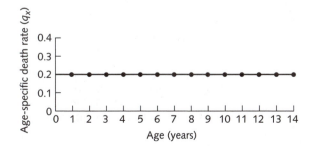

Figure 2.3 Plot of the age-specific death rate in a population of organisms that do not senesce, based on the q_x data of Table 2.1. (From Lamb 1977. © John Wiley and Sons.)

Table 2.2   **A Life Table for a Hypothetical Population of Organisms with a Constant Number of Deaths**

x	l_x	d_x	q_x	L_x	T_x	e_x
0–1	1000	200	0.20	900	2500	2.8
1–2	800	200	0.25	700	1600	2.3
2–3	600	200	0.33	500	900	1.8
3–4	400	200	0.55	300	400	1.3
4–5	200	200	1.00	100	100	1.0
5–6	0	—	—	—	—	—

Source: From Lamb 1977. © John Wiley and Sons.

tumblers have a constant but much lower number of "deaths" per time interval, and consequently have a higher e_0 (Witten 1984, 1987).

Such curves are often found in the biological world as well. Figure 2.6 shows the survival curve for wild lapwings in Britain. It is a clear-cut exponential survival curve with a value of e_x that is constant between 2.2 and 2.6 years throughout most of the life span. Similarly, it is not uncommon to find linear

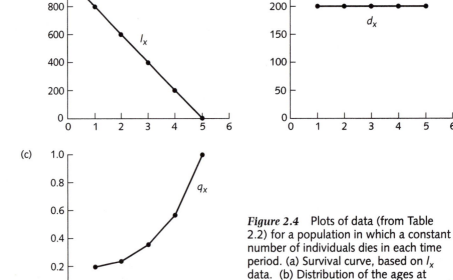

Figure 2.4   Plots of data (from Table 2.2) for a population in which a constant number of individuals dies in each time period. (a) Survival curve, based on l_x data. (b) Distribution of the ages at death, based on d_x data. (c) Plot of age-specific death rate, based on q_x data.

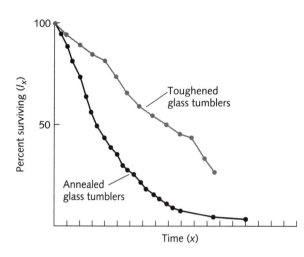

Figure 2.5 Survival curves for inanimate cafeteria tumblers. Each scale division equals 2 weeks. The lower curve depicts the (exponential) survival of 549 annealed glass tumblers. The top curve depicts the (linear) survival of 241 toughened glass tumblers. (Based on Comfort 1965, from data of Brown and Flood 1947.)

curves in the biological world, as Figure 2.7 illustrates. Should this observation be interpreted as meaning that these organisms are not subject to senescence? Obviously the answer is no, for most animals raised in captivity typically have an average expectation of life that far exceeds that observed in wild populations. The explanation for this apparent paradox is that in wild populations, the death rate from predation and other random events is so great that senescence has no chance to appear. Almost all members of the cohort are dead before vigor has declined significantly. The onset of senescence is impossible to detect from a life table if the mortality in early and adult life is very high. No individual has a chance to grow old.

If we measured the survival of a biological population maintained under laboratory conditions, we would construct a life table very similar to that shown in

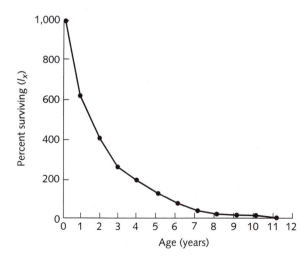

Figure 2.6 An exponential survival curve for lapwings, based on 460 birds banded as nestlings. Note the similarity of this empirical curve to the hypothetical curves depicted in Figures 1.5a and 2.1. The curve is based on data from Lack 1943. (From Lamb 1977. © John Wiley and Sons.)

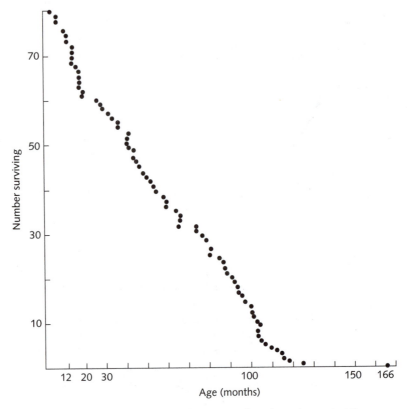

Figure 2.7   A linear survival curve for 77 mouflon sheep housed at the London Zoo. The data begin only after the first year of life and combine the male and female mortality information. (From Comfort 1979. © Holt, Rinehart and Winston.)

Table 2.3. In this case, a cohort of 750 newly hatched adult male *Drosophila* was reared and maintained under controlled conditions of temperature, light, humidity, and so forth. The animals were transferred to fresh food every 4 days and the number of flies that died in each time interval was counted. Note that this is a longitudinal study. The number dead at each age were multiplied by 1.33 (1,000/750) in order to normalize the d_x values to a standard population size. All of the subsequent calculations were based on these scaled d_x values. Note that the investigator chose to count the dead animals, but that she could equally well have chosen to count the living animals at each interval and thus constructed an l_x-based life table. If the counts were accurate, the two life tables would be identical. Figure 2.8a, b, and c illustrate the graphical plots for the survival curve (l_x), the distribution of ages at death (d_x), and the age-specific death rate (q_x), respectively.

Comparison of these curves to those illustrated in Figures 2.1 or 2.2 makes clear that this biological population differs markedly from our hypothesized nonaging populations in these three life table characteristics such that:

Table 2.3   A Life Table for Adult Male *Drosophila* Raised in the Laboratory

x (days)	$n_x{}^a$	l_x	d_x	q_x	L_x	T_x	e_x
0–4	750	1000	0	0	1000.0	11864	47.5
4–8	750	1000	1	0.001	999.5	10864	43.3
8–12	749	999	4	0.004	997.0	9864.5	39.3
12–16	746	995	7	0.007	991.5	8867.5	35.5
16–20	741	988	5	0.005	985.5	7876.0	31.9
20–24	737	983	7	0.007	979.5	6890.5	28.0
24–28	732	976	17	0.017	967.5	5911.0	24.2
28–32	719	959	23	0.024	947.5	4943.5	20.6
32–36	702	936	72	0.077	900.0	3996.0	17.1
36–40	648	864	116	0.134	806.0	3096.0	14.3
40–44	561	748	178	0.238	659.0	2290.0	12.2
44–48	421	570	125	0.219	507.5	1631.0	11.4
48–52	334	445	107	0.240	391.5	1123.5	10.1
52–56	254	338	111	0.328	282.5	732.0	8.7
56–60	170	227	83	0.366	185.5	449.5	7.9
60–64	108	144	39	0.271	124.5	264.0	7.3
64–68	79	105	51	0.486	79.5	139.5	5.3
68–72	41	54	29	0.537	39.5	60.0	4.4
72–76	19	25	17	0.680	16.5	20.5	3.3
76–80	6	8	8	1.000	4.0	4.0	2.0
80–84	0	0	—	—	—	—	—

Source: From Lamb 1977. © John Wiley and Sons.
$^a n_x$ is the actual number of animals present at the beginning of each time period; it is these raw numbers that are adjusted to yield the standardized numbers listed under l_x.

1. The survival curve is more rectangular; that is, very few individuals died early in life.

2. The distribution of ages at death reaches a peak value late in the life span of the population.

3. The further expectation of life decreases with increasing age.

4. The age-specific death rate increases with age.

These characteristics would be expected if the organisms were dying as the result of cumulative, progressive, intrinsic, and deleterious (CPID) changes that resulted in an increased susceptibility to death—that is, if they were dying of old age. After a certain age the organisms die from proximate causes that would not have killed them in their youth. Their susceptibility has increased. Therefore, the preliminary evidence for the presence of aging and senescence in a population is the presence of a more or less rectangular shaped survival curve.

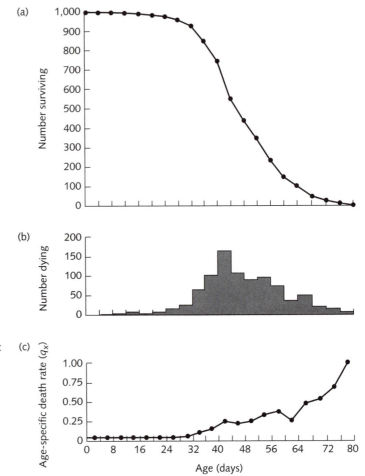

(a)

(b)

Figure 2.8 The survival
curve, distribution of ages at
death, and plot of age-specific
death rate for the population
of male *Drosophila melanogaster* whose life table is
shown in Table 2.3. Note the
similarity of these empirical
curves to the hypothetical
curves in Figure 1.5b and c.
(From Lamb 1977. © John
Wiley and Sons.)

(c)

A variation of this type of survival curve would result if the population were
subjected to an initial period of high juvenile mortality followed by a plateau with
very few deaths until the onset of senescence, when the age-specific mortality
would increase. A survival curve for such a population is shown in Figure 2.9.
This sort of curve is typical of many populations of large mammals such as
impalas, zebras, buffalo, and humans (Spinage 1972) (see Figure 2.16). Figure
2.9 is based on the analysis of 608 skulls of wild Dall mountain sheep that died at
an unknown time before being collected. The age of these sheep at death was
determined by a count of the annual growth rings on the horns. There was no
way of determining the cause of death of individual animals—whether illness,
predation, or natural causes. The corresponding life table (Table 2.4) and this survival curve are based on d_x data, for the investigator had no other recourse. All
other numbers in the life table were generated from this cross-sectional d_x data,
on the assumption that the population consisted of 1,000 individuals and had a
constant age structure. Of interest here is the existence of two periods of rela-

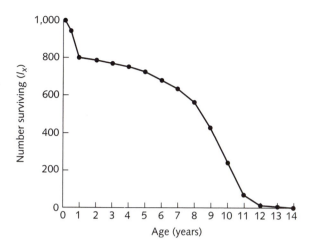

Figure 2.9 A survival curve for Dall mountain sheep, based on the remains of 608 sheep (see Table 2.4) whose age at death was determined from the annual growth rings on the horns. See text for explanation. (From Lamb 1977, based on data of Murie as given in Deevey 1947. © John Wiley and Sons.)

tively heavy mortality—very early in life and then again very late in life—with high survival rates in the intermediate years. As already mentioned, this type of survival pattern appears to be common in large mammals, including humans.

Another type of theoretically possible survival curve might be expected in populations characterized by an enormously high death rate in early life, followed by a lower rate later in life. Populations of trees or of various fishes, for example,

Table 2.4 **A Life Table for Dall Mountain Sheep Based on Estimated Age at Death**

x (years)	l_x	d_x	$1000q_x$[a]	e_x
0–0.5	1000	54	54.0	7.06
0.5–1	946	145	153.0	—
1–2	801	12	15.0	7.7
2–3	789	13	16.5	6.8
3–4	776	12	15.5	5.9
4–5	764	30	39.3	5.0
5–6	734	46	62.6	4.2
6–7	688	48	69.9	3.4
7–8	640	69	108.0	2.6
8–9	571	132	231.0	1.9
9–10	439	187	426.0	1.3
10–11	252	156	619.0	0.9
11–12	96	90	937.0	0.6
12–13	6	3	500.0	1.2
13–14	3	3	1000.0	0.7

Source: From Deevey 1947. © Williams & Wilkins.
[a]Mortality rate per 1000 animals alive at beginning of age interval.

are characterized by high egg and juvenile mortality. Once established, however, the adult organisms have a significantly higher life expectancy than they did as juveniles, presumably because they are now much less susceptible to environmental effects. A similar situation applies to *Drosophila*; thus, if we assumed that the 1,000 adult males alive at the start of the life table in Table 2.3 were themselves the survivors of a 90 percent mortality affecting the egg and juvenile stages (a not unrealistic assumption for wild populations), then we could construct an L-shaped survival curve for this population as shown in Figure 2.10. An individual that survived the period of high initial mortality would thereafter enter a period in which the further expectation of life would be very long. In some species, the further expectation of life for the survivors might even increase with age; this phenomenon is believed to be true of certain trees. In this case, the value of l_x would only very slowly approach zero.

The different types of survival curves we have discussed are summarized in Figure 2.11. Curve A represents a population that suffers very little from deaths until the onset of senescence, at which time all the members of the cohort die more or less simultaneously. Incidentally, the same sort of highly rectangular curve could be generated by a catastrophic environmental event acting on the entire cohort at one particular time. For example, a commercial herd of beef cattle would show such a sharply rectangular curve, with most members of the cohort dying at 2 years of age. It would be ludicrous to consider such a survival curve as indicating a synchronized senescence. Therefore, one could distinguish the abnormal from the normal by a comparison of the mean and maximum life spans measured in each group. Identical values for both groups, or a maximum value that is abnormally low, could indicate the truncation of the survival curve by cohort-specific environmental effects. Curve B of Figure 2.11 represents a typical survival curve for an aging cohort, such as that shown in Figure 2.8a. However, a similar curve was found to apply equally well to inanimate objects such as automobiles (Pearl and Miner 1930). Curves C, D, and E represent the previously discussed linear, exponential, and L-shaped curves, respectively.

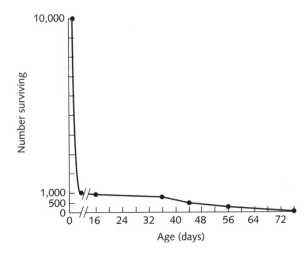

Figure 2.10 A survival curve for the *Drosophila* depicted in Figure 2.8a, based on the assumption that the 1,000 animals present at the start of adult life are themselves the survivors of a 90 percent rate of larval mortality.

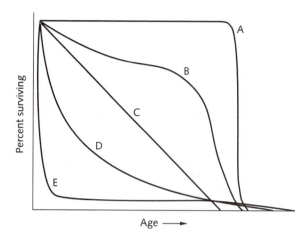

Figure 2.11 A compilation of the different types of survival curves observed in different populations. See text for explanation.

Our interest in life tables is prompted by the fact that the relationship between age and mortality that they display may tell us whether the population is senescing. Thus we would most likely be interested in studying further populations whose survival curve resembles either curve A or curve B in Figure 2.11. In addition, without the survival curve data, we would not be able to determine whether the life expectancy of an aging population could be improved and, if so, which portion of the life cycle should be the target of such interventions. Note that life expectancy can be calculated at any desired age. Although it is often used to denote the expected life span from the time of birth, it can also be used to estimate the life span expectancy given that an individual has lived to a specified age. What empirical basis do we have for implicitly concluding that the decreased probability of survival in these curves reflects an intrinsic biological process? Comfort (1979, p. 25) gave an excellent answer to this question, as Figure 2.12 shows:

> The accumulation of vulnerability with age is an all around and non-specific process. We can translate this into more concrete terms. The age distribution of pedestrian deaths in road accidents is similar in contour, excluding early infancy, to the general distribution of human deaths from all causes. This index is highly correlated with vigor, in its biological sense, for it represents a combination of sensory acuity, speed of avoidance, and power of recovery when hit.

Another consideration for the experimental gerontologist is the necessity of dealing with survival curves of different species, which may have similar shapes but very different absolute values. Such a comparative approach would be of value in discovering whether the "laws of mortality" are similar or different in different species. Is there a valid method of easily comparing such diverse data? One early approach to dealing with this problem was put forth by Pearl (1922), who proposed plotting the survivorship in equivalent life spans of different organisms versus percentiles of the life span. He defined equivalent life span as the period

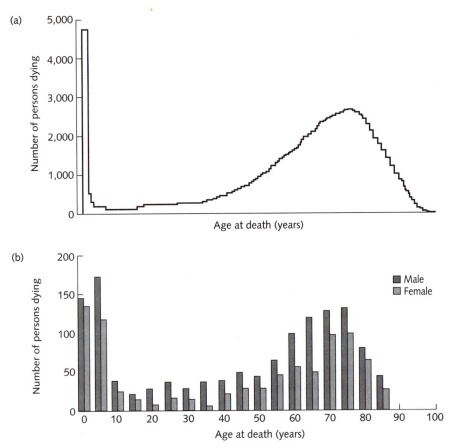

Figure 2.12 A comparison of survival curves for deaths due to aging versus deaths due to road accidents. (a) Distribution by age of all deaths in a privileged community, which thus presumably reflects mostly the deaths attributable primarily to aging. (b) Distribution by age of the deaths of pedestrians in road accidents. Note the similarity between the two curves. (From Comfort 1979. © Holt, Rinehart and Winston.)

between A, the point in the life history of each organism at which the value of q_x is at a minimum, and B, the point at which one survivor remains out of the 1,000 organisms starting at point A. Pearl then divided the span between these two points into 100 portions, thus measuring age in percentiles of the life span and not in absolute chronological terms. Pearl used this procedure to compare the survival curves of *Drosophila* and of humans, as shown in Figure 2.13, and thereby concluded that the laws of mortality are fundamentally the same in the two organisms. This comparison also allowed Pearl to suggest that 1 day in the life of a fly was approximately equivalent to 1 year in the life of a person. This procedure might well be the source of the other life span comparisons that we have all heard, such as the idea that 1 year in a human's life corresponds to 7 years in a dog's.

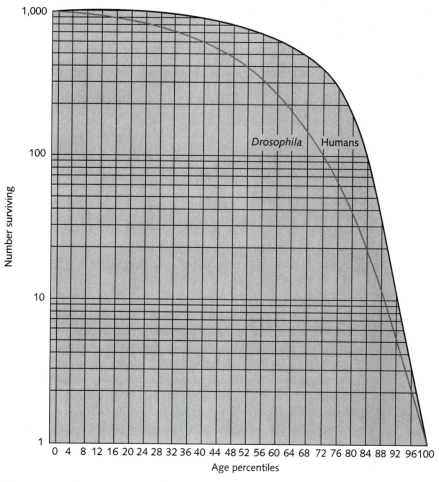

Figure 2.13   A comparison of the survival curves of *Drosophila* males and of human males during the equivalent life spans. See text for explanation. (From Pearl 1922.)

This method was subject to certain criticisms of a statistical nature. Seeking to improve on it, Pearl and Miner (1930) hit upon the idea of presenting the life table data not in absolute terms, but in terms of percentage deviations from the mean life span. Use of the mean has the advantage that all of the observed data play a role in its determination. The survival curves for three different species with very different life spans are shown in Figure 2.14. These l_x curves suggest that there is much more heterogeneity in the age at death in the herring gull population than in the other two populations. Applying the same process to the age-at-death (d_x) curves and to the death rate (q_x) curves yields similar comparisons. Interestingly, each type of survival curve depicted in Figure 2.14 is associated with its own characteristic sort of d_x and q_x functions. The similarities between

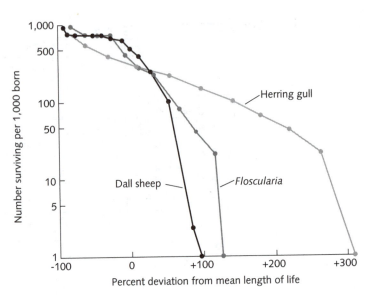

Figure 2.14 A comparison of the survival curves for three species with very different life spans, in which the age of the individuals within each species is expressed as the percentage deviation from the species-specific mean length of life. The mean life span for the Dall sheep is 7.09 years, for the herring gull 2.44 years, and for *Floscularia* (a sessile rotifer) 4.74 days. (From Deevey 1947.)

different species that have the same type of survival curve far outweigh the differences in absolute chronological periods characteristic of each. This observation suggested that the life history characteristics of various species are as much a species-specific characteristic as is their morphology. They also showed, however, that there are similarities of pattern in these life history characteristics of otherwise different species, thereby suggesting that the number of different biological processes involved in senescence and aging might be of a general nature and, therefore, that their number might be relatively small.

This conclusion was more important than was perhaps anticipated at the time, for if every species has a unique mechanism of senescence, it might prove very difficult to achieve any sort of general understanding. On the other hand, the possibility that there might be only a small number of ways in which organisms age would allow us to use a comparative approach to achieve the necessary insight. The similarity of fundamental biological processes has underlain much of our recent progress in biology. Eakin and Witten (1995a,b) have developed new methods for the uniform comparison of survival curves across species. The recent use of the "mortality rate doubling time," a concept derived from the use of the Gompertz plot of age-specific mortality (all of which we will discuss shortly), has simplified the comparison of the life history characteristics of different populations and species, and is now the major method by which such cross-comparisons are made.

● *Constructing Life Tables*

All of the life tables presented in the previous section were constructed on the basis of observations of a cohort of organisms born at the same time; the age of death of each individual was then recorded. Either the d_x curve or the l_x curve represents the primary data set; all other values in the life table are derived from this curve. Such cohort life tables can be constructed only for captive or laboratory populations. It is not possible to keep track of all individuals throughout their life in human or most other noncontrolled animal populations. In practice, then, human life tables must be constructed using data that have been obtained by other, indirect methods.

The differences between cohort and indirect life tables are essentially the same as those between longitudinal and cross-sectional studies, as discussed in Chapter 3. In the indirect approach, census data and death certificates for the same population are compared. Comparison of the age distribution of the population with the age distribution of deaths allows the value of the age-specific death rate, q_x, to be calculated for each age group represented in the original data. All other life table values are then derived from this secondary data set. This manipulation provides us with a cross-sectional sampling of the death rates for each age group in the population at the same time the data was originally collected. The age-specific death rates are those characteristic of the 1-year-olds, 2-year-olds, 3-year-olds, and so on, in that year. The result is not a true historical account of a cohort population. Given a constant environment and a constant age structure of the population, the two types of life tables would tend to approximate one another. These conditions do not apply to human populations. Not only do singular environmental events occur (such as the influenza pandemic of 1918–1919), but in human populations, there are at work long-term cultural trends (such as the introduction of antibiotics) that reduce the force of mortality. Figure 2.15 illustrates the indicated life table curves for an indirect human life table (Table 2.5) based on the population of England for 1960–1962.

A comparison of these curves with the corresponding ones derived from a cohort life table of *Drosophila* (see Figure 2.8) suggests that the general shape and pattern of the curves are quite similar. An indication of the long-term trends affecting this population is the alteration in the value of the age-specific death rate, q_x, for this population over a 50-year period (see Table 2.5). Note that the decrease in the force of mortality is age specific. There has been an 81 percent drop from 1910 to 1960 in the value of q_x at age 0, a 75 percent decrease at age 40, and only a 12 percent decline at age 80. These trends suggest that the forces responsible for the increase in life span noted during this half century have a larger impact on younger individuals than on older ones. The independently obtained set of human survival data shown in Figure 2.16 verifies this point while raising another issue. A comparison of the survival data for U.S. females in 1900 versus 1960 reveals that much of the increase in the mean life span was due to decreases in infant/child and middle-aged mortality. Comparing the 1960 data with the 1980 data shows that the latest increase in the mean life span was due to the postponement of elderly-adult mortality. Different forces must be affecting the mortality of different portions of the life cycle. We will return to this topic in the final section of this chapter and in Chapter 14. This last family of curves also shows that the large increase in human longevity known to have occurred in historical times was due to a decrease in premature death and not to any real increase in the maximum life span.

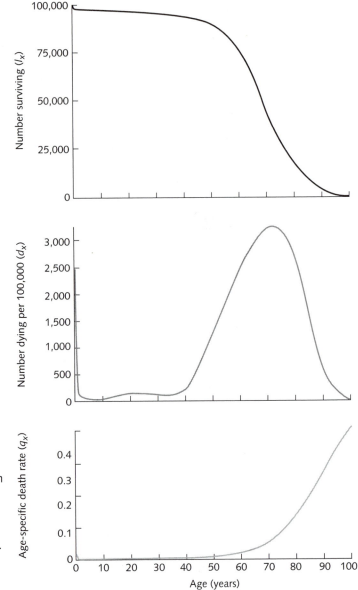

Figure 2.15   The curves illustrating the survival, distribution of ages at death, and age-specific death rate for human males in England in the period of time from 1960 to 1962, based on the data in Table 2.5. See text for explanation and discussion. (From Lamb 1977. © John Wiley and Sons.)

The difficulties in constructing a cohort life table for humans apply with equal force to obtaining accurate life tables for wild populations of animals. In certain cases, it is possible to ascertain the age of individuals directly—for example, by counting the growth rings in the scales of fishes, in the horns of ungulates, in the trunks of trees, or in the shells of mollusks. In these cases, a large random sampling of the population will allow its age structure (l_x) to be deter-

Table 2.5 **Secular Changes in the Force of Mortality (q_x) for English Males of Various Ages[a]**

Age (years)	1910–12	1920–22	1930–32	1940–42[b]	1950–52	1960–62
0	0.12044	0.08996	0.07186	—	0.03266	0.02499
10	0.00193	0.00181	0.00146	—	0.00052	0.00039
20	0.00348	0.00349	0.00316	—	0.00129	0.00119
40	0.00811	0.00688	0.00562	—	0.00290	0.00235
60	0.03042	0.02561	0.02415	—	0.02369	0.02287
80	0.14299	0.14002	0.14500	—	0.13629	0.12747

Source: From Lamb 1977, based on the Registrar General's Decennial Supplement, 1961.
© John Wiley and Sons.
[a]See text for an explanation of how these values are calculated.
[b]Records not available for these World War II years.

mined and an indirect life table to be constructed. If the indicator structures are stable and are not affected by postmortem changes, the remains of dead animals may be examined and the population's age at death (d_x) determined. The survival curve shown in Figure 2.9 (based on the data of Table 2.4) is of this type. Several of the more ecologically and statistically reliable life table data sets (such as that

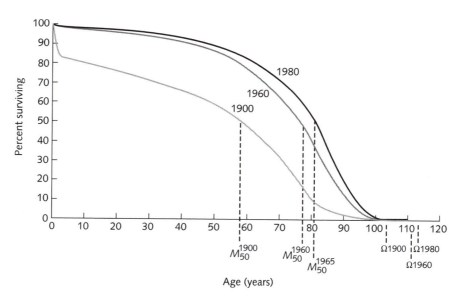

Figure 2.16 The survival curves for U.S. females in 1900, 1960, and 1980. M_{50} represents the age to which 50 percent of the individuals of each population survived. The symbol Ω represents the estimated maximum length of life for each population. (From Myers and Manton 1984.)

in Figure 2.9) have been reconstructed and reanalyzed by Miller (1988). These refined and empirically sound life tables will provide a rigorous test for any theory of aging as it manifests itself at the organismal and population levels.

• *Special Transformations of Survival Curves*

The preceding discussion makes clear that, in aging populations, the risk of death increases with age. This idea seems intuitively obvious, yet little could be done with this insight until it was quantitated. The mathematical relationship of that increase was first described by Benjamin Gompertz in 1825, and is an excellent example of the contributions of actuarial necessity to gerontology, for his motive in investigating this relationship was his need to be able to determine the future value of life annuities. This knowledge is crucial to the profitability of insurance companies, which must be able to adjust the premium charged to the risk entailed. Such information is useful in other ways to gerontologists today.

Gompertz found that the age-specific death rate increases as an exponential function of age:

$$q_x = (q_0)(e_x)$$

where

q_0 = further expectation of life at the time of birth, or the y intercept

q_x = further expectation of life at the beginning of an age interval, x

x = the slope constant

The equation can also be written in linear form as follows:

$$\ln q_x = \ln q_0 + x$$

which is, of course, a particular form of the general equation for a straight line:

$$y = b + mx$$

The discussion that follows reveals what is particularly interesting and useful about these equations. The age-specific mortality is defined as the probability of dying at a certain age among those individuals who have already survived to that age. Calculating these values for a given population, and plotting them versus age, produces curves of the types shown in Figure 2.17. When plotted in a linear fashion (Figure 2.17a), the rapid increase in the age-specific mortality over age 50 or so becomes very evident. The older you are, the greater the probability of death. This rapid increase is exactly what would be expected of an exponentially increasing function. In this kind of group, the rate of increase is so rapid that not much detail can be seen. It is inconvenient to make the scale of the graph much bigger than it is already, but when the same data are plotted semilogarithmically (Figure 2.17b), certain aspects of the curve stand out.

Ham and Veomett (1980) pointed out five distinct portions (labeled A to E in Figure 2.17) in the plot of human age-specific mortality. The very young are poorly adapted for survival and have a high mortality rate (A), due primarily to

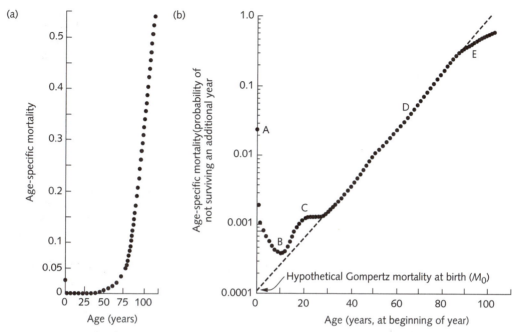

Figure 2.17 Plots of the age-specific mortality in the United States, 1959–1961. The mortality rates are plotted every 5 years up to age 75 and every year thereafter. (a) A linear plot. Note the great increase in mortality at advanced ages. (b) A semilogarithmic plot. The dots indicate the data points; the dashed line is an extrapolation of the data to age 100 and to age 0 in order to yield a hypothetical vulnerability to age-related death at the time of birth. The mortality doubles about every 8 years. The letters A through E are explained in the text. (From Ham and Veomett 1980, based on data from United States Life Tables 1959–1961, Vol. 1, No. 1, 1964. U.S. National Center for Health Statistics, Public Health Service, Department of Health and Human Services, Washington, DC.)

congenital defects and infectious diseases. Precisely because babies are so sensitive to environmental insults, infant mortality statistics are used as an index of the state of a community's overall health programs. For each year of life successfully completed, the probability of dying in the following year decreases, up to the age of about 10, when the probability of dying is lower than at any other time in the life span (B). The mortality rate increases among teenagers and young adults (C). This increase is due primarily to accidents, which are the major cause of death in that age range. From about age 30 until advanced old age, there is an almost perfect exponential increase in the age-specific mortality (D). At ages above about 95 years, the rate of increase in mortality for the few people who have survived that long appears to become less (E).

This slowing of the rate late in life could be due to the existence of a small subpopulation of individuals who age at a slower rate, and thus dominate the small group of survivors left at advanced ages. They could represent the differential aging characteristic of the long-lived portion of the population. An alternative hypothesis is that the decreased mortality rates observed in section E of the curve are the result of skewed data arising from a few individuals who, in reporting their age, exaggerated for some reason. Since accurate birth records are difficult to obtain for many centenarians, this scenario is a real possibility (see Chapter 6). However, the situation would be self-correcting since, as time passes, fewer and fewer centenarians will be included who do not have accurate contemporary records of their birth dates. If the decrease (E) is still apparent at those future times, the existence among us of a slower-aging, longer-lived subset of human beings becomes more probable. Is this implication true? And if so, does this decrease imply the existence among us of a subset of individuals in the population who differ from the rest of us in some genetic and/or environmental parameters? Or does it imply that senescence stops in old age, not continuing through the entire life span? If so, it might be useful to understand better what causes senescence to stop and to determine if we can manipulate such processes to make them occur earlier.

Another potentially useful aspect of this age-specific mortality plot is the observation that the largest portion of the human life span is adequately described by that portion of the Gompertz plot indicated in portion D of Figure 2.17b. Can this region be used for comparisons of mortality rates and/or other interesting demographic parameters between different human populations? Can these mathematical abstracts of the survival data be used for accurate comparisons of the mortality kinetics of different species? Is it possible to make logical comparisons of aging in long-lived and short-lived species? These are interesting questions, each with important implications regarding our ability to understand better the biology of senescence. We will devote the final section of this chapter to our search for the answers.

The Biological Meaning of Transformed Survival Curves

Interspecific comparisons of mortality kinetics   Given the curve shown in Figure 2.17b, one can extrapolate from the most prominent part of the curve, the linear portion (D) of this age-specific mortality, up to age 100 and down to age zero. The result is a straight line that can be described completely with only two components: the y intercept (q_0) and the slope (x). This feature represents one of the great values of the Gompertz function, in that it takes all the complex data contained in the life table and implicit in the survival curves and reduces it to just two numbers. The former, q_0, is a hypothetical value for vulnerability to death due to age-related causes at birth. Perhaps a better approach is to think of this value as representing the genetically determined vigor of the genotype. The latter value (x) measures the rate of increase in mortality and has been considered to represent the rate of aging. Although some information may be lost in this process of simplification, it also makes it easier to compare the longevities of different populations and gain some insight into the processes at work.

A change in either value will affect life span. A reduction in the value of q_0 would reduce mortality at all ages and result in a longer average survival (see

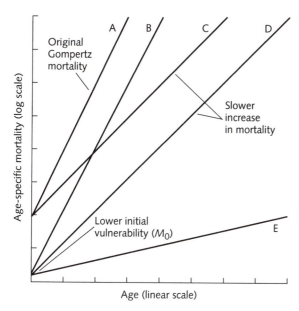

Figure 2.18 Effects of different values of the age-specific mortality (q_0) and of the rate of aging (x) on the Gompertz mortality. These terms and their interactive effects on mortality are described in the text. (From Ham and Veomett 1980. © C. V. Mosby Co.)

curves A and B or C and D in Figure 2.18). However, reducing the value of q_0 would have no effect on the rate of aging, since the slopes of the two lines would be identical. Changing the rate of aging (x), while leaving q_0 unaffected, would also decrease the age-specific mortality rate and hence increase life span (see curves A and C in Figure 2.18). Decreasing both values would result in a maximum increase in life span (curve E). The actual data tend to support this theoretical interpretation. Gompertz plots of rodent survival data show that the differences in species-specific life spans typically involve alterations in both parameters (Figure 2.19). Within a species, however, environmental interventions found to affect life span typically alter only one or the other of the constants of the Gompertz equation. Detailed analyses of the methods used in these estimates may be found in Shouman and Witten (1995) and in Eakin et al. (1995).

Subjecting people to highly adverse conditions, such as the malnutrition and confinement associated with war, often results in an increased mortality rate. The Gompertz plots for such populations show that the severe stress does not affect the rate of aging (the slope, or x) but does affect the initial vulnerability (the y intercept, or q_0) of the affected population (Figure 2.20). It is not known whether the rate of aging would be altered at some longer time after the stressful period was over. Other examples may be found in the various animal studies. Long-term administration of the anesthetic procaine to rats increases their life span by reducing their initial vulnerability (q_0), yet it has no effect on their rate of aging (x) (Figure 2.21). Conversely, caloric restriction also increases

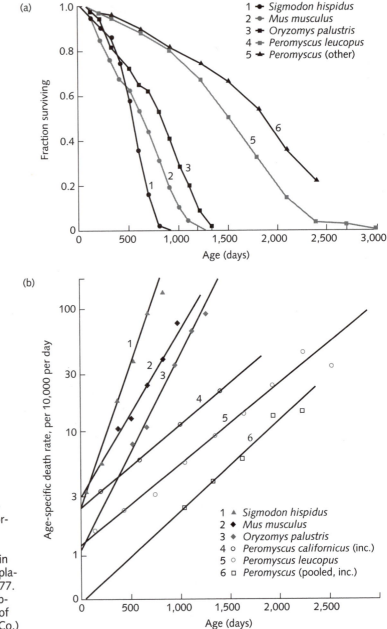

Figure 2.19 Survival curves (a) and the Gompertz plots (b) of the mortality data for wild-type populations of rodent species bred and reared in captivity. See text for explanation. (From Sacher 1977. © Litton Educational Publishing, with permission of Van Nostrand Reinhold Co.)

the life span of rats, but it does so primarily via a decrease in the rate of aging (x) coupled with a slight increase in the initial vulnerability (q_0) (Figure 2.22). Presumably these data tell us that these two different methods of prolonging the life span are bringing about their effects via very different mechanisms, even though they are affecting the same systems. These observations suggest that the

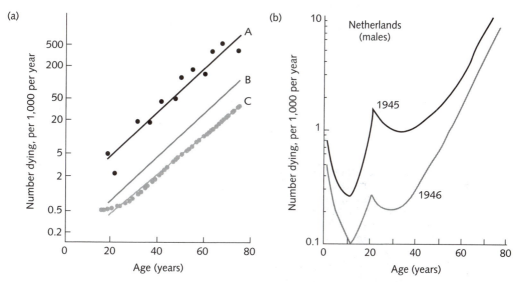

Figure 2.20 Mortality rates as a function of age in human populations subjected to prolonged dire stress duress, as analyzed by the Gompertz mortality rate model in which the logarithmic age-specific mortality rate is plotted against age. The rate of mortality (i.e., the slope) remains fairly constant, but the initial mortality rate (i.e., the intercept) changes significantly. (a) Curve A represents Australian prisoners of war held in concentration camps by the Japanese army during 1945; curve B represents civilians in Australia, 1944–1945; curve C represents white females in the U.S. 1980 census. (b) The initial mortality rate shifted without affecting the mortality rate slope in Netherlands male civilians in 1945 versus 1946 during and after World War II. (From Finch 1990, redrawn from Jones 1959.)

Gompertz transformations of the survival curve are somehow sensitive to the slight difference in mortality kinetics brought about by different methods of manipulating the same variable, such as antioxidant defense. Being aware of

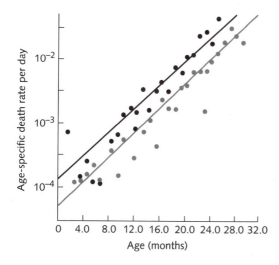

Figure 2.21 The effect of procaine on the mortality of rats. The long-term treatment of rats with procaine (gray circles) reduces vulnerability to death (q_x) at all ages as compared to controls (black circles) but does not alter the rate of aging (x). (From Sacher 1977. © Litton Educational Publishing, with permission of Van Nostrand Reinhold Co.)

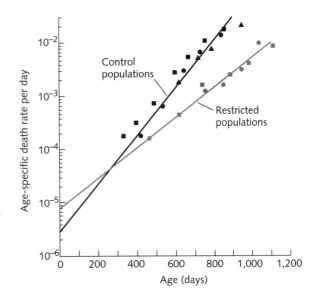

Figure 2.22 The effect of caloric restriction on mortality of rats. Two restricted populations (gray symbols) are compared with three control populations (black symbols). Note that in these populations, caloric restriction significantly reduced the rate of aging (x) but had a mildly adverse effect on the initial vulnerability (q_0). See text for discussion. (After Sacher 1977.)

this possibility will help us identify such situations and will keep us from inadvertently confounding disparate data.

Finch, Pike, and Witten (1990) have shown that, with a few modifications, the Gompertz parameters may be used for interspecific comparisons. One modification is to eliminate the neonatal and prepubertal periods (section A of the plot in Figure 2.17b) and compute the y intercept value (q_x) as if it occurred at puberty (section B), when it is at a minimum. This value is termed the initial mortality rate (IMR). Assuming puberty to take place at approximately 12 years of age, the IMR for Figure 2.17b would be about 0.00025 by inspection (alternatively, this value can be calculated from the linear form of the Gompertz equation (see page 46). The second interesting modification to this equation made by Finch, Pike, and Witten (1990) is the introduction of a new unit, the mortality rate doubling time (MRDT), which is related to the slope (x) of the Gompertz plot by the equation

$$\text{MRDT} = \frac{\ln 2}{x} = \frac{0.693}{x}$$

As Finch (1990) makes clear, the MRDT is derived from the slope but is more useful, since it varies in the same direction as the maximum life span does and is measured in the same units of time. It measures what it claims to measure—the period of time during which the probability of not living until the next time period doubles. It is more comprehensible to state that the MRDT of humans is 8.9 years than to state that the slope of the human age-specific mortality plot in Figure 2.17b is 0.087 units. What this MRDT value means is that when you are 36 years old, your chances of dying that day are only half what they will be when you are 45 years old, but twice as high as they were when you were 27 years old, and four time as high as when you were 18 years old. The MRDT quantifies in easily comprehended terms the increased probability of dying with age, which is one definition of aging (see Chapter 1).

Table 2.6 **Mortality Kinetics of Organisms with Different Senescence Patterns**

Species	MRDT IMR/year[a]	Senescence (years)[b]	Pattern	Maximum life span (years)
Humans:			Gradual	121
U.S. female, 1980	0.0002	8.9	—	—
Prisoner of war	0.0070	7.7	—	—
Horse	0.0002	4	Gradual	46
Rhesus monkey	0.02	15	Gradual	>35
Domestic dog	0.02	3	Gradual	20
White-footed mouse	0.06	1.2	Gradual	8
Lab rat	0.02	0.3	Gradual	5.5
Lab mouse	0.03	0.27	Gradual	4.5
Lab gerbil	0.1	0.9	Gradual	3.8
Pipstrelle bat	0.36	3–8	Gradual	>11
Herring gull	0.18	4	Gradual	49
Brush turkey	0.045	3.3	Gradual	12.5
Bengal finch	0.1	2.5	Gradual	9.6
Pea fowl	0.06	2.2	Gradual	9.2
Reeves pheasant	0.02	1.6	Gradual	9.2
Japanese quail	0.07	1.2	Gradual	5–8*
Broad-tailed hummingbird	0.25	—	Gradual	>12*
European robin	0.5	8	Gradual	12
Starling	0.5	>8	Gradual	20
Andean condor	—	—	Gradual	70–80
Guppy	0.07	0.8	Gradual	5
Lake sturgeon	0.013	10	Gradual	>150
Fruit fly	0.01–4	0.02–0.04	Rapid	0.3
House fly	4–12	0.02–0.04	Rapid	0.3
Honeybee worker:				
Winter	<0.001	0.03	Rapid	0.9
Summer	0.2	0.02	Rapid	0.2
Soil nematode	2	0.02	Rapid	0.15
Rotifer	6	0.005	Rapid	0.10
Nonfeeding moth	10	0.005	Rapid	0.03
Bamboo	—	—	Rapid	<120
Bristlecone pine	—	—	Negligible	>5000
Tortoise	—	—	Negligible	>150
Quahog	—	—	Negligible	>200

Source: Compiled from data presented in Tables 2.1, 3.1, 3.2, 4.1, Appendix 1, and Appendix 2 of Finch 1990, except items marked with an asterisk (*), which are from Holmes and Austad 1995.
[a]IMR, initial mortality rate
[b]MRDT, mortality rate doubling time

Table 2.6 presents representative values of mortality rate coefficients for a variety of different species with different types of senescence patterns. Humans have the slowest MRDT; the MRDT of a short-lived and rapidly senescing organism, such as the fruit fly, is about 500-fold greater. Note that the difference between humans and horses, or between monkeys and dogs, resides entirely in the MRDT, for their IMRs are equivalent. Thus the MRDT appears to serve as an empirical measure of senescence. In addition, flying vertebrates (bats and birds) have a longer MRDT than would be expected from their IMR values. Slow senescence appears not to be limited to animals with a large body size, as was once supposed. Finally, an inspection of the limited data available in Table 2.6 leads one to the suspicion that, since long-lived organisms with gradual senescence have low IMR and high MRDT values, a similar situation might well occur in these very long-lived species with negligible senescence.

Suppose we consider two species with comparable MRDT values, such as horses and brush turkeys (see Table 2.6). Is it valid for us to conclude that these two organisms, different as they are from one another, must necessarily undergo the same pathophysiological mechanism of senescence? Probably not. We must remember that the Gompertz equation and its various derivatives describe an empirical relationship. The equation is not dependent on a theoretical relationship between life span and some variable. So when we tinker with the equation and get it to fit some empirical data, what do we really know? We know only that the curve fits the data. But since we don't know why it fits, we can't logically deduce the nature of the underlying biological mechanisms. Another argument against overinterpreting these mathematical relationships is illustrated by Figure 2.23, in which inanimate electrical relays display a time-to-failure (survival) curve that is identical in form with that of an aging biological population. It seems obvious that relays and rhinoceroses senesce as a result of very different mechanisms, so the fact that different systems yield similar curves does not mean that similar mechanisms are operating in the two different systems.

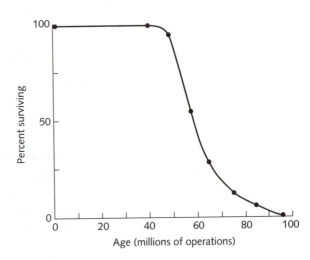

Figure 2.23 The survival of functions in electrical relays, plotted against the number of operations (events). (From Finch 1990, based on data of W. H. Lesser.)

Another interpretation of the same data is that what we are actually measuring in both animate and inanimate systems is simply the breakdown in connectiveness between compartmentalized but integrated systems (Finch 1990), wherein a subthreshold injury in one compartment increases the probability that another such injury, occurring independently in a connected component, will result in the breaking of the connection and the subsequent systemic failure of the machine or organism. In this deeper view, then, the important factor is the connectiveness of organisms and the failure that results from its loss. The nature of the particular components—whether copper switches or DNA repair systems—is of secondary consequence. We will return to this theme in later chapters, particularly Chapter 13.

Late-Life Mortality Kinetics

The implication of Figure 2.17b, that mortality rates may slow down at older ages, has been confirmed by several large-scale animal studies. An examination of the age-specific mortality of more than 1.2 million genetically heterogenous medflies showed that the mortality rate (q_x) slowed its rate of increase at about day 29 (about 16 percent survival), slowly rose to a maximum at day 58 (about 0.2 percent survival), and then decreased until the last fly died on day 172 (0 percent survival) (Figure 2.24) (Carey et al. 1992). It follows logically that such deceleration and eventual decrease in mortality rates should be accompanied by an increase in life expectancy, and that is what was found. The same deceleration of mortality rates was observed in genetically inbred *Drosophila* strains (Curtsinger et al. 1992; Fukui et al. 1993), as well as in genetically heterogenous (but not genetically inbred) nematodes (Brooks, Lithgow, and Johnson 1994). These observations have inspired a lively debate as to their reliability and interpretation (see, for example, the letters and technical comments in *Science* for June 11, 1993), yet several experiments explicitly designed to answer the question demonstrate that the mortality rate usually decreases among the very old individuals of these lab species.

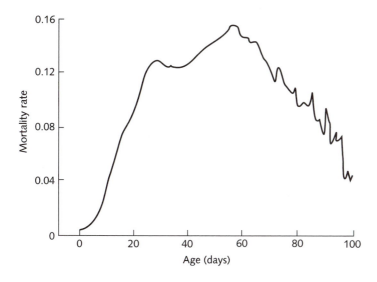

Figure 2.24 Mortality rates of a population of 1.2 million medflies maintained in cages of 7,200 animals each. Note that the age-specific mortality rates initially rose exponentially with age but then leveled off at about 20 days of age (16 percent survival), slowly increased to a peak at 58 days of age (0.2 percent survival), and declined thereafter. (Redrawn from data in Carey et al. 1992.)

What about humans? Evidence supporting the suggestion of Figure 2.17b can be found in the fact that multiple studies, done in developed countries with good living conditions and good data, show that the mortality rates among old (80+ years) humans have been steadily decreasing at an approximate rate of 1.5 percent per year since the 1960s (Kannisto et al. 1994; Manton et al. 1994) such that they now approximate a high but constant value. In effect, portion E of the curve in Figure 2.17b is now a straight line, and there is some indication that it might even be decreasing a bit. What might account for these observations? A recent study attempted to identify the physiological variables that affect the functional capacities of individuals and that thus underlie the late age-specific mortality (Manton, Woodbury, and Stallard 1995). The authors concluded that the deceleration in late-life mortality is brought about in part by the earlier death of frailer individuals, and in part because of changes (perhaps socially caused) in the age dependency of the important physiological parameters contributing to an individual's functional capacity. In effect, older people today are healthier and display significantly less morbidity or disabling conditions than did people of the same age a generation ago. This is a most interesting study, if only because it is one of the first to endeavor to replace the mere passage of time with documented alterations in the underlying physiological variables. We will discuss this study again in Chapter 6.

The inapplicability of the Gompertz plot to late-life mortality kinetics does not in any way invalidate the use of the Gompertz plot or of values derived from it, such as the MRDT, in the interspecific comparisons we have discussed. This situation arises because the MRDT is based on the linear portion of the Gompertz plot during the time period before the deaths of the most long-lived members of the population under consideration. (Note that this linear portion of the curve covers the deaths of about 85 percent of the popultion.) A recent analysis concluded that the Gompertz model gives a good approximation of the adult age-related mortality and generates a good fit between the expected and observed values of the maximum life spans for many different species (Finch and Pike 1995). Additionally, an analysis of genetically selected long- and short-lived strains of *Drosophila* showed that the Gompertz model could accurately summarize environmental and genetic alteration of longevity, despite the theoretical expectation of its failure to fit the observed data at very late ages (Nussbaum, Mueller, and Rose 1996).

Other Considerations

The Gompertz curve assumes that the level of nonsenescent deaths in a population, if there are any, is very low. As the frequency of such "accidental" deaths (age-independent mortality) increases, the result is a biphasic curve dominated by the constant mortality rate early in life and by the exponentially increasing mortality later in life. The shape of any particular survival curve is dictated by the relative contributions of both types of mortality to the survivorship of the population (Figure 2.25). Mathematical derivations of the Gompertz equation, as well as conceptually different equations, have been developed in an effort to fit the data better. Some sets of population data can be described best by a Gompertz plot, others can be best fitted by more complex transformations (such as a Weibull

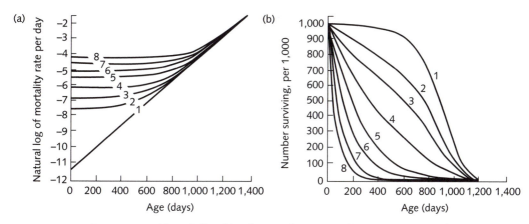

Figure 2.25 The relationship of survival curves to the Gompertz mortality curves, as depicted by demonstration of the effect of various amounts of nonsenescent deaths on the shape of mortality curves (a) and on survival curves (b). Lines with the same numbers in both panels represent the same populations. Population 1 represents the effects of only Gompertz mortality, where q_x increases exponentially with age. As age-independent mortality increases in populations 2 through 8, the survival curves progress from rectangular (1) to exponential (8), and the mortality curves approach a constant value. See text for discussion. (From Sacher 1977. © Litton Educational Publishing, with permission of Van Nostrand Reinhold Co.)

or logistic function), and there appears to be no obvious regularity as to which equation best fits any given population (Wilson 1994). However, a more extensive analysis of life tables showed that the Gompertz equation generally displays a better fit to the data than does the Weibull or other functions (Gavrilov and Gavrilova 1991), particularly when a two-stage model is constructed to account for the decreased mortality characteristic of very old individuals, as discussed earlier (Carey et al. 1992). The empirical basis of the mathematical treatment of mortality kinetics is shown clearly by the existence of the disagreement between theory and practice. In addition, we should keep in mind that the Gompertz equation assumes that q_0 and x are independent variables. This assumption has been challenged by an analysis based on the statistical comparison of theory with data (Witten 1988). Witten and his colleagues have compiled an extensive analysis of the methods and assumptions used in the Gompertz survival data, as well as a discussion of the validity of the conclusions that may be drawn (Witten 1985, 1988; Eakin et al. 1995; Shouman and Witten 1995).

Even though our lack of knowledge of the theoretical basis underlying the Gompertz equation prevents us from unambiguously interpreting the data, it has nonetheless greatly assisted us in better phrasing our questions regarding the kinetics of age-specific mortality. The continuing development of more accurate mathematical models should greatly assist us in making demographic predictions.

Distinguishing Between Development and Aging

In our attempt in Chapter 1 to define the terms "aging" and "senescence," it became apparent that most of the definitions contain no objective criteria that would allow a naive onlooker to unambiguously distinguish developmental processes from the processes of aging and senescence. Kohn's definition (see page 000) makes a qualitative but not a quantitative distinction. An inspection of Figure 2.17b suggests a simple objective criterion: Inasmuch as development is an adaptive process that enhances the functional capacities of the system, development may logically be considered to have ended when the age-specific mortality is at a minimum. This point is selected because it represents the age of maximum functional fitness of the population. The organisms will never be more healthy than they are at this point. Subsequent increases in the age-specific mortality rate of the system may be reasonably attributed to the onset and continuation of senescence processes. Thus, in the human data of Figure 2.17b, development ends, and senescence begins, just before puberty. Note that the MRDT in mammalian populations is usually determined beginning at the age of puberty; that is, the developmental period is omitted.

The Gompertz plot may be used to determine the age of sexual maturation when physiological data are nonexistent and the transition from developmental to adult forms is not clearly demarcated. In species that do show such demarcation, such as *Drosophila* and other holometabolous insects (insects that undergo complete metamorphosis), then the newly hatched adult represents the beginning of the postdevelopmental stage and the Gompertz plot should have its lowest initial vulnerability at this point in time. Not only is this definition based on objective quantitative data, but it is also in full agreement with the theoretical relationships posited to exist among reproduction, important life history features, and evolution (Rose 1991).

● *Are There Mathematical Limits to Longevity?*

Both the lay and the professional literature have commonly asserted that there exists a species-specific life span limit. The existence of such a limit seems so obvious at first that one might be excused for thinking that such a commonsense conclusion needs no further proof. But let's consider this proposition. It is tantamount to saying that for each species there exists a particular age that possesses certain unique properties such that no member of the species can live through that particular time period. According to this statement, if the maximum life span for humans is now 121 years, then it is impossible for another human being in the future to live 121 years and 1 day. Once reworded, it should be apparent that the statement is not only nonsensical, it also conflicts with the empirical data already presented that showed that the age-specific mortality rate decelerates and even decreases for very old individuals of several species, including humans. If the late-life mortality rate is constant, then the two constraints on the maximum age that any single individual might attain are (1) the size of the initial population and (2) the slope of the Gompertz plot (or the MRDT, as discussed earlier). Of these two, the latter is the more important and has by far the larger effect on maximum age (Finch and Pike 1995).

Altering the MRDT will alter the maximum life span. Maximum life span is, to a large extent, a probability function. There is no singular age beyond which it is impossible for any individual to survive. In addition, the concept of maximum life span conflicts with the idea that senescence is independent of time. Therefore, there is no reason to believe that there is a mathematical upper limit to life span, at least in species in which the late-life mortality rate decelerates and becomes a constant. (A more detailed discussion of this concept may be found in Gavrilov and Gavrilova 1991.) Yet even as we acknowledge the probabilistic nature of the maximum life span, we must also acknowledge the fact that species do have characteristic life spans. Flies, mice, cats, horses, people, and bristlecone pines represent a real continuum of mean and maximum longevities that we have to accommodate. And we can do so by remembering that these apparently fixed values are outcomes of each species' particular combination of Gompertz parameters, its initial vulnerability, its MRDT, and its population size. And these parameters are not immutable.

An understanding of this point is important, since important public-policy decisions often turn on demographic predictions, including that of the life expectancy of a particular portion of the population. If there were reason to believe that the human life span had a fixed upper limit, then it would logically follow that the continued increase in the mean life span (see Figure 2.16) would one day approach the unalterable maximum life span. This rectangularization of the survival curve (the transition from curve B to curve A in Figure 2.11) would compress mortality, since people would remain healthy for the greater part of their life, only to succumb to degenerative diseases and die within a relatively short time period (Fries 1980). Such a phenomenon would result in a decrease in the proportion of chronically ill people in the population. This potential decrease has been used to argue for a reduction in the amount of private and public resources spent on treatment of and research into the late-life degenerative diseases. The scientific basis for the argument has been disproven (Schneider and Brody 1983), but this example demonstrates the real-life impact of these supposedly abstract demographic numbers on each of us. There is every reason to believe that demographic projections of longevity will continue to play an important role in ongoing public policy debates. This example also shows that it is important for all citizens to understand the scientific assumptions underlying such public debate. We will return to the issue of aging and public policy in Chapter 14.

• *Summary*

The value of life tables and of the equations derived from them is that they enable us to determine whether aging and senescence are occurring in a population; they give us a crude idea of the timing and the rates of aging of one population relative to that of another, they allow us to test quantitatively certain propositions made about the kinetics of aging, and they provide us with the minimum parameters that any theory of aging must eventually explain. In particular, the Gompertz equation and the parameters derived from it have proven to be especially useful in simply but accurately describing the kinetics of aging of populations.

Measuring Age-Related Changes in Individuals

● *Actuarial Analysis of Age-Related Changes through Time*

We may analyze populations to determine whether the individuals within them will survive long enough to have a chance to grow old and age. Or we may study aging itself, a process in which the decrement of various physiological functions is coupled with an increase in the probability that any particular member of the population will die within the current time period. However, populations are composed of many diverse individuals, only some of whom display the expected age-related changes at the expected times. In this sense, therefore, we may conclude that aging is a very individual process and must be measured and studied in detail in individuals. The diagnosis of aging may be inferred from the population data, but the study of aging must ultimately refer to its expression in individuals.

Cross-Sectional Studies

Almost all the information available to us regarding age-related changes in animals, human or otherwise, has been drawn from cross-sectional, or "point-of-time," studies. In such studies the variable under investigation is measured for groups of subjects of different ages. The age-related changes are not measured directly; they are inferred from a comparison of the mean values for each cohort. They may also be inferred from a regression of the variable on age, made on subjects distributed over the total age span who are measured at about the same time. This experimental design allows us to capture a cross section of the population values in time; hence its name. Because this procedure is relatively simple and inexpensive, it is a very popular experimental approach. For long-lived species such as humans, this protocol is often the only feasible one. Even when working with a shorter-lived laboratory species, such as the rat, a single investigator could hope to do only a dozen or fewer longitudinal studies in his or her lifetime. Thus, longitudinal studies may not be a feasible or desirable approach. However, cross-sectional studies have at least four important drawbacks.

First, the cross-sectional approach assumes that the manner in which the average value changes from one age group to the next is an accurate reflection of the change that occurs in one individual with the passage of time. There is no *a priori* reason why this assumption must always be valid. Consequently, we must be aware of the probability that our interpretations of such data are incorrect. The problem is depicted in Figure 3.1. In this hypothetical example, the changes in a particular physiological function taking place in five individuals have been plotted as a function of age. Three conclusions can be drawn from such longitudinal data. First, the peak performance is reached in different individuals at widely different times. Second, there is no plateau value, for the rate of change in this variable is as great in one time period as in any other for each individual. Third, the individuals differ substantially in their rate of increase and decrease in this variable, but not in the absolute level of their peak values. Plotting the average value over time of all those values yields the thick-lined curve shown in Figure 3.1. By taking this average, we have converted the longitudinal data to a cross-sectional study. In the absence of other data, this cross-sectional curve might lead us to conclude that this variable plateaus at a peak level in the twenties, during which period its value changes little. Consequently, we might infer that individuals 1 and 5 (and possibly 2 and 4 in their older years) showed an abnormal age-related change in this physiological function. Clearly, such a conclusion is not warranted by the data. The consequences of making such a faulty decision go beyond impeding our understanding of the aging process if they lead to unnecessary worry, treatment, and expense for the individual concerned simply because he or she is a statistical outlier on a poorly interpreted test.

The second limitation of the cross-sectional approach is that it confounds the effects of environmental changes with the effects of age. For example, starvation affects young children differently from how it affects mature adults. If two such individuals lived through the same famine, the differences in average values of a

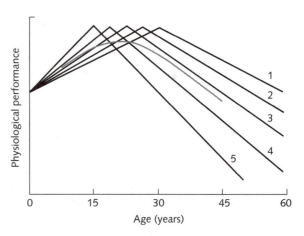

Figure 3.1 The relationship between individual rates of change (as indicated by the five black lines), and the average rate of change (as indicated by the gray line). Note that the average does not accurately describe any of the individual rates of change. See text for explanation. (From Lamb 1977. © John Wiley and Sons.)

particular variable measured after the event might erroneously be ascribed to aging. For example, the heterogeneity in peak values seen in Figure 3.1 may be the result of a general environmental effect, such as an epidemic or a famine. The age effect shown by the individuals could then simply be a result of the fact that they were at five different ages at the time of the event. In this case there would be no true age effect present, but our procedural error would have led us to infer one.

The third disadvantage is that the cross-sectional approach suffers from the effects of selective mortality. A population of 30-year-old males includes both individuals fated to die at relatively young ages and individuals fated to live a long time, whereas a population of 90-year-old males has been highly selected to include only individuals fated to live a long life. The two populations are not identical in the composition of the individuals within them, and hence comparisons between them may not be valid. For example, consider the situation that would arise if the population in Figure 3.1 consisted of all five individuals at age 45, only two of which (individuals 1 and 5) are still alive at age 60. The comparison of mean values for these two cohorts (1 through 5 versus 1 and 5) would suggest that no change occurred in this physiological parameter during this time period. This would be a deceptive conclusion, since survival (in this hypothetical example) was associated only with extreme changes in this variable.

The final problem with the cross-sectional approach is that it can provide no evidence regarding the rate of change of a particular variable within an individual, although the planned development of good biomarkers (which we will discuss later in this chapter) may alleviate this problem in the future.

Longitudinal Studies

The longitudinal method is characterized by repeated measurements of a specific variable(s) on the same subject. Thus the method measures primarily age-related changes in individuals. Such a prospective study makes possible statistical estimates of individual rates of aging for the specified variable(s), once sufficient observations have been collected over a long enough period of time. However, the individual records can be summarized to yield the average difference between groups of subjects of different ages. In other words, the longitudinal data can be reorganized to yield cross-sectional data, but the reverse operation is not possible. If the study subjects are of different ages, the cross-sectional data are yielded immediately after this transformation. If the study subjects are all the same age, the cross-sectional data will be obtained only when the study runs long enough that data can be collected from the subjects during several different age intervals. Subjects who are members of the same age class are often termed a cohort.

From a theoretical standpoint, the data from a longitudinal study are more reliable than the data from a cross-sectional study. However, the longitudinal approach is not free of drawbacks. The most obvious disadvantage of this method is the limitation of time and of money. Repeated measurements on a defined group of individuals over a long period of time require long-term commitment by subjects, investigators, institutions, and funding agencies. Such conjunction rivals alignment of the planets in its rarity and enhances the value of the several such studies that have been done (see Chapter 6, particularly Table 6.7).

The use of repeated tests may give rise to a "practice" effect, whereby subjects respond better in later trials than in earlier trials because they have learned the appropriate responses. The practice effect may be more of a problem with psychomotor tests than with more biochemical assays, although the effects of biofeedback on physiological processes cannot be ignored. In addition, the use of institutionalized subjects may render the logistics of a longitudinal study easier, but at the cost of making spurious comparisons from an institutionalized population to a healthy normal and mobile population. Even when longitudinal studies have been done on a normal population, it has been recognized that the population is not random but is highly selected with respect to socioeconomic and ethnic properties. The findings of the study should be generalized to the population at large only with caution.

Sources of Confusion

Three primary temporal factors may be responsible for chronological changes in a particular variable: age, period, and birth cohort. Cross-sectional studies tend to confound age effects with birth cohort effects. Longitudinal studies tend to confuse age effects with period effects. No statistical or design methods are available today that permit unambiguous distinction of the influences among these three effects on any variable. In the final analysis, our advances depend on the use of both cross-sectional and longitudinal data, buttressed by the interpretations of astute investigators.

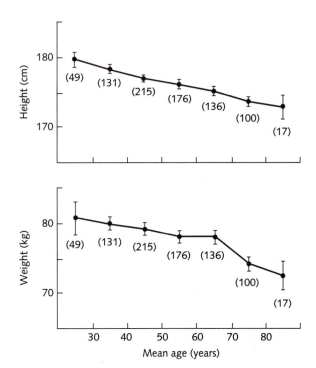

Figure 3.2 The regression of height and weight (mean ± standard deviation) in normal males, based on cross-sectional data. Numbers in parentheses represent sample sizes. Compare to Figure 3.3. (From Shock 1972. © Almqvist & Wiksell.)

Empirical Longitudinal and Cross-Sectional Comparisons

One advantage of longitudinal studies is that the data may be reconstructed into a cross-sectional format and the validity of the two approaches compared directly for the same set of data. Such comparison is very instructive and has been done by Shock (1985) for some of the data obtained from the Baltimore Longitudinal Study of Aging. This discussion will draw from Shock's observations.

Figure 3.2 depicts the cross-sectional regression of height and weight on age in healthy males. The simplest interpretation of these data is that a gradual reduction in height and weight over the age period of 30 to 85 years constitutes a normal age-related change. Figure 3.3 presents data from the longitudinal regression of height and weight on age for the same males as in Figure 3.2. It is clear that individual subjects tend to lose height as they grow older. It is equally clear that individuals younger than 55 years old tend to gain weight, even though the average weight value is falling. For these individuals, the cross-sectional and longitudinal data do not agree. For individuals 55 years and older, however, the two data sets agree. Thus, the cross-sectional interpretation of the height changes is verified by the longitudinal study, but the interpretation of the weight changes is upheld in part and falsified in part.

A phenotypic trait such as weight has a large environmental component, and it would not be wise to ignore this factor. How much, if any, of the weight gain observed with age is attributable to environment? Bouliere and Parot (1962) made a cross-sectional comparison between economically affluent Parisians and

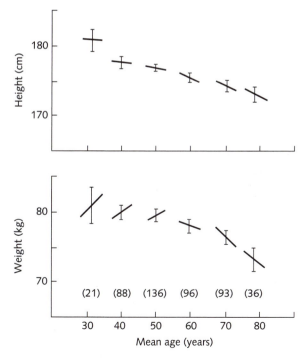

Figure 3.3   The regression of height and weight (mean ± standard deviation) in normal males during an 8-year period, based on longitudinal data obtained from repeated measurements on the same subjects as those represented in Figure 3.2. Numbers in parentheses represent sample sizes. See text for explanation and discussion. (From Shock 1972. © Almqvist & Wiksell.)

Kabyles, a North African group living a primitive life characterized by high energy expenditures and restricted food supply. In the Kabyles, weight changed little throughout maturity (ages 25–55 years) (Figure 3.4). This lack of change in weight was most likely due to a failure to deposit extra subcutaneous fat during middle age, as demonstrated by the differences in total weight (Figure 3.4) and in the thickness of skin folds (Figure 3.5). Past the age of 60 years, the lean body weight of human males of both groups appears to decrease markedly (see Figures 3.3 and 3.4). Taken as a whole, these data suggest that humans have the ability to gain weight via the deposition of subcutaneous fat, provided that their socioeconomic environment permits the purchase of extra calories. The catalogue of normal age-related changes must be considered in the context of the environment. This statement amounts to nothing more than the geneticists' concept that the phenotype is the result of expression of the genotype in a particular environment. The interplay of the genotype with the environment turns out to be of some importance in the study of aging, as we will discuss in Chapter 6.

In many instances, there is no discrepancy in the results achieved by the two different strategies. Figure 3.6 shows both longitudinal and cross-sectional data for age-related changes in creatinine clearance (a measure of kidney function) in humans. These data are charted in the same manner as in Figure 3.3. An inspection of this graph suggests reasonable agreement between the two sets of data, and thus in the conclusions drawn from them.

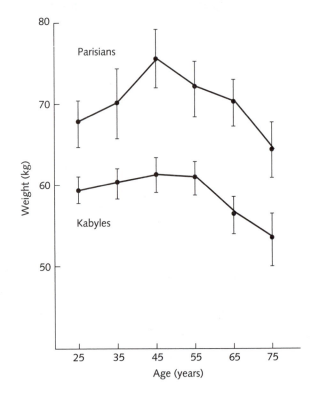

Figure 3.4 A comparison of the effects of environment on age-related weight changes between economically favored Parisians and the Kabyles, a North African group leading a primitive life. Note that the Kabyles display only minimal weight gain throughout adult life. (From Bouliere and Parot 1962.)

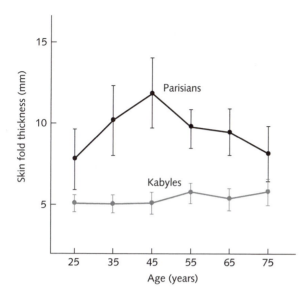

Figure 3.5   A comparison of changes in the iliac (pelvic regions) skin fold in the same two groups of men as in Figure 3.4. Again note the constancy in the Kabyles. (From Shock 1972. © Almqvist & Wiksell.)

An implicit assumption in the studies described here is that they represent traits universal among the individuals of the species. A later, more detailed reexamination of the problem led to a different conclusion—namely, that individual variability confounds these assumptions. Consider the case of creatinine clearance (Figure 3.7). This new longitudinal study demonstrates that both males and females show similar declines in this trait as measured by cross-sectional studies. It further shows a coincidence between the longitudinal and cross-sectional data for males. A reasonable deduction from these data would be that a decline in creatinine clearance should be observed in all humans over the age of 35. However, the population is actually quite heterogeneous.

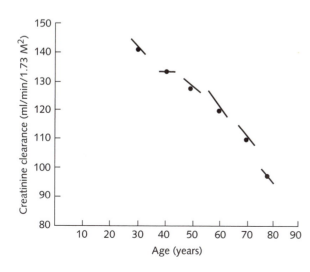

Figure 3.6   A comparison of cross-sectional and longitudinal age changes in creatinine clearance. The dots represent the mean values for each age decade as obtained from cross-sectional data. The short line segments indicate the mean slope of the change in creatinine clearance, as based on the longitudinal data for the indicated time spans. Note that the two sets of data agree. (From Rowe et al. 1976.)

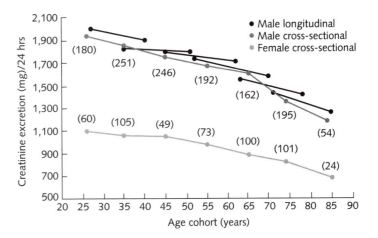

Figure 3.7   Cross-sectional and longitudinal creatinine excretion values by age and gender in subjects of the Baltimore Longitudinal Study on Aging. Numbers in parentheses represent sample sizes. (From G. T. Baker III and J. Frozard, Gerontology Research Center, National Institute on Aging.)

The individual longitudinal displays of serum creatinine clearance show that some individuals show large and rapid decreases in this trait (Figure 3.8, top panel), while others show only small decreases (Figure 3.8, middle) or no change at all (Figure 3.8, bottom). An analysis of the entire test population shows that substantial proportions of the test population are significantly differ-

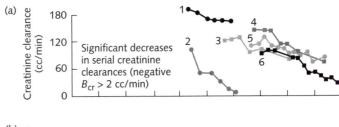

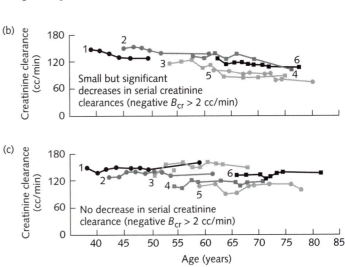

Figure 3.8   Individual longitudinal displays of serial creatinine clearances plotted against age for 18 representative subjects from the Baltimore Longitudinal Study of Aging. (a) Six subjects followed for 8–14 years. These subjects showed significant decreases in creatinine clearances. (b) Six subjects followed for 11–22 years and showing small but signficant decreases in creatinine clearances. (c) Six subjects followed for 15–21 years and showing no decrease in creatinine clearances. (From Lindeman et al. 1985.)

ent from one another (Table 3.1). Only about 58 to 71 percent of the study population showed a decrease in creatinine clearance rate during a 10-year period. Between 29 and 42 percent of the population showed no change. This finding is extraordinary, and illustrates how much individual variability may be hidden within our normal statistical procedures. Normally, we would have assumed that the agreement of cross-sectional and longitudinal data indicated universality of the trait. We now see that the assumption is not justified, and that the only factor we can count on is that most traits will display significant individual variability. These findings in humans are paralleled by findings in other species (for example, Draye and Lints 1995).

The next comparison confirms individual variability. Figure 3.9 summarizes cross-sectional data from nine different studies for maximum oxygen (O_2) uptake (see Norris and Shock 1974 for details). These data are an indirect measure of the maximum amount of metabolic work that an individual can do. Although the absolute values are different (perhaps as a result of methodological differences), the overall age-associated change observed in both sexes seems to follow the same pattern. The low value in childhood increases rapidly to a peak value in the teens and early twenties. This increase is succeeded by a slow decline until the forties, followed by a more rapid decline until the minimal values of childhood are once more attained. The heterogeneity of the several studies suggests that this trait is characterized by a great deal of individual variation. This suspicion is partly confirmed in Figure 3.10, which presents longitudinal studies of maximum O_2 uptake for two individuals over the age span of 35 to 87 years. Both individuals exhibit an age-related decrement in this variable, but the patterns are very different. Dr. Robinson displays a gradual, almost constant decrement in both factors throughout his life span; Dr. Dill shows only minimal age-associated changes

Table 3.1	**Percent Change in Creatinine Clearance over 10 Years in 412 Male BLSA Subjects[a]**			
	Percent of individuals showing indicated level of change in creatinine clearance			
Age cohort	No change	*Change of 10% or less*	*Change of 20% or less*	*Change of 21% or more*
20–29	42	27	18	13
30–39	39	29	19	13
40–49	42	29	23	6
50–59	30	26	42	2
60–69	29	22	37	12
70–79	31	7	31	31

Source: Data courtesy of George T. Baker III and James Frozard, Gerontology Research Center, National Institute on Aging.
[a]Data represent 412 male subjects followed over 10 years in the Baltimore Longitudinal Study on Aging (BLSA). Mean change from third to eighth decade equals 31 percent.

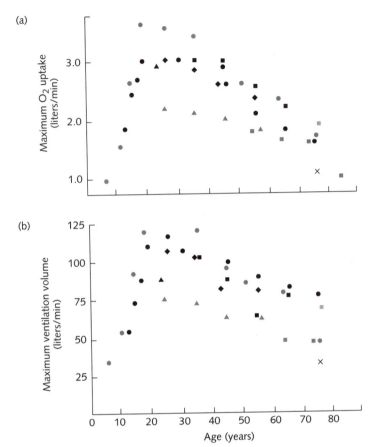

Figure 3.9   A comparison of the age-related changes in maximum oxygen uptake and in maximum ventilation volume, as observed in nine different studies of both men and women. Note that the several studies, although very heterogeneous, conform to the same general pattern. (From Norris and Shock 1974. © Harper & Row.)

until after age 65. This pattern would not have been predicted on the basis of cross-sectional data alone. Both men were very interested in exercise and sports, and their physical fitness was reportedly considerably better than that of most of their age peers. Thus the differences are not due simply to the effects of physical conditioning and training. Taken together, these data suggest that humans will undergo an age-related decrement in an important physiological factor such as maximum O_2 uptake, but that the great latitude in the individual pattern of this decrement suggests that factors other than age significantly affect this variable.

One other weakness affects cross-sectional and longitudinal studies equally: the dependence on time as a measure of the aging process. Although the idea may seem odd at first, using time units to measure age may be an imperfect compromise between accuracy and convenience. A good illustration is the example shown in Figure 3.11a, which depicts the growth rates of individual children between 5 and 18 years. Every individual reaches a peak value at some point, and the shapes of the several curves are very similar. Yet it is obvious that the *timing* of the pattern is different in the five individuals depicted. Knowing a child's age

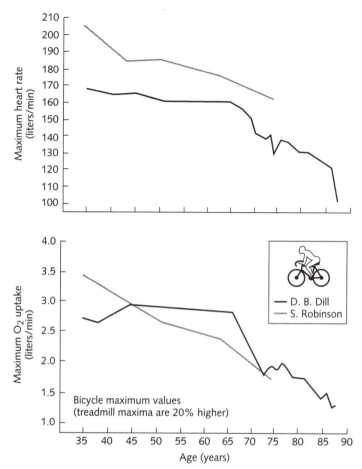

Figure 3.10 Differences in the longitudinal patterns for maximum heart rate and for maximum oxygen uptake of two individuals, D. B. Dill and S. Robinson. (From Horvath 1981. © Elsevier North Holland.)

would not allow you to make an accurate statement concerning that child's growth rate. In this instance, a chronological measure of age conveys very little information.

A better measure is shown in Figure 3.11b, where the curves have been arranged so that their points of maximum growth rate coincide and the other points for each individual are plotted as deviations in time from this event. This procedure suggests that measuring our age by the passage of years may not be as meaningful as measuring our age by the passage of certain significant events. We already use this concept in other areas—for example, when we talk about individuals passing through developmental stages that are functionally but not chronologically defined. We will return to this concept of the event-dependent nature of aging in our discussion of biomarkers later in this chapter and in Chapters 6, 12, and 13.

This brief survey of experimental design should leave you with the impression that aging is a highly individual process that requires the intelligent interpretation of both kinds of data in order to draw reasonable and testable conclusions.

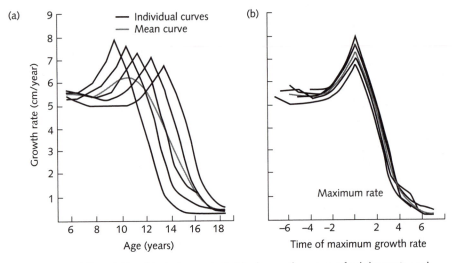

Figure 3.11   The relationship between individual growth curves of adolescents and the mean growth curve. In (a), the curves are plotted as a function of chronological age. Note that the average curve, which is based on the cross-sectional data, does not adequately describe any of the individual growth curves. Compare these empirical data to the hypothetical situation shown in Figure 3.1, and note the similarity. In (b), the individual growth curves are plotted as deviations from each person's age of maximum growth. Note the excellent agreement between the individual and mean curves in this instance. (From Tanner 1955. © Blackwell Science Publishers.)

Distinguishing Disease and Environmental Changes from Age-Related Changes

There are several different schools of thought regarding the relationship of diseases to aging. One group, perhaps expressing what has been the traditional medical model of geriatrics, views aging as the sum of the diseases to which we eventually succumb. In this view, aging is a disease. This point of view may have made sense in the past, when most people died young (see Figure 2.16), but it is no longer tenable now that we understand that people age even in the absence of disease.

A second point of view, perhaps arising as a reaction to the medical model, is characteristic of what we may term a gerontological viewpoint. This model disclaims any fundamental connection between diabetes or cancer or cardiovascular disease or other such age-related pathological syndromes and the processes of normal aging, except to assume that the increased incidence of these pathologies among the older members of the population is probably due to the fact that certain normal age-related changes are precursors to or precipitate disease, a concept that we will discuss in some detail. Consequently, much energy has been invested in the effort to distinguish "normal" aging from "abnormal" aging, by which is meant aging in the absence or the presence, respectively, of disease.

Adoption of this gerontological model in recent decades has allowed us to progress beyond the narrow study of geriatric disease to the identification, characterization, and manipulation of the aging processes that take place in the absence of overt disease.

An evolving third point of view suggests that there is a close relationship between aging and disease—that we may consider them two different aspects of the same process. This idea is not a return to the narrow geriatrics view of aging; rather it is a sophisticated broadening of the gerontological model. The study of age-related diseases is intimately linked to our increased knowledge of the normal aging processes. The linkage lies in the fact that the existence of these age-related diseases empirically delineates for us the aspects of the body's normal physiology and cell biology that are prone to failure as a consequence of the normal aging processes. A detailed molecular and genetic knowledge of the particular disease syndrome associated with such failures allows us to classify the weak points of our bodily machines, to sort out their modes of failure, and to try to determine which intervention strategies might delay or prevent these failures. Inherent in this proposition is the idea that using clinical tours de force to alleviate the *symptoms* of disease in older individuals is not as effective as is marrying the insights of basic research with the details of clinical knowledge to *prevent* the onset of disease, and thereby increase certainly the quantity—and probably the quality—of life. The aging process is not the sum of our diseases, nor is it totally divorced from our diseases, but it sets the stage for the possible appearance of particular syndromes of failure. In fact, Fozard et al. (1990) end their review of the future of longitudinal studies by concluding that ". . . an adequate description of aging must integrate an account of disease within it."

This viewpoint has been cogently expressed by Holliday (1995), who has termed the effects of aging as bringing about a condition of "incipient disease." When we age, a variety of deteriorative changes set in. These changes occur with some synchrony, but when deterioration of one organ system becomes more obvious, disease is diagnosed. Such disease is surely the result of aging to some degree, but it also accelerates the deteriorative changes in that organ system and thus contributes to the continued aging of that system and that individual. If an individual died before the diagnosis of the disease, some people would consider her to have died from "normal" aging; if she died after the diagnosis of the disease, most people would consider her to have died as a consequence of her disease—of "abnormal" aging. When phrased in this manner, the distinction between the two seems artificial. Aging, then, is not a disease but a cluster of incipient diseases affecting the functioning of a variety of tissues and organs in more or less predictable ways (R. Holliday, personal communication). The results of a recent conference (see Martin et al. 1995) suggest that this integrative point of view is becoming more widely accepted by scientists today (including the author of the book you have in hand). We will delve further into this point of view here and elsewhere in the text, particularly in the discussion of human aging in Chapter 5.

Despite the intellectually close relationship between disease and normal aging that is implicit in the latter point of view, we will not strive in this text to give detailed descriptions of age-related diseases. It is difficult enough to describe the usual progress of normal aging and senescense, simultaneously accounting for the usual individual heterogeneity in aging, without obscuring the main story with the diversionary tale of disease states. Diseases offer us the opportunity of identifying potential failure points; once we have identified them, we will turn our attention elsewhere. Of course, not all diseases are age-related, and we will have to distinguish between age-related and time-related diseases. In addition, not every person suffers from the same types or sequences of diseases, and we should be able to account for this phenomenon as well.

Diseases Associated with the Passage of Time

An example of this subtlety is illustrated by gray hair. The phenomenon of hair graying with age is documented in various mammalian species, including humans. Almost all humans possess some gray hair by the time they reach their late thirties or early forties, and all have gray hair by the time they reach their early sixties (Figure 3.12). No difference was observed between men and women nor between people of different hair colors. Not all hair is the same; the hair of the head, beard, and pubic area is different from the hair of the eyebrow and the armpit. The former set turns gray as indicated in Figure 3.12; the latter set is much more resistant to graying, especially in women (data of M. Isaki, as presented in Balin 1994b). Histological examination has shown that the loss of pigment is associated with a loss of tyrosinase acitivity and a production of imperfect melanin granules in the hair shaft (Orentreich and Orentreich 1994). Graying of the hair has occasionally been associated with severe emotional stress and/or certain disease states. Nonetheless, hair graying has been viewed as one of the more obvious and reliable signs of human aging. However, gray hair by itself is not deleterious in any obvious way, and logically we must conclude that graying of the hair does not fulfill the CPID criteria for an age-related change (see Chapter 1). The tendency of graying is said to be inherited, but very little else is known with any certainty (Kligman, Grove, and Balin 1985).

A similar situation holds in mice. Age-related graying has been reported in both wild and inbred mice and was suggested to be due to a single autosomal

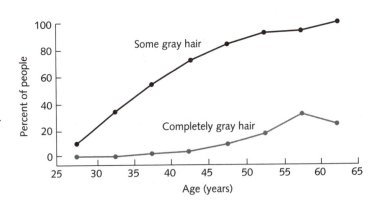

Figure 3.12 The rate of hair graying for 3,872 Australian men and women with medium-color hair. (From Lamb 1977. © John Wiley and Sons.)

dominant gene modified by various maternal influences (Kirby 1974). An alternative explanation substantiated by much persuasive evidence was presented by Morse et al. (1980). Their results suggest that graying with age, at least in certain strains of mice, results from melanocyte dysfunction that occurs after pre- or early postnatal infection with murine leukemia virus. The infected melanocytes gradually lose their ability to produce melanin, resulting in the appearance of white hairs, whereas uninfected cells continue to produce pigment. The distribution of the gray hair—"pattern graying" or "salt-and-pepper" graying—then reflects the original infection pattern. These data apply strictly only to certain mouse strains. In these mice, at least, graying of the hair is not an intrinsic change, but rather the defect produced by a viral parasite. Consequently, it does not fulfill the CPID criteria of Chapter 1 and cannot be considered an age-related change. If an analogous explanation eventually is found to hold for humans, we will be forced to conclude that hair graying is not a true age-related change, but is merely a symptom of a disease state associated with the passage of time. It should be noted that not all mouse strains gray with age; thus the differences between strains are likely to be genetically determined (Finch 1990).

A known example of a time-related disease in humans is polycystic kidney disease. In this disease, clinical symptoms are frequently not seen until the patient is in his or her fifties. It has long been viewed as a time-dependent disease, but until recently it was not clear in what ways a time-dependent condition is different from an age-dependent syndrome. Transgenic techniques have been used to produce a mutation in the mouse that gives rise to an animal model of this disease (Moyer et al. 1994). In these afflicted rodents, the normal function of this gene appears to be regulation of the cell cycle (see Figure 11.1) in the kidney epithelium. Inactivation of the gene in the mutant animals gives rise to an epithelial hyperplasia (overgrowth) via either abnormal activation of the cellular proliferative response or abnormal inactivation of cell death (apoptosis; see Chapter 11) in the kidney. Either mechanism will, if given enough time, cause enlarged epithelial cysts. This insight also provides a plausible explanation for the apparent time dependency of this syndrome (the hyperplasia has no ill effects until a certain threshold is reached after about 50 years of slow overgrowth). An age-related change, by contrast, might be viewed as one in which the hyperplasia would not be constant but would shift from a normal to an abnormal rate after the age-dependent failure of a cellular mechanism that regulated cell proliferation.

Age-Related Changes That Might Precipitate Disease

It is becoming obvious that it is increasingly difficult to distinguish clearly between normal age-related changes and pathological disease states. In part, this realization is founded on the observation that the normal deleterious age-related changes may be necessary preconditions for the development of an abnormal pathology. Let's consider the case of blood pressure and aging, particularly as it illustrates the diversity of age-related changes in humans (and probably in other species as well).

The major change that occurs with normal aging in the arterial wall is a slow, continuous, and symmetrical increase in the thickness of the inner layer of the artery, the intima. The thickening may be a response to a minor injury to the cells of the intima and may even involve the expression of particular oncogenes present in the cell. In any event, this thickening initially begins with a gradual accumulation of smooth-muscle cells and the subsequent proliferation of both these cells and the adjacent connective tissue. The thickening of this layer is coupled with the progressive diffuse accumulation in it of cholesterol and other lipids. This process is mediated by dynamics of blood flow, surface geometry, and heart rate. More recently, it has been shown that certain genetic alterations affecting lipoprotein metabolism can drastically alter the rate of intima thickening and endothelial injury. We are not concerned with these alterations at present, so we will defer our discussion of them until Chapter 5. The net result of these normal age-related changes is a gradually increasing rigidity of the arteries, as suggested by the data of Figure 3.13, which shows a decreased elasticity of the aorta with age. However, this decreased elasticity may result in an increased systolic blood pressure. In turn, this increased blood pressure is known to be a major risk factor for several vascular disorders, most notably cerebrovascular disease or stroke (Rowe and Minaker 1985, p. 944). In this manner a normal age-related change increases the risk of serious morbidity and/or mortality, and thereby obscures the definitive line once arbitrarily drawn between aging and disease.

To be fair, we must point out that this scenario of the normal age-related changes in arteries implies that an increase in blood pressure with age is a universal attribute. Is this correct? The cross-sectional data of Figure 3.14 suggests that it is. However, analysis of the data of Figure 3.15 shows that although most (about 75 percent) individuals show increases in both systolic and diastolic blood pressure, a small number (about 12 percent) show no change and a comparable number (about 13 percent) even show a decrease in systolic blood pressure with advancing age. This finding is consistent with the information shown in Table 3.1.

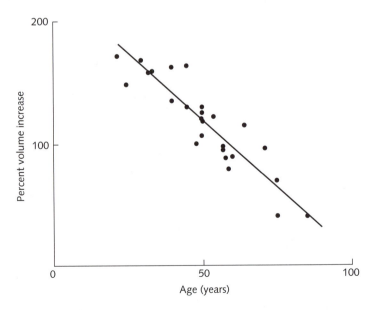

Figure 3.13 Age-related changes in the ability of the human thoracic aorta to expand when placed under standard pressure *in vitro*. (From Kohn 1978. © Prentice-Hall Inc.)

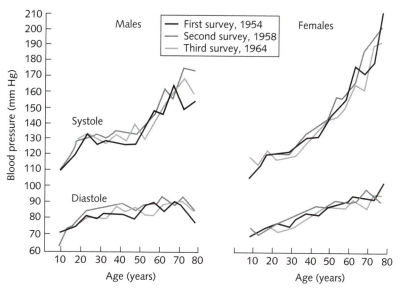

Figure 3.14 Age-related changes in the systolic and diastolic blood pressure in a Welsh population. Note how well the three repeated measurements agree. (From Miall and Lovell 1967.)

One could interpret these data as suggesting that the arterial changes described here are not normal age-related changes, because they are not universal within the species. This interpretation would then logically force the conclusion that the differences between the individuals might well be due to differences in the individuals' diet, health status, and other characteristics. In other words, the arterial changes might be environmentally induced pathologies. Some comparative cultural studies support this position. Alternatively, one could interpret the same data as suggesting that the population is polymorphic for this trait: Most individuals will display this trait of an age-related increase in blood pressure, and a small proportion of the population is genetically and physiologically different and capable of mobilizing various mechanisms that will compensate for the normal increase in arterial stiffness. This interpretation further suggests that these asclerotic individuals may constitute all or some of the long-lived fraction of the population, as evidenced by part E of the Gompertz curve depicted in Figure 2.17.

This conclusion is consistent with the evidence showing that not all individuals exhibit what are considered to be characteristic and normal age-related changes (see Figure 3.8 and Table 3.1). In addition, data now show that centenarians, relative to the general population, have significantly different frequencies of certain genes that are broadly involved in cardiovascular functioning (see Chapter 6); however, the observed genetic differences appear to explain only a subset of the cases of extended longevity. And it is well known that certain pathologies (such as diabetes) and certain environmental conditions (such as unlimited feeding) accelerate the rate of collagen cross-linking in arteries and hence increase blood pres-

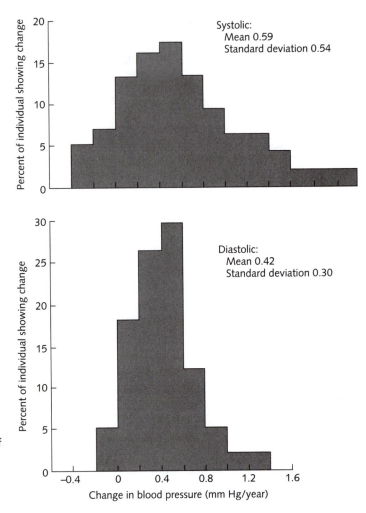

Figure 3.15   A distribution of changes in blood pressures in individuals of different ages. (From Harris and Forsythe 1973. © Grune and Stratton.)

sure. Thus neither of the above interpretations is exclusively correct, and there must be substantial interaction between the two parameters.

The classification of arteriosclerosis as a normal or pathological age-related change will, in the final analysis, depend on such difficult interpretation and will always be open to question. It seems much more reasonable to consider increased blood pressure as a normal age-related change that takes place in most, but not all, members of the human population and that can, in the presence of contributing genetic and environmental factors, act as a precipitating factor in the etiology of various cardiovascular diseases. (However, bear in mind that this presentation has simplified the argument by overlooking the fact that blood pressure is most likely under the control of other variables as well. A good discussion of the complexity of the mechanisms underlying hypertension appears in Lifton 1996.)

Resolving the ambiguities inherent in this interpretation may be of general import. An evaluation of the data obtained in the Baltimore Longitudinal Study on Aging by Rodeheffer and colleagues (1984) revealed that about half of the generally healthy people enrolled in the study had at least some covert signs of coronary heart disease, perhaps attributable to the mechanisms already discussed. Members of the study population who were free of such pathologies were also capable of maintaining a maximum cardiac output more or less comparable to that of much younger adults (see Chapter 5 for a more detailed discussion). This result suggests that the aging process in half the population induced no significant decrement in physiological cardiac function. In this instance, a strict insistence on the principle that age-related changes are identical in every member of the species would require us to eliminate the pathologies of coronary artery disease and its precursor stages from our list of normal age-related changes, or conversely, to conclude erroneously that cardiovascular disease is an integral part of the aging process of every person.

Either conclusion is too rigid an application of theory to reality, given the known genetic heterogeneity of the human population and our resulting polymorphic character. Both conclusions run the risk of blinding us to certain fundamental changes of great importance in understanding the biology of aging. The best procedure is to recognize that we are a heterogeneous and polymorphic species and that we must discard the notion of universal age-related changes, particularly when the genetic and phenotypic evidence suggests the existence of a polymorphic trait. If the disease pattern has accurately identified a polymorphic trait, then longitudinal investigations should reveal the existence of particular types or degrees of age-related changes in predisease individuals but not in individuals not fated to display the disease syndrome. Such appears to be the case with arteriosclerosis. The increased rigidity of the arterial wall over time, as described already, appears to be a normal age-related change. These structural changes bring about poorly understood fluid dynamic changes in blood flow. Whether these hemodynamic alterations are conducive to the eventual deposition of plaques appears to depend both on the individual's diet and exercise regime and on his or her genetic background, which establishes that person's capability of metabolizing, transporting, and excreting fats such as cholesterol. The phenotype of coronary artery disease therefore depends in part on a sequence of normal age-related changes that tend to put the individual at greater risk, in part on the individual's environmental situation, and in part on the individual's genetically determined physiological response mechanisms.

A similar situation pertains to age-related changes in the skeletal system; the relevant discussion in Chapter 5 is another attempt to come to grips with this difficult problem.

Environmental Changes That Modulate Aging

We have discussed in general terms the environmental plasticity of longevity (see Chapter 1). Given our discussion of mortality kinetics in Chapter 2, it should be clear that, for a cohort of long-lived creatures with negligible senescence, the environment determines the mortality of individual organisms. A more detailed account of specific examples is needed to discern the multiplicity of mechanisms by which environmental conditions affect aging and senescence.

The bristlecone pine, which has a documented maximum life span in excess of 5,000 years, is one of the longest-lived organisms in the world. But such longevities are attained only by trees that live in the harsh windswept peaks of the White Mountains in California. Individuals of the same species that live in more protected environments live substantially shorter times, on the order of about 1,000 years. This life span is still extraordinarily long by any standard, but the 80 percent reduction in longevity is striking. The harsh environment is conducive for extended longevity because it results in fewer fungi to parasitize the tree and smaller amounts of inflammable underbrush to bring about accidental death (LaMarche 1969; Finch 1990). The shortness of the growing season may also play a role, although much evidence suggests that these long-lived perennial trees have an apparently unlimited, or at least a very large, capacity for continuous cell division in their meristematic growth zones (Westing 1964).

Perennial trees such as the bristlecone or the beech, or other angiosperms such as the giant saguaro cactus, grow more or less continuously. Their increased size increases their vulnerability to exogenous risk factors, which increase their risk of sustaining vital damage. Such risk factors include the accumulation of underbrush that might harbor insect pests and/or serve as fuel for fires ignited by lightning strikes, the increase in the probability of severe wind and ice damage as the trees grow bigger and offer more resistance to the wind, the cumulative structural damage caused by commensal animals, and so forth. The longer these organisms live and are exposed to these environmental insults, the greater the probability that the accumulated structural injuries will someday result in a mortal wound. The mechanical senescence suffered by these long-lived plants is environmentally induced (Finch 1990).

An environmental effect common in organisms that display gradual senescence is the cumulative exposure of the organism to a ubiquitous environmental component that acts as a toxin for that species. The effect of this exposure often would be to gradually induce physiological dysfunction after a physiological threshold was exceeded. One example of such an effect in humans is the expression in later life of pathologies related to the accumulation of ultraviolet rays, such as the development of a skin cancer or the accelerated aging of the skin as a result of sun exposure. All else being equal, older individuals have a total exposure to the ultraviolet rays of the sun greater than that of younger individuals; thus, older individuals have a greater probability of having accumulated a level of UV-induced damage sufficient to bring about actinic aging or damage to the skin. This effect is so common in people that dermatologists examine only skin from usually protected areas, such as the buttocks, when they are trying to assess the effects of aging on skin structure. In this context, then, we can regard UV as an environmental toxin. The steps taken recently to curtail the production of common chemicals that are capable of destroying the ozone layer of the atmosphere and of increasing the UV flux at Earth's surface can be viewed in part as an anti-aging measure.

Social insects such as the honeybee provide us with a wonderful example of how environmental and developmental factors can interact to affect longevity in organisms that display rapid senescence (see Winston 1987 for references). Worker bees are sterile females. Those born in the winter have a mean longevity of about 140 days, although some individuals may live as long as 320 days; those born in the summer have a mean longevity of only about 15 to 38 days. Young worker bees of either seasonal group spend their first few weeks in the hive, attending the queen and nursing the brood. They then shift their activities to the field, where they forage for food. This shift is accompanied by large increases in juvenile hormone, decreases in vitellogenin levels, atrophy of the hypopharyngeal glands, and the onset of foraging flights. In winter bees, these physiological changes and the role change from nursing to foraging are delayed until late winter or early spring. The winter bees also have less energetically demanding hive duties than do summer bees. Thus senescence and death in the worker bee are not strictly determined by age, but are linked instead to the hormonally induced onset of foraging, with its increased risk of mechanical damage (broken wings, for example), energy depletion, and subsequent senescence. These environmental changes are capable of shifting the honeybee worker from the category of rapid senescence (summer bees) to that of gradual senescence (winter bees).

We could offer other examples, but the point is that the life span of an organism cannot be viewed as an intrinsic and unchanging quality. Rather it is the result of a complex series of interactions between the individual organism and its specific environment. In addition to the parameters already mentioned, such interactions often involve developmental modifications.

• *Developmental Changes That Accelerate or Retard Aging*

Development may end at the point of the life cycle at which the age-specific mortality rate of the population under consideration reaches a minimum, as described in Chapter 2. However, events that take place during the developmental period may well affect the longevity characteristic of the postdevelopmental, or mature adult, phase of the life cycle. It is thus important to our understanding that we be able to characterize the ways in which developmental events may modulate the aging process.

Let's focus again on the honeybee, which is a classic example of the fact that the presence or absence of particular hormonal changes during development can cause the same genome to adopt one of two alternative developmental paths, each leading to a morph with a characteristic and different life span. In the case of the honeybee, the basic observation is that females can develop either into sterile worker bees, whose longevity ranges from 1 to 12 months depending on whether they are winter or summer bees, as described in the previous section, or into fertile queens that may live for 5 years or more. The problem is to determine the mechanisms underlying this choice of alternative pathways. The evidence, as presented in Winston 1987, leads to the following conclusions.

Both queens and workers develop from fertilized eggs. The larva is multipotent with respect to its possible fates for the first 3 to 4 days of life. During this period, if the workers feed the larvae large volumes of food containing high concentrations of sugars, called royal jelly, stretch receptors in the larval gut initiate the secretion of juvenile hormone by the corpora allata glands in the head. This hormone brings about a higher growth rate, production of queen-specific proteins, and other responses that enable the larva to develop into a fertile queen. Failure to feed the larva this royal jelly leads to the development of a sterile worker. Experimentally administered subthreshold levels of food and/or hormonal manipulations lead to the production of worker–queen intermediates. Thus diet-induced neuroendocrine influences shunt development into a path that gives rise to a large fertile queen with a very long life span. Her longevity is limited primarily by the exhaustion of her sperm stores, which induces the worker bees to kill the queen, after which they bring about the development of a new queen. Old queens display few other signs of loss of physiological function. Thus queens appear to exhibit gradual senescence, while worker bees exhibit rapid senescence. We marvel at the long life of the queen, but we must also note the long life of her stored sperm, all 5 million of which were stored in her spermatheca on her nuptial flight and all of which drastically outlived the male drones from which they came.

In humans, females significantly outlive males, as is described in some detail in Chapter 6 (see also Smith 1993). This phenomenon is not generally widespread and is not found in many species (Gavrilov and Gavrilova 1991). However, in species that do display sex-based differences in longevity, we may view the process of sex determination as one that sets the fertilized egg on one of two developmental paths, each leading to the formation of a distinctive morph with a characteristic longevity. Since we do not fully understand the reasons underlying the longevity difference in humans, nor do we know when the sex-determining genes begin to exert their effect on life span, we cannot yet delineate the mechanisms responsible and characterize them as being developmental or postmaturational. Nor can we yet conclude whether the longevity difference is the summed result of many small differences in structural, physiological, and/or behavioral factors common to both sexes, or if it arises from a singular mechanism(s) intrinsic to only one sex. The evidence described in Chapter 6 suggests both possibilities. Solving this puzzle promises to be satisfying from both the intellectual and the practical viewpoint.

Dormancy and diapause are periods of slowed metabolism and growth that may occur during development and/or adult stages in many different types of organisms. They are often induced by specific signals characteristic of adverse environmental conditions. Dormancy and diapause are quite common in seeds, and one or the other is also found in worms, insects, fish, frogs, and various marsupial and mammalian orders. From an evolutionary point of view, such processes appear to have the function of delaying the onset of reproduction until the improvement of environmental conditions increases the probability of successfully transmitting one's genes to the next generation. Diapause and dormancy have two general effects on the life span, depending on the species involved: either none, or an inverse relationship between the time spent in dormancy and the subsequent life span (Finch 1990). The genes responsible for the control of larval diapause in the nematode *Caenorhabditis elegans* are intimately related to the genes that have been independently shown to be involved in the extension of adult longevity in this organism. Consequently, we will discuss genes, diapause, and extended longevity of *C. elegans* in more detail in Chapter 6.

Environmental and developmental effects merge together in our consideration of the intrauterine environment and its effects on life span and senescence. The literature summarized by Finch (1990) shows that both life span and senescence can be altered by the developmental effects of gonadal steroids or by the sex of the neighboring fetus. In mice, females flanked *in utero* by males are more agressive as young adults and enter reproductive senescence later than females that are flanked by other females characteristically do. In another inbred mouse strain characterized by an early onset of autoimmune disease and a short life span, implants of testosterone into the mother at day 12 during pregancy increased the life span of the unborn pups by 25 percent relative to untreated controls. Thus, the expression of immune dysfunctions that have a postmaturational onset can be significantly altered by the developmental effects of gonadal steroids during specific times of development. In addition, Iwase et al. (1995) have shown that in the rat, maternal diabetes significantly lowered the birth weight and shortened the life span of male offspring, leading the authors to suggest that the reduced fetal growth induced by the diabetic intrauterine environment may accelerate an age-related degenerative process. It is thus possible to have congenital or familial effects on longevity without any indication that these are primarily genetic in their causation. This result represents a possible confounding effect in our studies of the genetic determinants of longevity, as will be described shortly.

In humans, the particulars of fetal development also seem to permanently program the adult morphology, physiology, and life expectancy. It is well known that maternal malnutrition may adversely affect the developing fetus. What is new is the observation that certain cardiovascular and metabolic disorders may arise from such malnutrition; the specific type of disease observed in the adult depends on the trimester during which the fetus was undernourished (Figure 3.16). This situation presumably arises out of the interaction of nutritional factors with the tissue and time-specific patterns of gene expression involved in the development of the cardiovascular and other systems. Since adult life expectancy can be significantly affected by disease, this observation suggests that environmentally modulated developmental programming plays an important role in the plasticity of longevity in humans. In fact, some familial traits of disease and longevity may be explained in part by such a mechanism. Maternal undernutrition in the second trimester may result in diabetes in the offspring, and these diabetic daughters may then give rise to shorter-lived grandchildren. If identical twins are involved in any of these genealogies, their high concordance might well be due to both a shared common genotype and a shared common intrauterine environment. However, our current deterministic prejudices might cause many to interpret the data as indicating the effects of only the former, and thereby miss the point. We need a better understanding of the molecular changes that underlie these fetal adaptations and their persistence throughout later life.

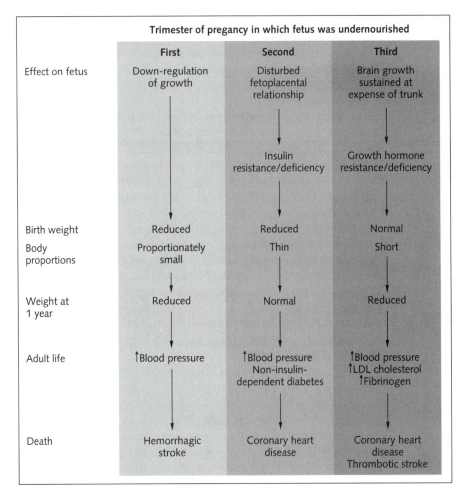

Figure 3.16   A schematic representation of the effects of fetal undernutrition, according to trimester of pregancy, on the probable health trajectory of the future adult. (Redrawn from Barker 1995.)

• *Postmaturational Changes That Accelerate or Retard Aging*

Most of the interventions known to be effective in modulating the rate of aging are postmaturational; that is, they are generally applied to the individual adult sometime after the developmental period has been completed. These interventions can have either positive or negative effects, and include smoking, nutrition, exercise, weight control, hormones, and other types of physiological interventions. We will discuss these in some detail in Chapter 7, in addition to pointing out some apparently ineffective interventions. For now, however, note that there exist, even in the adult organism, at least a few means of effectively and significantly modulating the individual's life span. It appears that the aging processes can be modified even while they are taking place, an observation that poses some constraints on the types of mechanisms potentially involved. At a minimum, the existence of postmaturational modification of longevity suggests that these mechanisms cannot be predetermined by the end of the developmental period, but must include some labile component(s) well into adulthood.

● *Individual Rates of Aging and the Use of Biomarkers*

One of the mandates of the National Institute on Aging is to explore and develop approaches for extending the vigorous and productive years of life. Evidence such as that described in Chapter 5 has been used to support the idea that aging is the cumulative result of multiple processes. These different processes appear to proceed at different rates within the same individual. Thus, a given individual may be functionally older than his or her chronological age in terms of one physiological process, such as hearing acuity, but not in terms of another one, such as muscle strength. A given intervention may affect only one of these processes.

Simply measuring the life span will not yield sufficient information as to the efficacy of a particular intervention. Clinicians and researchers alike want to know whether a particular "segmental intervention" (a treatment that affects only one or a few of these multiple aging processes) has successfully affected the physiological rate of aging of the system under investigation. This knowledge has practical importance, since postponing the onset of clinical dysfunction in a person's weakest physiological system may result in a substantial increase in both the quality and quantity of life for that individual. Continued progress in increasing the mean life span depends on this strategy. Consequently, the need has arisen to construct a panel of biological markers of aging—"biomarkers"—that can be used to test such segmental interventions both in humans and in laboratory animals.

The concept of biomarkers rests on the assumption that the passage of time is only indirectly related to age. If, in a biological sense, the life span of a mouse and the life span of a human are equivalent, then the passage of time is a very poor measure of age. Interventions into aging processes might produce equally significant differences in the rate of aging of individual members of a single species. Biomarkers would be measures that could be obtained in a small portion of the life span and that would accurately predict longevity. In effect, biomarkers of aging are constructs with which scientists are trying to forge a connection between the population-level phenomenon of increased mortality and the individual-level phenomenon of age-related changes in various physiological parameters.

The tests composing such a panel ideally should have all of the following characteristics (Reff and Schneider 1982; Baker and Sprott 1988):

1. The rate of change with time in a biomarker should reflect the rate of aging.

2. The biomarker should be monitoring a basic and important process.

3. The tests should be nonlethal and preferably noninvasive, and cause minimal trauma.

4. The tests should be highly reproducible and should reflect physiological age.

5. The function examined should display significant alterations during a relatively short time period.

6. The functions being measured should be crucial to the effective maintenance of health.

7. The biomarker should have a high cross-species correlation.

8. The biomarkers used should be able to function either as a prospective predictor of life span or as a retrospective marker of aging.

Others have pointed out that these desired attributes of biomarkers can be viewed as falling into three complementary classes:

1. Pragmatic: They should be simple and inexpensive to use.

2. Ethical: They should be minimally intrusive and cause the least possible pain and stress.

3. Methodological: They should be insensitive to the effects of prior measurements and robust over a wide range of laboratory and experimental conditions; above all, they must measure aging validly and reliably.

Given the idea that aging involves multiple processes, different panels of biomarkers may be needed in order to distinguish among interventions that affect maximum life span, those that affect mean life span, and those that have segmental effects.

By segmental, we mean treatments that (1) retard the aging process (and physiological deterioration) in a specific system without significantly affecting the overall survival characteristics, and/or (2) have this effect only during temporally restricted portions of the life cycle. In the former case, this means we are affecting morbidity but not mortality. In the latter case, the effects of the system on morbidity and/or mortality can be modulated only during a certain portion of the life span. The complexity and the rigor of these several demands raises a problem in terms both of their theoretical identification and characterization and of their practical implementation. All in all, the potential benefits of using biomarkers are matched by the difficulty of constructing them. It is fair to ask what progress has been made toward achieving this goal.

Results from Earlier Studies

Costa and McCrae (1980) critically analyzed four studies that attempted to devise a "functional" age scale for humans. They concluded that none of the studies to that date had yielded any statistically promising results, in part because of the heterogeneity of the variables used, in part because of statistical and methodological problems in measuring and comparing the results, and in part because of problems in concept and definition. The variables they examined included at least one (gray hair) that we have already concluded may not be a true age-related change. Others, such as weight or cholesterol level, may be subject to extensive environmental modulation, as we have discussed.

Some socioeconomic variables, such as expected age at retirement, show an arbitrary association with the aging process. The use of ambiguous variables such as these, particularly the uncritical mixing of genotypic and phenotypic characters, will result in poor statistical correlations with chronological age. Some of the less ambiguous and more widely used variables are listed in Table 3.2. The wide range of correlation coefficients for the same variable across multiple studies suggests the existence of one or more sources of uncontrollable variation in the test and/or the sample population. In other words, not all variation in a single measure can be ascribed to differences in biological age, since, as we have seen, such differences may exist for a variety of reasons.

This observation should make us pause before placing too much theoretical weight on any single variable. However, even if a particular variable showed a perfect correlation with chronological age, all we would have would be a perfect, and useless, alternative expression of chronological age. The problem here is that, if the intent of the effort is to find an alternative measure to chronological age, any approach that attempts to maximize the correlation of a particular variable to chronological age is logically flawed: A perfect model would merely be predicting the subject's chronological age.

A Potential Panel of Human Biomarkers

Table 3.3 lists 28 proposed human biomarkers (Reff and Schneider 1982). These markers are a diverse group spanning the physiological spectrum from molecule

Table 3.2	Some of the Physiological Variables Used in Studies on Aging	

Variable	Number of studies in which used	Correlation with chronological age
Systolic blood pressure	9	0.16 to 0.69
Hearing loss	8	0.42 to 0.66
Lung capacity	6	−0.77 to −0.40
Reaction time	5	0.26 to 0.52
Grip strength	5	−0.52 to −0.21
Diastolic blood pressure	4	0.10 to 0.51
Height	4	−0.68 to −0.09
Visual acuity	4	−0.57 to −0.42
Forced expiratory volume (1 second)	4	−0.70 to −0.38
Accommodation of eye	3	0.88 to 0.57
Tapping	3	−0.44 to −0.18
Weight	3	0.01 to 0.56

Source: From Shock 1981. © Oxford University Press.

Table 3.3   **Some Proposed Human Biomarkers**

Proposed biomarker	Shortest time period in which statistically significant change can be measured	Differences between males and females?
1. T lymphocyte proliferation mitogen	5–10 years	No
2. T cell levels	5–10 years	No
3. Thymic hormone levels	5–10 years	No
4. Sensitivity to DNA damage (lymphocytes)	5–10 years	No
5. Insulin resistance (glucose tolerance)	10–20 years	No
6. Racemization of proteins	10 years	No
7. Left ventricular mass and wall thickness	20 years	No
8. Rate of left ventricular filling	20 years	No
9. Response to cardiovascular stress	20 years	No
10. Lung capacity	5 years	Yes
11. Systolic blood pressure	20 years	Yes
12. Bone mass	2 years	Yes
13. Plasma norepinephrine levels	10 years	Unknown
14. Cardiac response to beta adrenergic stimulation	10 years	Unknown
15. Sleep disturbances: wave form	6 months	Yes
16. Sleep disturbances: lack of sleep	12 months	Yes
17. Sleep disturbances: air exchange efficiency	6 months	Yes
18. Brain ventricular and sulcal size	5 years	No
19. Psychomotor function (digit symbol substitution)	10 years	No
20. Hearing (pure tone threshold)	2–5 years	Yes
21. Pupil diameter	5 years	No
22. Visual contrast sensitivity	10 years	No
23. Accommodation of the eye	2 years	No
24. Glomerular filtration rate (creatinine clearance)	5 years	Yes
25. DHEA (an adrenal steroid) levels	5–10 years	Yes
26. Estradiol levels	2–10 years	Yes
27. Decreased heart rate variability	5–10 years	Yes
28. Glycosylated hemoglobin levels	20 years	Yes

Source: Adapted from Reff and Schneider 1982.

to psyche. They are equally diverse in the time they require to show a statistically significant change and in their ability to detect sexual differences. Let's examine several of these biomarkers in more detail in order to gain an appreciation of the benefits and problems associated with such representative biomarkers.

Protein Racemization

Our physiological functions reflect our structure. Any process that alters the structure of our proteins might well adversely affect the functions served by that protein. A good example is the racemization of our lens proteins that causes decreased visual acuity. The racemization of proteins (Table 3.3, item 6) is one example of an intrinsic molecular marker of aging. In racemization, a "left-handed" amino acid (L-amino acid) is converted to a "right-handed" amino acid (D-amino acid); this conversion is (usually) a nonenzymatic, spontaneous, water- and temperature-dependent posttranslational reaction (Masters 1982; but see Kreil 1994). When measured in bound amino acids in metabolically stable proteins, racemization has the potential to serve as a retrospective molecular indicator of aging. In the eye lens protein of normal individuals, the amount of converted amino acid increases steadily with time such that D-aspartic acid accumulates at a rate of 0.14 percent per year (Figure 3.17). However, the reaction proceeds at about half this rate in the protein in permanent teeth and appears to be delicately affected by temperature (Ohtani, Kato, and Sugeno 1996). These recently reported facts cast doubt on the potential utility of this reaction as an absolute molecular clock.

Changes in the structure of the lens protein are assumed to be correlated with the age-related decrements in visual acuity that take place during the same time interval. Pathological but non-age-related changes in the system, such as cataracts, are known to be associated with abnormally high values in the biomarker (see Figure 3.17). Similar processes are observed to take place in other proteins, such as the dentine of teeth (the proteinaceous layer immediately beneath the enamel) (Masters 1982). Calculations of actual ages based on the racemization of dentine show a good correlation with higher ages but not with lower ages. This type of test might be of value for assaying interventions that would prolong the high levels of protein synthesis characteristic of young organisms; it would be of only limited value in many other applications. The test suffers from the drawback that the process of obtaining the sample is invasive and might cause trauma and/or death. A major drawback is that it is of value only with

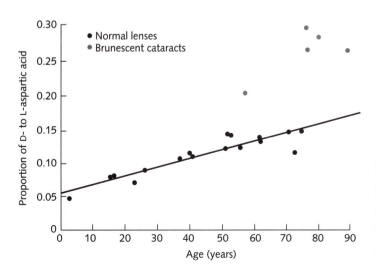

Figure 3.17 The extent of racemization of aspartic acid in the central portion of the lens, based on 17 individuals with normal lenses and 5 individuals with brunescent (brown) cataracts. (From Masters 1982.)

long-lived, stable proteins. The mosaic nature of the aging process suggests that such intrinsic molecular markers are not an accurate measure of aging for all the tissues and organs of the body. Finally, a recent report suggests that racemization is enzymatically controlled in some systems, and thus is not useful as a time-dependent biomarker (Kreil 1994).

Changes in Brain Mass

Anatomical changes within particular organs may be measured in different ways. For example, computerized tomography (CT) scans may be used to noninvasively measure atrophic changes in the central nervous system (see Chapter 5); thus this technique lends itself well to longitudinal studies. The nonlinear increase in ventricle and sulcus size with age begins at age 60 (Figure 3.18) and is consistent with a variety of reports suggesting that the brain atrophies and loses mass with age (see Figure 5.1). Such loss of brain mass appears to be of the sort that might well underlie a host of different segmental effects of aging on neurological and psychomotor functions. The problem here is that we do not quite understand what these gross anatomical changes mean, particularly since many individuals show no decline in particular psychomotor and/or memory tests and

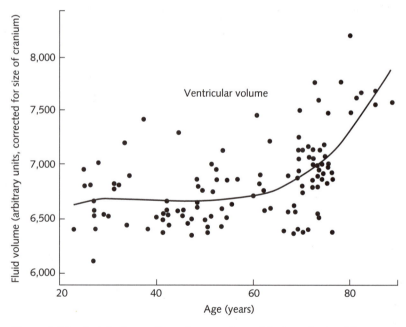

Figure 3.18   A plot of a nonlinear increase in ventricular volume of the brain, as determined by CT measurements in healthy individuals. The external fissures and sulci of these brains showed a very similar pattern of age-related increase in size. These changes are consistent with an age-related loss of brain mass. Note that the variance also increases with age, such that some elderly individuals have values that overlap those of much younger individuals. (From Alberts and Naeser 1982.)

different patterns of age-related changes in performance are found for different types of psychological tests (Arenberg 1978).

Forced Vital Capacity

One long-term (since 1948) longitudinal study of community residents in a Massachusetts town—the Framingham study—has yielded some very interesting information regarding a prospective predictor of life span that may lend itself to serve as an overall indicator of physiological age. This factor, the forced vital capacity (FVC), is defined as the maximum amount of air that can be exhaled in a given amount of time (see also Chapter 5). Measurement of this factor is a simple and noninvasive office procedure that lends itself well to longitudinal studies. The decline in FVC with age is shown in Figure 3.19. Smokers show a similar decline that exhibits a greater divergence from nonsmokers with time. The measured level of the FVC is a statistically significant predictor of premature mortality (see Table 3.2) and appears to be measuring a function that is more general than impaired pulmonary function. In the words of Kannel and Hubert (1982, pp. 157–159):

> In any event, an FVC determination would appear to be an efficient way to identify asymptomatic persons destined for a premature death. . . . FVC is one of the strongest predictors of mortality, second only to age itself. . . . It appears to be a measure of vigor, general musculoskeletal functional capacity and overall health; truly a measure of living capacity.

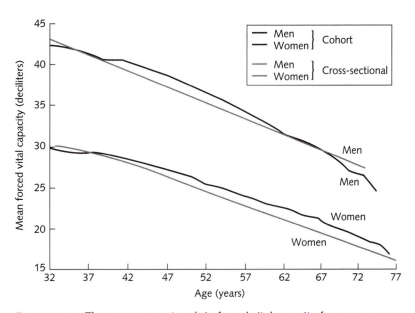

Figure 3.19   The average age trends in forced vital capacity for cross-sectional and longitudinal data obtained from the Framingham study. (From Kannel and Hubert 1982.)

Do People "Look Their Age"?

We should take note of the utility of a simple visual estimate of the whole person (preeminently the skin) as an indicator of biological age. As part of the Baltimore Longitudinal Study on Aging (BLSA), Borkan and Norris (1980) assayed the physiological age of 1,086 males using 24 different tests (Table 3.4).[*] They plotted these results for each individual as shown in Figure 3.20. This analysis demonstrates clearly that an individual may be older in some parameters than in

Table 3.4 **Mean Correlation with Age for Selected Biomarkers in 1,086 Males Studied in the BLSA**

Biomarker correlation coefficient (r)	
Forced expiratory volume (1 second)	−0.698[a]
Vital capacity	−0.606[a]
Maximum breathing capacity	−0.547[a]
Systolic blood pressure	0.538[a]
Diastolic blood pressure	0.368[a]
Hemoglobin levels	−0.223[a]
Serum albumin levels	−0.356[a]
Serum globulin levels	0.092[a]
Creatinine clearance	−0.602[b]
Plasma glucose levels	0.279
Auditory threshold (4000 cycles/sec)	0.549
Visual acuity	−0.306[b]
Visual depth perception	−0.232[a]
Basal metabolic rate	−0.337[a]
Cortical bone percent	−0.435[a]
Creatinine excretion	−0.538[a]
Hand grip strength	−0.501[a]
Maximum work rate	−0.511[a]
Benton visual memory test (errors)	0.502[a]
Tapping time (medium targets)	0.468[a]
Tapping time (close targets)	0.366[a]
Reaction time (simple)	0.287[a]
Reaction time (choice)	0.220[a]
Foot reaction time	0.222[a]

Source: From Borkan and Norris 1980.
[a]$p < 0.01$
[b]$p < 0.05$

[*]The set of biomarkers used in this study (Table 3.4) may also serve as an alternative to that shown in Table 3.3.

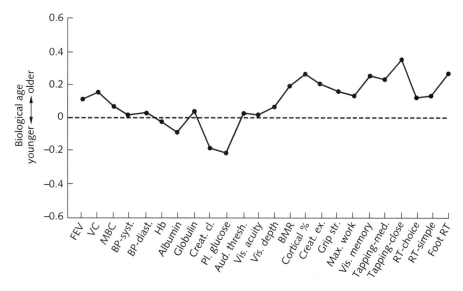

Figure 3.20 A biological age profile of a single individual, using the parameters given in Table 3.4. This profile demonstrates that an individual may be biologically older on some parameters than on others. Biological age is expressed as the twoscore transformation of the residuals obtained from a regression of the data for each biomarker on age. (From Borkan and Norris 1980.)

others and reinforces our earlier discussion of individual heterogeneity in aging. In addition, however, Borkan and Norris made a *visual* estimate of each individual's chronological age, which led to a most interesting conclusion. Their analysis of the data revealed that individuals who looked older were indeed biologically older (although we should note that the data in this example are taken from the two extreme ends of the population, as explained in Figure 3.21). A more generalizable aspect of their studies is that those subjects who had died since the start of the study were biologically older at the time the parameters were measured than those of the same age who had survived (Figure 3.22). Thus, an intelligent and informed visual appraisal of the whole individual may be as informative a prospective predictor of life span as are many more sophisticated biomarkers.

However, there are some contradictions that must be noted with respect to this mosaic biological pattern of aging. First, individuals judged as looking older and who died early were biologically aged in some functions but not in sensory measures or in body composition (see Figure 3.21). In fact, they were stronger than the younger-looking group and similar to them in terms of basal metabolic rate. Yet these are some of the factors commonly used in the layperson's assessment of age. Are they that wrong? Second, the doctors who estimated age in this study judged that larger individuals looked older than their actual age, raising the problem of the subjective interpretation of data, as well as a possible confounding of survival characteristics with body size. In fact, chest circumference is probably the best single predictor of FVC; thus one might reasonably expect larger individ-

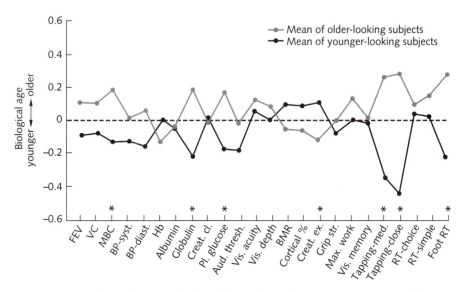

Figure 3.21   Biological age profiles based on subjectively estimated age, using the parameters given in Table 3.4. The dotted line represents mean biological age scores of subpopulations that appeared the most "old for their age" (the top 15 percent of the distribution). The solid line represents mean biological age scores of subpopulations that appeared the most "young for their age" (the bottom 15 percent of the distribution). The starred parameters represent significantly different mean scores by *t*-test ($p < 0.05$). Biological age expressed as in Figure 3.20. (From Borkan and Norris 1980.)

uals to be longer lived. The issue is not yet clearly understood, but there are some clues to the answer of this conundrum. For example, the work of Brant, Fozard, and Metter (1994) shows that most biomarkers bear only an age-specific, and not a general, predictive relationship to future mortality. This topic is discussed in more detail in the section on invertebrate biomarkers later in this chapter.

Age at Menopause

A longitudinal study of human females has shown that age at natural menopause is inversely associated with longevity (Snowden et al. 1989). Women who reported an early onset of natural menopause (less than 44 years) had a significantly elevated mortality relative to those who experienced the onset of menopause at ages 50 to 54 years. This observation suggests a correlation between ovarian aging and the aging of other tissues. The mechanisms involved are not clear, but age at menopause might serve as a prospective biomarker of aging for females. One implication of this observation is that there exists some sort of general aging "clock" that regulates all body systems. In an ongoing longitudinal study in mice, muscle function and immune function appeared to age in a coordinate manner (Miller et al. 1997). These two studies raise but do not prove the question of whether a general aging "clock" exists that governs the aging of all tissues.

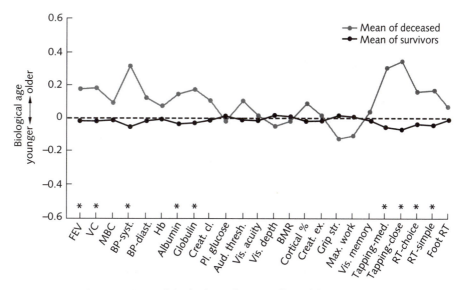

Figure 3.22 A comparison of the biological age profiles of deceased study participants with those of surviving study participants, using the parameters given in Table 3.4. The dotted line represents mean biological age scores of 166 men who had died since they were last measured. The solid line represents mean scores for all other (922) participants, who were still alive. The starred parameters represent significantly different mean scores by *t*-test ($p < 0.05$). Biological age expressed as in Figure 3.20. (From Borkan and Norris 1980.)

Is There a Single Indicator of Biological Age?

The literature records many attempts to construct a single numerical indicator of biological age (see Balin 1994a). While many of these studies present interesting and useful physiological data, none of them can escape one criticism or another. Does this mean that the attempt to quantify human aging is intrinsically impossible? Not at all. One can apply mathematical principles other than regression and correlation to chronological age in an effort to identify and quantify the aging process.

Nakamura (1994) used the technique of principal component analysis, which is designed to discern the underlying structure of interrelationships among the test scores measured in a complex system while retaining as much of the variation present in the data set as possible. His results were most interesting. Rather than constructing a single index of biological age, Nakamura identified 13 factors organized into three classes (Figure 3.23). The first factor (F1), a general aging factor, accounted for 13.5 percent of the total variance in test scores. The second set of 11 factors (F2–F12), the system-specific aging factors, accounted for 57.5 percent of the variance. The third set, termed uniqueness (the individual variance inherent in every variable but not necessarily related to any aging process), accounted for 29.0 percent of the variance. These results suggest that, while there may be a fundamental and unitary aging process, the system-specific

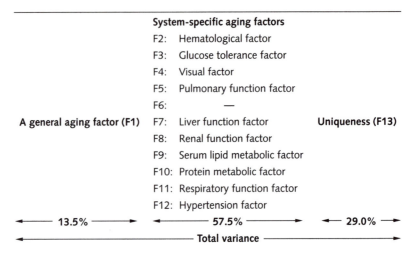

Figure 3.23 Nakamura's separation, based on the principal component analysis, of biological age changes into three categories: a general aging factor, system-specific aging factors, and uniqueness (the individual variance that is inherent in every variable). Note that the general aging factor constitutes a relatively small percentage of the total variance. Most of the variance in aging is accounted for by system-specific factors. (From Nakamura 1994.)

expression of this process is what is most easily detected and what accounts for most of the variance.

Building on this result, Nakamura (1994) incorporated the values of the 11 physiological variables listed in Figure 3.23 in a complex equation, constructed a biological score of the age-related changes in these physiological functions, and manipulated this score to yield a numerical biological age. When he plotted this biological age for 462 healthy men against their chronological age, he found that the former closely tracked the latter (Figure 3.24). When he performed the same procedure on diabetic or hypertensive adults, he found that both of these ill groups had physiological values that translated into biological ages about 4 years older than their chronological age (Figure 3.25). This significant discrepancy between biological and chronological ages was interpreted as due to a more rapid rate of aging in these ill individuals.

An analogous strategy was adopted by Hochschild (1989, 1994) who developed a suite of 12 noninvasive and automatically administered physiological tests, which he administered to 2,462 office workers in the United States. Hochschild used data transformation techniques to avoid the confounding of biological and chronological age already discussed, presented his data as a deviation about the mean in a manner analogous to that shown in Figures 3.20 through 3.22, and used these results to construct a unitary numerical index of biological age. He then proved the validity of his tests by demonstrating that they yielded a higher biological age for subjects who were known to have risk factors, such as smoking, for chronic disease.

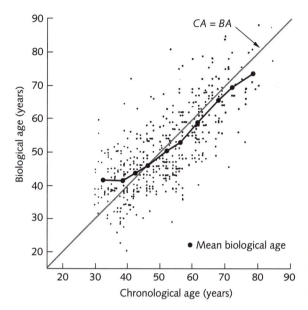

Figure 3.24 The relationship between biological age (*BA*) and chronological age (*CA*) in 462 healthy men. (Data from Nakamura 1988.)

Both Nakamura (1994) and Hochschild (1994) validated their protocols against people with chronic disease or with risk factors for chronic disease. However, as we have already pointed out, the medical model of aging is not valid, since aging progresses in the absence of disease. Both of these protocols may be accurate predictors of disease, but that fact does not validate them as predictors of aging. If either procedure is to fulfill the eighth criterion in the list on page 86

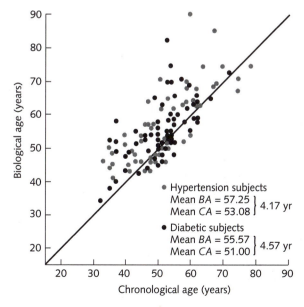

Figure 3.25 The relationship between biological age (*BA*) and chronological age (*CA*) in 62 hypertensive and 65 diabetic men. Note that in both groups of subjects, biological age is more than 4 years greater than chronological age. (Data from Nakamura 1988.)

(that the biomarker should function as a prospective measure of life expectancy or as a retrospective measure of aging), then it must be verified by longitudinal studies that follow each individual until the time of death. If the construct is valid, individuals with a biological age score higher than their chronological age generally should die earlier than individuals with a biological age score lower than their chronological age. In the absence of such information, we do not know exactly what we are measuring and thus we cannot reliably interpret what the observed relationship between aging and disease means.

In addition, compacting the excellent data of Figure 3.23 into a single number is probably an error. The use of a single or combined measure of functional age, such as those already discussed, could be profitable if there were a single process of aging. Yet many physiological data point in the other direction—that there are multiple processes of aging. The biomarkers would be of value if there were some correlation between the progression of different biomarkers in different systems of the same individual. Costa and McCrae (1984) have criticized the functional-age concept on the grounds that no evidence suggests that rates of aging covary across different physiological systems. Yet data such as those reported by Snowden and colleagues (1989) and by Miller et al. (1997) suggest a general covariance between aging processes in various different bodily functions. There seems to be a conflict in the data.

The resolution of this conflict may lie in the observation by Brant, Fozard, and Metter (1994) that many biomarkers are themselves only age-specific indicators of relative risk. Working with the excellent longitudinal data obtained from the Baltimore Longitudinal Study of Aging, these investigators statistically assayed several physiological factors collected over a 40-year period and correlated their values with the age at death of their subjects. They found that the predictive value of these biomarkers of mortality was highly age specific (Table 3.5). High levels of cholesterol, for example, were predictive of a high risk of mortality at age 40, but not at ages 60 or 80. Body build (body mass index) predicted mortality in different ways; obesity was a risk factor for mortality at age 60, but leanness was a risk factor for mortality at age 80. Quite independently, a study of Swedish twins led to the conclusion that the heritability of various cardiovascular risk factors had age-specific peaks and were much higher for people under age 65 than for those over age 65 (Row and Kahn, 1997). The fact that two different types of studies led to the same conclusion strengthens the case that some biomarkers are age-specific. This unexpected situation suggests the need for caution when using age-specific physiological values to construct a numerical measure of biological age. Does this mean that the concept of biomarkers is not useful? Not necessarily.

Brant, Fozard, and Metter (1994) have suggested that the various relative risk values for the traits listed in Table 3.5 could be combined to fit the particular profile of any individual, and the relative risk of mortality for that individual computed. The example given in Figure 3.26 shows that the individual with the higher risk factors has a higher probability of dying within a specified time period. Recall that in Chapter 2 we defined aging as the increased probability of dying within a certain time interval and quantified the definition with the Gompertz curve and the mortality rate doubling time (MRDT). By calibrating

Table 3.5	**Biomarkers Found to be Significantly Associated with Mortality at Specific Ages**
Age (years)	*Biomarkers significantly associated with mortality*
40	White blood cell count
	Cardiac diagnosis
	Diastolic blood pressure
	Total serum cholesterol
	Serum triglycerides
60	White blood cell count
	Cardiac diagnosis
	Systolic blood pressure
	Forced expiratory volume
	Visual acuity
	High body mass index
80	White blood cell count
	Low body mass index

Source: Adapted from Brant, Fozard, and Metter 1994.

their data against mortality, and not illness, Brant, Fozard, and Metter (1994) have constructed and validated a set of biological indices of aging that can predict the probability of dying within a specified time interval. The indices therefore are measuring aging. Do not overestimate the ability of these indices; they are restricted to a small subset of the population and are not capable of accurately

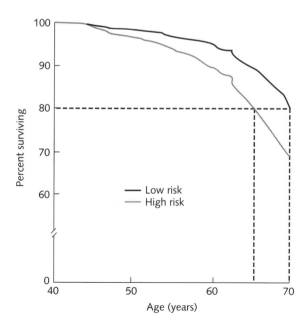

Figure 3.26 Estimated survival probabilities for males measured at age 40 with different levels of coronary risk factors: low (diastolic pressure 75 mm Hg, serum cholesterol 200 mg/dl, serum triglycerides 110 mg/dl) and high (diastolic pressure 95 mm Hg, serum cholesterol 250 mg/dl, serum triglycerides 140 mg/dl). Data are from the Baltimore Longitudinal Study on Aging. The vertical lines show the ages at which both the high- and low-risk groups have an estimated 80 percent chance of surviving the next year. The difference in the age at which the two groups reach this mortality level is about 5 years; in other words, there is about a 10 percent difference in survival rates at age 70 between the two groups. (From Brant, Fozard, and Metter 1994.)

predicting anyone's death date. However, this exercise does prove the concept of biomarkers in principle, and that is a very important advance.

In Summary

This survey should have made clear that, although panels of precisely calibrated valid and reliable biomarker tests suitable for general use do not yet exist, there are individual tests and different suites of tests, some of which appear to be more useful than others. A compilation of clinically feasible biomarker tests has been published (Dean 1988), as has a critical evaluation of such tests (Balin 1994). A good summation of the present state of the art and of its utility is offered by Heikkinen et al. (1994, p. 88):

> Our results . . . suggest that no single factor, but rather a combination of biological, psychological, and social factors . . . contribute to healthy aging. Therefore, any assessment of single or even multiple parameters of aging with the purpose of assessing an individual's biological age is pre-mature and the concept of biological age will have to be regarded as an empty abstraction. . . . However, as Mark Twain said of Wagner's music, "It is not as bad as it sounds." . . . Concepts of functional or biological age as statistical entities may be useful in making comparisons of different populations or between larger groups of individuals . . . [even though] a need exists for methodological development and more information is required. . . . [This] does not, however, necessarily mean that we should wait for the results of more conclusive studies before any intervention pro-grams can be initiated or any actions recommended to decision makers . . . aimed at promoting the physical and mental capacity of aging popula-tions and reducing inequalities in health.

A Potential Panel of Primate Biomarkers

Interventions with the potential to alter the maximum human life span must be tested experimentally before being considered for widespread use. This require-ment means that they must be tested in nonhuman primates. Macaque monkeys are the most commonly studied genus of nonhuman primates. Since they have a maximum life span of at least 29 years, it is not practical to use an extension of maximum life span as the assay for the effectiveness of such interventions. Assaying the effectiveness of these interventions will require the development of a panel of primate biomarkers. It would not be surprising if such a primate panel were also useful in assaying human aging.

A good start on sorting out the useful variables has been made in a cross-sec-tional analysis of biomarkers in a nonhuman primate, the pig-tailed macaque monkey. The goal of the experiment was to construct a battery of biomarkers for each age–sex class that would allow the assessment of the biological rate of aging in these monkeys, and to do this in a period of time significantly less than 29 years. From an initial list of about 290 candidate variables, Short, Williams, and Bowden (1987) empirically selected 72 variables for further study across young, middle-aged, and old animals. Of these, 20 were found to be significantly influenced by age and were therefore selected for inclusion in an initial longitudinal study (Bowden et al. 1990). Only eight physiological and three behavioral variables, listed in Figure 3.27, each showed a significant rate of change with time and were used to construct a biological index of aging (Short, Williams, and Bowden 1994). In addition, the investigators determined the rate of change of certain antioxidant levels, found that they varied in the expected direction (see Chapter 9) and included them in the model as protective mechanisms that might

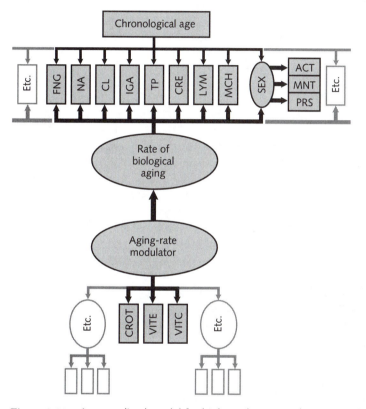

Figure 3.27   A generalized model for biological aging in the pig-tailed macaque monkey, a nonhuman primate. Eight factors were found to show significant age-related within-subject change: fingernail growth (FNG), serum sodium (NA), serum chloride (CL), immunoglobulin A (IGA), serum total protein (TP), serum creatinine (CRE), lymphocytes in white blood cells (LYM), and mean corpuscular hemoglobin (MCH). These factors were used as biological measures of aging. In addition, three measures of sexual behavior—activity level (ACT), mounting of female by male (MNT), and presentation of female to male (PRS)—were used to quantify sexual activity (SEX), which was then integrated into the model. Since more age-related factors may be found in the future, "etc." allows for an open-ended model. High levels of various antioxidants—carotenoids (CROT), vitamin E (VITE), and vitamin C (VITC)—were found to be associated with low values of biological aging, and vice versa. Therefore, these factors are thought to act as modulators of the age-related changes in the indicated biomarkers. (From Short, Williams, and Bowden 1994.)

modulate the animal's intrinsic rate of aging. The strategy of these investigators illustrates how one may move ahead and produce what appear to be useful biomarker panels even though the biomarkers cannot be definitively validated, in terms of prospectively predicting maximum life span, within the professional careers of the people involved. A similar time-saving strategy may well have to be adopted for translating this biomarker panel from macaques to humans.

A Potential Panel of Rodent Biomarkers

Recognizing the need to validate at least the short-lived rodent biomarker panels against longevity measures, the National Institute on Aging embarked on a large-scale, long-term, multiple longitudinal study of biomarker characterization and analysis using four mouse and three rat inbred strains (or their hybrids). Some of the animals were subjected to dietary restriction, the only intervention known that can significantly decrease morbidity and mortality and increase life span (see Chapter 7 for a detailed discussion of this longevity-enhancing process). Both the diet-restricted and the normally fed animals were subjected to an extensive battery of physiological and biochemical tests; at least 63 such variables were identified as being significantly altered as a consequence of dietary restriction, and thus presumably bear some relationship to the extended longevity (Hass et al. 1996).

Not surprisingly, many of these biomarkers can plausibly be related to the reduced body weight of the restricted animals. But many of the biomarkers that increase in the restricted animals (for example, antioxidant enzymes) have a protective function, while many of those that decrease (for example, free radicals and products of oxidative damage) are believed to have a harmful effect on the organism. This observation suggests that at least some of the biomarkers selected reflect diet-induced alterations in the body's long-term defense and repair mechanisms. Since they are calibrated against life span and are not being rolled together into a single numerical index of biological aging, these biomarkers should also have predictive value. It has also been observed that the changes in these rodent biomarkers generally parallel the changes noted in the corresponding primate biomarkers (see Figure 3.23) as well as in the human biomarkers reported by Walford, Harris, and Gunion (1992) for the residents of the Biosphere. As a result, these rodent biomarkers are believed to be anticipated indicators of human biomarkers. Plans are now being discussed for a future study on the effects of dietary restriction on humans (Hass et al. 1996). Such a study would depend heavily on our existing knowledge of biomarkers and would add immeasurably to that store of knowledge.

Panels of Invertebrate Biomarkers

Biomarkers have proven to be useful in deciphering the aging processes of some very useful models. In yeasts, the late-life increase in generation time can be viewed as a prospective biomarker of mortality (see Chapter 4). In the nematode *Caenorhabditis elegans*, the level of general motor activity is a good statistical predictor of mean and maximum life span (Johnson 1987). In *Drosophila*, the use of biomarkers enabled us to determine the time of action of the processes responsible for long life. It has proven possible to use artificial selection to construct long-lived strains of flies (see Chapter 6 for a more detailed discussion). Arking and

Wells (1990) measured five different variables in normal- and long-lived strains and plotted for each strain the survival rate versus the age at which each variable showed a significant decrement in its expression (see Figure 6.16). A remarkable relationship became apparent: The two strains of different life spans lose each biomarker in the same sequence and at a comparable portion of their life cycle. Since the long-lived animals lose their first biomarker at a later age than do the normal-lived animals, the events responsible for the delayed onset of senescence must occur just before the age when the normal-lived animals lose their first biomarker (for example, the positive phototaxis test at about 5 to 7 days of age; see Figure 6.16). In other words, the fly lives long because of events that take place early in its life. The validity of this deduction has been confirmed by the observation that the long-lived animal's antioxidant defense system is significantly activated relative to the control at 5 to 9 days of age (see Chapter 6) (Arking et al. 1998).

• *Criticisms of the Biomarker Concept*

The preceding discussion focused on two general types of studies, each of which strived to construct reliable, valid, and practical measures of the biological age of an individual. Implicit in this goal is the idea that one can define the functional age of a single organism as its relative rank among comparable individuals of the same chronological age with respect to a particular chosen suite of biomarkers of aging. The crux of the matter then becomes the selection of the measures that constitute the biomarker panel and the choice of the manner in which one expresses the biological age.

In one type of study, the goal was to arrive at a unitary numerical index of biological age, to be used in a manner analogous to our chronological age. In the other, the goal was to arrive at a multiple-factor panel of biomarkers, with no single index of biological age. Much evidence strongly suggests that biological aging involves more than one process, but other evidence suggests that some variables covary as the organism ages. What results are some conceptual problems, as voiced by knowledgeable commentators (Ingram, Stoll, and Baker 1995, p. 707):

> Although biologic age and biomarkers of aging are related concepts, a distinction should be made between them. The concept of biologic age emphasizes the construction of a single index derived from test results reflecting biologic function. These individual tests are referred to as biomarkers of aging. Research in biomarkers of aging, however, does not imply the need to compile different tests into a single index. Rather, biomarkers research can involve the examination of multiple aging processes to recognize the multidimensional nature of aging and the possibility of an intervention affecting specific aspects of aging (segmental effects), rather than general processes.

The comments of McLearn (1997, p. 87) independently yield the same conclusions:

> . . . [O]ur comprehension of aging will evolve iteratively from application of a diversity of biomarker variables. Each of these will have strengths and

shortcomings from methodological and measurement points of view. The siren song that a "gold standard" index of aging can be found should be ignored.

A second conceptual problem arises from the statistical procedures that are used to increase the validity with which various age-related variables measure aging by regressing them against chronological age. As was pointed out in the section "The Results from Earlier Studies," even if the variable showed a perfect correlation with chronological age, all one would have would be a useless alternative expression of chronological age capable only of predicting the subject's chronological age. However, some alternative mathematical methods do not fall into the same logical trap (Furukawa 1994; Hochschild 1994; Nakamura 1994) and appear to be reliable. But is the variable valid? Is it really measuring changes in aging and the implicit changes in mortality associated with aging? Only the data from the Baltimore Longitudinal Study on Aging have been formally subjected to the test of serving as a retrospective measure of aging (see Figures 3.21 and 3.22). Remember that the biomarker panel used in those reports (Borkan and Norris 1980) had predictive validity only for the individuals at the extremes (either alive or dead, or in the highest or lowest 15 percent of the test population). The restriction of predictive validity to the tails of the normal curve severely restricts the utility of such panels.

One possible reason for the restricted utility may lie in the observation by Brant, Frozard, and Metter (1994) that many biological biomarkers tested for their ability to predict future mortality behave differently with respect to age (see Table 3.5). These observations raise a third conceptual problem. The age specificity of such generally accepted biomarkers of aging means that the formulation of biological age is much more complex than a simple gathering together of a group of markers that are highly correlated across the entire age span. This does not mean that biomarker panels are not useful, for the data in Figures 3.24 and 3.26d illustrate their potential predictive uses. (This prediction, of course, still remains to be validated for all subsets of the population.) It does mean, however, that the panel of biomarkers used to assess life expectancy in 40-year-old individuals may be quite different from the panel used to assess life expectancy in individuals of other age groups. In addition, these data strongly suggest that the construction of a unitary numerical index of biological age, which has been the goal of many studies, is conceptually flawed. Forecasting biological age may well involve the monitoring of changing suites of physiological responses throughout the adult life cycle. It may be useful, but it does not promise to be simple. Practical approaches to overcoming many of these objections have been proposed (Bulpitt 1995).

Finally, there exists a school of thought, perhaps best exemplified by Masoro (1988a), that questions the whole concept of biomarkers by suggesting that we are in no position to use and interpret biomarkers at this time, since we have no good idea as to what constitutes the aging process(es). Although this objection is valid and cogent, a strict acceptance of this position appears to require that we not experiment with biomarkers until we fully understand the aging process. This restriction may be logical, but it is not practical. The evidence linking high blood sugar levels to increased glycosalation rates and more extensive cross-linking of collagen, for example, seems to be both persuasive and useful, even if we must admit that we do not fully understand each of the mechanisms involved. As Wilson (1988) pointed out, there are risks in not proceeding with the development of effective biomarkers. We need biomarkers not only to guide us in identifying interventions worthy of further study, but also to help keep at bay the charlatans with ineffective treatments.

• *Summary*

The measurement of aging in individuals is based on the analysis of cross-sectional and of longitudinal studies. Both experimental designs have strengths and weaknesses, which we should keep in mind when analyzing the data and the conclusions obtained from such studies. It is difficult but essential to be able to distinguish pathological disease changes and/or adverse environmental effects from normal age-related changes. Making this distinction is complicated by the fact that some normal age-related changes might themselves serve as preconditions capable of precipitating pathological disease changes in at least some members of the population. In addition, a complex interaction exists among certain environmental factors, aging processes, and disease states. Under these conditions, a too rigid or too lenient application of the CPID criteria would result in our identifying as a normal age-related change something that occurs in only part of the population.

Clearly, what is needed is a judicious interpretation. Much of the confusion might be alleviated if we were able to substitute functional age for chronological age. Research into developing biological markers of functional age is now in progress. The concept of biological age has great intuitive appeal, but the most promising approaches are those involving multiple markers that are not regressed onto chronological age but rather are calibrated against mortality. Although all the studies await a rigorous empirical demonstration of their validity and reliability, the data obtained to date are good enough to enable the development of some effective anti-aging interventions.

Part II

The Evolution and Description of Aging

4

Evolutionary and Comparative Aspects of Longevity and Aging

• *Why Have Long Life and Aging Evolved?*

Philosophical speculation as to the origin of senescence has been with us since at least the dawn of recorded history. Scientific inquiry into this question began in the middle of the nineteenth century. A complete scientific explanation should have two major components: an accounting of the origin of senescence and a characterization of the cellular and organismal mechanisms involved in the expression of senescence. In the terminology of Ernst Mayr (1961), the first component addresses the nature of the ultimate processes (the why of aging), while the second component addresses the details of the proximate mechanisms (the how of aging). In this chapter, we will concern ourselves with only the first component: Why should we age?

During the past 150 years, numerous theories dealing with this point have been put forth. What characterized much of the older gerontological writing was its lack of a systematic critical analysis and/or an empirical testing of the theory's predictions. In addition, these writings confused Darwinian selection acting at the level of the individual with group selection (Rose 1991). As Comfort (1964) points out in his classic text, most of these theories assumed that aging and senescence arose as a result of either a particular general property inherent to life (such as cellular wear and tear) or as the outcome of a specific process found in only some forms (such as toxins produced by intestinal bacteria). The first group of hypotheses could have been disproven by evidence of life forms that did not show senescence; the second set of hypotheses could have been falsified by evidence of senescence in life forms that did not possess the particular trait in question. But few people were concerned with critical testing, so many inadequate theories lived on.

The beginnings of our modern understanding have their roots in the work of August Weissman, who in 1891 first drew the attention of biologists to the distinction between somatic line and germ line and explicitly identified senescence as a property of only the somatic cells (Weissman, 1891a). The germ line is potentially immortal in the sense that one could trace an unbroken genetic continuum across generations only through the germ line cells (Figure 4.1). The somatic cells are derived from the germ cells and are fated to age and die. There is no cross-generational continuity between somatic cells. However, the germ cells are not totally resistant to aging processes, since older parents as a group often have a higher frequency of certain morphogenetic abnormalities. But these changes, whatever they might be, seem to affect no fundamental aging traits, for life expectancy is not diminished for the normal offspring of older parents, and this seems to be by far the most common observation. Thus the germ cells seem to be free of the effects of age (but see the results of Gavrilov and Gavrilova [1997], as discussed in Chapter 6, which suggest that there may be significant exceptions to this statement).

Both Medvedev (1981) and Bernstein and Bernstein (1991) have reexamined this situation and have concluded that the germ cells' capability of meiotic recombination and repair is what enables them to rejuvenate themselves continuously at the molecular and cellular levels, and thereby evade the deleterious age- and time-related injuries that eventually impede the functioning of the somatic cells. We now know that the meiotic cell contains various DNA repair functions that either are not present in somatic cells, or are present at a greatly reduced level. Avise (1993) points out that all gametes are structurally and functionally autonomous—cellular free agents as it were—and are thus diametrically opposed to the somatic cells from which they sprang, which are "trapped in a web of interdependencies" (Avise 1993, p. 1299). This observation prompted Avise to raise a question originally posed by James Crow: "Is passing through a single cell stage itself important?... Starting with a single cell, sexual or asexual, permits each generation to begin with a *tabula rasa* largely unencumbered by the somatic mutations for previous generations" (Avise 1993, p. 1299). The requirements for independent functioning, even for a short time, may have provided the selective

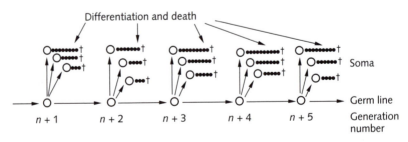

Figure 4.1 A diagrammatic representation of Weissman's (1891) concept that aging and senescence affect only the somatic cells, which differentiate and become specialized, while the germ line cells do not undergo this process and are potentially immortal. The concept has since been modified; see text for discussion.

pressure necessary for the germ line's high level of ability to repair DNA. Avise (1993) also extended the original domain of the concept to include the mitochondrial and chloroplast DNAs. These molecules are essential for organismal function yet appear to have only limited DNA repair systems, a paradox that will have to be resolved by future work.

In unicellular organisms, there is no distinction between soma and germ line at the cellular level, although forms such as *Paramecium* maintain a distinction between "somatic" and "reproductive" nuclei within the same cell (as we'll see later in this chapter). The distinction between soma and germ line is also blurred when regeneration creates an entire new organism from a smaller donor piece. In this form of asexual reproduction, the genetic identity of the original founder organism may be retained for thousands of years. Regeneration is particularly widespread in plants; many popular horticultural and fruit varieties are propagated by grafting or from sprouts. The mitotically reproducing somatic cells of plants can often give rise to meristematic cells, which in turn give rise to all other differentiated cells, including reproductive cells. Portions of this temporal and spatial clone may senesce and die, yet this process no more affects the identity of the original founding individual than cell turnover in the skin affects your identity.

In many cases, however, asexual reproduction does not involve a blurring of soma and germ line, but rather refers to organisms that have a clear distinction between the two yet are capable of parthenogenetically producing fertile eggs. It was once thought that asexual organisms would not senesce. However, it has been shown that senescence does occur in asexually reproducing organisms (Martinez and Leviton 1992). This observation suggests that the formation of somatic cells with a restricted potency is what leads to senescence, and not necessarily the sequestration of totipotent meiotically derived germ cells (Bell 1985). Our interest focuses on the processes that permit the onset of senescent changes in the somatic cells regardless of the mode of reproduction.

Modern gerontology may be said to have begun with the acceptance of the need for quantitative analysis and empirical validation. The mid-twentieth-century mark was conveniently chosen by Comfort (1964) as indicating the beginning of this period, perhaps because of the publication of Medawar's seminal essay on the topic in 1952. Yet we cannot overlook the early contributions of those few pioneers in the field who first glimpsed its future direction. Both Weismann and Wallace in 1891 and Bidder in 1932 had independently searched for and found evidence showing that not all life forms senesce. From this fact, they independently arrived at an evolutionary explanation for the occurrence of senescence in living organisms.

In addition to his work on the issue of soma versus germ line, Weismann (1891b) noted that unicellular forms show no signs of aging, and from this he deduced that senescence is inherent to metazoans (both views today are known to be only partly true, as we'll see shortly). Weismann (1891b, p. 24) postulated that senescence had evolved via the mechanism of natural selection, arising by chance but perpetuated as a positively beneficial adaptation because the "unlimited duration of life of the individual would be a senseless luxury.... Worn-out individuals are not only valueless to the species but they are even harmful, for they take the place of those which are sound." Weismann built on the much earlier argument of Alfred Russel Wallace (the codiscoverer of natural selection), which was written in about 1865 but published only as a footnote in Weismann's book (1891b) (and reprinted as Appendix 3 in Finch 1990).

The argument may be evolutionary, but it is both circular and flawed, for it assumes what it ostensibly tries to explain (that is, the decrease in the probability of survival with the increasing age of individuals) and then denies its own premise (by suggesting that older and less fit "worn-out" individuals can outcompete younger and fitter "sound" individuals). But it does have the honor of being the first explicitly evolutionary explanation of senescence to be put forth, and one that recognizes the existence of a link between reproduction and aging. Rose (1991) suggests that both Wallace and Weismann had the kernel of the central idea, that natural selection would favor the sacrifice of immortality in exchange for increased reproduction at the level of the individual.

Bidder (1925) noted that certain fish exhibit no signs of senescence or loss of vigor with age. These observations led him to postulate in 1932 a remarkably logical statement of the evolution of senescence: that the loss of function characteristic of senescence would have no effect on the organism's reproductive effort if the loss started after most of the usual individual's reproduction were completed. The loss of function would be invisible to the processes of natural selection. In Bidder's view, senescence is not the outcome of a particular process that positively selected for it, but of the organism's physiological processes operating in the absence of selective pressures. Although this argument was neither quantitatively presented nor empirically proven (Rose 1991), this is a correct encapsulation of our modern view that senescence occurs because the force of natural selection rapidly dwindles away when reproduction is over.

We asked, "Why must we age?" Perhaps we expected a more philosophical answer, so it may strike some as disconcerting to realize that the answer is, "Why not?" However, this is a liberating answer; for it implies that if a reason can be supplied, then senescence can be delayed.

Modern Evolutionary Models

"Nothing in biology makes sense except in the light of evolution." This famous quote by the well-known geneticist Theodosius Dobzhansky (1973) sets out the twin tasks before us: to make sense of the fact that organisms age and senesce, and to understand why closely related species may have very different characteristic longevities. Our current understanding is based on the solid fact that most organisms live in a hazardous natural environment—one where predators, disease, and starvation impose a heavy toll on the population. Since the individual members of any sexually reproducing population are genetically diverse, the environmental hazards are likely to impose a differential survival rate among the different genotypes present. As a consequence, genetic variants that have an enhanced survival rate will have the opportunity to leave more offspring in the next generation. Conversely, alleles that reduce the reproductive success of the individuals carrying them will occur in fewer individuals in the next generation. Over time, some genetic variants and the phenotypes associated with them will be favored while others are not. In short, natural selection is operating.

This situation is complicated by the fact that most known populations are structured by age; that is, the population is composed of individuals of different age classes, each of which represents a different proportion of the population. The high mortality rates common among wild populations mean that not many individuals live long enough to show signs of senescence and aging (see Chapter 2). As a result, in any population there are usually many more young breeding adults than old ones. One consequence of this age structure is that deleterious genetic variants that act late in life will not be selected against, since their carriers likely will have died from environmental hazards before then. Bidder (1932), Medawar (1946, 1952) and Williams (1957) independently achieved this insight. Medawar proposed that new mutations were always being generated at a low rate in any population. Most of these mutations would be stringently selected against. However, deleterious mutations that act late in life would not be selected against, because most of the organisms that carried them would have died at an earlier age from one or another of the environmental hazards. Consequently, natural selection could not act to decrease the frequency of such genes. They would accumulate and, if and when the high mortality was reduced by environmental manipulation, the larger numbers of older organisms would exhibit the effects of these late-acting deleterious mutations—senescence.

Williams (1957) proposed another proximal mechanism through which this ultimate process could be played out. He hypothesized the existence of pleiotropic genes that have beneficial effects early in life but deleterious effects late in life. Such genes would accumulate because they would be positively selected for on the basis of their early beneficial effects, while their late deleterious effects would escape the scrutiny of natural selection. Again, the outcome of this scenario would be the appearance of senescence in older, postreproductive organisms. The population geneticists, beginning with Haldane (1927), Fisher (1930), and Norton (1928) and continuing to the present day (Rose 1991; Charlesworth 1994a,b), have quantitatively described these models and verified their predictions.

Thus, unlike Weissman, we now have a coherent conceptual framework that allows us not only to understand how natural selection might operate to bring about senescence but also to empirically test the specific predictions of these evolutionary models. Medawar and Williams have completed Weissman's task of mechanistically explaining the existence of senescence and, in so doing, have tied the study of aging irrevocably to the central theory of modern biology.

Fecundity and Longevity: The Relationship Between Reproduction and Life Span

MacArthur and Wilson (1967) were perhaps the first to speak overtly of the role that fecundity plays in the life history of organisms. If we view evolution as a game in which the goal is to maximize one's genetic contribution to the next generation, we should realize that there are winning and losing strategies for the players in the game. Organisms may be viewed as adopting strategies that result in large numbers of offspring coupled with high mortality (prodigal, or, in the jargon of the field, *r*-selected, where *r* is the mathematical symbol for rate of population increase as used in equations describing population growth) or small numbers of offspring coupled with lower mortality (prudent, or *K*-selected, where

Table 4.1	Traits Characteristic of Alternative Life History Strategies	
Prodigal (r-selected)	*Prudent (K-selected)*
Many young	Few young
Small young	Large young
Rapid maturation	Slow maturation
Little or no parental care	Intensive parental care
Reproduction once	Reproduction many times

Source: From Curtis 1993. © Worth Publishers.

K is the mathematical symbol for carrying capacity of the environment in equations dealing with population growth). Table 4.1 lists the attributes of each strategy. These strategies should be viewed more as the two polar ends of an intergrading spectrum of strategies rather than as two discrete choices.

High fecundity is a necessary characteristic of r-selected organisms, but a long life span is not. A good example of an r-selected life history is that of the common meadow vole (*Microtus pennsylvanicus*). This small rodent matures at less than 1 month of age and produces litters of five young every 3 to 4 weeks throughout the year. In captivity, one vole produced 17 litters in 1 year! The average longevity of these voles in nature has been reported as less than 1 month, although some have lived several years in the laboratory.

At the extreme, the r strategy describes also those organisms that reproduce once in large numbers and then die. The young must fend for themselves with no parental care. Once the next generation has reached the age of reproductive maturity, there is no adaptive advantage for them to live any longer than is necessary to reproduce. The Pacific salmon (*Oncorhynchus* spp.) is perhaps the best-known example of this strategy. Another similarly extraordinary case is that of the so-called marsupial "mouse" of Australia (*Antechinus* and *Phascogale* spp.). In *A. stuartii* and *P. tapoatafa*, the males live no longer than 11.5 months. Near the end of their life, they stop eating and engage in a competitive, brief, and frantic mating period. All males die shortly thereafter, probably as a result of hormonally induced stress. For some period of time, the only males in the entire population are the male embryos being carried *in utero* by their mothers. The mothers live long enough to suckle their young and wean them. Very few females live long enough to breed a second time.

At the other extreme, the K strategy encompasses the behavior of mammals such as humans that have a low reproductive rate coupled with a higher degree of parental care. In this case, there is clearly an advantage for the adult to live a substantial length of time past the age of reproduction, if only to be able to deliver the parental care necessary for the survival of the offspring. A long life span is a characteristic of many K-selected organisms.

The distinction between the r and K strategies, then, revolves about the pattern of population growth. As illustrated in Table 4.2, r-selected organisms pro-

| Table 4.2 | Reproductive Capacity of an *r*-Selected Organism, the Housefly (*Musca domestica*)[a] |

Generation	Numbers if all survive
1	120
2	7,200
3	432,000
4	25,920,000
5	1,555,200,000
6	93,312,000,000
7	5,598,720,000,000

Source: Adapted from Kormondy 1969.
[a]In one year, about seven generations are produced. The numbers are based on each female laying 120 eggs per generation, each fly surviving just one generation, and half of these being females.

duce large numbers of individual offspring, each with a low individual probability of survival. If all the offspring survived, the population would grow exponentially and would shortly fill the universe. Even with a high mortality rate, there are more than enough young to ensure that sufficient numbers will survive to adulthood to maintain the population. Adults of species that adopt this strategy tend to be short-lived organisms whose major adult function is to reproduce. *K*-selected organisms, on the other hand, combine a lower reproductive potential with a higher probability of individual survival. They utilize parental care to maintain their population numbers at the carrying capacity of their environment (Figure 4.2). Adults of species that adopt this strategy tend to be longer-lived individuals for which reproduction per se constitutes only one of their adult functions.

In evolution, the name of the game is to play again. Individuals are competing with others of their species in an effort to maximize the number of copies of their genes that are represented in the next generation. The strategy employed by

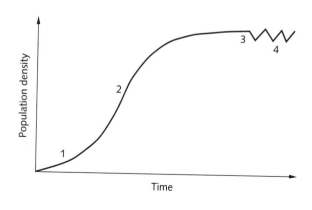

Figure 4.2 The growth curve of a *K*-selected organism. Biological growth curves are usually sigmoidal, or S-shaped. As with exponential growth, there is an establishment phase (1) and a phase of rapid acceleration (2). Then, as the population approaches environmental limits, the growth rate slows down (3 and 4), and finally stabilizes (5), although minor fluctuations around *K* (the mathematical symbol representing the carrying capacity of the environment) may continue. (From Curtis 1983. © Worth Publishers.)

the members of any given species is the outcome of their specific developmental and ecological characteristics, of which life history analysis suggests that the most important ones are those related to their reproductive practices. Empirical evidence of the close link between reproductive schedules and longevity, at least for mammals, is shown in Figures 4.3 and 4.4. In Figure 4.3, the age at first reproduction is strongly correlated with life expectancy at birth. Figure 4.4 shows that there is an inverse relationship between an organism's reproductive potential and its longevity. Taken together, these figures present the quantitative data underlying the concept of *r* and *K* life history strategies.

Two other examples, however, will suffice to show that organisms have some room to manipulate life history in view of changing environmental conditions. First, when parasitic wasps are raised under specific environmental conditions indicative of a decreased life expectancy (such as decreasing barometric pressure or photoperiod), they alter their reproductive behavior so as to lay many eggs early in life even in suboptimal environments. In the absence of these specific cues, and thus faced with the environmental conditions associated with a longer life span, the wasps lay fewer eggs early in life but deposit them in optimal environments. The simplest interpretation of these observations is that the wasps are sensitive to conditions that affect their potential longevity and alter their behavior to maximize their lifetime reproductive fitness (Roitberg et al. 1993). Second, it is now well known that diet-restricted animals live significantly longer than animals fed *ad libitum*, an observation that we will deal with in more detail in Chapter 6. The important point in this context is that diet-restricted animals become partly or fully sterile but can breed again once food becomes more plentiful, and can do so at a later age than can animals fed *ad libitum* throughout their life. Thus one can interpret these observations as showing that animals can reallocate their available energy to maximize somatic maintenance and individual

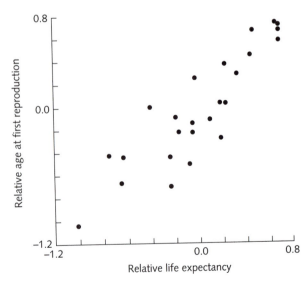

Figure 4.3 The relationship between relative age at first reproduction and relative life expectancy at birth for natural populations of mammals. Relative values refer to deviations from logarithmic regression lines of age at females' first breeding, or expectation of life at birth, on adult female body size. The correlation coefficient of *r* = 0.98 is only slightly decreased to 0.89 (*p* < 0.001) by removal of the effects of body size through partial correlation. The numbers refer to different mammalian genera. (From Holliday 1995.)

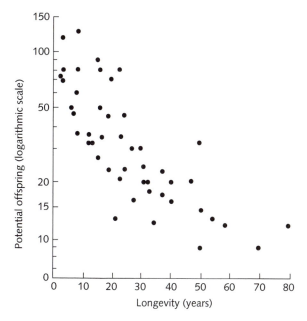

Figure 4.4 The relationship between reproductive potential and longevity of 47 genera of eutherian mammals. Reproductive potential is the maximum number of offspring that might be produced under ideal conditions. Longevity is based primarily on the maximum life span of limited numbers of individuals in captivity. (From Holliday 1995.)

longevity when their energy resources are so low as to jeopardize the probability of successful reproduction. The life history strategy that an organism adopts reflects a particular balance between somatic maintenance and reproduction, but this balance is not static. The organism apparently has the ability to modulate this balance significantly when environmental conditions change, and hence temporarily to adopt a more suitable life history strategy.

Although this point is controversial, not many animals appear to live long enough to age (Promislow 1991; Gaillard et al. 1994; Slade 1995; and see the discussion of birds below). One consequence of this fact is that aging cannot be considered a trait that has been directly selected for by evolution, contrary to Weismann's belief. There are simply too few old organisms (most of which are probably in a low reproductive or even a postreproductive state) in any feral population to have provided a selective advantage favoring the development of a genetic program for delayed aging and increased longevity. However, an organism of postreproductive age has a great selective advantage if it is able to maintain its physiological vigor for as long as the parents bear even some responsibility for the survival of the young (and thus for the transmission of copies of their own genes into the next generation). Thus there is reason to believe that the evolutionary trend toward increased postreproductive longevity seen in many groups of organisms is not separable from the processes that operate before the end of reproduction, but can be viewed as being part of the same life history strategy designed to ensure the survival of an organism's genes into the next generation (Holliday 1996a).

What, then, keeps *K*-selected organisms from living forever? Why doesn't a long-lived animal continue to reproduce and to live indefinitely? First, some parts of an organism, such as the heart, have no significant repair or regenerative mechanisms and thus constitute an inherent weak link. Of more general importance is a theoretical analysis by Kirkwood (1985, 1987) that points out that the organism must channel and apportion its energies into reproductive activities, as well as into the maintenance and repair of its soma. Although the energy cost of making an egg or sperm probably stays more or less constant over time, and is therefore the same for both young and old, this is not the only energy cost incurred in reproduction. The energy costs of courtship, as well as of pregnancy and child rearing, are high and represent a significant investment of energy by the organism. In addition, some energy must be devoted to the repair and maintenance of the soma if the organism is to survive. It is reasonable to assume that even a well-fed organism has only a certain amount of energy available to it. Thus the problem facing the organism is how best to allocate its finite metabolic energy to maximize both reproduction and survival.

Kirkwood (1985, 1987) has mathematically compared the success of different allocation strategies of investment in somatic repair and maintenance on reproduction and survival. As Figure 4.5 shows, increasing the amount of effort expended on somatic repair results in an increased survivorship but a decreased fecundity. One can use these results to calculate the joint effect of changing survivorship and fecundity on the evolutionary fitness of a genotype. The result, shown in Figure 4.6, leads to two conclusions: First, there is a clearly defined range of investment in somatic repair at which reproduction will be at a maximum. Second, this point of maximum reproductive effect will be at a level that is less than the minimum energy level needed for indefinite somatic repair (immortality). Reproduction requires less energy than repair. Therefore, allocating energy to maximize somatic repair will decrease the organism's Darwinian fitness. In most cases, a decreased fecundity over a longer life span yields fewer copies of an individual's genes in the next generation than does a higher fecun-

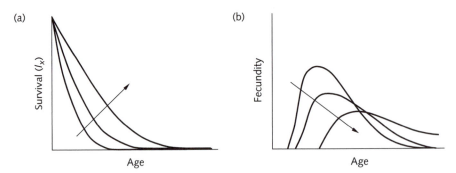

Figure 4.5 The effects of increasing the energy investment in somatic repair and maintenance on (a) survivorship (l_x) and (b) fecundity. The three curves in each group represent three different levels of energy investment. Note that survivorship increases and fecundity decreases as more energy is invested in somatic maintenance. (From Kirkwood 1987.)

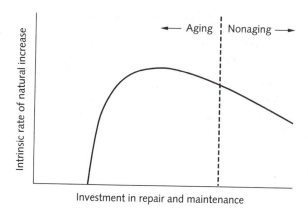

Figure 4.6 The relationship between the intrinsic rate of natural increase and the level of investment in somatic repair and maintenance. Note that the maximum reproductive fitness occurs at a lower energy investment than that required for indefinite somatic maintenance. Note also that reproductive fitness declines as more energy is invested in somatic maintenance. (From Kirkwood 1985.)

dity over a shorter lifetime. Thus fitness is maximized at a repair level lower than that required for indefinite somatic repair. Hence we die.

This process should not seem alien or far-fetched, for it is nothing more than the cost–benefit analysis that most of us have made when faced with the decision of whether to continue investing our hard-earned money in repairs to the old car or to invest our money in a new car. At some point, the cost of repairs exceeds the cost of purchase. Hence old cars are discarded (or traded in for newer ones). The important point is that this analysis implies that life span is modulated not by genes whose primary action is to shorten or extend life, but by the longevity-assurance genes that function in the processes involved in somatic maintenance and that alter life span as a pleiotropic result of this primary action (Williams 1957; Sacher and Hors 1978). This analysis of ecological and population genetics has summarized the reasons that lead us to believe that patterns of longevity are inseparable from, and flow out of, the life history strategy followed by the organism.

Ecology and evolutionary studies also suggest that there are a multitude of different organisms, each of which makes its living in its own distinctive manner. Yet beneath this obvious diversity lies a fundamental identity that links together all living creatures. This fundamental similarity shows itself in the fact that these diverse species accomplish important biological tasks in one of a small number of ways. For example, all eukaryotic organisms (and most prokaryotic ones as well) digest food molecules and extract energy from food using almost identical metabolic processes. The cells of a yeast and the cells of a human undergo the same process of cell division, which the two cells control by using almost identical genes. Neural circuits work in the same way in snails and insects and humans. This identity does not extend across the board, however. The evolutionary identities are most obvious at the cellular level and less obvious at the population level. For example, even closely related species, such as chimpanzees and humans, use a similar brain to organize widely divergent but adaptive behavioral and social responses. Since life history strategies are based on those adaptive behavioral and social responses, it is not surprising that phylogenetic relationships should be less obvious at these "higher-order" levels than at cellular and molecular levels.

The virtues of a comparative approach to the study of aging are threefold:

- It should allow us to survey the diversity of living creatures and determine how common and widespread aging is.

- It should allow us to identify the biological mechanisms that appear to play a causal role in regulating the rate of aging in different species. Uncovering novel methods of regulating fundamental processes may provide valuable knowledge.

- It should allow us to overcome the ethical, legal, financial, and temporal constraints associated with doing experiments with humans or any of the ordinary laboratory rodents.

The comparative study of aging has both theoretical and practical importance. In our comparative survey of aging, we will try to accomplish each of these three goals.

Strengths and Weaknesses of the Evolutionary Viewpoint

The overwhelming strength of the evolutionary viewpoint is that it has integrated the study of senescence into the mainstream of biological thought. It has allowed us to study longevity as just another phenotype and to separate its scientific analysis from our emotional reaction to it. The study of disease is important in its own right, but to conceive of aging and senescence in the context of only the medical model is to view them as an incoherent assortment of symptomatic bodily failures, with no obvious connection to the evolutionary principles implicit in genetics, in development, in physiology, in neuroscience, and in all other aspects of biology. Even diseases have recently been examined through an evolutionary lens (Nesse and Williams 1994). Adherence to the medical model implicitly relegated senescence to the sidelines, but viewing senescence through an evolutionary prism allows us to understand the Darwinian connection between aging and reproduction. This connection is not merely one of professional pride. The evolutionary model suggests testable and broad theories, something that the medical model has not done. It also makes clear the distinction between ultimate and proximal causes of senescence, to borrow the phrasing of Mayr (1961).

The empirical data collected as a result of inquiries into ultimate causes demonstrate that the life span of experimental animals can be significantly modulated as a result of alterations in reproductive behaviors, thus linking senescence to reproductive fitness. The data also provide us with a coherent idea of the interplay between repair and reproductive functions. Longevity is not a phylogenetically consistent trait, but its connection with species-specific life history strategies and the need of an individual to pass copies of its genes to the next generation enable us to understand why longevity isn't consistent.

The evolutionary theory is based on the analysis of gene frequencies in aclonal or sexually reproducing organisms. It is not surprising that the current concepts are somewhat less successful in explaining the existence of senescence in clonal forms. These genetically invariant organisms are potentially immortal, but at least some such organisms senesce (Martinez and Leviton 1992). One way to explain the paradox is to assume that deleterious mutations are inevitable in such forms because the repair processes present in germ cells are absent in these clonal somatic cells (Medvedev 1981b). In such a situation, one can show mathematically that the mean physiological and reproductive fitness of a finite population will decline because there is always a chance that the class of individuals with the fewest deleterious mutations will be accidently lost. Without the benefit of sexual recombination, there is no way to recover this class. This decline in fitness has been termed "Muller's ratchet" (Muller 1964) and has been postulated to lead to the evolution of senescence (Bell 1988; Maynard Smith 1988; Partridge and Barton 1993).

However, this situation also implies that the mean duration of existence of clonal species should be significantly less than that of aclonal species, since clonal species should succumb to this mutational load. The available data suggest that this prediction does not hold for a variety of different organisms. For example, the evolutionary persistence of the clonal species of corals is equivalent to that of aclonal species, both of which last about 9 million years (Finch 1990). Certain asexual freshwater crustaceans have a fossil record that extends back at least 268 million years (Butlin and Griffiths 1993). If mutations are accumulating, they do not seem to have a discernible evolutionary effect. One way to escape this paradox is to assume that asexual species are composed of large populations, a condition that may allow them to escape Muller's ratchet (Bell 1988). However, large populations for asexual species seem unlikely in at least some cases (Butlin and Griffiths 1993).

A recent extension of the basic evolutionary theory suggests that the population growth rate is important in determining whether or not senescence will evolve in an asexual population (Orive 1995). Although clonal reproduction does retard the evolution of senescence, it does not preclude it. Senescence in clonal species is not well understood, but it appears to be susceptible to continued analysis. Nor is it clear how programmed aging, indicated by a synchronous, nonrandom mortality among different "branches" of the colony, could have arisen in asexually reproducing colonial forms (Rinkevitch et al. 1992). All of the data, and their interpretations, are complicated by the fact that many clonal species retain the option to reproduce sexually at times. In sexually reproducing clonal species, reproductive fitness increases as the size of the colony increases; the fact that they become sexually mature when they reach the extrinsic limits of colony growth shows that the life history in these forms is still driven by their reproductive strategy (Harvell and Grossberg 1988). The loss of sexual reproduction may obscure but it does not obliterate the evolutionary connections between reproduction and longevity, since the major determinants of reproductive fitness in clonal organisms are colony size and organization.

Current evolutionary theory deals in general solutions and says little regarding the details of longevity and senescence in specific taxa. The one specific deduction one may make from theory is that there should be great diversity in the details of senescence in different life forms precisely because of the decreased force of natural selection in the postreproductive stages. However, a survey of mammals reveals what appears to be a common pattern of senescence over diverse species with a 30-fold difference in life spans (Finch 1990). In general, the force of natural selection on survival begins to decrease at the age of sexual maturity and drops to zero after the reproductive period. The result is an age-related increase in mortality rate (q_x) as discussed in Chapter 2, which gives rise to the commonly observed mortality pattern in most mammals.

This observation suggests three new possibilities. First, the common senescence pattern is a primitive mammalian trait that has persisted unchanged for at least 50 million years. Second, it may represent convergent evolution occurring in the absence of natural selection. Third, it may reflect the inevitable outcome in individuals of certain fundamental developmental constraints common to all mammals. These could include finite supplies of stem cells in the immune and other systems, the absence of repair and regeneration mechanisms in the heart, and so forth. I believe the third possibility to be the most likely, particularly because a similar argument is made to explain the longer life span of birds relative to mammals (as we'll see later in this chapter). Senescence patterns may well be constrained by developmental patterns that give rise to the body plan and to the distribution of rate-limiting molecules and cells.

One human weakness of some practitioners of the evolutionary approach is to assume that all creatures behave just as their favorite laboratory animal does. This may not be the case, particularly if one is arguing across different taxa and different environments. Another weakness is to assume that one's favorite theoretical genetic mechanism must be true, despite what someone else's data might suggest, especially if obtained with a different species. This problem has been particularly obvious in the technical discussions regarding which theory better explains the results obtained in experiments with laboratory animals—the mutation accumulation theory or the antagonistic pleiotropy theory (Schnebel and Grossfield 1988; Charlesworth 1994b; Clark 1994)—when there is some evidence to suggest that both sorts of mechanisms may be playing a role (Service, Hutchinson, and Rose 1988). In addition, the type of data obtained in an experiment may be highly dependent on the strains of organisms used and on the environmental conditions (Curtsinger 1995b, 1995c; Graves and Mueller 1995). Some participants in the debate suggest that neither theory is a complete explanation of the aging process, for both fail to predict the "oldest-old" mortality kinetics, thus leading to the suggestion that demographic and comparative methods should be incorporated into the study protocol (see Chapter 2; also see Curtsinger 1995a; Curtsinger et al. 1995). Others have suggested that methodological problems in data analysis may have contributed to the confusion (Promislow and Tatar 1994).

The continuing development of quantitative genetic models, which take into account the "ultimate" or evolutionary phenotypic trade-offs involved within the context of the "proximal" mechanisms of both the genetic architecture in the cell and the epigenetic interactions between the genomes of different cells, promise to reflect better the developmental genetic history of the organism and to predict better the magnitude and direction of evolutionary change in the expression of senescence (see, for example, Promislow and Tatar 1994, or Atchley, Xu, and Vogl 1994). The faults we have listed are those commonly observed when theory is being challenged robustly; these faults are not inherent in the evolutionary explanation of aging and senescence. The fact that the details of the theoretical mechanisms are still being worked out does not invalidate the entire theory. All in all, modern biogerontology is based on the concept that senescence makes sense only in the light of evolution.

• *Comparative Aspects of Aging*

At present, most biologists classify all living organisms as belonging to one of five different major groups called kingdoms. These kingdoms are distinguished from one another by their possession of certain structures, the presence or absence of which irrevocably casts their members into certain ways of life. The absence of a nucleus, of a discrete membrane-enclosed storage compartment for the genetic information, distinguishes the kingdom Monera (bacteria; also called prokaryotes) from all the other forms of life (eukaryotes). The eukaryotes themselves are divided into large groups depending on whether they consist of unicellular forms (kingdom Protista) or multicellular forms (kingdoms Plantae, Animalia, and Fungi). The multicellular forms are distinguished from each other by their method of obtaining food: Plants synthesize their own via photosynthesis, animals feed on other organic foodstuffs and digest them internally, and fungi feed on other organic foodstuffs but digest them externally. These relationships are shown in Figure 4.7.

Unicellular Organisms: Senescence Arising from Nucleocytoplasmic Interactions

The single-celled organisms are extraordinarily diverse, belonging as they do to both the Kingdoms Monera (bacteria) and Protista (unicellular algae and protozoans), and thereby comprising some species that are prokaryotes (cells without a nucleus) and others that are eukaryotes (cells with a nucleus and other organelles). No age-related changes have been observed in nonmutant bacterial cells. Normal prokaryotic cells exhibit an apparently infinite ability to replicate when grown under the appropriate culture conditions. They do not age, nor is senescence a normal part of their fate.

The protists, however, are another story. These single-celled eukaryotic organisms have been called "Nature's experiments," encompassing as they do an

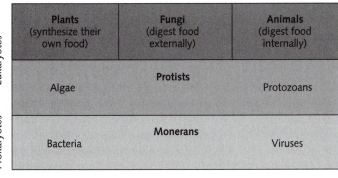

Figure 4.7 The five-kingdom classification scheme of living organisms.

almost bewildering variety of genetic organizations and mating behaviors. They can thus be viewed as a rich resource that one can use to decipher how different genetic systems interact with the environment to produce species-characteristic life spans. These life spans range from about 50 days for *Paramecium tetraurelia* to immortality for *Tetrahymena thermophila* (Smith-Sonneborn 1985). These, of course, are clonal life spans. A clone comprises the daughter cells that are derived from a single cell and that are genetically identical to their progenitor. These organisms can reproduce either sexually or asexually. Clonal offspring, which are genetically identical to one another, are produced only by asexual (mitotic) cell divisions. In most species, in the absence of sexual fertilization, the probability that a cell will give rise to viable progeny at the next cell division decreases as the time increases since the last sexual (meiotic) fertilization. The clone deteriorates, and eventually all members of the clone die. Thus, the clonal life span value is the sum of the life spans of all the mitotically produced, genetically identical but physically distinct cells that are descended from the single progenitor cell. This clonal life span concept is used in other aspects of studies on cell aging (this is the "Hayflick limit" that we will discuss in Chapter 11); it is the concept you would use if someone were to ask you the age of your skin. As discussed in some detail in Chapter 5, the individual cells that together make up your skin each have a life span of about several weeks. Yet your skin persists from before birth until death, despite the turnover of most of its component cells, much as a candle flame persists despite the rapid appearance and disappearance of the molecules undergoing combustion. The age of the skin is the summed age of all its component cells.

Let's briefly examine the aging process as seen in three of the better-known protists: the common *Amoeba* and the graceful ciliated *Paramecium* and *Tetrahymena* (Figure 4.8). We will also examine the patterns of aging of another interesting organism, *Volvox*, which appears to lie just over the boundary between unicellular and multicellular organisms (see Figure 4.11). Perhaps you have encountered these organisms in an introductory biology laboratory. If so, it is probably reasonable to assume that, whatever you thought of them at the time, you never considered them as undergoing aging. Yet some do. From these "simple" cellular organisms we might be able to detect some of the mechanisms operating within our own cells.

Amoeba

Amoeba (Figure 4.8a) appears to be immortal, provided it is maintained in an exponential growth phase. When its food supply is restricted for a substantial period of time (3 to 5 weeks), the organisms are induced to switch over to a finite life span ranging from 4 to 30 weeks. These mortal cells show two types of behavior. On cell division, Type A cells produce one viable daughter cell and one inviable daughter cell. Type B cells produce two daughter cells, both of which will live until all cells in the clone die. Experiments in which nuclei and/or cytoplasm from one cell type were transplanted to another were summarized by Muggleton-Harris (1979) and led her to suggest that this odd behavior is the result of a complex nucleocytoplasmic interaction. These experiments also suggest that the shift away from immortality is accompanied by the appearance of Type B factors in the

(a)

(b)

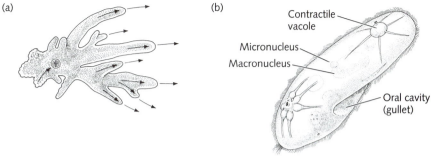

Contractile vacole

Micronucleus

Macronucleus

Oral cavity (gullet)

(c)

Figure 4.8 Drawings of three protists whose aging processes are discussed in the text. (a) *Amoeba*, a single-celled organism capable of changing its shape at will. (b) *Paramecium*, a ciliate that has a complex external and internal morphology. (c) *Tetrahymena pyriformis*, a ciliate that may have an unusual genomic organization. (a and b from Brusca and Brusca 1990; c from Grell 1973, courtesy of Springer-Verlag.)

cytoplasm or by the alteration of the nucleus from Type B to Type A. The molecular basis of these alterations is not known. The importance of these observations lies in their suggestion that the aging process in this simple asexually reproducing cell is under the control of certain molecular signals, that the presence or absence of such signals is dependent on the environment, and that these signals involve alteration of the nucleus via the cytoplasm. This information suggests that the aging process in higher organisms also has a molecular genetic basis.

Paramecium

Paramecium, unlike *Amoeba* but like many other ciliates, contains two kinds of nuclei (Figure 4.8b). The micronucleus is the germ line nucleus and shows little transcriptional activity other than at fertilization. The macronucleus controls somatic activities and is not only very active, but is often extensively restructured during somatic development and maturation. Transplantation of young or old macronuclei into short-lived hosts suggested that the macronucleus is capable of "remembering" its age (Aufderheide 1987), an observation suggesting that the aging process in *Paramecium* is accompanied by permanent functional changes in the nucleus. The macronucleus is destroyed during the next round of fertilization. Thus this little "animalcule," to borrow Antoni van Leeuwenhoek's term, has evolved an operational separation of germ line and somatic functions in a manner analogous to that seen in multicellular organisms. Both structure and function are altered with increasing age in *Paramecium* (see Smith-Sonneborn 1985, 1990).

Analyses of controlled crosses has revealed that the cytoplasm from aged parents is more likely to result in abnormal progeny and will eventually become incapable of supporting the existence of a normal nucleus. Very occasionally, such aged cytoplasm may be rejuvenated by a young nucleus. It is more common, however, to find evidence of young cytoplasm rejuvenating aged micronuclei. As the clone ages, the micronucleus appears to be progressively affected by the increasingly toxic effects of the aging cytoplasm. There is some reason to believe that this increased nuclear damage reflects the age-dependent loss in DNA repair capacity. What is clear is that we once again find evidence of a complex nucleocytoplasmic interaction, the molecular basis for which is slowly emerging (see Smith-Sonneborn 1990). In addition, however, the study of *Paramecium* first introduces us to the phenomenon of organelle damage. When a *Paramecium* divides asexually, the anterior daughter cell retains the original (parental) oral apparatus while the posterior cell receives the new oral apparatus. If the two newly formed daughter cells are separated from each other and their clonal life spans measured, the posterior cell line usually appears to be more viable than the anterior cell line. Both cells have received essentially identical nuclei and cytoplasm; thus it is unlikely that either of these are the important factors in this differential mortality.

It has been suggested that the increased vigor of the posterior cell line is due to its ability to repair any preexisting accidental damage to the gullet when it replicated it during cell division. This repair ability appears to reside in the micronucleus but can be transferred to the macronucleus in mutant strains that do not possess micronuclei (Smith-Sonneborn 1990). The anterior cell's inability to repair such damage, since it inherited the original or parental gullet, would result in a decreased viability. Thus the longevity of *Paramecium* is determined both by nucleocytoplasmic interactions and by organelle repair processes. As we'll see, this strategy appears to be common and may operate within humans as well.

Tetrahymena

Tetrahymena (Figure 4.8c) does not normally exhibit an age-related increase in somatic line abnormalities or in germ line abnormalities. It appears to be immortal. This does not mean that the organism does not make "mistakes." On the contrary. Even the immortal line produces defective (flawed and mortal) daughter lines, but at a constant rate. There is no increase in the frequency of defective daughter lines with increasing age of the parent cell. The lack of such age-dependent decrements in function is one sign that the cell is not senescing. Even within the defective lines observed in highly inbred strains, the defects can be "cured" or eliminated via successive inbreeding and stringent selection to eventually produce viable progeny.

As we've discussed earlier, aging is a phenomenon generally lacking among prokaryotic organisms. Prokaryotes such as bacteria are virtually immortal, probably because deleterious mutations are immediately expressed and subjected to stringent selection. Diploids, however, can carry recessive mutations of all kinds that are shielded from immediate selection by the normal allele. Smith-Sonneborn (1985) has made the interesting suggestion that *Tetrahymena*, although diploid, has retained a haploid genome subunit organization. This organization would subject each of the haploid genome subunits to immediate and stringent selection. It might also explain how *Tetrahymena* can repair organelles, such as its gullet, at any time during its life cycle. In this respect *Tetrahymena* stands in stark contrast to *Paramecium*, which can repair organelles only at fertilization. The molecular structure of any ciliate macronucleus is not yet known; therefore this suggestion has not yet been tested. However, certain otherwise anomalous genetic behaviors of *Tetrahymena* make sense if viewed in the light of this idea. The genome of *Tetrahymena* is known to undergo a controlled and complex process of molecular reorganization (Brunk 1986). Examination of this proposal may also lead us to insights applicable to other organisms and other systems. *Tetrahymena* is already known to contain odd but generally interesting molecules. Ribozymes, RNA molecules that can act like an enzyme (Zaug and Cech 1986), were first found in *Tetrahymena*, as was the hybrid RNA–protein enzyme telomerase—both of which have turned out to be present and important in other organisms generally. It will be interesting to see if this ciliate yields any other interesting molecules that may help us better understand the molecular biology of senescence in this and/or other organisms.

Yeasts

We are perhaps most appreciative of the important role that yeasts play in our life when we contemplate the fruits of their labors quietly aging in a wine rack. But yeasts are also useful for more mundane purposes, such as genetic investigations into the aging process. It is this aspect of their biology that we will discuss in this book. These unicellular eukaryotic fungi have been extensively investigated for many decades, in part because of their commercial importance. A large variety of mutants affecting various different basic cell processes have been collected over the years. These collections of genetic mutants have enabled yeasts to serve as excellent organisms for the genetic analysis of these processes. Because of this extensive genetic knowledge, the yeast *Saccharomyces cerevisiae* was selected as one of the genetic model organisms to be investigated as part of the Human Genome Project. The complete genome of this yeast has been mapped, and the complete sequence of the genome was released in 1996.

In order to use yeasts for studies on aging, it was first necessary to establish a method of measuring life span in these organisms. It was then necessary to show that their viability decreases in an age-dependent manner. One obvious marker is the "budding" of yeasts, a process by which a mother cell gives rise to a smaller daughter cell that eventually grows to the same size as the mother cell. The daughter cell is physiologically distinct from the mother cell but stays attached to it for some time before dropping off. Using the number of times that a given yeast cell buds during its life span as a measure of aging has the advantage of allowing the life span to be measured in physiological rather than chronological terms. This is a great advantage, as we will see. Using this criterion, several laboratories have independently demonstrated not only that *S. cerevisiae* has a finite life span but that its survival curve is rectangular (similar to that of curve 2 in Figure 2.24) and yields a linear Gompertz plot (Figure 4.9; Pohley 1978; Jazwinski, Egilmez, and Chen 1989; Kennedy et al. 1995). Since these are the identifying characteristics of an aging population, the exercise demonstrates the fundamental utility of the population measurements we discussed in Chapter 2; in their

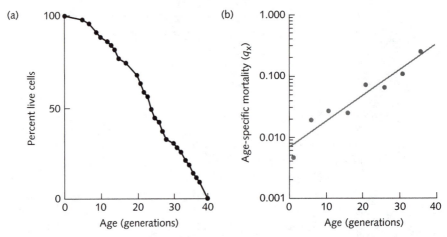

Figure 4.9 Survival characteristics of *Saccharomyces cerevisiae*, strain X2180-1A. Life spans were determined for 43 individual cells. Virgin cells that had never budded were used to start the experiment. Every time the cell budded, the daughter was removed and the mother was scored as being one generation older. In (a), the results are presented in the form of a survival curve. In (b), the age-specific mortality rate is presented in a Gompertz plot. (From Jazwinski, Egilmez, and Chen 1989.)

absence, it might have been difficult or even impossible to agree on whether or not yeasts age. It was further found that the mean and maximum life span values are characteristic for any given strain of *S. cerevisiae* but that they vary widely from one strain to another. Such evidence suggests the existence of strain-specific genetic mechanisms regulating longevity.

A detailed list of the morphological and physiological changes that occur during yeast aging was presented by Jazwinski (1993). Some of these changes can be used as biomarkers of aging; they include (1) increase in cell size, (2) increase in the number of bud scars, (3) increase in the chitin component of the cell wall, and (4) increase in the generation time. The increase in the generation time is the most interesting of these changes, and is perhaps the single best diagnostic biomarker of aging in this organism. The generation time of individual yeast cells increases with replicative age, accelerates as the cells enter the phase of exponential increase in mortality, and becomes acute two to three generations before the cessation of mitosis by the mother cell (Jazwinski 1993). Long-lived strains display a shorter generation time and a delayed increase in generation time when compared to strains that have shorter life spans (Egilmez and Jazwinski 1989). Some evidence suggests that a deficit in energy metabolism may lead to the increase in generation time with replicative age (Jazwinski 1993). These data have been encompassed in the cell spiral model of yeast aging (Figure 4.10; Jazwinski, Egilmez, and Chen 1989).

It was also demonstrated that young mothers, as well as daughter cells budded from young mothers, show a young (short) generation time. Old mothers, as well as daughters budded from old mothers, show an old (long) generation time.

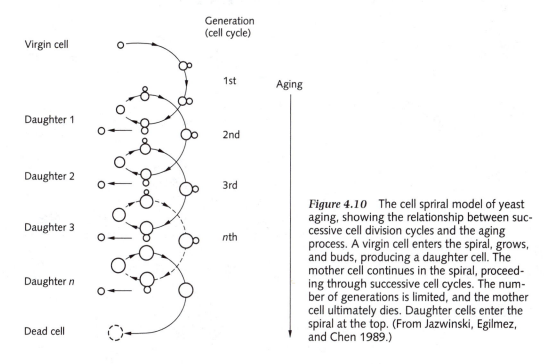

Virgin cell

Generation
(cell cycle)

Aging

1st

Daughter 1

2nd

Daughter 2

3rd

Daughter 3

*n*th

Daughter *n*

Dead cell

Figure 4.10   The cell spriral model of yeast aging, showing the relationship between successive cell division cycles and the aging process. A virgin cell enters the spiral, grows, and buds, producing a daughter cell. The mother cell continues in the spiral, proceeding through successive cell cycles. The number of generations is limited, and the mother cell ultimately dies. Daughter cells enter the spiral at the top. (From Jazwinski, Egilmez, and Chen 1989.)

Most interesting, however, was the demonstration that the generation time of these "old" daughters decreased to young (short) values within three generations after the daughter cell formed. Three conclusions can be drawn from this elegant experiment by Egilmez and Jazwinski (1989):

There exists a diffusible cytoplasmic factor(s) that is elaborated by aging cells and that can be passed on to daughter cells, but that can be diluted, destroyed, and/or replaced in young cells only.

The senescent phenotype (as judged by the presence of long generation times) is dominant over the nonsenescent, or young, phenotype.

The depletion of the senescence factor in a pedigree is not gradual but appears to be an all-or-none pattern, perhaps indicative of a particular threshold phenomenon.

It is not yet known whether the senescence factor acts catalytically or stoichiometrically within the cell. However, molecules regulating gene expression would fall in the first category and would be of great interest, given our current paradigms of the genetic regulation of longevity.

Another interesting finding regarding yeast longevity was the report that there is a direct correlation between the ability of a given strain to withstand stress (for example, starvation, heat shock) and the length of that strain's normal life span (Kennedy et al. 1995). This observation enabled Kennedy and colleagues to identify four genes responsible for extending life span by screening mutants for the ability to withstand stress. Mutations in the one gene they described in detail appear to involve a trade-off of fertility for stress resistance. We will discuss their data and the concomitant implications in some detail in Chapter 6. For the moment, note that this empirical connection between stress resistance and longevity is not unique to the strains of yeast that Kennedy and colleagues used.

Jazwinski and his group adopted a different strategy for identifying the genes involved in extending longevity in their strains. Using molecular biological techniques, they identified six genes that showed differential expression throughout the life span (Egilmez et al. 1990). Of these, five were preferentially expressed in younger cells and one was preferentially expressed in older cells, leading the investigators to conclude that aging in yeast is accompanied by defined alterations in the levels of certain gene transcripts. This conclusion is empirical evidence for the existence of nucleocytoplasmic (genetic) interactions that regulate aging. More recently, these researchers cloned three of these candidate longevity-assurance genes from yeasts (D'mello et al. 1994; Sun et al. 1994). One of these genes is called *LAG1*; the other two are the yeast homologues (termed *RAS1* and *RAS2*) of the well-known *c-H-ras* regulatory gene of vertebrates. We will discuss the possible role of these genes in more detail in Chapter 6; for the moment note that the *RAS2* gene is known to be important in regulating the response of the cell to ultraviolet irradiation (Engelberg et al. 1994). Kale and Jazwinski (1996) demonstrated that the age at which the *RAS2* gene is most highly expressed coincides with the age at which the yeast cell is the most resistant to UV-induced stress. This age corresponds to what we might call a "middle-aged" yeast. Interestingly, the expression levels of at least four of the longevity-assurance genes cloned by Kale and Jazwinski each peak in the same time period.

Thus, two groups working independently have each arrived at a similar conclusion: There is a strong correlation among specific forms of stress resistance, the expression levels of particular genes known to modulate the organism's response to stress, and the organism's longevity. This observation allows us to draw two major conclusions from the work done with yeasts. First, strong empirical evidence supports the existence of a correlation between stress resistance and longevity. In addition, this concordance appears to be inherently plausible—stronger organisms should live longer than weaker ones, everything else being equal. Second, the fact that the expression of the different longevity-assurance genes peaks in "middle-aged" yeasts suggests that the active life maintenance processes may operate only through that point and then shut down. This temporal pattern indicates that senescence may be due to the *absence* of specific gene products rather than to the *presence* of "old age"-specific gene products (Kale and Jazwinski 1996).

It would be most interesting if the diffusible senescence factor described by Egilmez, Jazwinski, and Chen (1989) turned out to be a diffusible molecule capable of repressing the transcriptional activity of various genes. As we will see, this situation of an active expression of life-extending activities is similar to that found in worms (Larsen, Albert, and Riddle 1995), in flies (Dudas and Arking 1995), and perhaps in other higher organisms as well (see Chapter 7). Although not yet formally proven, this conclusion appears to be consistent with the differential allocation of energy into maintenance or reproduction as specified by the "disposable soma" theory of Kirkwood (1987). But its molecular genetics was first worked out in the simple yeast.

In any event, the analysis of longevity and senescence in *S. cerevisiae* is currently one of the most advanced of any genetic model. The rapid increase in our understanding of the molecular basis of aging in this organism validates our faith in the genetic approach to answering these important questions.

Volvox and Other Simple Multicellular Organisms

The evolution of multicellular organisms was a major advance in that it made possible the division of labor and the differentiation of cells for particular tasks. There are several evolutionary paths by which such multicellular forms are thought to have arisen. One of them appears to have involved the coalescence, over evolutionary time, of individual cells into a colonial organism, with the subsequent specialization of the cells into somatic and reproductive cells. This process can be seen in the primitive green alga *Volvox carteri*, which consists of a hollow sphere of about 2,000 small, flagellated somatic cells (each of which resembles an existing, more primitive, free-living unicellular [protist] species of alga) (Figure 4.11). This sphere surrounds and encloses about 16 larger reproductive cells. The somatic cells can move but cannot divide; the reproductive cells can divide but cannot move. They are each specialized for different tasks. The reproductive cells divide and give rise to miniature adults, which are then released from the parents (Kirk 1988).

What is interesting from our point of view is that the somatic cells of the parent senesce and die shortly after reproduction is complete (Hagen and Kochert 1980). The terminally differentiated somatic cells show a characteristic pattern of morphological and biochemical changes (such as a loss of chlorophyll or a decrease in protein synthesis) that decreases their probability of survival and can thus be called senescent changes. These changes seem to be inherent in the somatic cell itself, for early surgical removal of the reproductive cells does not rescue the somatic cells from their fate. They can be rescued from death only by certain mutants that convert the somatic cells into reproductive cells. These observations lead us to the conclusion that aging in this species is an intrinsic part of a program of development. A somatic cell undergoes a series of specializa-

Figure 4.11　A young adult spheroid of *Volvox carteri*. The adult is composed of about 2,000 small somatic cells, all of which are embedded in a transparent glycoprotein matrix and which bear a strong resemblance to free-living unicellular algae. There are about 16 large, dark gonidia, or reproductive cells, which are contained within the central cavity of the adult. It is the somatic cells that will age, senesce, and die after the release of the reproductive cells. (Courtesy of David Kirk.)

tions and differentiations that allow it to perform a highly specialized function but that inevitably result in the death of the cell.

The decision of whether an embryonic cell will differentiate as a somatic cell or a reproductive cell appears to depend on the size of the cell. During development, asymmetric mitosis gives rise to daughter cells of unequal size. This difference in cell size is postulated to initiate a cascade of differential gene expression in the two types of cells, which then leads to their functional differentiation—the smaller cells becoming somatic cells and the larger cells giving rise to reproductive cells (Kirk et al. 1993). Not all species of *Volvox* use this mechanism of differentiation between soma and germ line; in some species the mitotic divisions give rise to equal-sized daughter cells in which presumptive somatic cells are indistinguishable from presumptive reproductive cells. However, these forms require a more prolonged period of development, and hence have a longer life cycle. Asymmetric cell division allows the organism to complete development more rapidly and enter reproduction earlier, which most likely confers a reproductive advantage (Freeman and Lundelius 1992; Kirk et al. 1993). The direct development of soma and germ line appears to be tied to the organism's reproductive fitness, which is consistent with the evolutionary concepts believed to underlie the aging process. (Note that this explanation is conceptually similar to the ontogenetic theory of senescence put forth by Jazwinski [1993] and described in Chapter 6.)

Aging, senescence, and death seem to be built into the multicellular way of life even from its very beginnings. In addition, these observations are entirely consistent with the idea that the senescence of the somatic cells is under genetic control. As we will see in succeeding chapters, the available evidence strongly supports this point of view.

Plants: Senescence as a Developmental Process

The area of plant aging and senescence has developed independently of the field of animal gerontology. This should not be surprising, considering that the former arose out of the needs of plant physiologists and the agricultural community, while the latter has its origins in medical science and evolutionary theory. There are both strong similarities and strong differences in the senescence patterns observed in plants and animals. Good reviews of this topic have been presented by Nooden and Thompson (1985), Nooden and Leopold (1988), Nooden and Letham (1993), and Nooden and Guiamet (1996); much of the following discussion is drawn from these sources.

In plants, as in animals, there seems to be a correlation between the pattern of reproduction and the pattern of senescence. Annual or biennial plants, which have a single reproductive phase closely followed by death, are technically known as monocarps (bearing a single fruit) and show a close link between the two processes. Perennial plants, which have repeated reproductive phases and are termed polycarps (bearing multiple fruits), decline more gradually and do not show such a tight linkage. The animal equivalents of "monocarpic" and "polycarpic" are "semelparous" and "iteroparous," respectively. Mechanisms of senescence may be different in the two categories of plants. For reasons of convenience, most of the research on this topic has focused on monocarpic senescence, so our discussion will also focus primarily on monocarps.

Since monocarpic plants senesce after their reproductive phase, any genetic alteration or environmental condition that delays flowering or seed production will postpone their senescence. Much of the research in this area has focused on determining which structures of the plant induce senescence and which structures respond to those regulatory signals. Gardeners have long known that removing old flowers or immature fruit will prolong flower production and/or the life of the plant, and this relationship has been confirmed by research. In monocarps such as soybeans, the reproductive structures appear to induce senescence and the leaves appear to be the primary target of these senescence-inducing signals, for they yellow and drop off before the plant dies.

Plant hormones called cytokinins (particularly the two dominant cytokinins—zeatin riboside and dihydrozeatin riboside) are synthesized in the root tips and transported to the leaves via the xylem. Early in the development of the seedpod, these two cytokinins show a marked drop in their flux through the xylem, a condition that is necessary but not sufficient to cause leaf senescence (Nooden and Letham 1993). Early removal of the pod restores the cytokinin levels and prevents leaf yellowing and abscission; late removal of the pod has no effect. An irreversible threshold seems to be involved. Experimental situations in which the cytokinin flux is artificially maintained at a high level not only prevent leaf senescence, but show that the cytokinins are actively metabolized by the leaf, suggesting that senescence is the response by that tissue to the removal of an active suppressor signal. Thus, the soybean plant dies because the development of the seedpod induces leaf senescence, the leaves no longer supply needed nutrients and hormones to the roots, and the whole plant withers (Nooden 1988a,b). Senescence in this organism is the result of the induced failure of a particular subsystem (the leaves) and not of the organism as a whole.

It should not be assumed that all leaf senescence is controlled by this one type of mechanism, for there appear to be multiple parallel regulatory signals involved in the process. For example, the breakdown of the chlorophyll molecule in the soybean can be inhibited by a certain nuclear gene that has, however, no effect on other aspects of leaf senescence (Guiamet, Pichesky, and Nooden 1995). Leaf senescence in another monocarp, *Arabidopsis thaliana*, which has been widely used in plant research, is caused by changes in light dosage, and reproductive development does not drive senescence directly in the way that it often does in other monocarpic plants (Nooden et al. 1995). Thus plant senescence appears to be regulated by specific, multiple factors. This conclusion is confirmed by the following fact: Although self-destruction is the hallmark of plant senescence, it is highly selective in its targets. Senescence is intimately associated with many phases of plant development. It is essential for the formation of xylem cells, the abscission of leaves in preparation for dormancy, the abscission of floral parts in preparation for fruit development, and so forth. Different floral parts located next to one another follow very different developmental courses. Such specificity may be observed even at the cellular level, where one cell may die and its neighbor (of another cell type) will live. This high degree of specificity must underlie the use of cell death by the plant as a developmental process, whereby floral structures will give rise to fruits, and so on. In this restricted sense we may view plant senescence as an integral part of the organism's developmental program.

The mechanisms underlying senescence in polycarpic plants are not as well understood. Many plants are capable of being vegetatively propagated for very long times, suggesting that passage through a sexual reproductive phase is not necessary in most species. Some polycarpic plants undergo clonal growth, whereby vegetative growth establishes linked parts that nonetheless have enough independence to continue growing after the parental parts have died. The concept of individuality is hard-pressed in such organisms, so two specialized terms are often used to assist us in making clear our meanings. The term "genet" refers to all the genetically identical products of a single zygote, no matter what size or however subdivided. The term "ramet" refers to a single shoot complex, which often appears to our eyes to be an individual organism but may actually be part of a larger clone or genet. In clonal organisms, a genet may contain many ramets, each existing more or less independently from other ramets. Some of these clonal plants are capable of very long lives, perhaps immortal or at least indefinite for as long as the plant's environment is compatible with the plant's requirements. Table 4.3 lists some such clones. A good animal analogue of these clonal plants might be coral reefs.

Senescence in plants is not linked only to the functional decline of the entire organism, but is also intimately involved with ongoing developmental processes involved in the production of flowers, fruits, and so forth. Corresponding selective differences are present in the control mechanisms that regulate senescence. Environmental factors that damage the roots will also cause foliage damage by prematurely shutting down cytokinin production. In general, the flux of cytokinin from the roots is high during vegetative growth and decreases during late reproductive growth, when many plants are adapted to focus their energy and nutrient resources on the growth of seeds. On the other hand, the senescence of the floral petals, known to be leaf derivatives, is triggered by ethylene and not

Table 4.3   **Long-Lived Plant Clones**

Species	Estimated age (years)	Size	Mode of propagation
Huckleberry	13,000+	1,980 m^2	Rhizome
Creosote	11,000+	8 m^2	Basal branching
Quaking aspen	10,000+	81 ha	Root buds
Velvet grass	1,000+	489 m^2	Rhizome
Lily of the valley	670+	83 m^2	Rhizome
Reed grass	400+	50 m^2	Rhizome
Black spruce	330+	14 m^2	Layering

Source: Data from Nooden 1988b, Table 12.2.

by cytokinins. In intact plants, the ovary and related structures synthesize and release ethylene. Bringing about the senescence of peripheral floral parts is a normal part of the normal growth pattern of the ovary. As a result of this evolutionary history, flower shippers and flower arrangers are very careful never to mix cut flowers with ripe fruits, for the ethylene gas produced by the fruit will cause the flowers to die. As the fruit ripens, it begins to produce much larger quantities of ethylene. These higher quantities induce the self-destruction or senescence of the fruit itself. The ethylene-induced senescence of the fruits causes the fleshy tissues surrounding the seed to undergo a series of complex changes that make them look, taste, and smell better to those animals that have coevolved with the plants, to aid in the dispersal of the seeds. In other words, the fruit ripens and becomes edible. We eat it and scatter the seeds far and wide. Some of these scattered seeds germinate and give rise to new individuals of the plant species. And the cycle begins again.

This discussion of plant senescence should illustrate that the result of senescence is not only the functional decrement of the organism but also the removal of structures whose job is done. Another major consequence of this selective senescence in polycarps is the redistribution of nutrients it makes possible. Key nutrients released by the senescence of one tissue (leaves or shoots) may be transferred to another tissue (such as roots or underground bulbs). This transfer of nutrients is probably an important factor in the ability of these organisms to become dormant and survive the harsh environmental conditions of winter.

Senescence in plants is an active and orderly process that requires both energy and protein synthesis. The orderliness is evident in the selectivity of target tissues, as well as in the regular sequence with which the process occurs in each tissue. Consider the regularity in the breakdown of leaf pigments as the leaf senesces—so regular that we may predict when different parts of forests will be showing different autumn colors. In general, mitochondrial activity is maintained intact until the later stages of senescence, presumably because energy is required to synthesize the catabolic enzymes needed to degrade the tissues and to transport the freed metabolites to other tissues. The DNA also appears to remain intact until very late in senescence. Although RNA synthesis declines much earlier, resulting in a net loss of RNA during senescence, the presence of polysomes in senescent leaves suggests that active translation of gene products is still taking place. Many of the new proteins thus synthesized are hydrolytic and will ultimately be responsible for the macromolecular degradation of the target tissue. Such enzymes must be compartmentalized, possibly in the vacuole, to prevent premature autodigestion.

The foregoing data suggest that senescence is under active nuclear control, being brought about by apparently programmed changes in gene activity and protein synthesis. These alterations in macromolecular metabolism are accompanied by changes in membrane structure that lead to an increased leakiness of the membranes and a decreased ability of the cell to effectively compartmentalize its contents. Such leakiness would have important physiological consequences, perhaps culminating in the release of the hydrolytic enzymes from the vacuole and the resulting death of the cell via autodigestion.

In many plants, senescence appears to be an active, energy-requiring endogenous process under genetic control. The senescing cells may generate free radicals, which may then stochastically react with the cell membrane and hasten senescence. Senescence is likely to be more complex than this brief overview may suggest, and probably consists of many integrated biochemical steps coupled into separate but parallel processes. Although used for developmental purposes, plant cell senescence also leads to a gradual decline in physiological functioning of the cell, tissue, or organ. In particular circumstances this decline may lead to the death of the whole organism.

Fungi: The Role of Mitochondria in Senescence

Many more species of fungi exist than those few we usually see in the markets. The two species most important to our survey of aging are *Neurospora crassa* and *Podospora anserina*, which are closely related ascomycetes. The ascomycetes constitute a very common group of fungi, comprising some 30,000 free-living species and including within their number the yeasts, many of the common black and blue-green molds, and the morels and truffles prized by gourmets. *Neurospora* and *Podospora* are well-established laboratory tools for investigation in biochemical genetics, and their analysis has allowed us to discern the roles that mitochondrial DNA (mtDNA) and antioxidant defense systems play in the extension of longevity in these species. We will discuss antioxidant defense systems in more detail in Chapter 6; mitochondrial DNA is what concerns us here.

Neurospora and *Podospora* have provided us with an interesting insight into an aging process that might have been overlooked if we had confined our attention to the traditional laboratory rodents (see Griffiths 1992 for review). The body plan of fungi is fundamentally different from that of most other organisms. Fungi usually do not have discrete cells; rather they contain mitotically derived nuclei contained within a more or less common cytoplasm. They usually reproduce vegetatively via mycelial or hyphal growth, and they can be widely dispersed via asexual cellular spores. These facts suggest that life span in these organisms can be measured either as the ability of the colony to continue growing or as the ability of the spores to survive for some time before germinating.

The growth of *Podospora* ceases at a time and a size characteristic of each geographic race. The nongrowing portions of a clone fuse, undergo meiosis, reproduce sexually, and produce ascospores. This process restores the growth potential of the clone. The old hyphae (somatic tissues) eventually die. Senescence is not transmitted to ascospores. Thus "life span" in this organism refers to the continued mitotic growth and vitality of the somatic cells constituting one clone, or individual. Genetic crosses have shown that the characteristic life span of any given race is inherited as a cytoplasmic factor localized to the mitochondria, cellular organelles that are essential to energy metabolism in all eukaryotic cells. All mitochondria contain their own DNA, but for proper functioning they rely on their own genome, as well as that of the nucleus. Cellular senescence in this fungal genotype is associated with the alteration of its mitochondrial genome into covalently closed, circular, head-to-tail multimers of a portion of the mtDNA. These elements are known as senescent DNA, or senDNA.

Different strains and even different cultures of the same strain may show different types of senDNA (Griffiths 1992). Regardless of their precise origin within the mitochondrial genome, these different senDNAs appear to act in much the same way. As senDNAs accumulate in aging cultures, mtDNA molecules change radically, in that complete wild-type molecules disappear. This transition is associated with a reduction of specific cytochromes, resulting in a disruption of energy production in the mitochondrion (Osiewacz and Esser 1984).

These senDNAs appear to be discrete mtDNA sequences that can autonomously excise and amplify themselves such that they may be found in very high concentrations in the mitochondria of senescent cells. The concentration of these senDNA molecules in the young hyphal cell appears to be positively correlated with the race-specific life span: very low in long-lived strains, and higher in short-lived strains (Wright and Cummings 1983). However, certain nuclear mutations confer "immortality" on their host. The existence of such genetically based suppression of the formation of senDNA suggests that senescence may be dependent on a certain sort of interaction between the nuclear and mitochondrial genomes, and a model to this effect has been proposed (Esser 1985; Kuck et al. 1985).

Neurospora shows a senescence pattern that is quite similar to that of *Podospora* both in its general progression and in its involvement of mtDNA (see Griffiths 1992 for full review). Extragenomic elements are progressively inserted into the mtDNA as the culture ages, causing cytochrome abnormalities and loss of growth potential, until at death intact mtDNA is barely detectable. The source of the extragenomic DNA appears to be one of several different strain-specific mitochondrial plasmids. Removal of the plasmids from a strain removes the senescent phenotype. Griffiths (1992) has suggested that the involvement of these plasmids in the senescent phenotype is a mistake, in that both the mitochondrial and plasmid genomes are probably sharing the same molecular machinery to carry out their own replication and so occasionally the two systems become entangled with one another, thereby setting off senescence.

This phenomenon may appear to be an odd evolutionary mechanism of senescence restricted to a few species of fungi and of no real consequence to us. Perhaps. Yet we must recognize that increasing evidence suggests that bioenergetic decline and the accumulation of mtDNA damage are associated with the degenerative effects of aging and age-related diseases in humans and other organisms (Wallace et al. 1995). Such damage is particularly noticeable in postmitotic tissues, and may be related to oxidative damage (Martin et al. 1995). We will explore this topic further in Chapters 6 and 9. Whether such a mechanism plays an important causal role in organismal aging is unknown, but it is now under active investigation. We cannot afford to overlook this clue revealed to us by the comparative approach.

Invertebrates: General Patterns of Aging

The varieties of senescence in invertebrates are exceeded only by the number of their species. Comfort (1979) has presented data on the maximum life spans of 282 invertebrate species; as Table 4.4 shows, the numbers span the gamut from 28 days to 90 years. In addition, more or less detailed descriptions of senescence

Table 4.4   **Maximum Recorded Longevities for Some Invertebrates**

Taxon	Species	Maximum life span	Evidence[a]
Porifera			
Demospongiae	*Suberites carnosus*	15 yrs	c
Cnidaria			
Anthozoa	*Cereus pedunculatus*	85–90 yrs	c
Platyhelminthes			
Cestoda	*Taeniarhynchus saginatus*	>35 yrs	h
Turbellaria	*Dugesia tigrina*	6–7 yrs	c
Aschelminthes			
Nematoda	*Wuchereria bancrofti*	17 yrs	h
Rotifera	*Callidina* sp.	5 ms	c
Annelida			
Polychaeta	*Sabella pavonina*	>10 yrs	c
Oligochaeta	*Lumbricus terrestris*	5–6 yrs	c
Arthropoda			
Arachnida	*Filistata insidiatrix*	11 yrs	c
Crustacea			
Cirripedia	*Balanus balanoides*	>5 yrs	w
Malacostraca	*Astacus*	15–25 yrs	?
Uniramia: Insecta			
Ephemeroptera	*Cloëon dipterum*	4 wks	c
Diptera	*Drosophila melanogaster*	9 wks	c
Isoptera	*Neotermes castaneus*	>25 yrs	w
Lepidoptera	*Maniola jurtina*	44 days	c
Coleoptera	*Blaps gigas*	>10 yrs	c
Hymenoptera	*Lasius niger*	>19 yrs	c
Echinodermata			
Echinoidea	*Echinus esculentus*	>8 yrs	w
Asteroida	*Marthasterias glacialis*	>7 yrs	c
Mollusca			
Amphineura	*Chiton tuberculatus*	12 yrs	w
Gastropoda			
Prosobranchia	*Patella vulgata*	15 yrs	w, g
Opisthobranchia	*Haminea hydatis*	4 yrs	w
Pulmonata	*Rumina decollata*	12 yrs	c
Bivalvia	*Margaritana margaritifera*	70–80 yrs	w, g
Cephalopoda	*Loligo pealii*	3–4 yrs	w

Source: After Lamb 1997, based on data from Comfort 1964.
[a]c = kept in captivity; g = age estimate based on growth; h = host case history; w = in wild conditions.

patterns were presented for about 20 different supraspecific groups. It is patently impossible to summarize the patterns of aging and senescence in such a diverse group of organisms. It is far more useful to describe in some depth the patterns of aging and senescence observed in a few experimentally important species. Provocative insights may be achieved perhaps more easily from a detailed but limited review than from an inclusive but superficial commentary. We will limit our observations on invertebrate aging to rotifers, nematodes, and insects because enough intensive work has been done on each of these groups to merit our study of the data.

Rotifers: The Power of Theory

The 2,000 species of the phylum Rotifera are very small aquatic pseudocoelomates. They are sometimes called "wheel animalcules" because the beating of a crown of cilia around the mouth causes them to spin like tiny wheels. These small animals have a muscular pharynx with hard jaws; they are omnivorous. Most species reproduce parthnogenetically, but many of these also reproduce sexually. The maximum life span is very specific, ranging from 12 days to 2 months. The nuclear number is fixed in rotifers; there is no cell division, and therefore they grow only via an increase in cell size. After a period of adult vigor, the aging animal enters a period of senescence, in which it becomes sluggish in its behavior, the tissues shrink and become opaque, pigment is deposited in the gut and associated organs, cells degenerate, and death soon ensues. (Note the similarity to the age-related changes observed in other invertebrates, such as *Drosophila* [see Table 4.7].) In many species, this senescent process begins while the female is still reproductively active. The conjunction of these two processes often results in a diminished rate of egg laying coupled with the production of apparently abnormal eggs.

This correlation of abnormal reproduction with the onset of senescence is by no means limited to rotifers, as we'll see. There is a considerable amount of individual variation in the length of the senescent period. An endogenous process of senescent degeneration appears to affect all parts of the animal's body at more or less the same time. There doesn't appear to be a pacemaker organ. As Comfort (1979) has pointed out, this pattern is fully consistent with the idea that some or all of the somatic cells have a fixed survival time. This then constitutes one of the theoretical attractions of rotifers to the experimental gerontologist, for their cells undergo a synchronous death. The other main attraction of rotifers lies in their alleged possession of deleterious parental age effects, and a review of this aspect of scientific history may teach us to be wary of being blinded by theory.

Lansing (1947, 1954) worked with two parthenogenetic species that reproduced via ameiotic divisions of the female germ line. What resulted were clones of genetically identical offspring with which Lansing could do his experiments. He found that eggs laid by old mothers had shorter life spans than did eggs laid by young mothers. Furthermore, if the strain was continuously propagated from older mothers for several generations, then the mean life span would decrease progressively and the strain would invariably become extinct. Given the genetic identity of the animals, these results suggested that death of Lansing's clonal lines was due to the existence of an extragenic, transmissible, and cumulative age factor. This hypothetical cytoplasmic factor, passed from generation to generation via the egg, was thought to influence longevity by accelerating the onset of senescence in later generations. Such "Lansing effects" have since been claimed to occur in many other organisms (see Lints 1978) and have been viewed by many as a general aspect of aging. Parental age effects do exist.

From studies on experimental animals, offspring of older parents are known to be quantitatively different from offspring of younger parents. But until Lansing's work, there was no reason to suggest that these effects were cumulatively transmissible over multiple generations. However, there may be a problem of overinterpretation here. First, this accelerated aging of subsequent generations is not found in other cases in which cytoplasmic factors are believed to be involved, such as *Paramecium* or *Podospora*. Second, Lints (1978) has pointed out what many readers of Lansing's papers have overlooked—namely, that all of the cloned lines eventually died out, regardless of the age of reproduction. Third, Lints also showed that both young and old mothers gave rise to offspring with shortened life spans. There appears to be a problem with oogenesis both in young and in old mothers, but not in middle-aged mothers. In other words, there is an optimal age for reproduction. Reproducing at suboptimal ages would allow the population to die out simply because of the reduced fecundity, not because of any effects of aging as such.

Even though the major experimental basis for the Lansing effects has been weakened by this analysis, the Lansing effects have since been claimed to exist in other organisms. Lansing effects are assumed to involve age-dependent alterations in the cytoplasmic factors that the mother contributes to the egg. Further, these factors are presumed to alter the patterns of gene expression in succeeding generations. The mechanisms involved are obscure, and there is some disagreement over the interpretation and the importance of the data. The topic was reviewed by Lints (1988b). It is possible that a maternal age effect is operating in the rotifers. An even more probable explanation is that the existence in the literature of descriptions of the Lansing effects may have persuaded other gerontologists to conclude that artificial-selection experiments for long-lived organisms were bound to fail, since one would have to breed continually from old mothers. Since the experiments were bound to fail, then what was the point of doing them? As Albert Einstein said, "It is the theory which decides what we can observe." If the theory is in error, what does that do to our observations and assumptions? The warning is pertinent whether you work with rotifers or with humans.

Nematodes: Genes and Altered Proteins

Nematodes are cylindrical, unsegmented pseudocoelomate worms, most of which are free-living microscopic forms. There are 12,000 described species. However, given their small size and inconspicuous habitats in the soil and elsewhere, it is not surprising to learn that some authorities believe that as many as 500,000 nematode species exist. Humans are hosts to about 50 parasitic nematodes, which cause diseases such as pinworm, hookworm, intestinal roundworm, filariasis, and others. These few diseases probably account for the bad reputation of nematodes as a group.

Several different species of free-living nematodes have been used in research on aging. In 1974, Sidney Brenner published a persuasive paper describing the genetic system of *Caenorhabditis elegans* and convinced many others of its experimental virtues (Hodgkin 1989). Most of the work being done today focuses on this species and, to a lesser extent, on *Turbatrix aceti*. *C. elegans* is easily cultured in dishes containing agar as a semisolid supporting medium and a layer of bacteria as a food source. Under these conditions, *C. elegans* lives to a maximum of 20 days. It is particularly suitable to genetic studies, and the heritability of the life span of this species is estimated at 20 to 50 percent (Johnson and Wood 1982). Several different mutants that confer long life have been isolated and described; several of them clearly have something to do with the aging process. The available data suggest that these mutants lengthen the life span by increasing the animal's resistance to oxidative stress. A more detailed discussion of their genetic control of aging appears in Chapter 6.

Senescence in nematodes is signaled by a progressive increase in mortality, a failure to respond to environmental stimuli, the accumulation of lipofuscin (the so-called aging pigment), and the deterioration of the internal anatomy. Senescence is also accompanied by a striking biochemical phenomenon in which structurally altered enzyme molecules accumulate in older animals. This phenomenon was first observed in 1970 by Gershon and Gershon in *Turbatrix aceti*. They found that a purified enzyme, isocitrate lyase, obtained from old animals had only 60 percent of the specific activity found in the pure enzyme obtained from young animals. The implication is that the enzymes from the older animals were altered in some way. This alteration might be due to inefficient protein synthesis in old animals or to some subtle physical changes taking place in old molecules. It is probably some sort of "wear and tear" phenomenon that affects old molecules, since it has been shown that these old molecules can be made as good as new simply by chemically unfolding them and allowing them to spontaneously refold in the test tube (Yuh and Gafni 1987).

Even though the processes that cause this structural change are still not clear, this initial observation has sparked an interest in determining whether other enzymes in the nematode are altered in the same way with aging and whether other species display such changes as they age. Perhaps the deterioration in our own physiological functions arises from altered, and hence less efficient, enzyme molecules. Five enzymes in *T. aceti* are known to be altered with age (Table 4.5). All of them demonstrate substantial differences (about 50 percent) in the age-dependent specific activities of these enzymes. This is a real process. However, the other fact not stated but implicit in Table 4.5 is that very few enzymes (only ten out of the several thousand present) demonstrate this age-specific alteration. Thus, either this process has little to do with aging, or the enzymes involved are rare limiting enzymes that regulate the activity of important metabolic pathways dependent on them. It will be an important task of future research to determine whether the facts support this alternative interpretation.

Table 4.5   Properties of Altered Enzymes from *Turbatrix aceti*

Enzyme	Altered specific activity[a]	Altered K_m[b]	Electrophoresis change	Antigenic difference	Immunological cross-reaction	Altered heat stability
Isocitrate lyase	Yes	No	—	No	Yes	Yes
Enolase	Yes	Yes?	No	Yes	Yes	Yes
Fructose-1,6-diphosphate aldolase	Yes	No?	No	No	Yes	Yes
Phosphoglycerate kinase	Yes	Yes?	No	—	—	No
Elongation factor 1	Yes	—	—	—	Yes	—

Source: From Russell and Jacobson 1985.
[a]Change in relative quantities of isozymes. All isozymes have altered specific activity.
[a]The term K_m refers to a measurement of the rate of an enzyme reaction. Each enzyme has a characteristic K_m when measured under standard conditions.

Whatever the nature of the mechanism involved, this phenomenon is not limited to nematodes but also appears in various different enzymes in both rats and mice (Table 4.6). Some of these structurally altered vertebrate enzymes, such as superoxide dismutase, are believed to be intimately involved in the protective aspects of the aging process; others, such as ornithine decarboxylase or glucose-

Table 4.6   Distribution of Altered Enzymes in Several Species

Enzymes	Species		
	Turbatrix aceti	Mouse	Rat
Isocitrate lyase	X		
Phosphoglycerate kinase	X		X
Enolase	X		
Elongation factor 1	X		
Aldolase	X	X	X
Tyrosine aminotransferase		X	
Ornithine decarboxylase		X	
Phosphorylase		X	
Glucose-6-phosphate dehydrogenase		X	
Superoxide dismutase			X
Lactic dehydrogenase			X

Source: Data from Rothstein 1982.

6-phosphate dehydrogenase, could be regulatory enzymes. The existence of thermodynamically nonrandom change that would alter the specific activity of certain key enzymes and hence initiate senescence is an interesting concept that should be examined further. We now know that the transcription of an important stress protein, hsp70, shows an age-related decline due to structurally altered transcription factors. Thus the concept needs to be broadened to go beyond enzymes in order to include all regulatory proteins. The existence of such a process would not have been found in the absence of a comparative approach. It will also be important for future research to determine if these structural alterations are merely the indirect consequences of an age-related decrease in protein turnover. An increase in the half-life of the protein molecules could result in nonspecific tertiary structural alterations simply as a result of increased exposure to environmental insult.

One of the most important aspects of the nematode for future work on aging is the fact that the complete cell lineage of *C. elegans* is known and described. The organism has a determinate and strictly programmed pattern of cell division and cell differentiation that leads to the development of an adult organism. The origin, position, and fate of every cell are known and charted. Another important advantage of this organism is the excellent assortment of mutant genes, mutant strains, and genetic tools that are available for use by geneticists. In addition, its genome is now being sequenced and should be completed in the near future. Current research has allowed the identification of two separate but interacting genetic systems controlling longevity in this species—one operating via regulation of stress resistance mechanisms and the other via regulation of metabolic timing. We will discuss these findings in more detail in Chapter 6. This organism therefore offers us an excellent opportunity to investigate which aspects of the aging process are genetically determined and which are stochastic.

Insects: Drosophila as a Genetic Model

Perhaps a million different species of insects are known to exist today, and more new ones are being named and described each year. In fact, it is likely that about 75 percent of all the animal species on Earth today are insects. They are the dominant terrestrial life forms on the planet, in terms of both number of species and number of individuals. As many apartment dwellers can testify, they also include among their number one of the toughest extant life forms: cockroaches.

As arthropods, all insects have an external skeleton, and their segmented body is divided into three main divisions: head, thorax and abdomen. The life history of insects is fundamentally different from that of the other invertebrates we have described. Immature forms of most insects have limited mobility and usually pass through their developmental stages close to the location where the adult female originally laid the egg. Young insects are voracious feeders. Their growth involves changes not only in size but also in form. In the holometabolous insects (about 90 percent of the extant species), this transition from immature to adult form involves a complete metamorphosis that is under hormonal and genetic control. This remodeling of the organism occurs within the pupal stage and results in the emergence of a sexually mature adult. The success and diversity of insects is reflected in the diversity of their life spans, ranging from 1 day for mayflies to more than 60 years for termite reproductives. Despite this rich diversity provided by natural selection, only a few insect species have been studied in relation to aging. These include several species of the fruit fly (*Drosophila*), the common housefly (*Musca domestica*), the mosquito (*Aedes stimulans*), a wasp (*Habrobracon serinopae*), and a flour beetle (*Tribolium castaneum*).

By far the overwhelming amount of this work has been performed on *Drosophila melanogaster*, the geneticists' favorite organism. Studies on aging are carried out on the adult form because the larval tissues show no signs of aging. Indeed, as pointed out in Chapter 7, the presumptive adult or imaginal disc tissue found in the developing larvae shows no signs of senescence but can be kept alive indefinitely and still give rise to normal adult tissue. One interpretation of these findings is that only organisms that are no longer in their developmental phase age.

Several obvious manifestations of senescence are detectable in aging insects; they are listed in Table 4.7. Extensive reviews of the aging process in *Drosophila* and other dipterans have been put forth by Lamb (1978), Sohal (1983), Arking

---

Table 4.7   **Age-Associated Alterations in *Drosophila***

External morphology
  Increased damage to external structures
  Increased melanin pigment in sternites

Behavioral changes
  Decreased geotactic and phototactic response
  Decreased ability to withstand environmental stress
    (starvation, insecticides, high temperature, low humidity, etc.)
  Decreased mating ability
  Decreased stamina, speed of locomotion and flight performance
  Decreased chemoreceptor sensitivity

Physiological, cellular, and biochemical changes
  Shrinkage of cortical area of brain, loss of basophilia, and vacuolation of neurophil
  Increase in lipofuscin content of brain, heart muscle, gut, fat bodies, and Malpighian
    tubules
  Cell structure changes within alimentary canal
  Cell structure changes/possible myofibrillar degeneration in "heart"
  Loss of glycogen granules and possible myofibril degeneration in flight muscle
  Mitochondrial enlargement and loss of cristae
  Decrease in functional capacity of the mitochondria
  Decreased amount of rough endoplasmic reticulum in Malpighian tubule cells
  Decreased fecundity:
    Decreased number of functional ovarioles in females
    Decreased number of spermatogonia/spermatocytes in males
  Various changes in steady-state activity of many enzymes
  Decline in protein synthesis ability

Source: From Arking and Dudas 1989.

and Dudas (1989), and Rose (1996). These age-associated alterations are quite comparable to the changes that take place in the human body (see Chapter 5). This fundamental biological similarity is what allows us to (cautiously) extrapolate from one species to another. An almost universal indication of aging in insects is the decline in the stamina, the speed of locomotion, and other behavioral parameters. Another common indicator is the decreased ability of the organism to resist stress, such as high temperature or insecticides. In fact, the investigation of different long-lived strains and mutants of *Drosophila* has led to the idea that resistance to stress is of particular importance. We will discuss this in more detail in later chapters. The beaten and worn appearance of wings and body parts is usually but not always a reliable indicator of aging. With the exception of the reproductive cells, the adult insect is postmitotic, yet cell death does not appear to be a major factor in insect aging, although insects do exhibit structural signs of degeneration and impaired function.

The adult organism dies while its component cells are still alive. Age-associated structural changes in the nervous system do not involve the loss of neurons as much as they involve a reduction in cytoplasmic volume, an accumulation of lipofuscin, and other degenerative changes. The age-dependent structural changes observed in the other tissues of the body all contribute to the physiological decrements associated with aging. The progressive accumulation of markers of damage, such as lipofuscin, carbonyl proteins, or peroxidized lipids, is probably the most consistent manifestation of aging in the postmitotic cells of the adult insect. There does appear to be a definite and marked decline in the ability of the aging insect to repair such damage.

The overwhelming advantage of using *Drosophila* is that one may draw freely on the multitude of mutant strains, genetic and molecular procedures, and the very large body of knowledge accumulated during the past 80 years or so. But this advantage is not as great as it initially seemed. Arking and Dudas (1989) have pointed out that not every mutant is well suited for studies on aging, but that one must develop suitable strains. And the unsuitability of ordinary strains was demonstrated some years ago by Ganetzky and Flanagan (1978), who compared two standard lab strains on numerous different characteristics and found so many differences that it was not possible to determine which ones were of potential importance and which were not. Another difficulty of using ordinary strains is that they are usually highly inbred. Crossing two such strains yields a hybrid that is usually more vigorous and longer-lived than either parent (Clarke and Smith 1955). These phenomena, known by the terms "inbreeding depression" and "hybrid vigor," respectively, provide difficult technical obstacles to the deciphering of the genetic and physiological mechanisms involved. The way out was shown some twenty years ago by several laboratories, which independently used long-term selection for longevity on moderately large outbred populations and thus developed stocks that did not exhibit inbreeding depression (Luckinbill et al. 1984; Rose 1984; Arking 1987b; Partridge and Fowler 1992). These are the suitable stocks alluded to earlier, and they will provide most of the data for this discussion. Additional information can also be cautiously obtained from genetically transformed stocks in which the techniques of genetic engineering have been used to introduce extra genes into otherwise normal flies. The caution arises from the many technical uncertainties inherent both in the technique itself and in the potentially confusing effects of introducing extra genes into an integrated response network.

The most important findings of the genetic studies in *Drosophila* thus far obtained are (1) that the life span can be genetically shortened or genetically prolonged; (2) that the physiological differences between the long-lived and normal animals are striking but are confined to a few particular traits; (3) that the strains developed in each laboratory appear to use different genetic and physiological mechanisms to bring about the expression of a very similar phenotype; and (4) that the genes involved in these proximate mechanisms have been or are now being identified. These findings will be described in Chapter 6, and their theoretical implications will be discussed in Chapters 10 and 13.

Vertebrates: General Patterns of Aging

The vertebrates are a large group of animals (41,700 species), and this is the group of animals that is probably the most familiar to us, since it includes humans and our close mammalian relatives. All vertebrates are characterized by a dorsal vertebral column, or backbone, as their main structural axis. The body is originally segmented, but the obvious evidence of this segmentation is lost in development, save for the muscle segments associated with the vertebral column. There are seven living groups of vertebrates: the jawless fish such as lampreys, the sharks and rays, the true fish, the amphibians, the reptiles, the birds, and the mammals. We are most familiar with mammals because we keep so many of them as pets; thus we tend to assume that all vertebrates show age-related changes and longevity patterns similar to those of mammals. This assumption may be true, but it would be best to review the relevant data.

Table 4.8 gives the maximum life spans recorded for various vertebrates. More extensive lists are presented in Comfort 1979 and in Table 2.6. A study of these data permits the following observations. First, even though we lament the shortness of our days, humans are one of the longest-lived species on the planet. Second, large animals tend to live longer than smaller ones. Third, on the basis of survival studies and morphological investigation, mammals and birds seem to senesce, provided they live long enough to demonstrate such changes. Comfort (1979) believes that reptiles, amphibians, and fish also senesce; however, the strength of this inference is blunted somewhat by the fact that the growth and life cycle patterns of these life forms may be so easily modified by diet, temperature, diapause, and so on, as to make it difficult to distinguish effects of aging from adverse environmental effects. In fish, for example, there is an inverse relationship between water temperature and life span. The bounds are set such that at too low or too high a temperature, the animal may live an exceedingly long or a very short life; but reproduction fails to occur at either extreme (Beaverton 1987). In both cases, the heritability of the life span falls to zero. Thus in these organisms under those conditions, longevity and its inheritance are matters of the temperature adaptations of the reproductive process. We will defer the detailed description of vertebrate aging to Chapter 5, where we will describe in detail the normal age-related changes in humans.

Table 4.8 **Maximum Recorded Life Spans for Selected Vertebrates**

Scientific name	Common name	Maximum life span (years)
Primates		
Papio ursinus	Chacma baboon	45
Macaca mulatta	Rhesus monkey	40
Pan troglodytes	Chimpanzee	53
Gorilla gorilla	Gorilla	54
Homo sapiens	Human	122
Carnivores		
Felis catus	Domestic cat	28
Canis familiaris	Domestic dog	34
Ursus arctos	Brown bear	47
Ungulates		
Ovis areis	Sheep	20
Sus scrofa	Swine	27
Equus caballus	Horse	46
Elephas maximus	Indian elephant	70
Rodents		
Mus musculus	House mouse	3
Rattus rattus	Black rat	5
Sciurus carolinensis	Gray squirrel	24
Hystrix brachyura	Porcupine	27
Bats		
Desmodus rotundus	Vampire bat	19.5
Pteropus giganteus	Indian fruit bat	31
Birds		
Streptopelia risoria	Ringed-turtle dove	35
Larus argentatus	Herring gull	44
Aquila chrysa'tos	Golden eagle	46
Bubo bubo	Eagle owl	68
Reptiles		
Eunectes murinus	Anaconda	29
Macroclemys temmincki	Snapping turtle	58+
Alligator sinensis	Chinese alligator	52
Testudo elephantopus	Galapagos tortoise	100+
Amphibians		
Xenopus laevis	African clawed toad	15
Bufo bufo	Common toad	36
Cynops pyrrhogaster	Japanese newt	25
Rana catesbiana	Bullfrog	16
Fish		
Gadus morhua	Cod	20+
Merluccius merluccius	Pike	40+
Hippoglossus hippoglossus	Halibut	60+
Poecilia reticulata	Guppy	6
Acipenser transmontanus	Sturgeon	82+

Source: Data from Comfort 1964 and Lamb 1978. Updated in 1997 by Steven N. Austad (personal communication).

Mammals: What Accounts for the Diversity?

Much of the early interest in the identification of factors that affect mammalian aging was motivated by the need to understand why human longevity should be so much greater than that observed for even our nearest relatives. The relationship between body size and longevity was examined by Sacher (1959). Although the two variables are well correlated, there is still a lot of scatter in the data, not to mention that the relationship utterly fails to predict the longevity of humans. We are much longer-lived than our body weight would predict when compared to other primates such as the gorilla (see, for example, Table 4.8). A much better correlation was obtained when brain weight, which often appears to be relatively larger in longer-lived species, was taken into consideration. Taking both body weight and brain weight into consideration gave a much tighter correlation with life span than did either one by itself and permitted a much better prediction of the human life span.

Sacher's interpretation of this finding rested on the observation that metabolic rate is inversely proportional to body weight. If one assumes that the frequency of metabolic errors is directly proportional to metabolic rate, then it follows that larger animals will have fewer metabolic errors and hence longer life spans. The brain size is important because animals with larger brains are assumed to have superior homeostatic mechanisms, which will tend to reduce the incidence of metabolic errors. Sacher reasoned that larger animals will live longer than smaller animals because of a decreased frequency in metabolic errors, but that for animals of comparable size, the ones with larger brains will live longer for the same reason. The two traits therefore reinforce one another. Hofman (1983) also explored this relationship and arrived at similar conclusions. Unfortunately, this relationship does not appear to be true. Not only are there serious logical problems inherent in a statistical analysis of correlations, and not only are other organs (liver, spleen, and so on) equally well correlated with longevity (Finch 1990, p. 278; Gaillard et al. 1994), but also the mortality coefficients of humans and other primates (e.g., rhesus monkeys; see Table 2.6) suggest that we live long primarily because of our lower initial mortality rate (IMR) and not because our rate of senescence (mortality rate doubling time, or MRDT) is so low.

An alternative explanation is that smarter behaviors may affect the IMR, which, if true, suggests that selection for more effective behaviors and for the brain structures associated with them might have played a role in the evolution of human longevity. In other words, the long life spans of large-brained mammals could be the secondary consequence of selection for increased brain size (Wilson 1991). Increased brain size would have a selective advantage because smarter individuals should have an increased reproductive fitness relative to dumb ones. However, in order for large brains to develop, gestation times have to be long and litter sizes small. The resulting decreased reproductive rate must be compensated for by an increased reproductive period. Of course, the width of the mother's pelvic girdle sets an upper limit to the size of the neonate's head, and thus sets an upper limit on brain size and function as well.

Humans have escaped this constraint by normally being born prematurely, at least in comparison with our closest relatives, the chimpanzees. This timing makes it possible for our necessary brain growth to take place after birth, free of the constraints imposed by the pelvic girdle. However, this strategy results in an even longer postnatal developmental period and a correspondingly increased span of time during which parental care must be given. Thus long life could be viewed as a pleiotropic consequence of selection for increased brain size taking place in *K*-selected species. This interpretation is consistent with the data, but is also heavily dependent on various unproven assumptions.

Holliday (1995) has pointed out that postreproductive factors might also affect longevity selection. He suggested that the selective advantage for parental care in humans led to the evolution of menopause as an adaption to ensure the survival of younger individuals, particularly since nonreproducing females cared not only for their own children but also for grandchildren or other young relatives (each of whom contain copies of their own genes and whose survival affects the reproductive fitness of the nonreproductive female).

A wide-ranging investigation of life span in various orders of mammals and birds was conducted by Prothero and Jurgens (1987). Their studies, summarized in Figure 4.12, show that many species of birds, bats, and primates have a substantially longer life span than do mammals of comparable body size. In other words, the relationships between body size and longevity that were developed by Sacher and Cutler do not appear to apply equally to all animals. Line F (aquatic mammals) in Figure 4.12 can be treated only as an approximation because of small sample sizes and indirect estimation of maximum life spans. The remaining data are reliable and show that birds, bats, and primates have life spans greater than those expected for mammals of comparable size.

We have already discussed the hypothesis that primate longevity increased as a result of selection for increased brain size. In the case of birds and bats, this increase cannot be statistically attributed to an increase in brain size but may be related to the metabolic demands of flight (see the discussion of birds that follows). Thus, that hypothesis may be a valid explanation only for primates, which might explain the inability of Gaillaird and colleagues (1994) to replicate it in a

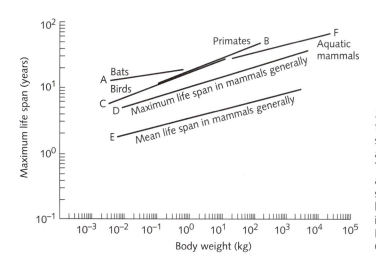

Figure 4.12 Regression lines for mean and maximum life spans in various vertebrates as a function of body weight. The lines labeled A, B, C, D, and F refer to maximum life span in the specific groups; line E refers to mean life span in mammals generally. (From Prothero and Jurgens 1987. © Plenum Press.)

variety of other mammals. If the data on aquatic mammals prove to be reliable, the explanation for their greater-than-expected life span may well involve their cardiovascular and respiratory adapations for long-term deep-sea diving. Other mammals may have other explanations.

If longevity is attributable to some sort of cellular function(s), then a general correlation between body size and length of life is not surprising. The fact that specific physiological and cellular specializations characteristic of particular species may interact with the animal's life history characteristics to indirectly result in a maximum life span that is greater than would otherwise be expected is also not surprising. In the case of primates, the explanation may involve behaviors and brain size; for aquatic mammals, it may depend on adaptations for diving; in birds and bats, the operative explanation may have something to do with the physiological requirements of flight.

Birds

For a long time birds were believed to be probably short-lived creatures, exhibiting a life span comparable to that of laboratory rodents and possessing no characteristics interesting enough to tempt biogerontologists to overcome the handicaps associated with studying them. The data of Figure 4.12 falsify this belief, which probably grew out of the fact that in the past the only birds studied in any detail by biogerontologists were chickens, quail, and other poultry. These birds were chosen probably for their economic importance as well as their convenience, but all of them are weak-flying, short-lived species. Thus the early conclusion was based on a small and skewed sample. Holmes and Austad (1995a, 1995b) recently reviewed the characteristics of a wide variety of different birds and concluded not only that many birds are very long-lived, but that they may be particularly well adapted for the study of retarded aging. Their data confirm and extend the conclusions of Figure 4.12: Birds are longer-lived and age more slowly than comparably sized mammals, both in nature and in captivity. For example, an inspection of Table 2.6 reveals that even the Japanese quail, which is the shortest-lived and most rapidly reproducing and senescing bird species yet documented (Holmes and Austad 1995a), nonetheless has a maximum life span of 5 to 8 years and an MRDT of 1.2. This MRDT value is about four times greater than that of the ordinary laboratory rodent and is indicative of a slower aging process than is found in the rodents. The MRDT of the European robin is equivalent to that of humans; only its high IMR value of 0.5 restricts it to a 12-year maximum life span.

Certain birds have life spans comparable to that of elephants, even though they are only a fraction of the elephants' size. Scarlet macaws have lived in captivity for more than 90 years, ravens for 69 years, and the royal albatross for more than 50 years. Hummingbirds are the smallest bird species and have the highest metabolic rate, yet they have maximum life spans in nature of more than 12 years, values that far exceed those predicted on the basis of their body weight. Each of these species reproduces slowly and is not fecund, in contrast to the reproductive strategies adopted by common poultry. These characteristics of *K* selection again illustrate the connection between reproduction and longevity.

What is most interesting is that birds attain these high longevities despite having metabolic rates equal to or much greater than those of comparably sized mammals. Since the production of potentially damaging oxygen free radicals (believed to be a major cause of senescent damage; see Chapter 9) is thought to be proportional to the lifetime energy expenditure, then it appears as if many birds have a more efficient means of coping with free-radical damage. In addition, birds generally have much higher blood glucose levels and higher body temperatures than do mammals, conditions that should accelerate the formation of glucose cross-linking of various macromolecules (thought to be a major cause of senescent damage; see Chapter 9). Again, the supposition is that birds may possess qualitatively different processes for coping with these potential mechanisms of senescence.

These unique processes may extend beyond the amelioration of senescence. For example, the genome size of birds is only one-third that of mammals; and among the birds, the genomes of strong flyers are smaller than those of weak flyers (Hughes and Hughes 1995). The origin of these interesting processes may be connected to the requirements of their life history strategies as expressed within the context of flight. Sorting out which of these unique avian properties are related to their delayed senescence, and thus may offer us some insights into the development of future interventions, promises to be an important future development.

● *Summary*

Species that exhibit an exponential increase in senescent changes and in mortality, and which are thus considered to undergo age-related changes, are found in four of the five kingdoms of living organisms. The comparative approach allows us to see that certain types of senescent changes and mechanisms are very common among aging organisms, perhaps indicating that aging involves a small number of basic aging processes, or that senescence patterns are constrained by developmental patterns, or some combination of both. In any event, the comparative approach also suggests that nucleocytoplasmic (genetic) interactions of one sort or another appear to be the predominant mechanism through which aging is expressed.

The comparative approach has also demonstrated that different aspects of aging may be more profitably studied in certain species than in others. The genetic analysis of aging, for example, is likely limited to the few species that have both a life cycle amenable to laboratory culture and a sufficient history of past investigative work that has developed the genetic tools necessary for the analysis. To pick an organism other than the fly or the worm or the mouse for genetic analysis would be akin to reinventing the wheel and would not be done in the absence of an extraordinarily compelling reason. The apparent ability of birds to withstand metabolic conditions that are thought to hasten senescence in mammals would provide one such reason for their analysis.

The comparative approach has also illustrated the fact that the study of diverse species has made it easier to identify particular age-related changes that would have been very difficult to identify in other species. Insects are particularly amenable to experiments designed to investigate the role of temperature manipulations on life span. Once altered proteins were found in the nematode, they were easily identified elsewhere. The role of mitochondrial DNA in aging might not have been discerned had it not been for the work done on the fungus *Podospora*.

However, another thing the comparative approach should have made clear is that not all living organisms age. Senescent mechanisms appear to be used by many plants as a developmental tool, an approach that is rarely found among animals. Many of the differences between different species are understandable in light of the species' particular developmental and life history strategies. The species' characteristic life span is but one component of the species' overall adaptability to its particular ecological and environmental niche, and it must be understood in that context. Both the life history approach and the population genetic approach have suggested that senescence arose as an inadvertent consequence of the fact that the force of natural selection diminishes sharply once the reproductive effort of the organism drops to a very low level.

The antagonistic pleiotropy and mutation accumulation hypotheses have been put forth as two possible broad outlines of the "ultimate" genetic mechanisms involved in bringing about the onset of senescence. Neither of these hypotheses address the identity of the specific "proximal" genetic mechanisms involved in the onset of senescence in various species. However, several fundamental processes of damage prevention and/or repair constitute the bulk of these proximal mechanisms. The disposable-soma theory offers a conceptual basis for understanding how organisms allocate their energy resources to maximize either reproduction or somatic maintenance, and allows us to comprehend better how some species are capable of reallocating these resources depending on environmental conditions.

This survey indicates that age-related and senescent changes may be widespread, but they are not universal. Many species may share common elements, but the actual mechanisms of aging may well be complex and there may well be considerable differences among species. The development of effective interventions for humans would be made immeasurably more difficult if we had not adopted a comparative approach to the topic of senescence.

We have focused on the scientific analysis of the evolution of aging, and of the close relationship between reproduction and senescence—in scientific terms. But to be fair, we must recognize that intimations of this strategy were earlier sensed by the artists among us. Consider, for example, Shakespeare's Sonnet Number 12:

> When I do count the clock that tells the time,
> and see the brave day sunk in hideous night; . . .
> Then of thy beauty do I question make,
> That thou among the wastes of time must go, . . .
> > And nothing 'gainst Time's scythe can make defence
> > Save breed, to brave him when he takes thee hence.

5

Human Aging

A Perspective on Human Aging

If we are fortunate, we will age. What do we have to look forward to? The popular assumption is that the end of our life will most likely be made up of physical disabilities, mental incompetence, familial rejection, loneliness, and poverty—that aging will inevitably lead to severe loss of physical, mental, and social functions. This pessimistic view has found its way into our life and our literature, as the following example of an anonymous piece (cited in Hall 1922) shows:

> Hard choice for man to die or else to be
> that tottering, wretched, wrinkled thing you see,
> age then we all prefer; for age we pray;
> and travel on to life's last lingering day,
> then sinking slowly down from worse to worse.
> Find Heaven's extorted boon our greatest curse.

It has been well understood for at least a century that the old in modern societies eventually succumb to degenerative diseases rather than to the infectious diseases that kill the young, and this understanding is probably what underlies the sentiments expressed in the preceding excerpt. Today it is becoming more and more clear that these assumptions and conclusions may not necessarily be either completely true or accurate. It is increasingly evident that, as Rowe and Kahn (1987) pointed out, the mere association of physiological and cognitive deficits with age is insufficient evidence for us to conclude that these deficits are determined by age. Hindsight tells us that research on aging has perhaps overemphasized losses. To some extent, this misplaced emphasis might have been a natural consequence of the fact that most early research on aging was carried out in medical schools as part of the geriatrics program and that aging thus may have been viewed as a special case of the disease process.

As was pointed out in Chapter 3, not only is aging an individual process that is easy to be inadvertently confounded with the pathologies of covert illness and disease, but it is superimposed on the very substantial heterogeneity characteristic of the human species. A good portion of this heterogeneity may be due to genetic factors, but an even larger proportion can probably be traced to environmental differences (Finch and Tanzi 1997). In theory, a variety of cultural and psychosocial factors can play a significant role in modulating the aging process. In fact, the Duke First Longitudinal Study found that such nongenetic factors could contribute as much as 16 years to longevity in men and as much as 23 years in women (see Chapter 6 for details). Furthermore, our social and physical lives do not exist in separate worlds with no communication between them. Rather, it now appears likely that these cultural and psychosocial factors work by affecting our neuroendocrine and immune systems and in this manner modulate the physiological and cellular levels of body function. The brown antichinus and the Pacific salmon, for example, die as a result of stress-related, hormone-induced physiological dysfunction. Our physical and social worlds are linked together by well-known biological mechanisms. These processes, in turn, provide the physical basis underlying the concept that people who have led a well-integrated life often demonstrate successful, as opposed to usual, aging.

An important aspect of future gerontology research will undoubtedly be the detailed characterization and analysis of the mechanisms and processes underlying successful aging. People who have aged successfully are individuals who display no or minimal physiological loss in any of many functions when compared to their younger counterparts. One example of such an individual is David Gill, whose exercise data are shown in Figure 3.10. These data show no age-related decrement in heart rate and oxygen uptake between the ages of 35 and 65 years. This is by no means an isolated example, as will become clear in the remainder of this chapter. These newer insights have shown us that aging is much more plastic and may be under more of our control than was previously believed possible. The logical conclusion, then, is that the number of programmed inevitable and decremental age-related changes that occur is probably much lower than we have previously believed possible. Aging is inevitable, but it need not be the tragedy envisioned by the anonymous poet cited earlier.

Two lines of evidence support these claims. One is the dispassionate description of age-related changes, which will fill the remainder of this chapter. The other is anecdotal and serves mainly to show us the possibilities. Many older people today are alive and vital and active at advanced ages; these people have aged successfully. Some are famous, most are not. Many of our fellows are old in their years, but young in their impact on our society. They have achieved their impact because they have remained professionally active and effective. They have not retired from life. There are numerous examples of successful aging, both in the past and in our own time—so many examples, in fact, that they should make us realize that the loss of our human potential is not intrinsic to the aging process. Such loss may be more common than is desirable, but it is not inevitable. On the other hand, this concept of successful aging should not be interpreted overoptimistically, thus suggesting that elderly individuals will show no decrease in capacity or function with age. Of course even individuals who have successfully aged are not as vigorous as they were in their youth. The point is not that age-related changes will not occur. They will. Rather, our focus is to describe the inevitable changes and to illuminate the mechanisms by which the other changes may be modulated so that we each may strive to age successfully and retain our effectiveness as individuals and as members of society.

● *The History of Human Mortality and Longevity*

The ancient Egyptians described the maximum human life span as 110 years (Smith 1993), which isn't too far off from our present measurement of 121 years. Roman funerary inscriptions describe individuals who lived into their eighties, and excavations from medieval cemeteries reveal skeletal remains from individuals in their sixties (Smith 1993). Although these values are similar to what might be found in our own society today, it would be a serious error to assume that the life expectancy and age structure of those early societies were similar to our own, as the quantitative data of Table 5.1 indicate. A 65-year-old man or woman is so common as to excite no attention today, but they would probably have been a rare spectacle in most early societies. Life expectancy at birth in most places in the past ranged from 25 to less than 50 years. Infants and children must have accounted for a large amount of the early dying, for this is the only logical explanation for the rise in the life expectancy between birth and 5 years of age in the Massachusetts of 1789. Presumably, children died of infectious diseases, women died in childbirth, and men died in accidents. Combining such short life expectancies with the high infant mortality rate explains why the human population had such a low rate of increase for such a long time. Altering the environmental conditions responsible for such conditions led to a slow increase in life expectancy, but still it took England about 300 years (from the mid-1500s to the mid-1800s) to increase the life expectancy by only 7 years. Change has since accelerated.

The more recent accomplishments are illustrated in Figure 2.16, which shows that during the twentieth century the median longevity for females has increased about 40 percent (from 58 to 81 years), while the mean life expectancy at birth for both sexes combined has increased about 50 percent (from 50 to 75 years) (Smith 1993). This progress has been uneven. In a demographic sense, undeveloped and poor countries such as Sierra Leone are lagging behind us by about 150 years. This difference reinforces the observation that longevity depends on the social environment. Had our ancestors been able to indulge in time travel, they would have been amazed at the increase in life expectancy and would have remarked about how this single phenomenon has transformed society. The more astute among them undoubtedly would have pointed out that this increase in life expectancy is really due to a striking decrease in premature mortality and not to any fundamental tinkering with the aging processes themselves. And they would have been correct, for the time being.

Table 5.1   Life Expectancies in Different Times and Places

| Place | Time | Sex[a] | Life expectancy | | |
			At birth	At age 1	At age 65 or indicated ages
England	1541		33.7		
	1661		35.9		
	1781		34.7		
England and Wales	1838–1854		40.9		
	1871–1880		43.0		
	1881–1890		45.4		
United Kingdom	1983–1985	Male	71.8	71.5	13.4
		Female	77.7	77.4	17.5
Massachusetts	1789		28	at age 5, 41	at age 60, 15
	1855		39.8		
	1890		43.5		
	1895		45.3		
	1901		47.8		
United States	1986	Male	71.3	71.1	14.7
		Female	78.3	78.0	18.6
Sweden	1816–1840		41.5		
	1851–1855		42.6		
	1871–1880		47.0		
	1881–1890		50.0		
	1891–1900		52.3		
	1985	Male	73.8	73.3	14.7
		Female	79.7	79.2	18.5
Canada	1984–1986	Male	73.0	72.6	14.9
		Female	79.8	79.3	19.2
USSR	1985–1986	Male	64.1	65.0	12.3
		Female	73.3	73.9	15.8
Japan	1987	Male	75.6	75.0	16.1
		Female	81.4	80.8	19.7
Bangladesh	1988	Male	56.9	63.7	12.2
		Female	55.9	61.5	12.0
Sierra Leone	1985–1990	Male	39.5		
		Female	42.6		

Source: Data from Tables 1.2, 1.3, and A-2 of Smith 1993.
[a]Where not specified, data represent both sexes combined.

• *The Relationship between Aging and Disease*

In 1900, the three leading causes of death in the United States were respiratory diseases, digestive diseases, and central nervous system diseases. In 1986, they were cardiovascular diseases, malignancies, and accidents (Smith 1993). In

1996, the prediction was made that coronary disease will no longer be a major public health problem by early in the twenty-first century (Brown and Goldstein 1996). Not only have the proximate causes of death been completely transformed during the twentieth century, but the current death rate is less than half its value in 1900. We all die eventually, but fewer of us die prematurely and we die from different immediate causes than was the case 100 years ago. Now that the norm is a full life, the question arises as to what insight—if any—an investigation of the diseases of the elderly may give us into the biology of aging. Human pathology is usually considered to be the province of geriatric medicine and is often overlooked in discussions of experimental biogerontology. Holliday (1995) maintains that the distinction between "natural" aging and "pathological" aging is artificial. No single individual suffers from all the age-related diseases, but no single individual exhibits all the manifestations of "normal" aging either. Therefore we must examine populations in order to assess the whole spectrum of age-related changes seen in humans. In this process, we usually exclude all people who are suffering from an age-related disease, presumably because we believe that there is something qualitatively different between normal aging and pathological aging. However, this distinction is arbitrary and a wasteful oversight of a huge amount of data.

It is useful to view the spectrum of age-related diseases as each representing a particular outcome of the failure to maintain a particular anatomical structure or physiological process, as indicated in Table 5.2. In this light, the utility of viewing diseases as *systemic failures that highlight the weak points of the evolved anatomical and physiological design of the organism and thereby allow us to identify and investigate them* becomes obvious. Would the biology of cell division have been a concentrated focus of research if no one had ever died of cancer? The answer is obvious. Note, for example, that the two leading causes of death in 1986 (cardiovascular diseases and cancers) are attributable respectively to failure to prevent damage to and otherwise maintain the linings of the blood vessels, and to the sig-

Table 5.2 **Relationship between Cell or Tissue Maintenance and Human Age-Related Diseases**

Structures/processes not maintained	Major resulting pathologies
Neurons	Dementias
Retina, lens	Blindness
Insulin metabolism	Type II diabetes
Blood vessels	Cardiovascular and cerebrovascular diseases
Bone structure	Osteoporosis
Immune system	Autoimmune disorders
Epigenetic controls	Cancer
Joints	Osteoarthritis
Glomeruli	Renal failure

Source: From Holliday 1995.

nal transduction mechanisms that regulate cell division. Both of these processes are in the forefront of modern biological research because of the social and political forces that provided research funding for the study of these common age-related diseases. And we study them to improve our understanding of the etiology of the disease in question and to develop procedures for better alleviating the disease or delaying its onset. So in one sense, studying the age-related diseases as individual entities apart from one another, as we do today, is part of modern geriatrics and biogerontology. But it is not enough.

In Holliday's (1996) view, this strategy is seriously flawed because the focus on disease keeps us from integrating our knowledge by studying all the cellular and molecular changes that precede and bring about the loss of reserve capacity that occurs in healthy people in the absence of disease, and that must also prepare the way for the overt onset of any disease. Holliday (1996b, p. 90) has explicitly stated that "the study of gerontology must have a central position in biomedical research" if we are to have a realistic hope of reining in the ever-increasing health care costs without adversely affecting quality of care or length of life. Whether biomedical science will be reorganized in this way cannot be foretold here, nor is it particularly germane to our central goal of understanding aging. However, Holliday's view that we should incorporate the study of disease into the study of gerontology by viewing diseases as systemic failures that identify biological weak points is germane to our goal. In fact, we have already discussed this problem along with a detailed presentation of one example in the section titled "Distinguishing Disease and Environmental Changes from Age-Related Changes" in Chapter 3 (see pages 75–79), which you may want to reread now.

Following Holliday's advice has allowed us to unify the biology of aging at a functional level instead of arbitraily continuing the division between normal and pathological aging. The mechanisms of aging identified in this chapter will be discussed in greater detail in many of the following chapters, as will the kinds of interventions necessary to prevent or delay the onset of these systemic failures. In addition, adopting this point of view integrates these functional levels with the evolutionary models discussed in Chapter 4, for here we confront the gory and personal details of what the disposable-soma theory, for example, implies when it states that selection pressures shift the allocation of energies away from somatic maintenance and toward reproduction.

• *An Overview of Theory*

In previous chapters we briefly described aging in selected experimental organisms. In this chapter we will describe the aging processes in mammals, using humans as the example. A multitude of changes take place with the passage of the years. Even if we had the space to describe every such change, we would still not chronicle all of them but would be selective in our characterizations. How, then, do we choose which variables to describe and which ones to ignore?

To a large extent, adherence to the CPID criteria outlined in Chapter 1 ensures that we will recount only the significant age-related changes and omit many interesting but probably unrelated time-dependent changes. A second factor that we must consider is the role of disease. If we regard disease as indicating the weak points in the body's structure and function, then some of the more common breakdowns should be examined, if only as an empirical test of our view as to the role of disease. A third factor influencing our narrative is the demands of theory. Theoretical explanations of the biology of aging make some facts more important than others. For example, knowing that extended longevity is hereditary in laboratory animals makes one sensitive to evidence suggestive of different patterns of gene action in long-lived animals as opposed to shorter-lived animals. Or being aware of the theories suggesting that cross-linking between important macromolecules plays an important role in the aging processes might indicate that the details of connective-tissue aging are to be given special significance. If you have not already done so, you may wish to skip ahead and look over the theories summarized in Tables 8.1 and 8.2 to gain a brief idea of the kinds of facts the theories require us to see.

• *Plasticity and Patterns of Aging*

We often talk about aging as if it were a unitary process that all members of the species undergo in the same manner. Perhaps this idea arose from the superficial resemblance of the old survivors to one another; they usually had grey hair and wrinkles and suffered from the slings and arrows of time's misfortune. Perhaps the idea arose by analogy with development, which all members of the species do undergo in the same manner. No matter how the idea arose, it is not correct, as suggested by the evidence presented in Table 3.1 and Figure 3.10, which you should review before reading further. Note the wide variability in the response of individuals for the single trait presented in Table 3.1: creatinine excretion. As we will see, aging occurs gradually, with some processes beginning to decline in a person's twenties or thirties, while other processes remain relatively untouched until the late sixties and beyond. Superimposed on this population heterogeneity is a substantial amount of individual heterogeneity (see Table 3.1), arising from the person's inheritance, development, and enrrironment, and suggesting that the preceding statement about the gradual nature of aging is not true for many, perhaps most, members of the species. If different traits can begin their decline at different ages in different individuals, and if most traits can change more or less independently of one another, then older adults are a heterogeneous group characterized primarily by their individual patterns of aging. In addition, the results from the Human Aging Study begun in 1955 by the National Institute of Mental Health found that much of what was popularly called aging is really a function of disease, sociocultural effects, and lifelong personality traits (Butler 1995). Once we correct for the confounding effects of such variables, we find that the age-related declines in function that occur in healthy adults are lower than the popularly assumed levels, although they are extraordinarily variable and individual. This individual heterogeneity must be kept in mind even as we present data based on statistical analysis of groups of people. The mean does not adequately describe the individual.

Age-Related Changes in Humans: Detailed Survey

Overall Anatomical Changes

Normal Changes

Table 5.3 lists changes in anthropomorphic measurements and indices that are believed to be probably related to aging. The relationships involved likely are not simple. In Chapter 3, we discussed in some detail the parameters affecting changes in weight with age. There is no reason to believe that the factors governing the other indices listed in Table 5.3 are any less complex than that one. A close examination of these indices yields no simple or overall detectable pattern of growth. Instead, one is faced with a mosaic of differential growth patterns, in which some features reach their peak values in the third decade of life (for example, facial index), a few reach their peak values in the eighth decade (for example, thoracic index), and the others are scattered throughout the intervening years. Since these indices are primarily skeletal measurements, postmaturational bone growth must be taking place. Furthermore, this highly localized growth is taking place not only against a background of slow overall growth through the fourth decade followed by decline thereafter, but also against the background of other

Table 5.3 Changes in Anatomical Measurements and Indices Probably Due to Aging	
Weight	Increase to 50; decline from 60
Stature	Increase through 30–34; decline from 40
Span	Increase through 30–34; decline from 40
Thoracic index	Increase through 70–74
Biacromial diameter	Increase through 35–39; decline from 55
Relative shoulder breadth	Increase through 45–49
Chest breadth	Increase through 50–54
Chest depth	Increase through 50–54
Sitting height	Increase through 35–39; decline therafter
Relative sitting height	Slow decline after 49
Head circumference	Increase through 35–39; slow decline after 54
Head length	Increase through 50–54
Head breadth	Increase to 40 and slight decline thereafter
Cephalic index	Decline from 35
Cephalo-facial index	Rise through 75–79
Total face height	Increase through 30–34; decline thereafter
Facial index	Increase through 25–29; decline thereafter
Upper face index	Increase through 30–34; decline from 55
Nose height	Increase through 55–59
Nose breadth	Increase throughout age groups

Source: From Rossman 1977. © Litton Educational Publishing.

complex age-related skeletal alterations, such as simple osteoporosis, and even more extreme abnormal alterations. These changes in the skeletal system are further confounded by ethnic and/or environmental effects.

This heterogeneity of growth patterns is not limited to the skeletal system. The cross-sectional data of Figure 5.1 show that about half the internal organs attain their peak weight in the fourth decade and then decrease in weight, while the rest of the internal organs attain their peak weight sometime between the fifth and eighth decades. Clearly there is neither a single nor a simple pattern of "normal" growth, but probably one that must be related to the normal functioning of each organ.

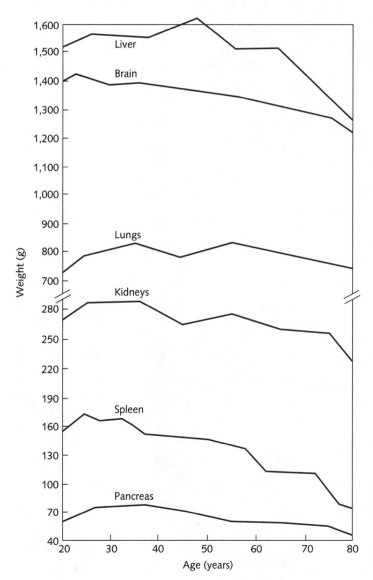

Figure 5.1 Alterations in the weight of body organs with aging. (From Rossman 1979, redrawn from Rossle and Roulet 1932.)

Accompanying these size and weight changes are changes in the composition of the body. We literally become a different person as we grow older. As Figure 5.2 shows, the amount of fat in the body increases with increasing age in both absolute and relative terms, and this increase in fat is accompanied by both absolute and relative decreases in the amounts of cell solids, bone minerals, and water. These changes are consistent with the longitudinal and cross-sectional, cross-cultural data in Figures 3.2 through 3.5, which demonstrate the reality of the changes in body build we will each undergo.

Summary

This quick and overall survey of gross anatomical alterations with age should leave the impression that the adult years are characterized by a complex interaction between growth processes and degenerative processes, that there is a mosaic pattern of growth changes in all parts of the body, and that there may well be no such thing as a single "normal" pattern of age-related changes. We must strive to keep this innate heterogeneity of the human species in mind despite the simplifying text of the discussions that follow.

Changes in the Skin and Connective Tissue

More money and effort are expended by individuals in the constant effort to hide and disguise the normal age-related changes occurring in the hair and skin than in any other organ system. The cosmetic industry thrives on our vain desire to remain young, and fortunes await those who can enhance the naturalism of our illusions. The importance of a discussion on skin in a gerontology text has little to do with morbidity or mortality numbers. No one dies of old skin or succumbs to

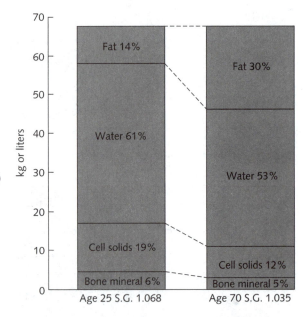

Figure 5.2   A comparison of major body components in males aged 25 years and 70 years. The relative decreases in the water and cell solids contents reflects the loss of muscle tissue; the decrease in bone minerals reflects the loss of bone mass; and the increase in fat content reflects the greater proportion of adipose tissue in aged humans and the decreased specific gravity (S.G.).(From Fryer 1962. © Columbia University Press.)

skin failure. Its importance is primarily psychological, for we read our mortality in our skin. This phrasing has literal as well as poetic meaning, as the discussion of human biomarkers in Chapter 3 should have made clear (see Figure 3.21). Since much of our communication with one another is nonverbal, we probably depend on subtle interpretations of each other's skin to tell us much about the other's health, social status, personality, and the like. The emotional impact of skin aging should not be underestimated, nor should we ridicule the serious attempts by cosmetic companies and health professionals to alleviate the impact of skin aging and maximize a positive self-image. It may be more true than we know that we must feel good about ourselves or suffer the consequences.

Normal Structure and Function

The skin is probably the largest organ of the body, constituting about 16 percent of the body weight (Bloom and Fawcett 1968). By contrast, a large organ such as the liver constitutes only about 2 to 3 percent of the body weight. The skin holds us in. It is the boundary between our bodies and the outside world, and we depend on it for our literal physical integrity. The skin is composed of several layers (Figure 5.3). The outermost layer is the epidermis, a specialized epithelial cell layer. Under the epidermis is the dermis, a vascularized layer of connective tissue. The innermost layer is a loose layer of connective tissue called the hypodermis.

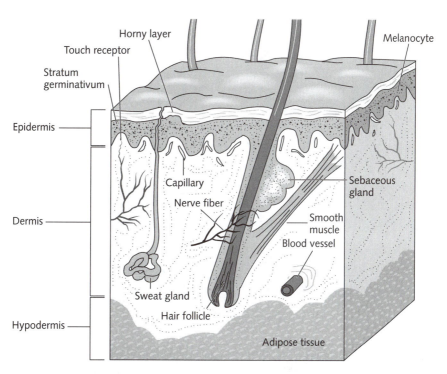

Figure 5.3 A diagrammatic representation of the structure of the skin. (After Spence 1989.)

Various structures penetrate these horizontal layers: hair follicles, sweat glands, sebaceous glands, and so forth (see Figure 5.3). The color of the skin depends on three factors. First, the skin itself is yellow, owing to the presence of the organic pigment molecule carotene. Second, the blood showing through from the underlying dermis implants a reddish hue. Finally, the presence of varying amounts of melanin granules, present in the epidermis, produces shades of brown through black.

We are constantly losing our skin, by the process shown in Figure 5.4. New cells are constantly produced by cell division in the basal layer of the epidermis and are moved upward by the subsequent appearance of newer cells beneath them. As they move up and outward, they synthesize huge amounts of the protein keratin, the same protein that forms our hair and nails. As the cell accumulates massive amounts of keratin, it becomes metabolically inactive, dies, and leaves behind only a flaky residue of a cell, which sooner or later is shed from the surface. The whole process takes between 2 and 4 weeks. The skin of the palms and soles is thicker than the skin of the rest of the body because of localized thickening of the keratinized dead cell layer of the epidermis in those regions.

The main function of the dermis is to provide an extensive and tough matrix both to support the many structures embedded in it (see Figure 5.3) and to provide a junctional base to which the epidermis may adhere. The dermis is composed mainly of connective-tissue fibers, most of which are collagen; the remainder are elastin. The collagen molecules are flexible but offer great resistance to a pulling force; they prevent the skin from being torn by overstretching.

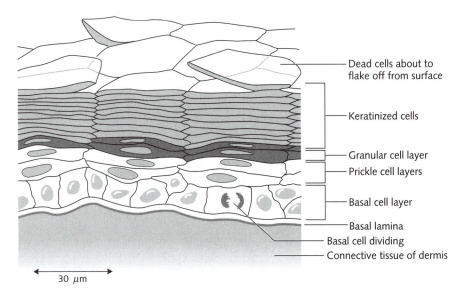

Figure 5.4   A detailed view of the cellular alterations that take place in the epidermis. The proliferating cells are found in the basal layer; one of the mitotic products of that division migrates upward, differentiates, and dies. See text for discussion. (After Alberts et al. 1983.)

Elastin, on the other hand, lives up to its name. It is a springy material that maintains normal skin tension, but that will stretch to allow movement of the underlying muscles and joints.

The hypodermis is a layer of loose connective tissue and is a deeper continuation of the dermis. Its collagen and elastin fibers are directly continuous with those of the dermis. Depending on the region of the body and the individual's nutritional state, variable numbers of fat cells are also found in this layer. This layer serves as a shock absorber against trauma to the internal organs, as a storage depot for high-calorie food reserves, and as insulation against excessive loss of body heat.

Finally, skin is an active element of the immune system (Edelson and Fink 1985). The keratinocytes produce not only the protective outer layers of dead cells filled with keratin, but also hormonelike molecules (interleukin and thymopoietin; see the section titled "Changes in the Immune System" starting on page 225),that are known to be capable of profoundly affecting lymphocyte function. In addition, the dermis contains small dispersed populations of two other types of cells that are thought to play a controlling role in immunological function. The Langerhans cells and the Granstein cells present antigens (foreign molecules) in the skin to specific helper or suppressor T lymphocytes, which tend to migrate into the epidermis from elsewhere in the body. Depending on the detailed characteristics of these intercellular interactions, the immune response will be either enhanced or suppressed. Both animal and human studies have shown that particular abnormalities of the immune system are closely associated with particular defects in the structure and/or function of skin cells.

Age-Related Changes

The skin's ability to function as an effective boundary layer depends on the maintenance of its structure. Unfortunately, regressive structural changes take place in all components of the skin with increasing age. The normal age-related changes encountered in human skin were described by Kligman, Grove, and Balin (1985). The epidermis itself does not become thinner with age; however, there is a marked decrease in the density of the dermal papillae. These stubby interlocking protrusions of the epidermis and the dermis hold the two layers in close contact with one another. The result of their loss is that the epidermis is held less tightly to the underlying dermis. This alteration accounts in part for the looser feel of aged skin. There are reported to be no significant changes in the fine structure of the epidermal cells themselves.

The dermis, on the other hand, does become thinner with age. This thinning is associated with a change in the weave of the collagen fibers located in this layer, resulting in less collagen per unit of surface area. The fiber bundles become larger and coarser, with larger spaces between them. The whole texture of the collagen becomes looser. There are several different varieties of collagen molecules, and this change in texture may have something to do with changing levels of synthesis of these different types. The fact that males have a thicker dermis than females may help explain why female facial skin appears to deteriorate more readily with aging, particularly after menopause.

In addition to the changes in collagen, transformations take place in the elastic fiber network. A significant number of such fibers are lost from the upper layers of the dermis, although a recent report suggests that this may not happen in all cases (Robert, Lesty, and Robert 1988). This fiber loss is accompanied by a disorganized increase in the elastic fibers in the lower dermis. The architecture of this localized increase is abnormal; the fibers are thicker, longer, more disarranged, and less elastic. The net effect of these fibril transformations is looser skin that is prone to wrinkle. The microvasculature also changes with age; capillaries and venules in the dermis and hypodermis become very sparse and irregularly formed.

Atrophy of the hypodermal layer is one of the factors that makes it more difficult for the aged to modulate their heat loss. However, this atrophy is not a generalized phenomenon occurring over the whole body. It usually occurs on the face and the backs of the hands; it usually does not occur about the waist or thighs, as all too many of us can testify.

One of the most obvious signs of skin aging is the formation of wrinkles. Kligman, Grove, and Balin (1985, p. 828) have pointed out that despite all the research done to date, "the wrinkle, the most telltale sign of aging, is still unexplained! Its anatomy does not distinguish it from surrounding tissue." Yet, it seems likely that wrinkles owe part of their origin to the decreased number of dermal papillae, part to the decreased and disorganized fibril network of the dermis, and part to the loss of the smooth padding provided by the fat cells of the hypodermis. The loss of this padding, the decreased elasticity, and the looser binding of the skin layers allow the skin to be pulled downward more easily by the force of gravity—and so it sags. A decrease in the muscle mass with age (see Figure 5.2) also contributes to the loss of firmness of the aging skin. However, if the wrinkle itself has no distinctive anatomy, then likely the formation of wrinkles in specific body locations is the result not of a specific localized anatomical defect, but perhaps of an overall pattern of stress lines resulting from the specific geometry of our muscles, bones, bumps, and depressions and their effect on the enveloping skin.

Summary

Our skin is the boundary between our bodies and the outside world. Consequently it is affected by both intrinsic and extrinsic factors. Intrinsic changes include a decrease in density of dermal papillae, which leads to a loosening of the epidermis from the dermis. Changes in the type, structure, and density of collagen and elastin fibers are very noticeable in the dermis. Actinic damage, brought on by excessive exposure to the sun, accelerates and amplifies these alterations. The net effect of these several transformations is looser skin that is more prone to wrinkles. The loss of the fatty tissue in the hypodermal layer and the increasingly sparse and depleted microvasculature are two of the age-related factors that interfere with the efficient modulation of heat loss.

Changes in the Skeletal System

Cartilage and bone are the specialized connective tissues that make up the skeletal system. Each of these tissues consists of cells and fibers such as collagen and elastin embedded in a nonliving matrix produced and secreted by the cells. Both the amount and the rigidity of this matrix distinguish these hard skeletal tissues from the "soft" muscles. In both cartilage and bone, the living cells are isolated in small cavities within the matrix, and most of the tissue bulk is made up of the matrix.

Cartilage

Normal structure and function   Cartilage has a capacity for very rapid growth. Its matrix imparts to it a considerable degree of stiffness. Together, these two properties—rapid growth and rigidity—make cartilage a particularly favorable skeletal element first for the embryo, in which the entire skeleton is first formed in a cartilage model and only later replaced by bone; second, in the growing bones of the young individual; and finally, in the joints and articulating surfaces of the bones in the adult. Because of its involvement in bone growth, cartilage is not an inert tissue, but a fairly delicate indicator of various metabolic disturbances, such as nutritional or hormonal deficiencies (Bloom and Fawcett 1968).

Age-related changes   With age, cartilage loses its translucence. Fewer cells are present, and the protein matrix undergoes some complex and still incompletely understood changes. The bluish color typical of young cartilage changes by age 20 to an opaque yellowish color. By age 30, cracking and fraying of the surface of cartilage joints begins to be visible. Although the aging cartilage cells retain the ability to make matrix, the rate of synthesis decreases and the types of fibrils present in the matrix are altered (Tonna 1977). The most important regressive change is that of calcification, in which minute granules of inorganic calcium salts are deposited in the matrix. As the granules become enlarged and merge with one another, the cartilage becomes hard and brittle. This calcification of the matrix interferes with the ready diffusion of nutrients and waste products to and from the cartilage cell, and the cells die. With their death, the calcified matrix subsequently is slowly resorbed (Leesen and Leesen 1970). This process of calcification and resorption is a normal part of the phenomenon whereby cartilage is transferred into bone or whereby broken bones repair themselves.

The alteration of fiber production leads to a regressive change known as asbestos transformation, in which short, closely packed, coarse fibers, totally unlike any collagenous fibers, are deposited in the matrix. These silky fibers may spread over large areas and may lead to a softening of the matrix or even to the formation of cavities within it (Bloom and Fawcett 1968). The cartilage cells themselves show a decreased level of biosynthetic activity and of proliferative ability. Dying cells are not often observed in growing cartilage but are quite common after growth has ceased. Cell death often leads to the formation of microscars.

The matrix of cartilage in particular, and perhaps of all connective tissues in general, has often been viewed as an amorphous, passive, and uninteresting tissue component. Although the older literature clearly indicated the existence of continuous and complex age-related changes in the matrix, the fundamental nature of these alterations was not understood (Balazs 1977). More recent studies shed new light on this topic (Caplan, Fiszman, and Eppenberger 1983). Other than collagen and elastin, the main component of the cartilage matrix is now known to be a very large and very elaborate protein molecule called proteoglycan. This molecule consists of a core protein, which is identical in animals of all ages and to which are bound many molecules of chondroitin sulfate. The chondroitin sulfate electrostatically binds large volumes of water to the proteoglycan molecule, and this hydrated structure accounts for the resiliency of young cartilage. As the cartilage cells age, they synthesize and secrete chemically different forms of chondroitin sulfate, the major characteristic of which is that they are smaller molecules and consequently can bind less water. This increasing inability to function as a cushion at the joints results in tissue damage, inflammation, and in some cases, symptoms of osteoarthritis. This changing biosynthetic pattern is part of the normal developmental program of the chondrocytes.

Programmatic alteration of the biosynthetic pattern is also seen in other tissues. The transition from cartilage to bone is marked by the cessation of cartilage-specific Type II collagen and its associated polysaccharides, and the onset of bone-specific Type I collagen and its associated calcium salts. Analogous changes occur in the connective tissues of muscles and, most likely, in other tissues as well. The potential complexity and variety of the different types of connective tissues are illustrated by the fact that there are at least nine known and different forms of collagen alone, each of which appears to possess different functional and tissue specificity (Table 5.4). The sequential replacement of these and other cellular components appears to be a normal and general phenomenon.

Bone

The adult human skeleton is composed of bone. Certain of the lifestyle alterations that we will likely encounter as we age stem from changes that take place in our bones. Although bone approaches cast iron in its tensile strength, it is less than one-third as heavy (Bloom and Fawcett 1968). The architecture of its construction ensures the greatest strength with the greatest economy of materials and of weight. Our bones are dynamic living structures, surprisingly responsive to metabolic, nutritional, hormonal, and mechanical factors. The state of our bones is a good reflection of the manner in which we have lived and will live.

Normal structure and function   There are two types of bone: the trabecular or spongy bone, and the cortical or compact bone. Spongy bone is characterized by numerous interwoven partitions called trabeculae. The trabeculae branch and unite with one another to form a meshwork or honeycomb, the intercommunicating spaces of which are filled with marrow. The honeycomb provides strength to the bone with a minimum of weight. The pattern of this meshwork is determined by the mechanical functions of the individual bones. Bones of the axial skeleton are mostly spongy bone. The vertebrae, the flat bones of the hips and pelvis, and the ends of the long bones are all spongy bone.

Compact bone, on the other hand, appears solid except for microscopic spaces. Compact bone has a layered bone matrix arranged in a manner determined by the distribution of blood vessels that nourish the bone (Figure 5.5). The

Table 5.4 **Collagen Types and Properties**

Type	Polymerized form	Distinctive features	Tissue distribution
Major forms			
I	Fibril arranged into highly organized arrays (cornea) or into irregular weave (bone)	Low hydroxylysine Low carbohydrate Broad fibrils	Major collagen (90%) of all connective tissues, including: skin, tendon, bone, dentine, ligaments, cornea, etc.
II	Fibril meshwork that contains proteoglycans	High hydroxylysine High carbohydrate Thinner fibrils than Type I	Cartilage, intervertebral disc, notochord, vitreous humor of eye
III	Fibrils	Low hydroxylysine High hydroxyproline Low carbohydrate	Skin, blood vessels, internal organs; absent from bone and dentine
IV	Meshwork	Very high hydroxylysine High carbohydrate Undergoes very little processing to arrive at finished form	Basement membranes
V	Unknown	High hydroxylysine High carbohydrate Function unknown	Present in small amounts in all connective tissue except cartilage
VI	Microfibrils formed from polymerized tetramers	Unknown	Blood vessels, uterus, placenta, skin
VII	Microfibrils formed from dimers	Unknown	Anchoring fibrils beneath basement membranes
Minor forms			
HMW and LMW	High and low molecular weight	Function unknown, but related to Type V fragments	Cartilage
SC	Short-chain	Unrelated to all other collagens	Cartilage only; may be involved in its calcification

Source: Data from Mayne 1984 and Alberts et al. 1983.

bone is traversed by a continuous and complex system of canals that contain the blood vessels and nerves of the bone. The skull, jaw, and shafts of the long bones are examples of compact bone. No sharp boundary may be drawn between the two types of bone; the differences between them depend on the relative amount of solid matter and the size and number of spaces in each. They both contain the same kinds of cells and calcified matrix. The bone cells themselves reside in small cavities (or lacunae) within this matrix. Radiating from each cavity are many

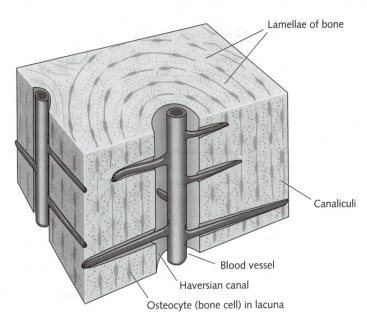

Lamellae of bone

Canaliculi

Blood vessel

Haversian canal

Osteocyte (bone cell) in lacuna

Figure 5.5   The Haversian system of compact bone, showing the osteocytes in their lacunae. (After Evans 1983.)

narrow channels that interconnect with neighboring lacunae to link all the bone cells together in an intercommunicating network (see Figure 5.5).

The matrix is secreted by the bone cells and consists of two main components, an organic protein phase and an inorganic salt phase. The organic phase consists of collagenous fibers embedded in an amorphous medium that cements them together and that contains various protein–carbohydrate complexes. The fibers are laid down in the gel in a distinct, probably helical, pattern. The inorganic matter of bone consists of submicroscopic salt crystals of calcium and phosphate apatite. These long, slender salt crystals are lined up alongside the collagenous fibers as if each were reinforcing the other—an efficient arrangement for resisting mechanical stresses. The bone mineral content increases during growth and development, reaching a maximum of about 65 percent of the dry weight of the bone in a healthy adult. In persons afflicted with rickets or other bone pathologies, the bone mineral content may be as low as 35 percent (Bloom and Fawcett 1968).

Age-related changes   Bone is a dynamic tissue that is constantly being remodeled throughout life. This remodeling results from the resorption of the bone in one location and the deposition of new bone elsewhere. Bone cells called osteoblasts are associated with the formation of new bone tissue and are invariably found on the advancing surfaces of growing bones. Closely associated with the process of bone resorption are morphologically different cells called osteoclasts. Osteoclasts are often found in small depressions on the bone surface, in cavities that arise as a result of their erosion of the bone surrounding the cell. Since the spongy bone accounts for 90 percent of the total surface area of bones, and since this remodeling takes place on the bone surfaces, it is not surprising that remodeling is more widespread in spongy bone than in compact bone.

Bone remodeling begins during the fetal period, accelerates to a peak during infancy and childhood, and continues throughout adult life at a much reduced level (Riggs and Melton 1986). The pattern of loss in spongy bone differs in several ways from that in compact bone. In both sexes, bone loss begins at least a decade earlier in spongy bone than in compact bone; and in women, the kinetics and patterns of spongy bone loss differ considerably from those of compact bone loss in both the premenopausal and the postmenopausal aspects of the life cycle.

Despite their dissimilar appearance, osteoblasts and osteoclasts are currently believed to represent simply different functional states of the same cell type. If we can one day understand how to specifically direct this reversible modulation of cell activity, we might be able to effectively abolish the most important age-related changes that take place in the bone. Recent events have made this goal appear more plausible than before. It has been known for some time that certain proteins can, when extracted from bone and applied into ectopic sites, stimulate the normal process of *in vivo* cartilage and bone formation. These proteins have recently been purified and sequenced, as have the DNA regions that code for them (Wozney et al. 1988). The three bone morphogenetic proteins (BMP) are members of the transforming growth factor beta superfamily. They promote the differentiation of bone and cartilage, both directly as well as by changing the terminal differentiation of other cell types so that they express an osteoblast phenotype. Their receptors have been cloned (Akiyama et al. 1997), but the details of their mechanistic involvement in normal and abnormal skeletal growth are still being worked out.

Age-related pathologies   Two bone pathologies—osteoporosis and arthritis—appear to be related to aging. We will examine each in turn. In general, beginning in our thirties, the bone resorbed by the osteoclasts exceeds the amount of new bone synthesized elsewhere by the osteoblasts (Figure 5.6). This shift in the balance between resorption and synthesis is the basis for the universality of bone loss with age. The progressive loss of bone mineral content during later adult life appears to be responsible for the simultaneous and progressive loss in bone strength. The cross-sectional data of Figure 5.7 illustrate the age-dependent changes in bone mineral content, which reaches its maximum value during our thirties and then declines beginning in our forties. (The statistically significant difference in the values for the left and right ulnae can be understood as the results of differential use of the bones by the predominantly right-handed population, a topic we will return to in our discussion of exercise as an intervention).

Neatly paralleling these changes in bone mineral are the age-dependent changes in bone strength (Figure 5.8). These data show that osteoporosis, defined as a decrease in bone mass with no change in the chemical ratio of mineral to protein matrix (Schlenker 1984), is not a disease entity separate from aging but is a more extreme version of the normal processes of bone loss. This bone loss is perhaps the most characteristic age-related change of the skeletal system. Although an intrinsic change, it is nonetheless one that may be successfully mod-

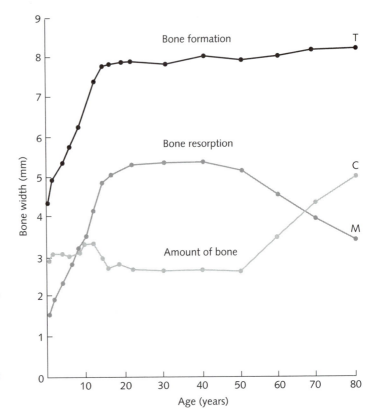

Figure 5.6 Age-related changes in the amounts of cortical bone formation and resorption in Ohio white females. Curve T is a measure of cumulative cortical bone formation. Curve M is a measure of cortical bone resorption. Curve C is a measure of the amount of bone, the net difference between formation and resorption. (From Garen 1975. © Academic Press.)

ulated by various environmental factors. Since the pathological effects of osteoporosis are associated with loss of strength and subsequent susceptibility to fractures, the more bone mass one has as a young adult, the better off one will be as an aging adult. The simplest way to increase bone mass is to use your body. "Use it or lose it" is one way to summarize the left–right discrepancy of the data in of Figure 5.7. Exercise, whether that of a professional athlete or that more typical of an ordinary person, is beneficial (Buskirk 1985).

The gonadal hormones play an important role in determining the rate of skeletal maturation. In normal human development, the progress of skeletal growth is intimately related to the developmental state of the reproductive system. This relationship is seen not only in conditions of precocious or delayed sexual development, with their corresponding effects on skeletal maturation, but also in pregnant women and postmenopausal women. The maternal skeleton is to some extent a calcium reserve during pregnancy for calcification of the fetal skeleton and during lactation to replace the calcium lost in the mother's milk. Such changes normally are very slight, but if they are superimposed on a severe nutritional deficiency or an impaired absorption of calcium, perhaps due to low levels of vitamin D, severe regressive changes leading to pathological fractures may result (Exton-Smith 1985). Diet is clearly an important modulating factor in the development of this age-related change.

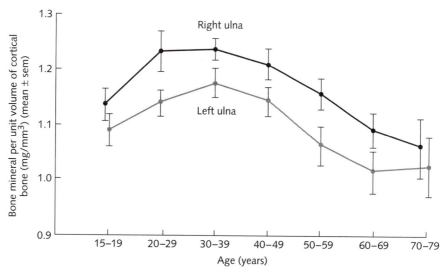

Figure 5.7   Age-dependent changes in the mineral density of cortical bone in women. The reduction in mineral density from age 40 on parallels the decrease in average mineral concentration. The values for the right ulna are significantly higher than those for the left ulna, highlighting the probable role of exercise in these predominantly right-handed people. (From Doyle 1969, courtesy of the British Postgraduate Medical Federation.)

Gender is important as well, for the sex differences in bone loss are dramatic (Figure 5.9). At any given age, bone mass is greater in men than in women. The rate of bone loss, however, is usually higher in women. A male with a 4,000-gram skeleton will lose about 450 grams (12 percent) during a 30-year period. Over an equivalent time period, a female with a 3,000-gram skeleton will lose about 750 grams (25 percent) of her bone mass, much of it in the years immediately following menopause.

These last two factors—hormones and gender—can be particularly synergistic, as in the case of postmenopausal women. Estrogenic hormones tend to protect bone from the stimulating effect of parathyroid hormone on the osteoclasts. When estrogen levels decline at menopause, bone resorption increases because of the increased sensitivity of the osteoclasts to the parathyroid hormone. Quantitative measurements of the amount of bone resorption in postmenopausal women have shown it to be about equal to 425 milligrams of calcium per day, while bone forms at a rate of only 387 milligrams per day. The result is a net daily loss of 38 milligrams. At this rate, an average female loses 1.5 percent of her bone per year (Schlenker 1984). Bone loss can be measured by a variety of different methods, each of which yields different numbers, but they all show the same patterns of age-dependent loss (Exton-Smith 1985). Estrogens also affect the levels of calcium absorption and excretion. Thus estrogens have a dual effect: indirect suppression of remodeling and improved efficiency in the utilization of dietary calcium.

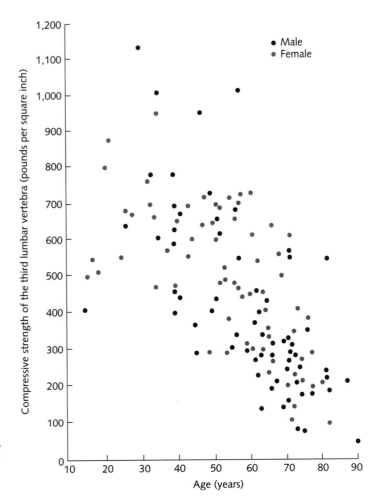

Figure 5.8 Age-related changes in vertebral compressive strength in 137 male and female cadavers. (From Weaver and Chalmers 1966.)

The loss of bone strength with age (see Figure 5.8) has been attributed to at least two different processes (Whitbourne 1985). An increased porosity arising from the continuous bone remodeling reduces the structural strength of the bone. The remaining bone also becomes more brittle with age—paradoxically via an increased mineralization of the remaining bone tissue. As a result, the bone of an elderly person, when subjected to pressure, is more likely to snap and cause a "clean" fracture. Such fractures are less likely to heal. The bone of younger persons is more flexible, because of the higher organic composition of its matrix. When subjected to pressure, it bends and cracks in such a way that a complete break is unlikely. Whitbourne (1985) instructively compared bones to tree branches. Young bone is like a green twig, which takes a great deal of bending before it breaks, and even when it does, it rarely snaps in two but sustains many small cracks and fractures. Old bone is like a dry stick, which snaps easily when bent.

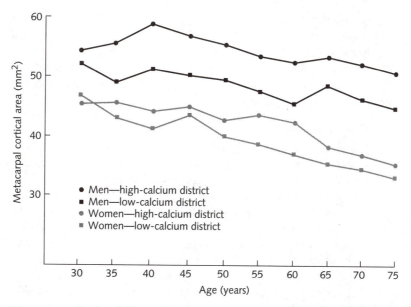

Figure 5.9   The loss of bone from the metacarpals in two populations with different peak adult levels. Calcium intake in the high-calcium group was about 1,000 mg in men and 875 mg in women; the comparable values for the low-calcium group were about 450 mg and 400 mg, respectively. Note that both groups lose bone mass at about the same rate, but that at age 75 the population with the highest peak value (the male population from the high-calcium area) had as much bone as the other male population had at its peak. Also note that gender differences overwhelm the dietary differences. (From Matrovic et al. 1979.)

Arthritis is an age-related bone pathology that attacks the joints. Our bones are joined to one another by our joints, whose smooth functioning is made possible by the strength and elasticity of the tendons and ligaments, by the smooth cartilage lining the opposing surfaces of the joint, and by the synovial fluid that lubricates the whole assembly. The age-related changes we have described thus far affect the entire joint system. The tendons and ligaments become less resilient and less able to transmit the forces that act through them as their component collagen and elastin fibers undergo degenerative changes in composition and overall geometry (see the next section, on muscle tissue, for a description).

The same processes affect the synovial membranes and make them less flexible. The synovial fluid becomes thinner and less viscous, and its biochemical composition is altered (Balazs 1977). The cartilage becomes scarred and calcified, thinner and less resilient. All of these intrinsic changes act both separately and together to decrease the functional efficiency of the joint (Tonna 1977; Whitbourne 1985). The description of osteoarthritis, a degenerative joint disease, greatly resembles the description of normal age-related changes in the joints; the distinction between normal and pathological age-related changes is very difficult to make (Tonna 1977; Whitbourne 1985). There is no doubt, however, that osteoarthritis itself is age-related, regardless of whether it originates with alterations in the bone or in the cartilage. Some evidence suggests that mechanical abnormalities of the joint, such as those that might arise as a result of injuries, poor posture, or immobilization, are the underlying predisposing factor that alters the course of normal age-related changes toward degenerative joint disease (Frymoyer 1986).

Summary

Cartilage undergoes intrinsic age-related changes that affect the types and amounts of matrix fibrils. The calcification of the matrix interferes with the ready diffusion of nutrients and waste products through the matrix.

Bone is a dynamic tissue; throughout life, old bone is constantly being resorbed and new bone is constantly being deposited. With increasing age, the amount of bone resorbed by osteoclasts exceeds that of the new bone synthesized elsewhere by the osteoblasts, so bone is lost with age. This process disproportionately affects the spongy bone. The loss of bone mineral content is responsible for the simultaneous and progressive loss of strength of the remaining bone.

Age-related pathologies such as osteoporosis and/or arthritis represent exaggerations of the normal aging process that have been amplified by intrinsic factors such as gender and by extrinsic factors such as diet or exercise.

Changes in connective tissue components such as proteoglycans, collagens, and elastins extend beyond the skeletal system, affecting the connective tissue components of almost all organ systems.

Changes in Muscle Tissue

Normal Structure and Function

Our muscles and our bones shape and define our bodies. There are three different types of muscle: skeletal (or voluntary) muscle, cardiac muscle, and smooth (or involuntary) muscle. We will limit our discussion of muscle aging to the skeletal muscles, in part because these constitute most of the muscle mass and in part because much is known about them. The structure of the skeletal muscle is a classic illustration of biological organization and one that clearly shows the interrelationships of one organizational level to another, from the molecular level to the gross anatomical level. Thus, a description of this tissue allows each of us to grasp the interrelationships between structure and function that lie at the heart of modern cell biology. A brief description of the normal muscle structure is also necessary in order to understand the origin and nature of the age-related changes and what can be done about them.

As Figure 5.10 shows (and as is familiar to anyone who has ever struggled with a portion of tough meat at dinner), the large individual skeletal muscles (Figure 5.10a) are made up of slender, stringy muscle bundles (Figure 5.10b). These bundles are associated in various patterns and held together with connective tissue to form the anatomically familiar muscle types such as the biceps or the gastrocnemius (calf muscle). Each bundle can move independently of its neighboring bundle. Each muscle bundle is composed of muscle fibers (Figure 5.10c), which are formed from individual muscle cells that have fused together.

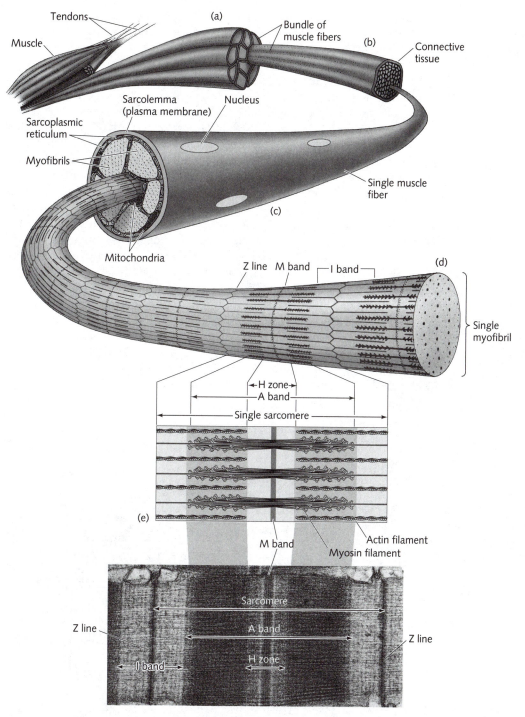

Figure 5.10 A diagrammatic representation of the organization of skeletal muscle, progressively enlarged in (a) through (e) from the gross anatomical level to the molecular level. See text for discussion.

The nuclei of the muscle cells are found on the outside of the muscle fiber. Since it corresponds to the cellular level, the muscle fiber may be regarded as the basic unit of organization in the muscle. The muscle fiber, in turn, is composed of many myofibrils (Figures 5.10d and 5.11). These myofibrils have a highly regular and periodic structure based on the ordered arrangement of two different families of protein molecules, the actins and the myosins. This ordered molecular arrangement is what gives rise to the periodic, or striated, appearance of the muscle fiber and underlies the muscle's ability to contract. Each of these repeating periodic units is called a sarcomere (Figure 5.10e). As Figures 5.10e and 5.11 show, the myosin molecules and the actin molecules are spatially situated within the myofilament in an alternating arrangement such that the two interdigitate. The muscle contracts and exerts a force via the tendon on the bone to which it is attached when energy is used to slide the thin actin filaments inward over the overlapping thicker myosin molecules. This process decreases the length of each sarcomere (see Figure 5.11). Since the muscle is composed of lengthwise repeating sarcomeres, the muscle as a whole shortens by the cumulative total decrease in length of all the sarcomeres. This contraction is initiated by a nerve impulse delivered by motor nerves to individual muscle fibers.

Although all the muscle fibers appear to have the same physical structure, it is possible to sort them into two distinct physiological types depending on their innervation and speed of contraction. The so-called fast-twitch and slow-twitch fibers differ from each other in their inventory of various enzymes; they consequently differ also in their appearance. The flight muscles of birds (the familiar "white meat" of the dinner table) are examples of fast-twitch muscles, while the

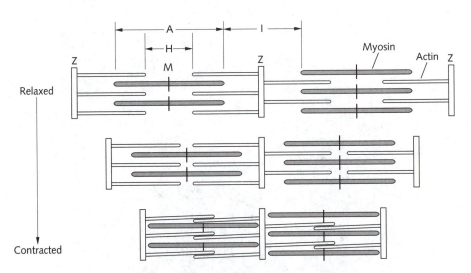

Figure 5.11   A diagrammatic representation of how changes are brought about in the length of individual sarcomeres by varying the degree of interdigitation of the thick (myosin) and thin (actin) filaments. (After Barrett et al. 1986.)

birds' legs and thighs (the "dark meat") are examples of the slow-twitch muscles. Fast-twitch muscle fibers develop the rapidly accelerating muscle contraction that we normally associate with strength. Slow-twitch fibers are involved primarily in activities such as postural adjustments, which require prolonged and enduring, but not necessarily quick, muscular exertion (Whitbourne 1985).

The two fiber types differ on the genetic level as well. Duchenne's muscular dystrophy is a disease caused by a sex-linked gene that eventually leads to the destruction of the skeletal muscles. The gene defect that causes this condition results in the absence of a particular protein, dystrophin, from at least one population of the fast-twitch muscle fibers—a situation that leads to their subsequent degeneration (Webster et al. 1988). Presumably the functional differences between the different classes of muscle fibers have their origin in gene-controlled structural differences.

The muscles exert their effects by contracting and thereby exerting a pulling force on the bone via the interposed ligaments or tendons. These connective tissue bundles increase efficiency and precision by allowing the muscle to be located at some distance from its site of action, as well as allowing for several muscles to exert different effects on the same bone. The tendons are composed of collagenous connective tissue (see Table 5.3); the ligaments contain substantial amounts of elastic fibers that allow them to act as a spring and thus permit heavy weights (such as the head of four-footed mammals) to be raised or lowered with very little muscle effort.

Age-Related Changes

The elderly commonly have less muscle mass than do younger individuals (see Figure 5.2). This muscle atrophy is thought to be brought about by a decrease in both the number and the size of the muscle fibers (McCarter 1978), although the decrease in size is disputed (Brown 1987). Muscle atrophy with age may take place somewhat differently in the fast-twitch and slow-twitch fibers, the former decreasing both in number and in size, the latter only in number (Gutmann and Hanzlikova 1972; Newton and Yernas 1986). The fast-twitch fibers are thought to atrophy because the nerves that innervate them die; the fibers apparently cannot be maintained without innervation. When muscle fibers die, they are not replaced.

The skeletal muscle is a nondividing tissue in humans. The number of our muscle cells is fixed during our fetal development, and this supply must last us an entire lifetime. Exercise is well known to stimulate the growth of skeletal muscle, which it brings about by causing an enlargement in the size of existing muscle fibers. On the other hand, disuse, malnutrition, or denervation cause the muscle structure to atrophy (McCarter 1978). This remarkable ability of the skeletal muscle to respond to environmental influences makes it difficult to determine the nature of the changes taking place during aging. In aging humans, the decreased motivation to exercise and the increased adaptation to a sedentary lifestyle by themselves would be expected to alter muscle function significantly. It is difficult to completely rule out such extrinsic factors affecting the aging process. However, some sort of an intrinsic age-dependent atrophy clearly takes place (McCarter

1978), and it involves at least some structural destruction (Figure 5.12). The deteriorated muscle fibril is replaced initially by connective tissue and eventually by fat (Inokuchi et al. 1975). The muscle fibers that do not atrophy appear to undergo some major metabolic changes, changes that appear to arise from age-dependent alterations in the neuronal regulation of the muscle fiber (Gutmann and Hanzlikova 1972). One result of these biochemical alterations is that the enzymatic differences between the fast-twitch and the slow-twitch muscle fibers are greatly decreased, and the functional differences in the speed of contraction between the two fiber types are consequently diminished as well (McCarter 1978). The energy metabolism of the muscle fibers also appears to decrease, possibly as a result of degenerative changes taking place in the mitochondria (which are the energy powerhouses of the cell). The decreased muscle strength brought about by these changes is complicated by concurrent neural, circulatory, and psychological changes in the aging adult, all of which may nonspecifically cause further decrements of muscle functioning.

Figure 5.12 A longitudinal section of fibers from the lateral omohyoid muscle of an 18-month-old male rat. Note the degenerating myofibrils (Z) alongside apparently normal myofibrils. Also evident are enlarged mitochondria (Mi), sarcoplasmic reticulum (SR), and a degenerated neighboring muscle fiber (C). (From McCarter 1978. © Raven Press.)

Alterations in the nerves innervating the muscle likely are a very important extrinsic aging factor. One indication that the intrinsic structural atrophy may not be primarily responsible for the decrease in muscular strength observed in aged adults is the remarkable fact that muscles isolated from old individuals and tested under laboratory conditions show no decrease in their dynamic properties when compared with the control muscles of younger adults. The dynamic properties are retained despite the presence of marked structural degeneration in the older muscles (McCarter 1978). These observations suggest that extrinsic factors play a major role in the aging of our muscle. It has been suggested that exercise-induced hypertrophy of the muscle fibers also brings about a reinnervation of existing muscle fibers that makes up for the fibers that have atrophied (Whitbourne 1985). The beneficial effects of exercise will be discussed in Chapter 7.

Inasmuch as muscle action is transmitted by means of our tendons and ligaments, it is reasonable to conclude that some of the effects of aging on muscle performance may originate in the age-related alterations that take place in these connective tissues. The elderly are particularly vulnerable to tendon rupture (Shephard 1982), in large part because of the loss of elastic tissue and the alterations in collagen structure that reduce the ability of the tendon to elongate. Following maturity, the collagen of our tendons and ligaments undergoes very little turnover and replacement. The basic aging process in these structures consists of alterations in protein structure (see Chapter 9) rather than changes in concentration. Aging of collagen is characterized by progressive insolubility in various reagents, increased chemical stabilization, and increased stiffness. These changes are assumed to be due to chemical cross-linking of the collagen fibrils to one another.

The mechanisms that underlie these age-related changes are just now being unraveled. One line of evidence came from studies of diabetes. The effects of this disease on many organs and tissues are similar to those that develop in the normal elderly. For this reason diabetes is sometimes described as accelerated aging. These and other observations led to the idea that the nonenzymatic attachment of glucose to certain proteins in the body gives rise to a series of chemical reactions that result in the formation of irreversible cross-links between adjacent protein molecules, the so-called advanced glycosylation end products (AGE products; see Chapter 9). Animal studies, described by Cerami, Vlassara, and Brownlee (1987), have shown that exposing collagen to high concentrations of glucose, either in the test tube or in the body of a diabetic mouse, leads to extensive cross-linking. Test tube studies have also shown that drugs such as aminoguanidine can block this cross-linking effect if the protein is incubated with glucose in its presence. AGE products are also known to stimulate the macrophages to produce and release tumor necrosis factor and interleukins, two growth factors with diverse effects. These factors then stimulate nearby cells such as fibroblasts to synthesize and secrete collagenase and other extracellular proteases that can digest the cross-linked AGE products (Vlassara et al. 1988; Brenner et al. 1989). Thus there appears to be an *in vivo* system that has as its function the remodeling of the connective tissue. These findings, as well as the observed effectiveness of caloric restriction (see Chapter 7), suggest that alleviation of normal aging of tendons and ligaments may not be impossible.

Summary

There is an age-related atrophy of the muscle fibers. Since the skeletal muscle is postmitotic tissue, this atrophy leads, in the absence of exercise, to a decrease in muscle mass with age. In addition, the physiological and biochemical differences between fast-twitch and slow-twitch muscle fibers are greatly decreased, and the functional differences between the two are also diminished. These intrinsic changes in the muscle are complicated by other neural and circulatory changes in the aging adult, which can also impinge on muscle function. Extrinsic factors such as exercise (or the lack thereof) can also play a major role in modulating muscle aging. For example, exercise induces hypertrophy of the muscle fiber and so can halt or even temporarily reverse the age-related decrease in muscle mass.

There is some reason to believe that age-related changes in tendons and ligaments also affect muscle performance. Such changes may be due to cross-linking of connective tissue molecules, an intrinsic process that can be modulated by extrinsic factors such as diet and exercise.

Changes in the Cardiovascular System

Normal Structure and Function

In vertebrates, the important function of distributing nutrients to the tissues and collecting waste products from them for transport to the appropriate excretory organs is carried out by the cardiovascular system. This system consists of a muscular pump (the heart) and two continuous systems of tubular vessels: the pulmonary circulation and the systemic circulation (Figure 5.13). The pulmonary circulation carries blood to and from the lungs; the systemic circulation serves all the other tissues and organs of the body. In both of these circulations, the blood pumped from the heart passes progressively through large and small arteries, capillaries, small and large veins, and back to the heart. Nutrients and waste products are exchanged primarily in the capillary network of each circulation. Most organs are also served by a network of capillaries belonging to the lymphatic system, which gathers up the fluids lost by diffusion from the blood during its passage through the capillaries, and returns those fluids to the bloodstream. During this return passage, the body fluids pass through a series of lymph nodes in which the immune system can detect foreign invaders in the components of the lymph fluids.

Figure 5.14 shows the tissue structure of these various vessels. The simplest vessel is the capillary, composed of a single layer of endothelial cells (a specialized form of epithelial cell). Since endothelial cells also line the inside of both arteries and veins as well as the heart, they provide a continuous lining throughout the cardiovascular system. Capillaries have an average diameter about equal to that of the red blood cell. They form a tubular meshwork in the organ (see Figure 5.13), the tightness of which is determined by the level of metabolic activity characteristic of the region. Nutrients and waste products are exchanged across and through the capillary walls. The flat, thin endothelial cells are highly adapted to

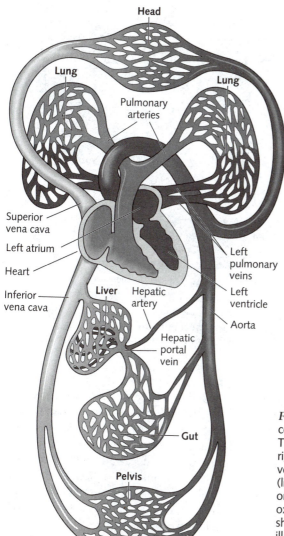

Head

Lung

Lung

Pulmonary
arteries

Superior
vena cava

Left atrium

Heart

Inferior
vena cava

Left
pulmonary
veins

Left
ventricle

Aorta

Liver

Hepatic
artery

Hepatic
portal
vein

Gut

Pelvis

Legs

Figure 5.13 The human circulatory system is composed of two complementary subsystems. The pulmonary circulation, originating in the right side of the heart, sends deoxygenated venous blood to the lungs for oxygenation (lighter shade), while the systemic circulation, originating in the left side of the heart, sends oxygenated blood to the body for use (darker shade). Each body structure is served by a capillary network that distributes the oxygenated blood to the cells and connects the two subsystems. (After Curtis and Barnes 1989.)

ensure that this process is quick and efficient. Capillaries in some organs, such as the kidney, contain pores that further enhance the process. Capillaries and their supporting cells in the brain appear to actively inhibit the transport of many molecules out of the vascular system into the nervous tissue; this inhibitory function has given rise to the concept of the blood–brain barrier.

Arteries and veins, regardless of size, show a common pattern of organization (see Figure 5.14a and b). Next to the endothelial lining is an elastic layer composed variously of branching elastic fibers and collagenous fibrils. The middle layer consists of smooth (involuntary) muscle cells, circularly arranged. The outer layer is composed mostly of various connective tissue elements, longitudinally arranged. The structural differences between the arteries and veins reside mostly in the dif-

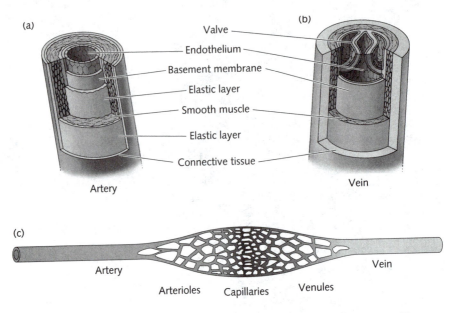

Figure 5.14   Structure of the blood vessels. (a) An artery. (b) A vein. (c) A capillary network connecting the arterial and venous circulations. Note that arteries and veins have a similar structural plan, although the artery has a much thicker muscle layer and possesses two elastic layers as well.

ferential contribution of each of these three layers to vessel. In general, the veins have a larger diameter than that of the arteries but their walls are much thinner. The larger internal volume of the veins allows them to accommodate the same amount of blood as do the arteries, but at a much lower pressure. As a consequence, venous walls can safely develop to be thinner than arterial walls (see Figure 5.14a and b). Arterial walls have significant amounts of both the muscular and the elastic layers. The muscular layer allows arteries to contract or dilate and thereby differentially regulate the distribution of blood to individual organs. The elastic layer makes the arterial walls flexible and expansible.

Only part of the force of contraction of the heart goes into advancing the column of blood in the vessels; the rest goes into expanding the arterial walls. The elastic recoil of the vessel wall during the interval when the heart is not contracting serves as an auxiliary pump, forcing the column of blood forward even during diastole. This process smoothes out the pulsatile nature of the blood flow, allowing a continuous flow with an intermittent pump (Bloom and Fawcett 1968). During its relaxation phase (diastole), the heart actively expands, in part because of a mechanical recoil action attributable to the arrangement of connective tissue in the heart. This recoil action creates suction and helps draw blood into the ventricles (Robinson, Factor, and Sonnenblick 1986).

The heart is the rhythmically contracting muscular portion of the cardiovascular system. It is composed of three main layers, each of which is homologous with the three layers of the blood vessels. These layers are the innermost endocardium; the middle myocardium, or muscular layer; and the outermost epicardium, or connective tissue layer. The cardiac muscle cells are similar in structure, although not identical, to the skeletal muscle cells described earlier. They differ primarily in that they are not under voluntary control. The myocardium is thinnest in the atria and thickest in the left ventricle. These structural differences probably stem directly from the functional differences between the two chambers: the highest pressures in the circulatory system are found in the left ventricle. The muscle bundles are arranged in sheets that wind about the atria and ventricles in complex patterns and are attached to the cardiac skeleton, a dense connective tissue structure that acts as the central supporting structure of the heart. Connective tissue fibers of collagen and elastin form a netlike structure around each cardiac muscle cell. It has been suggested that this meshwork actively contributes to protecting the muscle cell from either overcontraction or overextension and, in either case, to assisting the cell in moving back to its original or resting state (Robinson, Factor, and Sonnenblick 1986). This suggestion implies that the aging processes taking place in connective tissue can have a direct effect on the age-related changes in the performance of the heart muscle.

The motor impulse that triggers each heartbeat arises autonomously near the top of the right atrium. It is conducted throughout the heart in a coordinated manner by highly specialized cardiac muscle fibers. The heart is more than just a pump; it is also an endocrine organ. The atria secrete a protein hormone, atrial natriuretic factor, that plays an important role in the regulation of blood pressure, blood volume, and the excretion of water and salts (Cantin and Genest 1986).

Age-Related Changes

Structural changes with aging   Fewer age-related structural changes take place in the heart than one might naively suppose to be the case, given that cardiovascular disease is a leading cause of death. In fact, most experienced pathologists recognize that age cannot be accurately determined from an inspection of the heart. One of the major changes that can be observed is an increase in coronary artery *disease* with age. Various studies suggest that about half of the elderly population have symptoms of this cardiovascular disease; thus structural changes in the cardiovascular system must be interpreted with caution, since atherosclerosis is possibly the best example of an age-related disease. We discussed the problem of distinguishing between aging-related changes and disease-related changes in Chapter 3.

Each layer and region of the vascular tree is affected differently by the aging process. The endothelial cells of the intimal (innermost) layer (see Figure 5.14) become more irregular in size and shape. The elastic and smooth muscle layers of the intima increase dramatically with age, by up to 40 percent in the aorta. In the thoracic aorta, this thickening is due to an increase in the elastic layer; in the abdominal aorta it is due to the proliferation of smooth muscle. Much of the thickening in the elastic layer results from fragmentation, redistribution, and thinning of the elastic fibers. This process is accompanied by increased calcium-binding activity by the elastin. These changes may represent some sort of tissue response to prolonged stress, since the magnitude of these alterations is greater in the more highly stressed aorta than in the less stressed pulmonary artery. The relationship of such alterations to the genesis of atherosclerosis is a matter of current investigation (Bates and Gangloff 1986).

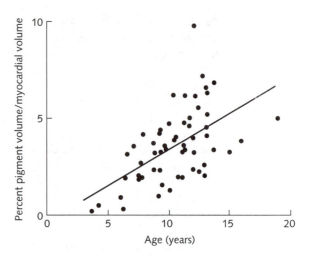

Figure 5.15 The percentage of the myocardial volume that is occupied by lipofuscin pigment as a function of age in dogs. (From Munnell and Getty 1968.)

In the heart itself, the only genuine age-related change observed is the approximately 30 percent increase in the thickness of the left ventricular wall, an increase that is due to cellular hypertrophy rather than to hyperplasia (Hangartner et al. 1985). The heart muscle cells do not have the capacity to divide; they are postmitotic cells that must last for the life of the individual. Such stable cells would be expected to display progressive morphological and/or chemical alterations reflecting age-related changes. In fact, one of the best-characterized age-related changes is the increase in cardiac lipofuscin pigment as a function of age (Figure 5.15; see also Chapter 11) (Kohn 1977).

Functional changes with aging   The importance of not confusing occult disease states with normal age-related changes is well illustrated by the data of Table 5.5 (Shock et al. 1984) and by the information of Figure 5.16 (Lakatta 1985). Most of

Table 5.5   **Effect of Adult Aging on Resting Cardiac Function**

	Population A Institutionalized Unscreened for occult coronary artery disease (Age range, 19–86)	Population B Active in community life Screened for occult coronary artery disease (Age range, 24–79)
Heart rate	Slight decrease	No effect
Stroke volume	Decrease	No effect
Stroke-volume index	Decrease	No effect
Cardiac output	Decrease	No effect
Cardiac index	Decrease	No effect
Peripheral vascular resistance	Increase	No effect
Peak systolic blood presure	Increase	Increase
Diastolic pressure	No effect	No effect

Source: From Shock et al. 1984.

(a)

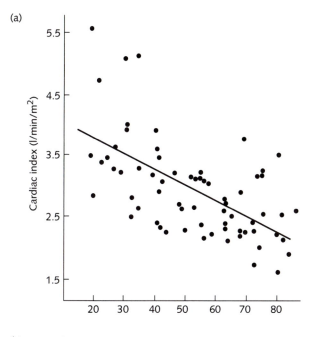

(b)

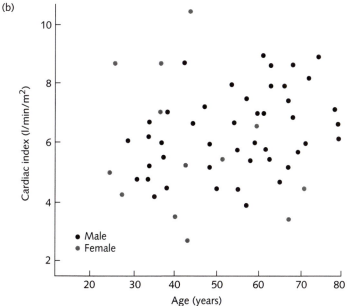

Figure 5.16 The relationship between age and cardiac index (the volume of blood passing through the heart per unit of time). In (a), the males had no apparent circulatory disorders but were recovering in the hospital from other ailments. A strong age-related decline in cardiac index is evident. In (b), the BLSA (Baltimore Longitudinal Study on Aging) male and female subjects were known to be free from cardiovascular problems. No age-related decline is seen in these healthy subjects. (a from Brandfonbrener, Landowne, and Shock 1955; b from Rodeheffer et al. 1984.)

the resting cardiac functions show no age-related changes, save for the systolic blood pressure. As noted in Chapter 3, it is both reasonable and plausible to attribute at least some of this change to the stiffening of the arterial walls as just described. The hypertrophy of the left ventricular wall can then be interpreted as an adaptive response of the heart muscle to this increasing load on the heart.

Cardiac output is the product of heart rate and stroke volume and is probably the most important single overall measurement of cardiac performance, for it represents the ability of the heart to meet the oxygen requirements of the entire body. Initially, cardiac output was believed to decline with age (see Figure 5.16a); however, populations screened for occult disease show no age-related change in cardiac output (see Figure 5.16b). When the same healthy subjects were stressed by exercise, however, their maximum workload did decrease with age (Figure 5.17). This decrease appears to be due to a decrease in the maximum attainable heart rate and thus may represent another true age-related change. This decrease in workload is not thought to be due to a decrease in the maximum contractility of the muscle fiber itself (Lakatta 1985). Animal studies have suggested that the decrease in workload may be the result of age-related alterations in the intrinsic pacemaker activity of the heart, and of significant decreases in the concentration of norephinephrine in the heart (Goldberg 1978). Norephinephrine is the principal neurotransmitter of the adrenergic system that innervates the heart. In any event, decrease in maximum heart rate presumably results in a failure of the heart to supply sufficient oxygenated blood to the leg muscles. This cardiovascular-induced muscle fatigue results in a significant reduction in the maximum attainable workload.

Age-Related Pathologies

One of the more serious age-related cardiovascular pathologies is atherosclerosis. If present, the atherosclerotic process usually begins early in life, progresses during the middle years, and culminates in clinical disease toward the later years of the life span. Age is a nonreversible risk factor for atherosclerosis. Since this is a multifactorial disease, it has proven difficult to sort out the intrinsic age-related

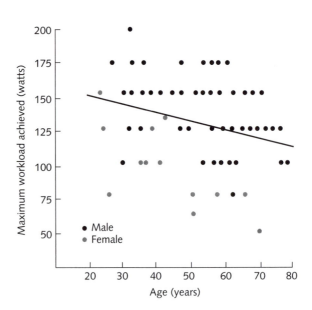

Figure 5.17 The effect of age on the maximum workload during upright bicycle exercise in BLSA participants (the same population as in Figure 5.16b.) The end point in all instances was muscle fatigue. (From Rodeheffer et al. 1984.)

changes from the environmental factors that exert their effects over a long time span. Nonetheless, substantial progress has been made. Bates and Gangloff 1986 offers a more detailed overview and references.

On the basis of extensive autopsy observations, Stary (1986) described the progression of this disease (summarized in Table 5.6). Not all thickenings of the arterial wall are pathological, for certain localized increases in the thickness of the intima (especially at branch points in the vessel) are found in all normal coronary arteries. The diffuse thickening of the intima is the hallmark of this pathology. Such lesions are composed of assemblages of macrophages and smooth muscle cells embedded in an extracellular matrix containing elastic fibers. These four components of the plaque—macrophages, smooth muscle cells, extracellular matrix, and elastic fibers—are unevenly distributed into two distinct layers (Figure 5.18). In the early stages, the innermost, or luminal, layer is rich in matrix and poor in elastic fibers. It contains a loose and irregular arrangement of the smooth muscle and macrophage cells. Conversely, the underlying musculoelastic layer is poor in matrix and rich in elastic fibers. In advanced lesions, this layer also contains dense and orderly arrangements of lipid-rich smooth muscle cells and macrophage foam cells layered above a thick extracellular lipid core (Figure 5.19). The foam cells are derived from macrophages that have become full of oxidized, low-density lipoproteins. This lipid or necrotic core is composed of the partly degraded lipid droplets of dead macrophage foam cells. Finally, other secondary processes also take place, such as the deposition of calcium in the core and the slow formation of a collagenous cap over the intima region above the core. The result is massive thickening of the intima and narrowing of the arterial channel to critical limits.

The mechanisms underlying this process are numerous and complex, but two observations stand out. First, the localized increased number of cells in the

Table 5.6 **Development Stages of Artherosclerotic Plaques**

Lesion type	Descriptive name of lesion	Characteristics
I	—	Macrophage foam cells as isolated cells in intima; no extracellular lipid
II	Fatty streak	Extracellular lipid layers of macrophage foam cells; lipid-rich smooth muscle cells; some extracellular lipid
III	Preatheroma; intermediate lesion	All of above, plus many small pods of extracellular lipid
IV	Atheroma; atherosclerotic plaque	All of above, plus large, confluent extracellular lipid pod replacing much of intima
V	Fibroatheroma; complicated lesion	All of above, plus collagen cap above core
VI	Ulcerated fibroatheroma	All of above, plus ulceration of surface
VII	Fibrous plaque	Massive thickening of intima by collagen layers; intra/extracellular lipid negligible

Source: Adapted from Stary 1986.

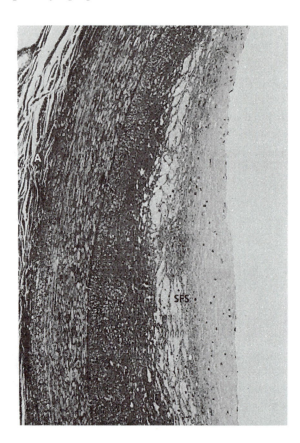

Figure 5.18   A Type II lesion (see Table 5.4) in the coronary artery of a 25-year-old woman who died in an automobile accident. Eccentric thickening contains a submerged fatty streak. (From Stary 1986. © Springer-Verlag.)

plaque suggests that an increase in cell proliferation is an important part of the disease process in atherosclerosis. Second, multiple lines of evidence strongly suggest that the involvement of high blood cholesterol (particularly the low-density lipoprotein, or LDL, fraction) is required for the initiation and formation of atherosclerosis. These two insights have been woven together into our current concept, according to which any one of several factors may injure the endothelial lining of the artery. Blood platelets adhere to the wound site and release platelet-derived growth factor (PDGF). This compound stimulates the smooth muscle cells to proliferate and heal the wound. At this point, the process is still reversible, unless something intervenes to convert this transient injury into a chronic situation with sustained release of PDGF. One of the most important sustaining factors (but not the only one) is the chronic elevation of LDL in the plasma. Animal studies have demonstrated that hyperlipidemic serum will stimulate the proliferation of arterial medial cells grown *in vitro*. Adding high-density lipoprotein (HDL) obtained from serum of normal animals to this *in vitro* system reduces the rate of cell division (Wissler and Vesselinovitch 1986).

Many important aspects remain to be understood, but the basic theme is clear: Atherosclerosis is an age-related pathology that depends on the dynamic

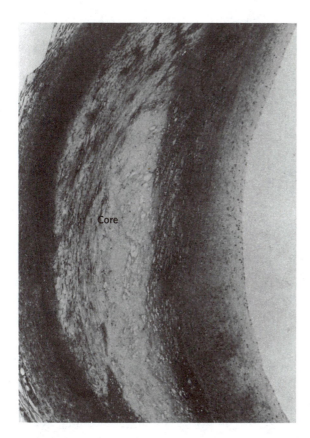

Core

Figure 5.19 A Type IV lesion, or atheroma (see Table 5.4), in the coronary artery of a 23-year-old male who died by violence. Note that extracellular lipid is concentrated at the core and replaces much of the musculoelastic intimal layer. Macrophage foam cells and lipid-laden smooth cells are layered above the core. (From Stary 1986. © Springer-Verlag.)

interplay of genetic and environmental factors affecting lipid metabolism, cell proliferation, cardiovascular hemodynamics, and other biological, social, and cultural variables. The complexity of the issue may be illustrated by two other observations. First, animal studies have shown that diets containing very high levels of lipids will produce only fatty streaks (Type II lesions; see Figure 5.18) when fed to prepubertal animals, but will yield coronary atherosclerotic plaques (Type IV and V lesions; see Figure 5.19) when fed for the same amount of time to young, sexually mature adults (Clarkson et al. 1987). This finding suggests that the sex hormones play an important role in modulating environmental insults.

The second observation concerns the longitudinal changes in serum cholesterol levels as determined in the Baltimore Longitudinal Study on Aging (BLSA). Figure 5.20 shows that serum cholesterol levels decline significantly as a result of social and cultural dietary changes, but that these decreases are superimposed on what appears to be an age-related increase in these levels. Theory predicts that these dietary changes will give rise to a decrease in serum cholesterol levels, and they obviously did—but the observed changes are much greater than the predicted drop. Clearly, other unknown factors are at work here as well. Incidentally, almost all the BLSA subjects shown in Figure 5.20 have elevated serum choles-

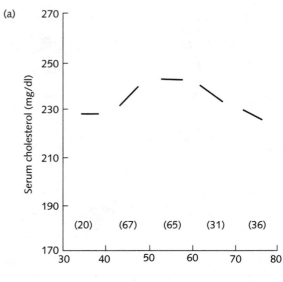

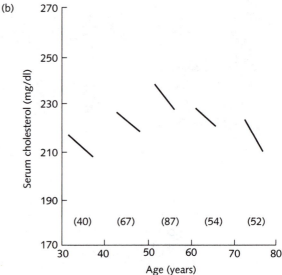

Figure 5.20   Longitudinal changes in serum cholesterol concentrations. Line segments indicate the mean slope of changes in serum cholesterol for each age decade. Each line is drawn with the midpoint at the mean cholesterol; the length along the *x* axis represents the mean time span over which the longitudinal data were gathered. (a) The longitudinal change during the period before the drop in cholesterol (1963–1971). (b) The longitudinal change during the period in which cholesterol levels fell (1969–1977). The number of subjects for each mean slope is given in parentheses. (From Hershcopf et al. 1982.)

terol levels relative to what is now considered normal (which is about 150 to 170 milligrams per deciliter). During the same period of time as shown in Figure 5.20, the age-related incidence of coronary artery disease began to decline, presumably as a result of long-term changes in diet, cigarette consumption, hypertension detection and treatment, and possibly other factors (Hazzard 1986a).

Third, it is a common assumption that atherosclerotic lesions, once formed, are permanent. This assumption is not correct. Significant regression of coronary atherosclerotic lesions has been observed in the Lifestyle Heart Trial (Ornish, 1993). In this clinical trial, participants were asked to make conventional (control group) or extraordinary (experimental group) lifestyle changes. The experimental group changes included a low-fat (10% of total calories) vegetarian diet without caloric restriction, no caffeine, limited alcohol, moderate exercise, and stress management techniques. Of the 22 patients in the experimental group, 82% showed regression of lesion size coupled with a significant reduction of symptoms (e.g., angina). Of the 19 patients in the control group, 53% showed a progression of lesion size coupled with an increase in symptoms. There is a suggestion in the data that women may show lesion regression more easily than men. The fact that lifestyle changes are capable of bringing about a significant reversal of atherosclerotic lesions strongly suggests that this condition cannot be viewed as an inevitable age-related disease, but rather as the outcome of socioculturally related diet and lifestyle habits acting on the background of different genetic or inherent susceptibilities.

Summary

Fewer age-related changes take place in the cardiovascular system than one might have expected. Intrinsic changes in elastic fibers lead to a normal thickening of the arterial wall, and this alteration indirectly leads to the normal thickening of the left ventricular wall. Except for blood pressure, most resting cardiac functions show no other age-related changes. Under stress, however, there appears to be an age-related decrease in the maximum attainable heart rate, a factor that results in a failure to supply sufficient oxygenated blood to the muscles. This effect may account for the age-related reduction in maximum workload.

Atherosclerosis is an important age-related pathology that is dependent for its expression on various intrinsic and extrinsic variables.

Changes in the Respiratory System

Normal Structure and Function

Figure 5.21 shows the anatomical structure of the respiratory system. The branching airways make up the main components of the bronchopulmonary system. These airways are as follows: nasal cavity; pharynx; larynx; trachea; primary, secondary, and tertiary bronchi; bronchioles; and finally, alveoli. The bronchi, bronchioles, and alveoli are contained within the lungs. The many series of tubes formed by the branching of the bronchi are known as the respiratory tree. The walls of the trachea and the primary bronchi contain cartilage and smooth muscle. The cartilage gradually disappears as the bronchi branch, so the bronchioles contain only smooth muscle. No muscle surrounds the alveoli. Gases are exchanged between air and blood in the alveoli, thin-walled sacs that are richly supplied with a dense network of capillaries. These blood vessels bulge out into the alveolar sacs, thereby presenting a large surface area to the alveolar air. Collagenous and elastic fibers form a tenuous supporting framework for these sacs and capillaries. The alveolar cells themselves are extraordinarily thin and present little obstacle to the free diffusion of gases throughout all parts of the alveoli and into the capillaries.

Ventilation of the lungs involves the inspiration and expiration of air. In the normal resting state, inspiration usually lasts about 2 seconds and expiration about 3 seconds. This rhythmicity is under the alternating control of inspiratory

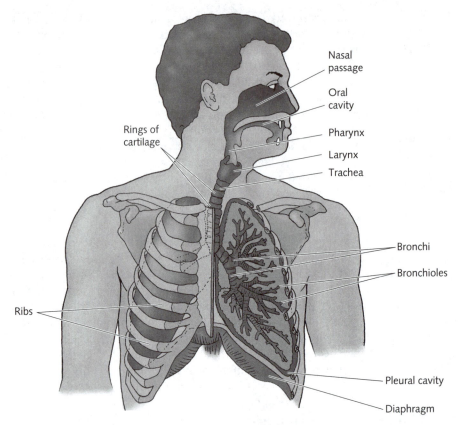

Figure 5.21   The structure of the human respiratory system.

and expiratory neurons located in the medulla. Various chemoreceptors monitor the oxygen, carbon dioxide, and hydrogen ion (pH) concentrations and transmit signals to the respiratory center to help regulate respiratory activity. The central chemoreceptor is located in the medulla and responds to the presence of excess CO_2 in body fluids (hypercapnia). The peripheral chemoreceptors are located in the neural tissue of the carotid body and the aortic body. These bodies are located at specific points on the arteries of the same name. They respond to reduced O_2 concentration in body fluids (hypoxemia). Thus, either hypercapnia or hypoxemia will normally increase the rate and depth of breathing.

Inspiration is an active process brought about by contraction of the diaphragm and elevation of the ribs. The increased volume reduces the intrapulmonary pressure to a level below the atmospheric pressure, so air flows into the lungs. Expiration is a passive process brought about by relaxation of the diaphragm and of the rib muscles. Relaxation of these muscles allows the elastic recoil of the chest wall to reduce the volume of the chest cavity. This action, when combined with the elastic recoil of the lungs, increases the intrapulmonary pressure and forces air to flow out of the lungs.

Several measurable volumes are important in understanding and measuring lung function; they are illustrated in Figure 5.22 and defined in Table 5.7. In normal individuals, the volume of air in the lungs depends primarily on body size and build. The different volumes and capacities also change with body posture, most of them decreasing in the sitting position and increasing in the standing position.

Age-Related Changes

The analysis of respiratory function is intimately involved with the functional ability of other systems, such as the cardiovascular and muscular systems, and varies as a function of body height. In addition, respiratory function can be readily impaired by disease states such as emphysema or by exposure to environmental pollutants, including those associated with smoking (Klocke 1977). Nonetheless, carefully designed studies make it possible to identify what appear to be the effects of age on respiratory function (Shock 1985). There seem to be very few, if any, changes in age-related respiratory functions at rest. Marked age effects appear, however, when the respiratory system is made to perform under stress.

Measurement of respiratory volumes is a convenient clinical test. The amount of air that can be forcibly expelled in 1 second (the forced expiratory volume, or FEV) is often used and has been found to possess some predictive value (see Figure 3.19). Even in populations screened for occult respiratory pathologies, the FEV decreases strikingly with age. This decrease in FEV occurs even though the total lung capacity is known to remain constant (Klocke 1977); therefore, the residual volume must increase. This increase in residual volume affects particularly the lower part of the lungs, leading to localized changes in ventilation.

Another measure of respiratory function is the ventilatory rate, or the minute respiratory volume, defined as the volume of air inspired in a normal breath (the tidal volume) multiplied by the frequency of breaths per minute. This

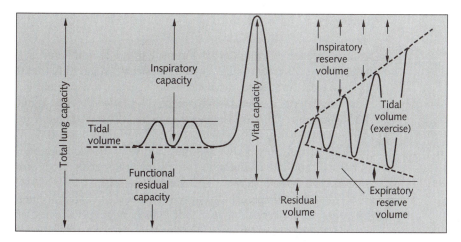

Figure 5.22 A diagrammatic representation of important pulmonary capacities and volumes. See Table 5.7 for explanation. (After Clarke 1975.)

Table 5.7 Pulmonary Volumes and Capacities

Type	Definition	Numerical value in normal young adult (ml)	
		Female	Male
Volumes			
1. Tidal volume	Volume of air inspired and expired during quiet normal breathing	500	500
2. Inspiratory reserve volume	Volume of air inspired during forced inspiration	2,100	3,000
3. Expiratory reserve volume	Volume of air forcefully expired at end of normal tidal expiration	800	1,200
4. Residual volume	Volume of air remaining in lungs after most forceful expiration	1,200	1,200
Capacities			
5. Inspiratory capacity	Sum of volumes 1 and 2; amount of air a person can breathe in beginning at normal expiratory level and distending lungs to maximum amount	2,600	3,500
6. Functional residual capacity	Sum of volumes 3 and 4; amount of air remaining in lungs at end of normal expiration	2,000	2,400
7. Vital capacity	Sum of volumes 1, 2, and 3; maximum amount of air one can expel from lungs after a maximum inspiration plus a maximum expiration	3,400	4,700
8. Total lung capacity	Sum of volumes 1 through 4; maximum volume to which lungs can be expanded with greatest possible inspiratory effort	4,600	5,900

Source: Adapted from data in Guyton 1966.

value averages about 6 liters per minute in males and females. At submaximal levels of work, a low ventilatory rate is desirable, suggesting that the lungs do not have to work hard to oxygenate the blood. There are no clear-cut age effects on this parameter at low levels of exertion (Whitbourne 1985). At maximal exertion, however, the ventilatory rate appears to decrease with age. Young adult males can sustain a maximum breathing capacity of about 125 to 170 liters per minute, but only for about 15 seconds. However, they can maintain a respiratory volume of 100 to 120 liters per minute for prolonged periods of time. This value represents a 20-fold increase over the tidal volume.

The maximum breathing capacity decreases to about 75 liters per minute at 85 years, a 50 percent decline. The elderly have lost their reserve. These age-related changes in respiratory function have been plausibly interpreted as arising from intrinsic age-related changes taking place in the connective tissue components of the lungs. We have previously described the intrinsic age-related changes in the structure of the elastin and collagen fibers. Such changes occur in the lungs and result in decreased elasticity of the alveoli. The elastic recoil of the lungs is its tendency to resist expansion as it becomes filled with air, and this property helps keep the airways open during expiration. A decrease in elastic recoil results in a decreased ability of the alveoli and associated structures to remain open during expiration, thereby causing air to be trapped inside them. As the residual volume increases, the FEV decreases. The entire process is accelerated by an increase in the size of the alveolar ducts and a decrease in the number of alveoli, thus decreasing the surface area available for gas exchange (Whitbourne 1985).

The same changes in connective tissue also affect the dynamics of the chest wall. The increased rigidity of the ribs and muscles makes it more difficult for the lungs to increase to their full volume. This rigidity increases the amount of work that must be done by the respiratory muscles during the breathing cycle. This increase in the amount of work combines with the loss of elastic recoil of the lungs themselves to further decrease the maximum volume of air that can be brought into the lungs.

As a result of these kinetic alterations, the lungs of older adults are less able to provide sufficient ventilation and gas exchange to meet the body's oxygen demands at maximum levels of exertion. Smoking adds chemical insult to these intrinsic age-related changes in the respiratory system. We worry a great deal about ways to offset these intrinsic changes, yet many of us tend to overlook the fact that one of the strongest predictors of a foreshortened longevity is smoking. It is an extraordinarily difficult addiction to break, as this author can testify, but the benefits of quitting are (eventually) worth the agony.

Age-Related Pathologies

Emphysema is an obstructive disease in which the lungs lose their ability to ventilate properly, excessive air accumulates in the alveoli, and the supply of freshly oxygenated air to the alveoli is sharply restricted (Spence 1988). This disease is believed to develop as a gradual response to chronic irritation of the bronchial tree by smoke, repeated infections, or another such irritant. The chronic irritation induces the production of excessive amounts of mucus within the airways. The buildup of mucus gradually restricts the airflow to the lungs. The trapped air causes the alveoli to remain inflated at all times, and this condition eventually damages the walls of the alveoli. In the repair process, damaged areas are replaced with fibrous tissues that are much more impermeable to gaseous exchange than alveoli are. This fibrous connective tissue also decreases the elastic recoil of the lung, making expiration less efficient and more difficult. People suffering from emphysema consequently have an increased residual volume, a decreased vital capacity, and a decreased minute respiratory volume. The afflicted individuals suffer from "oxygen hunger" and develop hypoxemia and hypercapnia. The disease also places an extra load on the heart as it attempts to compensate for the hypoxemia by pumping more blood to the lungs.

Summary

Changes in connective tissue components account for most of the age-related decreased elasticity of the lungs and the increased rigidity of the trachea, bronchi, and thoracic wall. As a result of these factors, the residual volume increases with age while the forced expiratory volume decreases. The number of alveoli decreases, adversely affecting the surface area available for gas exchange and further limiting the body's ability to oxygenate the blood sufficiently. These changes in respiratory function interact with concurrent changes in the cardiovascular and other systems. Although there are very few, if any, age-related changes in respiratory functions at rest, marked age effects appear when the person must perform under stress.

Environmental insults such as smoking often accelerate and amplify these functional decrements in the respiratory system.

Changes in the Digestive System

Normal Structure and Function

The primary function of the digestive system is to transform food into a form that the body's cells can use and to provide for the uptake of nutrients and the excretion of wastes. It also has secondary endocrine functions, which are intimately involved with its digestive and metabolic processes (Uvnas-Moberg 1989). The digestive system develops as a long tube, topologically outside of the body, with regional specializations for different functions. Components of this system include several highly specialized organs that may be viewed as belonging either to the alimentary canal or to the accessory organs. The normal functioning of each of these components is summarized in Table 5.8.

Although the digestive tube is regionally specialized, the structure of each region is fundamentally similar and consists of four concentric layers. The innermost layer, the mucosa, is made up of epithelial tissue, an underlying basement membrane, and connective tissue with a thin coating of smooth muscle in some places. The next layer is the submucosa, which is made up of connective tissue and contains nerve fibers and blood vessels. Then comes the muscularis, or muscle layer. In most regions the muscularis consists of a double layer of smooth muscle, with the inner layer arranged circularly and the outer layer arranged longitudinally. Coordinated contractions of these two layers produce the peristaltic motion that propels food along the digestive tract. At several points, the circular muscle layer thickens into a heavy band, or sphincter, which regulates the passage of food from one portion of the digestive tract to the next. The outermost layer is termed the serosa and is composed of connective tissue.

Food within the alimentary canal is digested by secretions that enter the tube from accessory glands and/or organs (see Table 5.8). Most of these secretions are different types of enzymes, but they also include nonenzymatic fluids such as hydrochloric acid in the stomach or emulsifying agents (bile) in the small intestine. A layer of mucus protects the stomach and small intestine from digesting themselves; failure of this mucus layer underlies the formation of ulcers.

The small intestine is approximately 6 meters (22 feet) long. Its effective length is much greater, however, because of the great increase in surface area provided by numerous tiny fingerlike projections, called villi, that line the mucosal lining of the small intestine. The surface area is further enhanced by the presence of microvilli, microscopic hairlike cytoplasmic projections on the surface

Table 5.8 **Normal Structure–Function Relationships in the Digestive System**

Region	Function	Characteristic enzymes, structures, and/or processes
Alimentary canal		
Mouth	Mechanical maceration	Teeth
	Moistening, beginning of carbohydrate digestion	Saliva, containing enzymes (salivary amylase)
	Stimulation of appetite	Taste buds
Pharynx and esophagus	Swallowing	
	Transport of food to stomach	Peristaltic motion of esophageal wall
Stomach	Killing of exogenous bacteria	Hydrochloric acid secreted by gastric glands; also pepsin enzyme
	Protein digestion	
	Conversion of chewed food to semiliquid form	Muscular contractions
	Production of gastric hormone	Stimulation of secretion of gastric juice
Small intestine	Completion of protein and carbohydrate digestion	Various enzymes from intestinal wall and from pancreas
	Beginning and completion of lipid digestion	Pancreatic enzymes plus bile from liver
	Absorption of food nutrients into bloodstream	Intestinal villi
	Production of secretin hormone	Stimulation of secretion of bile and of pancreatic juice
Large intestine	Absorption of water and salts	Microvilli of cells lining intestinal wall
Accessory glands and organs		
Pancreas	Two types of cells:	
	Acinar cells produce various enzymes	Pancreatic amylase, lipase
	Islet cells produce hormones that regulate blood sugar levels	Insulin, glucagon, somatostatin
Liver	Storage and release of carbohydrates; conversion of amino acids to carbohydrate	All processes carried out in all cells
	Packaging of fats for transport	
	Regulation of cholesterol levels	
	Synthesis of HDL and LDL	
	Secretion of bile	
	Storage of fat-soluble vitamins	
	Synthesis of blood plasma proteins	
	Inactivation of hormones	
	Inactivation of foreign substances (e.g., alcohol, drugs)	

of each epithelial cell making up the villus. It is estimated that because of these adaptations, the total surface area of the human small intestine is approximately 300 square meters, or about the size of a doubles tennis court. Most digestion takes place in the upper 25 centimeters of the small intestine, known as the duodenum. In addition to enzymes, the small intestine receives from the pancreas an alkaline fluid that neutralizes the stomach acid. This neutralization is essential because the pancreatic enzymes are inactivated by the acid environment of the stomach juices. The remainder of the small intestine is concerned mostly with the absorption of nutrients.

Age-Related Changes

Few true age-related changes are apparent in the digestive system, once the populations being examined have been screened for the presence of occult gastrointestinal diseases and/or pathological dieting habits such as high levels of alcohol ingestion and the like. Cultural and/or economic factors that may restrict the types of food available to the aging individual are another complicating factor. This topic was reviewed and summarized by Whitbourne (1985) and by Spence (1988); the discussion that follows is drawn from these sources.

At least two general changes affect the digestive tract: The muscle contractions become weaker, resulting in a slowing down of the peristaltic motion of the alimentary canal, and the glandular secretions tend to diminish somewhat. These alterations are themselves the result of more fundamental age-related changes, such as those already described affecting muscle performance or those affecting the rate of protein synthesis (see Chapter 10). The decrease in glandular activity leads to regionally specific alterations. The mouth becomes drier as the volume of saliva diminishes. Gastric secretion can diminish by as much as 25 percent by 60 years of age. In the small intestine, atrophy of the mucosal lining mildly reduces the absorption rate. All four layers of the large intestine atrophy, leading to a weakening of the intestinal wall and a concomitant increase in the incidence of diverticulosis.

The most significant of these few age-dependent changes in digestive function concern the relationship between vitamin D and calcium absorption. Calcium absorption in the intestine decreases after age 70. Normally calcium is absorbed via two different processes. One process is passive diffusion across the intestinal cell membranes from the high concentrations in the chyme (the liquid contents of the small intestine) to the lower concentrations in the cell. The other process is an active transport of calcium and is regulated by the blood levels of the active form of vitamin D (calcitriol). Thus, the decreased absorption of calcium might be due directly to reduced serum levels of active vitamin D. In this view, the decreased calcium uptake might be due to paradoxically higher blood levels of calcium as a result of bone resorption (see the section on the skeletal system, pages 170–172), which results in a decreased level of active vitamin D formation and a consequent continued low level of calcium absorption. However, this age-related change (if that's what it is) is capable of being modulated via appropriate nutrition and exercise (see Chapter 7).

Age-related changes in metabolic parameters or in energy production are discussed under "Metabolic and Hormonal Changes" (see page 240).

Summary

Age-related changes in the digestive system affect primarily components of the system such as connective tissue, muscle performance, or synthesis of glandular secretions.

Changes in the Excretory System

Normal Structure and Function

Healthy adult kidneys are about 12 centimeters long and 6 centimeters wide. Their weight ranges from 120 to 150 grams and is not appreciably correlated with body size. Internally, the kidney is divided into two distinct regions, the outer cortex and the inner medulla. The striated appearance of the medulla is due to the presence in it of many arrays of tubules and ducts that are more or less parallel. The renal arteries branch elaborately, giving rise to afferent arterioles that subdivide into a capillary bed, the glomerulus, contained within Bowman's capsule. Capillary convergence creates efferent arterioles that in turn subdivide into a network of capillaries surrounding the tubules before heading back into the venous circulation.

The nephron is the functional part of the kidney responsible for eliminating chemical wastes from the bloodstream, and for regulating the salt and water balances of the body. Each kidney is made up of millions of these functional subunits, the nephrons. As illustrated in Figure 5.23, the nephron consists of a very

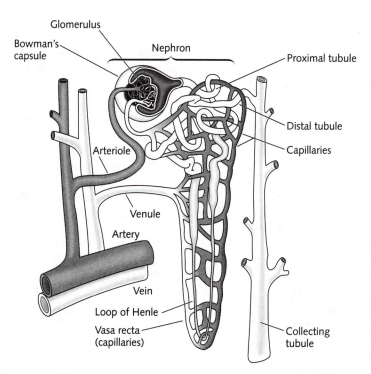

Figure 5.23 The structure of the nephron and its blood supply. About 20 percent of the liquid portion of the blood brought in by the arteriole filters from the glomerulus to the tubule system. The tubule system is composed of proximal and distal tubules, which are connected by the Loop of Henle. All regions of these tubules are surrounded by a separate capillary bed, the peritubular capillaries, which reabsorb much of the minerals, nutrients, and fluid from the filtrate. The resulting urine is transported out of the kidney to the bladder via the collecting tubules.

long, regionally specialized and coiled kidney tubule, intimately encircled by a network of capillaries connecting the arteriole and the venule. About 20 percent of the liquid portion of the blood is filtered out under pressure in the glomerulus and is then selectively reabsorbed throughout the rest of the tubule such that essential components are recovered by the blood while waste products are retained in the urine. The functional integrity of the nephron is directly related to the maintenance of this normal morphology.

The kidney filters an enormous volume of fluid. Approximately 125 milliliters of fluid per minute, or 180 liters per day, is filtered through the glomerulus into each Bowman's capsule. This filtrate contains digested foods, minerals, and waste products, but no blood cells or large protein molecules. Such components are essential for normal body functioning. Fortunately, about 99 percent of this fluid is resorbed in the renal tubules, so the body produces only 1 to 2 liters of urine each day.

The urine flows through the ureters to the bladder, where it is stored until excreted via the urethra. The bladder is a hollow muscular organ that can hold about 600 milliliters of fluid. Stretch receptors in the bladder wall initiate muscular contractions that will empty the bladder—usually when the bladder is only about half full.

Age-Related Changes

The aging kidney gradually loses mass (see Figure 5.1), most of this loss apparently from the cortex as a result of intrarenal vascular changes. These vascular changes take place independent of hypertension, although they are aggravated by that condition. The genesis of these changes is not clear, but one hypothesis suggests that they are due to a thickening of the visceral layer of the glomerulus (which is normally tightly opposed to the glomerular capillaries). This condition would then give rise to an impaired retention of proteins in the blood, resulting in proteinuria (Samly 1983). This proteinuria precedes and might then cause the glomerular sclerosis and vessel abnormalities. However, this point is far from settled.

One school of thought suggests that the loss of renal function is a disease process intitated by the high protein content of most human diets. The resultant high-solute load delivered to the kidney causes chronic renal vasodilation. This dilation initiates a series of reactions leading to progressive glomerular sclerosis. As glomeruli are destroyed, the solute load in the remaining nephrons is increased and a disastrous positive feedback cycle is initiated (Dworkin et al. 1984). What is clear is the widespread degeneration of the blood vessels that constitute the glomerulus, a change that effectively removes that nephron from any further role in renal function. Renal blood flow begins to decline by 10 percent per decade beginning at age 40. The glomerular filtration rate also declines from a steady value of 120 milliliters per minute at age 40 to 60 to 70 milliliters per minute at age 85. Tubular functions decrease at the same rate as glomerular functions, implying that the nephron fails as a unit (McLachan 1978). Since the kidney has tremendous reserve capacity, age usually has little effect on the body's ability to maintain fluid and electrolyte balances under normal conditions. When the elderly are stressed, however, their ability to cope is not as good as that of their younger counterparts, and their decreased number of nephrons begins to be evident in longer response times and a general failure to maintain homeostatic equilibrium.

Both cross-sectional (Tobin 1981) and longitudinal (Shock et al. 1979) studies have demonstrated that creatinine clearance (a measure of kidney function) declines with age (see Figure 3.6) and appears to be an intrinsic change. The longitudinal study also showed that there is a great deal of normal variability in this parameter between individuals. Some people show a remarkable maintenance or even improvement in some cases of their renal function. Interestingly, subjects who died during the study showed a greater rate of decline in renal function during the 10 years preceding death than did the survivors. These results bring to mind other data suggesting the existence of individual differences and the heterogeneity of the human population.

Summary

The main effect of aging on the kidneys is the widespread loss of glomeruli. The role that certain intrinsic or extrinsic factors play in this process is not settled, but it is clear that the degenerative vascular changes remove the affected glomerulus from any further role in renal function. Excretory functioning at rest is not affected, for these changes affect mainly the body's ability to maintain homeostatic equilibrium under conditions of renal stress.

Changes in the Nervous System

Normal Structure and Function

We each base our fundamental knowledge of ourselves as individual personalities on our conscious awareness. The complex actions, thoughts, perceptions, and emotions that constitute this awareness are made possible by the actions of the nervous system. Age-related changes that affect the functioning of the nervous system may well underlie changes in the processes that are most important to each of us. For this reason alone, we are not surprised by the high level of interest shown by both professionals and laypeople in this topic. The structural complexity of the nervous system and the not yet fully understood processes by which brain activity is transduced into mental processes repay our interest with more questions than answers. The best we can do here is offer a brief and partial summary of the neurological basis for some of these age effects as observed in the central nervous system (CNS), and to allude to some of their possible effects in intellectual functioning. More detailed and comprehensive reviews of the topic may be found in the writings of Whitbourne (1985), Finch and Landfield (1985), Duara, London, and Rapoport (1985), Cotman and Holets (1985), Rogers and Bloom (1985), Shock et al. (1984), and Brody and Vijayashankar (1977), among others.

Figure 5.24 shows the overall anatomy of the human CNS. The different regions of the brain are each involved with different aspects of sensory, motor, and/or mental activities. The human brain is the most complex living structure

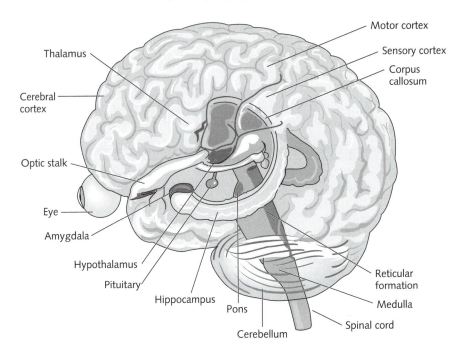

Figure 5.24   The brain, showing the major structures active in sensing and internal regulation. The eye and optic stalk are shown connected to the hypothalamus, from the lower surface of which the pituitary emerges. (After Bloom, Lazerson, and Hofstadter 1985.)

known to us; it is probably safe to say that it is the most complex structure on Earth. Much of the brain's ability to function normally depends on the high level of integration of these various components. The 50 billion or so neurons in the human brain do not function in isolated units the way the cells of the liver or kidney do; the brain is more than just 50 billion isolated nerve cells. Instead, the neurons are linked together in circuits, by means of which informational messages are passed from sending cells to receiving cells (Figure 5.25). An individual neuron may transmit messages to as few as one or two other neurons, or to as many as 1,000 or more other neurons. Thus these circuits are both complicated and overlapping. A message is transmitted from one end of a cell to the other as an electrical impulse. This impulse cannot jump the gap, or synapse, between individual cells, so it must be converted to a chemical signal at the start of the synapse and then converted back to an electrical impulse at the other side of the synapse before it can continue through the circuit. "Neurotransmitter" is the generic term for any of the diverse chemicals that regulate this intercellular transmission of the message across the synapse. Many of these different chemical transmitters are found only in particular nervous-system pathways.

Given the proper conditions, a nerve cell is either transmitting an impulse or not; it is either "on" or "off." It seems incredible that our complex thoughts and mental activities could be reduced to such a simple state. Yet it is instructive to

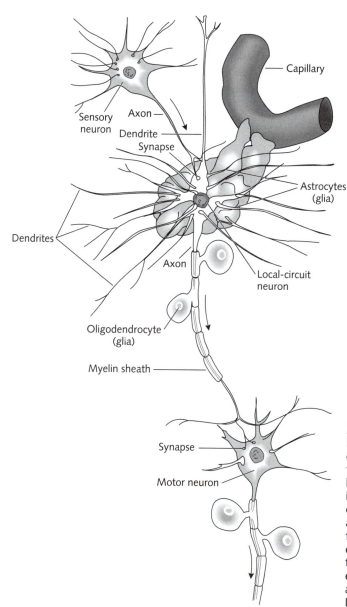

Capillary

Sensory neuron

Axon

Dendrite

Synapse

Astrocytes (glia)

Dendrites

Axon

Local-circuit neuron

Oligodendrocyte (glia)

Myelin sheath

Synapse

Motor neuron

Figure 5.25   A neural circuit. A large neuron with multiple dendrites receives synaptic contact from a sensory neuron (at upper left). The same large neuron sends its myelinated axon into a synaptic connection with a motor neuron at the bottom. These neural surfaces are shown without the extensive investment of glial cells that envelop the neural branch extending toward the capillary at upper right. (After Bloom, Lazerson, and Hofstadter 1985.)

remember that the most subtle and abstract written thoughts of humankind can be completely encoded in the equally simple dot–dash system of Morse code. It is just as instructive to realize that animal studies are now allowing us to describe learning in molecular biological terms (Black et al. 1987).

The gray matter of the brain is composed of the nerve cell bodies; the white matter contains no nerve cell bodies or dendrites and is formed by the myelinated nerve fibers. The gray matter is located on the surface portions of the brain and is known as the cerebral cortex, the cerebellar cortex, and so on. Most of the cells of the CNS are neuroglial cells and not neurons proper. The neuroglial cells are a diverse group of nonnervous cells that assist in supporting and maintaining the neurons, thereby contributing to their functional ability (see Figure 5.25).

Age-Related Changes

Gross structural changes   During the past century, at least a dozen studies of the changes in brain weight or volume as a function of aging have been undertaken. Some of these studies, particularly the early ones, appear to have been strongly biased in their methods of sample collection and/or measurement (see Gould 1981). The conclusions of such racially or ethnically biased investigations are of course suspect. Nonetheless, several objective studies, some rather recent, have established that the human brain loses both weight and volume from youth to old age (see Brody and Vijayashankar 1977 for review). Most studies agree on the general pattern: The brain increases in size from about 357 grams at birth to a peak size of about 1,300 grams at age 20 years. This weight is maintained until about 55 years, which marks the beginning of a progressive decline in weight through the age of 80 years (Davison 1987). The result can be as much as an 11 percent decrease in mean brain weight in the elderly relative to the young adult.

Several problems are inherent in such studies, not the least of which is the fact that such cross-sectional correlations might be spurious because the mean body weight of people has increased during the past century. Thus these studies would be confusing age effects and birth cohort effects. This problem can be resolved by statistically correcting for skull size. This standardization of brain volume neatly sidesteps these problems by expressing the volume in relative, not absolute, terms. The cross-sectional results, such as those shown in Figure 3.18, confirm that brain volume is relatively stable from the ages of 20 to 60 years but subsequently decreases rapidly. This pattern must be interpreted in consideration of the fact that the ventricles of the brain in normal individuals appear to enlarge slightly up to age 60, and more rapidly thereafter. Thus in some individuals the brain volume may be decreasing as a result of enlargement of both extracerebral and intracerebral spaces. There is no firm correlation between these changes and alterations in the intellectual capacity of the affected individuals (Duara, London, and Rapoport 1985). The use of computerized tomography (CT) scans should allow longitudinal studies, which might be of value in assessing the functional significance of such gross anatomical changes (Jernigan et al. 1980).

Microscopic structural changes   If the normal functioning of the brain is dependent on the normal architecture and arrangement of the cells which compose it, then we might expect that unusual cellular or subcellular level changes in that structure might give rise to abnormal mental functioning. A neural circuit may be substantively altered by the loss of its component cells and/or by a reduction in the number of other circuits it interacts with, so we'll now examine cell loss and morphological alterations.

The loss in overall brain weight and size through the life span (see Figure 5.1) may be due to the loss of individual neurons with age. Many studies have been undertaken to answer this question. Most of these studies indicate that neurons are lost in selected layers and regions of the aging human cerebral cortex, but not in most brain stem structures. However, losses in the number of interneurons in the lower spinal cord have been reported. The most extensive losses, which may range as high as 25 to 45 percent, appear to occur in the layers containing the associative neurons of the cerebral cortex. These regions are probably the ones ultimately associated with such mental processes as thought and memory (Duara, London, and Rapoport 1985).

This attrition does not take place on a daily basis, despite the popular folklore that we lose 100,000 neurons every day. Almost all the studies agree that the dramatic decreases in neuronal number occur mostly after the age of 60 years or so. Phrasing this as a daily rate is neither useful nor justifiable.

Morphological alterations may indicate of functional changes in the nervous system. The death of a neuron can affect, even disable, the functioning of a neural circuit; however, so can a decrease in the number of neurons participating in the circuit. The dendrites represent the major route for incoming nerve impulses to reach the neuron; thus, an alteration in their number may reflect an underlying functional change at the level of the synapse. Furthermore, since most synapses terminate on the dendritic spines, an estimate of their number provides us with an index of synapse abundance and distribution. In humans, the number of dendrites, and of the dendritic spines, decreases with age (Figure 5.26), although this decrease does not affect all brain regions in the same way. Some areas show no changes; some areas show decreases of up to 25 percent (Cotman and Holets 1985). In this manner, a functional decrement in our thought process may be brought about by means other than neuronal cell death. These progressive changes transform the delicate, multiply-branched neuron into a simple-looking, almost deformed, cell shorn of its many processes. Such changes are believed, but not yet proven, to lead to neuronal cell death.

Dendritic decreases have been shown to be associated with various dementias of middle and old age. However, the data are not robust enough to permit any strong inference regarding normal aging to be drawn from this correlation. Interestingly, several studies (summarized by Cotman and Holets [1985]) show that presumably normal individuals may display either no change or even an increase in the number of their dendritic spines with age. Animal studies have shown that new synapses, indicated by an increase in the number of dendritic spines, can form in the adult brain as a result of either partial denervation or various manipulations of the external environment. Although such synapse replacement is somewhat slower in aged animals relative to young ones, the older individuals end up with the same number of normal synapses at the end of the process as do young animals (Figure 5.27). This retained capacity for dendrite growth may compensate to some extent for the age-related decline in number of neurons. This neuronal plasticity in the adult brain appears to be enhanced if the animals are fed a choline-enriched diet and/or are raised in an enriched environment (an environment in which there are sufficient opportunities for exploration and activity; see Cheal 1986). These findings may have implications for human biology and society.

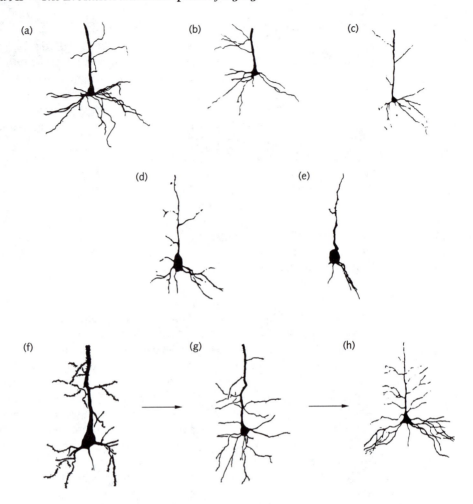

Figure 5.26 A comparison of Golgi-stained neurons from rats and humans. (a–c) Pyramidal cells from the auditory cortex of a 3-month-old rat (a), a 34-month-old rat (b), and a 36-month-old rat (c.) (d, c) A more detailed view of the rat neurons, showing the loss of the dendritic spines. The neuron in (d) is from a 3-month-old rat, the one in (e) from a 34-month-old rat. (f–h) Summary of the progression of senile changes in human cortical pyramidal cells. (a–c from Vaughn 1977; d, e from Feldman 1976. © Raven Press; f–h from Scheibel 1978. © Raven Press.)

More recently, animal studies have shown that in certain defined structures, adult neurons that are lost as a result of cell death may be replaced by the transplantation of certain fetal nerve cells to the affected site. This kind of surgical intervention is being explored as a possible clinical alleviation of Parkinson's disease in humans. The long-range outcome of such interventions is as yet unknown, in part because the time course of recovery in humans might be much slower than in rats (Lewin 1988). The implications of this strategy for gerontology and for society will depend on whether it proves to be clinically successful and whether the approach can be generalized beyond the bounds of a clinical allevia-

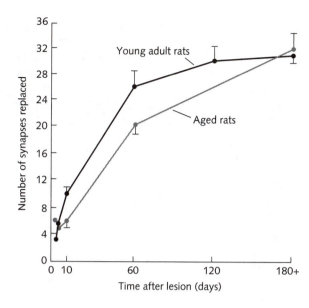

Figure 5.27 The time course for synapse replacement after an entorhinal lesion. Note that after an initial delay, synapse replacement in the aged animals proceeds at the same rate as in the younger animals, and an equal synaptic density is achieved. (From Hoff et al. 1982.)

tion for one particular pathological disease state. A potentially very interesting variant of this approach is the implantation of genetically engineered fibroblast cells into an affected organ (Rosenberg et al. 1988). This experimental approach might allow genetic tailoring of connective tissue cells, altering them so that they can synthesize desirable molecules not usually made by such cells. After transplantation, these altered cells might not only join in the structure of the particular organ, but might also supply necessary molecules to the organ. It has already been shown in animal studies that such grafted cells, genetically engineered to secrete nerve growth factor, survived and exerted a reparative influence on the CNS of surgically damaged rats.

The progressive accumulation of autofluorescent pigment within the cytoplasm of some long-lived cells is one of the oldest known manifestations of aging in the cell. Such age pigments have been found in many cell types of most eukaryotes and are discussed in more detail in Chapter 10. In general, the number of neurons that contain significant amounts of lipofuscin, a yellowish pigment, increases with age. It has been generally assumed that lipofuscin interferes with the normal activity of the neurons, and that the progressive accumulation of this pigmented waste product causes the malfunctioning and eventual death of the neuron. As a result, the amount of lipofuscin pigment is often used as a rough indicator of age. This interpretation is still far from being universally accepted, especially since certain neurons in the brain stem normally accumulate large amounts of lipofuscin and other pigments with no apparent deleterious effect (Whitbourne 1985).

Changes with age in the function of neurotransmitters One might suspect that many functional changes in the brain are not heralded by a visible morphological alteration in the neurons. Instead, one could plausibly postulate that even small biochemical changes bring about drastic changes in neuronal functioning. Neurotransmitters would be prime candidates as the targets for such masked changes. The neurotransmitters are a heterogeneous group of relatively simple molecules functioning as the chemical messengers that transmit nerve impulses from one neuron to another. In target cells, the neurotransmitters would also activate signal transduction mechanisms, and alterations in these latter systems could also contribute to a functional change in the nervous system (Fulop and Seves 1994). Alterations in neurotransmitter metabolism may decrease the functional ability of a neuron while leaving no structural lesion visible to the eye. Individuals who strive to understand just what kinds of changes with age neurotransmitters bring about are faced with an almost impossible task because of the many problems involved: The amounts of neurotransmitter involved are quite small; the quantities are localized at the synapse, which is microscopic; different neurons within the same nerve bundle may use different neurotransmitters; the same neurotransmitter may be used by nerves of very different specificity; different brain regions often show conflicting changes; and the neurotransmitter levels may change dramatically within minutes after death. Nonetheless, progress in this area has been made and has been reviewed by Rogers and Bloom (1985), Carlson (1987), Pedigo (1994), Roth and Joseph (1994), Goldman et al. (1994), and Sugawa et al. (1996).

As summarized by Whitbourne (1985), the most striking age-related reductions in neurotransmitter activity are seen in the hippocampus for acetylcholine, in the substantia nigra and the striatal pathway for dopamine, in portions of the brain stem for norepinephrine and serotonin, and in the thalamus for gamma-aminobutyric acid (GABA). These changes in neurotransmitter levels are often paralleled by changes in both the number of receptors (the membrane proteins to which the neurotransmitters associate; Pedigo 1994) and their binding affinity (Petkov, Petkov, and Stancheva 1988). Motor deficits in experimental animals are closely correlated with loss of striatal dopamine receptors, believed due to reduced rates of receptor synthesis (Roth and Joseph 1994). The regulation of receptor mRNA synthesis may not be entirely autonomous since it can be manipulated by diet, exercise, or hormone treatment (Roth and Joseph 1994). A decrease in neurotransmitter receptor density might lead to diminished prejunctional neurotransmitter reuptake, inhibition, or faciliation. Such a situation might result in only minor age-related changes in neurotransmission at rest, but yield a significantly diminished range of modulation of the nerve signal due to aging when the organism is stimulated (Docherty 1996). The activity of the neurotransmitter synthesizing enzyme, choline acetyltransferase, is known to be regulated by nerve growth factor (NGF) (Kerwin et al. 1993). Both animal and human studies indicate that the loss of cholinergic neuronal activity in the hippocampus is the earliest age-related deficiency observed, decreasing after the fourth decade (Araki et al. 1993; Kerwin et al. 1993). This suggests the possibility that regional changes in NGF receptor density may serve as an indirect but another level of neurotransmitter synthesis control. The cholinergic system is involved in neural systems that control memory and learning. Loss of cholinergic activity may have widespread effects on mental functioning. Work in rodents has indicated that transplants of cholinergic-rich fetal neural tissue can sometimes alleviate the behavioral effects associated with age-related cholinergic decline (Ridley and Baker 1993). More useful, perhaps, is the demonstration that adenoviral vectors are capable of transferring neurotransmitter receptor proteins to the brain (Ikari et al. 1995). The possible use of targeted gene therapy to reverse deficiencies in specific neurodegenerative disorders will command great interest in the near future.

The important conclusion from all these studies is that normal aging does not bring with it a universal decrease in neurotransmitter activity. However, the localized and specific decreases that we do see appear to play an important role in the development of age-related changes in behaviors.

Changes with age in cerebral metabolism   Another approach to identifying age-related functional changes in the brain is to monitor changes in the energy metabolism of the aging brain, the idea being that alterations in brain output might reflect changes in the amount of energy available to run the brain. This topic was reviewed by Duara, London, and Rapoport (1985). In humans, glucose is the main substrate for energy metabolism in adults eating a normal diet. Almost all the glucose taken up by the brain is oxidized and used for the production of ATP (adenosine triphosphate). The production of this energy-rich molecule is proportional to oxygen consumption and therefore to the rate of cerebral blood flow. One can use (quite safely) radioactive glucose or measure the magnetic spin of the phosphate molecule or measure cerebral blood flow in order to estimate the levels of these substances within the living brain. Thus researchers can noninvasively measure any of these three parameters and obtain an estimate of the brain's overall metabolic activity.

Up through 1989, at least 14 studies, involving 742 people of ages between 18 and 86 years, focused on age-related metabolic changes in the human brain. Since that time, there have been at least 56 (and probably more) additional studies involving many more people. These studies are consistent in showing that brain metabolism never increases with age: it either remains the same or it decreases. In subjects without covert disease, aging is not correlated with a decreased cerebral blood flow (CBF) while at rest (Atkinson et al. 1992). However, mental stimulation revealed significant age-related decreases in regional CBF and in regional glucose consumption, a correlation suggesting that regional hypometabolism may underlie the age-related increases in cognitive dysfunction seen in some people (Grady 1996; Grady et al. 1994; Eberline et al. 1995; Baron and Marchal 1992). Some support for this hypothesis is given by the rough correlation observed between the extent of cortical hypometabolism in an individual and whether that individual displays normal, subnormal, or severe levels of cognitive defects (Baron and Marchal 1992). Animal studies with the senescence-accelerated mouse (SAM) show that the early impairment of memory in these animals is closely correlated with the decrease in cerebral glucose metabolism but not with other metabolic indicators (Fujibayashi et al. 1994). In addition, there is some indication that there may be characteristic regional hypometabolic patterns associated with specific neural diseases as well as with healthy or normal aging

(Moeller et al. 1996). The regional metabolic declines may be the result of neuronal cell death (Meyer et al. 1994), degradative changes in the extracellular matrix of brain microvessels (i.e., the "blood–brain barrier;" Robert et al. 1997) an/or systemic changes in the cerebral blood supply as measured at the carotid artery. It may be significant to note that animals with few observable age-related neuropathologies, such as rats, exhibit little decline in brain metabolism, while animals with extensive age-related neuropathologies, such as humans, exhibit significant declines in brain energy metabolic indices. The studies discussed above are beginning to shed some light on the relationship of these two variables.

Changes with age in mental abilities   The anatomical and physiological evidence presented so far indicates that our neural circuitry changes and our rate of cerebral metabolism decreases as we grow older. Are these age-dependent decrements in structure and function correlated with age-dependent alterations of mental activity? One standard measure of mental activity in our society has long been the intelligence test. Intelligence is what scientists term a "soft" or "fuzzy" concept. We are not sure what it is, but we are sure that we know how to measure it. This attitude has engendered much unfairness and bad science in the past, as has been ably recounted by Stephen Jay Gould in his 1981 book *The Mismeasure of Man.* The now discarded stereotype that senility is an invariant accomplice of aging was based in large part on the misinterpretation of cross-sectional data.

The BLSA studies have shown the existence of a continual age-related quantitative decline in tests of memory and of decision performance (Shock et al. 1984). This is depressing, but it doesn't fully support the old stereotype, for the data also show that certain of the age differences (those having to do with learning new material) are strikingly lessened (but not abolished) if the older individuals are allowed to learn the test material at a slower pace. This observation suggests that the earlier cross-sectional results may have confounded intelligence with speed of test taking. Thus, the adoption of appropriate learning strategies by the elderly may substantially compensate for and alleviate any real decreases in learning performance. This effect may be particularly true in situations where a knowledge and appreciation of past events play a significant role in one's real-life performance. Wisdom and experience count for something. Perhaps Francis Bacon summed it up best when he wrote, "Young men are fitter to invent than to judge; fitter for execution than for counsel; and fitter for new projects than for settled business." And Jonathan Swift wrote, "No wise man ever wished to be younger." (But then, who has ever been given the option?)

We should be careful not to swing to the other extreme: maintaining that aging brings with it no decrement in mental function and that faculties such as memory, learning, and reasoning persist undiminished until late in life. In fact, the work of Jarvik over the years has documented the fact that people's mental faculties tend to diminish significantly shortly before death (Bank and Jarvik 1979). As we grow older, we experience a decrement in short-term memory ability. The anatomical structures involved in memory are known (Mishkin and Appenzeller 1987). The physiological basis of memory is not known, but it seems certain that here too the adoption of mnemonic aids can help. The important thing is that we remember; how we remember is not the issue. The loss of memory must be the saddest blow, as Loren Eiseley (1977) once wrote:

> They say that rats always leave a sinking ship.
> They say that after a certain age
> the gray cells, neurons, axons whoever they are sneak down
> trembling ladders
> in the brain's midcenter, carpetbaggers loaded
> with a lifetime's dreams.
>
> . . .
>
> In the raw mornings I can feel them missing.
>
> . . .
>
> In the night I feel things leaving
> I was sworn to keep.

The brain cannot function normally without a constant influx of sensory perceptions—perceptions that form our view of the world. It is now all-too-common knowledge that strong people in the prime of life can be broken and brainwashed by their jailer's manipulation of their sensory environment. If sensory deprivation can wreak such havoc on younger individuals, then it is fair to ask what sorts of functional decrements affect our sensory organs with age and what effects such decrements might have on our normal mental functional ability. Whitbourne (1985) reviewed this question in some detail, and much of the following discussion is drawn from that source.

Of the five traditional senses, only taste appears not to be affected by any well-characterized intrinsic age-related changes. This observation is consistent with the anatomical evidence, which shows no age-related decrease in the number or distribution of taste buds and receptors on the tongue. Although cross-sectional data show an age-related decline in salt and sweet taste detection, these results were probably confounded by other factors, such as smoking and denture use. In any event, even this possible decrement is far below the taste thresholds found in normal life.

Our sense of touch undergoes mixed changes. Sensitivity to touch on the skin of the hand decreases, even though this region is normally much more sensitive than the rest of the body surface. However, touch sensitivity decreases nowhere else on the body. These observations are consistent with the anatomical evidence, which shows that three out of the five different types of touch receptors undergo little if any age-related changes. Only the Pacinian corpuscles and Meissner's corpuscles seem to display structural and numerical changes with age. The ability to detect pain, an adaptive response of great value in the aged, is so confounded with extraneous cultural and personality factors that it is not possible to draw firm conclusions regarding the aches and pains of old age.

Smell is a chemical sense akin to taste. It has both a practical and an aesthetic role in informing us of the dangers and the pleasures of our environment and can, in some of us, trigger the release of specific memories. The way in which odors are transformed into neural signals by the smell receptors is not understood, except that this transformation must result from the interaction of the olfactory receptor molecule with the molecule responsible for that odor. We do not understand how to classify odors, nor do we agree on how to measure them. Nonetheless, the cross-sectional data appear to support the view that both the ability to detect odors and the ability to identify them experience an age-related decline from age 60 onward (Figure 5.28). There is a gender difference in these abilities, males scoring poorer than females in both categories. The data from 712,000 respondents enrolled in the National Geographic Smell Survey (Corwin, Lowry, and Gilbert 1997) suggest that enviornmental influences, such as factory work, adversely affected both men and women. The effects of age, sex, and exposure to noxious events or agents appear to interact so as to produce a progressive olfactory deficit.

The cross-sectional data of Figure 5.29 indicate that there is an age-related loss in hearing, which is especially pronounced at high frequencies. Superimposed on this loss is a gender difference in which men have poorer hearing at moderate and high frequencies than do women. Some or all of this gender difference may be due to the greater environmental noise that men used to be exposed to in their traditional occupations. Our hearing is known to be vulnerable to environmental insults. Thus we may expect to encounter an increased number of very deaf rock musicians (and perhaps concert goers) of both sexes in the decades to come. The anatomical site of this decreased sensitivity to high-frequency tones (termed presbycusis) lies in the inner ear. At least four different mechanisms (involving alterations in the sound receptors, their neurons, their blood supply, and the basilar membrane) are capable of producing presbycusis. Age-related anatomical changes also occur in the middle ear but these do not appear to result in a hearing decrement.

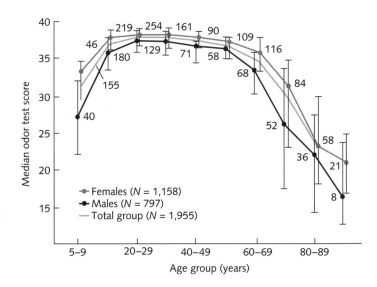

Figure 5.28   Changes in the ability to detect various odors as a function of age and gender. Numbers by data points indicate sample sizes. (From Doty et al. 1984.)

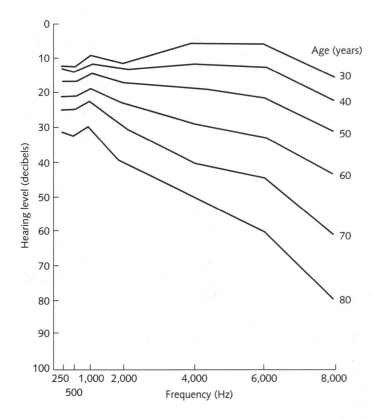

Figure 5.29 Changes in hearing level of various frequencies by age decade in adulthood. (Redrawn by Whitbourne 1985 from data of Lebo and Reddell 1972. © Laryngoscope Company.)

We are visual creatures. Most of us probably dread the loss of vision more than any of our other senses. Our language reflects this bias: When we understand something, for example, how often do we say, "I see"? Our eyesight is a critical feature of adaptation to the environment, for vision and memory combine to let us know how people and things are arranged in space and time. The eye makes vision possible by using the cornea, lens, and iris to focus a controlled amount of light onto the receptor cells in the retina. True age-related changes occur in various parts of the eye, the net effect of which is to reduce our visual acuity and our color discrimination, and to affect our sensitivity to light.

The cornea undergoes several age-dependent changes, the most important of which is its decreased curvature and thus decreased refractive power. These decrements can be a real problem, since the cornea is responsible for most of the refraction and focusing of the light entering our eye. The lens is the other structure involved in refraction. The lens capsule is elastic, and its shape can be altered from a spherical form to a more flattened form by the action of the ciliary muscle. This change in shape allows us to focus the light rays onto the appropriate region of the retina. The lens itself never stops growing, so it becomes thicker and stiffer with age. In fact, the mass of the lens triples from its original value by the age of 70. The greater density and stiffness of the lens make it more difficult for it to change shape. As a result, its refractive power drops considerably with age. By the age of 60, the lens is incapable of accommodating to focus on objects at close distance. So we hold the newspaper farther and farther away from our eyes—until we wear the glasses we so obviously need.

As the lens increases in thickness and density, it also becomes less transparent and thus transmits less light into the eye. This decrease is not uniform across the spectrum; it is aggravated by the increasingly yellowish tinge of the lens to selectively absorb the blue and violet portion of the spectrum. The result is impaired ability to discriminate colors and impaired night vision. This reduced transmission of light by the lens is further aggravated by the decreased ability of the iris to open to its widest, as a result of the atrophy of the iris muscles. The effect of this atrophy is to reduce the maximum size of the iris and hence to decrease the amount of light that can enter the eye.

These changes in our sensory functions appear to be true age-related changes. Most of them we can compensate for to some extent, either by prosthetic devices (glasses, hearing aids, and so on) or by adaptive changes in behavior.

The brain regulates and integrates all the activities of the body. Even small and localized changes in neural structure or function have the potential of bringing about far-reaching changes in the coordinated functioning of the body, should they affect the appropriate regions of the CNS. The deleterious effects on our thought processes that flow out of the localized death of certain cholinergic neurons that are characteristic of senile dementia of the Alzheimer's type (SDAT) are proof of the truth of this statement. These integrative activities of the brain are most easily observed in the neural regulation of endocrine functions and of immune functions. In recent years, it has become clear that the nervous, endocrine, and immune systems are functionally integrated. Rather than viewing them as three separate physiological systems, it now appears to make more sense to view them as three overlapping components of the body's intercellular communication system.

The awareness of the link between the nervous and endocrine systems is of long standing. The hypothalamus–pituitary axis constitutes the principal interface between the two systems (Figure 5.30). Together the two are usually termed the neuroendocrine system; this system is known to control a host of vital body functions. Thermoregulation is a good example. Body temperature is monitored by external thermoreceptors in the skin, as well as by internal thermoreceptors in the hypothalamus. The latter measure the temperature of the blood passing through the region. When a drop in blood temperature is sensed, peripheral autonomic nerves act to constrict the skin capillaries and shunt blood toward the core, to erect fur or feathers to trap a layer of warm air next to the skin (our "goose bumps"), and to induce shivering to generate heat. When the blood temperature exceeds the body's physiological set point, these heat gain mechanisms are inhibited and heat loss mechanisms (the reverse of the heat gain processes, plus evaporative cooling by sweating) are activated. Although the number of sweat glands is not noticeably reduced in the elderly, older people require a much longer time for the onset of sweating under conditions of moderate exercise than do students of college age (Finch and Landfield 1985). This impaired adaptive response of the

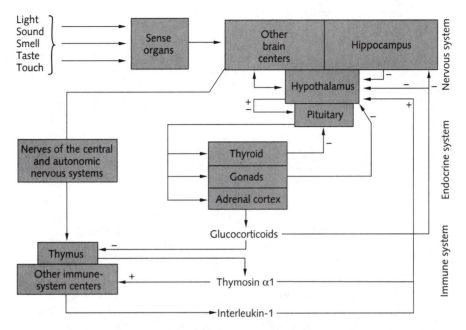

Figure 5.30   A schematic representation of the intercellular communication system. The hypothalamus–pituitary axis defines the neuroendocrine system, a key regulatory system composed of both neural and endocrine components. In a similar manner, the nervous system also overlaps with the immune system. The glucocorticoid pathway illustrates the role of negative feedback (–) on the nervous and endocrine systems. The thymosin $\alpha 1$ pathway illustrates the positive (+) and negative feedback effects of the immune system on the nervous and endocrine systems. Via these communication circuits, external stimuli, interpreted as stress by the brain, result in the pathophysiological effects of glucocorticoids, such as increased incidence of cancer, metabolic disorders, and so on.

heat loss mechanisms results in an increased heat load in the elderly, and the consequent increased morbidity and mortality.

This and other similar observations (Whitbourne 1985) suggest that the basic defect in thermoregulation resides in the delayed response of the peripheral structures (sweat glands, capillaries, and so on) to CNS signals and not in the neuroendocrine control mechanisms themselves. However, Shock (1977, 1985) has made the reverse argument, suggesting that the impaired adaptive response is due to a narrowing of the range within which the neuroendocrine control mechanisms can work effectively. The question as to the site of the defect(s) is still unresolved. In either event, the net effect is that the body's integrative and homeostatic mechanisms are impaired. The aging individual is less able to handle the stresses of daily living and is more likely to succumb to an environmental stress that he/she could easily have adapted to in the past.

The regulatory effects of the nervous system and the immune system on each other have only recently been appreciated and summarized, in Cooper 1984 and Cotman et al. 1987. The following discussion is drawn largely from these sources. The nervous system appears to communicate with the immune system directly via neuronal connections to the immune-related structures, such as the bone marrow and the thymus, and indirectly via the endocrine and neuroendocrine system. The most important aspect of biological communication, feedback regulation, has been demonstrated to occur among these several systems. A good example of feedback regulation is shown in Figure 5.30, which depicts the interactions between glucocorticoids (a product of the adrenal cortex) and thymosin $\alpha 1$ (a peptide hormone secreted by the thymus gland). Glucocorticoid production is under the proximate control of the hypothalamus–pituitary axis, which itself is under negative feedback control by the hippocampus (a part of the limbic system). The glucocorticoids have varied effects on other parts of the body, not the least of which is suppression of particular immune functions, especially after prolonged exposure to this secretion of the adrenal gland. The many observations that increased or prolonged stress increases the organism's susceptibility to certain diseases, such as cancer, may have their physiological basis in this immunosuppressive activity. The high glucocorticoid levels associated with prolonged stress also kill many of the regulatory neurons in the hippocampus, thereby reducing the effectiveness of the CNS control of glucocorticoid levels. Aging rats show a similar loss of neurons, and such impaired regulatory mechanisms may underlie the observed higher incidence of cancers in the elderly.

The thymic hormone thymosin $\alpha 1$ stimulates the immune system. This hormone is found in the hypothalamus, but with a circadian rhythm inverse to that of glucocorticoids. It is known to stimulate glucocorticoid production, probably by its stimulation of hypothalamic releasing factors, and is itself probably inhibited by glucocorticoids. Thymosin $\alpha 1$ completes the feedback cycle and ties all three systems into one. Furthermore, thymosin is known to stimulate the production of a substance called interleukin-1 by the macrophages (white blood cells). This substance is identical to the molecule used by the hypothalamus to regulate body temperature. Macrophages produce and secrete this substance only when actively engaged in fighting an infection. This signal induces the hypothalamus to increase the body temperature. The resulting fever decreases the viability of invading bacteria and hence contributes to our recovery.

The data are still being gathered, but it seems possible that some of the deleterious degenerative diseases and pathologies that characteristically affect the elderly have their origin in an upset of a particular aspect of this intercellular commication system.

Age-Related Pathologies

Alzheimer's disease   Individual neurons also exhibit other sorts of age-related changes, the etiology and significance of which are still being deciphered. Neurons normally contain very slender processes, known as neurofilaments. These neurofilaments are intimately involved with the internal transport of neurotransmitter molecules from their site of synthesis in the cell body to their site of usage at the synapse. Some older people display changes in these processes such that the slender filaments become transformed into thickened and twisted black fibrils of much greater prominence within the cell; these are termed neurofibrillary tangles. In intellectually normal old subjects, clusters of such affected neurons may be found at specific sites (the anterior temporal lobe, for example), although they may be very rare in other brain regions (such as the neocortex). Persons suffering from senile dementia may have a greater number of such neurofibrillary tangles in the anterior temporal lobe than do normal individuals. This phenomenon has been studied extensively in the case of Alzheimer's disease.

Alzheimer's disease (AD), also known as senile dementia of the Alzheimer's type (SDAT), is a degenerative disorder of the CNS that results in a progressive loss of memory and other intellectual functions of sufficient severity to interfere significantly with normal activities of daily living and social relationships. It is differentiated from benign age-associated episodes of forgetfulness by its inevitable, progressive, and irreversible declines in memory, time and space orientation, performance of routine tasks, language and communication skills, abstract thinking, learning ability, and, finally, personality changes and impairment of judgment (Katchaturian and Radebaugh 1996a).

Age, genetics, culture, and socioeconomic status are known risk factors for AD. This disease is a major health problem and promises to become worse in the future. The overall incidence of the disease is about 600 per 100,000 population or, to put it more realistically, about 5 to 10 percent of the people over the age of 65 (Evans 1996). The prevalence of AD increases with age, however, the percentage affected doubling for every decade that people live beyond the age of 65. Thus a study in East Boston determined a prevalence of 0.6 percent for people 65 to 69 years old, 1.0 percent for persons 70 to 74 years old, 2.0 percent for persons 75 to 79 years old, 3.3 percent for persons 80 to 84 years old, and 8.4 percent for persons 85 years of age and older (Evans 1996). This strong association of age with AD suggests two possibilities: first, that there might be an intimate coupling of the disease with an underlying process or processes of aging, possibly involving the age-related increase of damage processes coupled with the age-related decreasing efficiency of repair mechanisms (Martin et al. 1995); and/or second, that the disease might be dependent on some slow time-dependent processes that take a long time to reach a critical threshold. In the latter case, of course, AD might not fit the strict definition of an age-related change. Recall our description of polycystic kidney disease in Chapter 3 (p. 75), a time-dependent disease in which the long-term hyperplasia has no ill effects until a certain threshold is reached after about 50 years of slow overgrowth. Should AD actually be a similar sort of time-dependent process, then this would imply that individuals fated to develop AD should have characteristic abnormalities in their brains at an early, presymptomatic age.

Estimates suggest that more than 100,000 Americans die of AD every year. In 1980, approximately 2.9 million persons had the disease; in 1996, about 4 million persons were believed to have the disease; and it is projected that by 2050, approximately 10 million persons will be afflicted with AD. However, most of the increase in AD prevalence is projected to occur in the over-85 age group. The prevalence in the younger age groups will likely either stay constant or increase only moderately (Evans 1996). Clearly, the increase in our life spans and the consequent changing age structure of the population do not come without a price.

A natural history of AD indicates that the average patient first exhibits symptoms at about 72 years of age, is diagnosed at about 75, is institutionalized at about 77, and dies at about 81. The disease appears to progress faster in males (84 months) compared to females (108 months); the difference is most notable in the last, or institutional, phase (25 versus 52 months); however, this sex difference is not seen in all studies (Jost and Grossberg 1995).

Autopsies have shown that the brains of people who die with AD are abnormal (Gearing et al. 1995). At a gross level, there is an atrophy of the neocortex and often of the hippocampus and amygdala as well—all key sites involved in thinking and memory. In addition, the ventricular system is often enlarged, contributing to the atrophy. Finally, melanin-pigmented neurons are often much paler than normal. At a microscopic level, there are three more or less characteristic neuropathologies: neuritic plaques, neurofibrillary tangles, and amyloid angiopathy (Mirra and Markesbery 1996).

Neural, or senile, plaques are found in both intellectually normal individuals and people affected by the various dementias. Two major subtypes of these plaques are recognized: neuritic and diffuse. The neuritic plaques, which are the ones strongly associated with AD, are spherical structures about 80 μm in diameter, with thickened neuronal processes (or neurites) surrounding a central fibrillar core of an abnormal protein called amyloid (which we will discuss shortly). In addition, these neuritic plaques contain dense bodies thought to be the remains of lysosomes, mitochondria, and paired helical filaments. The diffuse plaques, on the other hand, lack the abnormal neurites, appear more amorphous, and contain little if any fibrillar amyloid (they do contain amyloid, but in a diffuse form). Diffuse plaques are often found in brains of cognitively normal individuals, as well as in brains of AD individuals. They may represent an early stage in the development of neuritic plaques; Selkoe (1997) has suggested that they represent very early lesions that may or may not progress to mature, symptom-producing lesions, depending on many factors, including the longevity of the host.

In individuals who suffer from AD, the number of neurofibrillary tangles (NFTs) in the affected brain areas is approximately six times greater than the number present in the most severely affected intellectually normal person. NFTs are found mostly in the hippocampus and the cerebral cortex; they have not been found in the cerebellum or the spinal cord. The tangle itself is intracellular and is composed mostly of paired helical filaments (PHFs), which, as their name suggests, are protein filaments helically twisted about each other in pairs. These PHF proteins are abnormally phosphorylated forms of the tau protein (which is usually associated with microtubules) and are complexed with another protein, ubiquitin, which is normally used by the cell to label proteins destined for degradation (Mori, Kendo, and Ihara 1987). Despite the tag, the PHFs are resistant to degradation in these patients. Note that although NFTs invariably are found in AD patients, they can be found at a lower density in cognitively normal individuals, as well as in the brains of patients suffering from other neurological disorders.

We can see these plaques and tangles. They must be important. But perhaps what we cannot see is even more important. We cannot see the loss of synapses and the death of neurons. The breaking of neuronal circuits and the isolation of important brain centers from their normal partners cannot be directly seen, although we can observe clearly the results of these losses in the transformed personality and diminished behaviors of our loved ones.

The third neuropathological feature of AD is amyloid angiopathy, or the deposition of amyloid protein within the walls of the blood vessels of the meninges and cortex. The severity of the deposition varies widely, and the same feature is sometimes found in the brains of older normal individuals.

What is the amyloid protein and what role does it play in the genesis of AD? Furthermore, what role do our genes play in the genesis of this disease? The answers to these two questions are intertwined. There are both inherited and noninherited forms of AD. Families have been identified in which the incidence is very high, affecting members of four or five generations (Wurtman 1985). The inheritance pattern is consistent with the idea that the defective aging is transmitted as an autosomal dominant. Thus individuals need inherit only one copy of the aberrant gene to develop full-blown AD. Estimates are that between 40 and 75 percent of AD patients suffer from some sort of a genetically transmitted form of this disease. The remainder of the affected individuals display a milder, nonfamilial form that tends to become apparent later in life; its etiology is not yet clear.

For reasons of convenience and accessibility, most of the research attention has focused on the inherited forms of AD, albeit with the understanding that the two forms of the disease may share some or even many common mechanisms. Four genetic alterations underlying the familial AD are now known; they are listed in Table 5.9. Note that all four mutations result in the increased production of amyloid protein or its variants. We will return to the genetics in a moment, but first let's describe the amyloid protein itself.

"Amyloid" is a generic term that describes proteins with a beta-pleated sheet structure. The amyloid proteins involved in AD are derived mostly from the *APP* (amyloid precursor protein) gene located on chromosome 21. The *APP* gene is a large gene (approximately 400 kilobases of DNA) that is alternatively spliced to yield several transcripts that code for a family of amyloid (Aβ) proteins ranging in size from 695 to 779 amino acids (Sandbrink et al. 1996). The *APP* gene is

Table 5.9 **Genetic Factors That Predispose to Alzheimer's Disease**

Chromosome	Gene defect	Age of onset	Aβ phenotype
21	*APP* mutations	50s	Increased production of total Aβ peptides or of Aβ1-42/43 peptides
14	*Presenilin 1* mutations	40s and 50s	Increased production of Aβ1-42/43 peptides
1	*Presenilin 2* mutations	50s	Increased production of Aβ1-42/43 peptides
19	*ApoE4* polymorphism	60s and older	Increased density of Aβ plaques and vascular deposits

Source: From Selkoe 1997.

expressed ubiquitously in mammals, by both neural and nonneural cells. It is highly conserved in vertebrates, and homologous proteins have been identified in the fruit fly *Drosophila* and the nematode *Caenorhabditis elegans.* In all these cases, the APP protein is a transmembrane protein apparently involved in cell–cell signaling processes. Significant amounts of newly synthesized APP protein appear at the cell surface; some of these molecules may be cleaved at particular positions by (unknown) proteases. It is not the APP protein itself that seems to cause AD but rather certain of these cleaved fragments. The cleavage normally yields a 40-amino-acid peptide (Aβ1-40); this fragment appears to play no role in the pathogenesis of AD. However, when cleaved so as to yield a 42- or 43-amino-acid peptide (Aβ1-42/43), these slightly larger fragments appear to nucleate rapidly into amyloid fibrils and apparently give rise to the structural abnormalities described above.

All four known genetic mutations (see Table 5.9) involved in familial AD cause an increase in the production of Aβ1-42/43 peptides and/or an increase in the density of Aβ plaques. Work done with transgenic mice containing a mutant *APP* gene leads to the same conclusion (Hsiao et al. 1996). Together, these results strongly indicate that the accumulation of Aβ-42/43 in the brain is an early and invariant event in the development of AD pathology (Selkoe 1997), yet the long time periods before the appearance of symptoms suggest that these pathogenic peptides accumulate very slowly. The *APP* gene is located on chromosome 21, the same chromosome that is involved in Down syndrome (Tanzi et al. 1987 and others). All individuals afflicted with Down syndrome develop symptoms indistinguishable from those of AD by age 50, and they show diffuse plaques as early as age 12. These observations were some of the earliest evidence suggesting an important role for the *APP* gene in the etiology of AD.

The *presenilin* genes (see Table 5.9) are located on chromosomes 1 and 19. They code for two homologous transmembrane proteins that are also involved in cell–cell signaling. Dewji and Singer (1996) have suggested that PS1 and PS2 (presenilin 1 and 2) normally interact directly with the APP protein in an evolutionarily conserved intercellular signaling mechanism. Mutations in either the *PS1* or the *PS2* gene apparently affect the manner in which cells handle the APP protein, and these mutations are believed to be responsible for the increased production of the pathogenic Aβ-42/43 fragments via the cell's ordinary protein-processing mechanisms.

Finally, the *ApoE4* gene plays a role in that individuals homozygous for that particular *ApoE* allele are significantly more likely to develop AD than are individuals with the *ApoE3* or *ApoE2* alleles. As described in more detail in Chapter 6 (see page 266), this situation might arise because the *ApoE4* allele is not capable of binding to the tau microtubule protein, thus allowing the unbound tau protein to be hyperphosphophorylated abnormally and thus give rise to the NFTs characteristic of AD. The *ApoE3* and *ApoE2* alleles are capable of binding to tau, so the NFT formation is delayed or suppressed (Schacter et al. 1994; Kamboh 1995). In addition, the *ApoE4* allele has a lower level of antioxidant activity, and this decreased protective effect probably also plays a role in the pathogenesis of AD (Miyata and Smith 1996).

These various genetic processes allow a local accumulation of the self-aggregating Aβ1-42/43 peptide. As it accumulates in its insoluble (plaque) form, this protein injures nearby neurons, either directly via neurotoxicity or indirectly via inflammatory reactions on the microglial cells. The mechanisms that produce this damage are becoming clear. We now know that the Aβ1-42/43 peptide can induce oxidative damage by binding specifically to a particular receptor protein that has a limited expression within the adult CNS (Yan et al. 1996). This specifically expressed receptor may well convey site specificity to an otherwise ubiquitous protein.

This receptor protein normally binds to molecules mediating neurite outgrowth, but it can also bind to the Aβ1-42/43 peptide. The Aβ1-42/43 peptide can by itself generate reactive oxygen intermediates (which cause oxidative damage; see Chapter 9); when bound to the receptor, however, it triggers within the cell an additional and sustained production of oxidants, resulting in oxidative stress and neuronal toxicity (Yan et al. 1996). The receptor–Aβ1-42/43 combination also activates the microglial cells, which react by secreting cytotoxic cytokines and by mounting other aspects of an inflammatory response (Yan et al. 1996). In either case, the resulting oxidative damage severely damages the neurons and decreases their ability to resist subsequent stresses. This decreased oxidative resistance is likely exacerbated by the low levels of mitochondrial activity (and therefore low energy levels) that are characteristic of AD patients (Davis et al. 1997); in fact, the low energy levels may be due to mitochondrial damage induced by the oxidative stress. Other metabolic changes likely include altered tau phosphorylation and PHF formation in neuritic plaques and NFTs.

The clinically important consequence of this train of events is eventual synaptic loss and/or neurotransmitter defects, both resulting in an altered neural circuitry and function (Selkoe 1997). However, there is no strict relationship between the level of damage and the extent of the observed behavioral modifications. Education, culture, and socioeconomic status allow for significant modulation of the outcome. The "Nun Study" (Snowdon 1997) combines a long-term, in-depth longitudinal study of the behavior and cognitive abilities of a large number of nuns with detailed autopsy data at death. The unselfishness of the nuns in contributing themselves (literally) to postmortem study has allowed the very interesting finding that high levels of education, verbal ability, and/or continuing mental activity allows at least some individuals to function at normal behavioral and cognitive levels, despite the ravages that AD unleashes on their brains. If mental activity stimulates complex neural circuits, the resulting redundancies may allow for multiple additional pathways by which information can get in and out. Using your mind may keep you from losing it.

This pathology most likely has a complex developmental history—more complex than was first thought when the amyloid gene (*APP*) was first discovered on chromosome 21 (Tanzi et al. 1987; Glenner 1988). Unraveling this etiology promises to be of prime importance in the near future, both for the insight it will give us into normal brain function and for the clinical interventions it will hopefully yield so that we may better alleviate or cure the multitudes otherwise doomed to the slow death of their memory and their personality.

Other disorders   The molecular genetics of the mind is not limited to the study of SDAT. New insights are being obtained into non-age-related illnesses such as manic–depressive psychosis (bipolar disorder) or schizophrenia. Genetic studies have suggested that bipolar disorder is due to any one of three different genes causing a predisposition to the psychosis (Robertson 1987). Three different populations yielded three different inheritance patterns, and hence three different locations, of the gene involved, thus indicating again the genetic heterogeneity of the human species. The gene on chromosome 11 might involve an enzyme responsible for the synthesis of the catecholamines, an important class of neurotransmitters. Schizophrenia has long been suspected of having a familial genetic basis. Recent reports suggest that this illness also is quite heterogeneous; in different populations the disease apparently involves different chromosomes.

The important point for us to gather from these early reports is that one day a more complete understanding of the molecular biology of the mind, and of how different biochemical processes, whether age-related or not, can affect our mental functioning, will be possible.

Summary

The human brain is the most complicated structure that we have yet encountered. Its functioning is uniquely related to our sense of self. Consequently, much research on aging over the years has concentrated on the characterization of neural structure and function and on how normal age-related changes affect our ability to function. The need to understand and alleviate certain age-related pathologies, such as Alzheimer's disease, has further heightened interest in neural aging processes.

The age-related loss in overall brain weight and size is likely due to the loss of individual neurons, particularly the associative neurons. Most of this loss occurs after about age 60. It is not clear whether this loss has any functional significance or whether it should be regarded more along the lines of sculpting away unneeded or unused material. Dendritic decreases, on the other hand, may well represent functional changes in neural circuits at the synaptic level. Other functional alterations probably involve neurotransmitter synthesis and cerebral energy metabolism. These sorts of changes may underlie the observed changes in our mental abilities with age. Note that the actual magnitude of the age-related changes in mental functions is significantly less than that portrayed by various stereotypes.

One of the more important roles of the brain is its integration of the body's activities via the neuro-endocrine-immune system. Some of the deleterious degenerative diseases and pathologies that characteristically affect the elderly may have their origin in the upset of a particular aspect of this intercellular communication system.

One of the more well-known age-related pathologies is Alzheimer's disease. AD is characterized morphologically by a very localized and much higher than normal level of abnormal structures such as neurofibrillary tangles and senile plaques. AD is frequently accompanied by the progressive loss of memory and other intellectual functions. The molecular basis of the pathology is being characterized and presently appears to involve, in part at least, an inherited defect in protein degradation.

The brain cannot function normally without sensory input. All of our senses except taste undergo intrinsic age-related changes that alter our perceptions of reality. Thus, to maintain our functional abilities, we must adopt prosthetic devices and/or adaptive changes in our behavior.

Changes in the Immune System

Our immune system saves us from certain death by infection. The various responses of this system destroy and eliminate invading organisms and any toxic molecules produced by them. The destructive nature of these responses makes it imperative that the system respond only to cells and molecules that are foreign to the host and not to those of the host itself. This ability to distinguish between self and nonself is a fundamental feature of the immune system. The immune system has mechanisms by which it first recognizes a large number of diverse and unrelated stimuli, then sorts them into self or nonself categories, and finally translates the detection of the latter group into an "on" signal for the appropriate type of immune response. The complexity of the system, and the abstractness of the foreign stimuli, are suggested by the similarity of the words used to describe the operations of both the nervous and the immune systems—for example, "learning," "short-term" and "long-term memory," "recall," and so forth. One reason for the delayed appreciation of the immune system mechanisms is that they are highly dependent on subtle biochemical signals rather than on more obvious morphological structures.

Normal Structure and Function

The bone marrow and thymus are the principal structures of the immune system and serve as the source of precursor cells. The spleen and lymph nodes are the secondary structures and serve as the sites at which immunity is initiated. Figure 5.31 shows the relationships among these several structures. The cells of the immune system consist mostly of B and T lymphocytes. These come in many specific subtypes, all of which have cell surface receptors that can respond to a limited group of structurally similar antigens. The antigen is the nonself stimulus molecule that triggers the highly specific immune response.

The B lymphocytes are responsible for the so-called humoral immunity, which they confer on the body by producing and secreting specific antibody molecules into the blood and lymph circulation. The immunoglobulin molecules then bind specifically to the antigen (such as a bacterium or toxin) that induced their formation and thereby inactivate that antigen (Figure 5.32). The T lymphocytes are responsible for the cell-mediated immune responses. This is a heterogeneous set of responses. One of these responses involves stimulation of the growth and differentiation of B lymphocytes (and thus regulates the humoral antibody response). Another response involves production of a T cell subpopulation that can directly recognize and destroy foreign, or nonself, cells (Figure 5.33). This recognition process is very important in graft and transplant rejection.

Age-Related Changes

The most obvious morphological change in the immune system is the age-related involution, or shrinkage, of the thymus, which becomes obvious at the

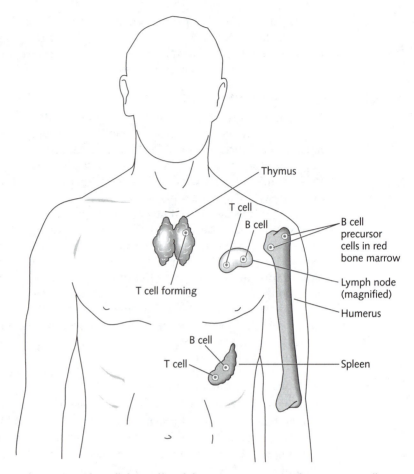

Figure 5.31   The cellular traffic of the immune system. The terms "T cell" and "B cell" refer to whether the particular lymphocyte originated in the thymus or in the bone marrow, respectively. (After Spence 1988.)

time of sexual maturity (Figure 5.34). This reduction in size is due primarily to the atrophy of the cortex, which is known to be responsible for the production of the various thymic hormones required for the maintenance of immune functions (see Figure 5.30). The resulting decrease in the levels of thymic hormones (Figure 5.35) is paralleled by the decrease in the number of component T lymphocytes (Figure 5.36). The relatively large number of immature T lymphocytes found within the involuted thymus suggests that the decrease in competent cells reflects the decreased capacity of the thymus gland to promote differentiation of the many immature lymphocytes contained within it. It is clear that immune senescene results in a selective decrease of some secretory factors, and that it is the lowered level of such factors which might give rise to alterations in the composition of immune cell populations, and hence in immune function (Table 5.10).

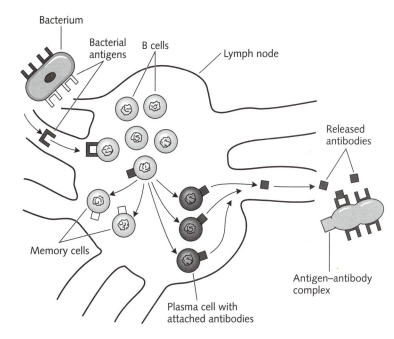

Figure 5.32 A humoral immune response. B cells stimulated by a foreign antigen develop into plasma cells, which produce antibodies against the specific antigen. Some stimulated B cells remain in the lymph nodes and serve as memory cells. (After Spence 1988.)

Oddly, the total number of circulating lymphocytes does not change significantly, despite the involution of the thymus. However, the proportions of the different subpopulations of T lymphocytes do change with age. These alterations may be responsible for the observed age-dependent decrease in natural antibody

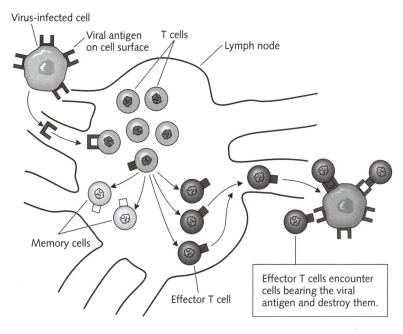

Figure 5.33 A cell-mediated immune response. T cells stimulated by a foreign antigen form effector T cells, which attack and destroy the cells bearing the foreign antigens. Some stimulated T cells remain in the lymph nodes and serve as memory cells. (After Spence 1988.)

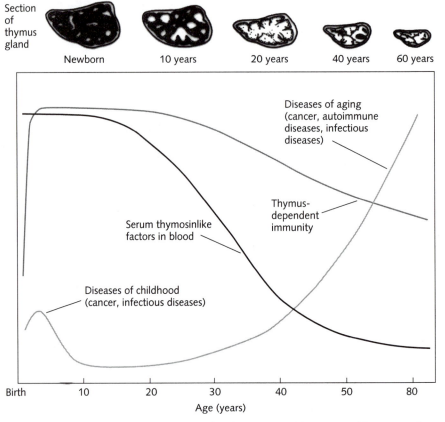

Figure 5.34 The relationship of thymus development and function to life span and the incidence of disease. (From Goldstein et al. 1979. © Raven Press.)

titers and the concomitant increase in autoantibody titers (Figure 5.37). The cell-mediated immunological reactions responsible for the rejection of foreign skin grafts and tissues also depend on T lymphocytes and show an age-related

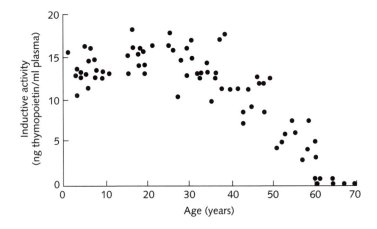

Figure 5.35 Age-related changes in thymic hormone activity in the plasma. (From Lewis et al. 1978.)

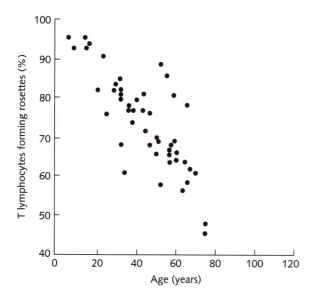

Figure 5.36 The percentage of human T lymphocytes from different age groups that form rosettes in sheep erythrocytes. The ability to form rosettes in this test is an indication of the cell's full maturity. (After Singh and Singh 1979.)

Table 5.10 **Immunologic Senescence**

Secretory factors:
1. Thymus
    Thymosin α-1   →   Decline in:
    Thymulin   Secretory factors
    Thymopoietin
    Thymic humoral factor
2. Stem Cell Differentiation
Influenced by:
    Bone marrow
      Thymosin   →   Decline in:
        Colony-stimulating factor   Helper T cell proportion
        Interleukin-3   Alloantigen-specific T_K
                                Natural killer cell number
                               Increase in:
                                T_S cell proportion
                                B cell/T cell ratio
                               Shift in:
                                B cell characteristics
                                Antibody production
3. Consequences of 1 and 2   →   Increase in:
                               Tissue graft tolerance
                               Cancer incidence
                               Autoimmune disease
                               Infectious disease

Source: From Sternberg 1994.

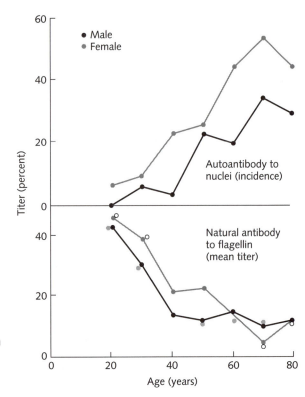

Figure 5.37 The age-related decrease in natural anti-*Salmonella* flagellin titer and the age-related increase in the incidence of antinuclear factor in humans of both sexes. Note that this increase in autoantibody titer is not necessarily correlated with the presence of clinical symptoms. (From Rowley, Buchanan, and Mackay 1968. © The Lancet, Ltd.)

decrease in their ability to perform these functions. For example, in the aftermath of a flu epidemic, the nonimmunized young and old individuals were examined to determine the levels of their immune response to this antigenic stimulus. Among the young individuals, 90 percent had antibodies against all three flu strains in their nasal fluids; only 63 percent of the older individuals attained the same level of protection. Furthermore, in a population of individuals examined for their ability to respond to a specific antibody (the yeast *Candida*), a disproportionate number of individuals who were unable to respond ("anergic" individuals) were greater than 65 years old. In addition, three times as many women as men displayed this defective response. After surgery, the infection and mortality rates for anergic individuals are four- and fivefold higher, respectively, than the corresponding rates for age-matched individuals with a normal immune response (Phair 1983; Hausman and Weksler 1985).

Perhaps not all of these defects result from intrinsic changes in the immune system. For example, the decreased proliferation of the B lymphocytes following an antigenic challenge might be at least partly due to a decreased level of mitotic stimulators arising from outside the immune system. At present, the mechanisms that initiate the involution of the thymus are not known. The fact that involution and atrophy are thought by some investigators to begin during the first year of life suggests that involution may be a hormone-independent intrinsic aging process. This is admittedly a minority view. In any event, it has been shown that the age-dependent drop in the immune competence of aged mice can be partly reversed by treatment with thymic hormones (Table 5.11). Clinical trials in humans are promising and suggest that the therapeutic use of thymosin enhances the body's ability to ameliorate immune defects. Nonetheless, although it seems plausible that age-related declines in immune function might contribute to the vulnerability of the elderly to disease and thus increase the risk of mortality, it must be admitted that much of the evidence to date is indirect or correlative.

Thus there is abundant evidence that the functional ability of the human immune system changes with age. The underlying cause(s) of this immunosenescence are not known, although the involution of the thymus may have all the characteristics of a true age-related change. The thymus, of course, occupies a key position in the continued functioning of the immune system. However, the very complexity of the immune system, coupled with its interactions with the nervous and the endocrine systems, suggest that not all aspects of immune senescence will be able to be traced back to this one root cause. In any event, it should be clear that intrinsic age-related changes in the neural, immunological, and/or endocrine components of the body's communication system will likely have profound effects on many of their target organs.

Summary

The involution of the thymus apparently brings about a decreased capacity of the gland to promote the full differentiation of lymphocytes, possibly because of its effects on the production of thymic hormones. These events are thought to be related to the age-related decreased ability of the immune system to detect foreign molecules, as well as to the increased frequency of autoimmune responses.

Changes in the Reproductive System

The reproductive systems of both sexes show age-dependent decrements in function. These changes are most obvious in the female, where they lead to a loss of fertility during midlife. These age-related changes as studied in the female rodent model by Finch and his colleagues have led to the development of the neuroendocrine model of aging (see Chapter 12). In males, reproductive aging is less dramatic and leads to a decrease in fecundity rather than an absolute loss of fertility.

Table 5.11   **Effect of Thymopoietin Administration on the Ability of Old Mice to Respond to a Specific Antigen**

Age of mice	Thymopoietin treated	No. of competent cells/spleen
2 mos.	No	5916 ± 2.3
24 mos.	No	385 ± 79
24 mos.	Yes	977 ± 102

Source: From Hausman and Weksler, 1985.

We will review reproductive aging primarily from the viewpoint of neuroendocrine control.

The reproductive system is strikingly different from other body systems with respect to the mechanisms controlling its development, its acquisition of function, and its loss of function. Furthermore, as discussed in Chapter 4, there appears to be a deep relationship between species-specific reproductive strategies and species-specific longevities. For the human female, this strategy means that she spends substantial portions of her total life span (about 45 percent) in either a prereproductive or a postreproductive state. Expression of the strategy depends on the proper functioning of the genetic and neuroendocrine mechanisms that control the reproductive organs. This will thus provide us with a focus with which to examine reproductive aging.

The primitive gonad *in utero* differs from other body tissues in that it contains the primordia for both ovary and testis and could potentially develop either male or female structures. The developmental decision to choose one alternative or the other is made at about the eighth week of gestation and is the result of an interplay between genetic and hormonal factors. Abnormal sexual development often results from breakdowns in these control processes.

In mammals, birth is followed by a period of gonadal quiescence until later activation of the gonads by pituitary gonadotropins. The final maturation of the reproductive system begins upon such activation. This period of growth and maturation is known as adolescence. Puberty defines the maturational state when reproduction is first possible, even if it is not feasible. The neural mechanisms that cause this activation are not yet clearly defined. One theory suggests that a hypothalamic mechanism holds gonadotropin mechanisms in check until puberty. Another theory suggests that small amounts of gonadal steroids inhibit hypothalamic production of the gonadotropins that activate the system and that puberty comes about as a result of the brain's decreased sensitivity to this inhibition. A third theory suggests that puberty is initiated by the removal of a local inhibitory effect on gonadal activity. Despite the absence of a definitive theory for the onset of puberty, once it is initiated, the neuroendocrine control of reproductive function is quite definitive, particularly in the female.

Female Reproductive Aging

Normal structure and function   Figure 5.38 shows the anatomical structure of the normal human female reproductive system. The two ovaries store and alternatively release a mature ovum each month into the uterine tubes for fertilization and transport to the uterus. A woman ovulates perhaps 500 or fewer eggs in her lifetime; this number represents only a tiny portion of the tremendous number of eggs that she was born with or that she had at the onset of puberty (Table 5.12). This atresia ("wastage") is a normal component of follicle development and probably represents a selection mechanism by which only the fastest-growing oocyte is chosen for ovulation. Likely the follicular store is exhausted or nearly so at the time of menopause. Women suffering from precocious menopause often have ovaries devoid of follicles. The functional life of the human ovary appears to be proportional to its follicular store and is not simply a matter of chronological age (Wise 1986).

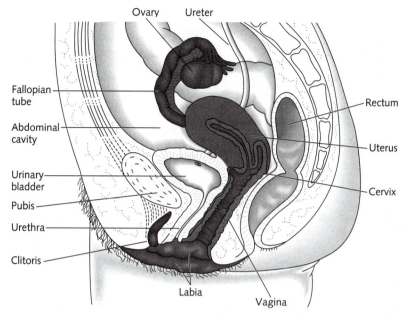

Ovary   Ureter

Fallopian tube

Abdominal cavity

Urinary bladder

Pubis

Urethra

Clitoris

Rectum

Uterus

Cervix

Labia

Vagina

Figure 5.38 A sagittal section showing the normal human female reproductive system.

Figure 5.39 shows the normal sequence of events during the menstrual cycle. The hypothalamus is the primary regulator of the reproductive system. The hypothalamus contains neurons that synthesize and secrete from their axon endings various protein hormones instead of neurotransmitters. These hormones, usually called gonadotropin-releasing hormones, travel via a special blood capillary network to the anterior pituitary immediately below where they stimulate

Table 5.12	The Effect of Age on the Number of Oocytes in the Ovary of the Human Female
Age	*Estimated number of oocytes*
4-month-old fetus	3,500,000
At birth	733,000
4–10 years	500,000
11–17 years	390,000
18–24 years	162,000
25–31 years	62,000
32–38 years	80,000
39–45 years	11,000

Source: After Talbert 1977.

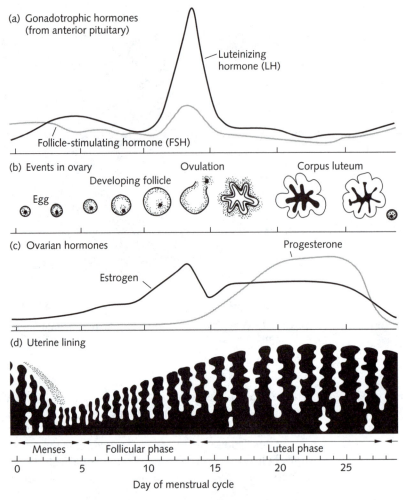

Figure 5.39 A diagram of the events that take place during the normal menstrual cycle. See text for discussion.

the pituitary cells to secrete the two primary gonadotropin-releasing hormones: follicle-stimulating hormone (FSH) and luteinizing hormone (LH). These two hormones are crucially involved in the regulation of ovulation. FSH stimulates the development of a number (10 to 20) of follicles and thereby brings about an elevation in the blood level of estradiol. Only one follicle grows fast enough and is mature enough to be able to respond to the signal next provided by LH. Blood levels of LH increase significantly just before ovulation. LH stimulates the rupture of the follicle and the extrusion of the "ripe" ovum from it. This process constitutes ovulation. The ruptured follicle continues to grow and is transformed into a corpus luteum, which actively produces progesterone, as well as estradiol. This action of LH and FSH on the ovaries is blocked by prolactin, a hormone that is usually produced at high levels only when the mother is nursing. Thus this inhibition underlies the contraceptive effects of nursing.

As the levels of the two ovarian hormones, estradiol and progesterone, increase, they act on the hypothalamus to inhibit the production of the gonadotropin-releasing hormones. The decrease in these factors brings about the curtailment of LH and FSH production by the pituitary. As a result of this drop in levels of gonadotropin-releasing hormones, the production of the ovarian hormones drops. If fertilization has occurred, implantation of the fertilized egg in the endometrium stimulates the production of progesterone independent of the hypothalamic–pituitary control axis, thereby maintaining the pregnant state. In the absence of fertilization and implantation, the production of progesterone ceases. Without hormonal support, the endometrium can no longer sustain itself, and a large portion of it is sloughed off in the menstrual fluid. Finally, as a result of the now low level of ovarian hormones, the level of the pituitary gonadotropin-releasing hormones begins to rise again, and the cycle begins anew.

The basic logic underlying this control mechanism is negative feedback: An excess of a substance acts to shut down its own production. This is the same logic as is found in the thermostat that regulates operation of the furnace in your home. The apparent complexity of reproductive control arises mostly from the fact that it comprises several interacting and cascading negative feedback cycles. However, there are still some important questions regarding the detailed operation of the cycle that remain unanswered.

Age-related changes   A discussion of sexual behaviors would involve us in many areas beyond the scope of this book, and so we must be specific. We will discuss the nature of age-related changes and how they affect the reproductive and/or the sexual functions in women.

The cessation of the menstrual cycle is the major age-related change in this system. Follicular deficiency is the most striking feature of the human ovary after menopause. The ovary is not completely afollicular, for at age 50 it still contains a few hundred or a few thousand follicles. The end of reproductive life is not due to the absolute absence of ova, but to a failure elsewhere in the system. In humans, this primary event appears to involve the failure to produce ovarian hormones. Clearly the depletion of follicles does result in a decreased level of ovarian estradiol secretion. This decrease in estradiol, in turn, might well account for the higher levels of FSH and LH seen in middle-aged premenopausal women. Even after menopause, normal levels of FSH and LH can be induced by exogenous estradiol (Finch and Gosden 1986).

The consequences of ovarian estradiol decline are widespread, since many other tissues depend on this hormone for their normal maintenance. The affected tissues include not only components of the reproductive system itself (uterus, vagina) and components of secondary sexual characteristics (breasts, external genitalia), but also nonreproductive organs such as skin, skeleton, and cardiovascular system. Tissue changes probably arise as a result of the cessation of various hormone-induced gene activities in these several tissues. The possibility that concomitant neural changes are taking place, particularly in the hypothalamus, and that these neural changes also act to bring about menarche (the onset of menstruation at puberty) must also be considered.

This hypothesis is supported by studies of hot flashes in women. Hot flashes occur in the vast majority (about 85 percent) of women at menopause. These are episodes of brief (average 2.7 minutes) increases in skin temperature (by an average of 7.5°F) accompanied by increases in pulse rate (by 9 to 20 beats per minute) and blood flow (Rebar and Spitzer 1987). Hot flashes are associated with a pulsatile release of LH, and they usually can be effectively abolished by estrogen therapy. The neurons of the hypothalamus that regulate the release of LH lie close to the neurons that are involved in thermoregulation. This juxtaposition suggests that some sort of neural change may have taken place in these neurons such that high levels of LH now stimulate the thermoregulatory neurons.

Since the proper functioning of the reproductive system depends on correct multiple feedbacks, a change in either the gonadal or the neural components will rapidly affect other parts of the system and result in a cascading deterioration of reproductive abilities (Wise 1986). Studies on the female mouse have elucidated the nature of hypothalamic involvement in reproductive aging in the female rodent (see Chapter 12). Mice and humans are known to differ in enough significant parameters that the same explanation is unlikely to apply in detail to both.

Humans use the reproductive system not only for procreation and childbearing but also for sexual pleasure and the expression of love and affection. It has been demonstrated not only that elderly persons have sexual needs and can enjoy sexual relations (Whitbourne 1985), but also that the enjoyment of sexual relations is a positive indicator of longevity (see Figure 6.6). The age-related physical changes that we have described affect the body's functioning. It is to be expected that these diverse changes would also affect sexual physiology. Masters and Johnson (1966) described these changes in the human female (Table 5.13) and male (see Table 5.15). There is no physiological reason for women to view themselves as asexual after menopause, and there appear to be important psychological reasons for individuals to continue appropriate sexual interest and activity. Whitbourne (1985) summarizes the literature on this topic.

Male Reproductive Aging

Normal structure and function   Figure 5.40 shows the anatomical structure of the normal human male reproductive system. Sperm are produced in the testes. Each testis is subdivided into about 250 compartments, and each of these compartments is tightly packed with highly coiled seminiferous tubules. The two testes together contain a total length of about 500 meters (1,640 feet) of tubules. Sperm are produced continuously within the tubules. The sperm is a highly differentiated cell specialized for the task of delivering one inactivated haploid set of chromosomes to the ovum. While in the testes, the sperm are immobile. They become partly motile only after they have spent about 18 hours in the epididymis. Interestingly, the sperm become fully motile and mature only after they have entered the female reproductive tract. Sperm are stored in the ductus deferens. The seminal fluid consists of the secretions of the seminal vesicle, the prostate, and the bulbourethral glands. Each ejaculate of 3 to 6 milliliters usually contains some 300 million to 400 million sperm. Of these, only one can fertilize the ovum.

Table 5.13　Comparison of Young and Old Women's Sexual Responsiveness, Reported by Masters and Johnson (1966)

Phase	Response or organ	Young women[a]	Old women[b]
Excitement	Time needed for lubrication of vagina after stimulation	15–30 seconds	1–5 minutes
Plateau	Vagina	Limitless capacity for expansion	Potential for expansion reduced but retained
	Uterus	Raised to allow greater expansion of vagina	Less elevation; less room provided for vagina to expand
	Minor labia	Redden as blood flow increases	No coloration change
	Major labia	Elevate and flatten against body	Hang in loose folds
	Clitoris	Elevates and flattens	No change
Orgasm	Vagina	8–12 contractions at 8-second intervals	4–5 contractions at 8-second intervals
	Uterus	3–5 contractions	1–2 contractions, which might include painful spasms
Resolution	Timing of return to prearousal state	Rhythmic	Rapid

Source: From Whitbourne 1985.
[a]20 to 40 years old.
[b]50 to 70 years old.

The other sperm cells may play an important, albeit accessory, role, since men who have fewer than 20 million sperm per milliliter of ejaculate are generally sterile.

The male reproductive system is under a less obvious form of neuroendocrine control than that of the female reproductive system. In addition to producing sperm, the testis secretes the male sex hormone, testosterone. This hormone is responsible both for the normal functioning of the accessory glands of reproduction and for the development and maintenance of the secondary sexual characteristics. Testosterone is produced by the Leydig's cells of the testis. These cells are activated by LH, and the effect is enhanced if FSH is also available. Maintenance of the structure of the seminiferous tubules and of sperm development in the tubules depends on the combined effects of FSH and testosterone. Thus the same hypothalamus–pituitary–gonad axis of control is active in both sexes.

Human males exhibit a daily, not monthly, rhythmicity in their testosterone levels (Figure 5.41). This variability in gonadal hormone secretion is paralleled by the finding that LH levels in normal young men vary in a pulsatile manner (Figure 5.42). Sleeping and waking states show a difference in the interpulse interval. It does not appear to be fully accurate to state that women have a cyclic

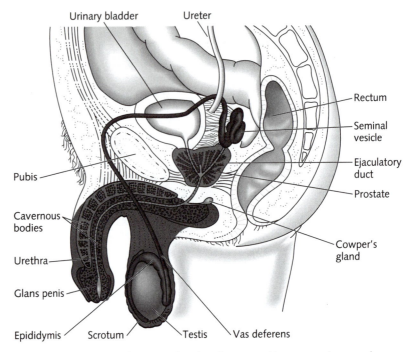

Urinary bladder   Ureter

Rectum

Seminal
vesicle

Ejaculatory
duct

Prostate

Pubis

Cavernous
bodies

Cowper's
gland

Urethra

Glans penis

Epididymis   Scrotum   Testis   Vas deferens

Figure 5.40   A sagittal section showing the normal human male reproductive system.

reproductive pattern while men do not. It is probably more realistic to say that both sexes have cyclic reproductive patterns but that their cycles are quite different from one another.

Age-related changes   Following the same logic as mentioned above for females, we will discuss the nature of aging-related changes and how they affect the reproductive and sexual functions in men.

Figure 5.41 reveals two facts. First, mean testosterone level appears to decrease with age. Second, and more striking, the circadian rhythm that is characteristic of testosterone production in young men is absent in old men. This decrease in testosterone level is accompanied by an increase in LH levels (Bremner, Viriello, and Prinz 1986) and by a loss of the pulsatile LH secretion characteristic of young men (see Figure 5.42). However, either because not enough LH is produced or because Leydig's cells cannot respond to the increased LH, the testosterone level in the blood does not increase. This situation is analogous to that of the postmenopausal female (Whitbourne 1985).

However, these age-related changes seem to make little difference in the functional aspects of semen in old men, compared to young men (Table 5.14). The decrease in normal motile sperm in old men appears to be compensated for by an increase in sperm density. The decreased fertility associated with increasing age appears to be associated more with cultural than with physiological events. In fact, it has been suggested that the drop in testosterone levels may have much to

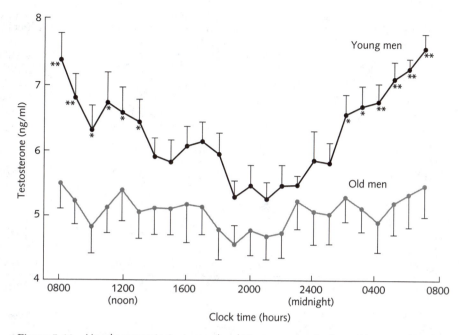

Figure 5.41   Hourly serum testosterone levels (mean ± standard error) in normal young and old men. Asterisks indicate statistically significant differences (* = <.05; ** = <.01) between age groups at that point in time. (From Bremner, Vitiello, and Prince 1983.)

do with a decrease in numbers of Leydig's cells arising from a decreasing frequency of sexual encounters. If confirmed, this may well be the primordial instance of "use it or lose it."

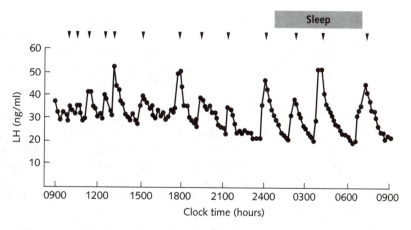

Figure 5.42   The time course of luteinizing-hormone levels measured every 10 minutes for 24 hours in a normal young man. Episodic LH secretion is less frequent in the evening and during sleep than in the morning. (From Bremner et al. 1986. © Plenum Press.)

Table 5.14   **Testicular Volumes and Seminal Parameters in Young and Old Fathers**

Phase	Young men (n = 20)[a]	Old men (n = 22)	Statistical significance (p)[b]
Mean age (years)	29.2 ± 3.2	67.0 ± 7.8	
Age range (years)	24–37	60–88	
Testicular volume (ml)	17.3 ± 4.0	19.0 ± 5.7	NS[c]
Ejaculate volume (ml)	4.0 ± 1.7	3.2 ± 1.9	NS
Sperm density (million/ml)	78 ± 51	120 ± 101	0.05
Percentage progressively motile sperm	68 ± 14	50 ± 19	0.0005
Percentage normally formed sperm	52 ± 13	48 ± 9	NS
Fructose (mg/ml)	3.2 ± 1.1	1.7 ± 1.1	0.0005
pH	7.28 ± 0.09	7.25 ± 0.15	NS
HOP test (percent penetrated ova)[d]	54 ± 20	54 ± 18[e]	NS

Source: From Nieschlag and Michael 1986.
Data are given as mean ± standard deviation.
[a]N = sample size.
[b]p = probability.
[c]NS = not significant.
[d]HOP = % penetrated ova
[e]N = 16.

There is no obvious correlation between levels of sexual activity and testosterone levels, suggesting again that eroticism may reside more in the mind than elsewhere. However, some real age-related changes take place in the sexual responsiveness of the human male, as Table 5.15 shows.

Summary

Female reproductive aging has long served as a model for the study of organ-specific aging. Follicular deficiency leads to lowered blood levels of ovarian hormones. The depletion of estrogens leads to secondary changes in all tissues, whether reproductive or not, that depend on estrogens for their normal maintenance. This process of female reproductive aging is accompanied by neural alterations in the hypothalamus and pituitary.

Male reproductive aging involves a decline in the testosterone level as well as a marked change in the rhythmicity of its secretion. However, these alterations do not seem to involve serious decrements in the male's reproductive ability.

Changes in the reproductive organs also affect the sexual functioning of both males and females, but they do not unduly hamper this aspect of our behavior. It has been demonstrated that for both sexes, the enjoyment of sexual relations is a positive indicator of longevity.

Metabolic and Hormonal Changes

Given the kaleidoscope of age-related changes surveyed in this chapter, it is to be expected that these morphological changes are paralleled by myriad biochemical

Table 5.15 **Comparison of Young and Old Men's Sexual Responsiveness, Reported by Masters and Johnson (1966)**

Phase	Response to organ	Young men[a]	Old men[b]
Excitement	Time needed for penile erection after stimulation	3–5 seconds	10–15 seconds to several minutes
	Degree of erection	Full	Reduced until close to ejaculation
	Elevation of testes	Occurs in late phase	Little or no elevation of testes
	Blood flow to testes and scrotum	Increases	No increase
	Bulbo-urethral gland	Secretes fluid	Less or no fluid secreted
Plateau	Increase of sexual tension	Rapid development of pressure for ejaculation	Can be prolonged, often indefinitely, before pressure for ejaculation is felt
	Glans at coronal ridge	Increases in circumference just before ejaculation	Increases in circumference just before ejaculation
Orgasm			
First stage	Subjective experience of inevitable ejaculation	2–4 seconds	1–2 seconds, not at all, or 5–7 seconds with irregular prostatic contractions
	Prostate	Begins contracting regularly at 0.8-second intervals	1–2 contractions; may be irregular
Second stage	Penile urethra	3–4 contractions at 0.8-second intervals, followed by contractions at longer intervals	1–2 contractions at 0.8-second intervals
	Expulsive force of seminal fluid, measured in inches from meatus	12–24 inches	3–5 inches
	Volume of semen after 24–37 hours of continence	3–5 ml	2–3 ml
Resolution	Return of full erection possible	Several minutes	Several hours
	Return to prearousal state	Two stages, lasting minutes to hours	One stage, frequently in several seconds

Source: From Whitbourne 1985.
[a]20 to 40 years old.
[b]50 to 70 years old.

alterations. An enormous number of individual metabolic reactions are involved in the formation and destruction of the literally thousands of chemical compounds necessary for our continued vitality. For any given compound, the rule seems to be that different sets of reactions are used for its synthesis and for its degradation. Thus there are multiple points at which any given reaction can be controlled. We will briefly review the important changes taking place in these major aspects of metabolic activity, with particular reference to humans.

Energy Metabolism

Measuring all the variables affecting energy metabolism in a cellular organelle such as a mitochondrion is daunting enough; to measure individually all the variables operative in an entire organism is impossible. However, a set of standard conditions has been developed under which a standard measure of metabolism, the basal metabolic rate (BMR), can be measured. Early cross-sectional studies showed that the BMR declines with advancing age; these results were contradicted by later longitudinal studies that controlled for the changes in body composition with age. It was later shown that the basal consumption of O_2 (BMR) per liter of body water is constant (Figure 5.43). The observed decline in the BMR unadjusted for water content is presumably due to the observed loss in muscle mass with age in humans (Tzarkoff and Norris 1978). There is no age-related decline in the overall resting metabolic activity of the body's cells and tissues. This conclusion is supported by the repeated findings that no age difference exists for mouth or axillary temperatures in the range of 20 to 100 years (Shock 1977).

The BMR is a laboratory measurement. In the real world, people expend a higher level of energy than is suggested by the BMR. Daily measurements of actual energy metabolism, unadjusted for changes in body mass, decline (Figure 5.44). This decline persists even when one adjusts the data to reflect changes in body mass with age (see Figure 5.44d). There appears to be a real age-related

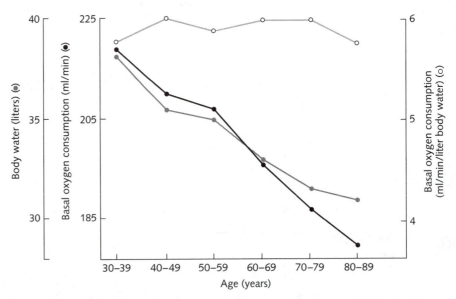

Figure 5.43 The relationship of age to basal oxygen consumption, total body water, and basal oxygen consumption per unit of body water. (From Gregerman 1967. © Charles C. Thomas.)

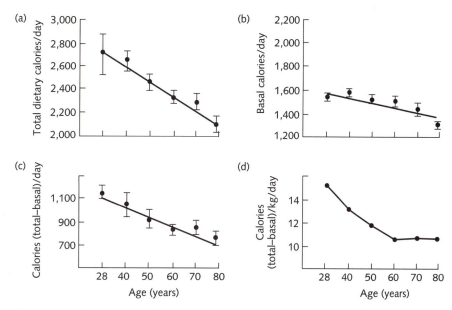

Figure 5.44 Energy expenditure by men. (a) Total caloric intake per day. (b) Basal metabolic rate. (c) Energy expenditure in addition to the basal expenditure. (d) Energy expenditure in addition to the basal expenditure, per kilogram body weight. (From McGandy et al. 1966.)

decrement in the body's ability to produce energy above the resting levels reflected by the BMR, at least between the ages of 28 and 60 years.

This apparent age-related decrease in maximum energy production in men (and presumably women as well) correlates well with many (but not all) studies showing that in various animal species, the older animals often have fewer mitochondria. Furthermore, these senescent mitochondria are usually less efficient in oxidative phosphorylation and other aspects of energy production (see Chapter 10). It is a well-known and verified observation that the maximum life span of any mammalian species is inversely proportional to its specific metabolic rate (calories/gram/month or year; see Chapter 4). It is another well-established observation that increasing the metabolic rate decreases the life span (Loeb and Northrop 1917). This observation is particularly well documented in poikilotherms, in which the metabolic rate varies according to the environmental temperature. The implication that there is a positive correlation between the metabolic rate and the rate of aging has led to the development of several theories of aging. These classic theories have recently been disproven in their strict sense, but modern versions of them appear to provide us with some good insights into the relationship between aging and energy. We will examine them in more detail in Chapters 7 and 10.

Fuel Utilization and Storage

Most of the body's energy stores are maintained in the form of triglycerides found in the adipose tissue; the remainder are mostly in the form of protein, and a trace (less than 1 percent) is found as glycogen. Age-related changes in fuel storage and utilization appear to parallel the shifts in energy metabolism. As Figure 5.2 shows, fat makes up an increasing fraction of total body mass with age. Animal studies suggest that aging has little effect on glycogen content or its utilization by the liver or muscles (Masoro 1985). Advancing age is accompanied by a large (31 percent) loss of body protein content, mostly from the skeletal muscles. Protein stores are not utilized for energy metabolism except under extraordinary (starvation) conditions. Very little is known regarding the role of aging in affecting the utilization of proteins for energy metabolism. The observed loss of protein mass may be caused by an age-related decrease in protein synthesis levels, a theory that we will discuss in some detail in Chapter 10.

There does appear to be a change with age in the body's ability to utilize both fats and carbohydrates—a change that is related to endocrine changes. In order to utilize fat as an energy source, the triglycerides stored in the adipose cells must be enzymatically converted to free fatty acids. This process is controlled in large part by the hormone glucagon, and there is an age-related decrease in the ability of the adipose cells to respond to that hormone. However, this age-related rate and pattern of the decline can be substantially modulated by diet, particularly by caloric restriction, such that the treated animals retain a "youthlike" response for a long time (Masoro 1985). We will return to this topic again in Chapters 7 and 10. It is interesting to speculate on whether this decreased lipolytic response of the individual cells is compensated for by the age-related increased mass of the body that is composed of fat.

Hormonal Changes Associated with Aging

Many metabolic reactions are controlled and/or influenced by a variety of hormones. A schematic diagram of an idealized endocrine system (Figure 5.45) illustrates its complexity and suggests possible control points. This diagram should be viewed as a detailed description of just one of the several components shown in Figure 5.30. In general, the different endocrine glands show a similar pattern of morphological changes with age. They lose weight and develop a patchy atrophic appearance accompanied by vascular changes and fibrosis (Minaker, Meneilly, and Rowe 1985). The basal levels of many hormones are not affected by age, even though the secretion rates of most hormones decrease. This situation necessarily implies that the clearance rates must have decreased in a compensatory manner. There appear to be no general systematic changes in the number or quality of receptors. The intracellular response to the hormone often appears to be diminished as a function of age.

The foregoing is a general description and does not apply to all cases. In fact, it has been known since the work of J. C. Spence in 1921 that there is an age-related decrement in the ability of the body to maintain carbohydrate homeostasis following glucose challenge. Cross-sectional studies have shown that there is no change with age of the fasting blood sugar level. What changes is the rate with which the blood glucose level is brought back to normal following a glucose overload. The oral glucose tolerance test, used to quantitate this process, measures the glucose level in the blood immediately after and 2 hours

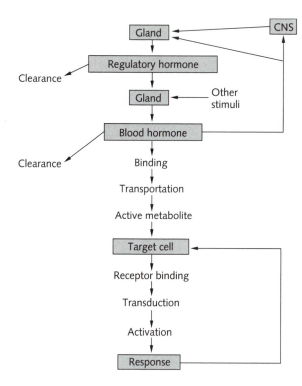

Figure 5.45   A generalized sequence of hormone action and regulation. (From Korenman 1982. © Elsevier.)

after the patient drinks a sickeningly sweet "cocktail." Normal individuals show a rapid drop; diabetic individuals do not. The intermediate values characteristic of an impaired glucose tolerance are characteristically shown both by large numbers of elderly persons and by younger individuals at risk of developing diabetes.

This age-related homeostatic impairment is due not to decreased levels of insulin released and/or circulating in the bloodstream, but apparently to a decrease in the sensitivity of peripheral (nonhepatic) tissues to insulin. The maximum response to insulin is the same in both young and old, but with age the dose–response curve is shifted to the right such that older subjects require twice the amount of insulin as do young subjects in order to attain a given level of glucose uptake. The change in rate does not appear to be associated with changes in number or quality of insulin receptors or the cell membrane. Thus this decrease must involve presently unknown age-related changes in the intracellular response of the cell to glucose. In addition, factors such as obesity, diet, and physical exercise are known to affect the extent of the decrement in glucose homeostasis.

Glucagon is involved in both carbohydrate and fat metabolism. Glucagon physiology does not change significantly with age, despite the changes occurring in insulin physiology and despite the age-related changes in glucagon-induced lipolysis. The two hormones and the two sets of metabolic reactions they regulate retain their autonomy despite the interconnectedness of metabolic reactions.

Pharmacological Changes Associated with Aging

Although some drugs are eliminated from the body largely unchanged, most are converted to a wide variety of metabolites before they are excreted. Given the wide-ranging nature of the physiological age-related changes already described, it should come as no surprise that some of these alterations are of pharmacological importance. This extensive topic was reviewed by Vestal and Dawson (1985) and by Beizer and Timiras (1994). A drug must be absorbed from the site of administration (usually the gastrointestinal tract) into the circulation, distributed via the circulatory system to both the central and the peripheral tissues, metabolized by the tissues, and excreted by the kidneys. Each of these processes may be affected by various factors.

Because of the broad physiological variations seen among the elderly, as well as the wide variety of drugs available, it is difficult to offer broad and valid generalizations on this topic. Nonetheless, it should be clear that many of the age-related changes discussed earlier will have profound effects. For example, the age-related decrease in total body water and increase in body fat will ensure that a constant dose of a water-soluble drug will have higher blood levels in the elderly, while a fat-soluble drug might have higher blood levels in the young. The changes in free drug concentrations in the circulation might be exacerbated by the 32 percent decrease in the weight of the liver from the fourth to the eighth decade of life (see Figure 5.1). If the intrinsic metabolic capacity of the liver to process such drugs were correspondingly reduced, one would expect these drugs to exhibit longer half-lives and a consequent reduction in clearance times. And, of course, age-related changes in the density and/or binding efficiency of the drug receptors would contribute to an alteration of drug effectiveness in the elderly.

These predictions appear to be upheld in various studies. In elderly patients, the drug propranolol exhibited a 28 percent longer half-life than in younger people, coupled with a clearance rate only 76 percent that of younger people. One might expect a similar variation in the symptomatic effects of this drug in people of different ages. Similar studies on another model drug, antipyrine, illustrate the large amount of individual variation in drug metabolism (Figure 5.46). The statistical analysis of these data substantiates the impression gained from a visual inspection—namely, that individual variation and environmental effects (such as smoking) far exceed the effect of age alone. Nonetheless, age has an effect on pharmacokinetics. In some cases, the expected increase in adverse reactions with age has been documented (Figure 5.47). The incidence of such adverse reactions is much increased at higher doses, a situation in which many older individuals might find themselves as a result of long-standing chronic conditions. Thus we may view these pharmacological alterations as a specialized but increasingly important aspect of the more general metabolic changes seen with aging.

• *Interactions Between Aging and Disease*

The preceding description of normal age-related changes in humans should have made clear that almost all age-related changes represent a decrement in function.

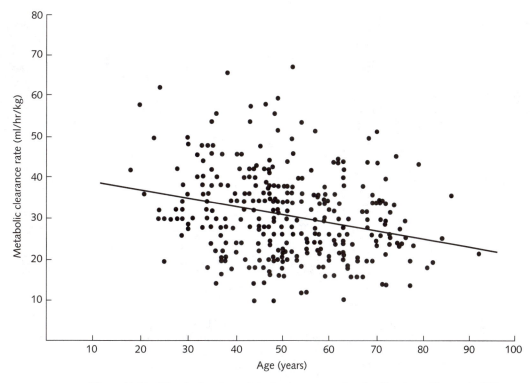

Figure 5.46 The decline in metabolic clearance rate of antipyrine with age in 307 healthy male subjects. (From Vestal 1978.)

We have also tried to distinguish normal age-dependent changes in structure or function from age-related pathologies. This distinction is not easy to draw, in large part because normal age-related changes are believed to be associated with the prevalence of age-related pathologies. We will explore this association in terms of the specific framework of the cardiovascular system.

Another conceptual area of interest regards the fit between the simple, clean, and rigorous definition of age-related changes as postulated by Strehler (see the CPID criteria in Chapter 1); and the complex, overlapping, and fuzzy descriptions we have presented of the actual age-related changes. We will explore this fit in the context of age-related changes in the skeletal system and suggest some possible alterations in these concepts.

Cardiovascular Interactions

Some aspects of the association between the normal and the pathological may represent the presence in some individuals of time-dependent processes (for example, changes in aortic elasticity) that may act as a predisposing factor to the development of the abnormality. Undoubtedly, the shift from normal to pathological may also represent situations in which the accumulation of many small quantitative changes may bring about a sudden, irreversible, and qualitative

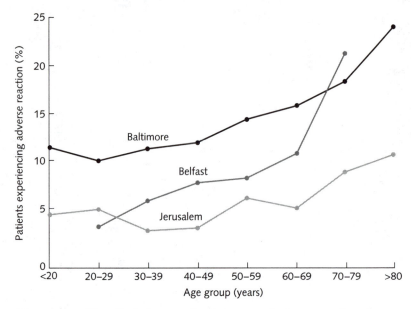

Figure 5.47 The effect of age on the frequency of adverse reactions to prescribed drugs. There is an age-related increase in all three populations; the quantitative difference between them may be attributed to socioeconomic factors. There were 714 people in the Baltimore population, 1033 in the Belfast population, and 2933 in the Jerusalem population. (Data from Vestal and Dawson 1985.)

alteration. The branch of mathematics known as catastrophe theory might be appropriate for the modeling of such situations.

The dynamic interactions between the aging process and cardiovascular disease can best be described as follows (Vessilinovitch 1986). The aging processes particularly relevant are those involved in (1) arteriocapillary fibrosis, (2) reduced elasticity of the vessel wall, (3) reduced blood flow, (4) enhanced endothelial injury, (5) defective endothelial repair, and (6) elevated blood lipids. Every one of these processes normally occurs in individuals not affected with cardiovascular disease and thus they cannot be regarded as pathological states by the CPID criteria. However, their presence will predispose and accelerate the course of the disease. In turn, the advancing disease state will enhance the progression of any of these age-related changes. The disease and the aging processes exert positive feedback effects on each other, thus creating a vicious cycle that leads to accelerated aging and increased debilitation. The goal of any effective segmental interaction would be to break, or at least minimize, the positive feedback signals accelerating this deleterious cascade.

Skeletal System Interactions

As already described, there is a wealth of knowledge regarding the age-related phenomenon of bone loss, and its role in both normal and abnormal aging. It will be an instructive exercise for us to compare Strehler's operational definition of aging (see Chapter 1 for CPID criteria), which we are using, with this rich data base in order to see how well (or how poorly) the definition fits the facts without confounding the normal and the abnormal. This comparison of principles and observation reveals a close but not complete congruence between the two (Table 5.16). It seems as if these defining criteria need to be reviewed so as to allow for the considerable heterogeneity of the human population (see point 2 of Table 5.16). We have elsewhere (see Chapter 3) dealt with this definitional problem of heterogeneity. It would also be useful if the deleterious effect (point 4 of Table 5.16) of the normal age-related change were viewed as arising from the fact that it serves as a precondition for the possible development of a pathological age-related change.

In the current example, we would want to make the following sort of statement: A decrease in bone mass is a deleterious age-related change initially brought about by changes in certain intrinsic factors and strongly modulated by certain extrinsic factors, all of which interact in a complex cascade to reach the end point of this pathogenic pathway, namely osteoporosis. This approach directs our attention to the necessary age-related changes that are a precondition to the pathology associated with senescence; it clarifies that the decreased bone mass and osteoporosis are not the same condition, but rather that the decreased bone mass is a precondition of the end point of osteoporosis. It would probably be useful if we could devise a statistical normalization procedure that would clearly distinguish between normal and pathological age-related changes. In addition, these age-related changes can be modulated to some extent, principally and most easily by appropriate exercise and nutrition. In that sense, then, their deleterious effect is not a fixed attribute.

Table 5.16 **Comparison of Theoretical Principles and Actual Observations**

Principle	Observations
1. Cumulative	The decrease in bone mass is cumulative over time.
2. Progressive	Significant differences in the rate of progression exist between men and women in general and between any two individuals of the same gender and are based on heredity and race. Progression rates differ for various dichotomous classes, such as spongy versus compact bone, pre- versus postmenopausal women and so on.
3. Intrinsic	The extent and kinetics of bone loss are significantly modulated by various environmental factors, some of which are extrinsic to the organism (diet, exercise, etc.) and others of which are intrinsic to the organism but extrinsic to the bone tissue (gonadal hormone status, for example).
4. Deleterious	There is no doubt of the deleterious effects that bone mass loss can have on an individual. But in and of itself, it is no deleterious. Not only do these losses not affect the death of the individual, but the majority of the elderly do not have symptomatic problems of the skeleton that can be traced solely to decreased bone mass.

Source: From Klebba-Goodman 1986.

There is no better way to end this discussion than with the words of Nathan Shock (1983, p. 137):

> Aging and disease are not synonymous. Aging is a normal part of the life span characterized by slowly progressing impairments in the performance of most organ systems .... The ability to adapt to stress also diminishes with age. There is mounting evidence to support the premise that aging in humans may be more than simply the summation of the changes that take place at the cellular, tissue or organ level. The essence of survival is the proper integration of responses of different organ systems to adapt to the stresses of daily living. Impaired effectiveness of these coordinating mechanisms may be the primary factor involved in aging.

6

Genetic Determinants
of Longevity

We each want to live a vital and vigorous life. Successful aging, as described in Chapter 5, may well be our individual and collective goal. But to age successfully requires, first and foremost, that we live long enough to age. It has long been a popular axiom that our inheritance plays a major role in delimiting our length of life. Indeed, an apocryphal saying prescribes that, if one wishes to live a long and happy life, one should first arrange to have parents who are long-lived and wealthy. And a major premise of certain of Robert Heinlein's science fiction stories and novels is that extraordinarily long life in humans can be attained via selective breeding among the longest-lived members of the population, who are themselves descended only from long-lived parents. If the genetic constitution of each organism determines whether it will be a fly or a mouse or a human, then it seems only reasonable that the characteristic life span of each species is genetically determined as well. Of course, this truism doesn't shed much light on the reasons underlying the variation of life spans within a single species, so it might conceal more than it illuminates. Impossible advice, fictional tales, and natural history do not constitute persuasive proof. Is the belief in our genetic predestination founded on fact or is it an old wives' tale? The quest to answer this question has resulted in the accumulation of much data, both in humans and in experimental animals.

Studies in Humans

Many human studies depend on the existence of accurate birth and death records. Rather than manipulating people in any way, the investigator selects certain of these records and examines them for any statistical signs of heritability of life span between related individuals. There are two types of such studies: (1) those based on genealogical records, either of one family alone or of several families collectively, and (2) those based on samples taken from special subgroups of the population, either in a retrospective study such as one that measures the life spans of insurance applicants and compares them to the life spans of their parents, or in a prospective study such as one that measures the life spans of descendants of unrelated long-lived individual members of one cohort. There are statistical and methodological objections to both procedures, but they are all we have. At least several dozen such studies have been reported in the literature; we will discuss only a representative few of them.

Genealogical Studies

Alexander Graham Bell, of telephone fame, did a genealogical analysis of longevity among the descendants of William Hyde of Connecticut, who died in 1681. Bell's analysis, published in 1918, of the 8,798 individuals listed in these family records revealed an excellent correlation between parental and offspring life spans (Table 6.1). The results show not only a substantial (about 40 percent) difference in the life span of offspring whose parents had both died before the age of 60 years as compared to offspring whose parents had died after the age of 80 years, but also that the offspring of parents with intermediate life spans also had intermediate life spans. However, it is equally clear that the mean life span of the progeny is always much less than that of the parents. There appears to be a high correlation but a low heritability, which seems paradoxical. In part, this phenomenon probably reflects the role of accidents, disease, and other environmentally dependent premature deaths; it certainly emphasizes the fact that not all children of long-lived survivors will themselves be survivors. In part, it probably also reflects the inadequacy of any single numerical measure, such as the mean, to describe a population. Perhaps a life table calculation such as is described in Chapter 2 would have been better.

It may be instructive to compare Bell's results to those of Yuan (Figure 6.1). Bell also concluded that the influence of the father on the offspring's longevity appeared to be somewhat greater than that of the mother. Yuan's data showed

Table 6.1   **Average Life Span (in Years) of Offspring in Relation to Parental Age at Death**

	Mother's age at death (years)		
	<60	*60–80*	*>80*
Father's age at death (years):			
<60	32.8 (N = 128)	33.4 (N = 120)	36.3 (N = 74)
60–80	35.8 (N = 251)	38.0 (N = 328)	45.0 (N = 172)
>80	42.3 (N = 131)	45.5 (N = 206)	52.7 (N = 184)

Source: After Bell 1918.

that a larger proportion of females than males lived to 95 years of age or more. On the face of it, these two statements appear to be paradoxical.

In 1932, Yuan analyzed the longevity records of 7,500 individuals who belonged to a single southern Chinese family and who were born and died in the 500-year span between 1365 and 1849. Yuan's life table analysis also showed a correlation between the life expectancy of sons and the longevity of their parents: The offspring of long-lived parents had a substantially greater (about 25 percent) life expectancy than did offspring of shorter-lived parents (see Figure 6.1). The virtue of a life table approach is shown by Yuan's calculation of life expectancy for sons at age 20. These individuals are already survivors of the high rates of childhood mortality (see Figure 6.3). Consequently, there is much better agreement between parental life spans and the surviving son's total expected life span at age 20. Comparison of the survivors at this age removes much of the early environmental effects, thereby highlighting the genetic similarities and/or differences.

One caveat should be mentioned regarding both of these studies. The degree of genetic relatedness (in the sense of sharing genes that are identical by common descent) between any two members of either genealogy decreases sharply as the number of generations separating them from their common ancestor increases.

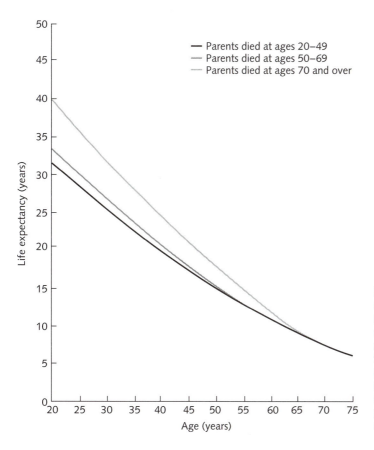

Figure 6.1 The further expectation of life in years for sons whose fathers and mothers both had short, intermediate, or long life spans. Note that the sons' life expectancy at age 20 has the same rank order as the parental life spans. This difference disappears as the sons survive to older ages. (From Yuan 1932.)

Barring inbreeding, there eventually arrives a point at which an individual may have the same degree of genetic relatedness to a stranger as to an ancestor. At this point, the genetic basis of "family" appears to lose its meaning. This objection does not apply when the correlation that enters the calculations is between only the parents and their immediate offspring, as in the example given here, and not between an ancestor and all of his/her descendants.

Jalavisto (1951) analyzed 12,876 individuals from Scandinavian genealogies of the middle class and minor nobility spanning 3 centuries from 1500 to 1829. Plotting the mean length of life of the offspring as a function of parental age at death revealed a striking linear relationship with the maternal age at death when the father's age was held constant (Figure 6.2). However, the relationship between the age of the offspring and increasing paternal longevity was much less obvious, becoming apparent only with very long-lived fathers. Jalavisto concluded, in contradiction to Bell, that the effect of maternal longevity exceeds that of paternal longevity.

A more recent genealogical investigation into human longevity, Mayer (1991) posed a rather different set of questions than its predecessors had posed. Mayer used a series of genealogies, including 14,549 useful individual data sets drawn from six white New England families covering the period of time from 1578 to 1963, and drew from it the answers to two questions: What proportion of the recorded longevity of these individuals could be statistically ascribed to

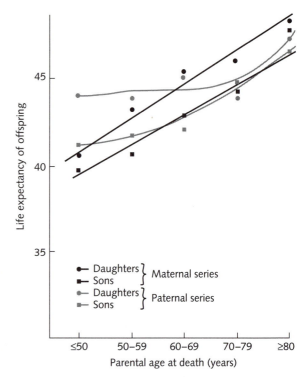

Figure 6.2 The mean length of life as a function of parental age at death. In the maternal series, the mother's age was held constant; in the paternal series, the father's age was held constant. Note that the expectation of life for both sons and daughters rises steadily with increasing maternal length of life, but that the increase in expectancy with increasing paternal longevity is much less, particularly daughters. (From Jalavisto 1951.)

their genetic inheritance? And did the value of this genetic inheritance of longevity change during the 300-year period of the study, or was it a constant? Technically, the genetic inheritance of this or any other trait is termed the heritability, and symbolized as h^2. Heritability is defined as the proportion of the total phenotypic variance that is genetic, and it is determined by dividing the genetic variance by the sum of the phenotypic and environmental variances.

Mayer found that the 95 percent confidence interval (the range of values between which we may be statistically certain that the true value falls) for the heritability of parents versus that of offspring was 10 to 30 percent. For sibs, he found a higher value: 33 to 41 percent (however, this value also includes the effect of common developmental environments). A subset of mildly inbred families showed a slightly (but not significantly) higher h^2 value. Finally, there was no evidence of significant alterations in the heritability values during the 3 centuries of the study, even though the U.S. population, including these families, changed dramatically from both a genetic and demographic viewpoint during the same period of time. The most reasonable interpretation of the data is (1) that a moderate genetic component determines about 10 to 33 percent of human longevity and (2) that this heritable effect is independent of populationwide environmental and social changes.

In a recent review of the topic, Finch and Tanzi (1997) surveyed heritability studies in various vertebrates and invertebrates. They concluded that, despite the evidence showing that some genetic variants or mutants can significantly affect senescence and longevity, in general the heritability of life span is relatively low, accounting for less than 35%. For humans, this low heritability implies that our choice of lifestyles probably has a profound and important influence on the outcome of our own aging. We cannot control our genetic composition, but we can decide, via our behavior, which risk factors we wish to minimize.

Gavrilov and Gavrilova (1997) undertook a different type of genealogical study. They used high-quality genealogical data from the Russian nobility of the seventeenth to nineteenth centuries and examined the longevity of the offspring as a function of the parental age at reproduction. They found that the mother's age at reproduction was not correlated with the longevity of either her sons or her daughters. The father's age at reproduction, however, was significantly correlated with the longevity of his daughters but not his sons. The daughters of older men (50 to 59 years old) showed almost a 4-year decrease in their mean life span, from 64.6 years to 60.8 years. The mechanisms involved are not clear, yet a change of such magnitude likely has many biological and social effects. Given the increase in the divorce rate since the 1800s and the probable increase in the number of second families started by older men, this sex-specific age effect may act as a countervailing force against the long-term trend of increasing longevity.

Thus, despite their substantial differences in time, place, and execution, all the genealogical studies agree with one another in showing a moderate genetic component to human longevity. It would be interesting to redo some of these genealogical studies in another century or two, by which time the life span will have undoubtedly increased, and see if the heritability values have decreased as we have learned and employed more effective nongenetic interventions.

Population Studies

The genealogical studies described in the previous section are generally consistent with the several population sampling studies that have been done. Raymond Pearl pioneered various different study procedures in his efforts to refine the simple genealogical surveys. In one study, he and his colleagues examined the longevity of offspring born to individuals identified as having lived to a very advanced age (90 or more years). The data from this ambitious undertaking were compiled and analyzed by Abbot et al. (1974) and Murphy (1978). Again, they show a striking positive relationship between the longevities of parents and offspring (Table 6.2). However, the data also show, in opposition to the results of Jalavisto (1951), a greater effect of the father than the mother on the longevity of offspring.

The insurance companies realized quite early that it would be beneficial to their future profitability if they could determine whether there was a significant positive relationship between parental and offspring longevities. Several different studies, summarized by Cohen (1964), have been conducted to address this question. The data from these investigations generally, but not consistently, are compatible with the conclusion that heredity counts—that a good predictor of your life span might be your parents' life spans.

All the studies we have cited here suffer from some sort of serious methodological or statistical shortcoming, as has been pointed out in some detail by Cohen (1964); thus no single study is entirely reliable. Yet the broad trend is clear enough: Parental age has some effect on the length of life of the offspring. The results appear to be more striking for sons than for daughters. The discrepancies in detail noted between the different studies may well have arisen as a result of the differences in structure or in reliability.

Twin Studies

To an incautious geneticist, the data patterns of these several genealogical and population studies immediately suggest polygenic and additive inheritance; that

Table 6.2 **Mean Life Span (in Years) of Offspring Who Had One Very Long-Lived Parent**

	Age of nonproband parent at death (years)		
	<60	*60–80*	*>80*
Sex of proband parent[a]:			
Male	67.6 ♂	71.4 ♂	73.2 ♂
	73.8 ♀	74.1 ♀	77.2 ♀
Female	67.0 ♂	69.3 ♂	70.9 ♂
	73.0 ♀	73.5 ♀	73.3 ♀

Source: After Murphy 1978.
[a]All proband parents lived to at least 90 years.

is, a large number of genes, each with a small but cumulative effect, could be involved. This conclusion would be premature, however, since not all familial effects must of necessity be genetic. For example, there is probably an almost perfect correlation between the language that the parents speak and the language that the child speaks, yet to argue that the high parent–child correlations are evidence of genetic transmission of this trait would be foolish. Many of the lifestyle choices we make that could reasonably be expected to affect our longevity, we likely learned at our mother's knee or table. A classic method of sorting out such familial environmental and genetic effects has been to study twins.

Kallman (1957) and his colleagues collected from various sources the histories on 1,739 pairs of twins in which at least one twin lived to age 60. They examined both the effects of parental life span on the longevity of twins and the similarity of life span between twins who are identical and twins who are fraternal. Although this study also has some statistical shortcomings, the data point in the same direction as do the results of the genealogical and population studies. There is a good positive correlation between parental life span and progeny life span (Table 6.3). More interesting, however, is the demonstration that there is less difference in longevities for identical twins (36.0 months difference) than for fraternal twins either of the same sex (74.6 months) or of different sexes (106.0 months). A similar pattern of longevities was observed among Danish twins (McGue et al. 1993). In other words, the possession of an identical genome by twins brings with it a much more nearly identical life span than is characteristic of other siblings.

This conclusion is supported by the observation that identical twins have a somewhat higher heritability of longevity (with values of h^2 ranging from 0.33 in McGue et al. 1993 to 0.50 in Yashin and Iachine 1995b). Recall that in the general population, h^2 ranges from 0.10 to 0.33 (Mayer 1991). In addition, identical twins appear to show a statistical association between middle-aged and senescent deaths (McGue et al. 1993), since the life expectancy of one twin was significantly less than predicted if his or her co-twin died in middle age. The behavioral and psychological findings also suggest that identical twins undergo a qualitatively similar, if not almost identical, pattern of aging as they grow older (Bank and Jarvik 1979; Jarvik 1979). This last set of findings is entirely consistent with the results of several more recent twin studies, all of which show that the genes play a dominant role in personality development—with heritabilities

---

Table 6.3　**Effect of Parental Age on Mean Life Span of Senescent Twins and Their Siblings**

	Mother died			Father died			Both parents died		
Parental age at death (years)	<55	55–69	>69	<55	55–69	>69	<55	55–69	>69
Mean life span of offspring (sexes combined)	58.5	59.8	62.1	58.5	60.0	61.5	55.9	59.4	62.9

Source: After Kallman 1957.

for a general cognitive factor of 81 percent early in life, decreasing to 51 percent in later life (Plomin et al. 1994; Finkel et al. 1995).

Together these results suggest that heredity is a significant factor in determining the human life span. The apparently low magnitude (about a 2- to 5-year increase in offspring life span for every 10-year increase in parental life span) might reflect the possibility that what we inherit from our parents is not a tendency to long life but the absence of a tendency to short life. The identity of the patterns of aging in identical twins, apart from any considerations of the correlations in familial longevities, suggests that the manner in which our individual behavior and physiology change and adjust with age may be under more of a positive genetic control than we had previously thought possible. Our genes give us not just the absence of deleterious conditions, but also the unique temporal reaction patterns that identify us as surely as our fingerprints do (see Figure 3.20). Most human studies rely heavily on the length of life as an indication of the influence of our genes on our life span.

One important conclusion afforded us by these twin studies may be the insight that our reliance on life span measurements alone may be seriously qualitatively underestimating the role that our genes play in shaping our days. A better estimate would perhaps pay more attention to quantitative and qualitative biomarker measurements, as exemplified by the work of Manton, Woodbury, and Stallard (1995), in which the specific physiological variables affecting the functional capacities of individuals were identified and these variables underlay the late age-specific mortality. Knowing which of these variables are under strong genetic control and which are subject to environmental modulation would likely facilitate rational and targeted interventions.

Sex Differences and Longevity

In the past, men may have proclaimed themselves the stronger sex and convinced many people of the truth of this proposition. But they could fool neither the geriatric physicians, the bulk of whose practice was composed of women, nor the demographers, who counted the survivors. In fact, mortality rates are higher for males than for females through every part of the life cycle (Figure 6.3). At conception, it has been estimated that the male:female sex ratio may be as high as 170:100. The excess male mortality clearly is responsible for reducing this ratio to about 130:100 at the first trimester, about 106:100 at birth, about 100:100 during adolescence, and about 60:100 at age 75 years and older. However, Figure 6.3 also shows that the sex differential in mortality rates is far greater in young adulthood and middle age than it is in old age. This observation suggests "that the major basis for the sex differential in longevity lies not in old age once achieved but before old age" (Hazzard 1986b, p. 457). In other words, women live longer than men not because old women are healthier than old men but because younger men are not as healthy as younger women.

Another interesting but still unexplained observation is that, in general, women have more illnesses than men, but their disorders are less likely to be fatal (Holden 1987b). Perhaps this finding is related to the observation that the immune response of women is quantitatively greater than that of men. This

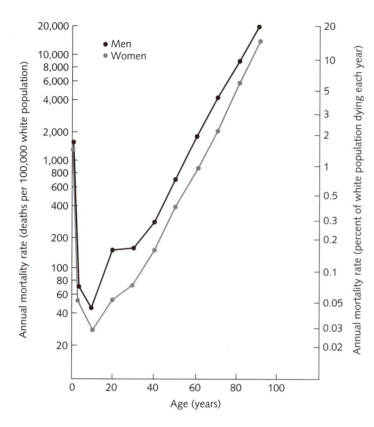

Figure 6.3 Sex-specific mortality rates in the United States in 1976. (From Hazzard 1986b; compiled by Hazzard with data from Gee and Veevers 1984.)

observation has been seen in a variety of other species as well and suggests that females can combat disease more efficiently than males. We know that hormones affect the immune system (see Chapters 5 and 12), and it has been shown that treating female mice with male hormones reduces their immune response. Postpubertal castration of mentally deficient men indicated that eunuchs live slightly longer than normal controls, possibly because of the reduction of their initial mortality rate (IMR) in a Gompertz analysis (Hamilton and Mestler 1969). One possible explanation for this effect is the inhibitory effect of androgens on immune functions (Finch 1990).

The data in Figure 6.3 are taken from a developed country. It is fair to ask if all human populations show this same gender difference in longevity or whether it is a particular attribute of only certain populations. Some data suggest that this is a general human trait. Regardless of the actual mean life span, Gavrilov and Gavrilova (1991) found that males lived longer than females in only six out of 157 populations. However, Smith (1993) has shown that the actual size of the gender gap varies widely among human populations. In developing countries, the gender gap varies from about 4 to 10 years (Table 6.4), but the size of the gap varies for widely different and usually society-specific reasons. Among developed nations, Japan has the smallest gender gap, presumably because both men and

Table 6.4   **Sex-Specific Differences in Mean Life Expectancy at Birth**

Country	Female	Male	Gender gap (female–male)
Developed Nations			
Greece	76.3	72.1	4.2
Japan	80.4	74.8	5.6
Iceland	80.2	74.0	6.2
United States	78.3	71.4	6.9
France	79.2	71.0	8.2
Finland	78.5	70.1	9.8
Former Soviet Union	72.7	62.9	9.8
Developing Nations			
Guatemala	59.4	55.1	4.3
Pakistan	59.2	59.0	0.2
Bangladesh	54.2	54.9	−0.2
Nepal	48.1	50.9	−2.8

Source: Data from Table 5.1 of Smith 1993.

women live so long there. The former Soviet Union has the largest gender gap, apparently because both sexes—but especially males—are showing a dramatic decrease in mean life span there. The small gender gap in Greece seems to stem from the fact that women there do not appear to live as long as women in other developed countries do, and the identical gender gap in Guatemala seems to stem from the fact that everybody dies prematurely there. The cases in which the gender gap disappears or even reverses itself are societies characterized by high rates of premature mortality and/or a devaluation of female children.

In the United States the gender gap has approximately doubled since the turn of the twentieth century, suggesting that women have benefited more than men from the advances in living standards (Smith 1993). Within the United States, the data suggest that most different ethnic groups exhibit the gender gap even as their longevities change in response to societywide changes (Table 6.5). Note that 22 of the 24 possible comparisons in Table 6.5 show that women of different ethnic and (presumably) socioeconomic groups live longer than the males in their cohort. So considering all the data, it is reasonable to conclude that the gender gap is a consistent but modifiable human trait. Incidentally, this gender gap is not a general law of biology. In some species, females live longer than males, in others the reverse occurs, and in some there is no difference between the two (Gavrilov and Gavrilova 1991). Since it is not a general case, the gender gap in each species might well have its own particular causation and consequent explanation.

This gender-specific mortality has been attributed to all sorts of biological phenomena, not the least of which is the fact that males have only one X chromosome whereas females have two. However, the situation is not as simple as it might seem, since one X chromosome is normally inactivated in human females.

Table 6.5   **Mean Age at Death of Different Ethnic Groups at LT 50 and 75 during Three Decades in California**

Group	LT[a]	Female			Male		
		1970	1980	1990	1970	1980	1990
White	50	83.4	85.9	87.0	78.2	79.9	81.1
	75	87.8	89.6	91.3	83.7	85.7	86.4
African-American	50	73.9	78.0	81.0	68.3	72.0	73.4
	75	81.2	84.4	87.2	76.7	78.9	80.5
Hispanic	50	76.1	79.1	81.2	72.7	72.8	71.1
	75	83.3	85.6	87.4	80.2	80.8	80.7
Asian/others	50	77.9	81.7	82.5	78.4	79.5	80.0
	75	84.2	87.6	88.3	84.2	84.2	84.7

Source: From Tables 3 and 4 of Go et al. 1995.
[a]The mean age of the population at which the indicated percentage (50 or 75%) of individuals have died.

Thus both sexes have the same number of functional chromosomes. However, some human data taken from a study covering four generations of an Amish family suggest that gender-specific mortality might have something to do with the presence of a certain portion of the Y chromosome. In this study (K. Smith, cited in Holden 1987b), the average longevity of normal males was found to be about 70 years, of normal females about 75 years. Proband males who carry a Y chromosome with a partial deletion in one arm had a mean longevity of 82.4 years, while females in the same family (who obviously have no Y chromosomes) had a mean longevity of 77.4 years. The association of a particular gender-specific chromosome region with what appears to be a gender-specific longevity difference is both fascinating and provocative. Although the general question of chromosome composition has been reviewed, the data are not firm enough to allow a definitive answer (Smith and Warner 1989; Smith 1993).

More recently, attention has focused on physiological factors. It has been known for a long time that women have lower indices of coronary artery disease than do men. An examination of the epidemiological and clinical evidence led Hazzard (1986a, p. 464) to conclude that a major cause of the increased mortality of younger males can be attributed to the clinical consequences of coronary artery disease: "The sex differential in sex hormone levels gives rise to the sex differential in lipoprotein metabolism which in time (given our Occidental lifestyle) leads to the sex differential in atherosclerosis and this in turn to the sex differential in longevity." In addition, the data of Ornish (1993) suggests that lifestyle changes may lead to a faster regression of coronary artery disease in females than in males, which implies the possibility of a hormonal basis.

In a quantitative estimate of the factors contributing to the sexual difference in mortality, Waldron (1987) estimated that about 18 percent of the sex differential in total mortality is due to these sorts of sex-specific hormonal effects on the cardiovascular system, and thus may well represent an intrinsic and perhaps unchangeable risk to the male sex. However, Waldron also estimated that at least 55 percent of the sex differential in total mortality can be attributed to destructive behaviors such as smoking, as well as to accidents due to reckless use of guns, cars, and alcohol. Whether such sexually characteristic behaviors are themselves the product of hormonal influences is a moot point. What is important is the conclusion that much, perhaps even most, of the sex differential in total mortality may represent modifiable behaviors.

Ethnic and Social Differences

In recent years much attention has focused on the measurable differences between different ethnic groups with respect to various social and cultural activities. The age-adjusted mortality rates show large racial and ethnic differences, almost all of which can reasonably be attributed to social and economic factors. But the important question for us is whether there is a significant difference in the manner in which different ethnic groups age. The data of Tables 5.1 and 6.5 suggest that the answer is no. The different ethnic groups represented in these tables seem to age in a more or less identical manner, at least as judged by the demographic and survival data. All groups except Hispanic and Asian men (see Table 6.5) showed substantial increases in mean longevity during the past 3 decades. And the failure of these males to emulate their sisters and wives can probably be attributed to the high-risk behaviors of young males (see Figure 6.3). By 1990, the differences between like sexes of any two groups seemed to be approaching the magnitude of the difference between the sexes of any one group (see Table 6.5). This finding suggests that the intergroup differences are not intrinsic, but may be due largely to socioeconomic and cultural factors. There are some minor differences that may be intrinsic, such as a greater sensitivity of African-Americans to renal disease or a greater life expectancy for older (85 years) African-American men and women relative to whites of comparable age, but these differences do not contradict the interpretation of the data of Table 6.5 that the variation in patterns of aging within any single group are comparable to the variation in patterns of aging between groups.

There are socioeconomic differences within and between different groups. It is a general finding, exemplified by the data of Tables 5.1 and 6.5, that survival curves are to a large extent a function of social conditions. That is, an individual's life span is the result of a complex interaction between his/her genome and the environment, a finding obtained in numerous population and twin studies (for example, Finkel et al. 1995). Improving the environment is the fastest and most efficient method of increasing mean life span, as implied by the data of Table 6.5. And degrading the environment, as is the case in much of eastern Europe and the former Soviet Union and developing countries (see Table 6.4), is an effective way to shorten our lives. As we discuss the genetic components of life span, keep in mind that our genes do not operate in a vacuum; they interact with our environment in complex and still poorly understood ways. The adoption of a deterministic social policy is not justified by the available genetic evidence. There may be varied and debatable reasons for adopting a particular public policy, but one certain reason for rejecting such a policy would be if it contradicts biological knowledge.

One can subdivide a population by identifying characteristics other than race and see whether longevity is affected by that variable. Income is a major factor. There is a twofold difference in the age-adjusted male death rates between the richest and poorest residency areas such that mortality rate is related to family income up to a level of about $20,000, beyond which mortality rate changes very little with income (Sorlie et al. 1992). Harmful behaviors such as smoking are more prevalent in low-income groups, and protective behaviors such as moderation in the use of alcohol are more prevalent in high-income groups (Smith 1993). It is reasonable to speculate that harmful and beneficial dietary practices, respectively, follow the same pattern. These observations suggest that the effect of income on longevity is due in part to the physiological implications of dysfunctional behaviors, and cannot be ascribed entirely to the shortage of money per se. Educational level is another variable that affects longevity. The progression in educational level attained from primary to secondary to postsecondary is associated with a significant reduction in mortality rate for both blacks and whites and for both men and women (Christenson and Johnson 1995). Another factor is marital status. Married people live longer than do never-married, divorced, separated, and widowed people at every age over 20 years, and mortality rates are as much as 50 percent higher for the unmarried groups (Smith 1993).

"Lifestyle" is an ambiguous word, but it seems to apply in this case. Both Mormons and Seventh-Day Adventists follow more or less closely a religiously based way of life that proscribes certain behaviors (smoking, drinking alcohol, consuming caffeine) and encourages certain other behaviors (strong family life and education for both groups, and vegetarian diet for Seventh-Day Adventists). When compared to the general U.S. population, both of these groups show an increased longevity and a decreased mortality from many common age-related diseases. All in all, these different factors may well exert their effect on longevity and mortality via the differential physiological effects of behaviors that have a strong socioeconomic bias.

Himes (1994) made an observation that supports this suggestion. As we have seen, the human life span has increased as a result of the elimination of premature deaths. An examination of the age patterns and causes of death in three different developed societies (Sweden, Japan, and the United States) indicates that Sweden and Japan have similar age patterns of mortality, which are, however, quite different from the pattern in the United States, which shows higher mortality at younger ages. Different national groups appear to achieve a long life span in different ways, and this difference may be related to the cultural and ethnic homogeneity of the society. In a heterogeneous society such as the United States, the various factors and their behavioral correlates (which we have described) may have differential effects on population subgroups sufficient to skew the general response of the population as a whole relative to that of a homogeneous society.

Superlongevity: Myth or Reality?

There is an urge to believe the reports that, somewhere in the world, human beings have discovered the secret of longevity. This idea appeals to a certain wishful side of our natures, especially since these "fountains of youth" are most often located among unsophisticated peoples leading simple rural life in the Ecuadoran Andes, in northern Pakistan, and in parts of Soviet Georgia. Several decades ago, reports began to reach the Western world not only that there were disproportionately high numbers of centenarians in these areas, but that some of them had reached the fantastic ages of 150 years or more. For example, reports from Caucasia claimed that Shirali Muslimov was the oldest man in the world when he died in 1973 at the alleged age of 168, and that Khfaf Lasuria was the oldest woman in the world when she died in 1975 at the alleged age of 142 (Pitskhelauri 1982).

The enticing thought was that these people had discovered, either by inbreeding or by their way of life, the genetic and/or environmental factors capable of strongly modulating life span. Alas, objective investigations such as those of the expatriate Russian gerontologist Zhores Medvedev (1986), now at the National Institute for Medical Research in London, have shown by analysis of the official Soviet census data that the maximum life span in these areas is probably no more than the expected 115 years or so that is characteristic of the human species. For example, the mortality rates in these areas are higher than in other parts of the Soviet Union until the ages of 79. Only after that point in the life span can one discern the lower mortality rates one would expect to be characteristic of a long-lived population. The geographic distribution of the centenarians is spotty; they are absent or very rare in many areas and yet relatively common (six or more) in some villages. Such villages become famous for the extraordinary ages of their select inhabitants. As Medvedev has pointed out, these particular villages, rather than the more realistic statistical figures for the whole region, provide the main contribution to the public awareness of this superlongevity phenomenon.

There are other statistical and methodological reasons for doubting the accuracy of the reported ages, not the least of which is the fact that there are twice as many superlong-lived men as women, a ratio completely opposite from that found in all other age groups of the population. Either something extraordinary happens to old men in Caucasia, or something extraordinary happens to the data. The tales probably had their origin in a little pious fraud. After all, in a culture where age is esteemed and respected, adding a few years surreptitiously to your real age is obviously a winning strategy. In the absence of documentary records and given a parent with the same name, it probably also wasn't very difficult.

Leaf (1984) demonstrated that a similar explanation applies to the Ecuadoran and Pakistani reports: that social and economic factors have unduly influenced these tales of extraordinary longevity. These rural Edens do not possess the secret of the Fountain of Youth. We should not judge these people too harshly, especially since many of us accede to the demands of our own culture and surreptitiously remove some years from our real age with the help of hair dye and faulty memory. In fact, Leaf (1984) pointed out that the raw and unverified data on the number of centenarians in the U.S. census for 1970 overstate the real (verified) numbers by a factor of 17, a factor more or less similar to that seen in the popularized overestimates of these three other societies. A large part of Jack Benny's long-ago fame as a radio comedian was based on this age-denying behavior, to say nothing of the profits of present-day cosmetic firms. We each react to aging in the manner that our culture teaches us.

Segmental Progerias and Premature Aging Syndromes

If life span had a simple genetic basis, one would expect to find a strong correlation between parental and offspring life spans. The studies we have discussed in this chapter consistently show a strong familial component, but one that does not account for as large a proportion of longevity as do our social and environmental factors. The human genetic data are consistent with these parent–offspring studies. Although more than 3,000 specific human genetic conditions are known, no single mutation appears to lead to a significantly longer life span. This finding has been interpreted to mean that the evolution of increased life span may be the result of the modification of numerous genes. Estimates of the maximum number of genes involved range from 70 to 7,000. Even if only a fraction (about 10 percent) of this number were involved in the determination of longevity, one would not expect such a polygenic trait (especially one so susceptible to environmental modulation) to display a strong one-to-one correlation between parent and offspring longevities.

On the other hand, various single-gene genetic traits have a segmental feature characteristic of accelerated biological aging. "Segmental" means that the pathologies of these several traits are each limited to one or a few organ systems. Thus they mimic the aging process, but only in part. George Martin (1978) has combed through the human gene catalogue and identified at least 162 single-gene defects and numerous chromosome disorders, each of which displays a segmental aspect of this accelerated-aging phenotype. Such mutations constitute about 7 percent of the human genome. In many cases, the effects on aging were most likely tangential, as would be expected for the many life-shortening diseases such as diabetes, arthritis, cystic fibrosis, and the like—all of which have a genetic component. In ten syndromes, however, the effect on the aging process was believed to be of fundamental importance (Table 6.6). Of these ten, Down syndrome, progeria, and Werner's syndrome have been most often viewed as offering useful caricatures of normal aging. A good clinical description of these conditions may be found in Brown 1985.

Table 6.6   **Premature Aging Syndromes**
1. Down syndrome
2. Werner syndrome
3. Cockayne's syndrome
4. Progeria
5. Ataxia-telangiectasia
6. Cervical dysplasis, familial
7. Seip's syndrome
8. Klinefelter's syndrome
9. Turner's syndrome
10. Myotonic dystrophy

Source: From Martin 1978.

Down syndrome is caused by a chromosomal disorder, most often an extra copy of chromosome 21. Patients with this syndrome are characterized by (1) a delay in the rate of normal development, (2) a failure to achieve full development, and (3) a more rapid onset of apparent aging, with various organ systems degenerating earlier than normal. Patients with this syndrome have a shortened life expectancy (only 8 percent survive to age 40) and suffer from premature graying and hair loss, increased tissue lipofuscin, increased neoplasms, variable adipose tissue distribution, amyloidosis, increased autoimmunity, hypogonadism, degenerative vascular disease, and cataracts. In addition, they suffer from a precocious dementia, which appears to be accompanied by neuropathological changes indistinguishable from that of SDAT (senile disease of the Alzheimer's type, or Alzheimer's disease; see Chapter 5).

The gene responsible for the amyloid precursor protein (APP) composing the neuritic plaques characteristic of SDAT and of Down syndrome has been mapped to chromosome 21, the one causing the chromosome imbalance. This result first engendered a lot of speculative excitement that the two diseases might have the same dysfunction. In fact, patients with trisomy 21 overproduce APP from birth and show diffuse APP plaques as early as 12 years of age, long before they develop other SDAT-type lesions. However, continued research has shown that the story is more complex. As described in Chapter 5, it has been shown that an increased production of APP, particularly the more harmful $A\beta$-42 peptides, may be brought about by mutations on chromosome 21, on chromosome 14, or on chromosome 1; the age of onset of $A\beta$-42 plaque deposition is accelerated by the *ApoE4* gene on chromosome 19 but is delayed by the *ApoE2* allele of the same gene, as we will see in the next section.. Thus, overlapping but different genetic mechanisms seem to govern the production of these plaques in patients with Down syndrome and with SDAT. This observation reinforces the viewpoint that similar if not identical phenotypes may be produced by very different processes. Down syndrome may be brought about via subtle changes in timing of the developmental events induced by the chromosomal imbalance, particularly involving other genes on the chromosome that are known to be expressed in the facial and neural structures usually involved in Down syndrome (Hopkin 1995). If so, the etiological relationship of this syndrome to the normal aging process is not clear.

Progeria is a rare genetic disease caused probably by the spontaneous and sporadic production of a dominant mutation in one parent's germ line. Patients with this condition have striking clinical features that superficially resemble nothing so much as premature aging. Patients usually appear normal at birth but begin to lose their hair and subcutaneous fat beginning sometime in the first year. Growth slows and finally ceases. These children characteristically attain the height of an average 5-year-old and the weight of an average 3-year-old. The skin becomes thinner, making visible the superficial veins. "Age" spots appear over the body. Bone mass is resorbed. Sexual development is limited. The progeric head, with its beaked nose and underdeveloped jaw, is characteristically unusual. Patients have normal to above-normal intelligence. No neurofibrillary tangles appear in the central nervous system. The median age at death is 12 years. The cause of death is almost always very severe coronary artery disease. Differences have been noted at the cellular and molecular levels between progerics and normal controls. For example, the progeria patients seem to have elevated growth hormone levels and an elevated basal metabolic rate (Abdenur et al.1997), an altered signal sequence region in their manganese superoxide dismutase gene (Rosenblum, Gilula, and Lerner 1997), shorter than normal telomeres (Allsopp et al. 1992), and reduction in DNA repair synthesis (Wang et al. 1991; Sugita et al. 1995).

However, other aspects of the syndrome point to the involvement of connective tissue. Fibroblasts in these patients have abnormal expression of collagen and elastin (Colige et al. 1991; Giro and Davidson 1993), high levels of glycoproteins (Clark and Weiss 1993), high levels of collagen-digesting metalloproteinases (Millis et al 1992), and elevated levels of hyaluronic acid excretion (Brown 1992; Sweeney and Weiss 1992). The continued study of this pathology likely will give us some insight into normal processes of connective tissue aging. However, it is unlikely that this disease represents an acceleration of normal aging, so it is best viewed as a pathology with segmental applications to normal connective tissue functions and aging.

Werner's syndrome is an autosomal recessive trait that is sometimes called progeria of the adult. Patients generally appear normal during childhood but cease growth during the teenage years. Premature graying of the hair and baldness occur, as does skin and muscular atrophy, hypogonadism, poor wound healing, atherosclerosis, osteoporosis, soft-tissue calcification, juvenile cataracts, and a tendency toward diabetes. The median age at death is 47 years. Death appears to result from complications involving the cardiovascular system or from malignancies. Basic research at the cellular level has revealed that cells from patients with either Werner's syndrome or progeria exhibit particular defects in connective tissue metabolism. Furthermore, their fibroblasts (a type of connective tissue cell) have a significantly shorter life span potential *in vitro* than do normal fibroblasts (see Chapter 11). They also have a significant increase in their chromosome abnormalities relative to the controls.

The gene responsible for Werner's syndrome was localized on the short arm of chromosome 8 and recently has been precisely located and identified by positional cloning (Yu et al. 1996). The product of this gene has been tentatively identified as a helicase, one of a class of enzymes involved in unwinding DNA in preparation for any one of various different DNA-specific activities, such as replication, repair, or recombination. At least four different mutations of this gene are found in patients with Werner's syndrome. Derangements in any one of the helicase-dependent activities could cause the cells to function poorly, and thus precipitate a premature aging syndrome. Certainly much of the pathology of Werner's syndrome can be understood in principle as the result of a failure of DNA repair or replication.

It will be the task of future research to determine the effects of the mutations in the gene on these DNA processes and to illuminate the causal sequence leading from the gene to the phenotype. In addition, it will be of great interest to determine whether ostensibly normal individuals carry different alleles of the gene that might affect their life span in either direction. The development of a unitary explanation for this syndrome will be of great value in advancing our understanding of at least some of the mechanisms involved in aging.

The Genetics of Human Aging

As the preceding discussion of the segmental progerias indicates, all the known mutants that affect longevity in humans do so by reducing life span. The impact of other genetic factors on the incidence of age-associated diseases and disabilities is becoming more clearly defined. These genetic factors might act either by extending longevity in the individuals who carry them or by promoting disease and/or premature death in the individuals who carry them. Given the nature of medical research, more is known about the latter category than the former, so our account may be unbalanced. What we do know suggests that the eventual explanation of the genetics of human aging will include a complicated series of physiological and evolutionary interactions.

As an example of genetic factors that promote disease, let's consider the apolipoprotein E (*ApoE*) gene. This gene encodes a protein that is synthesized in the liver, brain, lungs, spleen, kidneys, and macrophages. The *ApoE* gene is located on chromosome 19 at position q13.2. Human populations are polymorphic for three common alleles (*E2*, *E3*, and *E4*), which encode three major ApoE isoforms with different molecular and physiological characteristics (see Kamboh 1995 for references). When the frequencies of the three different *ApoE* alleles were measured in centenarians and in noncentenarians, the results showed a decided shortage of people bearing the *ApoE4* allele among the centenarians (5.2 percent) compared to the normal controls (11.2 percent), coupled with an excess of the *ApoE2* allele among the centenarians (12.8 percent) relative to the normal controls (6.8 percent) (Schacter et al. 1994). The *E2* and *E4* alleles seem to have a positive and negative effect, respectively, on longevity. We have some insight into the nature of these effects.

Individuals homozygous for *ApoE4* alleles are significantly more likely to develop late-onset Alzheimer's disease than are those homozygous for *ApoE3* alleles. Individuals homozygous for *ApoE2* alleles are even less likely to develop Alzheimer's disease, and heterozygous individuals demonstrate intermediate risks. The rare individuals who are completely deficient in the protein (because of a null mutation of some sort) are at very high risk of atherosclerosis and hyperlipidemia. Note that the presence of the *ApoE4* alleles does not necessarily mean that the individual will develop Alzheimer's disease, nor does its absence offer complete protection against Alzheimer's, for this allele is neither absolutely necessary nor sufficient for the expression of the disease. Thus the presence of a functional ApoE protein is necessary to avoid very early death, but the particular isoform(s) present each have different probabilities of bringing about different effects in late-life morbidity for the individuals who carry them.

Individuals who carry the *ApoE4* allele are strongly predisposed to developing late-onset Alzheimer's disease and are also likely to respond poorly to current therapies (Poirier et al. 1995). The latter observation opens the possibility of using genetic identity to subdivide a heterogeneous disease group into more homogeneous subsets of patients who can respond differentially to various therapeutic interventions. In addition to its role in neural impairment, the *ApoE4* allele appears to be involved in the etiology of ischemic heart disease, or atherosclerosis, a leading age-related disease and cause of death. The frequency of the *ApoE4* allele varies among different populations, ranging from a low of 0.07 in Oriental populations to a high of 0.37 in New Guineans (Kamboh 1995), and these frequencies are inversely proportional to the frequency of ischemic heart disease observed in the different groups. In addition, fewer older individuals carry the *ApoE4* allele than younger individuals, suggesting that fewer bearers of this allele survive to old age (van Bockxmeer 1994).

How can one protein be involved in two syndromes as disparate as neural degeneration and atherosclerosis? A plausible, although unproven, scenario follows. The ApoE protein participates in all three known pathways involved in lipoprotein metabolism: transport of dietary lipid from the intestine to the liver, from the liver to extrahepatic cells, and from extrahepatic cells back to the liver. In this process, the ApoE protein binds to the surface of different types of cholesterol-rich lipoprotein particles and causes their uptake by liver cells, which have receptors on their surface that recognize and bind the ApoE protein. It has been suggested that the major difference among the three isoforms (E2, E3, and E4) is their differing number of cysteine residues. In fact, the three proteins are defined by whether they have cysteine or arginine at codons 112 and 158. The ApoE2 protein has cysteine at both sites, the ApoE3 protein has cysteine at codon 112 and arginine at codon 158, and the ApoE4 protein has arginine at both sites. The lack of cysteine in the ApoE4 protein and its consequent inability to participate in disulfide bond formation might result in a protein that has an altered binding capacity for a variety of intra- and extracellular components, and this condition may give rise to different disease syndromes, depending on the organ system involved (Schacter et al. 1994; Kamboh 1995).

The lack of disulfide binding in ApoE4 causes it to fail to bind to a particular microtubule protein (tau; see Chapter 5), and the unbound tau protein is consequently hyperphosphorylated and gives rise to the neurofibrillary tangles that are characteristic of Alzheimer's disease. ApoE2 and ApoE3, on the other hand, can bind to the tau protein and thereby prevent or slow the formation of tangles. The same lack of disulfide binding capacity of the ApoE4 allele for lipoprotein particles has been put forth as a plausible explanation for its association with atherosclerosis and ischemic heart disease (Kamboh 1995). Indeed, it has been shown that Alzheimer's patients that have the *ApoE4* allele also have abnormally high levels of cholesterol (Giubilei et al. 1990). More recently, the three *ApoE* alleles were shown to differ in their antioxidant activity, and thus in their ability to protect cells against oxidative insults (Miyata and Smith 1996). As might be suspected, the antioxidant ranking of the three alleles is *E2 > E3 > E4*. The differential antioxidant activity probably is also due to the differential ability of the three resulting proteins to bind metals (which have pro-oxidant activities) and to remove them from the cell's environment.

Thus we have outlined what appears to be a plausible and unitary (but still unproven) explanation for the role of the *ApoE4* allele in two seemingly disparate diseases. (But the reader will know from the material presented in Chapter 5 that this hypothetical explanation, even if true, is only one part of the complete story for each of these diseases). The apparent underlying simplicity is masked by the complexity of the pleiotropic interactions stemming from this one protein. The fact that the presence of a particular allele does not guarantee the presence or absence of a particular syndrome suggests that there are probably substantial interactions taking place between gene and environment, resulting in phenotypic plasticity. Such interactions could, if defined, lead the way to potential interventions.

Similarly complex stories probably underlie the involvement of other genes, such as the angiotensin-converting enzyme (*ACE*) gene or the vitamin D receptor gene, both of which are also known to be associated with the promotion of age-related disease morbidity and mortality. Such studies will continue to reveal much about the biological basis and the nature of the genetic contribution to middle- and late-life morbidity and mortality, and their consequent effects on life expectancy and individual longevity. In the ApoE story, we can tentatively conclude that defective protein-binding capacity leads to tissue-specific cascades of grave and abnormal consequences. Note that there is no gene for short life per se, but rather a gene that simply affects protein binding. All the rest is the result of a pleiotropic cascade. Perhaps most diseases will reduce eventually to similarly simple explanations.

This does not necessarily mean that genes that enhance longevity do not exist in the human species. Such genetic conditions would be much less obvious in the population. A child dying of progeria or a man dying of heart disease at the age of 35 is much more noticeable and commented on as being caused by something out of the ordinary than is an elderly person living to an extraordinarily old age, particularly before the advent of careful population statistics to serve as an objective marker (see the discussion of ethnic and social differences earlier in this chapter). In fact, certain centenarians and nonagenarians were shown to have a statistically significant association with certain alleles at the HLA (human leukocyte system A) locus, which is known to be responsible for much of our immunological defenses (see Chapter 12) (Takata et al. 1987). There is evidence in human nonagenarians and centenarians of an excess frequency of some HLA alleles, but the data also indicate that there are important ethnic or geographic differences. For example, elderly Chinese in the Shanghai area seem to have an excess of the *HLA-A9* allele and a deficiency of the *HLA-A30, Cw3, Cw6,* and *C27* alleles, all relative to the middle-aged control group (Ma et al. 1997). However, elderly French Caucasians showed an excess of the *HLA-Cw1* allele in females and the *HLA-Cw7* allele in males (Proust et al. 1982). Thus there are mostly differences between the two groups but some similarities as well. It seems reasonable to suppose that certain HLA halplotypes are probably associated with extended longevity, but that more work will be needed to positively identify the particular alleles.

Such alleles might be considered longevity-enhancing genes. Other longevity-enhancing genes probably exist, but they have not yet been identified and characterized, since they likely require similar sorts of statistical and biochemical clues to be recognized. In addition, there is no reason to believe that humans are fundamentally different in this respect from laboratory animals that are known to have such genes. Thus it is reasonable to believe that the human genome contains a diversity of genes that affect life span in both positive and negative directions.

As already mentioned, Martin (1978) concluded from his survey of genetic disorders affecting life span that there are a large number of genes at which variation could modulate aging. However, many of these genes might be expected to be involved only indirectly, and not causally. As discussed in Chapter 4, the approach taken by Cutler (1975) and by Sacher (1975) to derive the rate of evolution of the modern human life span led them to conclude that longevity has evolved rapidly by means of relatively few mutational alterations, most if not all of which are thought to operate at the regulatory-gene level and not at the structural-gene level. However, there is no firm independent evidence to support or falsify these statements.

Until now, genetic investigations into human aging have had to restrict themselves to clinical or statistical studies, for obvious ethical and empirical reasons. However, a revolution has taken place in human genetics within the past two decades. In 1968, the chromosomal location of only one gene was known with any certainty. In 1978, the chromosomal location of about 120 genes had been painstakingly deduced (McKusick and Ruddle 1978). By 1988, more than 1,600 genetic markers had been mapped (Martin and Turker 1988), and a complete linkage map of the human genome had been published (Donis-Keller et al. 1987). The policy decision to sequence the human genome was made at that time, and it now appears very likely that the genome will be completely sequenced by its target date of 2005 (Olson 1995). Enough progress has been made in mapping the genome that it is possible to begin serious investigations designed to expand our theoretical understanding of human genetics (Fink and Collins 1997). It should soon be possible to associate particular enhanced-longevity pedigrees with particular DNA regions and with their gene products, thereby adding a very powerful tool to the analysis of longevity in humans.

One procedure that could be used to accomplish this goal is quantitative trait loci (QTL) mapping. If one has a dense array of detectable markers spread across each of the chromosomes, then one can make the appropriate crosses (or in the case of humans, assay family members who differ in the trait of interest) and determine which sets of markers are preferentially associated with the phenotype of interest. The genes of interest lie somewhere between, and are linked to, the non-randomly assorting markers. (See the December 1995 issue of *Trends in Genetics* for reviews of this topic.) The most convenient markers to use are known DNA sequences such as are being churned out by the Human Genome Project. As the project continues and the map increases in resolution, the identification of genetic regions associated with particular syndromes will accelerate. At some point, our increased genetic knowledge will allow us to shift from a statistical and general approach to the genetics of human aging, to a genetic and causal approach. Thus, instead of calculating heritability (h^2) values for longevity on the basis of the analysis of long- and short-lived populations, we will be able to identify the chromosomal regions—and eventually the genetic loci—involved in the trait of interest.

This qualitative shift in our knowledge is one of the outcomes that will eventually fully justify the cost of the Human Genome Project. We are already using such procedures to identify genes of interest in commercially important organisms such as pigs, cattle, and trees. The qualitative advances in our knowledge brought about by the application of these procedures to ourselves promises to be inextricably entwined with some serious ethical and social problems. Reflect on the ApoE protein described earlier. Should people with the *ApoE4* allele be refused health insurance? Should they be denied long-term and expensive education because they might not live long enough to make it worthwhile? Or should they be shunned in romance by prospective spouses? These and other difficult questions are being addressed at both institutional and personal levels by both scientists and laypeople. It would be useful to have some guidelines in place before we are once again surprised by the unexpected social and personal impact of our quest for knowledge (see Kevles and Hood 1993 for review and references to bioethical issues).

Once the genes that are believed to be mechanistically involved in a particular aspect of human aging are identified and sequenced, we can be sure that the desire to use these genes in some sort of intervention strategy will not be long in coming. In fact, the discussions have already begun (Dykes 1996). The potential type of intervention most often discussed is somatic gene therapy: the introduction of normal genes into all or some of the somatic cells of an individual in order either to replace genetically defective functions or to alter pathological disease processes. Somatic gene therapy does not alter the heritability of the underlying mutation; such a change would involve germ line gene therapy, which is not currently practiced in humans. Somatic gene therapy for humans is in its infancy, with more failures than successes in its record to date. Nonetheless, much effort and hope are being invested in it, and it is worthy of at least a brief discussion here.

The diseases currently targeted for somatic gene therapy include such disorders as immunodeficiency, hypercholesterolemia, hemophilia, cystic fibrosis, and muscular dystrophy. None of these conditions are intimately involved in the aging process. If we assume that the goal of biomedical research is to increase the mean life expectancy of the population, then somatic gene therapy should be targeted on heart disease, cancer, and stroke. If, however, we assume that the goal of biomedical research is to maintain the health and decrease the portion of the life span during which aging people are disabled, then somatic gene therapy should be focused on alleviating Alzheimer's and other neurological diseases, such as arthritis, diabetes, osteoporosis, and immunosenescence. The question is academic at the moment, since the genes for none of these disorders are yet characterized, nor are the roles of such genes understood well enough to construct rational gene therapies. A more important consideration is that the probable polygenic nature of many of these conditions guarantees that effective somatic gene therapy will be some time in coming. This delay may give us time to debate the issues and decide how we should utilize this future therapy.

Physiological and Other Predictors: Conclusions from Longitudinal Studies

Although expensive and tedious, a relatively large number of human longitudinal studies have been done during the past half century or so (Table 6.7). Together they provide a substantial data base against which various generaliza-

| *Table 6.7* | **Selected Longitudinal Studies of Aging** | | | | | | | |

Study	Began	Ended	Nature of sample	Sample size (N)	Sex and ages at entry	Test interval	Variables measured	Health criteria for admission
Longitudinal Studies of Individuals								
Minnesota	1947	1977	Professional and business men	281	M 45–54	Annual	Anthropometry Behavior and personality	Yes
Duke I	1955	1976	Community residents	260	M&F 60–94	2 years	Psychiatry Psychology Physiology Anthropometry Blood chemistry Social history	Yes
Duke II	1968	1976	Community residents selected from register of health insurance plan	502	M&F 45–69	2 years	Psychology Social history Personality	No
Normative Aging	1963	Continuing	Community residents in Boston	2,032	M 25–75	5 years	Biochemistry Special senses Anthropometry Psychology Sociology	Yes
1000- Aviator	1940	1970	Cadets and officers in fight training	1,056	M 20–30	Irregular	Physiology Psychomotor (rigorous) Psychology	Yes
NIMH[a]	1955	1967	Community residents in	47	M 65–91	5 years	Psychiatric interview Cerebral physiology Psychological tests Social history	Yes
Basel	1955	1965	Community- residing CIBA employees and retirees	121	M 8–85 (Most 26–56)	1–2 years	Anthropometry Physiology Sensory tests P.W.V.	No
Bonn	1965	1976–77	Community residents in West Germany	220	M&F 60–75	2–4 years	2- to 4-hour interviews Intelligence Personality	Yes
Framing- ham	1948	Continuing	Community residents	5,209	M&F 30–59	2 years	Blood chemistry end points-CV disease	No

(continued on next page)

Table 6.7   (Continued)

Study	Began Ended	Nature of sample	Sample size (N)	Sex and ages at entry	Test interval	Variables measured	Health criteria for admission
Tecumseh	1959 1969	Total community	8,641	M&F Birth to 70+ (45% under age 20)	3 years	Anthropometry Physiology Blood chemistry Activity questionnaire	No
ABCC[b] Adult Health	1958 1972	Nonexposed residents of Hiroshima	12,123	M&F Birth to 70+	2 years	Anthropometry Physiology Blood chemistry	No
BLSA[c]	1958 Continuing	Community-residing males[d]	1,142	M 17–96	1–2 years	See Table 3.4	No

Longitudinal Studies of Twins

SATSA[e]	Like-sexed twin pairs, ages 50–85 years, reared together and apart; primary purpose: to identify etiologies of behaviors that characterize successful aging; tests include: measures of physical and mental health status, daily living activities, health-related behaviors.
MTSADA[f]	Upwards of 600 twin pairs will eventually be incorporated into the study; designed to study upper age range (60–85); testing similar to SATSA, therefore together will provide an excellent cross-cultural comparison; extension of Minnesota Twin Study.
BETS[g]	Getting under way; large number of twins within the black population have been identified; should provide an excellent cross-racial comparison with other twin studies.

Source: Adapted from Shock et al. 1984.
[a]National Institute of Mental Health.
[b]Atomic Bomb Central Commission.
[c]Baltimore Longitudinal Study on Aging.
[d]Women have been recruited to the study since 1978.
[e]Swedish Adoption/Twin Study of Aging.
[f]Minnesota Twin Study of Adult Development and Aging.
[g]Black Elderly Twin Study (University of Illinois at Chicago).

tions can be tested. Unfortunately, the very real differences in their structure and methods make it impossible for data bases of these studies to be combined, so each study must be understood on its own terms. Yet their results are generally compatible. We will briefly examine certain selected results of the Framingham, Duke I, and BLSA studies of Table 6.7, as well as some early data from the Alameda County study.

A wealth of data in this text and elsewhere indicate the change in a particular physiological variable with age. But these variables do not operate in a vacuum.

They interact with other physiological variables over time, and some are greatly influenced by gender. The data from the Framingham study were analyzed by Manton, Woodbury, and Stallard (1995) and used to construct a more realistic model of the gender changes in several physiological variables and how they affect functional capacity and mortality. Some of these variables change in complex ways (Figure 6.4). For example, what does the alteration in cholesterol levels with age say about the activity or changing roles of the *ApoE* alleles in these individuals? Cutting through such idle speculations, Manton, Woodbury, and Stallard (1995) used these observed data to construct mathematical models of the optimum values of the 10 variables studied that would yield the lowest mortality, highest life expectancy, and highest degree of function (Table 6.8). The optimum values for males and females are often quite different, and the difference between the observed and optimum values translates into apparently substantial amounts of unrealized life expectancy. In addition, Manton, Woodbury, and Stallard (1995) concluded that the individual's functional capacity explains more of the age dependency of mortality than do risk factors. We will pick up this point again in Chapter 13. A complete description of the important physiological factors seem-

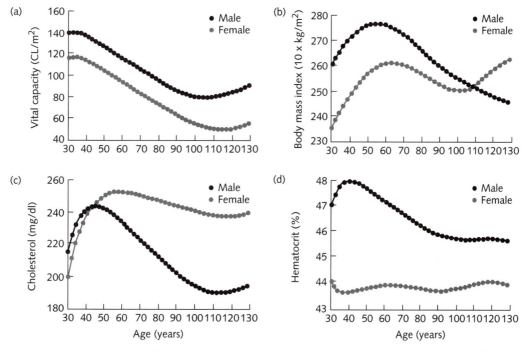

Figure 6.4   The predicted gender-specific age trajectories of four risk factors calculated using risk factor dynamics and mortality equations estimated from the 34-year follow-up data from the Framingham Heart Study. Note that the predicted risk factors are not constant but change throughout life. Also note that the risk factor may be similar (a) or different (b–d) in males and females. (From Manton, Woodbury, and Stallard 1995.)

Table 6.8   **Values Producing Lowest Mortality in Gender-Specific Mortality Functions**

	Male		Female	
	Observed means at 30	*Optimal values*	*Observed means at 30*	*Optimal values*
1. Pulse pressure (mm/Hg)	48.5	31.0	43.8	46.8
2. DBP (mm/Hg)	82.0	75.8	76.6	78.0
3. BMI (10 x kg/m^2)	254.1	241.9	233.0	267.6
4. Cholesterol (mg/dl)	212.3	176.8	195.2	221.7
5. Blood glucose (mg/%)	79.5	84.1	77.9	124.4
6. Hematocrit (%)	47.1	46.7	42.2	44.6
7. VCI (CL/m^2)	136.8	159.7	114.0	121.6
8. Smoking (cigarettes/day)	15.0	0.0	8.0	0.0
9. LVH (%)	2.0%	0.0	1.0%	0.0
10. Heart rate (per minute)	72.4	67.8	75.6	55.5
Life expectancy remaining at age 30 (years)	43.7	81.0	49.6	73.2

Source: From Manton et al. 1995.

ingly would yield a complex pattern of interactions that change with age and that have extensive pleiotropic effects on the functional status of the individual.

The BLSA has performed an extensive number of physiological, cognitive, and psychological tests on hundreds of subjects over a 30-year period. The results to date have been thoroughly summarized (Shock et al. 1984). Most of the subjects are still alive, so many of the conclusions are still open-ended. One of the goals of this study is the construction of physiological indices of aging. An example of such an endeavor is provided in a report by Tobin (1981) in which he chose four physiological variables that are considered to be clinically important measures of individual health. Age-adjusted standard scores were developed for each test such that a score of 50 equaled the mean value of the physiological variable for any age group. These scores were then compared between study subjects who were still living ($N = 860$) and those who had died ($N = 162$). As Figure 6.5 shows, the dead individuals before their death had displayed lower-than-normal scores in three out of four of these physiological functions. An expanded version of this biomarker index is presented in Figures 3.20 to 3.22 and illustrates the potential value of this approach toward constructing a physiological index of aging.

The first Duke study revealed a general stability over time in an individual's activities and traits. We change less than we might fear or our teachers might hope. This study also made clear that many individuals do not show the functional decline in particular traits that were predicted by cross-sectional data; thus, the results of this study emphasize the value of the longitudinal approach. In brief, the results show that in that particular study population, the strongest predictors of longevity were physical health, not smoking, work satisfaction, and happiness (Palmore 1982). The study controlled for age, sex, and race by measuring the divergence between the number of years the subject lived and the sub-

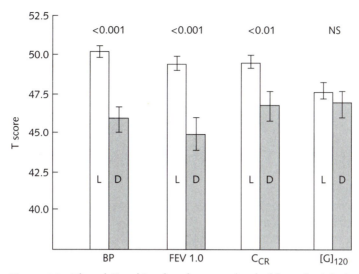

Figure 6.5 The relationship of performance level of four physiological tests to survival on subjects in the BLSA project. Gray bars (D) represent results for subjects who have died; open bars (L) represent results for the survivors. The T score is an age-adjusted scoring system that allows for the relative comparison of the different tests. For the first three tests, T scores of survivors were significantly different from those of nonsurvivors. BP, systolic blood pressure; FEV 1.0, forced expiratory volume in 1 second; C_{CR}, creatinine clearance; $[G]_{120}$, glucose concentration 2 hours after administration of oral glucose. Values across the top represent probabilities (NS = not significant). (From Tobin 1981. © Oxford University Press.)

ject's theoretical life expectancy based on the actuarial table appropriate for his or her age, sex, and race. This value is termed the longevity difference (LD), is not significantly correlated with the subject's age, and is normally distributed around a mean of +1.6 with a range of −14 to +15 (Palmore 1982). This means that the average subject would have lived about 19 months longer than actuarial analysis would have predicted. Of 50 variables examined, 22 (divided into 8 groups) were found to be statistically significant predictors of the LD for men or women or both (see Table 6.9). Figure 6.6 shows a theoretical model for the interrelationships of these various predictors. As a result of the statistical analysis, the investigators were able to identify a limited number of different strong predictors for each sex. For men, the three most important of these were found to be the health self-rating, work satisfaction, and performance intelligence. For women, the three most important, independently significant predictors were health satisfaction, past enjoyment of sexual intercourse, and the physician's health rating.

Finally, the results from the Alameda County study (Guralnie and Kaplan 1989) suggest that the following variables can function as statistically significant predictors of healthy aging: race, higher family income, absence of hypertension, absence of arthritis, absence of back pain, being a nonsmoker, having normal

Table 6.9 **Statistically Significant Predictors of the Longevity Difference**

Predictor	Comments
1. Father's age at death	Men only
2. Intelligence, both verbal and performance	Men and women
3. Socioeconomic status: education, finances, occupation	Men only
4. Activities	
a. Physical mobility	Women only
b–c. Social activities	Women only
d. Group acitivites	Men and women
e. Self activities	Men and women
5. Sexual relations	
a. Frequency of intercourse	Men only
b. Past enjoyment of intercourse	Women only
c. Present enjoyment of intercourse	Women only
6. Tobacco use	Negative predictor for both sexes
7. Satisfaction	
a–c. Work, religion, usefulness	Men only
d. Happiness	Men and women
8. Health	
a. Physician's rating	Men and women
b. Self-rating	Men and women
c. Health satisfaction	Women only

Source: From Palmore 1982.

weight, and drinking only moderate amounts of alcohol. Several of these variables have been statistically implicated in other studies, as described earlier in the section on ethnic and social differences.

How does one interpret these different findings? The BSLA and Framingham results document the role of physiological factors, while the Alameda County and Duke I studies appear to involve an interesting mix of physiological and behavioral factors. There is no contradiction between these disparate conclusions, for, as discussed in Chapter 5, the neuro-endocrine-immune system together translates physiological factors into behavioral traits, and vice versa. The same factors are affecting each of us, but in different ways. Some of these differences might be due to real physiological differences between the sexes, others might reflect more of a sociocultural influence on our perceived sex roles. Men and women appear to live differently. No wonder it proves so puzzling when we live together.

Studies in Experimental Organisms

Many studies on the biology of aging cannot, for obvious ethical, legal, and practical reasons, be done with human beings. Accordingly, animals are often used as

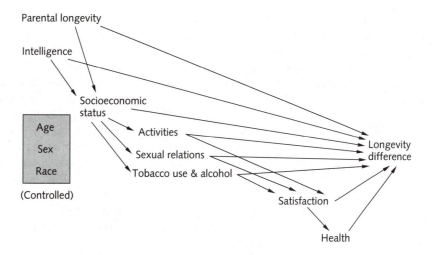

Figure 6.6 A simplified theoretical model showing the nature and the interrelationships of various predictors of the longevity difference (LD) as determined in the Duke First Longitudinal Study of Aging (see Table 6.8 for details). The LD is the difference between the actual and the actuarially calculated life span of the subjects. (From Palmore 1982.)

surrogates. The information that is obtained through research on animals provides scientists with an objective basis for identifying possibly important physiological mechanisms in humans, as well as a basis for comparative studies on aging, which are important in their own right. Scientists study different species for a variety of reasons, not the least of which is the suitability of the particular animal for the particular question. The animals should have a reasonably short life span and be available in adequate numbers, and there should be sufficient information available for that species that the research can be profitably continued at any level desired—from molecular to organismic. In particular, the animal system chosen should be amenable to genetic analysis to take full advantage of the power and resolution of genetic approaches to complex phenotypes.

There are two different ways in which one can use genetics to learn about the regulation of aging. First, one can identify age-specific changes that occur in normal animals and then use molecular genetic techniques to determine if the particular change has a causal relationship to the aging process; that is, does alteration of the age-specific change bring about a corresponding change in the aging process? Second, one can identify genes that might regulate aging by searching for mutants that have an altered rate or process of aging. We will discuss examples of both approaches. One virtue of the genetic approach is that it is not tied to the preconception of the investigator. It does not matter whether aging is strictly regulated or whether it is stochastic and dependent on chance. From the types of mutant genes identified or not identified, it is possible to make rational inferences about the architecture of the mechanisms of aging.

However, once a genetic approach has been chosen, considerations of convenience, cost, and custom probably influence us more than we might like to admit. In Chapter 1, we discussed the limited range of animal systems that have been extensively investigated, and we noted that there are other models, such as birds, that may be very informative but have not yet been investigated in depth. The first part of this chapter has tried to make clear that our heredity is a major influence on, and good predictor of, our longevity. It should be equally clear that much of the future information regarding the genetic control of aging will have to come from animal studies, given the necessary constraints on human studies. Much of the little we do know about the genetic aspects of aging has come from investigations undertaken on an unlikely quartet of species—flies, mice, fungi, and worms—that superficially appear to be very dissimilar to humans. What genetic insights have these studies given us? Are they applicable to humans? Can any of these diverse species teach us anything regarding the existence of genetically based predictors of longevity?

The obvious and fundamental biological differences between insects such as *Drosophila* and vertebrates such as humans do not necessarily constitute a major disadvantage to using the fruit fly as a model for the genetic analysis of aging. Of course, some of these differences are quite important. When we translate results from one species to the other, we must keep in mind that the cells of the adult insect are, with the exception of the germ cells, entirely postmitotic. Yet from another point of view, this restriction is an experimental virtue, for it allows one to examine senescent processes uncomplicated by the effects of cell division and replacement (Figure 6.7). Many of the cellular and subcellular age-related changes that take place in the insect are similar to those that take place in vertebrates. The experimentally verified phenotypic expressions of aging in *Drosophila*

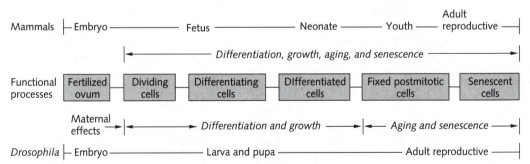

Figure 6.7 A diagrammatic representation of the pathways of cell differentiation and aging in *Drosophila* and in mammals, correlated with the sequence of the developmental stages that constitute the life cycle in these different types of organisms. Mammalian models contain heterogeneous tissues because at any given point in time or developmental stage there are a variety of functionally different cells at various points along the differentiation pathway within almost every structure. *Drosophila* contains only terminally differentiated cells in the adult individuals; thus they are a simpler model in which to investigate the mechanisms of senescence in differentiated cells. (After Miquel and Fleming 1984.)

listed in Table 4.7 bear a striking resemblance to the age-related changes that take place in humans, as described in Chapter 5. This similarity is probably a reflection of the fact that biological mechanisms fundamentally important in one species are generally fundamentally important in most species. For example, the now famous homeobox-containing genes were first identified as developmental mutants in *Drosophila*. Homologous multigene families are now known to regulate mammalian development and to be responsible for certain human congenital malformations (Gilbert 1994). Finally, the gene products from both vertebrate and invertebrate homeobox loci appear to possess fundamental similarities to the lambda phage repressor (Ptashne 1988).

This sort of molecular homology validates the usefulness of animal research on aging. Such genetic research may not tell us directly how to manipulate human aging, but it does promise to tell us what physiological systems and which organizational levels we should investigate. A very common strategy today is to ask interesting questions regarding aging in systems amenable to genetic manipulation such as *Drosophila* and then later to translate these findings to a vertebrate model such as mice and, if the results warrant, translate the results to humans.

Mice and Other Rodents

The laboratory rat and mouse have many characteristics, such as small size, short life span, and a physiological similarity to humans, that have endeared them to laboratory scientists. One indication of their popularity is a bibliography that lists about 750 references to studies of aging done with genetically defined strains of rodents between 1977 and 1988 (Hazzard and Soban 1988). Probably as many, if not more, such studies have been done since 1989. A much larger variety of inbred strains and mutants is available in mice than in rats, so we will concentrate our genetic inquiries on the former. In fact, during the past half century and as a result of the meticulous accumulation and study of genetic variants, the mouse has become one of the world's better organisms for genetic research. It has proven to be very useful as a genetic tool for exploring mammalian developmental genetics; its value in studies on aging has probably not yet been fully realized. Historically, investigations into the genetics of aging in the mouse began with a comparison of longevity among different strains. There exists a wealth of survival data for the mouse, a portion of which is presented in Table 6.10.

First, almost all the strains have a mean or median life span of about 2 years or so. None of the inbred strains have a value higher than 2.3 years, although some may have a significantly lower mean life span. In some strains, this decreased life span is associated with a high incidence of pathology that has nothing to do with aging. In the AKR/J strain, for example, leukemia is the principal cause of death.

Second, there are moderate but consistent differences in life span among the several strains. However, these modest differences in mean life span do not always reflect the survival course of older animals. For example, the C57BL/6J strain has been repeatedly shown to have a slightly longer mean life span (by about 18 percent) than the Balb/cJ strain. Yet there is no difference between the two strains

Table 6.10   **Life Spans of Inbred Mouse Strains**

Strain	Mean life span (days)		Cause of death
	Male	Female	
C57BL/6J	827	818	Nonspecific pathologies in both sexes
DBA/2J	722	683	Nonspecific in male, but 34% of females have breast tumors
AJ	622	688	Nonspecific, but 30% of females have varied tumors
Balb/cJ	648	816	Nonspecific, but 29% of females have varied tumors
AKR/J	326	276	90% leukemia in both sexes
F_1 hybrids of AJ x C57BL/6J	945	861	—

Source: Data from Goodrick 1975.

regarding the survival characteristics of their longest-lived one-sixth of the populations. Thus the median survival differences may result because of genetic influences on processes other than aging, such as a lower incidence of early or premature death in the C57BL/6J strain.

Third, the females generally but not always (12 out of 20) have a modestly higher life expectancy than do the males within the same strain. This finding suggests that certain mouse strains might serve as a good model for exploring these gender differences.

Fourth, hybrid offspring, derived from a mating between two inbred strains, have a longer mean life span than do either set of parents. This phenomenon is called heterosis, or hybrid vigor, and is thought to be due to the breaking up of the deleterious gene combinations brought about by extensive inbreeding. The same phenomenon is seen in many other species, including *Drosophila*. This concept is very difficult to translate into human terms, for we as a species are largely composed of outbred populations.

Fifth, it has proven possible to make statistical comparisons between the longevity of a long-lived inbred strain (such as C57BL/6J) and that of a short-lived inbred strain (such as AJ or DBA/2J), and of their F_1 and F_2 hybrids as well, to estimate (1) the proportion of the variance in the life span that is due to inheritance (the heritability, or h^2) and (2) the minimum number of genes involved. The results are interesting. They suggest that between 48 and 79 percent of the variability in life span of these strains is due to genetic determination. Not a very large number of genes are involved in the regulation of longevity, perhaps contrary to one's initial suspicions. An early estimate by Goodrick (1975) indicated that as little as one gene might be responsible for longevity differences between the C57BL/6J and the AJ strains. Although one should be skeptical about that number, the result certainly points in the direction of a small number of genes. A more recent investigation (Gelman et al. 1988), based on the analysis of 20 recombinant inbred hybrid lines derived from the mating of the C57BL/6J and DBA/2J strains, suggests that at least six regions on four different chromosomes are statistically associated with the increased longevity of the longer-lived inbred strain. Of course, more than one gene might be involved within each chromosome region. Since these two studies involved three different strains, they are not necessarily contradictory; the hereditary mechanisms might well differ depending on the strain. Gelman et al. (1988) suggest that complex patterns of gene interaction are taking place that may make the analysis of longevity in outbred populations such as humans difficult. Genetic analysis will have to be performed on inbred strains and mutants especially constructed for those purposes. QTL mapping will be of great value in furthering these studies.

Sixth, it has proven possible to create a series of recombinant inbred strains that undergo genetically mediated accelerated aging (Takeda et al. 1981). Such senescence-accelerated mice (SAMs) were created via an accidental outcrossing of AKR/J mice with AJ (and perhaps other) mice to yield a series of genetically and phenotypically distinct lines, each of which display a variety of senescence-associated pathological phenotypes (Kitado, Higuchi, and Takeda 1994a). Some of the lines no longer display the lymphomas characteristic of their parent AKR/J strain, suggesting the loss or lack of expression of certain parental genes. They exhibit no obvious alteration in their developmental processes; they simply senesce significantly earlier than does the AKR/J strain from which they were derived. It has been speculated that normal mice have both senescence-accelerating and senescence-repressing genetic factors, but that the crosses that gave rise to the SAM lines accidentally yielded animals with only the senescence-accelerating factors but none of the senescence-repressing factors (Kitado, Higuchi, and Takeda 1994a).

Future validation of this speculation would indicate that the aging process in mice (and other mammals presumably) is probably under both positive and negative genetic control. (You may wish to speculate about whether a human homozygous for the *ApoE4* alleles is in any way analogous to a SAM strain.) Once again, the future value of QTL mapping as applied to this system should be obvious. Note that there is a strong consensus among biogerontologists that the study of animal models with reduced life span, such as the SAMs, eventually will prove to be unrelated to the mechanisms of normal aging (Harrison 1994). The researchers working with the SAMs disagree (Kitado, Higuchi, and Takeda 1994b). For our part, we might consider viewing the SAMs within the same conceptual framework that we view disease: as indicating the weak points and failure modes of the evolved animal model, the study of which may indicate by default the processes that need to be modulated if longevity is to be extended. In fact, one might view most of the inbred mouse and rat strains in the same light; most of them are probably a good model for the study of a particular disease complex. John Phelan (1992) has compiled data illustrating well that each of these inbred strains has a unique qualitative and quantitative pattern of nonfatal lesions. Some strains are very susceptible to certain lesions; other strains are not (for example, 30 percent of the DBA/2NNia mice show amyloidosis of the kidney glomeruli, compared to 0 percent of the A/HeNNia mice).

Together, these results unequivocally demonstrate that there is a strong genetic component governing longevity in both inbred and outbred strains. The genetic mechanisms likely involve moderate numbers of both positive and negative control elements affecting several physiologically important variables. The potential complexity of the results obtained from these comparisons of longevity among strains has led investigators to focus their attention on strain comparisons involving age-dependent changes in specific organ systems, with the hope of relating these genetic and physiological indices to the aging process.

One example of the utility of the mouse for this type of study is shown by a study involving important age-related changes, such as atherosclerosis (Bulfield 1988). It had been assumed for many years that mice do not develop atherosclerosis. However, when the fat content of their lab chow is tripled, thereby simulating our high-fat diet, some mouse strains develop widespread atherosclerotic lesions. By crossing the susceptible strain (C57BL/6) with each of the three resistant strains (AJ, C3H, and Balb/cJ) and inbreeding the offspring in a controlled manner for 20 generations, the resulting recombinant inbred lines can be assayed for the pattern of appearance of normal or abnormal conditions in the inbred offspring. From this pattern, the number of genes involved and their chromosomal location may be deduced. When this procedure was applied in this particular case, only one gene was found to be responsible for resistance or susceptibility to atherosclerosis. There is some reason to believe that this gene codes for a particular plasma lipoprotein in the mouse. If so, this finding might open the door to understanding how and why atherosclerotic lesions in humans and mice are correlated with low levels of plasma high-density lipoprotein. In any event, this finding shows that understanding the nature of a hereditary pathology such as atherosclerosis may allow one to improve life expectancy by eliminating premature deaths but may not shed direct light on the mechanisms underlying extended longevity.

A second purpose to which the mouse is being used is the development of biomarkers of aging. These efforts have culminated in the initiation of an expensive and lengthy process in which the National Institute on Aging and the National Center for Toxicological Research are cooperating in sponsoring an organized search for accurate, reliable, and feasible biomarkers of aging in mice and rats (see Chapter 3 for a discussion of biomarkers). Examination of biomarker functions in different genotypes over time should allow investigators to correlate particular traits with particular genetic markers. It is hoped that this approach will provide the information needed to do genetic analysis of basic aging processes in particular organ systems of the mouse, as already described, and eventually to relate this analysis to an understanding of the genetic events that bring about the age-dependent change. Some of the initial results of this study are now available and are discussed in the next chapter.

Podospora

The fungus *Podospora* ages and senesces by means of a rather different sort of genetic control mechanism. The mitochondrial genome also plays a major role in determining the life span of this organism, except that what causes the damage in this case is not an extraorganismic parasite, but rather a piece of its own genome.

The first clear evidence for the role of extrachromosomal genetic traits in the control of aging was derived from the analysis of the aging process in *Podospora*. This result both directs our attention to the role that the extranuclear genomes may play in the aging process, as well as alerting us to the interactions between nuclear and mitochondrial genomes.

Chapter 4 briefly described aging in *Podospora anserina*; that description will be recapitulated here for convenience. It has been known for some 30 years that the growth of each race of this fungus ceases at a characteristic time and size. The nongrowing portions of a clone reproduce sexually, producing ascospores that, when released, will give rise to new individuals elsewhere. The old somatic tissues eventually die. The important point is that the onset of aging varies according to the geographic race of fungus involved, ranging from a minimum of 7 days to a maximum of 106 days. This observation is consistent with the view that longevity is dependent on the genome. It has not yet been possible to uncover the genetic or molecular processes underlying these interstrain variations.

Studies within one strain, which had a normal life span of about 25 days, showed that this fungus has a second genetic system that exerts a negative control on longevity. It was discovered that there is a series of mutant genes that postpone the onset of aging indefinitely, through the synergistic action of at least two genes (Esser 1985). Only the double mutant shows this extraordinary prolongation of life span; the single mutants each exhibit a mildly prolonged life span relative to the wild type, but one that is several orders of magnitude shorter than the life span that results when the two are combined (Figure 6.8).

It was later found that even the wild-type fungi of this particular strain could indefinitely delay the onset of senescence if they were grown on media contain-

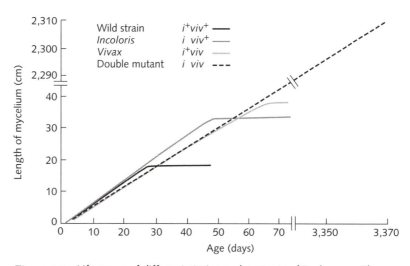

Figure 6.8 Life spans of different strains and mutants of *Podospora*. The wild strain is indicated by $i^+ viv^+$, the two different single mutants by $i\ viv^+$ and by $i^+ viv$, and the double mutant by $i\ viv$. The mutants differ in their color, growth habits, fertility, and life span. (From Esser and Keller 1976.)

ing chemical inhibitors of mitochondrial DNA and protein synthesis. But once the fungi were removed from the inhibitory media and placed on standard media, aging resumed and proceeded normally. These observations suggested that the mitochondrial DNA was doing something that normally brought about senescence. A series of other experiments (summarized in Esser 1985, Benne and Tabak 1986, and Osiewacz 1995) showed that a noncoding portion, or intron, of a vital mitochondrial structural gene is, under certain circumstances, capable of liberating itself from the mitochondrial genome and forming a small circular plasmid that can replicate autonomously. This excision process appears to begin the breakup of the mitochondrial genome.

These plasmids are capable of entering other mitochondria and the nucleus, and so may be thought of as infectious. It is thought that these plasmids can also integrate themselves back into the mitochondrial genome in such a manner to inhibit the expression of the vital mitochondrial gene (cytochrome *c* oxidase) from which they arose. The general breakup of the mitochondrial genome that is due to the gross DNA rearrangements occurring as a result of the excision and integration, as well as the lack of this specific gene product, will certainly inhibit energy production by the mitochondrion, adversely affect the physiological functioning of the fungal cells, and possibly bring on the onset of senescence and death. This explanation of senescence in *Podospora* has been termed the "mobile intron" model and is supported by recent data (Osiewacz 1995).

Some of the *Podospora* mutants that are resistant to senescence have an altered and inactive cytochrome *c* oxidase gene from which the intron has been excised differently. The alteration in the DNA structure of the intron renders it noninfectious, and the mutant strain does not senesce. The mutant fungus is thought to survive despite the inactivation of this key mitochondrial gene, by employing other metabolic pathways that bypass this biochemical block. But not all plasmids cause senescence. One linear plasmid is causally related to an increase in life span, even though it has the ability to integrate into the mitochondrial genome (Hermanns et al. 1995).

However, the ability of the senescence-causing plasmid to excise itself from the mitochondrial genome and to express itself afterward is under the control of the nuclear genome. The *i viv* double mutant (see Figure 6.8) inhibits the expression of the plasmid in the mitochondria. There is no damage, and senescence is delayed forever. In this case, then, longevity is a recessive trait, for the normal functioning of the nuclear genes promotes mitochondrial destruction, senescence, and death. The nuclear gene system involved in suppressing the mitochondrial plasmids may be a genetic system that controls the normal processes of cell death (Bernet 1992). If so, perhaps the mutations in key genes of this system suppress this normal cell death process and somehow maintain the integrity of the mitochondrial plasmids. The longevity-promoting plasmid mentioned here is not suppressed by the double nuclear mutant of Figure 6.8, perhaps because the plasmid's effects do not touch the normal cell death process.

In this fungus, at least two different genetic systems regulate longevity. The regulatory system responsible for the life span variations among geographic races apparently involves only the nuclear genes. The other system involves both nuclear and mitochondrial genes as already described. Understanding the interplay between the two systems should prove to be an interesting and fruitful topic for future research.

Neurospora

The red bread mold, *Neurospora crassa*, is a free-living fungus that has been popular and useful in genetic investigations since the pioneering studies of George Beadle and Edward Tatum a half century ago won them the Nobel prize for the conceptual advances they made in biochemical genetics using this unlikely organism. Some of the reasons for the popularity of *Neurospora* are that it grows quickly, takes up very little space, and is quite amenable to biochemical analysis. In one portion of its life cycle, the fruiting body of this multicellular eukaryote produces up to 1 billion spores, called conidia (Figure 6.9). Each conidium is a separate cell. These conidia will grow and give rise to new organisms when exposed to conditions favorable for growth. If the environmental conditions are not favorable, the conidia will remain dormant. The conidia are mortal and eventually lose their ability to germinate. They die.

Kenneth Munkres and his colleagues were perceptive enough to identify this stage of the *Neurospora* life cycle as possessing the major attribute of an aging system (the time-dependent loss of viability) and have been very active in working out the details of the genetic system that controls aging in this fungus (Munkres and Furtek 1984; Munkres, Rana, and Goldstein 1984; Munkres 1985, 1990, 1992). They started with the observation that the conidia of wild-type or normal strains have a mean life span of about 22 days (Figure 6.10). They were then able to create different short-lived strains (which they designated *age⁻*) by mutageniz-

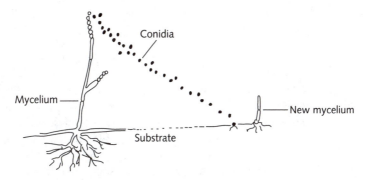

Figure 6.9 The asexual portion of the life cycle of *Neurospora crassa*, a fungus that has played an important role in research on aging. The organism reproduces both sexually and asexually; our interest lies in the life span of the asexual conidia. The conidia are produced by mitosis in the parent fungi, are released, and can, if exposed to the proper environment, germinate and give rise to another vegetative mycelium that is genetically identical to that of the parent. The conidia retain this germination ability for a limited amount of time. This time-related functional decrement has been used as an indicator of aging in this organism.

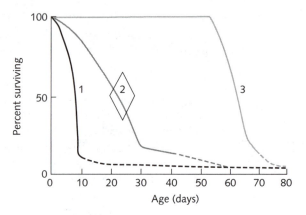

Figure 6.10 Survival curves of the asexual conidia of *Neurospora* assayed under standard conditions. Curve 1 represents the mean survival data obtained from 13 selected short-lived (age⁻) mutants. Curve 2 represents the mean survival data obtained from 20 wild-type, or normal, strains. The lozenge on curve 2 indicates the standard deviation of the mean normal life span. Curve 3 represents the survival data for an extended-longevity (age⁺) variant. See text for discussion. (Based on data in Munkres and Furtek 1984.)

ing the wild type and collecting the resulting short-lived variants. These *age⁻* strains had a mean life span of about 9 days. In addition, a small proportion (about 5 percent) of the wild-type population seemed to have a longer-than-normal life span. By applying the principles of selective breeding to this portion of the population, the investigators were able to create a long-lived variant (termed *age⁺*) with a mean life span of about 60 days (see Figure 6.10). Both the *age⁻* and the *age⁺* strains are clearly produced as heritable traits, illustrating that life span in this organism is under both positive and negative control. The genetic analysis by Munkres and colleagues of 28 different *age⁻* strains showed that, with one exception, they could be mapped to a single complex of 17 genes located in a particular region of one chromosome. This functional clustering of genes is not common in eukaryotes. Later these genes were found to code for various different enzymes known to be essential in combating the deleterious effects of oxygen on living systems. These enzymes (superoxide dismutase, catalase, glutathione peroxidase, cytochrome *c* peroxidase, and ascorbic free radical reductase) are among those known collectively as the antioxidant defense system enzymes (see Chapter 10). Perhaps the most remarkable finding of Munkres's group was their observation that the *age⁻* short-lived mutants are associated with significant decreases in the activity levels of these enzymes, while the *age⁺* mutants are associated with significant increases in the activity of these enzymes. The increased enzyme activity can serve as a good genetically based predictor of longevity. This is a very important observation, for it provides a possible enzymatic mechanism tying together genes and life spans. In fact, these genetic investigations showed that the genes coding for 12 different antioxidant enzymes are under the common control of one regulatory network, termed the oxy-regulon. Similar networks are known in bacteria; this was the first demonstration of such a network in eukaryotes. Its existence suggests that global changes in antioxidant resistance might be mediated through factors affecting only the oxy-regulon itself, without having to act on all 12 enzymes independently.

It was also shown that mutants deficient in any one of the 12 antioxidant genes, such as superoxide dismutase, were also very sensitive to oxidative stress. The findings with both the mutant lines and the selected strains are consistent with one another and lend credence to the oxidative damage theory of aging (see Chapter 9). They also strongly support the idea that life span is under a strong form of genetic control (see Chapters 10 and 13) and are consistent with genetic data obtained from other eukaryotes (as we will see shortly).

All of the studies we have described here were done with conidia. Investigations have also been done with other *Neurospora* strains, using as an index the senescence of the entire fungal culture. As mentioned in Chapter 4, these results have implicated the involvement of the mitochondria and a senescent mechanism that is quite different from that operating in the conidia (Griffiths 1992). In the Kalilo strains of *N. intermedia* from Hawaii, senescence is inherited maternally. The longevity of sexual progeny from crosses of senescent females by nonsenescent males depends on how close to death the maternal culture was, suggesting the transmission of a gradually accumulating deleterious factor by the mother.

Many of these senescent strains are defective in one aspect or another of energy metabolism. The mitochondrial DNA (mtDNA) of these strains has an extragenomic plasmid DNA molecule inserted into it. In juvenile stages, the plasmids can be found free in the cytoplasm. Eventually, they begin to insert into the mtDNA, and in the process of insertion they destroy vital mitochondrial genes. Insertion continues until almost no normal mtDNA is left, and the fungal culture eventually stops growing permanently and soon dies. In this case, then, a parasitic molecule integrates into its host's DNA, taking over the host's functions to promote its own replication, and in the process it destroys the host. The phenomenon is not limited to this one Hawaiian strain; certain Indian and Indonesian strains have been shown to senesce as a result of infection with different plasmids. These appear to represent the independent evolution of senescence arising as a result of molecular parasitism.

Hundreds of eukaryotic plasmids are now known, and these are likely only a small fraction of the total plasmid diversity. Do they cause senescence only in fungi? Or can they infect mitochondria in other life forms as well? Does the difference in energy levels between 2-year-old and 90-year-old people have anything to do with this phenomenon?

Saccharomyces cerevisiae

This budding yeast is probably the fungus with which we are most familiar. As described in Chapter 4, each cell has a finite, age-dependent life span and undergoes a series of characteristic age-related changes. The fact that the mean and maximum life spans are characteristic features of any given yeast strain, even while these parameters may vary considerably from one strain to another, suggests that the yeast life span has a strong genetic component. This fact, as well as the observation that the senescence phenotype is dominant and is determined by soluble cytoplasmic factors (Egilmez and Jazwinski 1989), suggests that there are differences in the expression of specific genes during the yeast life span, and that the expression of such genes late in life may bring about the production of the hypothesized senescence factors.

This interesting genetic hypothesis was tested directly by means of molecular techniques. Egilmez et al. (1989) used a differential hybridization procedure to identify yeast genes that are preferentially expressed in either young or old cells.

In this procedure, a yeast genomic DNA library was separately probed with cDNA (complementary DNA) prepared from the poly-A$^+$ RNA of young and old cells. (The poly-A$^+$ RNA represents the cytoplasmically localized gene transcripts; probing with cDNA is simply a procedure for converting these unstable transcripts into a stable form that can withstand the rigors of experimental manipulation.) Most of the genes are expressed at the same level in both young and old cells; six were not and appear to be age-specific. Five of these were found preferentially in young cells, and one was expressed preferentially in old cells. Since these investigations, 14 genes that display differential patterns of expression have been isolated; we will discuss the role that three of these genes appear to play in regulating yeast longevity.

The first gene analyzed was named the *LAG1* gene, or Longevity Assurance Gene 1 (D'Mello et al. 1994). *LAG1* is expressed predominantly in younger cells and shows a marked decrease in its expression as aging proceeds, finally disappearing at about generation 18 (Figure 6.11). The gene was mapped to the right arm of chromosome VIII. Sequencing revealed that it is a unique gene that lacks significant sequence homology to any other known genes and that appears to code for a transmembrane protein containing clusters of putative phosphorylation sites. Humans appear to have a homologous gene. Its precise function is not yet known, but it may well be a rapidly replaced membrane protein involved in signal transduction. Whatever it does, null mutants of the gene have no observable effect on cell growth or metabolism, but they have a dramatic effect on the longevity such that the mutants live significantly longer than the wild type (Figure 6.12).One possible explanation for this behavior is that the *LAG1* gene is regulating longevity by setting a threshold or limit to the number of divisions the cell may undergo. A gene deletion eliminates its effect on life span, and then a new gene or gene hierarchy becomes limiting for longevity. The result is the resetting of the threshold, leading to an increase in the mean and maximum life spans of the cells (D'Mello et al. 1994).

The other two genes analyzed by Jazwinski and his colleagues are the two yeast homologues of the mammalian proto-oncogene *c-ras*, called *RAS1* and *RAS2* (Jazwinski 1993). Knowing that the *RAS* gene plays a key role in regulating

Figure 6.11 The mRNA transcript levels of the Longevity Assurance Gene 1 (*LAG1*). When measured in yeast of different ages, these data show that the gene has an age-related pattern of expression. The expression of this particular gene peaks in young yeast cells and then declines. (From D'Mello et al. 1994.)

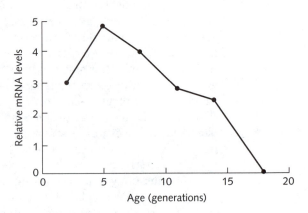

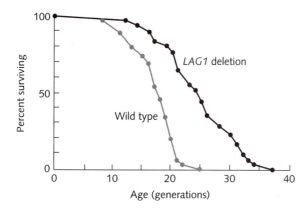

Figure 6.12   The life span of yeast cells with a deletion in the *LAG1* gene. These yeast cells live longer (a mean of 25 generations) than do normal controls with a complete *LAG1* gene (a mean of 17 generations). This observation suggests that the normal gene is acting as a negative regulator of longevity. (From D'Mello et al. 1994.)

many important cell and metabolic processes in both mammals and yeasts, Chen et al. (1990) transformed yeast cells with the Harvey murine sarcoma virus gene, v-Ha-*ras*, and found that both the mean and maximum life span of the cells almost doubled when the transformed genes were expressed at a moderate level. The phenomenon disappeared at very high levels of expression, indicating the existence of dose-dependent regulatory effects. The *RAS1* and *RAS2* genes are highly pleiotropic and affect a large number of different cellular processes.

As described in Chapter 4, there is some reason to believe that the *RAS* genes are affecting the cell's ability to resist certain types of stress. In any event, expression of the *RAS2* gene was found to decrease with replicative age in normal yeast in a manner similar to that seen with the *LAG1* gene, and a moderate overexpression of the gene results in a 30 percent increase in mean and maximum life span. No life span extension was observed after overexpression of the *RAS1* gene; however, deletion of *RAS1* prolonged the life span (Sun et al. 1994). These observations suggest that the two genes may play reciprocal roles in modulating yeast longevity, perhaps in a manner similar to the *age*⁻ and *age*⁺ factors observed Munkres in *Neurospora* and described earlier.

On the basis of these observations, Jazwinski (1993) proposed an ontogenetic theory of longevity in which he brought together several observations regarding yeast longevity, as well as some general aspects of eukaryotic biology that are most easily seen in single-celled organisms such as yeasts. In brief, he notes that stem cells reproduce via asymmetric cell division, while cells with a limited life span, such as ordinary somatic cells, reproduce via symmetric or binary fission. The same phenomenon was noted in *Volvox* (see Chapter 4). Consequently, genetic determinants and molecular mechanisms, such as the *RAS* genes, that play a role in regulating cell division also play a role in determining longevity. This hypothesis has the virtue of offering a fresh way to examine the genetic control of longevity in the context of fundamental cell and developmental processes. If this hypothesis proves to be true, then it implies that there are no genes for aging as such. There are only genes that control various sorts of cellular processes, some of which may play the role of a limiting factor to cell longevity in certain species under certain conditions. Thus there may well be many different sets of longevity-determining genes in different species under different conditions, and the major genes in one system may be the minor genes in another. This last conclusion is a strong argument for a comparative approach to the study of the genetic determinants of longevity.

The stress-resistant, long-lived mutants in *S. cerevisiae* that were discussed in Chapter 4 may offer an example of how the major longevity-determining genes may vary from one strain to the next within the same species. By taking advantage of the correlation between life span and stress resistance noticed in several lab strains of *S. cerevisiae*, Kennedy et al. (1995) generated stress-resistant mutants that had significantly increased mean and maximum life spans when raised under normal conditions. One of their more interesting mutants, termed *sir4-42*, increased both life span and stress resistance at the cost of inhibiting mating and making the organism sterile.

Yeasts have a complex set of genes controlling their mating response. Part of this response requires the silencing of particular mating-type genes, for the simultaneous expression of different mating-type genes can lead to sterility. An elaborate mechanism exists for the repression of certain yeast genes. The function of the wild-type allele of the *SIR4* gene is to silence certain reproductive loci (HML, HMR); the gain-of-function *sir4* mutants reverse this gene silencing and allow the transcription of specific genes in old cells. Guarente and his colleagues (Smeal et al. 1996) propose that genes other than those at the HM loci are also repressed by the *SIR4* gene, and that one of these hypothesized genes must enhance stress resistance. Mutations in the *SIR4* gene would be expected to derepress this gene, enhance stress resistance, increase longevity, and make the organism sterile.

A molecular mechanism possibly linking aging in yeasts and humans is that the yeast cell's nucleolus undergoes a progressive enlargement and fragmentation due to the accumulation of extrachromosomal rDNA circles, or ERCs. The involvement of similar sorts of self-replicating molecules fragmented from the genome has also been implicated in the aging of *Neurospora* and *Podospora*, as discussed earlier. Yeasts normally accumulate ERCs during aging; accelerating the accumulation of such molecules results in a shorter life span, whereas delaying ERC accumulation yields an increased life span (Sinclair and Guarente 1997). As postulated by Jazwinski (1993), it is presumed that ERCs are distributed asymmetrically between the mother and daughter cells at mitosis, conceivably accounting for the different physiological ages of the two cells. Presumably ERC accumulation is somehow repressed by the *SIR* gene. In humans, the gene involved in Werner's disease is a DNA helicase that brings about a shortened life span. Its yeast homolog, the *SGS1* gene, shortens yeast life span and brings about nucleolar enlargement and fragmentation. It is possible the accumulation of ERCs may be accelerated in the absence of a functional helicase. It is not known yet whether ERCs are involved in human aging, although the potential role of genomic instability and fragmentation has been discussed (Strehler 1986).

Thus we now have several plausible explanations for aging in yeast. Which of them is correct? They each may be an accurate reflection of reality. A failure to silence certain genes, or to inhibit genomic fragmentation and partial overreplication, or to regulate precisely certain genes, may each be an operative proximal mechanism bringing about a decrease in the cell's ability to handle stress. And it is the increasing probability of succumbing to stress—no matter what the proximate cause of the loss of stress resistance—that may be the important and fundamental mechanism involved.

The connection between stress resistance and longevity has been observed in other strains of long-lived yeasts, such as those that use the *RAS* genes to enhance the resistance to ultraviolet irradiation stress (Kale and Jazwinski 1996). In addition, the close genetic and functional relationship between stress resistance and extended longevity has been observed in both the nematode and the fruit fly (as we'll see shortly). Together, this evidence suggests that the study of particular strains across a wide array of species will allow us to identify both general processes important in the regulation of longevity and different genetic mechanisms that function in different systems to bring about the same functional result, namely, enhanced resistance to one or more particular stresses and extended longevity in particular environments.

Caenorhabditis elegans

C. elegans is a harmless, small, soil-dwelling, free-living nematode that was deliberately chosen by Sidney Brenner in 1964 to be an organism of genetic study (Brenner 1974). Brenner persuaded enough other scientists of the wisdom of his choice that today this little worm is one of the world's more widely used organisms for genetic research. Nematodes are no stranger to research on aging; we have already discussed their usefulness in uncovering the role of altered proteins (see Chapter 4). Several investigators searched for and obtained genetic variants that shorten life span and others that extend life span. Most attention has focused on the latter phenotype, for the genes that cause a lengthened life are most likely the ones that are affecting the normal aging process.

As illustrated in Figure 6.13, Thomas Johnson (1987) showed that these recombinant-inbred strains show as much as a 70 percent increase in their mean and maximum life spans when compared to their wild-type progenitor strains. Furthermore, the Gompertz plot (Figure 6.13d) suggests that the increase in life span is brought about by a decrease in the rate of aging of the long-lived strain relative to the controls (Figure 6.13c). However, the increase in life span did not occur as a result of stretching out the entire life cycle like a rubber band. The life cycle of the normal animal contains a developmental period, an adult reproductive period, an adult postreproductive period, and a senescent period that culminates in death. Friedman and Johnson (1988a, 1988b) found that the extended life span in the long-lived strain is due to a lengthened postreproductive period only, which occurs with no change in the length of the developmental and reproductive periods or any alteration in the organism's fertility. They named this gene the *age-1* locus and mapped it to chromosome II.

Since the recessive mutant brought about the extended longevity, it seemed reasonable to conclude that the normal allele was doing something to repress longevity and thus that the mutants are "loss-of-function" alleles. But the nature of the processes was not clear until two different labs uncovered the relationship

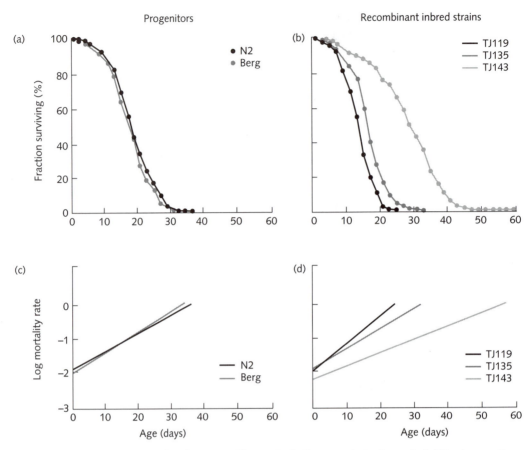

Figure 6.13 The alteration of longevity in the nematode *Caenorhabditis elegans*. Survival data (a, c) and Gompertz mortality data (b, d) for the wild-type parent strains (a, b) and for three different recombinant inbred strains (c, d). The strain designated TJ143 is a long-lived strain. The differences in its survival and mortality curves when compared with the other strains are obvious. See text for discussion. (From Johnson 1987.)

between extended longevity and dauer larvae. The nematode responds to conditions of overcrowding and limited food by arresting its development early in the life cycle and molting into a nonfeeding, stress-resistant, developmentally arrested, and sexually immature dauer larva stage. The dauer larva can survive adverse conditions for months and then, when conditions improve, resume development and become a normal adult. The dauer larva is the nematode's version of a spore—its way of riding out bad times. The genetic analysis of dauer larva formation had been performed some time earlier (Riddle, Swanson, and Albert 1981), and the animal's ability to enter the dauer larva stage was known to be under the coordinate control of a complex genetic pathway. It was also known that null mutants for certain of these genes (*daf-2, daf-23*) force the animal to enter the dauer larva stage, but that when the activity levels of these genes are only partly lowered, the animals become not dauer larvae, but instead become adults with extended life spans (Kenyon et al. 1993; Larsen, Albert, and Riddle 1995).

This result was the first clue that the dauer larva genes are not just involved in the development of the organism but are also active in the mature adult. The other key observation was that the *age-1* and the *daf-2* genes function in the same pathway, are dependent on the same two downstream genes (*daf-16* and *daf-18*), and generally appear to act in the same manner (Dorman et al. 1995). In the model shown in Figure 6.14, the wild-type *age-1* and *daf-2* gene products act to accelerate the aging process. But when either gene is defective and its activity thereby lowered, life span is increased by a mechanism that depends on the downstream activities of both *daf-16* and *daf-18*. Some evidence suggests that the *age-1* gene is a negative regulator of the activity of the copper–zinc superoxide dismutase (*CuZnSOD*) gene, the gene product of which is a well-known antioxidant enzyme (Duhon and Johnson 1993). If this is true, then a loss-of-function mutation would weaken or abolish the negative regulation of the *CuZnSOD* gene and increase the amount and/or activity of this antioxidant enzyme in the adult

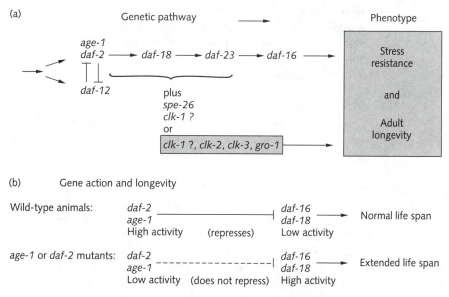

Figure 6.14 Genetic circuits regulating longevity in the nematode. (a) Two separate and complementary pathways. The first path involves the *age-1* and *daf* genes that are known to regulate a pathway leading to stress resistance in both the larval and adult stages. The second path involves the *clk* genes, which are thought to slow the biological events by which the organism marks the passage of metabolic time. The two paths are different and complement each other; double mutants have an extraordinarily extended longevity. (b) The details of the manner in which a negative regulator gene, such as *age-1*, is thought to operate. (Adapted from Dorman et al. 1995 and Jazwinski 1996.)

animal. Inhibiting an inhibitor leads to an increased activity of the final gene product. Increased antioxidant activity is known in many systems to be causally associated with extended longevity. It has recently been shown that the *age-1* gene codes for an enzyme, also found in mammals, called phosphatidylinositol-3-hydroxyl kinase (PI3K) (Morris, Tissenbaum, and Ruvkum 1996). This enzyme is thought to function as a membrane-localized molecule that transduces signals from upstream receptor molecules to downstream effector molecules via a protein kinase cascade. Thus the putative function of the gene is consistent with its observed effect in the animal.

Genes of another group increase life span in the nematode by altering processes other than stress resistance. The *clock* (*clk*) genes control the rate of the worm's development, the pace of its behavior, and the length of its life. The *clk* mutants live about 50 percent longer than normal, apparently because the timing of a wide range of physiological processes is deregulated and appears to run at a slower pace (Lakowski and Hekimi 1996). One of these genes, *clk-1*, has recently been cloned and sequenced (Ewbank et al. 1997). This gene is homologous to a gene in yeast termed *CAT5/COQ7*, which is thought to be involved in controlling multiple metabolic processes. This presumed function of the *clk-1* gene is consistent with its apparent ability to extend longevity by slowing the metabolism, and thereby bring about an attendant reduction in the rate at which detrimental by-products such as free radicals are produced. It is of more than passing interest to note that the *clk-1* gene is highly conserved in eukaryotes and is found in humans. The potential effects of a mutation in this gene in a homeothermic organism are not clear. Perhaps a "knockout" mutation in the mouse will reveal the answer.

Many of the genes that extend life span in *C. elegans* do so by virtue of their ability to alter development and/or regulate the physiological processes necessary to protect the organism against stressful conditions. Some of them, such as the *age-1* or *daf* genes, act directly to increase the level of stress-resistance (protective) gene products. Others, such as the *clk* genes, act on the metabolism and thereby indirectly lower the rate at which harmful products are produced. Thus the life span of the organism may be viewed as arising from a balance between the level of production of damaging products and the level of protection that the organism can muster in response to damage. The nematode data show us that long life can be obtained by alteration of either side of this balance, or both sides together, as in the *daf–clk* double mutants (Lakowski and Hekimi 1996). Thus we have a unitary conceptual framework in which to view the activities of these genes: They are not special kinds of "gerontogenes"; rather they are genes that are normally involved in regulating the organismic and cellular physiology in a highly coordinated manner. We have already noted the close relationship between stress resistance and longevity in yeasts and *Neurospora*, and we will see it again in *Drosophila* and, in a highly modifed form, in mammals as well. The fact that the genes involved are often (but not always) conserved suggests that this relationship represents a general strategy among eukaryotes. Note, however, that the different species we have examined appear to resist stress by means of mechanisms that differ in their details—a general theme individually played.

Two other experimental approaches are now being tried in the nematode. One is the identification of genes that are differentially expressed during the aging of the organism. Twelve such differentially expressed genes have been identified by Fabian and Johnson (1995), of which nine decrease in abundance with age, two increase slightly in abundance with age, and one peaks in abundance during the middle portion of the life span. The expression patterns of six of these genes were examined in both wild-type and *age-1* mutant strains, and no difference was observed. This finding suggests that the genes examined are not associated with the aging processes altered by the *age-1* (that is, *daf*) genes. The second experimental approach is QTL mapping. Both Ebert et al. (1993) and Shook, Brooks, and Johnson (1996) have used this technique and reported finding three loci strongly associated with mean life span, with one locus each on chromosomes II and IV and on the X chromosome. The relationship between these QTLs and the other mutationally defined loci known to affect life span is not yet defined but is being vigorously pursued.

Drosophila melanogaster

The fruit fly is the geneticist's favorite organism (Lints and Soliman 1988). For almost 9 decades this organism has been researched in investigations that have yielded the multitude of special strains, mutants, and knowledge needed to perform extraordinarily sophisticated experiments. We probably tend to think that little of applicability to humans can be learned by studying fruit flies. Appearances, however, can be deceiving. As dissimilar and as evolutionarily remote as a fruit fly appears to be from a human, nonetheless we and they use related genes to guide related processes. The genetic insights gained from studying fruit flies may well help us understand ourselves better.

Most of the existing *Drosophila* mutants had their life spans shortened as a result of deleterious processes unrelated to aging (for a review of the literature, see Arking and Dudas 1989). Thus it was not possible to study existing mutants; instead, long-lived strains had to be created for studying the aging process. Beginning in 1979, several different groups of investigators decided to use artificial selection to create extended-longevity strains, and to use these as a model with which to examine the mechanisms underlying aging and senescence. This approach has been more successful than those of the earlier studies. One implication of this approach was the transformation of longevity into just another phenotype. As such, it is as variable as any other quantitative trait. Thus we have learned that the species-specific maximum life span, a value that was once treated as though immutably set in our genes (see Chapter 4), can be altered and exceeded by genetic means.

Experiments conducted independently by several different groups have shown that it is not so difficult to breed extraordinarily long-lived fruit flies by artificial selection, using the same principles that have guided animal breeders for centuries and geneticists for decades. In most cases, different investigators have indirectly selected for extended longevity by directly selecting for delayed female fecundity (Luckinbill et al. 1984; Rose 1984; Arking 1987a; Partridge and Fowler 1992). In this approach, a cohort of sibling males and females is established at day 1 of adult life, and the animals are maintained under optimum conditions. Although they are allowed to breed freely, their eggs are not used to give rise to the next generation until 75 percent of the initial cohort have died. This procedure is repeated each generation; thus we breed only from the longest-lived quartile of the population. It usually takes several generations of such selection before the longevity changes significantly in response to this selection regime (Figure 6.15). Rose and his collaborators (Rose and Charlesworth 1981; Rose 1984) independently used similar techniques.

In addition, it has been shown possible to directly select for desiccation resistance (Hoffmann and Parsons 1989) or starvation resistance (Graves et al. 1992; Rose et al. 1992) and thus indirectly select for extended longevity. In these cases, stress resistance gives rise to extended longevity. Each of these different selection scenarios seems likely to give rise to similar but not identical phenotypes, and this variability in selection paradigms might also account for some of the genetic plasticity of longevity in *Drosophila*. A different approach was taken by Zwaan, Bijlsma, and Hoekstra (1995), who directly selected for long-lived individuals. The significance of the 40 to 60 percent increase in both mean and maximum life spans that is commonly observed as a result of such selection pressures can perhaps be better understood if we keep in mind that the mean life span of the long-lived animals exceeds the maximum life span of the normal animals (Figure 6.16). This is a significant and robust result, not due to transient causes, and strongly suggests that the increased life span came about as a result of a significant genetic alteration of the mechanisms involved in aging.

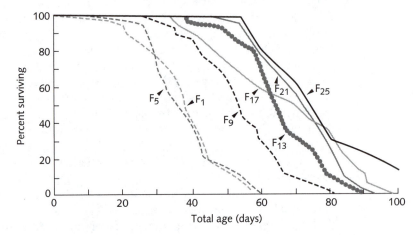

Figure 6.15 The alteration of longevity in *Drosophila*. Shown here are the survival curves for the seven generations measured before (F_1), during ($F5$–F_{21}), and at the end (F_{25}) of selection for an extended adult longevity. The F_1 life span values are identical to those of normal-lived control strains. The F_{25} values identify the appearance of an extended-longevity strain. The temporal directionality in the onset of senescence is obvious. See text for discussion. (From Arking 1987b.)

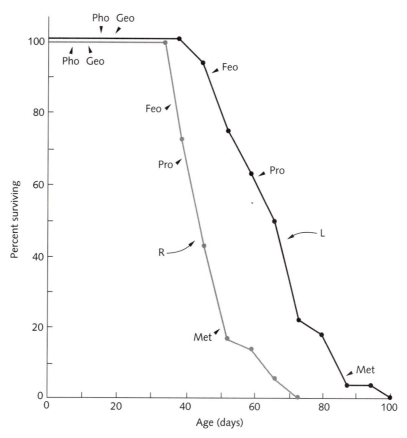

Figure 6.16 The age-dependent loss of behavioral and physiological traits in adult females of the long-lived (L) and control (R) lines of *Drosophila*. The traits observed are positive phototaxis test (Pho), negative geotaxis test (Geo), fecundity (Fec), amino acid incorporation *in vivo* (Pro), and mean daily metabolic rate (Met). The arrows indicate for each trait the point in time at which half of the animals can no longer perform to meet defined quantitative criteria for each test. Note that both strains show the functional loss of each trait in the same sequence and at approximately the same portion of the life cycle. The aging process in the L strain is extended but entirely normal by comparison with the control strain. See text for discussion. (From Arking and Wells 1990.)

Our results, as well as those of others, showed that this increase in the life span did not occur as a result of stretching out the entire life cycle like a rubber band. The life cycle of the fruit fly can be viewed as consisting of a developmental period, an immature adult phase, a mature adult reproductive phase, and a postreproductive senescent phase that culminates in death. The use of biomarkers (see Chapter 3) has allowed us some insight into the timing of gene action in our long-lived strain and has enabled us to validate the logic underlying this comparative genetic analysis. We have examined two behavioral (geotaxis and phototaxis) and three physiological and/or biochemical (female fecundity, metabolic rate, protein synthesis) functional-age biomarkers. These diverse indices are likely under the control of diverse mechanisms. When we plot, for each strain, the survival rate versus the age at which each population shows a significant decrement in the expression of each of these five biomarkers, a remarkable relationship becomes clear (see Figure 6.16). Not only do the long-lived and the control strains lose these five different biomarkers in the same sequence (albeit at different chronological times), but both strains lose each particular biomarker at comparable physiological states. Whatever these genes are doing, they seem to be acting to delay the onset of senescence. Therefore, they can act no later than the time at which we notice the first delayed biomarker—in this case the first biomarker (Pho in Figure 6.16). It seems reasonable to conclude that these biomarkers are exerting their protective effects early—not late—in the adult life span. In fact, we estimated that, whatever the long-lived strains were doing, they were doing it sometime between 5 and 7 days of age. This estimate suggests that aging is dependent on events that take place early in the adult life.

What are these genes doing? As a result of our studies on the biochemistry and stress resistance properties of the long-lived strain, we knew that the only predictive factor clearly and significantly associated with extended longevity in our strains was an enhanced resistance to paraquat observed early in adult life (Arking et al. 1991; Force et al. 1995). Paraquat is an herbicide that kills both animals and plants by its ability to generate free radicals (see Chapter 9), and resistance to this chemical usually indicates that the organism has a high level of antioxidant resistance. Thus it seemed logical to conclude that the long-lived animals probably live long because of higher-than-normal activity of the antioxidant defense system genes early in life. To test this hypothesis, we assayed the quantitative changes in the mRNA levels and the antioxidant enzyme activity levels of several loci during the development and early adult life of our normal-lived (R) and long-lived (L) strains (Dudas and Arking 1995). In addition, we used antibodies to measure the actual amount of CuZnSOD protein present in the R and L strains (Hari et al. 1998). Figure 6.17 summarizes many of these changes in gene expression. The mRNA data demonstrate that, at day 5 in the L strain, there appears to be a coordinately regulated significant increase in the mRNA levels of CuZnSOD, CAT, and xanthine dehydrogenase (XDH). There is a nonsignificant increase in glutathione-S-transferase (GST) mRNA during the same time period. These increases in mRNA levels are accompanied by significant increases in the enzyme activity of CuZnSOD, CAT, and GST. In addition, our ongoing work shows that the amount of SOD-specific protein is proportionately increased in the L strain during the same time period (Hari et al. 1998). Thus it seems reasonable to conclude that these alterations in gene expression are probably the result of a transcription-level change that alters the enzymatic arsenal available to the organisms.

It is well known that all four of these gene products are involved in antioxidant defense, and that null mutants at each locus render the organism very sensitive to paraquat-dependent oxygen stress (see Phillips and Hilliker 1990 and Weinhold et al. 1990 for review and references). Accordingly, one would expect

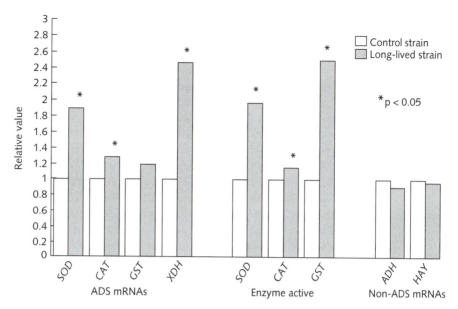

Figure 6.17 Relative levels of expression of antioxidant genes in young (5-day-old) normal-lived and long-lived strains of *Drosophila*. The data are presented such that for each item listed, the left-hand bar represents the normalized value of the normal-lived strain and the right-hand bar represents the relative value of that item in the long-lived strain. Note that three of the four antioxidant defense system (ADS) mRNAs are significantly elevated in the long-lived strain even at this early age, as are all three of the ADS enzymes. It is significant that none of the non-ADS mRNAs are elevated, thus suggesting that the ADS is specifically up-regulated in these long-lived strains. (Data from Dudas and Arking 1995.)

these increased defenses against oxidative stress to be accompanied by a greater resistance to such stress. And that is exactly the case. That these changes in antioxidant gene expression are important to the expression of extended longevity is suggested by the fact that the long-lived strains have both a delayed onset and a lower level of oxidative damage to their proteins and lipids relative to the normal-lived controls through the 3-week period during which they have elevated antioxidant levels (Arking et al. 1998). It seems reasonable to conclude that these animals developed the ability, as a consequence of artificial selection, to turn on a regulatory process that coordinately activates the antioxidant defense genes early in life, thereby protecting the animals against the oxidative damage to vital molecules and thus delaying the onset of senescence until their antioxidant defenses fall to normal levels. Reverse-selecting these long-lived strains for shortened longevity reverts their antioxidant gene expression patterns to control levels. Only the antioxidant genes, and not various other metabolically important genes, show these correlated and coordinate changes in gene expression. Thus this experiment reveals a causal relationship between antioxidant levels and longevity in these strains of *Drosophila* (Arking et al. 1998).

While analyzing another group of long-lived strains (known as the O strains), Rose and his colleagues (Tyler et al. 1993) found that these strains contained a known high-activity allele of the *SOD* gene. However, although enzyme activity measurements have been reported for this allele in other genetic backgrounds, there has been no report of their activity in the O strains' background. Their analyses have led these investigators to consider other metabolic and biochemical factors as constituting proximal explanations for the expression of extended longevity in *Drosophila*. In particular, they find that the O strain animals are significantly resistant to desiccation and starvation, and they suggest that these traits enable the animal to live significantly longer than the normal-lived strains from which it was derived. More important is the idea suggested by these and related results: that the O strains' energy metabolism has been altered in such a manner as to allow these strains to sequester calories early in life, which allows them to survive stresses applied to them later in life by dipping into their caloric reserves (fat) for the energy needed to repair and maintain themselves in the face of various insults (see Service 1987 for review). The same techniques of artificial selection operating on two different progenitor stocks may well have operated to bring about two generically similar extended-longevity phenotypes, each of which is dependent on different proximal mechanisms. As was noted in our discussion of yeast aging, there appears to be more than one mechanism that organisms may use in order to regulate their longevity. Some of the observed plasticity of longevity may have its origins in this situation. Both the O and the L strains have each been shown to have some alterations in one aspect or another of their energy metabolism. This is a newly found commonality, and only future work will tell whether it represents a deep biological similarity between these otherwise different strains.

Transgenic experiments on *Drosophila* have specifically tested the antioxidant theory of aging (Harman 1956). Reveillaud et al. (1991) made transgenic animals carrying an extra copy of the bovine copper-zinc superoxide dismutase (*CuZnSOD*) gene under the control of a constitutive (actin 5c) promoter. The resulting animals expressed both mammalian and *Drosophila* SOD proteins. Some, but not all, of the transgenic strains exhibited an increased resistance to exogenous paraquat along with a modest increase in the mean life span. No effect on maximum life span was observed in the experimental and control lines, suggesting that the effect of the treatment was to decrease premature mortality. This conclusion was confirmed by a later experiment showing that the bovine *SOD* gene had the ability to rescue a *SOD* null mutant from early lethality (Reveillaud et al. 1994).

An essentially identical result was obtained by Staveley, Phillips, and Hilliker (1990) when they used a chromosome duplication to create a fly with three copies of the *Drosophila CuZnSOD* gene. These animals had a 50 percent increase in SOD activity, a significantly increased resistance to ionizing radiation, and a minor increase in the adult life span. The animals were unexpectedly sensitive to paraquat, presumably because the higher levels of CuZnSOD enzyme gave rise to excessive H_2O_2 concentrations within the cell.

A similar result was reported by Orr and Sohal (1992, 1993) as a result of their construction of animals transgenic for either a *Drosophila SOD* gene or a *Drosophila* catalase (*CAT*) gene. However, constructing an animal transgenic for both the *SOD* and the *CAT* genes, each under the control of their own promoter, gave rise to three independently constructed strains that, relative to the controls, (1) had significantly higher levels of CuZnSOD and CAT enzyme activity, (2) were significantly more resistant to exogenous paraquat, and (3) exhibited a significant increase in both mean and maximum longevity (Orr and Sohal 1994). In addition, the Gompertz curve for these doubly transgenic strains had the same intercept but a lower slope compared to the controls, suggesting that the extended longevity of the transgenic animals might result from a slower rate of aging (an increase in the MRDT). Both CuZnSOD and CAT are important antioxidant enzymes, and this experiment has shown that the overexpression of just these two genes is sufficient to extend longevity.

Comparing this transgenic experiment with our selection experiment discussed earlier (Arking et al. 1997) reveals that the important thing is to increase the antioxidant levels, and not the particular process by which they are raised (selection or transgenes). But there are other important antioxidant defense genes that have not yet been tested but for which selective overexpression is likely also to extend longevity. Given this assumption, it seems reasonable to conclude that even though there are several different strains that appear to rely on the antioxidant defense system for their extended longevity, the mechanisms by which this enhanced antioxidant gene activity exerts its physiological effects may well be quite different in these several strains. This difference in the genetic mechanisms underlying the expression of a common phenotype is likely to manifest itself as a genetic plasticity of longevity in *Drosophila*.

We do not know with any certainty how many genes are involved in regulating the extended longevity of *Drosophila*. However, there are enough data to make a broad estimate. One can determine the number of genes involved by actually mapping them, or one can estimate the number of genes involved using statistical analysis of the mean life spans of long- and short-lived strains plus their hybrids. The latter procedure is technically easier than the former, but it is based on several assumptions.

The transgenic experiments we have discussed led to the conclusion that altering the expression of as few as two particular genes, *SOD* and *CAT*, can lead to the expression of an extended-longevity phenotype that is superficially similar to that produced by artificial selection. The transgenic experiment of Orr and Sohal (1994) also provides strong support for the involvement of free radicals in governing the rate of aging. Their data are consistent not only with our molecular data, but also with our genetic estimates suggesting that although extended longevity is a polygenic trait, it probably does not involve a large number of genes (Buck, Wells, et al. 1993). On the face of it, this experiment, with its minimalist number of genes, stands opposed to the concept that aging is a highly polygenic phenotype, dependent on the integrated functioning of a large number of different genes, such as has been proposed by Rose and his colleagues (see below). Our own selected strains also seem to depend on an enhanced antioxidant defense system response, but as we'll see, in a somewhat different mode.

Luckinbill et al. (1987) initially reported that at least one gene was involved in the expression of extended longevity in sister stocks to our strains. This minimum estimate was later discarded in favor of a polygenic mechanism involving primarily the third chromosome (Luckinbill et al. 1988). Although chromosome localizations were not performed, Rose and his colleagues (Hutchinson and Rose 1991; Hutchinson, Shaw, and Rose 1991) used two different types of quantitative genetic analyses to show that the transmission and expression of the extended-longevity phenotype in their selected strains could be adequately explained as being due to the effects of additive genes averaged over an unspecified number of loci. On the basis of their analysis of the mobility and expression patterns of 321 proteins of the long-lived O strains of Rose (1984), Fleming et al. (1993) concluded that about six proteins (about 2 percent of the total) had statistically different expression patterns in the long-lived and control strains. Given the assumption that this is a representative number that one may extrapolate to the whole genome, they then estimated that perhaps 200 to 400 loci that can postpone aging exist in their strains. If the Orr and Sohal (1994) experiment sets a lower limit on the number of genes involved in extended longevity, then the experiment of Fleming et al. (1993) can be viewed as setting an upper limit. The resolution of this debate is important, driving as it does both our concepts and our experimental strategies of identifying the genes involved.

Data obtained from the analysis of our selected strains supports the concept of a hierarchy of regulatory genes involved in the expression of a long-lived phenotype but suggests (1) that the number of structural genes involved may be substantially smaller than the estimate of Fleming et al. (1993) and (2) that selection acted to alter the nature of certain key regulatory genes in the experimental strain relative to its baseline control. (Note that this explanation suggests the existence of a genetic pathway not unlike that presented in Figure 6.14 for the nematode.) Our genetic and chromosomal analysis of the long-lived strain led us to the following conclusions. First, the genes essential to the expression of the extended-longevity phenotype are located on only the third chromosome of the L strain (c3) and map somewhere to the left of the gene called *ebony*. Second, these genes are recessive. Third, there exists a complex pattern of gene interaction in which the longevity-enhancing recessive genes on c3 are regulated by genes on the other chromosomes (Buck, Wells, et al. 1993). These facts can be better represented in the form of a regulatory circuit (Figure 6.18).

The circuit is supported by independently obtained data. The negative effect of c2 on c3 is supported by the report of Graf and Ayala (1986), in which they showed that the levels of *CuZnSOD* activity on c3 are under the control of (unknown) loci on c2. In a similar manner, Bewley and Laurie-Ahlberg (1984) have shown that the expression of *CAT* activity on c3 is also regulated by (unknown) loci on c2. The report of Graf and Ayala (1986) further suggests that one such difference between the c3 of the R and L strains involves a cis-acting element, such as their SOD^{CA1} mutation, which was shown to significantly reduce SOD protein levels.

We have isolated a number of insertional mutants on c2 that significantly modulate the flies' CuZnSOD and/or CAT activity. Most of these exert a negative effect on these antioxidant levels, but several mutants exert a significant up-regulation of the CuZnSOD and CAT activity levels (Arking, unpublished data). The important point is that the regulatory mutants predicted by our prior chromo-

Figure 6.18 The hierarchy of regulatory genes involved in the expression of a long-lived phenotype, represented as a circuit. In our selected long-lived strains of *Drosophila*, extended longevity appears to be the end product of a complex process of interactions taking place at various organizational levels. The extended longevity is due to the enhanced levels of antioxidant activities (see Figure 6.17 and text), and these structural genes are located on chromosome 3 (c3). These ADS genes may be negatively regulated by other genes on chromosomes 1 (c1) and/or 2 (c2). In addition, the effects of larval density can also modulate the expression of the ADS genes, low densities having an inhibitory effect and high densities having a stimulatory effect. If the chromosomal and environmental factors interact appropriately, the enhanced ADS activity leads to a delayed onset of senescence and thence to the full expression of the extended-longevity phenotype. See text for further discussion. (From Arking et al. 1996.)

some manipulations actually do exist. This suggests, of course, that the genetic regulation of longevity in *Drosophila* may have similarities to the situation in *C. elegans*, where regulatory genes control the operation of complex gene pathways (see Figure 6.14). The validity of this suggestion will have to be proved by ongoing research. Curtsinger (1996) has reported using QTL mapping to detect a putative locus on chromosome 3 of *Drosophila* that accounted for about 30 percent of the longevity difference observed between long-lived and control strains similar to those of Figure 6.16, but in only one sex. The nature of the proximal mechanisms in this mutant promise to be most interesting.

Finally, while the molecular genetic regulation of antioxidant systems is one important and confirmed approach to extended longevity, other hierarchies of regulatory genes controlling systems that may act in conjunction with antioxidant systems are likely to exist. We have already mentioned that selection for extended longevity in our strains is accompanied by fixation of certain alleles of metabolic genes; the products of these genes may have a rate-limiting effect on antioxidant activity. Caloric restriction is a good example of an experimental paradigm that is known to enhance longevity and overall physiological vigor and that undoubtedly has its own regulatory hierarchy. The effectiveness of different proximal mechanisms suggests additional sources of genetic and environmental plasticity affecting the expression of the extended-longevity phenotype. Eventually, we want to be able to integrate these interactions of biological macromolecules and the flow of regulatory information into a genetic network of functional paths in which the nodes are the genes or their RNA and protein products, while the connections between them are the regulatory interactions (Loomis and Sternberg 1995). At the moment, we are at a rudimentary state in being able to delineate the network that controls aging and longevity (but see Kowald and Kirkwood 1996; see also Chapter 13). A well-analyzed network, such as the lysis-lysogeny decision circuit of the bacteriophage lambda, can integrate conventional biochemical kinetic modeling within the framework of an electrical circuit simulation (McAdams and Shapiro 1995).

Explaining the complexity of the phenotype in terms of a genetic circuit should be our goal, for it forces us to describe the phenotype accurately even as it provides us with a powerful test of our hypothesis. We do not yet have a complete explanation of the genetic and physiological mechanisms involved in the expression of the extended-longevity phenotypes, but the application of sophisticated genetic and molecular tools to the several different specially constructed longevity strains appears about to yield much interesting and informative data.

In addition to the genetic extension of life span in *Drosophila*, there is a large number of single-gene mutants that cause premature death of the adult. Most of these mutants are the result of a non-age-related cause and are of no further interest to us. However, there is at least one such mutant that appears to cause premature death by accelerating the rate of aging of the adult (Leffelaar and Grigliatti 1984). This mutant was identified by the fact that animals carrying this gene display a normal but accelerated pattern of age-related decrements in their adult behavior patterns. Interestingly, this effect on the biomarkers is the reverse of what appears to happen in the long-lived strain depicted in Figure 6.16. This age acceleration mutant appears to bring about its effects by causing an accelerated physiological dysfunction in the central nervous system. In addition, our selected short-lived strains do not appear to live short lives because of an absence of antioxidant activity. In fact, their antioxidant activity is similar to that of normal-lived animals. So we cannot view short life as the symmetrical opposite of long life. Something else is involved.

Thus it appears that in *Drosophila* there are several different and separable genetic systems, at least one of which accelerates aging and shortens the life span, and at least two (and probably more) that extend the life span through any one of a variety of proximal physiological mechanisms. However, note that all of the proximal mechanisms explored so far appear to involve some aspect of specific stress resistance. The similarity with *C. elegans*, *S. cerevisiae*, and *Neurospora* may not be coincidental.

What Proximate Mechanisms Are Implicated and How Many Genes Are Involved?

The answers to these questions are important, since one sort of experimental approach will be required if we decide that aging is under the direct control of a large number of genes, while quite another type of approach will be needed if we decide that aging is under the direct control of a small number of genes. Some data regarding the number of genes and/or chromosomes is available from the several laboratory studies discussed in this chapter.

In *C. elegans*, it has been shown that there is a genetic pathway comprising some 23 genes that appears to be responsible for the extended-longevity phenotypes in that organism (Larsen, Albert, and Riddle 1995). In *Neurospora*, the genes responsible for the extended longevity of conidia map to two loci, one of which contains a functionally reiterated and related cluster of about 16 genes (Munkres and Furtek 1984). In *Podospora anserina*, the shift from short-lived to long-lived status is governed by two nuclear mutations that are thought to affect certain mitochondrial genomic functions (Esser 1985). A statistical genetic analysis of the inheritance of life span in different inbred strains of the mouse led to the conclusion that there are at least six different chromosomal regions, scattered over four different chromosomes, that are statistically correlated with longevity (Gelman et al. 1988). In addition, it has been suggested that the H-2 locus in the mouse (located on still another chromosome and homologous to the HLA locus of humans) might also play a major role in the regulation of longevity in this species. Our own data on *Drosophila* suggest that there is a common genetic pathway that regulates the expression of the individual antioxidant genes, and that comprises a moderate number of different loci. Finally, the analysis of the protein data in the O strains of *Drosophila* led Fleming et al. (1993) to suggest an upper limit of about 200 to 400 genes involved in their extended-longevity phenotype.

Not all of these numbers are definitive, for a variety of reasons. Thus they should not be overinterpreted. Yet the interesting thing about these numbers is that they are uniformly low—lower than would have been intuitively guessed as being involved in a quantitative trait such as life span. The numbers are especially interesting if one is operating under the assumption that life span is a continuously varying polygenic trait in the classic genetic sense. Thompson (1975) has shown that quantitative traits, such as height, that are generally considered to be due to the effects of many genes, each of which has only a small effect (polygenes), can just as accurately and empirically be considered to be due to the effects of only a few genes, each of which has a large effect (ordinary or major genes). Evidence to support this contention is being obtained from QTL mapping (Paterson et al. 1988; Shrimpton and Robertson 1988; Curtsinger 1996) and shows that traditional quantitative traits in several different organisms are each under the control of only a few major genes, although their expression may be modified by the major genes of other interacting systems.

The assumption that longevity must be under the control of a very large number of genes has not been disproved, but it does not seem to be supported by the data so far available. One source of uncertainty in making these estimates of gene numbers arises from the difficulty of distinguishing among all the genes that vary their expression with aging and the smaller number of genes that initiate the variable expression of the other genes. Of course, it must be recognized that the total number of genes *potentially* capable of regulating life span would increase dramatically if we considered that there is more than one proximal mechanism that the members of a given species might utilize to extend longevity. This multiplicity of mechanisms is particularly true for humans in light of our genetically polymorphic composition. But even so, the number of genes *actually* being used in any single individual genotype would likely be much lower than the total number potentially available to the species.

How are the activities of these genes, whatever their number, integrated with the rest of the organism's physiology to alter longevity? We first need to understand what these genes do, what processes they affect, and how these processes can interact with one another before we can begin to give a comprehensive

7 Altering Aging: Interventions Known to Modify Longevity and Aging

• Introduction

The ability to significantly increase longevity or delay aging by manipulating a particular variable has obvious theoretical and practical interest. The philosophy underlying this approach is that even though aging may well be a mosaic of different processes, it may be possible to develop a segmental intervention that has a significant impact on the overall aging process. Few of us care much for the more deleterious aspects of aging, so there is a large popular market for the latest insights and offerings. Until recently, science and the marketplace offered only palliatives or nostrums. But our biological knowledge of the processes leading to loss of function has broadened greatly, and our ability to intervene in the aging process, while limited, has nonetheless increased dramatically. The current combination of high individual expectations, instantly publicized research, and lack of sufficient knowledge is unstable and leads to situations in which market pressures often result in unprovable and extravagant claims. Far and away the best course is to ground our analyses in verifiable animal and human studies and only cautiously extrapolate past the data.

Before discussing this experimental work, we must emphasize again the difficulty of deciphering anything regarding the nature of the aging process(es) based on treatments that yield only simple changes in life span. Given an intervention that either shortens or lengthens the life span, the diagrams of Figure 7.1a–c suggest that there are at least three possible different interpretations of the data: a change in the rate of aging, a change in the threshold of mortality, or a change in the type of pattern of aging. On the face of it, all of these interpretations are logical, yet the reasons why the life span is altered differ in each case. Given the simple fact of a life span alteration, deciphering the physiological mechanisms involved requires much careful, skeptical, and well-formulated scientific inquiry. Answers

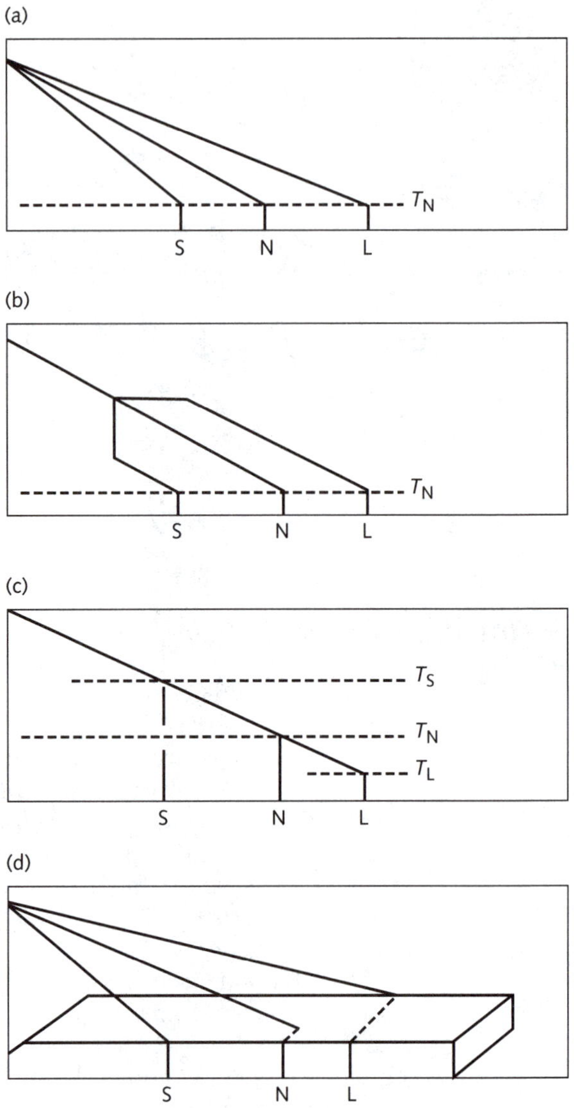

(a)

(b)

Figure 7.1   Four different explanations of how differences in mean life
span may be accounted for by differences in rate of aging. S, N, and L
denote the mean life span and T_S, T_N,
and T_L the death threshold of short-
lived, normal, and long-lived strains,
respectively. (a) The three different
strains age at different rates throughout their life spans. (b) The three
strains age at the same rate until a
particular change is made in the environment. Aging is accelerated or
delayed immediately after this alteration, but the subsequent rate of
aging is not affected. (c) A particular
environmental change does not alter
the rate of aging but raises (T_S) or
lowers (T_L) the death threshold from
the normal value (T_N), and thus cuts
short or extends the life span. (d) A
particular environmental change initiates a new direction of aging such
that the three strains are now aging
in a qualitatively different manner
from one another. (Modified from
Lamb 1978.)

(c)

(d)

must be not only plausible, but true, particularly since these answers will form the
basis of the effective anti-aging interventions that will be available to us.

A view to another field may be instructive here. Cancer is another area in
which, like aging, hope and desire outpace knowledge. Nostrums and palliatives—false interventions—are common. The Laetrile affair is an instructive
example. Unscrupulous marketing of this folk medicine, accompanied by anecdotal evidence and fed by despair, led to popular pressure forcing the National
Institutes of Health into conducting a clinical trial. The scientific test confirmed
the uselessness of this nostrum. But the process caused the needless waste of lives
and money. Perhaps a dispassionate review of the evidence might prevent that
scenario from playing out once more.

A discussion of anti-aging interventions is sure to arouse interest. But our enthusiasm for intervention should be tempered by the facts. It is important to understand whether a proposed treatment is based on animal studies only or includes human data as well. And if the latter, is the evidence anecdotal or is it of the quality associated with a serious clinical trial? Our emotions often lead us to ascribe more weight to a favorite intervention than it may deserve. So in an effort to help sort out the different types of data, this discussion of anti-aging interventions will be divided into two sections: one dealing with laboratory interventions on animals, the other with interventions tested on humans. The division between the two is more apparent than real; some of the same studies are considered in both sections.

Experimentally Proven Laboratory Interventions

Caloric Restriction as a Dietary Intervention

Effects on Longevity

Caloric restriction has been the single most consistent method of extending life span in vertebrate laboratory animals. The experiments of McCay and his colleagues, which we will discuss shortly, grew out of the idea that longevity is inversely proportional to developmental rate. This idea was derived partly from the works of philosophers such as Aristotle and partly from the experimental work of Osborne, Mendel, and Ferry (1917), whose data suggested, but did not prove, that underfed rats live longer. McCay, Crowell, and Maynard (1935) demonstrated that rats that were fed a nutritionally complete but calorie-restricted diet from the time of weaning on had significant increases in the values of their mean, median, and maximum life span when compared to animals that were fed a normal diet conducive to rapid growth (Table 7.1). The animals provided with unlimited calories grew and matured normally. In the restricted group, maturation was greatly slowed, although these animals held their weaning weight and suffered from no other nutritional deficiency, since their diet included adequate amounts of protein, vitamins, and minerals. Growth and development in the restricted animals resumed only after they were given additional calories at about 2 years of age. The restricted animals never attained a normal body size or body weight; they remained about 15 percent smaller than their normal controls.

These observations have since been confirmed and extended by a host of other investigators. The results of a particularly well controlled experiment are shown in Figure 7.2. Examination of such data in terms of their Gompertz parameters (see Chapter 2) reveals that calorically restricted animals live longer and have a longer MRDT (mortality rate doubling time) than do their *ad libitum*–fed sibs (Yu et al. 1985; see also Figure 2.22). In fact, caloric restriction is the only known environmental means that has been shown to significantly slow the mortality rate of any mammal. The basic observation has been found to apply to other species, both vertebrate and invertebrate, and its hallmark is its ease of repeatability. It is a robust intervention.

Table 7.1   **The Effect of Calorie-Restricted Diet Longevity in Rats**

	Life span (days)				Percent change in median life span	
	Mean		Median			
Diet	♂	♀	♂	♀	♂	♀
Normal	483	801	522	820	—	—
Deficient from time of weaning	820	755	797	904	+53	+10
Deficient from 2 weeks after weaning	894	826	919	894	+76	+9

Source: After McCay and Crowell 1934, and McCay, Crowell, and Maynard 1935.

Effects on age-related pathology

Are these animals that live longer also healthier, or are they sick and feeble? Is the boon of extended longevity a blessing or a curse? What, in other words, is the effect of caloric restriction on age-related pathologies? Many studies have shown

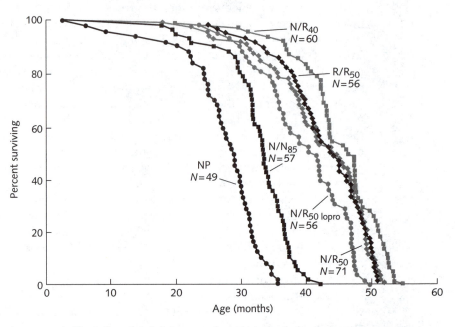

Figure 7.2   The influence of diet on survival. Each symbol represents an individual mouse. Diet groups are as follows: N/N$_{85}$, purified diet fed after weaning, at about 85 kilocalories (kcal) per week (this is the reference group); NP, nonpurified diet fed *ad libitum* at about 113 kcal per week; N/R$_{40}$, diet restricted after weaning to about 40 kcal per week; N/R$_{50}$, diet restricted after weaning to 50 kcal per week; N/R$_{50\ lopro}$, diet restricted after weaning to 50 kcal per week, with a decreased protein content; R/R$_{50}$, diet restricted before and after weaning. (From Weindruch et al. 1986, reproduced with permission of the American Institute of Nutrition.)

that the dietary history of the rodent has a major effect on the age of onset and the incidence of the various age-related pathologies (see Weindruch and Walford 1988 and Merry and Holehan 1994b for references).

First, tissue integrity is maintained well into old age (Figure 7.3), and the incidence of chronic tissue inflammations (for example, chronic glomerulonephritis, myocardial fibrosis) and of endocrine hyperplasias is significantly reduced.

Second, it appears to be a general but far from absolute rule of thumb that tumor incidence is reduced, disease progression is slowed, and onset is delayed. For example, several studies assayed the effects of caloric restriction on four endocrine tumors (pituitary, adrenal, pancreas, and testes) and leukemia in rats of one strain (Shimokawa et al. 1993; Higami et al. 1994, 1995). The incidence and time of onset of all five types of cancers were favorably affected by caloric restriction, but only the pituitary and adrenal tumors showed a progression that

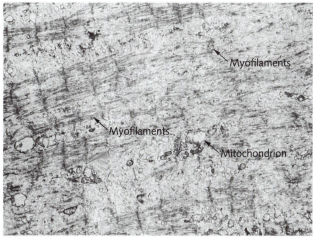

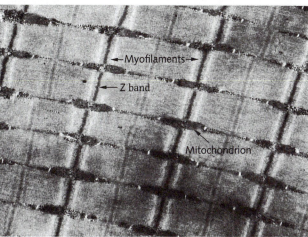

Figure 7.3 The influence of diet on tissue structure. (a) A longitudinal section through the gastrocnemius muscle of a control male Wistar rat aged 1,010 days. Myofibrillar breakdown is significant; only thin, diffuse Z bands remain to support the sparse, degenerated myofibrils. The sarcoplasm contains few mitochondria, vesicles, and fine filamentous remnants. (b) A longitudinal section through the gastrocnemius muscle of a food-restricted male Wistar rat aged 1,284 days. There is no evidence of myofibrillar breakdown or structural abnormalities in mitochondria or T tubules. Abnormal amounts of lipid were not detected. (From Everitt et al. 1985.)

was significantly delayed relative to the *ad libitum*-fed controls. And the incidence of some tumors is significantly increased by caloric restriction (Tucker 1979; Maeda et al. 1985). This unexpected result may be the consequence of extended longevity, since the increased life span also increases the time during which the events leading to tumor formation might occur. The mechanisms by which caloric restriction exerts its antitumor effects are not known, but the incidence and age of onset of leukemia appear to relate only to the total cumulative energy intake (that is, age × mean daily energy intake) of the rat (Higami et al. 1994). Long-term limitation of energy intake is known to lead to lower incidence of breast cancer in both animal and human studies (Willett 1994). Similar conclusions may be drawn about other human tumors (for example, gastrointestinal cancer).

Third, the restricted animals have a greater degree of protection against exogenous carcinogens; these rodents showed significantly fewer tumors after exposure to any of several different carcinogens tested. The mechanism underlying this effect is not yet known with any certainty, but it may involve specific sorts of alterations in particular DNA repair enzyme activities or, perhaps more generally, in a more rapid mobilization of the body's detoxification and repair processes.

Related in some way to the effects on tumors that we have described here must be the effects of caloric restriction on the immune system. The early effects of restriction seem to depend on the strain, but a general response to the restriction of calories seems to be a decrease in antibody production coupled with an enhanced cell-mediated immunity. Certainly the proliferative response of spleen cells to three commonly used antigens was maintained or enhanced in all ages of the restricted groups, while it decreased dramatically in the animals fed *ad libitum* (Fernandes and Venkatraman 1994)—a result consistent with the treatment's protective effect against the incidence and prevalence of tumors with age. In addition, autoimmune diseases can be significantly postponed in susceptible strains.

A large body of data (reviewed by Masoro 1988a, 1992a; Weindruch and Walford 1988; Finch 1990) shows that caloric restriction, in addition to having an effect on the age-related pathologies, delays or eliminates the onset of many normal age-related physiological changes. Examples of delayed normal changes range from retardation of the loss of crystallin proteins from the lens, to prevention of the decline in the mouse's learning ability, to delayed reproductive senescence in female rats. An example of a normal trait that is eliminated in restricted animals is the normal increase in the number of fat cells found in particular fat depots in the rat. Not only does caloric restriction eliminate the increase, but it brings about a significant decrease in the fat depot mass, as a result of a reduction in the number of fat cells (Masoro 1992). Restricting the amount of fat without restricting the total energy intake did not have this effect. The variety of traits affected in the different species examined suggests that the dietary restriction is affecting the basic aging process(es) and thus may not be a superficial type of segmental intervention. The same conclusion is drawn from observations on the delayed appearance of strain-specific age-associated pathologies.

Although not age-related pathologies in the strict sense, a delayed onset of puberty and/or an inability to maintain normal estrous cycles are often shown by calorically restricted animals and humans. These effects seem to arise as a result of neuroendocrine changes induced by caloric restriction, a topic to which we will return in some detail shortly, when we discuss the evolutionary origins of the caloric restriction effect.

Physiological Responses to Caloric Restriction

It seems reasonable to assume that caloric restriction is affecting, either directly or indirectly, some fundamental process(es) involved in the regulation of biological aging. But what might these processes be? And what specific aspect of dietary manipulation is involved? At a minimum, one could hypothesize that the critical variable is the amount of body fat, or the total amount of food eaten, or the total amount of calories taken, or the decreased intake of specific (toxic?) food components such as fats or carbohydrates or proteins, or perhaps more subtle effects, such as the lack of exercise in well-fed laboratory animals or the delayed onset of degenerative diseases in the restricted animals.

The amount of body fat is not what is important. The mice in one genetically obese strain eat more, gain weight very rapidly, live a shorter time than other mice, and have a high percentage of fat in their body weight (Table 7.2). Yet when these animals are calorically restricted, they exhibit a median and maximum life span comparable to that of their long-lived, calorically restricted controls, even though they still have about 3.5 times as much body fat as do the controls. The increased longevity appears to be related to food consumption as such in these animals, and not to body composition.

Conversely, the enhanced longevity of diet-restricted animals does not seem to be due to leanness *per se*. A survey of data from various laboratories has shown that the coincidental losses in body weight that often accompany diet restriction are not consistently related to the effect on the life span (Ingram and Reynolds 1987). Ingram and Reynolds concluded that a curvilinear relationship exists between body weight and life span such that different genotypes will react in different ways to this environmental modulation (Figure 7.4). For example, if male

Table 7.2 The Effect of Genetic Obesity and Food Restriction on Aging and Longevity in Mice

Treatment	Food (g/day)	Body weight (g)	Fat (percent of weight)	Immune response of old mice (percent of young value)	Collagen denaturation value of old mice (min)	Renal function (percent of young value)	Longevity (days) Median	Longevity (days) Maximum
Fed obese	4.2	59	67	13	80	113	552	890
Fed normal	3.0	30	22	49	52	71	799	970
Restricted obese	2.0	28	48	8	30	75	814	1300
Restricted normal	2.0	20	13	50	35	86	810	1280

Source: Data from Harrison, Archer, and Astle 1984.

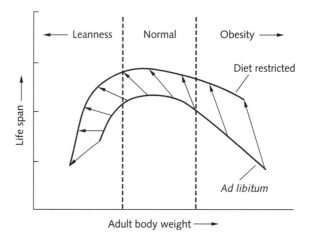

Figure 7.4   A hypothetical model relating body weight to life span on the basis of the response of the rodent species subjected to dietary restriction. The model is not based strictly on data, but rather provides a conceptual framework with which to view the data. Some genotypes are leaner and some are more obese than others; these trends are indicated by the tripartite division along the top of the figure. The curves represent *ad libitum*-fed animals and diet-restricted animals. Any one of the arrows connecting the two curves suggests the response of any single particular genotype to dietary restriction. Not all genotypes react in the same manner to the same dietary regime. The model predicts that for genotypes prone to obesity, body weight should be negatively correlated with life span; these animals should show a significant increase in life span when their diet is restricted. For genotypes prone to leanness, body weight should be positively correlated with life span; these animals should show a decrease in life span when their diet is restricted. Most of the genotypes intermediate between these two extremes should show an intermediate response; as drawn, most would show some increase in life span when their diets were restricted. (From Ingram and Reynolds 1987. © Plenum Press.)

mice of the B6 inbred strain are subjected to caloric restriction, their mean and median life span values drop by about a third (Harrison and Archer 1987). As these investigators thus concluded, thinner is not always better.

Furthermore, the diet restriction does not appear to work if it consists of the elimination of any single deleterious component of the diet. The individual restriction of any single food component (such as protein, fats, carbohydrates, fibers, or minerals) to the same extent as observed in the complete diet restriction regime does not markedly affect longevity (Iwasaki et al. 1988; Masoro, Katz, and McMahan et al. 1989). It now appears unlikely that diet restriction experiments extend the life span by reducing the intake of a particular single component of the food. This observation suggests that our life span is not shortened as a result of toxic components in our diet, but it does support the idea that longevity is affected by the daily amount of food (calories) eaten.

What about the timing of the restriction? In the early experiments, diet was severely restricted beginning shortly after weaning. Is this the only effective strategy? The complexity of the process is illustrated by the fact that this lifelong diet restriction regime can be mimicked by manipulation of the preweaning nutrition alone. Rat pups were allowed to nurse at normal or enhanced quantities of milk until after weaning, when both were fed *ad libitum*. The results, shown in Table 7.3, suggest that infant overfeeding is not conducive to enhanced longevity. They also suggest that the deleterious effects of this preweaning overfeeding can be partly overcome by daily exercise throughout most of the adult life span. Exercise itself seems to have no enhancing effect on the life span in these particular normally fed animals, which is consistent with the finding that *ad libitum*-fed rats kept slender by exercise show no increase in their maximum life span.

This conclusion regarding the deleterious effects of early overfeeding is supported by other studies, such as that done by Stuchlikova, Juricova-Herakiva, and Deyl (1975), which showed that the maximum extension of life span was observed in animals whose diet (caloric intake) was restricted by 50 percent throughout their first year of life and who were fed *ad libitum* thereafter. Animals given the reverse treatment had a somewhat shorter mean life span, although the life span was still significantly greater than that of animals allowed to feed freely throughout their life. Dietary restriction extends life span to the greatest extent when applied throughout life (Yu et al. 1985; see Figure 7.2).

The severe growth retardation that results from the imposition of severe caloric restriction regimes initially made this form of segmental intervention unattractive for human applications. It has been found, however, that a milder caloric restriction is still an effective intervention. This observation applies if the regime is one of moderate caloric restriction that is begun in early life or even in midlife. When the regime is begun in early life, the increased life span appears to be the result of a prolongation of the growth period rather than of the adult period. The data of Figure 7.5 demonstrate that a gradual caloric restriction to about 70 percent of *ad libitum* calories, started in midadult life, is capable of significantly increasing the mean and maximum life spans of mice. The success of the intervention is enhanced if the caloric restriction is applied gradually. It is rarely too late to start eating sensibly.

The mechanisms underlying the effectiveness of caloric restriction are not clear. Caloric restriction has different effects on different systems; some parame-

Table 7.3	**Longevity in Rats as a Function of Preweaning Nutrition (Mean ± SEM, in Days)**	
	Postweaning treatment	
Preweaning nutrition	*None*	*Exercise*
Normal	748 ± 38	720 ± 27
Enhanced	544 ± 41	669 ± 53

Source: Data from Drori and Folman 1986.

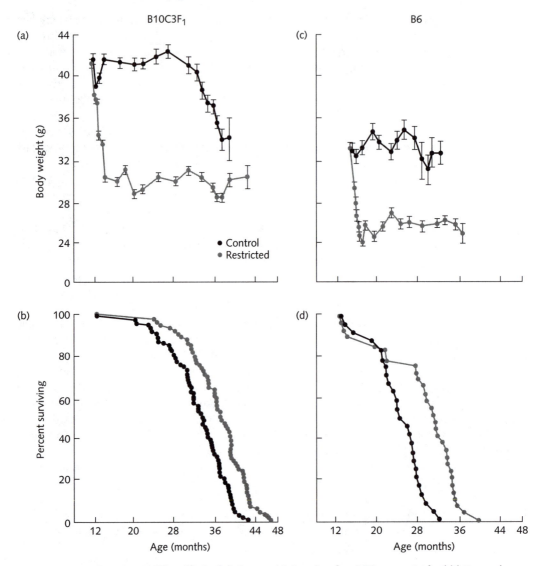

Figure 7.5   The effect of dietary restriction (to about 50 percent of *ad libitum* calories) on life span when started at 1 year of age. Plotted here are the body weights (a and c) and survival curves (b and d) of strain B10C3F$_1$ mice (a and b) and of strain B6 mice (c and d) fed on control or restricted diets. Weights are plotted as mean ± standard error. Each point on the survival curves represents one mouse. Note the gradual introduction of the restricted diet, as indicated by the gradual loss of body weight. (From Weindruch and Walford 1982. © AAAS.)

ters are altered while others are unaffected (see, for example, Table 7.2). As Masoro (1988a) has pointed out, recent studies have eliminated two hypotheses regarding the mechanism of action of dietary restriction, and forced the reconsideration of a third. First was the idea put forth by McCay, Crowell, and Maynard (1935) that food restriction increases life span by retarding growth and development. If the diet is properly adjusted so that the amounts of nutrients are adequate but the amount of calories is reduced, no deleterious effect is seen in the animals' growth and development. Second was the idea that food restriction increases life span by decreasing body fat. The data in Table 7.2 show that this is not the case, although we need to keep in mind that restricted normal animals have fewer fat cells (Masoro 1992a). The third hypothesis was the idea that dietary restriction increases life span by decreasing the metabolic rate. This idea was particularly attractive, since it has an obvious theoretical connection to the oxidative-damage theory of aging (see Chapter 10).

Recent information suggests that this third hypothesis is too simple to be entirely correct, but it is also not entirely wrong. Dietary restriction does affect metabolism, but not in the simple manner envisioned by this theory. Data obtained from the National Institute on Aging–National Center for Toxicological Research (NIA–NCTR) joint biomarker study have shown that caloric restriction induces a major metabolic reorganization in animals (Duffy et al. 1989; Feuers et al. 1991, 1995). This reorganization includes a lowering of core body temperature, a shift away from fat synthesis and toward glucose synthesis, a change in motor activity such that it is concentrated about the feeding time, and an alteration in the body's metabolic rate such that the restricted animals have a lower-than-normal metabolic rate before feeding but a higher-than-normal metabolic rate after feeding. One result of such a metabolic shift would be the lowering of the organism's steady-state production of harmful metabolic by-products that result in oxidative stress and damage (Sohal and Weindruch 1996). This situation is analogous to what is assumed to be happening in the *clk* mutants of the nematode, as discussed in Chapter 6.

Calorically restricted animals seem to be metabolically efficient in more ways than the one just mentioned. Let's consider one example of this metabolic efficiency that may give us an idea of the complexity of the mechanisms involved, while also pointing us in the direction of some likely causal mechanisms (Feuers et al. 1995). Pyruvate kinase is an important "gatekeeper" enzyme that catalyzes an irreversible ATP-generating step in glycolysis. The enzyme is activated by insulin-induced dephosphorylation and inactivated by glucagon-induced phosphorylation. It is thus controlled by the hormones that regulate glucose metabolism. When pyruvate kinase is activated, even low levels of carbohydrate can be metabolized via glycolysis to yield energy; when it is inactivated, the pathway is shut down and the organism must rely on gluconeogenesis for energy production. Young animals can activate or inactivate this enzyme with efficiencies approaching 100 percent. Old *ad libitum*-fed animals have lost as much as 90 percent of this ability while aging. Thus they must make available for metabolism via glycolysis significantly more carbohydrate and more enzyme if any ATP is to be produced. This need results in much wasteful synthesis. Old calorically restricted animals, however, have a much lower loss and maintain at least 60 percent of their ability for efficient regulation of the enzyme as they age, so they avoid this wasteful synthesis.

It is not just the wasted synthesis that may be important. The ability of calorically restricted animals to satisfy energy requirements with low levels of blood glucose implies that they can minimize the age-related effects of glycosylation. And maintaining an efficient flow of glucose through glycolysis enables calorically restricted animals to modulate their NADPH pools better. These latter cofactors are known to play an important role in maintaining some of the enzyme systems responsible for the detoxification of free radicals. Thus the ability to maintain "youthful" regulation of this enzyme may spare the organism the harmful effects of glycosylation and free-radical, or oxidative, damage, two processes that are harmful by themselves and that can interact synergistically in contributing to the degeneration that is characteristic of old age (Kristal and Yu 1992).

There is evidence consistent with this supposition. Caloric restriction has been shown to reduce the age-dependent accumulation of advanced glycosylation end products (AGEs) in both red blood cells and skin collagen (Cefalu et al. 1995). In addition, calorie-restricted animals have, in some but not all tissues, a higher level of superoxide dismutase enzyme activity and a lower level of superoxide and/or hydroxide radicals throughout their life span (Lee and Yu 1990). Remember that the key element in regulating the pyruvate kinase enzyme is the insulin–glucagon hormonal system, a fact that should focus our attention on the effects of caloric restriction (and aging) on the endocrine system, and to which we will return in Chapters 10 and 12. The same data should also remind us that the endocrine system regulates many enzyme systems, some of which may be important in the aging process.

In addition to these changes in energy metabolism, a multitude of other enzyme reactions are affected by diet restriction, including liver enzymes known to be involved in drug metabolism and elimination (Leakey et al. 1989). The complexity of these changes is illustrated by the observation that DNA repair activity increases in diet-restricted rodents (Lipman et al. 1989), while the same treatment simultaneously decreases both normal DNA synthesis and the binding of a chemical carcinogen to the DNA *in vivo* (Chow et al. 1990). The observation that caloric restriction also brings about various alterations in brain neurotransmitters also suggests neuroendocrine involvement (Kolta et al. 1989). Finally, persuasive evidence suggests that many other age-related changes are either slowed or reversed by caloric restriction (Weindruch and Walford 1988). A unifying explanation for these diverse effects would be useful.

A likely working hypothesis is that caloric restriction acts on the organism by modulating the neuro-endocrine-immune system. This regulatory system would indirectly couple food restriction with the aging processes of the various tissues and organs of the body, possibly by coupling hormonally mediated changes in metabolic gene activity to beneficial alterations in metabolic balances within the organism as just described for the pyruvate kinase enzyme system. Caloric restriction has been found to alter the levels and patterns of certain growth control genes (Nakamura et al. 1989). This finding empirically ties together the environmental, physiological, and genetic levels and suggests that the putative effects on the neuro-endocrine-immune system are eventually transduced into genetic signals.

One unexpected beneficial outcome of diet restriction is its effect on learning performance in mice (Ingram et al. 1987). Both middle-aged and old mice were tested for their learning abilities in a standard maze test. The control and diet-restricted middle-aged adults had comparable learning levels, as indicated by their number of errors per trial. However, the old diet-restricted animals, exhibiting scores comparable to the middle-aged mice, were clearly superior to the old controls. This study is very important because it indicates that the delayed growth and maturation characteristic of diet-restricted animals have no deleterious effect on adult learning abilities but instead maintain these abilities well into the aging process.

Measurement of the longevity of mice that had been made transgenic for the urokinase-type plasminogen activator (*uPA*) gene revealed that these animals have extended longevity and reduced body weight comparable to the values obtained in normal mice with caloric restriction (Miskin and Masos 1997). Further work showed that the animals' behavior had changed so that they now ate less. However, these transgenic mice also exhibited significant deficiencies in their learning behavior, suggesting that procedures designed to mimic the effects of caloric restriction may do so in an undesirable segmental (partial) manner.

Another unexpected outcome of caloric restriction is its negative interaction with antioxidant feeding programs (see, for example, Harris et al. 1990): The life span is significantly shorter in calorie-restricted animals that are fed particular antioxidants than in animals treated with a restricted diet only. One should not overgeneralize from these studies, because each antioxidant may have its own strain-specific effect, yet the data suggest that these two treatments are not necessarily complementary. The fact that diet restriction reduces free radicals *in situ* does not mean that feeding the restricted animals extraneous antioxidants further improves their health, even though such antioxidant supplementation may be of value to nonrestricted animals, as we will see shortly. The relationship between these two interventions is not simple.

Caloric restriction works wonders for rodents, but what about other mammals? How does caloric restriction affect primates in general and human beings in particular? At least two ongoing studies are focusing on the effects of caloric restriction in rhesus monkeys—one located at the National Institute on Aging (Ingram et al. 1990), the other at the University of Wisconsin (Kemnitz et al. 1993). In both studies the treatment is a reduction in caloric intake of about 30 percent. At the end of the first 5 years of the studies, this level of caloric restriction appears to be well tolerated by the animals, and the treatment outcomes identified so far resemble those of the rodent studies (Weindruch 1995b). These results include decreased blood glucose and insulin levels, increased insulin sensitivity, and increased HDL ("good cholesterol") levels. Interestingly, long-term caloric restriction appears not to affect the animals' energy metabolism, percent lean body mass, or percent body fat (Lane et al. 1995).

The restricted animals also show a slower decline in DHEA and DHEA-S (the most common steroid hormone in the body) levels than were observed in the controls. The importance of this observation is that DHEA levels are generally agreed to serve as a good biomarker of aging rate. It would appear that caloric restriction slows the rate of aging and reduces the rate of morbidity; a definitive answer needs to await the conclusion of these ongoing studies. Combining these results with the ongoing primate biomarker studies (see Chapter 3) may be especially informative.

No well-controlled, long-term studies deal with the effects of caloric restriction on humans. The severe malnutrition too often practiced on prisoners and refugees in time of war clearly has devastating short- and long-term effects on the health of these unfortunates (Mohs 1994a), but such data cannot be used as evidence one way or the other in this question. There is, however, some anecdotal evidence. In the past, the caloric intake of much of the population of Okinawa was much lower than the norm in Japan, but the nutrition of the Okinawans was otherwise adequate. Okinawa has a high incidence of centenarians: 2 to 40 times as many as may be found on any other Japanese island. Other anecdotal evidence suggests that very few, if any, centenarians or other long-lived people have been obese. Finally, the seven people who voluntarily entered Biosphere 2 for 2 years and reduced their caloric intake while there are reported to have shown physiological changes similar to those observed in calorically restricted rodents. However, anecdotal evidence and results from small-scale studies are by their very nature suggestive but not unambiguously persuasive. This is particularly obvious when we consider that a variety of controlled studies have shown that moderately overweight individuals have the highest survival rate (Casper 1995; see also Figure 7.12 and the related discussion). However, most human studies deal with populations that have either normal nourishment or malnourishment; a nourishing but calorically restricted diet is not common among the peoples of Western societies that are likely to engage in scientific examination of themselves.

Figure 2.22 illustrates the effect of caloric restriction on the Gompertz parameter. As mentioned earlier, the restricted groups have a lower slope and consequently an increase in the MRDT, and thus a decrease in the apparent rate of aging, accompanied by an increase in the initial mortality rate (IMR). Sacher (1977) suggests that this shift indicates the potential deleterious effects of caloric restriction, especially since the increase of the life span is proportional to the severity of the diet regime (at least in the early studies that he considered). In these terms, the life span represents the outcome of a dynamic balance between the increased IMR and the decreased rate of aging, as is implicit in the model shown in Figure 7.4.

Of course, the validity of such a statement depends on the assumption that caloric restriction affects the same processes as normal aging does. Some data argue against such an identity. The NIA–NCTR joint biomarker study has shown that calorically restricted rodents are metabolically different from the "normal," *ad libitum*–fed controls. Certain enzymatic changes that occur in the kidneys and liver of restricted rats are not identical to those seen in control animals. Hypophysectomized animals have growth curves similar to those of restricted animals, yet their lives are significantly shorter. Other hormonal treatments appear to retard growth and delay senescence in some mouse strains but not in others. It is possible that diet restriction acts through physiological processes other than those involved in normal aging (see Chapter 10). This may be the reason underlying the segmental nature of diet restriction.

One body of opinion holds that all the food restriction experiments are fundamentally flawed in their design. According to this view, the appropriate control is not an *ad libitum*–fed animal, for normal animals in the wild are probably usually calorie restricted anyway. Thus the increase in life span revealed by the food restriction experiments is more apparent than real, for it flows from comparison of a pathological state (the control) with the organisms' evolutionary normal state (the experimental). This objection is certainly logical and in one sense is practically unanswerable, for a resolution would mean conducting survival and nutrition studies on wild animals in their natural environment. In another sense, however, this objection is answerable, for the final conclusion is the same no matter what labels one assigns the two groups of animals: Caloric restriction enhances longevity. Reinspection of Figure 7.2 should reveal the unambiguous nature of this statement.

Evolutionary Origins of Caloric Restriction

Clearly, caloric restriction works. But why should mammals come equipped with a mechanism that enables them to live long if they stay hungry? What is the evolutionary sense behind this concept? One proposal suggests that caloric restriction is best viewed as a special application of the disposable-soma theory (see Chapter 4), which is based on the premise that an organism can devote its excess calories, beyond the amount needed for basic and essential functions, to reproduction and/or somatic maintenance. In this view, caloric restriction evolved as the set of mechanisms by which an organism adjusts its reproductive strategy to the conditions of its environment by shifting from rapid reproduction over a short time period to a reduced rate of reproduction over a longer life span (Holliday 1989; Richardson and Pahlavani 1994). How might an organism accomplish this change? The data in Table 7.4 are instructive. Caloric restriction has a major effect on the endocrine system, causing rapid and significant decreases in the plasma levels of most hormones. Many of the changes

Table 7.4 **The Effect of Caloric Restriction on Hormone Levels in Rodents**

Hormone	Effect of caloric restriction
Insulin	Decrease
Glucocorticoids	Increase
Thyroid hormones (T_3)	Decrease
Growth hormone	Decrease
Ovarian/testicular hormones	Decrease
Catecholamines	Increase (?)
Calcitonin	Decrease
Parathyroid hormone	Decrease

Source: From Richardson and Pahlavani 1994.

recorded in Table 7.4 are consistent with the idea that the affected animal is shifting resources away from growth and reproduction and toward survival. The brain is generally believed to have a central role in regulating both appetite and reproduction, probably via certain integrative centers in the hypothalamus and limbic system (Finch 1990). Therefore, the effects of caloric restriction on life span and reproduction likely begin via an unknown sensory input to the integrative centers of the hypothalamus, are probably transduced into hypo-thalamic-pituitary-endocrine organ trophic signals or changes in gene expression, and finally manifested in the form of hormonal alterations such as presented in Table 7.4. These hormonal alterations then probably bring about coordinated alterations in gene expression in their affected target cells. From this point of view, we might consider the integrative centers of the brain to be acting as if they were the pacemaker regions for senescence and longevity in vertebrates (Finch 1990). In fact, Masoro and Austad (1996) have presented a scenario for the evolution of the caloric restriction effect based on data suggesting that short-term unpredictable food shortages bring about changes in the glucocorticoid system and, through it, the systemic alterations characteristic of caloric restriction. We will return to this theme of neuroendocrine-based changes in gene expression in Chapter 12.

If this general view of the process is correct, one might predict that the only species that will show an increase in their life span as a result of caloric restriction are those that show a shift in their reproductive strategies in response to a decrease in calories. There are no firm data on this point for humans, but it is interesting to note that well-nourished women who engage in hard physical exercise often stop menstruating. In rural China, where caloric intake is often restricted, the age at menarche is approximately 18 years (Willett 1994). This time of onset represents a significant delay when compared to the U.S. age of about 13 years.

Investigations by Lints and his colleagues on *Drosophila* have shown the existence of a relationship between growth rate and life span in invertebrates that is somewhat similar to that presented for vertebrates. The earlier work of these researchers had demonstrated a good correlation between developmental speed and life span: Slow rates of development were associated with long life spans (Lints and Lints 1971). Further analysis has elucidated the existence of an optimum growth rate for maximum life span; at both lower and higher values of growth rate, life span is progressively shorter (Economos and Lints 1984). The growth rate depends on the amount of food (yeast in this example) that is present up to a limiting level. This aspect of the data is similar to the vertebrate data insofar as an excessive amount of food is clearly correlated with both a rapid growth rate and a shorter life span. Dietary restriction to an optimum yeast level will increase the life span; severe restriction will diminish the life span. However, the failure to observe any simple correlation between duration of development and life span suggests that there is no single, simple relationship between these two variables. In nutritionally complete media, there is a biphasic correlation between development time and life span: Maximum longevity appears to arise from a moderately short development time.

Some other investigators (David, Van Herrewege, and Fouiller 1971) failed to find any evidence to suggest that dietary restriction in *Drosophila* adults enhances life span. More recent work has shown that dietary restriction in the adult can significantly influence the adult life span (Chippindale et al. 1995). In addition, dietary restriction in the larval period has been shown to enhance the life span and the resistance to oxidative stress of long-lived strains of *Drosophila* (Arking et al. 1996). This effect is not limited to flies. Austad (1989) showed that dietary restriction significantly increases the life span of adult spiders in the laboratory. These results suggest that adult longevity in some invertebrates is also mediated via caloric restriction. The evolutionary reasons for the existence of this caloric effect in invertebrates may be similar to those presented earlier for its existence in mammals; but certainly the operative proximal mechanisms must be quite different in detail. In fact, Masoro and Austad (1996) suggest that invertebrates, lacking the vertebrate-type neuroendocrine system, have instead evolved the ability to use their heat shock protein system to respond to food shortages by reducing their mass-specific metabolic rate.

Taken all together, then, the results obtained from vertebrates and invertebrates strongly suggest that diet restriction is an effective intervention across a wide variety of animal species.

Toxicity Studies and Caloric Restriction

Chemicals that have the potential to affect human health are routinely tested for their toxicity in rodents, and such tests play a key role in the regulatory process for new medicines, food additives, and other such chemicals that are designed to enter the human body. The animals used in these tests must be in good health at the beginning of the tests. Over the years, the rodents used in such tests have usually been allowed to feed *ad libitum*; moreover, they have been inadvertently selected for fast growth and reproduction. The application of these evolutionary principles has led during the past several decades to the expected outcome; namely, the rodent models used for testing have shown a progressive increase in their mortality and morbidity during this time period. These alterations have brought about a possible confounding of toxicity data with the effects of diet on longevity. Investigators recognizing this problem have incorporated the control of dietary intake into the experimental design and conduct of animal studies, and they now consider the role of caloric restriction in carcinogenicity, toxicity, and pharmacology studies (Hart, Neumann, and Robertson 1995).

Caloric restriction and reproduction

Caloric restriction of a pregnant animal leads to malnutrition of the fetus, with stage-specific deleterious effects on its longevity and other traits (see Figure 3.16). But how does caloric restriction affect the reproductive behavior and performance of nonpregnant animals? The answer appears to be species-specific (Schwetz 1995). No significant effect on reproductive performance was noted in Sprague-Dawley rats under 10 or 20 percent restriction and only minor effects were noted at 30 percent restriction. Swiss mice are another matter. Significant effects, including a reduction in the number of live pups per litter, were observed in both genders and at all levels of restriction.

Manipulations of Metabolic Rate in Laboratory Animals

The data presented in Chapter 4 suggest that one reason for the interspecific differences in life spans might involve differences in basal metabolic rates; mammalian species with high metabolic rates tend to have short life spans and vice versa. Within any single species, however, there is often extensive individual variation in life span. It would be interesting to know how much, if any, of this individual variation is due to metabolic differences. The usual experimental procedure is to alter the metabolic rate of the animals and then to measure life span.

Altering metabolic rate in homeotherms is a difficult task, since their body physiology is designed to yield a body temperature and basal metabolic rate that is relatively independent of the environment. However, Kibler and Johnson (1961) apparently succeeded in altering the metabolic rate of rats by raising them at 48°F (9°C). This temperature approximates the environment of a refrigerator. The refrigerated animals had a higher food intake, a higher O_2 consumption, a lower body weight, normal core body temperatures, and a shorter life span compared to normal controls. The extra energy generated by the animals' reputed (but not measured) higher metabolic rate probably was being channeled into shivering to maintain body temperature rather than being devoted to growth. This reduction in life span took place despite the concomitant reduction in growth rate, suggesting again that the connection between these two variables is not simple. Note that these animals were not pathogen free, so they may have suffered also from the effects of cold stress on chronic infections. In a study of the effects of intermittent cold exposure (animals kept in 23°C water for 20 hours per week), the exposed rats ate 44 percent more food than did the controls but had a lower body weight than that of the controls. The exposed animals showed no significant difference in their mortality pattern or their mean longevities (Holloszy and Kohrt 1995).

Changes resulting from the alteration of ambient temperature are not the only way in which metabolism may interact with longevity. For example, hibernating homeotherms can down-regulate their body temperature during hibernation. If they are prevented from hibernating, their life span is significantly reduced. These observations suggest that extraordinary manipulation of metabolism affects longevity, but it is difficult to determine if the effect on aging is direct or indirect. Caloric restriction increases life span while simultaneously increasing metabolic rate, at least for that part of the day immediately before and for some time after the feeding time (Barrows and Kokkonen 1982; Duffy et al. 1989). But this finding must be balanced against the observation that calorically restricted rats and monkeys have slightly lower body temperatures, implying a decreased metabolic rate during at least part of the day. There may well be a relationship between metabolic rate and aging, but it need not be simple.

Temperature manipulation as a way of altering life span is much more easily effective in a poikilothermic animal, whose body temperature is not physiologically preset, than in a homeotherm. Loeb and Northrop (1917) were the first to demonstrate that the life span is markedly increased in *Drosophila* raised at low temperatures (about 16°C) but markedly decreased in *Drosophila* raised at higher temperatures (28°C). This observation has been confirmed many times since Loeb and Northrop's investigation. The data in Figure 7.6 show that flies responded in the expected manner to temperature, living significantly longer at low temperatures than at high temperatures, but these data also show that temperature manipulations of the normal-lived (R) strain cannot overcome the inherent

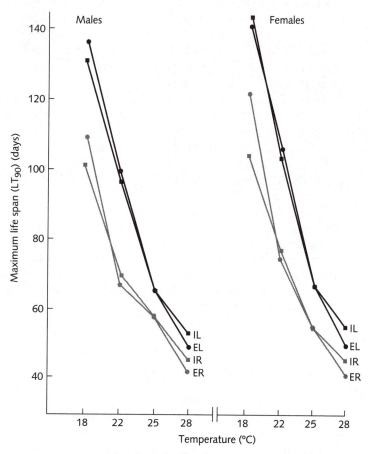

Figure 7.6   The effects of ambient temperature on the maximum (LT$_{90}$) adult longevity of a long-lived (L) strain (black graphs) and a normal-lived control (R) strain (gray graphs) of *Drosophila*. The strain-specific longevity is plotted against the particular temperature at which each population was raised. Each population was further subdivided according to what portion of the life span was spent at the indicated temperature: "E" individuals spent both their developmental and adult life at the indicated temperature; "I" individuals were allowed to develop at 25°C before being shifted to the indicated temperature. Note that (1) developmental temperature has little effect on the life span within each strain; (2) there is not much difference between males (left side of figure) and females (right side); (3) lower adult temperatures greatly increase life span within each strain; and (4) this environmentally mediated extension of life span does not overcome the genetically mediated superiority of the L strain. (From Arking 1988.)

genetic factors responsible for the extended longevity of the long-lived (L) strain. Temperature cannot be the only explanation of life span in this organism.

The later finding that the metabolic rate of a poikilotherm depends on the ambient temperature became one of the key observations underlying Raymond Pearl's "rate of living" theory, which he put forth in 1928. This concept originally stated that there is an inverse relationship between metabolic rate and aging (see Chapter 11 for discussion). One problem with this approach is that some data suggest that the effect of temperature on metabolism involves something more than a simple alteration of metabolic rate. The L and R strains depicted in Figure 7.6 have the same metabolic rates but very different longevities (Arking et al. 1988).

Experiments on fish, in which the eggs were allowed to develop at different temperatures, showed that both life span and body size were affected: The lower the temperature, the larger the body size attained. Since the fish eggs had a constant and fixed amount of food stored inside them in the form of yolk, the increased body size must be due not only to an increase in the time available for growth but also to alterations in the levels and ratios of synthesis and degradation reactions. Both the rate and the quality of metabolism appear to be altered.

Another problem with this approach is that the animals raised at lower temperatures usually show an extension of every phase of their life cycle, which is why this treatment has been called the "rubber band" mechanism of life extension. Thus, although the animals' chronological age was greatly extended, it is not at all intuitively clear that the animals' biological age would also be extended. This ambiguity is simply another reflection of the fact that chronological time is a poor measure of biological age. Finally, Lints (1989) reviewed the data supporting the rate-of-living theory and concluded that it rests on a weak theoretical basis and is not supported by several thorough studies. We will review this evidence, or lack of it, in Chapter 10.

Perhaps because of the abstraction of data, it is easier to draw conclusions when comparing metabolic rates across species than within species. Cutler (1982) plotted the maximum (LT_{90}) life span and the daily metabolic rate for 77 mammalian species (Figure 7.7). In general, these interspecific comparisons support the idea of an inverse relationship between these two variables, as first stated by Pearl (1928). Cutler (1984) interpreted the data as showing that every species has a lifetime energy potential (LEP), which is a measure of the amount of energy that individuals of that species will, on average, expend per gram of body weight during its life span. In other words, each species has a fixed amount of energy to expend on living. Cutler's statistical analysis shows that these 77 species can be statistically divided into three groups with different LEP values. But there are obvious exceptions. Humans, for example, are way off the scale, having a maximum life span that is twice as high as indicated for animals with a comparable LEP (for example, orangutans and red deer). Note that the data of Figure 7.7 yield three identifiable hyperbolas. Since hyperbolas approach their limits asymptotically, at low metabolic rates a small difference in the metabolic rate may be associated with a large difference in life span. In the same manner, a small difference in longevity may be associated with a large difference in metabolic rate. Despite these caveats, the data in Figure 7.7 show that in general, mammals show an

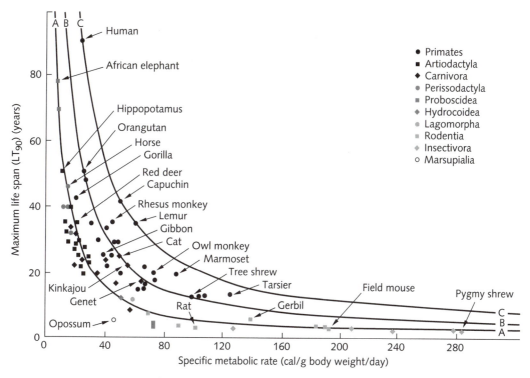

Figure 7.7   The total amount of energy estimated to be used by each of 77 mammalian species during their lifetime, based on data taken from the literature (see Cutler 1984 for references). Each symbol represents the intersection of the estimated maximum life span (LS) and specific metabolic rate (SMR). There is a strong inverse correlation between these two variables. Note that the data can be grouped into at least three similar but different categories according to lifetime energy potential (LEP), which is calculated as LS x SMR. The LEP values for the three groups shown here are as follows: 220 kcal/g for most nonprimate mammals (curve A), 458 kcal/g for most primate species (curve B), and 781 kcal/g for humans, capuchins, and lemurs (curve C). (From Cutler 1983a. © Alan R. Liss.)

inverse relationship between life span and metabolic rate. Does this prove to be the case? The relationship may be real, but it need not be causal. Our review of the *Drosophila* data (see Figure 7.6 and Chapter 10) illustrates that the maximum life span can be significantly altered without any measurable change in metabolic rate. Thus, this species at least either has no fixed LEP or the LEP value must be very plastic. If the LEP were fixed, we would have a very difficult time explaining the decrease in mortality rates with increasing age in the medfly or in humans (see Chapter 2). After all, to claim that the LEP is fixed is tantamount to claiming the existence of a fixed species-specific maximum life span. Much of the data presented in Chapters 2 and 3 argue against such a conclusion.

Austad and Fischer (1991) suggest that the theory is fundamentally flawed and that the explanation lies elsewhere. The fact that larger animals live longer than smaller animals may be a consequence of the survival value of increased body size, and not an effect of decreased metabolic rate. This explanation allows us to rationalize the very long life spans of birds and bats (see Chapter 4), which have very high metabolic rates per unit mass, and understand them as arising as a consequence in part of the survival value of their lifestyles. The high longevity of large terrestial mammals can then be understood as a consequence of reduced environmental vulnerability rather than decreased metabolic rate per unit mass. Not many predators want to irritate an elephant. Finally, the difference in longevity between island and mainland varieties of the opossum can be best explained in terms of their difference in body size (Austad 1993). In effect, the logic of Austad and Fisher's argument is that we have been looking at the wrong variable.

This explanation has the virtue of letting us resolve the apparent contradictions in the metabolism data simply by shifting our approach to an evolutionary point of view and, in so doing, rediscover that the animals' life history strategy plays an important role in determining life span. But this does not mean that metabolism plays no role. It is simply not possible to understand the long life of birds, for example, without also taking into consideration the fact that they exhibit a decreased amount of oxidative damage because of their low rates of mitochondrial free-radical production (Sohal and Weindruch 1996; Herrero and Baja 1997). Clearly, although we do not yet fully understand the role of metabolic rate in regulating life span on either an interspecific or intraspecific physiological basis, we can nonetheless conclude that its role is perhaps best understood if we realize that the metabolic rate is linked to the levels of oxidative stress suffered by the organism over time, and that a full explanation of the organism's life span is likely to involve factors other than metabolic rate.

Exercise in Laboratory Animals

Numerous studies have investigated the effects of exercise on laboratory rodents. The initial impetus for these investigations was to test the prediction of the rate-of-living theory that an intervention such as exercise will use up calories, accelerate aging, and decrease longevity. Early studies (Slonaker 1912) showed that exercised rats died younger than sedentary controls, but more recent studies do not show such an effect. It is believed that the earlier studies did not use pathogen-free rats and that what was observed was that exercise stress worsens chronic infectious diseases of these rats and hastens their death (Holloszy and Kohrt 1995).

One complication in conducting exercise studies on rats is that exercised rats tend to lose weight and their growth may be stunted. Thus, the experiment must be very carefully controlled to ensure that the effects of exercise are not being confounded with the effects of caloric restriction. When these conditions are met, one can see that lifelong exercise improves the mean life span but has no effect on the maximum longevity (Figure 7.8). In these experiments, rats subjected to both caloric restriction (by about 30 percent) and exercise showed the expected increase in maximum longevity ascribed solely to the dietary intervention. In other words, exercise by itself does not increase the maximum life span, but it doesn't interfere with the one intervention that does.

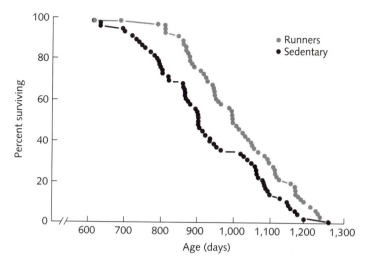

Figure 7.8 Survival curves of rats that were allowed to exercise every day (runners) or not (sedentary). The mean longevity of the 64 sedentary rats was 924 days ± 155; of the 60 runners, 1,009 ± 132 ($p < 0.001$). The age of the longest-lived 5 percent of each group was not significantly different (1,199 ± 44 versus 1,239 ± 14). Thus, exercise reduced premature mortality but did not increase maximum longevity. (From Holloszy 1993.)

Other studies, such as that by Goodrick (1980), suggest that both mean and maximum life spans may be extended by exercise. The reason for the disagreement is not known. This study also showed that when a regular exercise regime is begun early in life, it appears to increase both the mean and the maximum life span. Exercise regimes begun late in life have variable effects on life span values, suggesting the existence of some sort of threshold age (Edington, Cosmos, and McCafferty 1972). An alternative hypothesis, given that older rats do not exercise as hard as younger rats, is that there is a level of exercise below which no beneficial effect may be detected.

A more recent study addressed the effect of reduced physical activity on the longevity of female mice (Mlekusch et al. 1996). The inactive animals were housed in small cages constructed to permit little physical activity. These mice were compared to littermates housed in large cages equipped with running wheels and other aids to physical activity. The inactive group showed an 11 percent reduction in longevity, despite a significant voluntary decrease in food intake. Caloric restriction in the absence of physical activity appears not to be beneficial. In contrast, another study examined the effects of lifetime physical exercise on the thermal stability of the rat's tail tendon (Viidik, Nielsen, and Skalicky 1996). The results are consistent: Exercised animals have thermal stability values characteristic of chronologically younger animals.

If begun early enough, exercise also seems to have beneficial effects on the normal age-related decrements in the physiological functioning of various organ systems in the mouse, such as a slowing of collagen cross-linking in the tail tendon, improved cardiac contractability, prevention of decline in the energy stores of skeletal muscle, and the like.

Perhaps the most fascinating benefit of exercise is the effect on the neurotrophic factors of the brain. Neurotrophic factors protect neurons from damage, promote their growth and function, and generally serve in maintaining the long-term plasticity of the nervous system. Brain-derived neurotrophic factor (BDNF), nerve growth factor (NGF), and fibroblast growth factor (FGF) are common neurotrophic factors. BDNF and NGF are expressed at high levels in the cerebral cortex and hippocampus, areas important to memory and higher mental functions. In rats, even short-term exercise significantly increases BDNF mRNA in these brain areas (Cotman and Neeper 1996). In fact, there is a tight correlation between the distance the animal runs and the level of BDNF mRNA detected in its brain. This is not an isolated effect; similar stimulatory effects of exercise have been noted in other neural characters (see Cotman and Neeper 1996 for references). As Cotman and Neeper point out, the exercise-dependent increase in these neural factors may provide a fundamental molecular mechanism for use-dependent changes in the cellular structure of the brain, and the resulting enhanced neurons may strengthen the initiating exercise behaviors.

Exercise seems to have no effect on several other age-dependent factors, most notably the number or synaptic activity of neuromuscular junctions in skeletal muscle. The reduced capability of old animals to adapt to vigorous exercise may be due to this unrelieved age-related decline. However, studies have shown that exercise also has some adverse effects. In mice, for example, a strenuous exercise regime was found to induce both cardiac microdamage, such as loss of myofibrils and increased deposition of collagen, and the formation of giant mitochondria in the myocardium (Coleman et al. 1987a, 1987b). Such abnormalities were not observed in sedentary animals. In addition, this exercise regime appeared have an adverse effect on the glomerular integrity of the kidney (Lichtig et al. 1987). Thus, exercise is not an unconditional blessing. These animal studies seem to indicate that exercise can have both positive and negative effects, but that long-term training begun no later than midlife maximizes the beneficial effects of exercise.

Genetic Manipulations in Laboratory Animals

The selection and mutagenesis experiments done on fungi, nematodes, and fruit flies and described in Chapters 6 and 10 have clearly and conclusively demonstrated that the species-specific life span is under positive genetic control. This finding opens an avenue for potential interventions. Manipulation of the genome produces statistically significant increases and decreases in the life span of these laboratory organisms. The twin studies pioneered by Kallman (1957) (see Chapter 6), which have been confirmed and extended by more recent studies (Jarvik 1979, 1988), suggest that in humans, both the number and the pattern of our years have a strong genetic component.

Although these genetic studies are still in their beginning stages, it is only realistic to expect that they will take full advantage of the extraordinarily powerful techniques of modern molecular genetics. The first edition of this text stated:

> It has been shown that a laboratory animal's genome may be experimentally altered by adding and/or substracting specific DNA sequences to produce some significant alteration in aging and longevity. Only time and data will tell whether the experiment will prove feasible and successful. . . .

Should it pass these twin hurdles, we will be entering the era of somatic gene therapy.

The experiment has been done by Orr and Sohal (1994) and was described in Chapter 6. Other transgenic experiments affecting longevity are in progress or have recently been reported (for example, Miskin and Masos 1997). So we have entered a new era without much fanfare or appreciation by the press.

By its nature, gene therapy is likely to be targeted to specific tissue sites where a needed factor or two can be produced to restore, maintain, or optimize function. Although all tissues and cells are potential targets for gene therapy, this approach may be particularly effective in the brain, which presents certain limitations to other treatments or interventions. Recent investigations offer evidence that the adenovirus-mediated transfer of cDNA from the dopamine D2 receptor directly into brain cells is possible (Ikari et al. 1995). The loss of dopamine D2 receptors, one of the most robust features of mammalian aging, is associated with diminished motor control with age and is implicated in various neurodegenerative diseases, such as Parkinson's disease or Huntington's chorea. The possibility of restoring losses due to age or to disease is exciting.

Another very exciting prospect is the use of genetic therapy to control weight. Recall the obese mouse strain discussed in Table 7.2. Mice of this strain are strikingly overweight because they are homozygous for the *obese* (*ob*) gene. Humans have a homologous gene. The mutant mice have been known for about 40 years, but the gene was identified only recently and its protein product is now being tested (Barinaga 1995; Campfield et al. 1995; Halaas et al. 1995; Pelleymounter et al. 1995). To sum up the data, the obese protein (Ob; now known as leptin), when injected into mice, causes the animals to lose weight and to maintain their weight loss. (Maintaining a reduced weight is what most human dieters find impossible to do. The prospects of transferring this technology to humans is so rosy that Amgen, a biotech company, paid Rockefeller University $20 million for the exclusive license to develop such products.)

The initial studies show that lectin has a dual action: It simultaneously decreases the animals' appetite and increases their energy use. As a result, the animals become more active, further increase their energy use, and thus lose more weight than is accounted for by their lower food intake alone. When lectin is injected into mice of another nonmutant strain that are lean in their youth but put on weight as they age, these "maturity-onset" obese mice also lose weight. The Ob protein also works on mice made overweight by the inclusion of high amounts of fat in their diet ("diet-induced" obesity). Lectin appears to control body weight through a negative feedback system. This protein is made by the fat cells and presumably acts on a brain structure, possibly the hypothalamus, that measures lectin levels and instructs the body either to gain or to lose weight via adjustments to appetite, physical activity, metabolic rate, and so forth.

There is much yet to learn before we understand how the Ob protein brings about its effects. It is already clear that leptin does not function alone (Ezzell 1995). The *fat* gene, thought to be responsible for maturity-onset obesity in mice, has been cloned, and mutations in a human gene (β3-adrenergic receptor) that is responsible for the same phenotype have been identified. In addition, the *tub* and *diabetic* genes in mice have been cloned and are also thought to be involved in obesity and weight control.

Screening of about 200 obese people has failed to detect any individuals who have mutations in the *obese* gene, suggesting that obesity in humans involves defects in the putative brain receptor for the Ob protein rather than a failure to make the protein itself. With all these genes around, it is clear that obesity in humans is a polygenic phenotype, the genes for which act in conjunction with diet and exercise. However, anti-obesity drugs that stimulate the β3-adrenergic receptor are being tested, apparently successfully (Ezzell 1995). To the extent that obesity is a risk factor for the onset of certain age-related chronic diseases (for example, non-insulin-dependent diabetes mellitus) and/or for the failure to age successfully, the control of obesity may be viewed as an anti-aging intervention.

Debates on such therapies should and do include examination of the social and political, as well as the scientific, realities (see, for example, Kevles and Hood 1992). But the debate should be based on facts and not on slogans. There is much talk in modern society of doing the "natural" thing. But we do not extend this talk to depriving people with diabetes of the insulin they need to live. In principle, somatic gene therapy is no more detrimental to the individual or to society than is providing an internal source of insulin to a diabetic. If we forbid the one, should we not logically forbid the other? And if we allow diabetics to have insulin or severely obese people to have the Ob protein, then on what basis do we forbid the use of gene therapy (for example, the Ob protein for pleasingly plump people) for extending life span? And if we grant that our perception of our appearance can affect our physiological status, then should we forbid the use of gene therapy for cosmetic purposes?

Finally, we should not overlook the aspect of this line of genetic research that will have perhaps the most widespread effect—namely, drugs. It is unlikely that Amgen paid $20 million so that they could engage in gene therapy on people. It is much more likely that they plan to dissect the system both genetically and molecularly, detect the key control points, and devise drugs that can safely interact with people's normal body components to bring about the safe loss of weight and perhaps even a state in which many of the beneficial effects of caloric restriction can be expressed without forcing the individuals onto a permanent involuntary diet.

Hormonal Interventions in Laboratory Animals

The ability of hormones to coordinately affect diverse body functions is well known, and their role in the aging process has long been suspected. In fact, a substantial body of work describes the role of the endocrine system in bringing about various types of age-related loss of function, and we will discuss these data in Chapter 12. The question to address here is whether there are hormonal interventions that can extend the life span of a healthy laboratory animal. Such claims have been made for several hormones; we will focus here on melatonin.

Melatonin is produced by the pineal gland and plays a role in maintaining circadian rhythms and in helping to regulate the output of other endocrine glands. It is well known that melatonin levels in mice and humans peak at night and decline dramatically during the day. However, this nightly hormone spike

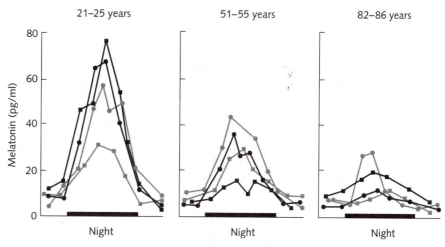

Figure 7.9 Representative blood levels of melatonin during the day and at night in four humans in each of three different age groups. As humans age, the amplitude of the melatonin rhythm and the duration of the nighttime peak of melatonin diminish. The animal studies purporting to show that administration of exogenous melatonin is an effective anti-aging intervention are seriously flawed. (From Reiter 1995.)

decreases dramatically with age (Figure 7.9), giving rise to speculation that there is a causal link between the drop in hormone levels and aging. Pierpaoli and Regelson (1994, 1995) claimed that exogenous melatonin added to the drinking water of mice increases the median life span of the mice by about 20 percent and the maximum life span by about 11 percent. Furthermore, they claimed that transplanting the pineal gland from young mice into the thymus of old mice also increases survival, as well as rejuvenating the host's thymic and immune functions. On the face of it, these treatments appear to constitute an effective intervention on aging. These claims have received wide attention, particularly in the popular press, but they are seriously flawed.

The three mouse strains used in the transplantation study of Pierpaoli and Regelson (1994) have a well-described defect in pineal melatonin synthesis and cannot make the hormone. Thus any assertion that young pineal glands transplanted into old mice of these strains keep the old mice from aging by restoring youthful melatonin levels cannot be correct (Reppert and Weaver 1995). To be sure, treatment of these strains with pharmacological levels of melatonin led to a 20 percent increase in life span in two of the three strains. However, administration of comparable amounts of melatonin to a mouse strain that can synthesize the hormone resulted in a decreased life span as a result of the induction of reproductive-tract tumors (Reppert and Weaver 1995). Thus, the evidence that melatonin is an effective anti-aging intervention in mice ranges from nonexistent to inconsistent. Extrapolation of these data to humans is premature at best and harmful at worst. Nonetheless, the claims are being prematurely popularized in the press and in health stores, suggesting that factors other than good science are involved in this process.

Transplantation of Tissues and Organs in Laboratory Animals

Transplantation of aging tissues from a young organism to an older organism was once touted as an aging intervention for humans; we now classify it in the category of "unlikely interventions" (which we discuss at the end of this chapter). Nonetheless, there remain two major reasons for seeking knowledge regarding the age-related changes observed in organs that have been transplanted from a donor of known age to a host of different age. First is the quest for fundamental insights: Is the aging process controlled by tissue- or organ-specific clocks? In other words, is the rate of aging intrinsic to the tissue, or can tissues perform their normal functions for periods of time greatly exceeding the maximum life span of the species? The second motivation is pragmatic: the desire to know what causes and can control age-related diseases. Is there any benefit to be gained from using organs (such as kidneys) from donors of advanced age? Or should we restrict ourselves to donors of younger ages? In this discussion, we will focus primarily, though not exclusively, on the first objective: Are age-related changes autonomous or nonautonomous in relation to the tissues in which they are expressed?

Transplantation experiments are simple in concept but more difficult in execution (see Harrison 1985 for review). There are five major sources of confusion. First, there should be a way to measure the extent of the inability of the transplanted tissue to perform its function. Second, there must be a way of conclusively identifying the transplanted tissue, as opposed to the host tissue, as the one performing the function being measured. Gene markers are probably the most convincing biomarkers in these cases. Third, the necessary controls needed to distinguish the effects of aging from the effects of transplantation must be performed. Fourth, the old tissue must not have been irreversibly damaged by its stay in the aged host. And fifth, the problem of immune rejection may severely limit the number and kinds of feasible donor–host combinations.

Assuming that these problems can be overcome, the basic concept of a transplantation experiment is as shown in Figure 7.10. If the loss of normal function with age in a tissue is caused by something intrinsic and irreversible (somatic mutations), the tissue will malfunction in an age-characteristic fashion even after transplantation to a young host. If, on the other hand, the aging defect is not autonomous (that is, it is due to a pacemaker effect from some other tissue or tissues), the transplanted tissue will function normally, perhaps even attaining the performance levels of a young tissue. Of course, a moment's reflection should convince the reader that this last case represents negative data in the sense that it imparts no information about what caused the aging process. These experiments are designed to identify cases of autonomous aging, not to identify the nonautonomous sources. With appropriate modification of the experimental design, they could be used to identify such sources.

Mammalian Studies

Krohn (1966) transplanted skin and ovaries within inbred lines of mice in order to avoid histocompatibility problems. His data suggest that the skin can function

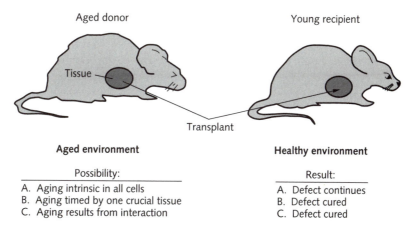

Aged donor   Young recipient

Tissue

Transplant

Aged environment   **Healthy environment**

Possibility:	Result:
A. Aging intrinsic in all cells	A. Defect continues
B. Aging timed by one crucial tissue	B. Defect cured
C. Aging results from interaction	C. Defect cured

Figure 7.10 The basic design of a transplantation experiment. If aging is intrinsic to a particular tissue (A), the transplanted tissue will exhibit the same age-related defects as if it had been left *in situ*. If aging is not intrinsic (B or C) , the transplanted tissue will not show these defects and could function as well as transplanted older tissue would. B and C can be distinguished by means of more precise transplantation/ablation experiments. See text for discussion. (From Harrison 1982.)

normally for periods in excess of the organism's maximum life expectancy; one such serially transplanted skin graft survived for 10 to 25 years (Daniel 1977). In line with these data are the results of experiments showing that the slower hair regrowth associated with aging is a nonautonomous property (Horton 1967) and appears to reside in the neuroendocrine system. Harrison (1985) discusses the technical ambiguities surrounding this experiment. That the phenomenon of tissue aging may be more complex than thought at first is suggested by the observation that old skin is intrinsically more sensitive to certain carcinogens than is young skin (Ebbesen 1973, 1974). This increased sensitivity may well be due to autonomous changes within the older cells. These two sets of results raise the possibility that tissue- and organ-specific age-related changes are a mosaic of autonomous and nonautonomous properties.

In many mammals (although not in humans), the ovaries fail to function at a certain age even though plenty of oocytes remain. Transplantation experiments in mice have shown that old ovaries transplanted to young hosts generally begin cycling again, whereas the reciprocal experiment—inserting young ovaries into old mice—does not cause estrous cycles to resume. Hence, the factors that bring about ovarian aging in this species appear to be nonautonomous in relation to the ovary. These findings are consistent with Finch's hypothesis (1987) that the hypothalamus and pituitary, which normally regulate the estrous cycle, can respond to only a certain limit of long-term estradiol exposure. Attainment of this limit then inhibits the neuroendocrine regulatory system, and the ovary shuts down. This topic and its implications are discussed in more detail in Chapter 12.

The age-related changes characteristic of the thymus at first appear to be autonomous, for infant thymuses transplanted into aged hosts display normal growth patterns. However, aged thymuses grafted into young thymectomized, lethally irradiated hosts function almost as well as those from young donors. This observation suggests that nonfunctional thymuses from old animals can be rejuvenated by some factor(s) present in younger animals, which in turn implies a nonautonomous control of thymic function. In support of this idea, thymus-dependent immune responses of older animals can be rejuvenated and their thymic growth pattern partly reversed by means of interventions affecting the hypothalamus–pituitary axis. Consequently, we must conclude that the initial impression is in error, for the thymic age-dependent changes appear to be nonautonomous and centered in the neuroendocrine system (Harrison 1985). This topic is explained in greater depth in Chapter 12.

All age-related changes in kidneys are believed to stem from the death of long-lived postmitotic cells and the consequent progressive decrease (by about 30 percent) in the number of functioning nephrons. In laboratory animals, the data strongly suggest that old kidneys function worse after transplant than do young kidneys. This reduced level of function may have something to do with the fact that young kidneys can enlarge by means of hyperplasia (an increase in cell number via the division of glomerular and tubular cells), whereas old kidneys can enlarge only by hypertrophy (increase in the size of existing cells). However, there is a great deal of individual variation; some old kidneys function as well as the best of the younger ones. For example, in humans, a renal transplant patient with a kidney obtained from a 75-year-old donor had a subsequent successful pregnancy, which is a stressful test of kidney function. Several authors believe that the results implicating autonomous kidney aging probably arise from the fact that older kidneys are more likely to be damaged by anoxia and operative shock during the transplant operation itself than are younger kidneys (see Harrison 1985 for review). This lessened physiological reserve capacity would be a direct reflection of the smaller number of nephrons in older kidneys. If this generally held interpretation proves correct, then the age-related changes characteristic of kidneys appear to be nonautonomous in relation to the nephron.

Insect Studies

A very dramatic illustration of the ability of tissues to live indefinitely with no signs of aging is shown by the results of transplantation experiments in *Drosophila*. In this organism, the future adult tissues are set aside as small nests of cells within the body of the growing larvae. These nests, called imaginal discs, will not develop into the adult tissues unless they are signaled to do so by a particular hormone stimulus. The imaginal discs can be removed from the growing larvae and maintained in culture under conditions where they never see the signal. Under these conditions, the imaginal-disc cells can live healthy and continuously for at least 10 years, 100 times longer than the normal life span of *Drosophila* (Hadorn 1978). In this case, then, the factors controlling aging are not intrinsic to the cell, for the cultured imaginal discs can give rise to normal young adult tissues even after 10 years in culture. Very clearly, whatever the nature of the cellular clocks that measure age, they are not working during this extended growth period.

Other Factors Affecting the Longevity of Laboratory Animals

There are various other factors that some data show are potentially effective in modulating the aging process, including various antioxidants, as well as nutritional, hormonal, and immunological interventions. These factors will be discussed in later chapters in the context of the various theories with which they are closely associated. In addition, recall the evidence we have already put forth showing that prenatal and developmental factors are capable of altering the rate and manner in which the organism ages.

● *Individually Useful Methods of Modulating Aging Processes in Humans*

Manipulating the life spans of mice and rats and flies is all very interesting, but what, you may ask, are real people to do in the here and now, today? Are there any segmental interventions to the aging process that an ordinary person can practice without withdrawing from the modern world or without becoming a guinea pig for an unproven regime? Strategies that fulfill these criteria do exist. In one sense, they are based on recently confirmed scientific investigations; in another sense, they date from the origins of Western civilization. As the Greeks put it: "a sound mind in a sound body," and "all things in moderation." There are no magic bullets that can stop aging in its tracks, but there is also no biological necessity to become decrepit.

Avoiding Premature Death

Though this suggestion may seem obvious, the first thing to do to age successfully is to avoid dying prematurely. Engaging in activities that carry a high risk of catastrophic injury or death, as is the wont of teenage boys, decreases the probability of surviving to middle age (see Figure 6.3). More important but not as obvious is the necessity of avoiding behaviors that will bring on a progressive disability and lead to death in middle age or early old age.

Consider the data presented in Figure 7.11, which tabulates the factors contributing to the causes of death in the U.S. population. Tobacco is implicated as a causative agent in about 40 percent of all deaths. Its role in bringing about heart disease and cancer, which together account for 57 percent of all deaths, is well documented. Tobacco use is an addictive but otherwise wholly avoidable high-risk behavior. The conclusion seems obvious: If you smoke, you are significantly increasing your risk of having a premature and unpleasant death. In fact, the single most important life extension step is to eliminate the use of tobacco. We will all die of something, but delaying the age of onset of major diseases will inevitably lead to an increase in the mean life span (see Figure 2.16), to say nothing of improving the quality of life. But smoking is not the only culprit. Note that poor diet and/or lack of exercise are listed as a contributory cause of death in almost 30 percent of the deaths (see Figure 7.11). We will discuss the interventions of restricting diet and of exercising in the next section. The point to be garnered from these data is that you are one of the most powerful influences on your

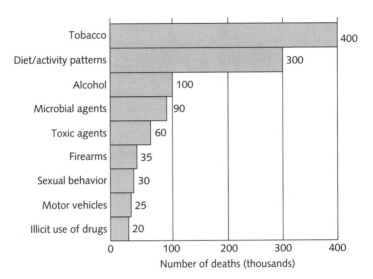

Figure 7.11 Contributory causes of death in the United States, 1990 estimates. (From G. T. Baker III and J. Frozard, Gerontology Research Center, National Institute on Aging.)

own rate of aging. I am nonplussed when friends and students ask me about anti-aging interventions while holding a cigarette. What's the point of hoping to live a long life if your own behaviors make it likely that you will die prematurely?

Physiological Interventions Suitable for Individuals

Nutrition Data in Humans

The animal studies indicate that caloric restriction is the single most effective intervention yet known. Although rigorous proof of the efficacy of diet restriction in humans is not yet available, enough other evidence has been gathered to suggest that dietary restriction would have similar effects in humans. The feasibility of a controlled caloric intake study on humans is now under discussion (Hass et al. 1996), and perhaps "hard" data on this topic will be available in the future. For now, however, we must be satisfied with only indirect answers to this question.

First, although it has now been established that the populations of Soviet Georgia, Ecuador, and Pakistan have no super-long-lived individuals, who live past the maximum human life span of 120 years (as we discussed in Chapter 6), the fact remains that some of these populations contain sizable numbers of physically active individuals of advanced age. Analyses of their traditional diets (Schlenker 1984) suggests that they are generally low to moderate in calories and that complex carbohydrates are the primary source of energy. The intake of proteins and saturated fats varies considerably, from very high and based on animal foods (meats and dairy products) among the Georgians, to very low and based on vegetable foods among the Hunzas (in Pakistan) and the Vilacambians (in Ecuador). The latter two groups live on the edge of their food supply and are probably slightly underfed every winter. Aged individuals in all three societies are usually slim. The results of studies on the food-restricted animals lead us to suspect that their moderate caloric intake, continued physical activity, and avoidance of weight gain may play major roles in the enhanced longevity and delayed aging observed in these populations. Evidence for this position is now available.

The "Mediterranean paradox" refers to the relatively long life spans of the Greeks and Italians, despite their high total fat intake and high rates of smoking. The explanation of this paradox is believed to be the Mediterranean diet, which is high in fruits, vegetables, cereals, and legumes, but low in animal fats, and which enables the people who eat it to avoid cardiovascular disease. Retrospective studies of elderly rural Greeks suggest that those who followed the whole traditional diet were only half as likely to die as were those individuals who adhered to only a portion of the traditional diet. Thus each of these societies may have found their own versions of a healthy, life-enhancing diet.

An 11-year follow-up study of a group of German vegetarians revealed that the mortality from all causes was reduced by one-half compared with the general population (Chang-Claude, Beyme, and Eilber 1992). The lowest mortality was obtained for cardiovascular diseases, but significant declines were also noted in deaths from cancer and from respiratory and digestive diseases. These data are comparable to those noted elsewhere, for example among Seventh Day Adventists, Mormons, and other groups whose traditions promote the practice of good nutrition and health habits. It has been suggested that the health benefits of the dietary practices of each of the several groups discussed above are sufficiently well documented as to be an important public health recommendation, even if it adversely affects the beef industry (McMichael 1992).

A second line of study has to do with nutritional deficiencies. Faulty eating habits, poor appetite, difficulty in chewing or swallowing food, loneliness, and hospitalization are all risk factors for malnutrition. Protein-calorie malnutrition has been termed the most undiagnosed nutritional disorder in the world today (Gambert and Kassur 1994); it develops in cases where a prolonged diet is very low in protein and high in carbohydrates. This condition is often found in the elderly, for reasons such as those just described. Supplemental nutrition may be justified by physiological changes, which may account in part for a decreased efficiency of nutrient absorption or waste product excretion, as well as by nonphysiological factors such as a change in income or an increased consumption of sweets and a decreased intake of protein.

A great deal of evidence suggests that aging is statistically associated with the development of glucose intolerance, by which is meant the inefficient uptake of glucose from the blood by the peripheral tissues (see reviews by Ruhe and McDonald [1994] and Halter [1995]). Glucose homeostasis is maintained largely by the insulin-mediated uptake of glucose by the peripheral tissues. When this process becomes inefficient, the result is a high blood sugar level. In severe cases, the afflicted person may be said to have developed non-insulin-dependent diabetes mellitus (NIDD), a pathological syndrome that may have severe and adverse effects on the aging process. Obesity and lack of physical activity may be the most important factors contributing to the development of glucose intolerance in the aged, since nonobese individuals who exercise show no decrease in insulin sensitivity (Kahn et al. 1990).

Overnutrition is a major factor in modern society and may be one reason why the incidence and prevalence of glucose intolerance is so widespread. It has been estimated that almost 45 percent of Americans between the ages of 65 and 74 have severe or impaired glucose tolerance (Halter 1995). In addition, the average annual incidence of NIDD triples between the ages of 50 and 70, compared to only a 25 percent increase between the ages of 30 and 50 (Ruhe and McDonald 1994). NIDD is an age-related disease that does and will continue to affect a large number of individuals. In addition, there is a variable association between glucose intolerance and hypertension in some, but not all, groups of people (Halter 1995). Obesity may be one confounding variable, and ethnicity may be another; the association can be detected in some Caucasian populations and is absent in other racial or ethnic groups.

Altering the dietary carbohydrate intake can modulate the development of glucose intolerance. Healthy elderly people demonstate an improved glucose tolerance, an enhanced tissue sensitivity to insulin, and improved pancreatic beta-cell function when placed on a restricted diet in which their carbohydrate intake was limited to 85 percent of the prior *ad libitum* diet (Chen et al. 1987). The effects of aging on glucose and insulin action were reduced but still persisted as a result of this treatment. The fact that improvement was observed after a mere 3 to 5 days of carbohydrate restriction suggests that a longer-term dietary restriction might prove at least as beneficial. It may be instructive to recall the effects of dietary restriction on the rodent's ability to maintain efficient regulation of its pyruvate kinase enzyme, as discussed earlier, and its subsequent effects on the animal's ability to age in a healthy manner.

Along the same lines, other studies (cited in Schlenker 1984) indicate that animals that are fed diets consisting of highly processed foods also have a higher incidence of degenerative diseases. Comparable longitudinal studies of people who are fed mostly fast foods are not yet complete, but the high calorie, fat, protein, and salt content of the typical fast-food meal does not bode well for the continued metabolic efficiency of the people who eat them. If you routinely partake of such fare, you are a member of the experimental group. Good luck. If the animal studies are any guide, you will need it.

Studies of U.S. and British populations (cited in Schlenker 1984) have indicated that diets deficient in various vitamins and minerals are associated with a high rate of mortality that often involves degenerative diseases. (Interestingly, the long-lived survivors in some of these studies adjusted their diets as they aged to decrease the quantity but not the quality of their foods.) Deficiencies of certain such micronutrients lead in some cases to recognizable physical symptoms. Swollen and bleeding gums or capillary microaneurysms of the fundic region of the eye are often indicative of a vitamin C deficiency, while a magenta tongue might be indicative of a riboflavin deficiency (Mohs 1994b).

The need for micronutrients is currently under discussion and represents an evolution in our thinking on the topic. For example, the minimum recommended daily allowance (RDA) for vitamin C (ascorbic acid) was originally based on the knowledge that the prevention of scurvy requires at least 10 milligrams per day. It is now known that our bodies require higher doses for the maintenance of good health and for the prevention of various pathologies. Linus Pauling strenuously championed the preventive health benefits of vitamin C "megadoses" of as much as 10 grams (1000 milligrams) per day. Studies revealed no ill side effects in healthy individuals taking up to 5 grams of ascorbic acid per day (Cohen, Cheng, and Bhagavan 1994). And high levels of plasma ascorbic acid have been associated in some but not all studies with a lower incidence of hypercholesterolemia, cancer, and certain other age-related pathologies (Cohen, Cheng, and Bhagavan 1994). Perhaps most germane to the normal aging process are the antioxidant effects of vitamin C on supposedly normal aging processes such as glycosylation and oxidative damage; we will discuss these topics in more detail in Chapter 9.

Vitamin E is an essential fat-soluble compound with antioxidant activity that is found in biological membranes and is considered to be a major protection against lipid peroxidation. Persons having conditions that interfere with the normal processes of fat digestion, absorption, or transport often have low serum vitamin E levels (less than 0.5 milligrams per deciliter). Severe and chronic vitamin E deficiency can result in various neurological symptoms. The minimum daily intake of vitamin E that is necessary to avoid these deficiency syndromes is set by the Food and Drug Administration (FDA) at 15 international units (IU). But perhaps more important to our purposes are the results of several epidemiological studies that generally indicate an inverse relationship between the incidence of various cancers and the level of serum vitamin E (and/or of other antioxidants as well).

An increasing amount of evidence, discussed in Chapter 9, suggests that these beneficial effects may be modulated via the known antioxidant effects of vitamin E and its ability to assist in countering free-radical promulgation and damage. For example, healthy adults taking a daily supplementation of 1,000 IU of vitamn E for 10 days had a significantly decreased level of pentanes in their breath, which is a reliable index of lipid peroxidation taking place *in situ*. A review of 19 studies done in different countries on different populations suggests that significant increases in the risk of heart disease are associated with lower blood levels of vitamin E and/or other antioxidants. Although some foods are rich in vitamin E (for example, vegetable oils, whole grains, wheat germ), it is not usually feasible to obtain from the diet alone the high values of vitamin E needed for disease prevention, which are commonly in the range of 300 to 1,200 IU per day. Oral vitamin E is well tolerated by the body and is relatively nontoxic. Animal studies suggest that huge doses over a long period of time, equivalent to a the consumption of 35,000 milligrams per day for 2 years by a man weighing 70 kilograms, are necessary before chronic toxicity can be detected (VERIS 1991). Human studies show that high daily doses (100 to 800 IU) of vitamin E taken for a 3-year period yielded no observed side effects (Farrell and Bieri 1975). In view of these facts, large doses of vitamin E probably have no adverse effects and this antioxidant certainly appears to play an important role in preventing certain diseases associated with oxidative damage.

Other vitamins besides ascorbic acid and vitamin E are needed, including thiamine (vitamin B_1), folic acid, and vitamins B_{12}, D, A, and K. All of these micronutrients are available in a well-planned natural diet. Some healthy people might be persuaded to take larger-than-recommended doses of one or two of them for preventive means, and an increasing number of studies indicate that such supplementation is of value. Deciding to supplement your diet with vitamin(s) means that you are banking on a mechanism of aging that hasn't been proven yet, so you could be wrong. But, of course, by the time this approach is proven efficacious, it might be too late for you to do anything about it. So you must accept responsiblity for your own treatment. Remember, though, that there is no evidence that taking megadoses of *all* of these micronutrients is of value, and some recent studies have shown that supplementation of certain of them (vitamin A, beta-carotene) can be detrimental in certain populations. For example, the current RDA for vitamin A is 1,700 IU. Consumption by women in early pregnancy of more than 10,000 IU per day was found to be associated with a high level of birth defects. There may be a fine line between enough and too much. A simplistic approach to nutrition—popping a pill while continuing to eat your cheeseburger, smoke your cigarette, and sit on your duff—will simply not work. Even the ultimate bible of consumers, *Consumer Reports*, agrees with this pronouncement in its report on practical methods of living longer (see the January 1992 issue).

Adjusting your diet as you age is clearly important. However, the most effective intervention would be to manipulate your diet as a young or middle-aged adult to delay or minimize the deleterious effects of aging. In other words, if we don't practice some mild form of caloric restriction, we should at least ingest a low-fat, nutrient-dense diet. Guidelines for such a diet, released by the National Research Council in 1989, are summarized in Table 7.5. These recommendations, if followed, are expected to reduce the incidence of cardiovascular disease, cancer, and obesity. More people are becoming increasingly aware of the linkage between diet and health, and the U.S. food industry has responded to this heightened concern with an array of new nonfat products. However, many of these products have substituted the fat with sugar, diglycerides (which do not count as

---

Table 7.5   Summary of National Research Council Recommendations for a Healthy Diet

1. Reduce total fat intake to 30 percent or less of calories. Reduce saturated fatty acid intake to less than 10 percent of calories and cholesterol intake to less than 300 milligrams daily.
2. Every day eat five or more servings of a combination of fruits and vegetables, especially green and yellow vegetables and citrus fruits. Also, increase starches and other complex carbohydrates by eating six or more daily servings of a combination of breads, cereals, and legumes.
3. Maintain protein intake at moderate levels.
4. Balance food intake and physical activity to maintain appropriate body weight.
5. Limit alcohol consumption to the equivalent of 1 ounce of pure alcohol per day.
6. Limit total daily salt intake to 6 grams or less.
7. Maintain adequate calcium intake.
8. Avoid taking dietary supplements in excess of the RDA in any single day.
9. Maintain an optimum intake of fluoride, particularly during the years of primary and secondary tooth formation and growth.

Source: From Willett 1994.

fat on food labels), artificial sweeteners, and sucrose polyesters (Willett 1994). It is not clear that these substitutions are in fact healthful. It is clear, however, that optimum health can be achieved from a diet that emphasizes generous helpings of vegetables and fruit.

Dr. Roy Walford, an internationally respected immunologist and gerontologist, described in practical terms a high-nutrient, low-calorie diet in his book *How to Double Your Vital Years: The 120 Year Diet* (1986). The diet contains a variety of foods, is relatively practical to implement in today's society, and is based on the principles elucidated by past decades of research on animals and humans. Readers interested in pursuing this effective intervention for themselves or others may wish to read this or another similar text.

Weight Control and Caloric Restriction in Humans

We live in a society that glorifies thinness. This attitude is certainly reinforced by our very real concern with avoiding pathologies such as cardiovascular diseases, diabetes, and the like—conditions for which excess weight and obesity are considered to be risk factors. Several studies that examined the relation between weight and mortality produced diverse findings, ranging from no association to a J-shaped or U-shaped relation to a direct association to an inverse relationship. One retrospective study used data obtained from the life insurance industry (Andres 1984). When mortality was plotted as a function of weight, the surprising result was a U-shaped curve (Figure 7.12) instead of the continuous linear relationship implied by the popular expectation that thinner people always live longer than

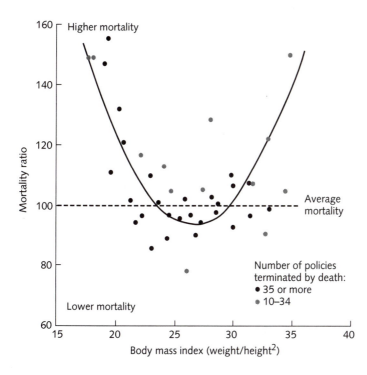

Figure 7.12 The U-shaped relationship between body mass index (BMI) and mortality ratio. Data are derived from the Build Study (1979). The curve was constructed from the quadratic relationship between the two variables. A mortality ratio of 100 represents the average or expected mortality for the specific age–sex group—in this case, for men 60 to 69 years of age. The nadir of the curve represents that BMI that is associated with minimal mortality. The two points at which the curve intersects the mortality ratio line (at 100) represent BMIs associated with mortality less than the average; those BMIs can, therefore, be used to define a recommended weight range. (From Andres 1985. © McGraw-Hill.)

plumper people. The portion of the U-shaped curve that falls below this level defines the body builds associated with a less-than-expected mortality, and the two points at which it intercepts the expected mortality line can then be used to define a recommended weight range for that group.

Plotting and summarizing many such age-specific curves yield the age-related range of optimum weight relationships for a given height and gender, as is illustrated in Figure 7.13 for men 5 feet 11 inches tall. Not only do these results differ from the standard tables of the life insurance companies (which have themselves been modified upward as shown in the figure), but Andres's recommended weight range increases dramatically with age. The standard weight–height tables are age-invariant. Table 7.6 presents both data sets for a wide range of heights to enable personal comparison. According to these newer data, an unthinking attempt to maintain one's weight at its former level might be dysfunctional.

On the other hand, the data should not be interpreted as giving the scientific imprimatur to obesity. A more recent prospective study investigated body weight and mortality among 115,195 U.S. women enrolled in the prospective Nurses' Health Study (Manson et al. 1995). Interestingly, the relationship between these two variables changed as the subjects were sorted according to various health parameters. A J-shaped relationship was observed for all women before sorting

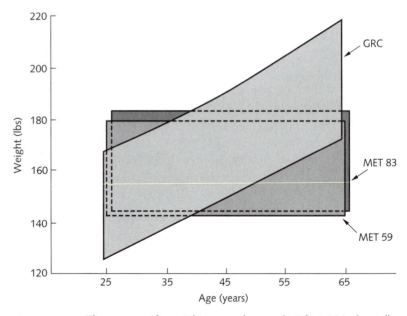

Figure 7.13   The age-specific weight ranges for a male 5 feet 11 inches tall, as recommended by the Metropolitan Life Insurance Company Tables in 1959 (MET 59) and in 1983 (MET 83), and by the Gerontology Research Center (GRC), as based on the findings of Andres (see Table 7.6 and Andres 1985). Note that the optimum weight ranges are age-invariant in the life insurance tables but are positively age-dependent in the GRC data. (From Andres 1985. © McGraw-Hill.)

Table 7.6   **Comparison of the Weight–Height Tables from Insurance Data and from the Gerontology Research Center Recommendations**

Height	MET 83 weights[a] for ages 25–59 Men	MET 83 weights[a] for ages 25–59 Women	Weight range for men and women by years 25	Weight range for men and women by years 35	Weight range for men and women by years 45	Weight range for men and women by years 55	Weight range for men and women by years 65
4'10"	—	101–131	84–111	92–119	99–127	107–135	115–142
4'11'	—	101–134	87–115	95–123	103–131	111–139	119–147
5'0"	—	103–137	90–119	98–127	106–135	114–143	123–152
5'1"	123–145	105–140	93–123	101–131	110–140	118–148	127–157
5'2"	125–148	108–144	96–127	105–136	113–144	122–153	131–163
5'3"	127–151	111–148	99–131	108–140	117–149	126–158	135–168
5'4"	129–155	114–152	102–135	112–145	121–154	130–163	140–173
5'5"	131–159	117–156	106–140	115–149	125–159	134–168	144–179
5'6"	133–163	120–160	109–144	119–154	129–164	138–174	148–184
5'7"	135–167	123–164	112–148	122–159	133–169	143–179	153–190
5'8"	137–171	126–167	116–153	126–163	137–174	147–184	158–196
5'9"	139–175	129–170	119–157	130–168	141–179	151–190	162–201
5'10"	141–179	132–173	122–162	134–173	145–184	156–195	167–207
5'11"	144–183	135–176	126–167	137–178	149–190	160–201	172–213
6'0"	147–187	—	129–171	141–183	153–195	165–207	177–219
6'1"	150–192	—	133–176	145–188	157–200	169–213	182–225
6'2"	153–197	—	137–181	149–194	162–206	174–219	187–232
6'3"	157–202	—	141–186	153–199	166–212	179–225	192–238
6'4"	—	—	144–191	157–205	171–218	184–231	197–244

Source: Data taken from Table 3 of Mohs 1994b (courtesy of R. Andres and the National Institute on Aging, 1992).

Note: Values in this table are for height without shoes and weight without clothes. The weight range is the lower weight for small frame and the upper weight for large frame.

[a]See Figure 7.13.

(Figure 7.14a), but this relationship became direct when smoking, weight gain, and preexisting conditions were taken into consideration (Figure 7.14b). Perhaps the difference between the data presented in Figures 7.13 and 7.14 can be attributed to an undetermined prevalence of smokers among the leaner people in the retrospective study and to the inability of the study design to sort those people into subsets.

A third study, involving above 325,000 nonsmoking people 30 years of age or older and enrolled in the American Cancer Society's Cancer Prevention Study, also detected a significant association between greater body-mass index and mortality (Stevens et al. 1998). Interestingly, the relative risk associated with increased BMI decreased with age—although it is also interesting to note that there are apparently no obese men above the age of 85 (Figure 7.15). Presumably it is this decrease in age-specific mortality associated with high BMIs that under-

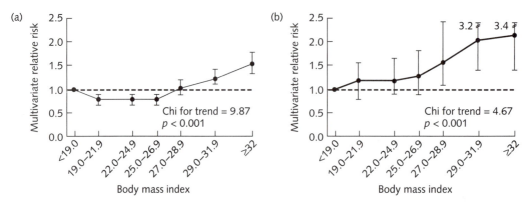

Figure 7.14 The relative risk of death from all causes, 1976 through 1992, according to body mass index for (a) all women (4,726 deaths) and (b) women who never smoked and had stable weights (531 deaths). All relative risks have been adjusted for age in 5-year categories. The reference category is that of women with a BMI less than 19.0. See text for discussion. (From Manson et al. 1995, courtesy of the Massachusetts Medical Society.)

lies the increase in the body weights recommended by the Gerontology Research Center of the National Institute on Aging (see Figure 7.13 and Table 7.6).

All three studies, when considered against the background of the animal studies involving caloric restriction, can be interpreted as showing that there is, quite literally, no free lunch. The anecdotal data obtained from interviews with centenarians suggests that such individuals generally follow rational and moderate dietary practices. The most obese individuals have a mortality risk 30 to 100 percent higher than that of thinner individuals. Approximately one-third of the U.S. adult population is overweight (defined as more than 20 percent above the desirable level), and the studies suggest that these people are at a significant risk of premature mortality. If so, then the long-term trend of increase in the U.S. life expectancy may slow or even decline. According to an old folk saying, after the age of 40, every person is either a fool or a physician. That saying might be a useful guide to the behaviors we should adopt.

Exercise in Humans

The effectiveness of exercise as an anti-aging intervention has been the focus of many studies. Very few of these investigations have been longitudinal studies, so the interpretations are sometimes open to question. However, the story told by the various studies is reasonably consistent.

The data suggest that the maximum oxygen uptake (VO_2 max) declines at a rate of about 1 percent per year. This measure of respiratory function is a good indicator of aerobic capacity and often has predictive capability (see Chapter 3). The reasons underlying this age-related reduction are not known, although the decreased cardiac output and the changes in the connective tissue of the lungs

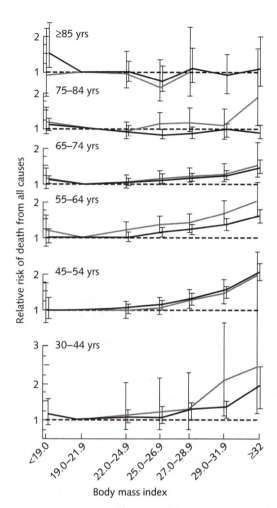

Figure 7.15 The relative risk of death from any cause according to age group and body mass index category among healthy white men and women who have never smoked. All relative risks were adjusted for age, education, physical activity level, and alcohol consumption. The reference category was made up of subjects with BMIs of 19.0 to 21.9. The bars represent 95 percent confidence limits. Relative risk estimates are not shown for age-BMI groups with fewer than five deaths. (From Stevens et al. 1998.)

and respiratory muscles (see Chapter 5) must play a part. This decline is not inexorable, however; the VO_2 max value increases as a result of habitual strenuous exercise (Table 7.7). In addition, healthy older men who were given a year of endurance training exhibited statistically significant increases in their VO_2 max values, a result that confirmed earlier reports in the literature regarding the beneficial effects of regular, moderate exercise (Buskirk 1985). The exercise must be regular or deconditioning will set in and all the hard-won gains will disappear within a few months, as Table 7.8 shows. It has been observed that adaptation to exercise is itself an age-dependent phenomenon, for a given effort will produce greater effects at younger ages than at older ages. The reasons underlying this change probably involve many factors, two of which must be the intrinsic structural and metabolic changes taking place in the cardiovascular system, as well as in the skeletal muscle fibers and the nerves that innervate them (see Chapter 5). Successful exercise regimes for older individuals take these changes into

Table 7.7   **The Effects of Habitual Physical Activity on Selected Physical Variables**

Variable	Marathoners	Joggers	Sedentary people
Age (years)	48.2	48.7	48.3
Weight (kg)	72.4	76.2	86.0
Triceps skin fold	8.4	9.5	12.5
Distance run/year (km)	2,644	1,488	0
VO_2 max (ml/kg/min)	57.2	49.2	42.5
HDL/total cholesterol	0.36	0.31	0.18

Source: Data from Hartung, Farge, and Mitchell 1981.

account by altering the type and the pace of the prescribed physical activities (Buskirk 1985).

Loss of skeletal muscle mass with age is well documented. This loss decreases the strength available to do the tasks of daily living. Since lean body mass represents the most metabolically active compartment of the body, its loss must certainly contribute to the decreases in the VO_2 max and in the resting metabolic rate. In one study, elderly individuals who engaged in resistance training increased their muscle mass and their resting metabolic rate, decreased their fat body mass, and increased their caloric intake (Evans 1995). We pointed out in Chapter 5 that the bones respond to the stresses placed on them by muscle use. The expectation that exercise benefits the skeleton is borne out by the data. Strength training has a beneficial effect on bone density: A group of elderly women who exercised for a year increased their bone mineral density, while the nonexercising control group showed a significant decline (D. Evans 1995). We also pointed out the association of glucose intolerance and its consequent effects with age. Exercise has been shown to improve glucose tolerance in previously sedentary subjects and to prevent the onset of NIDD (Holloszy and Kohrt 1995). It has been shown that the improvements in carbohydrate metabolism occur pri-

Table 7.8   **Changes in Selected Variables as a Result of Short-Term Physical Conditioning and Deconditioning**

Variable	With conditioning	With deconditioning
VO_2 max	11.7%	−7.2%
VE_2 max	15.1%	−3.5%
Maximum heart rate	15.1%	−13.9%

Source: Data from Miyashita, Haga, and Mozota 1978.

marily in skeletal muscle, brought about in part by the increased muscle mass and in part by physiological changes that improve the muscles' uptake of glucose in response to insulin (D. Evans 1995).

Finally, exercise induces significant alterations in plasma hormone concentrations in all age groups, without regard to the subject's accustomed activity levels beforehand (Table 7.9; Silverman and Mazzeo 1996). Certain of these hormones (for example, growth hormone) are known to have significant anti-aging metabolic effects, as we'll see in the next section. The observation that the old, trained men demonstrated a greater hormonal response than did the young, sedentary men suggests that the neuroendocrine mechanisms underlying the hormonal responses are enhanced with endurance training. The data further suggest that the normal age-related diminution in these neuroendocrine mechanisms can be delayed or attenuated by exercise.

Weindruch (1995) has pointed out that skeletal muscle accounts for a large share of the body's oxygen consumption. This fact, coupled with the low repair capacities of muscle, suggest that some of the age-related changes seen in muscle reflect oxidative damage to muscle cells (Luhtala et al. 1994). This correlation raises the possibility that caloric restriction coupled with moderate exercise is an effective intervention (see, for example, Figure 7.8). Such an effect has now been demonstrated in rats: A 10 percent caloric restriction combined with a mild daily exercise regime led to a significant extension of maximum longevity, which was, however, less than that seen with a standard 40 percent caloric restriction without exercise (McCarter et al. 1996). In these animals, the age-retarding effects of caloric restriction were mobilized by the combination of two low-level interventions. Note, however, that there are major gaps in our knowledge of these processes in humans, so no firm recommendations can be made.

Physical frailty arising from severely impaired strength, mobility, balance, and endurance significantly diminishes the ability of many older persons to con-

Table 7.9   **The Effect of a Maximal Exercise Test on Plasma Hormone Concentrations**

Hormone	Young		Middle-aged		Old	
	Sedentary	*Trained*	*Sedentary*	*Trained*	*Sedentary*	*Trained*
Lactate[a] (mM)	4.8 ± 0.3	6.0 ± 0.4	3.9 ± 0.5	5.2 ± 0.4	3.7 ± 0.4	3.8 ± 0.6
Norepinephrine (ng/ml)	2.0 ± 0.4	7.5 ± 1.3[b]	3.1 ± 0.3	8.6 ± 2.5[b]	4.1 ± 1.0	6.0 ± 1.1[b]
Epinephrine (ng/ml)	0.4 ± 0.04	1.2 ± 0.3[b]	0.4 ± 0.12	1.3 ± 0.5[b]	0.3 ± 0.05	0.7 ± 0.3[b]
Growth hormone	5.6 ± 1.8	21.9 ± 4.0[b]	8.6 ± 3.2	19.0 ± 4.4[b]	2.8 ± 1.0	11.3 ± 3.5[b]
Cortisol (ng/ml)	19.8 ± 2.3	26.8 ± 2.2[b]	14.9 ± 0.9	21.6 ± 1.8[b]	16.3 ± 2.4	19.5 ± 2.4

Source: Data from Table 4 of Silverman and Mazzeo 1996.
Note: Data are given as mean ± SEM.
[a]Lactate levels indicate metabolic effort.
[b]Significant training effect.

duct the activities of daily living. It also significantly increases the risk of falls and their associated trauma (for example, hip fracture), as well as the risk of mortality. Between 10 and 62 percent of the elderly, depending on their sex and age, need help with the activities of daily living and cannot live independently (Guralnick and Simonsick 1993). Physical frailty is a negative predictor of active life expectancy, with all the personal and public costs thus implied. Although physical frailty was once thought to be an inevitable part of aging, it now appears that it can be reversed by exercises designed for endurance training and for muscle strengthening.

The success of the intervention in the laboratory appears to depend on the intensity of the exercise stimulus. The high-repetition, low-intensity stimulus of aerobic training leads to only minimal strength gain when compared to the low-repetition, high-intensity stimulus of resistance training (Fiatarone et al. 1993). Nonetheless, any exercise is better than none. A community study showed that elderly people who walked 30 minutes or more every day performed significantly better in both laboratory and community than did those who did not walk (Svanborg 1993). In fact, regular walking in physically capable older men is not only associated with a lower overall mortality rate than among nonwalkers, but the distance walked is inversely related to mortality (Hakim et al. 1998). The musculoskeletal system seems to retain its plasticity at all ages. The fact that our reserve capacity goes down with age means that the need for adopting preventive or postponing measures becomes more obvious.

There seems to be no clear relationship between athletic competition done as a college youth and subsequent longevity (Schneider 1985), although many former athletes can perform aerobic walks later in life with less effort and strain when compared to age-matched nonathletes (Buskirk 1985). However, when men habitually active in endurance-type recreational sports (such as cross-country skiing or jogging) were compared to habitually sedentary men, the active men scored better on several (but not all) physiological parameters than did the inactive men (see Table 7.7).

As with any other intervention, carrying exercise to an extreme may be detrimental. When 20 men engaged in vigorous exercise (10 hours per day for 30 days), the rate of oxidative DNA damage products detected in their urine increased by 33 percent (Poulsen, Loft, and Vistisen 1996). Human cells exposed to extreme oxidative stress *in vitro* are not capable of repairing the DNA damage that occurs in their mitochondria, although they are capable of repairing nuclear damage (Yakes and Van Houten 1997). Thus extreme exercise may preferentially expose one's mtDNA to increased oxidative damage, thereby potentially damaging one's health instead of improving it.

The conclusion of Buskirk (1985, p. 924) seems appropriate: "Thus, functional alterations wrought by regular exercise blunt the downward trends commonly associated with aging." Properly used, exercise can be an effective intervention.

Hormonal Interventions in Humans

Growth hormone   The ability of hormones to stop or reverse the aging process is well established in the popular mind as a result of the indiscriminate commingling of modern hormone replacement therapy for postmenopausal women with the older attempts of Brown-Sequard (1889) to rejuvenate older men with testicular extracts from dogs and guinea pigs. But what of the facts? The regulatory role of the endocrine system has long been recognized, particularly the central integrative role of the pituitary and hypothalamus. The anterior pituitary gland directly regulates several peripheral endocrine organs (for example, adrenal cortex, thyroid, gonads) and indirectly regulates a host of other tissues via its secretion of prolactin and growth hormone. The cells of the anterior pituitary itself show very few structural changes with aging (Timiras 1994). Attention has focused on the role of growth hormone in aging, in part because growth hormone deficiencies in children are associated with reduced lean body mass, increased fat mass, reduced protein synthesis, reduced skin thickness, and a self-perceived loss of energy (Nelson 1995). Because the same deficits are usually seen in aging adults, several groups hypothesized that the age-related decline of 50 percent in growth hormone levels observed in aging adults (see Table 7.9) bears a causal relationship to these observed age-related changes. The evidence suggests that this hypothesis is correct.

The level of growth homone itself is regulated positively by growth hormone-releasing hormone (GHRH) and negatively by somatostatin. All three hormones are secreted throughout life, growth hormone exerting metabolic effects and GHRH and somatostatin regulating the secretion of growth hormone. Growth hormone has both direct and indirect effects on target tissues. Many of the indirect effects are mediated through the insulinlike growth factor 1 (IGF-1) molecule, which is synthesized in the liver in response to stimulation by growth hormone. IGF-1 acts as a classic endocrine molecule when secreted into the circulation. Its serum level falls in conjuction with that of growth hormone, so it is often used as a surrogate measurement for growth hormone.

Rudman et al. (1990) treated 21 healthy men over 60 years of age, each of whom was deficient in growth hormone, with doses of recombinant human growth hormone (rHGH) designed to restore their IGF-1 levels to those of young adults. The treatments lasted 6 months and showed no adverse side effects. The men showed a threefold rise in plasma IGF-1 levels, a 9 percent increase in lean body mass, a 14 percent decrease in fat tissue mass, a 1.6 percent increase in lumbar vertebral bone density, and a 7 percent increase in skin thickness. These effects disappeared within 3 months after the treatments were stopped. A larger follow-up study was carried out for 12 months (Cohn et al. 1993) and found that significant numbers of the participants developed potentially serious side effects ranging from carpal tunnel syndrome to hyperglycemia. Other investigators discovered the same phenomenon (Schwartz 1995). Many of the subjects dropped out of the studies.

This finding lent importance to interventions based on indirect stimulation of the growth hormone levels. Both Iovino, Monteleone, and Steardo (1989) and Corpas et al. (1992) found that administration of GHRH increased levels of growth hormone and IGF-1 in older individuals, giving hope that alternative routes would provide an effective intervention strategy without side effects. This concern cannot be minimized, given the seriousness of the side effects so far observed and the pleiotropic effects of the growth hormone on many tissues.

A comprehensive review by Wolfe (1998) of the role of GH in slowing aging processes emphasizes the variable outcomes of GH therapy and the possibility of deleterious side effects arising from its unregulated use. People who suffer from hypopituitarism can benefit from GH replacement therapy, but GH supplementation of normal elderly people yielded either no functional change or adverse side effects after extended use. Elderly men who exercised vigorously showed no noticeable effect of GH on body mass or muscle size, presumably because exercise itself induced more GH than the supplementation provided (Table 7.9). GH is now known to be regulated by an entirely new signaling pathway involving hexapeptides administered either orally or nasally (see Wolfe 1998 for review and references). Such GH-releasing peptides (GHRPs) have already been demonstrated to induce the normal pulsatile nature of GH secretion. The effect of increased GH, however induced, on the aging process still needs to be rigorously confirmed or disproved. Wolfe suggests that the popular enthusiasm for GH and other "anti-aging" comounds will lead to unregulated self-administration and all sorts of potential damage. In addition, prudence requires us to note that a chronic excess of GH in young adults is associated with eventual diabetes, osteoarthritis, hypertension, and, possibly, cancer—the very problems that characterize normal aging and that the use of exogenous GH is intended to avoid (Rudman and Shetty 1994; Wolfe 1998).

Thus, at the moment, the use of trophic factors to improve muscle mass and glucose metabolism must be viewed as a research tool only. Important questions remain to be answered.

DHEA   Dehydroepiandrosterone (DHEA) is the adrenal steroid hormone that is found in the highest concentration in human plasma. Its serum levels are known to decrease as a function of age in humans. The levels begin to rise with puberty, peak in the late teens (teenaged males have about 50 percent more DHEA than teenaged females), and then decline in a linear fashion at a rate of about 10 percent per decade until low and equivalent levels are reached in both sexes at age 75 (Orentreich et al. 1984). The levels in normal human serum can be modified by various metabolic, physiological, and behavioral factors. DHEA is believed to have no specific effect of its own; rather it is transformed within the body's cells into a variety of active androgens and/or estrogens, and this presumed steroid interconvertibility is postulated to underlie its varied physiological and pharmacological effects (Orenteich et al. 1984). The hormone can be bought in health food stores and is written about from time to time in the popular press. So what are its effects?

Some evidence suggests that administration of DHEA suppresses the incidence of tumors in rodents, but these results are confounded by questions about whether caloric restriction was the operative mechanism in these experiments. Recent evidence suggests that DHEA acts as a physiological regulator of interleukin-2 biosynthesis (Yu 1995). If so, its ability to regulate such cytokines may be a plausible mechanism by which the molecule exerts its antitumor effects and putative anti-aging action. In any event, lifetime feeding of DHEA to healthy mice has no effect on their median or maximum life span (Orenteich et al. 1984). Some evidence suggests that short-term administration of DHEA to older humans improves their feelings of well-being in both objective and subjective terms (Orenteich et al. 1984). Women already on estrogen replacement therapy who experience a positive effect with DHEA supplementation may wish to discuss the potential of steroid hormone overload with their physician before embarking on a long-term supplementation regime.

Hormone induction via exercise   This intervention may appear to be out of place in this category, but a serious inspection of Table 7.9 will indicate that exercise can induce a fourfold increase in the levels of endogenous growth hormone, even in elderly individuals. This increase is comparable to the threefold increase in IGF-1 levels noted when older adults were given growth hormone directly. The beneficial and anti-aging effects of growth hormone have already been enumerated. It stands to reason, therefore, that the simplest and cheapest way to induce your own growth hormone levels to the point where you can enjoy their anti-aging effects is to exercise. At the very least, you can do this now while you wait and see if a safe and effective trophic response can be developed.

Antioxidant Supplementation in Humans

Chapter 9 pointed out that dietary supplementation of antioxidants to various laboratory animals is only occasionally effective in prolonging life, although such treatments are believed to be effective in reducing morbidity. Certainly, individuals with deficiencies in serum levels of various antioxidants are at a significantly increased risk for cardiovascular disease, cancer, and other age-related pathologies. Recent epidemiological studies showing that supplementation with specific types of antioxidants offers the potential for slowing the onset of some age-associated diseases and for retarding physiological declines. As discussed earlier, several studies have shown that individuals who consume high levels of antioxidant vitamins, primarily vitamin E, either through their normal diet or by supplementation, are at reduced risk for cardiovascular disease (Rimm et al. 1993; Stampfer et al. 1993). There is also evidence that vitamin C provides some protection against non-hormone-dependent cancers (Block 1991) and may lower blood pressure of borderline hypertensive subjects (Troute 1991).

These studies are encouraging but not definitive. It is possible, for example, for a compound to have more than one effect *in vivo*. Ascorbic acid is usually a free-radical scavenger, but in the presence of excess iron it becomes a free-radical generator. Tocopherol (vitamin E) may act as a procoagulant. Thus, predicting the *in vivo* results of pharmacological doses of these natural products is difficult. Data from a recent double-blind, placebo-controlled prevention trial of the effect of daily supplementation of alpha-tocopherol, beta-carotene, or both on almost 30,000 Finnish smokers over a period of some 5 years underscore this caution. This study reported that participants who received alpha-tocopherol showed an 18 percent increase in the incidence of cancer as compared to participants who did not receive this supplement (Alpha-tocopherol Study Group 1994).

The disappointing findings of the Finnish study were recently reinforced by two, now discontinued, large-scale studies in the United States: the Beta-Carotene Retinol Efficacy Trial (CARET) and the Physicians' Health Study. In one study involving more than 18,000 people, people who smoked and people who were exposed to high levels of asbestos were given daily doses of beta-carotene, vitamin A, or a placebo for approximately 8 years. The individuals taking beta-carotene experienced a 28 percent increase in the incidence of cancer and had a 17 percent greater rate of mortality as compared to the control group. There were no differences between the groups on the incidence of cancer or cardiovascular disease. While one may raise serious questions regarding the experimental protocol of the Finnish and CARET studies, such as the inclusion of only individuals already at high risk and chosen from a population that has one of the highest mortality rates in Europe, these results, combined with the negative findings on beta-carotene in the Physicians' Health Study, clearly demonstrate that vitamin supplementation needs to be much better understood before sound recommendations can be made.

Deprenyl is a specific inhibitor of monoamine oxidase B (MAOB), a key enzyme involved in the metabolism of dopamine, an important neurotransmitter. Deprenyl also has the ability to counteract the neurotoxic effects of certain illegal "designer" drugs and is a very effective therapeutic agent in the treatment of Parkinson's disease. Parkinson's is thought to arise as a consequence of neurotoxic metabolites produced from endogenous dopamine in the brain. Deprenyl not only inhibits the age-related increase in MAOB activity in the brain, but also blocks dopamine uptake. From our point of view, the interesting finding is that lifetime treatment of rats with deprenyl showed significant increases in their mean and maximum longevities, and this effect was observed without the confounding effects of dietary restriction (see Yu 1995 for references).

A summary of life span studies with rodents given L-deprenyl shows that the treated animals in all the studies exhibited an increased longevity (Archer and Harrison 1996). The major side effect was a significant decrease in the fecundity of old, treated male mice. The antioxidant activity of deprenyl, and its ability to induce some of the body's other antioxidant defenses, are assumed to underlie the effectiveness of deprenyl in treating Parkinson's and in extending life (Shoulson 1992). There are no data regarding the effects of deprenyl treatment on the longevity of healthy humans.

The use of synthetic compounds to chelate heavy metals or the use of certain organic compounds to trap or otherwise neutralize free radicals offers another means of reducing the body's exposure to oxidative stress. Injecting a known "spin-trapping" compound (PBN) into accelerated-senescence mice (SAMP8 strain) reversed the signs of oxidative stress damage to brain membranes (Butterfield et al. 1997). This experiment offers encouraging evidence that age-related cellular damage and age-associated neurodegenerative conditions resulting from oxidative reactions can be ameliorated (Carney et al. 1991; Floyd and Carney 1993).

Psychological Interventions

For most of us, our individual autonomy—our individual ability, real or perceived, to exert some control over our life—is important. Several studies in gerontology suggest that the lack of such control may be one of the factors that spells the difference between usual aging and successful aging (Rowe and Kahn 1987). When individuals in a variety of communal environments were given small measures of control or autonomy over their lives, such that they were able to order or at least predict future events, they perceived themselves to be more in control and they scored higher in life satisfaction parameters and lower in parameters measuring stress. This is consistent with classic studies on worker satisfaction. The stress-reduction factor is what interests us, especially in view of the large number of studies in the literature that link psychological factors, immunological functions, and susceptibility to infectious diseases (Rodin 1986; Rowe and Kahn 1987). The physiological mechanism involved in this linkage is clearly the neuro-endocrine-immune system, as described in Chapter 5.

The transformation of stress into biochemical factors that increase the incidence of degenerative pathologies such as coronary disease or tumor growth and proliferation speeds up the deleterious effects of aging. Shock (1983) has defined aging as the progressive loss of the organism's ability to adapt to stress. We can never remove stress from our lives, but if we can retain some measure of effective control and autonomy, then the probability of our aging successfully is much enhanced, for the probability of suffering from a degenerative pathology is reduced.

Cosmetic Interventions

If looking good makes one feel good, then one should try to look good. Presumably our own satisfaction with our appearance is translated by our neuro-endocrine-immune system into favorable biochemical signals. Dermatological changes are the first and the most obvious outward signs of advancing age. In some societies, such change might be welcomed. In our society, with its emphasis on youth and its consequent need for laws prohibiting age discrimination, such changes are all too often met with despair. Older men and women who want to retain a youthful appearance increasingly are seeking treatments for wrinkles, graying hair, and the like.

Skin Creams

As we age, the skin undergoes intrinsic changes that result in thinning of the dermis, a decrease in the microcirculation, and alterations in the type and patterning of connective fibers (see Chapter 5). These changes are accelerated by exposure to sunlight. In a society that worships sun and youth, the paradox is obvious. Most skin creams act like moisturizers, trapping water in the top cells of the epidermis. The trapping of water beneath the cosmetic barrier plumps up the skin and smooths the fine wrinkles. The moisturizers, however, disappear during the course of the day, so their effects are transient and noncumulative. They may make us appear more youthful and thus help us feel better about ourselves, but they will not arrest the aging process. The large difference in the price per ounce of the many different products may have more to do with psychological and marketing factors than with dermatological ones, a supposition supported by product testing reports (see *Consumer Reports*, May 1988).

The first anti-aging ingredient that was approved by the FDA was the nonglamorous sunscreen. Products that claim to alter only superficial appearance can be classified as cosmetics, unless their advertising claims something more than a transient or superficial effect. In that case, they must be considered drugs and meet much more stringent scientific standards. But cosmetics, by definition, cannot be advertised as having any anti-aging effect. The market demand for anti-aging formulations has tempted many cosmetic companies into making claims that skirt this boundary, and this blurring of the distinction between fact and fiction has led to increased public concern.

At present, the only skin creams that might fulfill the FDA's stringent demands required of an anti-aging agent are those that are based on Retin-A®. Retin-A is a patented vitamin A derivative that has long been used as a prescription treatment for acne. Its effects on the skin were noted as a result of medical observation in the course of the original treatment. Retin-A appears to be helpful in retarding photo-aging of the skin by stimulating it to increase cell production in the epidermis, enhancing the microcirculation and increasing collagen production in the dermis. Retin-A also compacts and smooths the stratum corneum, the dead outer layer of the skin. These several changes appear to account for the reported diminution of fine wrinkles and the reappearance of a rosy glow to the complexion. The effect on the coarser wrinkles that start in the dermis is a bit harder to explain. However, some evidence suggests that retinoic acid reprograms the intrinsic patterns of gene activity in the epidermal cells, turning off the synthesis of certain proteins and inducing the synthesis of certain others (Roberts 1988).

Retinoic acid is known to be intimately involved in the development of the normal patterning of the vertebrate limb and is thought to be a normal inducer of gene activity. It is possible but not yet proven that the drug acts on the dermis by reprogramming the cells so that they synthesize different types of connective tissue molecules. By so doing, the retinoic acid might alter the three-dimensional changes in the dermis as discussed in Chapter 5. A drug that would reverse the intrinsic program of gene expression might truly deserve to be labeled an anti-aging compound.

The effect of Retin-A appears to be region-specific; initial reports suggest that the drug is less effective on facial skin than on forearm skin, which is probably not the result desired either by us or by the cosmetic companies. The drug is probably safe, given its prior history, although the question of its long-term effects remain to be determined.

Hair Dyes and Restorers

Hair dyes and coloring agents are cosmetics and are rarely marketed as anything but that. Hair restorers are another matter. Male pattern baldness accounts for most of the market demand. This condition is apparently due to a combination of genetic predisposition, age, and hormonal factors. Various strategies have been devised to cope with it. The only ones that could be considered potential anti-aging drugs are vasodilators that work by increasing the blood supply to the hair follicles. Minoxidil® is one such agent that has been approved by the FDA; it appears to restore hair growth in some but not all individuals. Minoxidil appears to be most effective when used as a preventive and thus requires lifetime use. Its effects disappear within several months after treatment stops.

• *Unlikely Interventions*

The desire for immortality is a common one. Most people settle for achieving it through their works or descendants, but some optimists try to achieve immortality by not dying. The preference for personal immortality is probably the initial and most common response of every individual at the time when the concept of death suddenly becomes a real and future event. The failure to obtain our wish in this life provides one of the major foundations on which our sense of religion rests. The wish may be sublimated into a concern for the future of our children and grandchildren, but it probably doesn't entirely disappear. Under these circumstances, it is not surprising that some miraculous "cures" for aging still abound; the wonder is that there are so few of them. We will briefly consider three such claims simply to highlight their unlikely scientific basis.

Cell Therapy

This treatment originated in Switzerland during the 1930s and is still practiced in certain luxuriant health spas there. The FDA has strictly forbidden its use in the United States. The treatment consists of the intramuscular injection into the patient of fresh, living cells taken from a near-term sheep fetus. The sheep cells are taken from the fetal organ corresponding to the organ that is functioning poorly in the particular aging human patient. The theory is that the young sheep cells impart to the failing human organ the ability to function again at a more youthful, or more normal, level. Not only is there no scientific basis for this belief—which is perhaps closer to sympathetic magic than to science—but it also contravenes a host of confirmed scientific observations and facts regarding the fate of foreign cells in our body.

The transplantation of human fetal adrenal gland cells into the brains of adults suffering from Parkinson's disease should not be misconstrued as simply a modern version of this sheep cell therapy, for it does not contradict modern immunological theory by the use of interspecific transplants nor does it attempt to "cure" aging. It attempts only to transplant certain human cells from one part of the donor's body to a place in the recipient where similar cells are normally located but have died as a result of the disease.

Gerovital

Gerovital, also known as GH3, is a mixture of procaine, benzoic acid, and potassium metabisulfite, all dissolved in a saline solution and buffered to a pH of 3.3. Dr. Ana Aslan of Romania championed this mixture as an anti-aging formulation. Patients would come to her clinic for a series of intramuscular injections over a period of time. She reported a variety of anti-aging effects, none of which were supported by independent investigations in this country (see Ostfeld, Smith, and Stotsky 1977). Procaine is the local anesthetic commonly used by your dentist. In addition to its anesthetic properties, it has a mild inhibitory effect on the enzyme monoamine oxidase; this latter effect is allegedly responsible for the anti-aging effects of Gerovital. Gerovital appears to affect the same mechanism as does deprenyl, but much less effectively. The treatment may not be totally without merit (for example, see Figure 2.21), but there does not appear to be sufficient scientific evidence in support of its claim as an anti-aging compound, so the FDA does not permit the use of Gerovital in the United States.

Vitamin and Chemical Therapies

It may appear incongruous for us to include vitamin supplementation under the headings of both effective therapies and unlikely therapies. But this is not an error, for it can be both effective and ineffective. Several theories of aging postulate that the decrements in physiological function that we call aging are the results of intrinsic cellular damage. Each theory usually has it own particular explanation of how this damage comes about. One of the more plausible and popular of these explanations is the oxidative-damage theory (see Chapter 9), which postulates that various oxidants cause the damage. Antioxidant molecules are known and they should be able to retard or inhibit the damage. The data discussed earlier in this chapter and in Chapter 9 tend to support the theory.

Studies such as those cited in our earlier discussion of vitamin supplementation, for example, are usually rigorously done and critically interpreted. The conclusions drawn from such studies are then compared to those of similar studies, and the data are examined for agreement or disagreement. But this is a long drawn-out process, one that can be frustrating to someone who "knows, just knows" that the data are right and the effect exists. This impatience can be satisfied by the conclusion that whatever is plausible must also be true. And such unfounded conclusions have given a great impetus to individuals suggesting that we ingest various antioxidants, vitamins, growth factors, certain amino acids, specified types of lipids, and so on, all of which are believed—but not proven—to have some sort of anti-aging effect. Each recommendation usually has some factual basis, although good science is more than just a collection of odd facts and good scientists are intelligent skeptics. In many cases, the recommendations are taken out of context or are overinterpreted. Not surprisingly, much of the popular support for such supplemental therapy comes from individuals and firms associated with the health food and/or vitamin industry—a field in which substantial profits are possible.

Now, vitamins and other such nutrient supplements are good for us, and we have spent considerable time so far discussing the data and their implications. I take vitamins. In fact, they are essential to our health, and we can become ill or die in their absence. What could be wrong with taking them or following the hucksters' advice? There are two problems. The major problem comes about when people are persuaded that an inappropriate lifestyle—their being overweight, their malnutrition, their smoking, their lack of physical exercise, their personal and professional stress, their dysfunctional social and work relationships—can be discounted simply because they also consume the "right" anti-aging chemicals. This point of view is exceedingly simplistic and mechanistic. Perhaps that is part of its appeal. It is, unfortunately, all too common and can cause harm to the extent that it lures people into thinking they are taking steps to protect their health by adopting such a simplistic approach.

The second problem arises when negative data are ignored in the rush of enthusiasm and a person takes a pill that actually hurts him or her. Consider the case of male smokers who have been persuaded to take beta-carotene supplements. Given the outcome of the Finnish smoker study, we would have to conclude that their enthusiasm was misplaced and they may actually have harmed themselves. Alternatively, a high intake of antioxidants may usually decrease the possibilities of oxidative damage, but in certain circumstances may actually *increase* such damage. For example, ascorbic acid becomes a pro-oxidant in the presence of excess iron, or if added during the propagation phase of the oxidation process (Otero et al. 1997). "Usually" is not "always."

The third problem comes about when a modicum of standard advice is wrapped up in a coating of salemanship and/or mysticism, leading to a waste of money and/or a confusion of scientific fact with what one wishes were true. The January 1992 issue of *Consumer Reports* contains an instructive account of one reporter's visit to an "aging control clinic" where, for the sum of $3,500 paid in advance, her biomarkers were measured and she was put on an anti-aging diet. Follow-up visits cost $1,500 for further tests and $500 an hour for consultation. Outside experts rated the advice as having some "very reasonable elements and authentic advice mixed in with some marginal science and outlandish claims." Some of the information given was just wrong, some was "paranoid," and some was dubious. And the dietary supplements prescribed for the reporter were unlikely to be effective but generated additional profit for the physician. As the magazine points out, the same tests and advice could be obtained from a good primary-care physician for a total cost of about $600—without the false pizzazz of pretending to know what no one knows yet.

Or consider two of the more popular of the many anti-aging books on the market. One advocates taking all sorts of pills every day in order to delay the aging process. The prescriptions it recommends for the various anti-free radical chemicals are based on facts but overlook all sorts of negative data, restrictions, side effects, and other such nuisances. The book was a best-seller. The other book buries nuggets of standard and reasonable advice under a candy coating of pop psychology and New Age mysticism. It became a recent best-seller and book club selection, and the author is introduced as an "expert" in the field. There isn't much harm in this, but there isn't much good either. And encouraging a belief in mystical science is not the best way to educate one's readers or to enable them to make responsible decisions for their own future. It is the educational equivalent of encouraging your children to eat candy and thinking you've taught them good nutrition. But at least it wastes less of your money than a clinic visit does. Perhaps the only thing that these nostrums prove is that a fool and his or her money are soon parted.

• *Summary*

There are effective interventions that can significantly manipulate longevity and aging. Nutritional intervention in the form of dietary restriction is by far the single most effective factor with which to extend the life span in both vertebrates and invertebrates. Dietary restriction delays or eliminates the onset of both the normal age-related physiological changes and the abnormal age-associated diseases. The mechanisms involved are not clear but probably include the modulation of cellular gene activity via the neuro-endocrine-immune system. The effect of caloric restriction on glucose metabolism is an especially important illustration of the mechanisms through which these modulations are translated into real physiological changes.

Exercise is another effective and beneficial intervention, particularly in its ability to modulate signs of cardiovascular aging. In addition, its ability to raise growth hormone levels and thereby induce many of the anti-aging effects associated with that hormone cannot be overlooked.

Finally, transplantation experiments have shown that many tissues are capable of performing their normal function for periods of time longer than the donor's life span. The whole may be greater than the sum of its parts, but it does not live as long. This observation means that theories predicting that the aging process proceeds at a uniform pace in all cells and tissues will have to be modified to accommodate these facts.

Although it has been proven that longevity and aging are under both positive and negative genetic control, at present no significant interventions are designed to manipulate this factor in humans. The lack of genetic anti-aging interventions stems in large part from the complexity of the mechanisms involved in the several effective interventions of which we are aware, and in part from our present ignorance of how to genetically manipulate any of the component processes of these mechanisms. This situation may change in the long-term future as a result of the effort being put into sequencing the human genome, but it would be foolish to pass up the present effective but ordinary interventions in favor of a future glamorous possibility.

Research has illuminated the importance of both body build factors and psychological factors as determinants of mortality acting through our neuro-endocrine-immune system. Cosmetic interventions may not contain any anti-aging "magic bullets," but if they make us feel better about our appearance and subsequently alter our neuro-endocrine-immune system, then there is no harm in them and there is likely to be some small but beneficial psychological effect. Unlikely interventions not only waste our time and our money, but to the extent that we accept the lure of a specrum of "magic bullet" pills we substitute pill-popping for the proven benefits of good nutrition, exercise, and the other known (albeit sometimes difficult to follow) life processes that can delay the onset of senescence and disability. There really is no free lunch.

Part III

Theories of Aging

8

Concepts and Theories of Aging: An Appreciation

● *The Role of Theory in Gerontology*

Aging is a biological process. We observe organisms and see that certain more or less predictable changes occur in a more or less predictable sequence. Changes that appear to lead to an increased or enhanced level of functioning of the organism are often defined as "development," while changes that appear to lead to a decrement in functional ability of the organism are often defined as "aging." Yet simply providing an operational definition of the symptoms by which we recognize the presence of an underlying process does not at first appear to be a method by which we can increase our understanding of the process itself. A descriptive account of frog embryology gives us no insight into the nature of the mechanisms regulating and controlling each phase of the frog's development. However, at least the embryologist has a good idea of what she or he is trying to explain, which is perhaps more than can be said about the gerontologist.

The embryologist empirically knows that development begins at the moment of fertilization. With this knowledge, she or he can describe the events that eventually give rise to the adult frog and can logically relate them to the initial event. But when does aging start? Even if we agree that it starts at puberty (see Figure 2.17 and related text), does this mean it starts at the same time in every cell? Or does each part of the body have its own schedule of aging? Almost every aspect of the organism appears to undergo deleterious changes with time. What, exactly, is happening? In fact, one can make a reasonable case that the central problem of gerontology is to define aging.

We cannot be sure that we understand the mechanisms of aging until we have a fairly good idea of what we are trying to explain. Historically, however, gerontology has been characterized, even by its practitioners (Hayflick 1985), as lacking a strong data base even while it simultaneously abounds in theories purporting to explain the fundamentals of biological aging. This situation appears to be paradoxical. How can we deduce and understand the mechanisms of aging if we cannot agree on the kinds of observed phenomena that constitute aging? The solution lies in our being able to develop a knowledge of facts and of theory simultaneously, for "Theory without fact is fantasy, but facts without theory is chaos" (Whitman 1894).

Nonetheless, there are many theories of biological aging. Almost all of them are plausible, many have some firm or at least provocative data to support them, and a few may even tie into other broad concepts of biological theory. Why, then, has there been so little agreement among the investigators about the biological causes of aging? One reason is that organisms are complex, hierarchical, and interacting systems of subsystems. Murphy's Law ensures that the more complex the system and the more functions it can discharge, the more things there are that can go wrong with it. As a result, any biological change one might postulate could, with time, affect almost all components of the living system and could logically (albeit not reasonably) be a candidate for the cause of aging. This fact accounts for the common failing of "transforming the changes found in one narrow aspect of the plethora of age changes into a generalized theory of universal applicability" (Hayflick 1985, p. 146). Another reason for the lack of agreement could be the naive assumption that any particular age-related change can be brought about by only one particular cause, an assumption that contradicts the very notion of hierarchical interacting systems. A further reason might be the difficulty in critically testing many of the postulated theories, in part because of the constraints of time and money and in part because of technical constraints. Finally, of course, is the problem that the word "aging" is often used by different investigators in differing and sometimes contradictory ways, as pointed out by Esposito (1987, p. 26):

> Sometimes aging is presented as a *result*, a process that occurs because of the passage of time. At other times, it is presented as a *cause* that alters normal physiology and function . . . Do wrinkles cause aging? Or does aging cause wrinkles? Even elementary propositions are open to doubt.

An emphasis on the theoretical constructs works well in other disciplines, but until recently it has not proven profitable in the study of aging. Part of the reason is the fact that, until recently, no single one of the various theories put forth was that much more useful (predictive) than any of its competitors. Without the ability to make *testable* predictions, it is operationally impossible to make a scientific judgment as to which one of several theories most closely describes reality. For example, the atomic theory in one guise or another has, since the time of the Roman poet Lucretius 2,000 years ago, played a role in the history of chemistry. Yet plausible as this theory might have sounded to alchemists and chemists alike, not until 200 years ago were the first precise descriptions, measurements, and definitions of observed chemical changes made. This reliance on observation and empirical modifications of theory led to the development of the periodic table of the elements by Dmitry Mendeleyev in 1869, an innovation that allowed chemists to predict the existence and properties of hitherto unknown elements. Today we take it for granted that chemists can manipulate molecules, yet this mastery rests on the predictive ability of their theories.

What, then, explains the historical lack of success of theory in gerontology? One part of the answer must lie in the cultural framework in which the science is practiced. Gregor Mendel first presented an accurate description of the inheritance patterns of genes in 1865. Yet his work was ignored by the scientific world because the concepts then accepted by most people did not and could not include the idea of inheritance via discrete factors. It took a generation before the preconceptions and biases held by the scientific community changed sufficiently that other scientists could understand and appreciate the clarity and insight of Mendel's ideas.

Biological gerontology is a young discipline and has only within the past several decades or so been able to attract the serious interest of sufficiently large numbers of scientists. The reasons for this neglect are not clear, but they probably have a lot to do with the scientific-cultural idea that aging is not a fundamentally interesting biological process. And this conception probably stems from the fact that one of the two central questions in biology for the past century has been the unraveling of development, of how an egg transforms itself into an adult. (The other question was that of deciphering the mechanisms involved in the process of evolution.) Aging was probably assumed to be an uninteresting sort of eroding away of the end product of development. But our concepts have now changed, in part because of demographic data and in part because we are beginning to understand that the failure to maintain function is an inherent—and potentially modifiable—part of the evolutionary design of organisms.

Another reason for this past failure of theory in gerontology might be that gerontology is not a scientific discipline based on its own fundamental and cohesive constructs, as are chemistry and physics, but is instead a field of investigation that cuts across many different disciplines. It is a synthetic discipline. The investigators themselves come from different disciplines, and each one approaches the study of aging with his or her own set of professional biases and opinions. Thus the theories that each gerontologist proposes usually are faulty in that they view only the portion of the field that corresponds to what that individual's background allows him or her to recognize. (Remember Einstein's caution: "It is the theory that decides what we can recognize.") Accordingly, many theories utilize only part of the data and consequently often are biased, unidimensional, and nonpredictive.

Recent gerontological theory shows signs of becoming more predictive, using evolutionary theory to provide a unifying conceptual framework for the field and integrating it into the mainstream of biological thought. Certainly the response to the publication in 1991 of Michael Rose's book *Evolutionary Biology of Aging* marked the general acceptance of this point of view. The disposable-soma theory (see Chapter 4) views aging and longevity as the inevitable outcome of an evolutionarily derived equilibrium between the amount of resources devoted to repair and the amount devoted to reproduction. This theory subsumes many other observations of a valid but limited nature, each having to do with detailed biochemical mechanisms leading to cell, tissue, and/or organism failure, while simultaneously organizing them into a framework consistent with the fundamental biological principles of evolution and cell biology. At the very least, this theoretical synthesis allows us to see order where very little was apparent before and to provide a coherent explanatory basis for both the similarity and variability of aging across different species. Quantitative computer simulations of the theory yield believable and interesting results, thus building confidence in the correctness of its assumptions (Kowald and Kirkwood 1994, 1996; see also Chapter 13).

Another integrative theoretical step has been the abandonment of the dichotomy between "pathological" and "normal" aging. It was long customary to consider the study of age-related diseases as a distracting hindrance to the study of "real" aging. But an extension of the evolutionary theory of aging led Bellamy (1988), Holliday (1995), and others to consider that the common age-related diseases are not just random occurrences of physiological breakdown, but are the systemic failures that highlight the weak points of the evolved anatomical and physiological design of the organism. Thus, studying the etiology of these diseases allows us to identify these evolutionary weak points and to characterize the mechanisms involved in them. And adoption of this point of view allows us to integrate into modern biogerontology all of the huge host of medical studies bearing on these age-related pathologies, with a concomitant increase in our detailed knowledge of the processes underlying the loss of function that is characteristic of aging.

This does not mean that we must abandon gerontology and study only the care of the ill and aged. That province of geriatrics is not included in our curriculum. But geriatrics is organically connected to gerontology via the study of the etiology of age-related systemic failures. This connection also means that the mechanisms underlying aging are no longer different from those usually encountered in the rest of biology, but are continuous with them. This widening of our conceptual views and the increase in our detailed knowledge should give second thoughts to skeptics who were persuaded that the problem of aging is presently insoluble and that the field is not yet ripe for investigation. The adoption of an evolutionary point of view is not limited to gerontology; an exposition on Darwinian medicine has recently been published (Neese and Williams 1994).

In the next few chapters, we will discuss various different theories and categorize them as either stochastic or systemic. By "stochastic" I mean an explanation based on the occurrence of single random events, such as gene mutation. The term "systemic" here denotes an explanation based on the occurrence of a hierarchical cascade of interconnected events. By this I do mean an interrelated series of biological processes linked together by a web of feedback signals that often operate so as to yield a progressively unstable positive feedback cycle. I most emphatically do *not* mean an explanation based on the idea of determinative and sequential gene action designed to produce aging. Such an explanation would constitute an adaptive theory of aging (that we age because there is a particular reason for us to age), and, as we saw in Chapter 4, aging has evolved not because it is adaptive but because the force of natural selection declines with age (we age because there is no reason not to age). By "systemic," I mean simply interlocking or cascade mechanisms that can give rise to one or more common aging phenotypes.

There is an obvious temptation to view these two terms as denoting opposing viewpoints—as being antithetical to each other—but that would be a mistake. Applying evolutionary principles allows us to understand that the life span of an organism is shaped by its genes but that the details of its senescence will flow from the interaction over time of those gene products with the organism's internal and external environment. An integrative approach to the study of biogerontology leads to the breakdown of the apparent dichotomy between stochastic and systemic theories as it makes clear that the difference between the terms depends on one's point of view, but that the terms make useful pedagogical pegs on which to hang a lesson or two. We will, at the end of our review, attempt to integrate these two concepts into a network view of a homeostatic system.

There are many existing theories of aging. They implicitly color our preconceptions and influence the structure of our experiments. Many of them are probably wrong or inadequate or redundant, but one or two of them are probably correct or nearly so. We need to review each of these theories and critically examine the evidence marshaled both for and against them, for each theory probably has captured only one aspect of the complete explanation. Our final understanding will depend on an integration of the best of these theories. In particular, we should pay some attention to how well each theory explains the occurrence of all the phenomena known to occur during aging. It is highly unlikely that aging has a single mechanism or can be fully explained by a single theory, any more than one can state today that embryological development has but a single mechanism. The geneticists and the developmental biologists have profited by their reliance on description and on fact-based, testable theories. We would do well to follow their example.

● *An Overview of Current Theories of Aging*

There are several different methods by which one can organize the different theories of aging. Hayflick (1985) grouped the theories according to their level of action, writing of organ-based, physiology-based, and genome-based theories. Hart and Turturro (1983) wrote of cell-based, organ system-based, population-based, and integrative theories. Esposito (1987) wrote of causal, systematic, and evolutionary theories. In addition, theories of aging could be reasonably sorted according to whether the causes each one postulates are supposed to arise from systemic cascade processes, or from stochastic and random processes.

There are probably other ways to sort the theories of aging. None of these systems is fully satisfactory, in large part because the complexity of the aging processes suggests that the mechanisms involved can be sorted into more than one valid scheme. However, the origin of the change and its level of action both appear to be reasonable and logical pegs from which to hang our descriptions. We will employ a dual classification scheme. We will consider whether the theories suggest that their particular effects are exerted within all or most cells (intracellular theories) or whether they are exerted mostly on the structural components and/or regulatory mechanisms linking together groups of different cells (intercellular theories). In addition, we will simultaneously consider whether the effects postulated by each theory are conjectured to take place accidentally (stochastic theories) or are the result of the hierarchical feedback cascades characteristic of the species (systemic theories). As we will see, there are classification difficulties even with this simple scheme. Finally, we will introduce the evolution in our thoughts that now leads us to construct a smaller number of much more inclusive theories, such as the stress theory of aging (Parsons 1995).

Table 8.1 presents a classification of the 14 theories that we will examine in some detail in Chapters 9 through 12. These theories have been classified according to how they fit best into the dual criteria of the location of the changes and the nature of their effects. These criteria are useful empirical guides; they are not exhaustive theoretical principles. Accordingly, you may suggest that a particular theory can just as logically be assigned to another cell. For example, we have classified DNA damage theories as stochastic, but you might logically counter that the amount of damage is a function of the species' DNA repair ability, and that these theories appear to be genetically determined and therefore systemic. Or you might suggest that the free-radical, or oxidative-damage theory can be viewed equally well as affecting the biochemical processes within each individual cell (and therefore should be classified as intracellular), or as affecting the regulatory processes that affect the metabolic relationships of various cells, tissues, and organs (and therefore should be classified as intercellular).

The fact that this little exercise reveals how difficult it is to unequivocally file our theories into little pigeonholes suggests that the theories are larger than the somewhat arbitrary compartments into which we are forcing them. But the classification scheme does have the advantage of allowing us to engage in a simple linear discussion of the several theories, postponing our integration of them until the end. This integration will involve the concept that the body normally is maintained by a network of processes that operate in parallel with one another and

Table 8.1   **A Classification of Aging Theories**

Level at which effect of change is executed	Origin of change	
	Stochastic theories	*Systemic theories*
Intracellular	Altered proteins	Metabolic theories
	Somatic mutations	Genetic theories
	DNA damage and repair	Apoptosis
	Error catastrophe	Phagocytosis
	Dysdifferentiation	
	Oxidative damage	
	Waste accumulation	
Intercellular	Posttranslational	Neuroendocrine theories
	Protein changes	Immunological theories

together provide a homeostatic system (Kristal and Yu 1992; Kowald and Kirkwood 1994, 1996; Parsons 1995).

Table 8.2 summarizes these theories. The original cell-based theories viewed aging as the gradual wearing down of the somatic cells to the point at which they could not adequately discharge their functions. This failure was viewed as leading directly to the functional decrements that are characteristic of aging. In the early twentieth century, the experiments of Alexis Carrel (1912) were thought to demonstrate that somatic cells grown *in vitro* are immortal, so the earlier "wear and tear" theories fell into disfavor. Hayflick and Moorhead (1961) corrected Carrel's work and demonstrated that normal cells grown in culture can undergo only a limited number of mitotic divisions. This observation has been confirmed repeatedly and has inspired the development of numerous genetically oriented, cell-based theories of aging—theories that use either stochastic or systemic mechanisms to explain the observed impairment of cell function. The metabolic theories that postulate intrinsic changes in metabolic rates as the cause of aging also imply that their particular mechanisms must be operative in all cells of the organism. And some of the conceptual foundations of the various genetic theories also have their origins in the concept of autonomous systemic gene action within each cell of the organism.

The homeostatic, integrative, or intercellular theories are all based on the assumption that there are one or more "pacemakers of aging"—particular tissues or organs that initiate the onset of the events characteristic of senescence. (The term "pacemaker" is derived by analogy with the pacemaker cells of the heart, which initiate each heartbeat and are responsible for its rhythmicity.) In principle, such initiation could stem from either a positive or a negative signal. In either case, Nathan Shock's empirical observations that aging is characterized primarily by the body's failure to maintain homeostatic equilibrium among different organ systems seems to lend much weight to this class of theories. The highly integrated state of our neural, hormonal, and immunological functions (see Chapter 5) is certainly consistent with (but does not prove) this point of view.

Earlier we identified a major paradox of gerontological theory: If one postulates stochastic causes, then one must account for the apparent predictability and systemic aspects of aging; yet if one postulates systemic causes, one must also account for the extraordinary variability one sees in the course of aging among different individuals. It has been apparent for some time that certain of these theories are less different from one another than our classification scheme might suggest. For example, the rate-of-living theory was early recognized as more or less congruent with the metabolic theories, and these latter theories have been recognized as being but restatements of the free-radical theory. And the free-radical theory has been recognized as one component of a generalized stress theory of aging. Many of the theories could be organized in a hierarchical scheme. In addition, it has been recognized that the mechanisms postulated by these different theories do not take place in separate test tubes but rather interact within the organism. Thus the free-radical and the posttranslational protein change, or glycosylation, theories are seen to interact in a synergistic manner such that oxidative damage enhances the probability of glycosylation taking place (because the

Table 8.2 **An Overview of Some Theories of Aging**	
Theory	*Major theoretical premise and current status*
Altered proteins	Time-dependent, posttranslational change in a molecule that brings about conformational change and alters enzyme activity, cell's efficiency.
	Proven, but exact role not clear.
Somatic mutation	Somatic mutations alter genetic information and decrease the cell's efficiency to subvital level.
	Disproven in a few cases, but the occurrence of age-related neoplasms at least is apparently due in part to somatic mutation.
DNA damage and repair	The cell contains various mechanisms that repair constantly occurring DNA damage. The repair efficiency is positively correlated with life span, and decreases with age.
	Proven, but exact role not clear.
Error catastrophe	Faulty transcriptional and/or translational processes decrease the cell's efficiency to subvital level.
	Disproven, but modern reformulation has empirical support.
Dysdifferentiation	Faulty gene activation–repression mechanisms result in the cell's synthesizing unnecessary proteins, thus decreasing the cell's efficiency to subvital level.
	Possible.
Oxidative damage/Free radical	Longevity is inversely proportional to the extent of oxidative damage and directly proportional to antioxidant defense activity.
	Proven in a few cases, probable in many others.
Waste accumulation	Waste products of metabolism accumulate in the cell and will depress the cell's efficiency to subvital level if not removed from the cell or diluted by cell division.
	Possible, expecially in a modern reformulation, but unlikely.
Posttranslational protein changes	Time-dependent chemical modification of important macromolecules (e.g., collagen) impairs tissue function and decreases the organism's efficiency to subvital level. Protein cross-linking is one subset of this theory.
	Proven.
Wear-and-tear	Ordinary insults and injuries of daily living accumulate and decrease the organism's efficiency to subvital level.
	Proven in restricted examples (e.g., loss of teeth, leading to starvation), but modern reformulations are part of other theories.
Metabolic theories	Longevity is inversely proportional to metabolic rate.
	Disproven in its original form, but reformulated into a form of the free-radical theory, and that reformulation appears to be correct.
Genetic theories	Changes in gene expression cause senescent changes in cells. Multiple mechanisms are suggested. Changes may be general or specific. May function at intra- or intercellular level.
	Proven, but there are multiple genetic pathways.
Apoptosis	Programmed suicide of particular cells is induced by extracellular signals.
	Proven. Failure to induce or repress apoptosis probably responsible for a variety of diseases. Role in nonpathological aging changes not clear.

Table 8.2 *(Continued)*	
Phagocytosis	Senescent cells have particular membrane proteins that identify them and mark them for destruction by other cells, such as macrophages. Proven, but only in restricted cases.
Neuroendocrine theories	Failure of cells with specific integrative functions brings about homeostatic failure of the organism, leading to senescence and death. Proven for female reproductive aging and other specialized cases. Probably involved in many other cases. Exact role needs to be ascertained as a general case.
Immunological theories	Life span is dependent on the types of particular immune-system genes present, certain alleles extending and others shortening longevity. These genes are thought to regulate a wide variety of basic processes, including regulation of the neuroendocrine system. Failure of these feedback mechanisms decreases the organism's efficiency to subvital level. Probable.

processes described in Figure 9.1 are accelerated by free radicals; Kristal and Yu 1992). Thus, consideration of the interaction of different mechanisms acting at different organizational levels within the organism leads us inevitably to an integrative outcome. Chapter 13 will present a more detailed description of these and other integrative models that have been proposed in the past few years.

Much of the evidence we will consider in the following chapters is correlative. There are good practical reasons for this, but the convenience comes at a price. Such data can suggest only that two variables (for example, life span and something else) are linked; it cannot prove the causal nature of the relationship. Another complication arises from the nature of much of the genetic evidence. The absence of a factor (as in a null mutation) will often result in an abnormal pathology and a drastically shortened life span, but such evidence cannot be construed as proving that the factor is therefore sufficient to extend life span. Not many mutations result in the overexpression of the factor of interest, but this is exactly the condition needed in order for us to determine if a surplus of the factor will result in a slowing of the MRDT (mortality rate doubling time) and an extension of the life span. Many variables may be necessary for life but not be sufficient by themselves to bring about an extended life span. Our final estimation of any theory will depend in part on the acuity of our analysis of the data and in part on our perception of how well the theory allows us to integrate data obtained from different levels of analysis.

Finally, any good theoretical explanation should also account for the failure of a complex self-repairing organism to overcome the structural and functional defects that characterize aging. We are likely to solve this conundrum only by an unwavering reliance on empirical observations and on critical testing of our several theories. And the answers we develop should be consistent with evolutionary data, bearing in mind Dobzhansky's famous statement: "Nothing in biology makes sense except in the light of evolution."

9

Stochastic Theories of Aging

• *Can Predictable Events Be Brought About by Stochastic Processes?*

There is, as we have seen, a predictable regularity in the aging process, both in the sense of a maximum life span that is characteristic of each species and in the sense of a certain pattern of describable physiological changes that can be expected to occur with advancing age. Against such a background, it may seem improbable that a process as orderly as is aging is due to random, or stochastic, factors. Yet this idea is the basis of theories of aging postulating that the deterioration associated with old age is due to the accumulation of random molecular damage. Such faulty macromolecules could accumulate through two somewhat different mechanisms: failure to repair stochastic damage or stochastically caused error in macromolecular synthesis. In either case, information vital to the cell is lost. These "information loss" theories state that the progressive accumulation of faulty macromolecules eventually reaches the point at which some or all cells of an organism are so metabolically crippled that systemic death results.

Although these theories provide a mechanistic explanation for the observed age-related declines, two additional assumptions must be made if one is to rationalize how stochastic damage brings on systemic changes. First, it is necessary to postulate that the cell or tissue or organism in question has specific classes or types of molecules that are particularly sensitive to certain types of damage. Second, it is necessary to conjecture that long-lived species are better able to tolerate such damage than are short-lived species; in other words, long-lived species have either a better repair system or greater functional redundancy than do short-lived species. Given these latter assumptions, it should be clear that one could equally well classify such information loss theories as systemic, for they view the organisms as formulated to fail in a predictable and species-specific manner as a result of exposure to random insults. This discussion of the hidden assumptions highlights the complexities of the processes that are implicit even in what superficially appears to be a simple concept of aging.

Stochastically Based Theories

Wear-and-Tear Theory

The "wear and tear" theories of aging are probably the oldest precursors of the concept of failure to repair. Although dated, these theories persist probably because they are unconsciously reinforced by our everyday observations. All organisms are constantly exposed to infections, wounds, and injuries that are likely to cause minor damage to cells and tissues and organs. A broken limb can heal, but it might not be as strong as it was before the fracture occurred. Loss of a tooth might impair an animal's food-gathering ability. As an animal gets older, it will likely have accumulated progressively more of the type of minor damages associated with slight diseases and injuries. Such structural erosion and minor injuries might contribute incidentally to an age-related decline in functional efficiency. August Weismann (1891) thought this gradual wearing down of the somatic cells as a result of use to be the major cause of aging.

Today we would strenuously disagree and could present three very logical reasons for doing so. First, animals raised in an environment that protects them from such minor insults and pathologies not only still age but also fail to show any improvement in their maximum life span. Second, many of the minor damages postulated by the wear-and-tear hypothesis are time-dependent changes only, and while they can certainly increase the probability of death for any individual, they cannot logically serve as a causal mechanism of the aging process. A lost tooth does not initiate aging. Finally, and most important, the theory is outdated. Advances in our knowledge of cell and molecular biology have generated the need to explain cellular and organismic aging in more precise terms.

The modern reformulations of the failure-to-repair hypothesis more completely and more convincingly explain particular aspects of biological aging than does the unmodified wear-and-tear hypothesis. For example, alterations in the texture of the cartilage of our joints (see Chapter 5) might be ascribed to wear and tear, but pigeonholing those changes gives us no conceptual framework of how to understand the process better or how to intervene in it. However, thinking of this alteration in cartilage texture as being, in part, the result of age-related changes in the expression of the genes that code for proteoglycan may help guide our thinking to a deeper level of understanding. As we shift from considering gross anatomical levels of organization to considering a more cellular and molecular level, discarding the wear-and-tear idea for more mechanistic explanations will be increasingly supported by the data. However, to the extent that these modern theories contain some aspect of the wear-and-tear idea, one could view all of the intracellular stochastic theories as conceptual descendants of this original idea.

Posttranslational Protein Modification Theory

One variation of the "failure to repair" class of theories is the idea that the time-dependent accumulation of irreparable chemical modifications in important macromolecules could prevent the affected tissues from functioning normally and thereby is a plausible mechanism of aging. This idea was first put forth by Bjørksten and Champion (1942) and independently by several others. Such post-translational modifications are known to occur in both proteins and nucleic acids, so their effects could be widespread.

It has been known for quite some time that extensive age-related chemical changes leading to cross-linking of once separate fibrils take place in connective-tissue components such as collagen and elastin. These changes also appear to be associated with well-described functional decrements in skin and other tissues (see Chapter 5). In fact, our discussion of cardiovascular aging suggested that one of the few intrinsic age-related changes in that system is the increased stiffness of the connective fibers in the arteries, causing an increase in systolic blood pressure, which leads to other pleiotropic effects on the cardiovascular system. Several different techniques have been devised to show that the properties of connective tissue fibers such as collagen change with age; studies using these various techniques have been reviewed by Sell and Monnier (1995). Since one-third of the protein content of a typical mammal is collagen, the age-related changes that take place in this family of molecules have intimate effects on every aspect of our being. The aging of connective tissue changes our shape, our size, our nimbleness, and our ability to live independently. Collagen isolated from old rodent and human donors is more difficult to digest enzymatically than is collagen from young donors, probably because of cross-linking between the different collagen strands. Tail tendons of rats and mice contract after being heated and denatured in a warm salt solution. The rate of contraction, as well as the amount of weight needed to inhibit this contraction, increases with age. Such observations can be understood as being the result of the greater stiffness and structural complexity imparted to the collagen fibers by the cross-linking. Observations such as the fact that denaturation continues even in collagen fibrils removed from the organism and stored *in vitro* (but in air) suggest that collagen cross-linking is an intrinsic oxygen- and time-dependent process. *In situ*, however, the process can be significantly modulated by the physiological state of the animal (for example, diabetic or nondiabetic). Comparison of rodent strains with different longevities shows that collagen tends to age faster in the shorter-lived strain than in the longer-lived strain, and it generally seems to correlate well with either the animal's chronological age or the strain's maximum life span, but not with its mean life span (Harrison et al. 1978).

There are several different chemical types of cross-links. One type consists of intermolecular cross-links between lysine residues in different collagen helices. These cross-links likely serve as precursors to even more complex cross-links among the several molecules, and some of these derivatives are among the most abundant species in human skin. Not all cross-links increase in number with age.

Reducible cross-links such as those involving certain histidine residues are most numerous in the fetus or young organism and decrease thereafter. Nonreducible cross-links, which are formed by oxidation and include much of the fluorescent material seen in collagen *in situ*, tend to increase significantly with age in most organisms tested (Sell and Monnier 1995). Other forms of collagen cross-links may arise as a side effect of the noxious products formed as a result of lipid peroxidation. But perhaps the best-known process that has been shown normally to give rise to cross-linked proteins *in vivo* is the nonenzymatic and irreversible reaction of proteins with glucose to form advanced glycosylation end products (AGE products, or AGEs; Figure 9.1) (Cerami 1985; Cerami, Vlassara, and Brownlee 1987; Vlassara et al. 1988). It may be best to view these structures as constituting a posttranslational modification of collagen by sugar. This modification begins with the nonenzymatic condensation of a sugar aldehyde by means of a free amino group of a protein to yield a Schiff base. This base then is rearranged to yield the more stable Amadori product, which can react further with other such proteins to form the cross-linked AGEs. Despite certain technical concerns, it is generally accepted that the levels of AGEs increase significantly with age in humans and in experimental animals (Sell and Monnier 1995). Type I diabetics also appear to have significantly higher amounts of such AGEs than would be expected on the basis of their chronological age alone, thus implying that their elevated blood glucose levels are accelerating the rate of production of the cross-

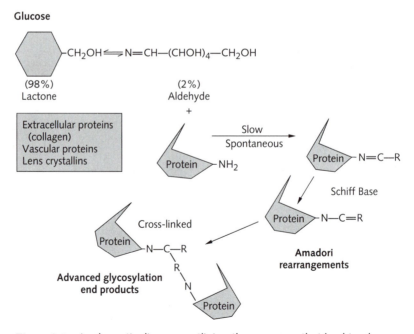

Figure 9.1 A schematic diagram outlining the processes that lead to glucose-based cross-linking of individual protein molecules. See text for discussion. (Drawing by G. T. Baker III. Used with permission.)

linked AGEs. On the other hand, excepting diabetes, the available evidence suggests that these age-related changes in long-lived proteins predispose rather than cause age-related diseases (Sell and Monnier 1995). Nonetheless, this predisposition likely arises because the old and damaged tissue is now more vulnerable to trivial insults than is young and undamaged tissue.

Such AGE structures can be recognized and destroyed by macrophages as part of a process that also induces neighboring tissue cells to replace the destroyed structures with non-cross-linked molecules. This process of normal tissue remodeling is thought to become unbalanced with time, resulting in the age-related accumulation of cross-linked proteins and the accompanying functional deficits. We know that many age-related disorders that involve collagen cross-linking occur at a younger age in diabetics, and Cerami (1985) has suggested that the reason is the chronic high glucose concentrations of diabetics. Moreover, there is good evidence to suggest that extrinsic factors such as caloric restriction (see Table 7.2) or exercise can impede the cross-linking process in the extracellular collagen fibers. Thus the external and internal environments can modulate the rate of connective-tissue aging.

The connective tissue that holds us together and gives us shape contains molecules other than collagen; the most prominent are elastins and proteoglycans. Similar sorts of age-related posttranslational modifications seem to be taking place in these molecules as well, although there are major differences in the protein structure and chemistry involved, to say nothing of the difficult technical problems in analyzing them. We will not explore those aspects further (see Sell and Monnier 1995), except to note that the general precepts developed for collagen appear to apply to these other molecules as well.

Similar nonenzymatic cross-linking reactions take place between glucose and intracellular proteins such as hemoglobin. Of particular interest, food-restricted rats show a statistically significant slower increase in their level of glycosylated hemoglobin than do *ad libitum*–fed controls (Masoro, Katz, and McMahan 1989). Other important intracellular macromolecules, in particular DNA, are also susceptible to glucose-mediated cross-linking (Bucala, Model, and Cerami 1984). This process might underlie the DNA damage that we will discuss later in this chapter or the age-related changes in gene expression that we will discuss in Chapter 10. However, in contrast to the extracellular collagen molecules, genetically important macromolecules such as DNA possess an efficient system of repair processes, and an understanding of genetically based age-related changes must take that into account as well.

Altered Protein Theory

We discussed this theory in Chapter 4 when we pointed out that work with the nematode had first shown that various purified enzymes obtained from older animals appeared to have been altered in certain of their immunological and thermal-stability properties (see Tables 4.5 and 4.6). An abundance of evidence shows that these alterations do not involve errors in the sequence of their component amino acids, nor do they involve the types of covalent changes that would accompany the chemical modification and cross-linking of the preexisting protein (Rothstein 1983). Since the enzymes are made correctly, and since they are not irreversibly chemically altered thereafter, the only other reasonable explanation must be a conformational change in the old enzyme—in other words, a change in its shape.

The available evidence shows that this is the case. Altered enolase was extracted from old nematode donors and was assayed by standard procedures for enzyme activity, heat sensitivity, resistance to protease digestion, and immunotitration. The altered enolase was then denatured in a strong salt solution to break the hydrogen bonds on which its shape depends, allowed to renature in a physiological solution so that hydrogen bonds would form spontaneously, and then retested for the same factors. The renaturation product was found to be very similar to the young enzyme (Sharma and Rothstein 1980). The old enzyme has undergone a shape change that can be reversed by denaturation. Similar procedures done with other altered enzymes (for example, phosphoglycerate kinase) in other species (for example, the rat) have yielded comparable data and comparable conclusions (Hardt and Rothstein 1985; Yuh and Gafni 1987; Gafni and Cook 1988). Presumably, the altered enzymes are "long-lived" molecules (that is, have a low turnover rate) and reside in the cell for such a long time that they are subtly denatured by the cytoplasmic environment.

Comparisons of enzymes purified from young and old animals show that they may also vary in their carbonyl content, the older animals having a higher level of these oxidized protein products. Berlett and Stadtman (1997) have calculated that the oxidized protein content in an old animal might represent 30 to 50 percent of the total protein content. In addition, the catalytic activity of many enzymes is known to decrease by 25 to 50 percent in older animals. Since the actual amount of protein usually remains unchanged, the level of inactive enzyme agrees roughly with the level of oxidized protein. In Berlett and Stadtman's view, oxidative modification is a unifying concept that allows us to understand the alterations of proteins during aging. Altered proteins, then, can be viewed as representing a special case of the cross-linkage concept, involving conformational changes that are either reversible (use hydrogen bonds to change shape) or irreversible (use covalent bonds to attach extraneous groups).

Protein processing appears to slow down with age, apparently because of unknown changes in the cytoplasmic pathways of degradation (Van Remmen et al. 1995). Given that the probability of a long-lived protein's undergoing a posttranslational modification and becoming an "altered" protein increases with time, and given that the rate of degradation decreases with time, it stands to reason that abnormal proteins will accumulate with age. Finch (1990) suggested that the accumulation of inactive proteins also might be influenced by genetic variants in the cytochrome P450 detoxifying system. In contrast, an alternative explanation for the age-related increase in altered proteins is that the altered enzymes are normal intermediates in protein degradation and accumulate only because of slowed protein degradation during aging (Gershon 1979). The evidence to support this view generally takes the form that altered proteins are present in both young and old animals but their level is higher in the latter. The evidence is plausible but certainly not persuasive, particularly since erythrocytes and lens cells, both of which have no capacity to synthesize new proteins, accumulate a variety of altered proteins during their lifetimes. In fact, the removal of old erythrocytes from the circulation depends on the spontaneous addition of tyrosine residues to a particular membrane-spanning protein, which then acts as a molecular signal for macrophages to destroy the old cell (see Chapter 11).

Only some of the cell's enzymes are affected by this process (see Table 4.5). Many of the enzymes that do undergo these conformational changes appear to play a regulatory or gatekeeping role in controlling the flux of metabolism. Thus the alteration of their enzymatic properties may affect the cell in more pervasive ways than their small numbers would otherwise indicate. Finally, the existence of these altered proteins provides us with excellent evidence in support of the concept of molecular aging.

Somatic Mutation and DNA Damage Theories

The idea that chromosomal abnormalities might underlie the aging process is a more specific version of the failure-to-repair concept. This idea dates back to the influential paper by Szilard (1959) in which he postulated that species-specific life spans might be the result of species-specific rates of random "hits" that inactivate large chromosome regions or even entire chromosomes. This concept itself flowed out of the earlier work done on the effects of radiation on cells. Szilard's suggestion renewed interest in the genome as a controlling factor in the aging process. Of course, mutations affecting the germ line cells—the sperm and ova—might well result in abnormal offspring, but they could have nothing to do with the aging process in the parent, since only the parents' somatic cells age. Hence this group of theories focuses on damage done to the genomes of somatic cells only.

It seems reasonable to assume that processes that act to destroy the integrity of the somatic-cell DNA will also cause a loss of function in the affected cells and tissues. DNA may suffer two basically different types of damage: mutations and damage. The two are not synonomous. Mutations are changes in the polynucleotide sequence such that the standard AT or CG base pairs are deleted, added, substituted, or rearranged. These mutational changes often affect, sometimes seriously, the information coded into that portion of the genome. For example, the difference between a normal hemoglobin and an abnormal sickle-cell hemoglobin is due entirely to the effects of a single substitution of an A for a T at the seventeenth base position in the beta-hemoglobin gene that encodes that protein. Regardless of the type or extent of the mutational alterations, and regardless of its effects on the informational content of the genome, the affected DNA molecule retains its characteristic double-helical structure and still consists of an uninterrupted sequence of nucleotide pairs. It still looks like a normal molecule.

DNA damage, on the other hand, refers to any one of many chemical alterations in the double-helical structure of the molecule. The damage may be caused by either exogenous or endogenous sources; the latter are perhaps more important. These alterations produce structural irregularities that interrupt, modify, or break the double helix. Examples of such irregularities include but are not limited to pyrimidine dimers, apurinic sites, single-strand breaks, adducts, covalent cross-linking of the DNA strands to one another or to other molecules, and so forth.

Even if none of these forms of damage alter the informational content of the DNA molecule, they do structurally interrupt the DNA molecule.

The effects of mutations and DNA damage are similar but not identical, and the processes by which they achieve their results are different. Both can interfere with gene expression; on this basis they have been independently proposed as possible mechanisms of aging. We will discuss them as independent theories.

Somatic Mutations

If mutational mechanisms play a role in the aging process, they could arise through a germ line mutation in the parent that would then give rise to an offspring in which all body cells contained a somatic mutation. The realization that several inherited pathologies believed to mimic certain segmental aspects of aging, such as Down syndrome, are caused by chromosome abnormalities contributed to this restored interest in genetic causes (but see Chapter 6). With very few exceptions, such abnormalities arise from stochastic damage that results in either an alteration of chromosome number or the formation of lesions in the existing chromosomes.

Jacobs and her colleagues conducted the first investigation of the effect of aging on human chromosomal number and found a significant increase in the number of lymphocytes that exhibited visible chromosomal abnormalities as a function of donor age. A large number of later studies verified these initial observations (Jacobs and Court-Brown 1966). Similar sorts of chromosome abnormalities have also been observed among "old" (late-passage) cells grown *in vitro* (Saksela and Moorhead 1963). Jarvik (1988) suggested that cells of individuals afflicted with Alzheimer's disease might have chromosome abnormalities. Chromosomes from older humans appear to be more fragile than are those from younger individuals, since the rate of aminopterin-induced breakage is higher in older chromosomes than in younger ones (Esposito et al. 1989).

All aneuploid human embryos are lethal. In fact, most aneuploids are cell lethals because the loss of one or more chromosomes usually alters a cell's functions so severely that it is no longer viable. Thus, it might appear plausible to postulate that such stochastically caused chromosome damage causes the observed age-related declines in function. However, the frequency of aneuploid cells is low even in aged donors. For example, the most common abnormality found in lymphocytes is the loss of a chromosome. In one study, such affected cells increased from a frequency of 3 percent in youths aged 5 to 14 years to more than 9 percent in the 65+-year-old group. Though the threefold increase is certain, it is not clear whether that difference is sufficient to explain the difference in functioning between a 5-year-old and 65-year-old. Moreover, the missing chromosomes often involved the cytogenetic set, which includes the X chromosome, an interesting observation since the loss of one sex chromosome often has no deleterious effect in females, and such hypodiploidy is most often found in females (Schneider 1985). In addition, such chromosome loss is not necessarily seen in other body cells (Finch 1990). Taken together, the available data suggest that such chromosome loss does not play a substantial causal role in bringing about the aging phenotype.

Somatic chromosome lesions can be most easily recognized in dividing cells, and this fact made such cell studies a popular experimental approach. H. J. Curtis (1963) and his colleagues (Curtis and Miller 1971) demonstrated the existence of an inverse relationship between the rate of increase of chromosomal lesions in regenerating liver cells, and the species-specific life span of the three species (mouse, guinea pig, and dog) examined. More recently, Martin, Fry, and Loeb (1985) examined the chromosomes from the enzymatically dispersed kidney cells shortly after they were added to culture (early-passage cells) obtained from young (8 months) and very old (40 months) mice. Their results showed that the frequency of a variety of chromosomal lesions is substantially elevated in the older animals.

Cells taken from individuals afflicted with progeria (a segmental mimic of aging; see Chapter 6) are known to have a very limited life span in culture (Martin et al. 1965). The reason for this shortened *in vitro* life span may be related to the fact that the chromosomes of these cells are extraordinarily unstable and undergo particular chromosome rearrangements and/or loss (Salk et al. 1981). The relationship of this finding to the clinical picture is not clear, although it has been hypothesized that all the myriad chromosome aberrations are due to a defect in the Werner's syndrome gene that is thought to code for a helicase involved in DNA repair. However, studies on other normal tissues *in vivo* have revealed that many tissues show no evidence of visible chromosome damage, yet they still age. Visible chromosome abnormalities are not widespread, so it is difficult to entertain them as potential causative factors of the aging process. In fact, a review on this topic concluded that the chromosomal aberrations must be considered the effect, not the cause, of aging (Sen, Talukder, and Sharma 1987).

Not all chromosome damage need result in visible abnormalities. Many, perhaps most, somatic mutations involve molecular alterations of the DNA that are sufficient to irreversibly alter the information coded therein but that are invisible even with the microscope. Such a mutant gene would be incapable of producing a normal gene product. The topic has recently been reviewed (Ames, Shigenaga, and Hagen 1993; De Flora et al. 1996). Leo Szilard proposed in 1959 that the accumulation of such somatic mutations constitutes the elementary step in the aging process. This hypothesis was based on an analogy with the known effects of radiation. Indeed, H. J. Muller received the Nobel prize because he demonstrated that exposure of experimental animals to X rays induces both germ line and somatic mutations. How could one detect such mutations and critically test the hypothesis? There are several viable approaches, four of which we will discuss here.

First, one could attempt to detect the abnormal gene products directly and see if there is an age-related increase in their frequency among all members of the test population. In humans, a very clever utilization of existing data was adopted by Popp and colleagues (1976). The human alpha- and beta-hemoglobin chains have been completely sequenced, and their amino acid composition is known. The amino acid isoleucine is not normally encoded genetically in either of these polypeptide chains. Inclusion of isoleucine into the hemoglobin molecule thus would be indicative of a synthesis error that was due probably to a somatic muta-

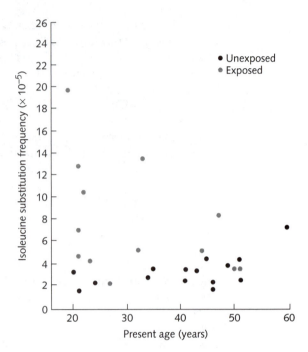

Figure 9.2   The average content of isoleucine in highly purified human hemoglobin, shown as a function of age at the time of assay for persons from the Marshall Islands who were unexposed or inadvertently exposed to an estimated radiation dose of 69 or 175 rads. (From Popp et al. 1976.)

tion occurring in a few cells of that organism. Figure 9.2 shows the results of isoleucine assays done on the hemoglobins of two groups of individuals: those accidentally exposed to radiation (from an atomic bomb test) as youths and those who had no known exposure to radiation. The unexposed individuals show no significant age-related increase in isoleucine content. The exposed individuals, on the other hand, show significantly higher levels of isoleucine content in their hemoglobin. These data suggested that somatic mutations are readily induced by high levels of irradiation but do not increase with age, as demanded by the theory.

Clark, Bertrand, and Smith (1963) took another clever approach with the wasp *Habrobracon*. These wasps have an unusual genetic system that allows the construction of males that are either haploid (*n*) or diploid (*2n*); that is, they differ only in the number of chromosome sets each contains. This fact allowed Clark to set up a critical test of the theory. If the accumulation of somatic mutations is the cause of aging, the haploid animals should age faster, and have a shorter mean and maximum life span, than the diploid animals. This relationship should hold whether or not both sets of animals have been irradiated. This situation would arise because a somatic mutation occurring in the haploid organism would inactivate the animal's only copy of that gene, but would still leave a "backup" copy of the gene in the diploid animal. The results are quite striking. The nonirradiated haploid males had the same life span as that of the nonirradiated diploid males. However, the irradiated haploid males had a significantly shortened life span when compared to the irradiated diploid males. These data are consistent with the human hemoglobin data already discussed, but they contradict the predictions of the somatic mutation theory.

Woodruff and Nitikin have re-investigated the somatic mutation theory using the newer technique of P-element insertional mutagenesis (Nitikin and Woodruff 1995; Woodruff and Nitikin 1995); this technique has the advantage over radiation in that it allows the experimenter to induce defined and controllable numbers of random single mutations. They find convincing evidence that the inducation of somatic genetic damage can reduce life span in *Drosophila* but that the effect is dependent on the particular species of fly involved and the type of transposable element used. Their conclusions suggest that a close relationship between somatic genetic damage and aging might in fact exist, but that the earlier work of Clark and his colleagues may have been too broadly generalized.

Metaplasias occur when one type of tissue is transformed into another type. It is not uncommon to find such small nodes of metaplastic tissue in different organs of older individuals. The organs of the elderly often seem to exhibit transformation of related cell types, such as intestinal metaplasia in the stomach or gastric metaplasia in the small intestine. Although they are often benign, metaplasias are suspected to give rise to transformed cells under certain conditions. Hartman and Morgan (1985) showed that certain types of metaplasias may be induced in laboratory rats after treatment with known mutagens. These mutagens cause heritable changes in somatic cells. The treatment is believed to have given rise to somatic mutations, although no cytogenetic analyses were performed in this study. Many of the induced mutations presumably inactivate the normal functioning of mature, normally differentiated cells. These mutations probably have little effect on the organism's ability to function, because of the normal reserve capacity of the remaining cells. However, mutations that are presumed to affect a stem cell and alter the final differentiation pathway of that cell and of all its descendants are likely the ones that give rise to the observed metaplasias. Thus a stem cell normally destined to give rise to gastric cells would be altered such that it would now give rise to intestinal cells. High numbers of metaplasias in any single tissue could disrupt the integrity of that tissue and lead to the physiological decline that is characteristic of aging. Although this approach is intriguing and tends to support the somatic mutation theory, we must recognize that (1) somatic mutations have not been proven to be the cause of tissue metaplasias and (2), the deleterious effects of metaplasias are seen only after mutagen treatment, a procedure that raises anew questions about the relationship of the pathological to the normal aging process.

A final approach to the topic is based on the behavior of cells in culture. As is discussed in Chapter 11, human cells grown *in vitro* follow a predictable pattern of loss of proliferative potential that is widely thought to reflect cellular aging. One can compute the levels of somatic mutation that must take place if such mutations cause the observed cellular senescence. Both the predicted mutation rate and the predicted cell division time conflict with the empirical data (Holliday and Kirkwood 1981). The theory is not capable of explaining cellular aging.

This survey suggests that there is an age-related increase in certain types of chromosome abnormalities, particularly in response to radiation and mutagen treatment, but that there is no firm evidence that such alterations have fundamental functional effects. There are two exceptions to this statement. First, the development of certain cancers late in life is very likely tied to the occurrence of particular aberrations and mutations affecting specific DNA repair and cell cycle control genes (see Chapter 11); and second, gene inactivation via transposable elements results in a reduced life span. But when we consider the aging process as a whole, we must conclude that there is currently little evidence to support the idea that the diseases and dysfunctions of aging are caused by somatic mutations or chromosomal aberrations, or that differences among species in rate of aging are linked to alterations in mutation and aberration.

DNA Damage and Repair

DNA damage is not a rare event in mammalian cells. The data in Table 9.1 suggest that the number of damaging events is so high that without repair mechanisms, within a few years or so the affected cells would not be able to transcribe or to replicate their DNA accurately or completely. More recent and independent measurements made by Ames, Shigenaga, and Hagen (1993) also indicate that there are probably more than 10,000 oxidative hits of DNA per cell per day in humans, a value in general agreement with those of Table 9.1. Fortunately, the specific DNA repair mechanisms that exist within the cell are normally more than sufficient to repair the ongoing damage (see Table 9.1). For example, the typical neuron would lose in its lifetime about 3 percent of the total number of adenine or guanine (purine) bases in its DNA solely as a result of depurination, were it not for the existence of an apurinic (AP) repair system that specifically attacks and repairs AP sites in a whole variety of organisms (Gensler and Bernstein 1981).

Table 9.1   **Damage and Repair Kinetics of Mammalian DNA**

Type of damage	Rate of appearance of damage in DNA of mammalian cells (no. events/hour)	Rate of repair of damage in DNA of mammalian cells (no. events/hour)
Pyrimidine dimers in skin (noonday sun)	5×10^4	5×10^4: normal cells 5×10^3: xeroderma pigmentosum group C cells
Thymine glycols	13	1×10^5
O_6-methylguanine	130	1×10^4 to 1×10^5
Depurination (cleave out A or G)	580	—
or		
Depryrimidation (cleave out T or C)	29	—
both of which lead to		
Single-strand breaks in DNA	2,300	2×10^5

Source: Data from Tice and Setlow 1985.

Each type of damage usually has a specific type of repair system that enzymatically recognizes and removes the damaged portion of the DNA and synthesizes a new patch using the nonaltered opposite strand as a template; these systems are reviewed in detail by Demple and Harrison (1994) and by Dusenbery and Smith (1996). However, these systems do not constitute the cell's only level of repair. The general repair mechanisms associated with recombination can also play a role in repairing nonrecombinational damage such as interstrand cross-links and double-strand breaks. In addition, more recent studies have shown that DNA repair is linked to its transcription; actively transcribed strands are repaired at a higher rate than are nontranscribed strands (Bohr and Anson 1995). This mechanism is an additional safeguard against the possibility of damaged DNA being allowed to generate damaged gene products. Since unrepaired lesions are potential mutation sites in replicating DNA, it is important that DNA damage be repaired before cell replication. Such repair is accomplished by a block in the cell cycle before DNA replication that involves activation of the *p53* tumor suppressor gene, as well as other antiproliferation genes. Extensive DNA damage can activate apoptosis, the intrinsic cell death program that eliminates potentially neoplastic cells, which we will discuss further in Chapter 11.

As depicted in Figure 9.3, cells and organisms normally exist in a dynamic equilibrium between the rate of DNA damage and the rate of DNA repair. Should the net rate of damage increase for any reason, then the balance will be reset to a new, perhaps dangerously high, level of DNA damage. The major predictions of the DNA damage theory of aging are (1) that there is a positive correlation between DNA repair ability and life span and (2) that a systemic, age-related shift in repair activity is the major event underlying the appearance of the functional decrements characteristic of aging.

The underlying assumption of the theory is that all DNA damage is related to levels of DNA repair and/or to levels of functional performance. This relationship may be true in many cases, but it need not be true in all cases. For example, DNA damage might occur in a critical cell type, yet not be related either to an age-related functional decline or to changes in the level of DNA repair. This situation might arise when the affected cell is embedded in a network of functional redundancy such that the cell's loss of function would be compensated for by other

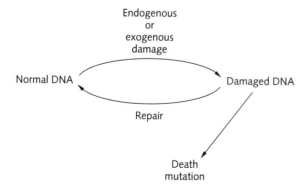

Figure 9.3   A schematic representation indicating that the level of damaged DNA depends on the relative rates of input of damage and repair. (From Tice and Setlow 1985. © Van Nostrand Reinhold.)

members of the network. The loss of function of the particular cell might well impinge on the organism's level of functional redundancy, but this would be noted only as a loss in cell number or as a decrease in future performance, neither of which is being measured. Thus the theory, in its simplest form, cannot encompass all age-related changes.

In mammals, the daily rate of DNA damage can be conveniently determined by an assay of the animal's urine for DNA damage products. Ames (1994) has shown that the species-specific urinary output of thymine glycol and thymidine glycol is directly proportional to the species' oxygen consumption: Humans have the lowest damage rates, mice the highest. Since oxygen consumption and free-radical production are related (Sohal and Weindruch 1996; see also the discussion on this topic later in this chapter), it seems likely that oxidative damage is the major cause of DNA damage. This hypothesis provides a plausible mechanism of DNA damage, but it does not address the question of DNA repair.

Evidence supporting the first prediction was first put forth by Hart and Setlow (1974). Their interspecific data (Figure 9.4) showed a striking correlation between the species-specific repair ability and the characteristic species life span. Subsequent work by others has generally (Cortopassi and Wang 1996), but not always (see Kato et al. 1980), tended to support this initial observation. The relationship appears in groups other than mammals as well, for DNA repair systems have been found in representatives of all five kingdoms of living organisms.

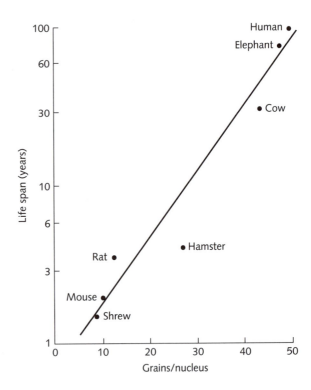

Figure 9.4 The correlation between life span and the ability of fibroblasts from various mammalian species to conduct unscheduled DNA synthesis (that is, DNA repair), as represented by the average number of grains per nucleus. (Data from Hart and Setlow 1974, as redrawn by Tice and Setlow 1985. © Van Nostrand Reinhold.)

Smith-Sonneborn (1979) showed that the clonal life span of unicellular *Paramecium* is reduced when these organisms are exposed to ultraviolet (UV) light, a known inducer of thymine dimerization in DNA. However, when UV irradiation is followed by photoreactivation, a process that reverses the dimerization, the clonal life span is not only restored but even increased. These results suggest that the DNA repair enzymes are induced by UV and are capable, once the excess dimers are removed by photoreactivation, of subsequently repairing other unspecified but accumulated DNA damage that is acting to limit the life span.

This interpretation is supported by the finding of Holmes and Holmes (1986) that there is a positive and linear correlation between the number of AP sites in the *Paramecium* genome and the clonal age of the population, thus indicating that the accumulation of DNA damage is age related. Since we may regard the mitotic cells in our bodies as spatial or temporal clones, the findings on *Paramecium* may have a wider relevance. Prevention and/or repair of DNA damage may result in an extended clonal age, which, if the cells involved play a critical role in the organism, may translate into an alteration of the aging phenotype. UV photoreactivation may not play a major role for cells that are embedded in the darkness of our bodies, but an analogous situation of inducible DNA repair may occur in multicellular forms as well. *Drosophila* contains an enzyme called recombination repair protein 1 (Rrp1) that, when experimentally overexpressed, reduces the frequency of somatic mutations and repairs certain types of DNA damage induced by oxidative stress (Szakmary et al. 1996). There are no data regarding the effect of Rrp1 on the animal's longevity, yet it is not too great a speculative leap to conclude that inducible DNA damage and/or repair activities may play a role in modulating the aging phenotype.

What evidence supports the second of the theory's predictions—namely, that a systemic, age-related shift in repair activity is the major event underlying the appearance of the functional decrements characteristic of aging? The data of Holmes and Holmes (1986) just described have been cited. Other evidence suggesting the validity of this assumption is the finding that DNA obtained from fibroblasts of old human donors has a molecular weight that is lower than that of DNA extracted from fibroblasts of younger donors (Williams 1983). The difference is thought to be due to the higher incidence of unrepaired single-strand breaks in the genomes of the older cells, giving rise to larger numbers of smaller DNA molecules relative to the young controls. Similar observations have been made with rodents, although there are areas of disagreement. For example, several researchers (Ono, Okada, and Sugahara 1976; Polson and Webster 1982) found that, although there was the expected difference in single-strand breaks between the DNAs obtained from old and from young mouse livers, no such difference was observed in their spleen, thymus, or brain DNAs. Thus in some organisms, the age-related DNA fragmentation appears to be tissue specific, while in other organisms, such as *Drosophila*, there is no evidence of age-related DNA fragmentation. On the other hand, human fibroblasts obtained from healthy young individuals and kept in culture showed lower levels of chromosome breaks and micronuclei than did fibroblasts from healthy old individuals (Weirach-Schwaiger et al. 1994). In turn, the same investigation showed that cells obtained from younger patients suffering from premature aging syndromes (for example, Werner's syndrome, Cockayne's syndrome) showed evidences of DNA damage as high or higher than those of the older healthy controls. The relationship between age and DNA damage exists but does not appear to be very tight or universal.

One interesting set of interspecific data, depicted in Figure 9.5, shows an inverse correlation between the species-specific life span and the cell's ability to convert harmless substrates into DNA-damaging agents. One interpretation of this data set is that metabolic activities that ordinarily detoxify harmful chemicals can on occasion convert those chemicals into active substances that may bind to DNA and cause a pattern of age-related damage. These data also suggest that this trend is evolutionarily selected against in long-lived species. Such detoxification systems may be a pleiotropic component of a long life. A review of various such interspecific studies indicates that there is a good but not excellent relationship between relative DNA repair activity and maximum life span potential (Cortopassi and Wang 1996). This finding led Cortopassi and Wang to suggest that DNA repair is a necessary but not a sufficient condition for long life, a view in agreement with other independent studies, as we have discussed.

One cogent objection that has been raised to interspecific studies that measure a particular variable against the species' maximum life span is based on the observation that the latter is the outcome of the annual rate of mortality and the annual rate of increase in the population and as such constitutes a poor measure of the extent of senescence present in the population (Promislow 1993). However, the interspecific studies are implicitly trying to correlate a particular variable (for example, DNA repair) with the extent of senescence in the populations. The studies' conclusions may still be correct; the point is that they often use

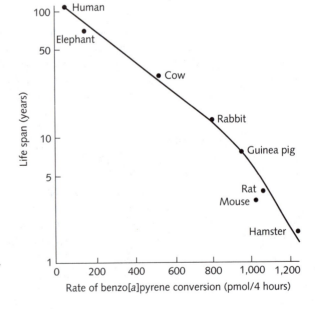

Figure 9.5   The abilities of fibroblast cultures from various mammals to convert benzo[a]pyrene to a water-soluble form. This metabolic activation of the hydrocarbon gives rise to a potentially dangerous molecule. Note the inverse relationship between life span and the activation ability. (Data from Moore and Schwartz 1978, as redrawn by Tice and Setlow 1985. © Van Nostrand Reinhold.)

an inaccurate measure of senescence, in part because the better measure (annual change in the age-specific rate, or q_{x}) simply is not known for many species. Thus we need to accept the results of most interspecific studies with a measure of uncertainty.

The story is also unclear at the intraspecific level. There appears to be an age-related increase in DNA damage in some individual organisms, but this may well be the result rather than the cause of aging (Sen, Talukder, and Sharma 1987). For example, Vijg and colleagues (1985) conducted a 9-month longitudinal study of UV-induced DNA repair in early-passage fibroblasts obtained from skin biopsies of inbred rats varying in age from 6 to 44 months. These excision repair results showed (1) that there is very little difference in the DNA repair values of individual animals, regardless of age, and (2) that there is very little difference in the DNA repair values of cells taken from the same animal at different ages. As these investigators concluded, the lack of pronounced inter- and intraindividual differences in fibroblast excision repair makes it unlikely that this particular DNA repair system is an important determinant of individual longevity. This lack of variability may be the consequence of using an inbred strain. Nonetheless, similar results have been reported in human fibroblasts (Goldstein 1971; Painter, Clarkson, and Young 1973). However, late-passage human fibroblast cells *in vitro* do show a decreased level of DNA repair, a phenomenon that we will deal with in Chapter 11. In summary, the cross-sectional data show differences between young and old individuals and suggest that aging affects the DNA repair parameters measured, but they do not address the question of individual variability in these parameters and its relationship to age-dependent changes in cell and tissue function. The longitudinal study addresses but does not answer that question.

Other tissues appear to behave quite differently. Niedermuller (1985) measured the ability of the various internal organs of the rat to perform four different types of DNA repair. The results, shown in Table 9.2, show that there is a complex pattern of age-related changes in DNA repair ability. Some repair systems show no or a slight age-related decrement; others show extensive change. Furthermore, the different organs show different patterns of change for each type of repair system. (Note that other investigators—Wheeler and Lett [1974]; Ono and Okada [1978]; Hanawalt [1987]—have reported results that do not fully support those of Table 9.2.)

DNA damage can result in significant physiological deficits in certain pathological situations. Individuals afflicted with particular types of xeroderma pigmentosum, a group of rare inherited diseases, have defects in the AP repair enzymes: Their repair activity is much lower than normal. These individuals show a 10- to 30-fold increase in the number of AP sites in their fibroblasts relative to normal controls. They are also defective in the repair of many other forms of DNA damage, and they exhibit neurological abnormalities. The observation that the ill individuals most deficient in repair capacity die at an early age suggests, but by no means proves, that there is a causal relationship between their defective repair system and their defective physiology. The recent cloning and conceptual identification of the gene responsible for Werner's syndrome as possibly a helicase, a particular type of DNA repair gene, strengthens the plausibility of a

Table 9.2   **Organ-Specific Age-Related Decreases in DNA Repair Ability**

Type of DNA system	Tissues that show an age-related decrease in DNA repair ability in rats of age[a]	
	18 months	*28 months*
Excision repair	Spleen, lung	Spleen, lung, liver, testes, kidney, heart
Single-strand break repair	No change	Testes, brain
Double-strand break repair	No change	No change
Gamma-irradiation repair	Kidney, lung, testes, brain	Liver, kidney, lung, testes, duodenum, brain muscle

Source: Data from Niedermuller 1985.
[a]In all cases, the ability of the 9-month-old animal to repair damage in each specific organ is taken as the standard, and the values for the 18-month-olds and the 28-month-olds are expressed relative to that standard.

causal link between rates of aging and levels of DNA repair (Yu et al. 1996; see also Chapter 6).

Genetic studies afford better insight into the relationship between DNA repair and longevity. If DNA repair ability were essential to normal longevity, one would predict that mutants that decrease or abolish DNA repair activity would decrease the animals' life span. Such a relationship was reported in *Drosophila* (Whitehead and Grigliatti 1993). Whitehead and Grigliatti used temperature-sensitive (*ts*) alleles of three mutagen-sensitive (*mus*) genes. Animals carrying such mutations are very sensitive to mutagens, usually because of defects in DNA repair pathways. The interesting attribute of *ts* mutants is that the affected gene product performs normally when the organism is raised at the permissive temperature (22°C) but is inactivated at the restrictive temperature (29°C). The authors found that the *mus* mutants raised and/or maintained at 29°C had shorter life spans than those raised at 22°C, showing that the loss of normal DNA repair capacity leads to a reduction in longevity.

To determine whether DNA repair ability by itself is sufficient to affect longevity, one would need to repeat this experiment, but using *ts* mutants that, when raised at the restrictive temperature, would exhibit higher-than-normal levels of DNA repair. If such mutants existed, one could directly test this question. But they do not, so we are left to devise indirect ways of testing our questions. Cross-sectional studies of rats indicate that the levels of a common by-product of DNA damage, 8-hydroxyguanine (8-OHG), show no significant age-related changes between the ages of 5 months and 30 months, even though there are significant baseline differences among different organs (Hirano et al. 1996). In addition, there are no age-related differences in the repair enzyme activity, indicating that the lack of age-related differences in 8-OHG cannot be attributed to this factor. For the moment, we must conclude from the intraspecific data that DNA repair ability is a necessary but not a sufficient condition for a long life span.

It has been suggested that this heterogeneity of results dealing with overall DNA repair ability is misleading in the sense that the ability of a cell to function properly may depend on its ability to selectively repair only those genes that are essential to its survival and the accomplishment of its differentiated task. This explanation may underlie the fact that the excision repair ability of rodent cells is much lower than that of human cells (see Figure 9.5) but that the rodent cells are about as resistant as human cells to killing by ultraviolet light.

In recent years, an endogenous type of DNA modification was found that does not appear to represent DNA damage. The compounds that reflect this modification appear to be indigenous to the normal DNA and have been termed I (indigenous) compounds. Although their level in the cell increases with age, it also increases in response to treatments such as caloric restriction that increase life span, and these compounds display a positive correlation with median age. Their function is not known, although it has been speculated that indigenous compounds play a role in protecting the cell against transformation (De Flora et al. 1996). However, most of the DNA modifications found in the aging animal appear to be harmful and result from either oxidative damage or are induced by pro-oxidant carcinogens. De Flora and colleagues (1996) have concluded that the patterns of DNA damage are consistent with the oxidative-damage hypothesis of aging, which we will discuss at the end of this chapter.

Many data suggest that damage to mitochondrial DNA plays an important role in some aspects of aging. We discuss the relationship between mitochondrial damage and aging in Chapter 10, where it is considered under the rubric of metabolic theories.

Damage to nuclear DNA likely contributes to the aging process, at least in certain tissues. Tice and Setlow (1985) prudently concluded that aging does not appear to be the direct or causal consequence of a decline in DNA repair capabilities alone. Other factors, such as resistance to oxidative stress, undoubtedly play an equally critical role. Age-related increases in DNA damage may be an important contributory process, but one that may also be the result of systemic alterations in other processes (for example, decreased levels of protein synthesis), which then bring about an age-related alteration in DNA repair processes. Other authors (for example, Bernstein and Bernstein 1991) argue for the opposite case—namely, that failure to repair DNA damage is the proximate cause of aging. Our sampling of the data suggests that the latter position is plausible but unproven. It is reasonable to conclude from the current data that DNA repair ability is necessary but not sufficient for the expression of extended longevity.

Error Catastrophe Theory

This concept was originally developed by Leslie Orgel in 1963 and differs from the somatic mutation and DNA damage theories in that it generally postulates an error in information transfer at a site other than in the DNA. The basic idea behind this theory is that the ability of a cell to produce its normal complement of functional proteins depends not only on the correct genetic specification of the various polypeptide sequences, but also on the competence and fidelity of the protein-synthesizing apparatus. Even if the genome contains neither somatic mutations nor DNA damage and the organism has an accurate copy of the correct species-specific information for a particular protein, the organism will reap no benefit if it garbles the information in the process of translating it.

Consider the general path of information flow in biological systems, as shown in Figure 9.6. Errors in Type I products would yield a somewhat lower average efficiency in a particular aspect of metabolism or of structure but would leave no lasting trace once the product was turned over. An example of this situation might be a person in whom some hemoglobin had inadvertently suffered a one-time error and had been made with isoleucine instead of leucine, as in Figure 9.2. Such abnormal molecules probably would be less efficient, perhaps strikingly so, in binding oxygen and carbon dioxide than would normal molecules. However the abnormal molecules would be cleared from the body when the old red blood cells that contained them were destroyed in about 90 days. They would have no lasting effect.

Errors in Type II products can be subdivided into two categories: those that lead to a complete loss of function (Type IIa) and those that lead to reduced specificity of an information-handling enzyme (such as a DNA or RNA polymerase) (Type IIb). An error in the Type IIa class is similar to the Type I error in that it affects the efficiency of the information transfer process by reducing the number and kinds of molecules replicated. The extent of damage depends on which part of the translation process is affected, but such an error does not affect molecules that do become synthesized. If the molecules that fail to be synthesized are absolutely required for life and cannot be substituted for by other molecules, and if their concentration in the cell falls below a minimum threshold, then cell death will likely ensue. Errors in Type IIb products, giving rise to a reduced fidelity or specificity of translation, are very different; even one such error inevitably leads to an exponentially increasing error frequency. Many, if not all, of the molecules synthesized by defective Type II enzymes are themselves defective. A single defective enzyme molecule in the cell amplifies its effects throughout the cell with every round of synthesis. These errors are transmissible and cumulative and might ultimately lead to what Orgel termed an "error catastrophe." An error catastrophe results when the error frequency reaches a value at which one of the processes necessary for the existence of a viable cell becomes critically inefficient. A vital threshold has been crossed, and the cell dies. If sufficient cells die, the result is a decrement of physiological function that is characteristic of aging.

This theory is both logical and reasonable, but its best virtue is that it makes a specific and testable prediction: Proteins obtained from cells of old donors

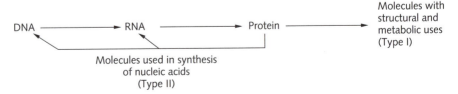

Figure 9.6   The flow of information from genome to gene products. Gene products are classified into one of two categories depending on whether they are involved in information replication.

should exhibit a significantly higher frequency of errors than would proteins extracted from cells of young donors. Such protein populations are easily and accurately examined experimentally by means of a molecular separation technique called two-dimensional polyacrylamide gel electrophoresis (2D-PAGE). This procedure sorts out the proteins by molecular weight and by electrical charge, depositing the isolated proteins on an *x*–*y* grid. It is very sensitive, allowing investigators to accurately detect even small numbers of proteins that contain a change in charge and/or molecular weight. Such changes are indicative of errors in synthesis. This procedure made the error catastrophe theory one of the few theories of aging that could be critically tested at the time it was put forth.

The 2D-PAGE test has now been applied to a wide variety of different species and cell types, including *E. coli, Drosophila, C. elegans*, and human fibroblasts, among others. The results are quite clear: There is no evidence of the predicted electrophoretic heterogeneity that is characteristic of synthesis errors in the proteins obtained from older donors. Not only is there no difference in error rate between young and old, but all cells show remarkably good fidelity in synthesis, and all have error rates that are so low as to be almost undetectable. It is unlikely that such transcriptional or translational errors are one of the mechanisms responsible for aging and senescence (Rothstein 1987).

However, this evidence does not necessarily rule out errors in the replication of the DNA itself. Murray and Holliday (1981) showed that certain DNA polymerases obtained from older cells have an increased error rate relative to those from younger cells. The loss in fidelity is less severe in calorically restricted mice than in *ad libitum*–fed animals (Srivastava et al. 1993). This observation is formally consistent with the error catastrophe theory, and Holliday (1984) skillfully supported it by wedding this theory to the disposable-soma theory (see Chapter 4), whereby with aging the cell must divert an increased proportion of resources from reproduction to error correction.

Dysdifferentiation Theory

It has been suggested that the normal aging of an organism results because its component cells drift away from their proper state of differentiation. Differentiated cells are characterized by their ability to selectively repress the activity of genes not necessary to the survival of the cell and its particular functions. Understanding how the cell activates a relatively few selected genes and represses all the others is a major research goal of developmental geneticists. In any event, a decrease or alteration in the specificity of these activation–repression mechanisms, perhaps brought about by time-dependent changes in the cell's internal milieu, could theoretically interfere with the cell's finely tuned ability to carry out its specified function. Richard Cutler (1985) coined the term "dysdifferentiation" to denote this process and suggested that the resulting lack of stringent gene control might result in the cell's synthesizing proteins other than those characteristic of its differentiated state. Other authors have spoken of a loss of homeostasis or an alteration in gene expression. Regardless of the name, the decrements in physiological function that are characteristic of aging might thus have their origins in an impaired genetic control mechanism. This concept imposes stochastic errors on a theory of programmed gene expression.

Like the error catastrophe theory, the dysdifferentiation theory possesses the virtue of making specific and testable predictions, for it postulates that cells from old donors will synthesize more proteins that are uncharacteristic of its particular differentiated state than will similar cells from young donors. This is not the same thing as stating that the same tissue type taken from animals of different ages will display a different panorama of proteins. For example, one might be tempted to interpret the fact that senescent rat liver shows an age-dependent alteration in the synthesis of normal liver proteins (Roy and Chatterjee 1984) as evidence of a programmed change in gene expression that supports the theory. The dysdifferentiation hypothesis, however, rests on the assumption that the stochastic changes taking place in the genetic regulatory system result in disorderly changes in gene expression, changes that might best be detected by the presence in one tissue of proteins that are usually characteristic of another tissue.

An early indication that the theory might be correct was obtained by Ono and Cutler (1978), who showed that there was a twofold age-dependent increase in the amount of alpha- and beta-globin RNA synthesized by mouse brain and liver. Other uncharacteristic proteins also showed an age-dependent increase. However, no such age-dependent increase in the uncharacteristic globin gene expression was noted when young and old cultures of normal human fibroblast cells were examined (Kator et al. 1985). Thus, at least in these cultured cells, the genetic control mechanisms do not appear to relax their stringent control of gene expression. Despite the absence of strong positive data, this approach remains of interest, in part because its predictions are easily testable at the molecular level and in part because it allows for the stochastic modulation of a programmed process by means of a known genetic mechanism.

Oxidative-Damage Theory

Except for those few organisms that are specially adapted to live under anaerobic conditions, all animals and plants require oxygen for the efficient production of energy. About 95 percent of our total metabolic energy is produced in the mitochondria, the cellular organelles that combine the carbon molecules obtained from the digestion of our food with the oxygen obtained from our breathing. If these reactions are blocked, we lose consciousness and die very quickly. Oxygen is essential to the energy-producing reactions that keep us alive.

However, it has long been known that oxygen supplied at concentrations greater than those of normal air is toxic to many plants and animals. Exposing *E. coli* to pure oxygen causes them to stop growing immediately. Oxygen is known to enhance the damaging effects of ionizing radiation on living cells: A threefold higher dose of radiation is needed to kill cells in a nitrogen atmosphere than is needed to kill the same cells in an oxygen atmosphere. Exposure of humans to pure oxygen for as little as 6 hours causes chest soreness in some individuals, and longer exposures eventually lead to irreversible damage to the alveoli of the lungs. There are many other known examples of oxygen damage, for almost all tissues of many organisms are affected, as Table 9.3 shows. The damaging effects of oxygen on organisms vary depending on the species, on the particular tissues examined, and on the individual's age, physiological condition, and diet.

Table 9.3 **The Effects of High Oxygen Concentrations on Animal Tissues**

Species	Nature of exposure	Organ examined	Results
Rats	Pure O_2 at 5 atm for 75 minutes	Heart	Mitochondrial swelling followed by myofibril damage
	Pure O_2 at 0.33 atm for 3 days	Liver	Mitochondrial damage
Hamsters	70% O_2 for 3–4 weeks	Testes	Degeneration of seminiferous epithelium; cessation of sperm production
Guinea pigs	70% O_2 for 6–36 weeks	Bone marrow	Inhibition of red blood cell development
Monkeys	Pure O_2 at 0.5 atm for up to 22 days	Liver	Proliferation and abnormality of smooth endoplasmic reticulum; decrease in glycogen content
Humans	Hyperbaric oxygen therapy	Ear	Hemorrhages of inner ear; deafness

Nonetheless, oxygen toxicity appears to be a general phenomenon and may reflect a fundamental biological mechanism.

Ironically, the molecule on which we depend for our life is also the molecule that can harm us. Various explanations have been put forward to explain oxygen toxicity. The widely accepted current explanation states that most of the damaging effects of oxygen are the results of cellular damage caused by free radicals. These highly reactive, naturally occurring chemicals are induced to form in the presence of oxygen and have been implicated in more than 60 disorders, including heart disease, cancer, and cataracts. They also appear to be one of the major factors responsible for the changes in body structure and function that are characteristic of aging and senescence. The initial proffering of this theory (Harman 1956) was based in large part on the observed inverse relationship between life span and metabolic rate for mammals and the inverse effect of temperature on the life span of poikilotherms, as described in Chapters 6 and 10. The data that have been obtained during the 4 decades since the theory was first stated are always plausible, usually convincing, and almost definitive. The oxidative-damage hypothesis is one of the major theories providing a probable and testable biological mechanism for the aging process. Thus the topic warrants our close and critical examination.

A free radical is defined as any chemical species that has an odd number of electrons. Most chemical compounds have paired electrons and thus are only moderately reactive; they require specific starting conditions or enzymatic assistance to react chemically with another substance. Molecules that have an unpaired electron, however, are thermodynamically unstable; they are highly reactive as they seek to combine with another molecule to pair off their free electron. Free radicals are produced in the cell by various mechanisms, including exposure to toxic agents (such as oxygen, radiation, and pollutants or drugs such as ozone or paraquat), enzymatic processes that produce and release free radicals *in vivo*, and others. Common to all of these mechanisms is the ability to provide enough energy to break the covalent bond that holds the two atoms or molecules together.

If A and B are two atoms covalently bonded, and : represents the pair of electrons constituting the bond, the result of normal breakage of this bond—that one atom receives both electrons—can be represented as follows:

$$A:B \rightarrow A:^- +B^+$$

The products are two ions, one with a positive charge (due to the absence of an electron) and one with a negative charge (due to the extra electron). This is the normal situation, for example, in pure water:

$$H:O:H \rightarrow OH:^- +H^+$$

The hydrogen and hydroxide ions are not very reactive. However, if the covalent bond is broken such that each atom receives one electron:

$$A:B \rightarrow A \cdot +B \cdot$$

then two free radicals have formed. If this process took place in water:

$$H:O:H \rightarrow \cdot OH+ H \cdot$$

the resulting hydrogen and hydroxyl radicals would be quite reactive and dangerous.

Free-radical reactions have three biologically important stages: initiation, propagation, and termination. The details of the initiation phase vary depending on the particular atom or molecule involved. For example, the mitochondria of the cell usually reduce oxygen (O_2) in a series of one-electron steps. The result is the frequent formation of univalently reduced oxygen ($O_2 \cdot$), or superoxide radical. This superoxide radical is capable of damaging biological structures, but usually it reacts with hydrogen peroxide (also formed normally in the cell) to yield a hydroxyl radical, a hydroxyl ion, and oxygen:

$$O_2 \cdot^- H_2O_2 \rightarrow \cdot OH+OH^- +O_2$$

In this particular situation, the hydroxyl radical is what enters the next phase and causes the cellular damage. No matter how it is initiated, however, once it is formed, the free radical (represented here as R·) can propagate itself indefinitely:

$$R \cdot +O_2 \rightarrow ROO \cdot$$

$$ROO \cdot +RH \rightarrow ROOH+R \cdot (\text{which can recycle})$$

or it can undergo any of several other possible chemical rearrangements of existing molecules. The rearrangement depicted above is similar to a lipid peroxidation, a process that causes great damage to cell membranes. This continuous cycle of cell damage and free-radical propagation can be terminated by various different processes:

$$R \cdot + R \cdot \rightarrow R{:}R$$

or

$$R \cdot + ROO \cdot \rightarrow ROOR$$

or

$$2ROO \cdot \rightarrow ROOR + O_2$$

or

$$\text{Antioxidant } H + ROO \cdot \rightarrow \text{Antioxidant} \cdot + ROOH$$

This last category of termination reaction is of great interest because it suggests that exogenous antioxidant molecules provide protection against the deleterious effects of free radicals.

To sum up, the reaction of O_2 with four electrons yields three high-energy free radicals and eventually a termination product such as water, and can be visualized as follows:

$$O_2 \rightarrow O_2 \cdot^- \rightarrow H_2O_2 \cdot OH \rightarrow H_2O$$

Cytochrome oxidase efficiently adds four electrons during energy generation in the mitochondria, but some of these toxic intermediates leak out of the inner mitochondrial membrane and can initiate their damaging propagation reactions in the mitochondrion itself (such as causing damage to mitochondrial DNA; see Chapter 10) or perhaps in the membrane lipid components of the cytoplasm (causing lipid peroxidation; see Chapter 11).

Multiple cellular defenses exist to protect the cell against the continual oxidative and free-radical stress to which it is exposed. In general, these can be broadly categorized as compartmentalization, protective enzymes, and antioxidant molecules.

Compartmentalization is the structural segregation of free-radical production sites and substances from other parts of the organism. Most oxidative metabolism, and thus most free-radical production, occurs in the mitochondria, which are structurally isolated from the rest of the cell. Furthermore, many of the naturally occurring defense mechanisms are concentrated about or in the mitochondria, although the cytoplasm and the extracellular fluids also contain antioxidant defenses (Table 9.4). The net effect of this distribution is to create a layered defense concentrated near the sites at greatest risk. In addition, the cells are normally exposed to oxygen concentrations far below those present in air (Table 9.5).

Table 9.4   The Distribution of Cellular Defenses against Free Radicals

Type of defense	Location
Catalase and Mn-SOD	Mitochondrial matrix space
Membrane-bound vitamin E	Mitochondrial inner membrane
Cu–Zn SOD	Mitochondrial inner membrane, matrix space, and cytoplasm
Glutathione peroxidase and catalase	Cytoplasm
Various antioxidant molecules, such as vitamin C, quinon, etc.	Blood plasma, serum, and cytoplasm

Source: From Lippman 1983.

There are many protective enzymes. Two of the more common ones are superoxide dismutase (SOD) and catalase (CAT), which often work together:

$$2H^+ + O_2 \cdot \xrightarrow{\text{SOD}} O_2 + H_2O_2$$

$$H_2O_2 + H_2O_2 \xrightarrow{\text{CAT}} 2H_2O + O_2$$

Another important antioxidant defense enzyme is glutathione peroxidase, which is capable of reducing many peroxides besides the simple H_2O_2 molecule. H_2O_2 is the only peroxide against which catalase can protect the cell.

In addition to these several enzymes, some nonenzymatic molecules are capable of termination reactions with free radicals. The resulting oxidized antioxidant molecules are then either regenerated, or excreted and replaced in the diet. Vitamin E (alpha-tocopherol) is one of the most important biological free-radical quenchers, because of its ability to insert itself into the cell membranes and thereby protect the unsaturated fatty acids (which compose much of the membrane) from oxidative damage. Vitamin E is regenerated, at least *in vitro*, by reaction with ascorbic acid. Unfortunately, the more vitamin E we consume in our

Table 9.5   Oxygen Pressure in Localized Environments of the Body

Location	Partial pressure of O_2 at that location (mm)
Ambient air	158
Tracheal air	149
Alveolar air	100
Arterial blood	95
Venous blood	40
Tissue fluids	1–20

Source: From Balin 1983.

diet, the less we absorb as a proportion of the amount ingested. The rate of absorption appears to be self-limited to about 10 mg per day. Until it can be circumvented, this homeostatic mechanism might limit the usefulness of dietary vitamin E as a segmental intervention. However, continued high levels of vitamin E in the diet do allow for a slow buildup of the compound in various parts of the cell, thus circumventing the absorption limit to some extent.

Vitamin C, or ascorbic acid, is an effective scavenger of the superoxide radical in cells and has been shown to reduce lipid peroxidation in experimental animals. It may have a particularly important role in the lungs, where it is found in high concentration in the extracellular fluid of the respiratory epithelium. (We discussed the value of dietary supplementation of these vitamins in Chapter 7.)

Finally, there are a large number of synthetic antioxidants, most of which were developed for industrial use as stabilizers of rubber or petroleum products. The "BHT" that one often sees on the ingredient list of packaged foods stands for butylated hydroxytoluene, one of the synthetic antioxidants that is widely used to prevent oxygen-based food spoilage. Some others are ethoxyquinone and mercaptoethylamine.

The oxidative-damage theory of aging postulates that all or much of the physiological decrements characteristic of true age-related changes can be ascribed to the intracellular damage done by the various free radicals. Several different cell components are known to be damaged by oxygen-derived free radicals (Table 9.6); lipid peroxidation and DNA damage are probably the most important examples of such damage. The net damage done is the net result of several complex variables, such as the types of free radicals present, their production rate, the structural integrity of the cells, and the activity of the several different antioxidant defense systems present in the organism. Figure 9.7 outlines the interacting systems of oxidative damage in human fibroblasts; note the cascading and pleiotropic effects of a pro-oxidant such as H_2O_2.

An age-related increase in cellular damage due to free radicals might be caused by age-related alterations in any of these several variables. It is an inher-

Table 9.6 **Cell Components Damaged by Reactive O_2 Species**

Component	Damage[a]
Lipids	Peroxidation of unsaturated fatty acids in various membranes
Proteins	Oxidation of SH-containing groups, cross-linking, enzyme inactivation
Carbohydrates	Polysaccharide depolymerization
Nucleic acids	DNA damage, including strand breaks, cross-linking, base hydroxylations, base excision

Source: From Frank 1985.
[a]Also, there is an inhibitory effect on the biosynthesis of proteins, nucleotides, and fatty acids.

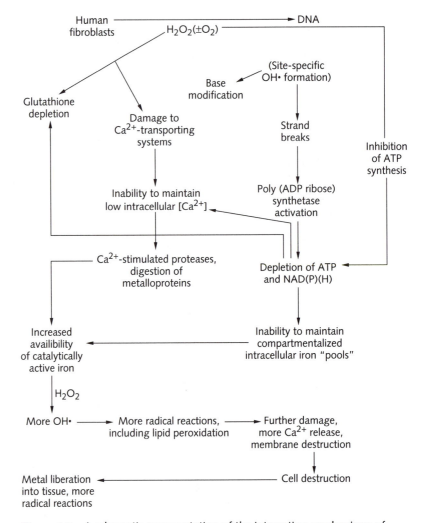

Figure 9.7 A schematic representation of the interacting mechanisms of oxidative damage as exemplified by the action of H_2O_2 on human fibroblasts. H_2O_2 can produce DNA damage, by site-specific generation of hydroxyl radicals and/or by activation of Ca^{2+}-dependent nuclease enzymes. H_2O_2 can also directly inactivate some enzymes involved in ATP synthesis and cause cascading effects by that mechanism. (From Halliwell and Gutteridge 1989.)

ently complex and very plausible concept, but one that most likely cannot be cleanly proven or disproven on the basis of a single experiment. Accordingly, several different types of evidence have been gathered in the testing of this theory.

The interspecific, or evolutionary, approach is to examine the mean levels of various antioxidant defenses in different species and the mean levels of species-specific life spans to determine whether there is any statistical correlation between the two. There appears to be an excellent statistical correlation between

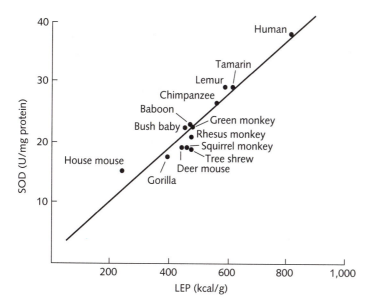

Figure 9.8 The correlation of the species-specific SOD activity in liver tissue (expressed as units of enzyme activity per mg of protein) with the species-specific lifetime energy potential (LEP), or the total lifetime amount of energy per unit of body weight that the species expends. (From Cutler 1983b.)

species-specific life span and species-specific content of molecules such as SOD (Figure 9.8) or other known antioxidant defense system molecules (see Cutler 1984). This analysis is open to the same criticisms regarding the use of life span as a measure of senescence that apply to the interspecific DNA repair studies discussed earlier (Promislow 1993).

An evolutionary comparison more interesting than simply comparing different mammals (as in Figure 9.8) is to compare mammals and birds. As Holmes and Austad (1995) have pointed out, birds live significantly longer than mammals of comparable size, despite having a much higher metabolic rate and blood glucose levels—two traits that are usually associated with accelerated senescence in mammals. This paradox suggested that birds must have specialized protective mechanisms against oxidative damage, and this suggestion turns out to be true. A biochemical investigation of heart mitochondria in rates (life span ca. 4 years) and pigeons (35 years) showed that the pigeon mitochondria leak only 30 percent of the level of free radicals as do the rat mitochondria (Herroro and Barja 1997a,b). This low level of free radicals probably translates into a lower level of oxidative damage. The decreased leakage is apparently due to a number of different changes in the pigeon relative to the rat, suggesting the incremental evolution of a more efficient energy production system.

Another interspecific study that might escape Promislow's (1993) criticism is that of Agarwal and Sohal (1996). Their comparison of five species showed an inverse relationship between the brain's susceptibility to X ray–induced oxidative damage and the maximum life span potential. In other words, the tissues of the longer-lived species appear to be less susceptible to oxidative damage. Agarwal and Sohal also measured the same damage parameter at two different ages within one species and showed that there was an age-related increase in oxidative damage to proteins, suggesting that the parameter was measuring a senescent change and not simply a change due to a variable other than aging. It would have been better to take these measurements in all five species tested, but the point is proven in principle.

There are several different types of intraspecific approaches. One strategy consists of administering antioxidants to experimental animals and then determining whether the treatment has had any effect on their life span. The addition and withdrawal of vitamin E to and from the diet of the nematode yielded clear results that are in excellent agreement with the predictions of the theory: Both the mean and the maximum life span shifted in accordance with the exogenous vitamin E supplied (Table 9.7). Vitamin E supplementation in the diet of *Paramecium* (see Chapter 4) resulted in a significantly increased clonal life span, regardless of whether the life span was measured chronologically (in days) or functionally (in number of fissions) (Thomas and Nyberg 1988).

Some very interesting data were obtained by vitamin E supplementation of the diet of the banana fruit fly, *Zapronius paravittiger* (Kakkar, Bains, and Sharma 1996). Every dose tested increased longevity above the normal control value. The optimum dose for extension of longevity in either sex was 5 µg/ml of food. Higher doses yielded intermediate median and maximum life spans; doses greater than 25 µg/ml yielded longevities that were significantly decreased relative to the longevities of the controls. Furthermore, at the optimum dose, the animals exhibited a significantly decreased level of malondialdehyde (an end product of lipid peroxidation) and significantly increased levels of antioxidant enzymes (catalase and peroxidase) throughout their life span. The mechanism by which vitamin E acts to increase enzyme activities is not clear. It is clear, though, that the beneficial effects of vitamin E are mediated through its effect on the antioxidant defense system. The banana fruit fly responds in a similar manner when its diet is supplemented with 100-millimolar methionine, an essential amino acid that can inhibit

Table 9.7   **The Effect of Exogenous Vitamin E on Nematode Life Span**

Treatment	Day added or withdrawn	Life span (days) Mean	Maximum
None	—	36	53
Vitamin E added	1	49	73
	10	41	62
	20	33	62
	30	35	62
Vitamin E withdrawn	Always present	46	70
	10	39	66
	6	36	63
	0	31	57

Source: From Balin 1983.

production of the superoxide radical (Sharma, Sharma, and Kakkar 1995). Taken together, these two experiments suggest that higher levels of antioxidants are sufficient to increase longevity in this laboratory invertebrate.

However, when the same type of experiment was tried with rodents, but using antioxidants other than vitamin E (because of the homeostatic limits on its absorption), the results were very different. Table 9.8 compiles the results of several of these experiments. In Experiment 1, median but not maximum life span increased, suggesting that the antioxidants delayed or prevented some of the early deaths. In Experiment 2, both mean and maximum life span increased considerably over the control values. However, the control values appear to be abnormally low when compared to those of Experiment 1, and these mice show no effect if compared to the best available control data. The same analysis applies to Experiment 4. In Experiment 3, the additives appear to have decreased the mean but not the maximum life span, suggesting that they brought about some early deaths—a result that contradicts the result of Experiment 1.

Only in Experiment 5 was there any apparently significant increase in both the mean and the maximum life span of the treated group relative to the controls. However, these last results are confounded by the fact that the treated animals weighed significantly less than the controls. Thus it is impossible to determine which factor—the additive or the caloric restriction—caused the increase in life span. None of the synthetic additives were developed for their palatability, so they may have imparted a bad taste to the mice, who thereupon might have voluntar-

Table 9.8 **The Effect of Dietary Antioxidants on the Life Span of Mice**

Experiment strain number	Additive	Life span (months)		Mean weight (g)
		Median ± SD	Maximum	
1. LAF$_1$ ♂	None	20.0 ± 8.1	42	30.2
	MEA (1%)[a]	22.9 ± 10.8	42	27.0
2. LAF$_1$ ♂	None	14.5 ± 4.6	26	31.6
	BHT (0.5%)[b]	20.9 ± 4.7	30	29.2
3. Swiss ♂	None	22.0 ± 4.4	29	—
	MEA (1%)[a]	18.0 ± 3.7	29	—
	Cysteine (1%)	19.0 ± 4.0	29	—
4. C57BL ♀	None (range of 3 experiments)	20.6 ± 27.7	28.4 ± 33.9	40–42
	BHT[b]	27.2	33.6	37
	MEA[a]	26.3	33.2	40
5. C3H ♀	None	17.7 ± 0.8	23.6	1X
	EQ (0.5%)[c]	21.2 ± 0.9	29.6	≈0.75X

Source: Data from Balin 1983.
[a]2-Mercaptoethylamine HCl.
[b]Butylated hydroxytoluene.
[c]Ethoxyquinone.

ily decreased their dietary intake. Note that on average, the treated animals weighed less than the controls in each of the experiments.

An increased life span due to underfeeding has been reported in a wide variety of organisms. Perhaps the nematodes of Table 9.7 and the fruit flies mentioned here simply have less-sensitive tastes than do the mice, or perhaps they have no homeostatic limit on vitamin E absorption. In any event, the data are confusing, for they both support and contradict the theoretical expectations. They do, however, strongly indicate that dietary supplementation of these synthetic antioxidants, for whatever reason, is not an effective antioxidant intervention for mice, at least with respect to increasing life span. The strong epidemiological and prospective data indicating the protective effects of dietary vitamins C and E with respect to prevention of morbidity in humans (see Chapter 7) is an observation consistent with the results of Experiment 1 (see Table 9.8). On speculation, it seems possible that the beneficial effects of vitamin supplementation are species-specific, increasing both mean and maximum longevity in some forms but only abolishing premature mortality in other forms. It is also possible that the protective effects of vitamin E are much greater than those of the synthetic antioxidants, and this disparity may account for the differences in the data.

Another intraspecific approach to testing the oxidative-damage theory is to raise animals under conditions known to increase or decrease the production of free radicals and to determine the effect on their life span. Exposing different strains of nematodes to high concentrations of either oxygen or paraquat, both of which are known to generate high levels of free radicals *in situ*, gave the following results: Development was inhibited and mean life span decreased, suggesting that both of these complex processes could be adversely affected by oxidative damage (Hartman, Childress, and Beyer 1995).

Another approach is to measure the reactants or the products of oxidation. It is very difficult to measure free radicals directly, especially *in vivo*. It is much more feasible to measure the end products of free-radical formation. One easily measured end product is the group of intracellular pigments collectively known as lipofuscin. A detailed description and analysis of this pigment and its significance in research on aging is contained in Chapter 11. For the present, suffice it to say that the lipofuscin granules accumulate slowly within the cell. They are believed to be the end product of a variety of processes, of which free radical–induced lipid peroxidation is believed to be the major one.

Working on the assumption that the formation of free radicals in poikilothermic houseflies is proportional to the amount of their physical activity, Sohal and Donato (1978) raised male houseflies under spatial conditions in which they could fly about freely (the "high activity" group) or could only walk but not fly (the "low activity" group). The low-activity animals showed not only a significant increase in their mean and maximum life spans relative to the high-activity controls, but also a much lower rate of lipofuscin formation, thereby suggesting that the rate of oxidative damage is modulated by the rate of physical activity and has something to do with the rate of aging. This suggestion was supported by Sohal and Donato's observation that there is an inverse relationship between catalase activity and inorganic peroxide concentrations over the life span of the housefly:

The catalase activity was high at young ages and then steadily decreased; the peroxide concentration was initially low and then increased (Sohal et al. 1983).

In a related experiment, Sohal, Toy, and Allen (1986) found that they could identify at midlife, by means of their activity, certain potentially long-lived and short-lived individuals of the same housefly population. Biochemical assays done on these individuals showed that the short-lived animals had lower levels of antioxidant defense activities (such as SOD and catalase activities or glutathione levels) and higher levels of inorganic peroxides and other biochemical indicators of free-radical activity. These data again lend themselves to the same interpretation and are consistent with the theoretical predictions of the oxidative-damage theory.

Methionine is an essential amino acid and is capable of inhibiting production of the superoxide radical. Feeding this compound to a certain species of fruit fly led to a significant increase in mean and maximum life span, an increased level of catalase and peroxidase activity, and a decreased level of lipid or inorganic peroxides (Sharma, Sharma, and Kakkar 1995).The induction of antioxidant defenses by feeding will be of some interest if it turns out to be a general finding.

Genetic studies with *Drosophila* have shown that there is also a very clear inverse relationship between the levels of antioxidant defenses on the one hand, and the levels of oxidative damage on the other hand. The long-lived (L strain) animals are known to live long because they delay the onset of senescence (Arking and Wells 1990). The data in Figure 9.9 show that delayed onset appears to be due to the presence in the L animals of a "protective phase" characterized by high antioxidant defense (Cu–Zn SOD) levels and low oxidative damage (carbonyl protein) levels. This period begins at about 5 days of age, when the L animals exhibit a coordinate up-regulation in the gene expression of their antioxidant defense system (Dudas and Arking 1995), and ends at about day 33, when the defense system begins to fail and oxidative damage begins to accumulate. This "damage phase" is presumed to bring about senescence and the loss of function. Note that the normal-lived (R strain) animals do not exhibit a protective phase; rather they move right into the damage phase. Thus, the extended longevity that is characteristic of the L animal is due to early life events involving the early activation and later inactivation of the antioxidant defense system.

A transgenic experiment by Orr and Sohal (1994) showed that increasing the number of the genes encoding Cu–Zn SOD and catalase led to a significant increase in the activities of these enzymes in the genetically altered animals, a corresponding decrease in their oxidative damage, and an increase in both the mean and maximum life span. In Chapter 10 we will discuss some important caveats regarding this experiment. The point, however, is that three experiments using very different approaches (feeding, selection, gene dosage) to manipulate the fly's antioxidant defense system nonetheless led to very similar conclusions regarding the role of the free radicals and of antioxidant protection in determining life span.

These conclusions are not restricted to flies. A cross-sectional biochemical study done on gerbils showed that the level of molecular oxidative damage to proteins and to DNA increases with age, and that the increased oxidative damage is due both to an elevation in the rates of oxidant generation and an increase in the

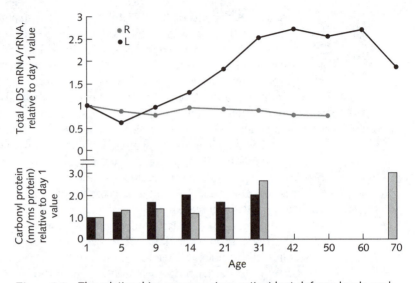

Figure 9.9 The relationships among aging, antioxidant defense levels, and oxidative damage in a normal-lived strain (R) and a long-lived strain (L) of *Drosophila*. The lifetime antioxidant defense levels are exemplified by the total measure antioxidant (ADS) mRNAs measured in each strain, expressed relative to the day 1 values, and are represented by the line graphs. The lifetime oxidative damage levels are exemplified by the nM/mg of carbonyl protein levels measured in each strain, expressed relative to the day 1 values, and are represented by the bar graphs. Note that during the first six weeks of adult life, the ADS levels in the L strain animals increase, whereas they stay low and steady in the R strain animals. During the first three weeks at least, the oxidative damage levels in the L strain animals stay at a relatively steady level that is lower than the level in the R strain. By the fourth week of adult life, this protective effort does not seem to be effective (for reasons that are presently unknown) and the L strain animals undergo senescence (Data from Arking et al. 1998.)

susceptibility of the tissues to oxidative damage (Sohal, Agarwal, and Sohal 1995). Thus the age-related increase in oxidative damage might be attributed to higher levels of free-radical generation, presumably by the mitochondria in aerobic muscles such as the heart, as well as to a decreased antioxidant protective ability on the part of the animals' defense mechanisms. Similar data have been compiled for many different organisms (for example, see Halliwell and Gutteridge 1989). For example, the short-lived senescence-accelerated mice (SAM-P) are reported to have a higher rate of lipid peroxidation than their SAM-resistant (non-short-lived) controls (SAM-R) (Park et al. 1996). Interestingly, the increased rate of oxidative damage is thought to be associated with a decreased rate of transport of Cu–Zn SOD into the mitochondria. Note that this association represents a life span-limiting control at a posttranslational step. When the SAM-P mice were treated with an injectable free radical-trapping compound for 1 month, they showed a significant decrease in their levels of oxidative damage (Butterfield et al. 1997). In addition to demonstrating the existence of intraspecific baseline differences in antioxidant defense activity in mice, these studies demonstrate that injectable chemicals can, in principle, alter these baseline levels. When combined with the data regarding dietary guidelines and vitamin supplementation (Ames, Shigenaga, and Hagen 1993), this observation suggests that the presumably genetically set baseline levels of antioxidants can be altered by environmental modulation. This possibility offers hope of eventual practical interventions (see Chapter 7).

Macaque monkeys are being used to determine biomarkers of aging (see Chapter 3). The factors being used in constructing the biomarkers, and in estimating the rate of biological aging derived from them, include no measurements of antioxidants. Thus the observation that the levels of seven circulating antioxidants in the blood of the monkeys showed an inverse relationship with the calculated rate of biological aging is particularly persuasive, especially when it was also shown that the antioxidant level influenced the animal's susceptibility to disease (Short, Williams, and Bowden 1997).

Finally, note that high blood glutathione levels in humans are correlated with high self-rated health scores, while low blood glutathione levels are statistically associated with low self-rated health scores (Julius and Lang 1988). Furthermore, a prospective longitudinal study involving 2,900 men over an 18-year period revealed that significantly elevated blood levels of vitamins C and A are associated with significantly lower risks of death due to ischemic heart disease, while low levels of vitamin C and beta-carotene are associated with a significantly higher risk of death due to cardiovascular disease (Stahelin et al. 1989). These epidemiological findings have been amplified in recent years by several other studies, as discussed in Chapter 7. Although these correlational data do not address causation, and might well suffer from various confounding effects, they do suggest that the laboratory findings to date—namely, that intraspecific variation in antioxidant levels is correlated with various indices of morbidity—are applicable to humans.

These findings are not limited to animals. Senescence in the plant leaf (see Chapter 4) has been shown to be correlated both with decreases in catalase activity and with increases in lipid peroxidation and membrane permeability (Strother 1988). We have pointed out that the senescence of annual plants begins with the death of their leaves; thus the processes of leaf abscission are connected to organismic senescence. In a similar fashion, a strain of the common bacterium *E. coli* that has an enhanced capacity for glutathione synthesis is more resistant to the lethal effects of gamma irradiation (and the free radicals produced by that treatment) than is the control strain. The resistance is abolished when glutathione synthesis is inhibited (Moore et al. 1989). These findings suggest that environmental damage in representatives of other kingdoms also depends on oxidative damage, and thus senescence in a variety of other forms may use many of the same mechanisms as are characteristic of animal senescence.

It is much more difficult to manipulate life span in homeothermic vertebrates than in poikilothermic invertebrates such as houseflies, so comparable experiments are not done on mammals. However, other approaches are possible. For example, 28-month-old mice fed a diet high in vitamin E throughout their life were shown to possess the same concentrations of lipofuscin in their heart muscle as did 22-month-old control mice, even though no extension in life span was noted (Blackett and Hall 1981a, 1981b). Such data might relate more to the quality of life than to the length of life. Other experiments in which various antioxidants were fed to mice also showed a decrease in the lipofuscin levels, but showed no effect on other life span parameters (Tappel et al. 1973).

These findings are consistent with the observations that high levels of lipofuscin are characteristically found in animals with vitamin E deficiencies, and are part of the information that has led to the conclusion that lipid peroxidation is positively correlated with the polyunsaturated fatty acid (PUFA) concentrations in the membrane and negatively correlated with the concentrations of antioxidants such as vitamin E (Lippman 1983). Our cells depend on high PUFA levels for normal membrane functioning and elasticity, yet the same PUFAs subject our cells to peroxidative damage arising from oxygen metabolism. In the absence of sufficient antioxidants, the PUFAs of the cell membrane, which are part of the compartmentalization antioxidant defense system, are susceptible to oxidative damage. Different regions of the brain undergo complex age-related declines in various different antioxidant enzymes (Benzi et al. 1989). This fact may take on particular importance in view of the fact that the brain uses about one-fifth of the total oxygen demand of the body. The spatially distinct antioxidant enzyme patterns could provide the structural basis for the spatial and temporal pattern of cellular damage and/or decrement observed during the aging process.

The best approach to testing the oxidative-damage theory is the genetic strategy, in which one can either (1) construct long-lived and short-lived animals and then assay them to determine if their antioxidant defense systems have been altered in the expected manner, or (2) construct animals that have genetically altered levels of antioxidant defense systems and then test them for their effect on life span and rate of aging. Both of these experiments have been done and were first discussed in Chapter 6. They will be discussed at greater length in Chapter 10. In general, the results of both types of experiments are entirely consistent with the predictions of the oxidative-damage theory. The available data from *Drosophila*, *C. elegans*, and *Neurospora* indicate that life span is positively correlated with the levels of antioxidant defenses, and the *Drosophila* data further demonstrate that manipulating the levels of antioxidant defenses brings about a corresponding alteration in the life span. This is a very exciting and promising lead.

Parsons (1995) suggested that resistance to oxidative stress is the fundamental trait through which long life is expressed. The work of our laboratory has shown that antioxidant resistance is the only factor causally involved in the expression of extended longevity in our strains. We have reason to believe that there is some relationship between an organism's ability to resist oxidative damage and certain aspects of its energy metabolism. If these preliminary thoughts are substantiated by subsequent data, we may be approaching a deep level of biological mechanisms. At the last Dahlem Conference on the Molecular Biology of Aging, one of the major conclusions was that oxidative damage plays a pivotal role not only because of its direct effects on the cell's components but also because it can react synergistically with other processes so as to accelerate other molecular mechanisms of aging, such as mitochondrial dysfunction, altered protein processing, and nuclear genome instability (Martin et al. 1995). The observation that the appearance of many signs and symptoms of aging are coordinated is not new; the idea that they may be linked at a deep biological level through the intervention of a common mechanism such as oxidative damage is an interesting and challenging concept (Parsons 1995; Martin, Austad, and Johnson 1996).

Taken as a whole, the data demonstrate the existence within organisms of a genetically programmed response to limit stochastic damage arising from oxidative stress. Such damage may not be the only mechanism involved in the aging and senescence of various kinds of organisms, but it is certainly a major component in many species. Equally important is the organism's response and its genetic modulation of the oxidative stresses it faces. This variable response may well account for the heterogeneity in life histories.

• *Summary*

Our cells are thermodynamically unstable structures. Their highly ordered molecular structure is under continual attack by a variety of stochastic (random) degradative events and processes. We have examined several such processes that have been suggested as being major mechanisms in the aging processes. All of them occur in living systems, and all of them might have serious ramifications in bringing on the diseases associated with aging, but not all of them fulfill the theoretical predictions expected if they are causal, or even just major, processes in aging. On this basis, the wear-and-tear, somatic mutation, DNA damage, and error catastrophe theories are each no longer considered to be the sole potential candidate for a mechanism of aging, although the experiments that were involved in their proof and/or disproof are now an essential part of the intellectual history of the field.

The somatic mutation, error catastrophe, and DNA damage theories may well describe important but secondary mechanisms involved in the aging process. The cross-linkage theory is partly substantiated, since cross-linking clearly plays a major role in connective tissues, but it is not clear if cross-linking might also be a major mechanism in other cells and tissues. The oxidative-damage theory has a large amount of persuasive evidence supporting its main points, although it is not yet critically proven. In particular, it remains to be demonstrated in detail how important oxidative damage is in bringing about the types of damage that lead to age-related dysfunction in key organs and tissues. At this time, this particular theory appears to be both a promising theory that can guide us to develop more effective interventions and a plausible and probable mechanism through which the other factors regulating the aging process may be expressed.

The cell can maintain itself in the face of these insults only by focusing substantial amounts of energy on defense and repair processes. Since stochastic processes are time dependent and thus might be presumed to occur at a constant rate, and if we assume that repair processes are generally not 100 percent efficient, then we expect the amount of damage to increase with age. Under these circumstances, at first glance the age-related decrease in the organism's defense and repair activities seems suicidal, because any decrement in these activities will inevitably bring about the eventual senescence and death of the organism. Yet the factors that govern the life span of any species are based on evolutionary, not teleological, criteria. As discussed in Chapter 4, these evolutionary factors are intimately involved with the species' particular life history and reproductive strategy.

The energetic costs of reproduction probably increase little with age. However, the decreasing efficiency of the organism reduces the amount of energy available to it. Therefore, with increasing age, the energetic costs of repair begin to outweigh the energetic costs of reproduction; this appears to be the point at which the force of natural selection begins to decrease. Evolutionary theory suggests that at this point the repair activities of the aging organism should decrease, and they do. In this context one can view these stochastic theories as systemic theories: It is not so much that the incidence of damage has increased as it is that the ability to repair cannot be maintained and the resulting damage spills out in a cascade of interrelated pleiotropic events. If so, our attention should be focused on whatever underlies this decreasing ability to repair.

10

Systemic Theories of Aging

If Aging Is Systemic, Why Is There So Much Variability?

Systemic theories of biological function often invoke thoughts of an organized program designed to bring about the function in question. The word "program" means different things in different contexts, but to biologists the term is probably thought to derive from and refer to computer science, where it means a set of coded instructions that the computer must follow in order to complete the task assigned to it. One implication of this concept is the idea that there is a very tight and very precise linkage between the coded instructions and the operation of the computer; the computer can do nothing that is not accurately written down in the instructional sequence beforehand. "Garbage in, garbage out" is the motto of those who are all too familiar with the mindless computer's inability to adapt to even a small deviation or error in the instructions. Molecular biologists use terms such as "genetic program" or "developmental program" as a convenient short-hand way of describing the coordinated and sequential events that all together constitute organismic development. This adoption of a metaphor originally developed in cybernetics makes it easy to assume that the rigor and precision of the computer term is equally valid of the biological term. This is not correct.

Wilkins (1986), in an excellent review of developmental genetics, pointed out correctly that many of the processes upon which normal plant and animal development depends—for example, the cell–cell contact and communication that is absolutely vital for the normal induction and formation of most of our internal organs—are not directly specified by the nucleotide sequence in the genome. These absolutely essential processes are emergent properties, implicit perhaps in our definition of what we expect normal ectodermal or mesodermal cells, for example, to do, but not explicitly set down (Edelman 1988). For example, there are many instances in embryonic development when different cells predictably migrate to certain regions of the body and meet up with another population of distinct cells originating elsewhere that have predictably migrated to the same area, and the two populations interact in such a way that they form a new tissue type that was not previously present. To the best of our knowledge, no gene directs an ectodermal cell to migrate to a specific position and there interact in a certain way with a mesodermal cell type that bears complementary instructions. Since these are emergent properties that are not precisely spelled out in any single DNA strand, we should not be surprised if any two organisms show significant environmentally modulated variation in the timing and manner with which these higher-order interactions are expressed.

As a result of this "noise in the system," the developmental program of humans, for example, gives rise after about 266 days to a baby. But as any obstetrician and most mothers know, very few infants are born after exactly 266 days of development. Most (about 75 percent) are born sometime within 252 to 278 days, and a substantial minority are born at even more extreme times. These differences amount to more than a 10 percent variation in normal developmental rate. Our own developmental program yields not a precise result, but a normal probability distribution of results. Now, if aging is due to some sort of systemic cascade of interactions between gene and environment, why should we be so surprised when human adults—subjected to considerably more environmental modulation than is any fetus—show comparable variation in the times at which individuals display various biomarkers of aging? The presence of variation in aging is not an argument against systemic theories, nor is it an argument for stochastic theories. It simply exists.

For the purposes of this discussion, it will be helpful to reiterate what we pointed out in Chapter 8. The term "systemic" is being used here to denote an explanation based on the occurrence of a hierarchical cascade of interconnected events. I most emphatically do *not* mean an explanation based on the idea of determinative and sequential gene action designed to produce aging. That would constitute an adaptive theory of aging (that we age because there is a particular reason for us to age), and, as we saw in Chapter 4, aging has evolved not because it is adaptive but because the force of natural selection declines with age (we age because there is no reason not to age). By "systemic," we mean simply interlocking or cascade mechanisms that can give rise to a sequential series of common aging phenotypes.

We will consider two classes of systemic theories of aging, both of which are fundamentally genetic. The difference between them lies more in the incomplete state of our knowledge than in a fundamental difference in their biology; thus the distinction is based on pedagogical convenience, and the blurry boundary between them may disappear in future. In the first case, the aging process is postulated to be under the influence of a general process, such as metabolism, which itself is known to be under the control of a large number of genes. Metabolism is a complex process, but one that has been intuitively felt to be consistent with the complexity of the events involved in the aging process. In the other case, the aging process is defined to be more or less directly under the primary control of one or more (but some small number of) certain specified genes. In many ways, this situation is similar to the standard sort of gene-controlled developmental process in which a given gene is shown to synthesize the molecules involved in a particular process or structure. This relatively small number of primary events is then thought to give rise, by a cascade mechanism, to the complexities of the aging process. But a caveat is in order here: When we talk about metabolism, we are using one word to describe an incredibly complex interplay of hundreds, if not thousands, of individual gene-controlled and environmentally modulated reactions with multiple feedback loops that impart robust homeostatic properties to the network. Evidence of strong genetic control is difficult to discern at this level.

"Metabolism" is an all-inclusive term. When we shift our focus to a subset of metabolism—oxidative damage, for example—and discuss the effects of alterations in specific gene activities, it is much easier to find evidence of strong genetic control of the aging processes that are dependent on oxidative stress and damage. There is probably no conceptual difference between these two topics of discussion. As we learn more about the details of general processes such as metabolism and can talk with meaning about its components, eventually our discussions will shift entirely to talk of specific processes and how they interact with one another.

• *Systemic Theories*

Metabolic Theories

It has long been known that bigger animals have a longer life span than do their smaller relatives (see Figure 4.12) and that metabolic rate is inversely proportional to body weight. The early coupling of these related facts led to the belief that longevity and metabolism are bound together in a causal relationship—that high metabolic rates lead to, or are associated with, short life spans. In Chapter 7, we briefly reviewed some of the information suggesting that experimental alterations of metabolic rate are capable of producing, in some organisms, corresponding alterations in life span. In addition, we have presented data showing that the metabolic rate appears to decline with advancing age (see Figures 5.43 and 5.44). These and other similar observations led to the widespread concept that longevity can be best understood as a function of metabolic decline. The two theories we will discuss in this section propose rather different mechanisms to account for the metabolic decline. As a result, they give rise to rather different predictions.

The Rate-of-Living Theory

This particularly venerable theory was first proposed by Buffon in 1749 and was effectively popularized by Pearl in 1928. It states that longevity is inversely proportional to metabolic rate. The concept was based on the earlier observations of Rubner (1908), who noted (erroneously, as it later turned out) that mammalian species with very different species-specific life spans nonetheless expend a similar amount of metabolic energy per gram body weight per lifetime. This was equivalent to saying that all animal cells had the same fixed amount of calories available to them. Later, Loeb and Northrop (1917) reported that poikilothermic animals, such as *Drosophila*, show an inverse relationship between adult life span and ambient temperature. They inferred (but did not prove) that this situation arises as a result of the temperature-dependent breakdown and/or accumulation of various metabolites critical to the organism's health. Pearl (1928) then wove these observations, among others, into his rate-of-living theory.

The original theory makes two strong predictions: (1) There is a predetermined amount of metabolic energy (a metabolic potential) available to the organism that can be expressed equally well in terms of oxygen consumption per life span or kilocalories expended per life span, and when this amount of energy is gone, the organism dies. (2) There is an inverse relationship between metabolic rate and aging. The theory sounded plausible and was widely accepted, despite the confused and circular logic that Pearl used in writing about it (Lints 1989). However, recent findings indicate that the theory is incorrect as commonly stated, although some data do support it. We will discuss both sides of the issue.

The first prediction has been disproved by the comparative analyses of metabolic rates in different species of animals. For example, the data obtained from the analysis of 77 species of mammals (see Figure 7.7) show that these different mammals have not just one predetermined metabolic potential but a spectrum of lifetime energy potentials with values ranging from 220 to 781 kilocalories per gram per lifetime. Experiments on invertebrates have shown that different species of insects also have quite different metabolic potentials. Thus different species have different metabolic potentials, in contradiction to the theory's predictions. However, other available data logically suggested that within each species there is no variability in the metabolic potential—and that different populations and individuals of the same species have the same potential value. The demonstration by Sohal and Donato (1978) that low-activity flies live longer than high-activity flies (see Chapter 9) was widely interpreted as showing that the total amount of calories a fly can expend (or of oxygen that it could consume, which is just another way of measuring the same thing) is fixed and that the length of its life depends on whether it spends them quickly or slowly. This interpretation seemed to be substantiated by the many observations showing that poikilothermic animals, whose metabolic rate was known to be proportional to the ambient temperature, live longer when kept at low temperatures than when kept at high temperatures. In fact, such results were thought to support the theory's second prediction, of an inverse relationship between metabolic rate and life span.

However, more recent data show that the metabolic potential not only differs among species, but does not even stay at a constant value for different populations of the same species. In one study, individuals from a genetically selected long-lived (L) strain of *Drosophila* and individuals from their progenitor normal-lived (R) strain were raised at different temperatures, and their metabolic rates were measured (Figure 10.1). The mean daily metabolic rates of the two strains were statistically equivalent to each other across the range of tested temperatures. The long-lived organisms spent about the same number of calories per day and in much the same manner as did the normal controls, yet they lived significantly longer. As a consequence, during their entire life span the long-lived

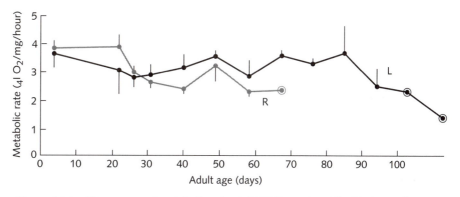

Figure 10.1 The measured metabolic rate at 22°C throughout the lifetimes of a normal-lived control strain (R) and a long-lived strain (L) of *Drosophila*. (From Arking et al. 1988.)

strains expended about 40 percent more calories than did the normal-lived strains, simply because they lived longer. The L strains have a significantly higher metabolic potential. The conclusion is inescapable that the long-lived *Drosophila* strains do not bring about their increased longevity simply by husbanding their calories (Arking et al. 1988). Another mechanism must be involved.

Conclusive evidence that at least two different physiological functions are involved in the aging process of these *Drosophila* is shown in Figure 7.6. Within each strain, temperature can alter life span. However, these environmental treatments are clearly incapable of overcoming the genetically based interstrain differences. Not only do the environmental and genetic treatments exert their particular effects on life span by affecting separate physiological compartments, but their effects are probably additive. Metabolic rate appears to be only one of several factors that regulate the life span of an individual organism. The theory is plausible, but it oversimplifies aging by reducing it to the manipulations of a single dependent variable. The predictions made on the basis of this simplistic model have not been upheld by the data.

In the nematode, recent studies have shown that there is a class of genes that alter the length or timing of diverse biological cycles such as the cell cycle, embryonic and postembryonic development, activity periods, and life span (Hekimi, Boutis, and Lakowski 1995; Wong, Boutis, and Hekimi 1995). Because of their effects on biological timing, these genes are called *clock* (*clk*) genes. The most interesting observation is that four of these *clock* genes interact genetically to significantly extend life span. For example, the *clk-1 clk-2* double mutant has a life span of 28.2 days, which is significantly greater than the life span of either single-gene mutant by itself (about 19 days) (Lakowski and Hekimi 1996). (This finding is similar to the observation of Orr and Sohal [1994] that their transgenic flies require both the catalase and *CuZnSOD* genes for their life span to be extended; see Chapter 6.) Furthermore, the *clk* genes interact with the *daf* genes (a class of developmental stress-response genes that also extend longevity; see Chapter 6) such that an animal containing both types of genes (*clk-1* and *daf-2*) lives at least three times as long (49.1 ± 1.9 days) as either single-gene mutant by itself (8.6 to 15.9 days). The importance of this finding is that it demonstrates for the first time the interaction of two different genetic pathways in extending longevity in any organism.

The empirical demonstration of the existence of more than one pathway verifies the assumptions of many people and illustrates how a small number of genes may have widespread pleiotropic effects. The discovery of the *clock* genes and their role in extending longevity via what appears to be a general slowing of various physiological events lends new support to the rate-of-living hypothesis. Although the mutants may have a lower metabolic rate, more likely they have an altered control of metabolism. It is not known how this altered control leads to a longer life span, but an altered control of metabolism might well lead to a reduced rate of oxidative damage and thus to a more gradual rate of aging. The involvement of the *daf* genes, at least one of which (*daf-2*) is thought to be identical to the *age-1* gene, which is likely to be a negative regulator of superoxide dismutase activity (see Chapter 6), lends credence to this hypothesis. These investigations may shed some light on the manner in which caloric restriction alters energy metabolism in rodents and primates.

It has been proposed that the rate-of-living theory should be updated in light of new knowledge and its prediction restated as follows: "The rate of aging is directly related to the rate of unrepaired molecular damage inflicted by the by-products of oxygen metabolism, and is inversely related to the efficiency of antioxidant and reparative mechanisms" (Sohal 1986, p. 41). This redefinition clearly equates the rate-of-living theory with the oxidative-damage theory of aging (see Chapter 9). The oxidative-damage theory is very plausible and offers a good working hypothesis as to the nature of the mechanisms involved in aging. However, translating the one theory into the other seems to serve only to keep alive a (mostly) discredited theory by metamorphosing it into something else. It seems best to leave the simplistic theory behind us and focus our attention on the very plausible and probable mechanisms underlying the more complex and more sophisticated oxidative-damage theory. The framers of the rate-of-living theory may well have been correct in their assessment that metabolic processes are controlling aging and longevity, but they probably erred in their effort to reduce all aging phenomena to alterations in a single parameter. There is no reason for us to continue the error.

Mitochondrial-Damage Theories

Another approach that seeks to lay an updated metabolic framework under the aging process is exemplified by theories suggesting that the cause of the physiological senescence that is characteristic of aging cells resides in the cumulative effects of oxidative injury to the mitochondria. In this view, the sequence of events that lead to aging, as postulated by Miquel and Fleming (1984) and by Wallace and colleagues (1995), is as follows. First, as we know already, as embryonic cells differentiate they usually lose the ability to divide (see Chapter 11). Second, in the same process, cells lose the ability to rapidly repair and replace their mitochondria. Even though the mitochondria in irreversibly differentiated nondividing or very slowly dividing cells can divide, they do so at a very reduced turnover time (about 1 month) when compared to nondifferentiated and rapidly replicating cells. Thus the mitochondria of nondividing differentiated cells must last much longer than the mitochondria of rapidly dividing cells.

The third, and key, point is that, as is well known, all of the oxygen consumption by the cell takes place on the inner membrane of the mitochondria. This is the site where oxygen-induced free radicals form—in fact, the production of these free radicals is a mandatory side effect of mitochondrial respiration—and where they might be most likely to cause peroxidative damage to the structural and functional components of the mitochondrial membrane. The molecules involved in the final steps of energy production are located within and are part of this mitochondrial membrane. Therefore, the accumulation of peroxidative damage to the mitochondrial membrane would be expected to impair the mitochondrion's ability to produce energy. This impairment alone might account for many of the metabolic and physiological declines, such as the decreased metabolic rates (see Figure 10.1) that are almost always observed in aging cells and organisms. It is well known that damaged mitochondria are often (but not inevitably) found in aged cells (see Figure 5.12).

Finally, the free radicals may also cause irreparable damage to the DNA (see Chapter 9) of the mitochondrial genome (which is separate from the nuclear genome)—damage that could well result in an accelerated loss of the organelle's energy production and that might lead, in turn, to further decreases in the cell's replicative and repair abilities. It is speculative but plausible to assume that such decreases lead to the pleiotropic onset of at least some common age-related dysfunctions; however, hard evidence of this connection is still needed.

This "oxygen radical–mitochondrial injury" theory has the advantage over the older rate-of-living concept in that it postulates that aging is due to certain specific and measurable reactions, taking place in defined structures, that bring about particular types of molecular damage and physiological senescence. In this sense, the new theory is certainly more susceptible to precise testing than were the older concepts. It is also attractive inasmuch as it ties all of the many observations on decreased metabolic functioning together with the high plausibility of the free radical–oxidative damage theory. But attractiveness is one thing, and proof is another. What does the evidence say?

Mitochondria are self-replicating organelles that have their own DNA (mtDNA). In humans, the mtDNA is a closed circle of 16,569 nucleotides that encode the genes for 13 proteins of the electron transport chain, as well as 2 RNAs and 22 tRNAs. Each cell can contain hundreds or even thousands of mitochondria, and each mitochondrion can contain numerous mtDNA molecules (Wallace 1992). Mitochondria replicate even in nondividing cells such as brain, heart, and skeletal muscle; the turnover time in rats is about 1 month (Menzies and Gold 1972). It has been estimated that the amount of reactive oxygen species, or free radicals, generated by the mitochondria is as much as 4 percent of the oxygen they consume. Probably because of the proximity to such high levels of very reactive radicals, oxidative damage to mtDNA has been estimated to be more than ten times higher than the damage to nuclear DNA. Somatic mtDNA mutations in humans—consisting of deletions, duplications, and base substitutions—are preferentially found in certain regions of the brain (basal ganglia, cerebral cortex), skeletal muscle, and heart. All three of these nondividing tissues have a high rate of oxidative metabolism.

The temporal association of mutant mtDNA with certain types of damage by-products is consistent with the view that the mutations are the result of oxidative damage (Wallace et al. 1995). During aging, the mtDNA damage appears to accumulate exponentially, and this rapid rise late in life suggests that the mutant mtDNAs are preferentially replicated. We need a mechanism to explain this preferential replication. One explanation suggests that the nuclei in the vicinity of mutant mtDNA detect the cell's energy deficiency and signal the surrounding mtDNAs to replicate in an effort to alleviate the deficiency. There are theoretical reasons to believe that the mutant mtDNAs, which are smaller than normal mtDNAs, would replicate faster and thus be favored in this expansion. They would be overreplicated relative to their initial proportion in the cell. However, this particular explanation depends on a preferential stimulation of the replication of some but not all mitochondria. No hard data support this view.

An alternative mechanism leading to the same outcome was proposed by de Grey (1997). His hypothesis is based on the assumption that mitochondria with reduced respiratory function caused by a deletion or mutation will consequently inflict less damage on their own membranes than will normal mitochondria. As a result, the mutated mitochondria will suffer less frequent lysosomal degradation than the normal mitochondria, and hence the defective mitochondria will preferentially survive and replicate. Eventually, de Grey proposes, once such a deletion or mutation occurs in a mitochondrion of a nondividing cell, it will rapidly populate that cell and thereby destroy the cell's respiratory capability.

This hypothesis, termed the "survival of the slowest," is unproven and needs to be critically tested. However, as discussed by de Grey (1998), its implications are consistent with observed effects of other oxidative-damage models (see, for example, the MARS model discussion in Chapter 13). Cells with destroyed respiratory capability must rely on glycolysis for ATP production and can only stabilize their $NAD^+/NADH$ ratio by expelling electrons from the cell. If the rate of electron efflux exceeds the electron-accepting capacity of the electron acceptors in the plasm, then reactive free-radical species are likely to be formed and to give rise to increased peroxidation of serum lipids such as the low-density lipoproteins (LDL). When damaged LDL is imported into a healthy mitochondrion, the LDS is destroyed by the organelle's antioxidant defenses. But this task is thought to overload the mitochondrion's ability to degrade the pro-oxidants that it is itself generating as a result of aerobic metabolism. This increases the oxidative stress on the cell and sets off an unstable positive feedback system in which the increase in the number of damaged mitochondria causes the oxidative stress to increase even more, further increasing the number of damaged mitochondria. The hypothesis is plausible and consistent with much known data, but it does need to be critically tested.

The generation of mtDNA molecules that have large deletions of their coding sequences has been much studied in an attempt to correlate the levels of deletions with the loss of function and/or the presence of pathologies. The evidence is inconclusive. In patients with particular syndromes of muscle degradation (for example, "ragged red fiber disease"), particular deletions can be found in very high levels, approaching 50 percent of the patient's mtDNA, yet the patients remain reasonably functional (Wallace et al. 1995). This finding implies that (1) mtDNA mutations are not of primary importance in aging or (2) the combination of various different mtDNA mutations is responsible for the decreased mitochondrial function with age or (3) the mtDNA mutations are one of several processes that act to decrease the reserve capacity of the organism.

The first implication is contradicted by the finding that some normal aging people have the same mtDNA mutation as is found in people with a mitochondrial genetic disease, and that this deletion accumulates with age (Arnheim and Cortopassi 1992; Zhang et al. 1992). The second implication has not been critically tested yet. The last implication is supported by the phenomenon of mosaicism. It is thought that the damaged mtDNA molecules are unevenly distributed among the cells in a tissue, and the function and survival of cells that have high numbers of damaged mitochondria may be reduced. This mosaicism has been shown in the adult human brain (Corral-Debrinski et al. 1992). More recent evidence in muscle from older monkeys also points to a mosaic of normal and abnormal myofibrils. The abnormal myofibrils have been shown to contain as much as 15 percent of mtDNA with deletions (R. Weindruch, personal communication). Such a deficit might easily compromise tissue or organ function, reduce the animal's reserve capacity, and leave it less able to cope successfully with additional stress. In addition to the mtDNA damage, the high levels of oxygen-derived free radicals would be expected to cause cumulative oxidative damage to the lipid and protein components of the mitochondria. Agarwal and Sohal (1995) have shown that the high-molecular-weight proteins in their animals are preferentially oxidized with age. This oxidative damage to mitochondrial protein is thought to contribute to the age-related loss of energy function.

Not all species show the same patterns of mitochondrial damage with aging. In the nematode, Melov and colleagues (1995) have shown that the frequency of mtDNA deletions increases with age. Interestingly, the deletions increased more slowly in the *age-1* long-lived mutant, which is known to have higher levels of antioxidant resistance; and this finding certainly supports the oxidative-damage origin of mtDNA mutations. A very different pattern of damage is seen in a standard laboratory strain of *Drosophila* (Calleja et al. 1993). No age-related increase in mtDNA frequency is observed; the level of deletions is low (about 1 percent) and constant throughout life. However, there was a significant decrease in the steady-state levels of several important mitochondrial RNA transcripts, including those for both rRNA and certain oxidative enzymes. Such a change would clearly affect the efficiency of mitochondrial energy production, albeit via a different mechanism than that observed in mammals and nematodes. In this case, the loss in energy production appears to be the result of an age-dependent metabolic alteration. This observation is not only interesting in and of itself, but it also warns us not to blindly and without hard proof attribute all mitochondrial dysfunctions to an mtDNA mutation. There is more than one way of bringing about a specific phenotype.

In Chapter 4 we discussed the case of birds, in which a high rate of oxygen consumption is combined with a high maximum life span, and pointed out that an investigation of their physiology might offer insight into previously unsuspected protective mechanisms. Studies have been done on rats and pigeons, since the two animals are of similar body size but differ significantly in their maximum life spans (4 years for rats, 35 years for pigeons). It has now been determined that pigeons convert significantly less oxygen into free radicals in the mitochondria than do rats, even though pigeons have the higher rate of oxygen consumption (Barja et al. 1994; Herrero and Barja 1997). The high longevity of birds relative to mammals must be due in part to the capacity of the bird mitochondria to decrease free-radical leakage at the respiratory chain. Understanding the underlying mechanism will be of some interest, for both its theoretical and its practical implications.

Mitochondrial dysfunction is known to increase with age in some organisms, including humans (Arnheim and Cortopassi 1992; Gadaleta et al. 1992; Munscher, Muller-Hocher, and Naplwotzki 1993; Kadenbach et al. 1995). In most, but not all, cases it is believed but not yet proven to be the result of oxidative damage that is due to the leakage of reactive oxygen species from the mitochondrion (Kappus 1985; de Grey 1997). Many specific types of mutations have been associated with certain diseases or syndromes, and they are often tissue specific in their distribution. The loss of energy production probably decreases the organism's reserve capacity and may contribute to its inability to function normally under stresses that would not have affected it at an earlier age. However, the data show that the association of mtDNA damage with certain rare neuromuscular diseases is much stronger than is its association with ordinary aging. It has been suggested that this lack of an association with aging is a technical shortcoming, arising from the inability to detect small and/or multiple mutations within the same mitochondrion. Perhaps the deployment of more sensitive techniques will resolve this question. Mice lacking the mitochondrial form of superoxide dismutase, and thus rendered susceptible to oxidative stress and damage, display extensive neural degeneration in the cerebral cortex and specific brainstem nuclei (Melov et al. 1998). The existence of this animal model should permit examination of the relationship between free radicals and age-related neurodegenerative diseases.

At the moment, however, the mitochondrial-damage hypothesis remains an intriguing mechanism that needs critical testing so as to unequivocally establish its causal or correlative relationship to aging. Despite this lack of critical proof, it is generally believed to be a valid and fruitful theory; it is, for example, the centerpiece of the MARS model described in Chapter 13 (Kowald and Kirkwood 1994, 1996).

Genetic Theories

In Chapter 6 we discussed at length the results of the genetic studies of aging that have been done on worms, flies, molds, and mice. The data presented there clearly demonstrated that aging and longevity are under strong genetic control. The old question as to whether the genes play a detectable role in the aging process has been effectively answered in the positive. In addition, the minimum number of genes necessary to significantly extend the life span apparently does not need to be very large, ranging from one locus in *C. elegans* to two in *Neurospora* and *Drosophila* and up to at least six or more in the mouse. Of course, this does not mean that only one (or six) genes is responsible for extended longevity. A more realistic interpretation is that within the context of a given genotype with a particular longevity, alterations in the activity of these few genes are sufficient to shift the equilibrium of the genome to yield an extended longevity. Given a somewhat different background genome, it is not clear whether altering the same genes would result in the same modulation of the life span.

The maximum number of genes involved in an extended-longevity phenotype is estimated to be much larger than the small number we manipulate experimentally. Such estimates range up in the hundreds or thousands of loci. Keep in mind that we are dealing with genetic networks—sets of genes and signal pathways bound together in a gene circuit that is analogous to an electrical feedback circuit (McAdams and Shapiro 1995). When we ask a question regarding the characteristics of the circuit, the answer we obtain depends to a large extent on how our query was framed. For example, there is good evidence that modulation of antioxidant defense activity affects longevity in *Drosophila*. But there is equally good evidence suggesting that other genes, such as those that confer the ability to resist desiccation and other sorts of stresses, are also capable of shifting the equilibrium of the *Drosophila* genome to extend longevity.

It may turn out that the important concept is the detailed description of the genetic network and the magnitude of the shift in activities needed to reset the network's equilibrium to a different value, and not the identity of the several stress-response genes that we today know how to manipulate. There may be more than one way to shift the network's equilibrium, and the genes that constitute each of these shift mechanisms are the ones that yield data indicative of a strong genetic component: antioxidant genes in one case, desiccation-resistant genes in the other. But they cannot do it by themselves; these genes exhibit their controlling behavior only in the context of the particular genetic network. The deep biological identity between these different longevity gene sets would reside in the underlying network. Now, however, we cannot even identify, let alone characterize, a genetic network that is important in modulating aging, so we will turn our attention to the genetic mechanisms for which we have empirical data, recognizing that we are examining only part of the process.

Because we have no firm idea of the genetic networks involved in aging, it would be silly to set up defining criteria *a priori* that would force us to reject any genetic process that extends longevity. We are not particularly interested in genes that shorten longevity (with certain exceptions; see Leffelaar and Grigliatti 1984), but we will regard genes that significantly extend longevity relative to an appropriate control as being of great interest. After some deliberate reflection, we might revise our sense of their importance, but we do not initially reject them.

At this level there are three very interesting mechanisms—any, all, or none of which might eventually prove to be correct. These are (1) antioxidant defense enzymes, (2) protein synthesis, and (3) gene activity changes induced by caloric restriction. We will discuss each of these topics in turn. We will conclude the chapter by considering a fourth category consisting of several other genetic mechanisms (telomeres, signal transduction, and so on) that are interesting but that at the moment have a less well defined role in the aging process.

Antioxidant Defense Enzymes

Physiological investigations into the nature of the genetic mechanisms involved in regulating the aging process have been done on *Neurospora* and on *Drosophila*. In *Neurospora*, Munkres and Furtek (1984) were able to select for both long-lived and short-lived strains such that the mean life spans of the several strains ranged from about 7 days to about 60 days, compared to a control value of about 21 days (see Figure 6.10). Assaying these strains for the activity of superoxide dismutase (one of the more important antioxidant defense enzymes; see Chapter 9) showed an almost perfect positive correlation between the strain-specific enzyme activity and the strain-specific life span (Figure 10.2). Furthermore, similar positive correlations were found for other important antioxidant enzymes, such as catalase, glutathione peroxidase, cytochrome *c* peroxidase, and ascorbate free-radical reductase. In all of these cases, decreases of life span were accompanied by a decrease in enzyme activities; increases in life span were accompanied by an increase in enzyme activities. Although correlative, the evidence is highly suggestive of a causal relationship between the two variables.

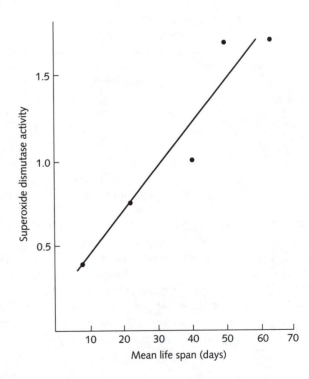

Figure 10.2 The correlation of superoxide dismutase activity with life span in conidia of various strains of *Neurospora*. The value of the correlation coefficient, *r*, was 0.96. (From Munkres, Rana, and Goldstein 1984.)

Munkres and Furtek (1984) suggested that the two gene loci (*age-1* and *age-2*) that they determined to be responsible for these alterations in life span are loci that regulate the amount of synthesis of the several different antioxidant enzymes. This empirically based suggestion agrees well with the theoretical discussions predicting that evolutionary alterations in life span, such as are characteristic of selection experiments, most likely would be brought about by changes in the regulatory genes rather than in the structural genes (Cutler 1975; Sacher 1975; see also Chapter 6). In this view, then, populations would usually be polymorphic at many different loci, some of which might confer a minor increase in the organisms' reproductive fitness as a result of the variant's effects on antioxidant resistance. Subsequent application of the appropriate selection pressures to this population might lead to the isolation of genetic variants that have alterations in their regulatory genes such that they have intrinsically higher (or lower) activities of the several antioxidant enzymes. Isolation of these genes, in turn, would lead to a more (or less) effective defense against the stochastic damage caused by the oxygen-induced free radicals. The resulting slower (or faster) accumulation of such peroxidative damage would decrease (or increase) the rate of aging of the fungal cells, and hence extend (or shorten) the strain-specific life span. This is a very plausible genetic hypothesis, the proof of which lies in determining the nature of the mechanisms by which the *age-1* and *age-2* loci effect changes in the antioxidant enzyme activities.

Evidence obtained from *Drosophila* studies points in the same direction. First, the data shown in Figure 6.16 illustrate that the normal-lived R strains begin to lose function at about 5 to 7 days, while the long-lived L strains do not lose function until about 18 days or so. We interpreted that data as meaning that the L strain animals do something at about 5 to 7 days of age that preserves their functional ability—something that the R strain animals are not capable of doing. What do they do? The answer is summarized in Figure 6.17, which shows that at day 5 in the L animals there is a coordinate up-regulation of the mRNA levels and the enzyme activities of certain major enzymes and nonenzymatic free-radical scavengers of the antioxidant defense system. What effect does this increase in antioxidant activity have?

The data portrayed in Figure 9.9 demonstrate the existence in long-lived and normal-lived animals of a correlated and inverse relationship between the antioxidant enzymes on the one hand and the harmful by-products of oxidative reactions on the other. Could another factor have been responsible for the extended longevity observed in the L strain animals? One can never prove a negative statement, but in an analysis of various biochemical and stress-resistance factors, the only factor that robustly differentiated all long-lived animals from all normal- or short-lived animals was antioxidant resistance (Force et al. 1995).

What causes the "protective phase" to end? We don't know yet, but we are certainly trying to find out. The cause does not appear to be a decrease in the amount of antioxidant enzyme present, so another more subtle mechanism may be at work. Another interesting phenomenon is that the molecular changes described earlier cause a change in the survival curve that is characteristic of the normal-lived animals such that the Gompertz curve of the L strain animals has a lower slope, and hence a longer MRDT (mortality rate doubling time), than does the Gompertz curve of the R strain control animals.

Orr and Sohal (1994) earlier performed a conceptually very different sort of experiment, but one that yielded data pointing to the same conclusion. They took a standard laboratory strain of *Drosophila* that has a mean life span of about 40 days. Being normal diploids, each of these animals had two copies of the Cu–Zn superoxide dismutase (*CuZnSOD*) gene and two copies of the gene that encodes catalase. Using standard molecular genetic techniques, they constructed a DNA fragment containing each of these genes and its own promoter region. This construct was then used to transform normal embryos, and several lines of flies were obtained, each with three copies of the *CuZnSOD* and catalase genes (and, of course, two copies of all other genes). In effect, these investigators created several lines of flies that had a 50 percent increase in the number of these two key antioxidant genes. The question was whether the extra genes would be active, and if they were, whether they would have an effect on the animals' longevity.

The transgenes were indeed active, as judged by the fact that the transgenic flies had about 50 percent more Cu–Zn SOD and catalase activity than did the normal controls. Of more importance, their life span was about 40 percent longer than that of the controls. This last result was particularly interesting, in view of Orr and Sohal's prior experiments, in which they had made flies transgenic for either Cu–Zn SOD or for catalase but not for both. Such single-gene transgenic flies showed a large increase in either Cu–Zn SOD or catalase as appropriate, a variable but moderate alteration in the mean life span, and no change in the maximum life span. Cu–Zn SOD and catalase work together as a coupled enzyme system; the products of the Cu–Zn SOD reaction become the reactants of the catalase reaction. Increasing the gene dosage of one component without increasing the dosage of its partner is not effective. In fact, it is believed that an overdose of Cu–Zn SOD without a compensating increase in catalase might yield cytotoxic effects. Each of the single transgenic strains showed either no or only moderate levels of enhanced resistance to oxidative stress agents. However, the double transgenic animals had a lower rate of oxidative damage. In addition, the Gompertz curve of the double transgenics had a lower slope than that of the controls but it had the same intercept, suggesting that the MRDT was increased.

Some negative data reported in the experiment also need to be examined. Not every transgene that successfully integrates into the genome will be normally expressed. There are several possible reasons for this phenomenon, the most important of which is position effect: the integration of the transgene into a portion of the genome that does not permit the normal qualitative or quantitative expression of the transgene. In their successful experiment, Orr and Sohal (1994) actually generated 15 different transgenic lines containing both the *CuZnSOD* and the catalase genes. Of the 15 lines, in only eight did life span increase; in one it decreased, and in six it remained unchanged. It was presumed, but not proven, that the six lines with an unchanged life span did not express their transgenes. It was also presumed that all of the eight lines with an increased life span were expressing their transgenes; confirmatory data were acquired for only three lines, which we discussed earlier. The decreased life span in the one line might present an interesting exception (threshold effects?) to the expected results, if the transgene was being expressed.

Thus the data obtained and reported lead us to conclude that the increased expression of the transgenes increased the animals' antioxidant defense activity while lowering their rate of oxidative damage, and this phenomenon is what led to their extended longevity and longer MRDT. However, the fact that we do not know if the transgenes were equally well expressed in the other 12 lines that displayed all three possible alterations of longevity means that we cannot draw a robust conclusion that the manipulation of the antioxidant variable directly led to the alteration of the longevity variable. In addition, the control flies used were not the most robust available, and this fact casts some doubt on a robust interpretation.

A more traditional type of genetic approach is to mutagenize the antioxidant genes and observe the effect on the animals' longevity. The *CuZnSOD* gene in the fruit fly may be either inactivated by a particular mutation or completely deleted from the genome by means of certain chromosome deletions (Campbell, Hilliker, and Phillips 1986). In either case, the homozygous animals have no measurable superoxide dismutase activity. They also die at very early ages, even though they appear to be morphologically normal. None of the affected adults lives more than a week or so. A similar event transpires when the catalase gene of *Drosophila* is mutationally inactivated, the affected animals dying within a week or so after eclosion. Several different mutant catalase strains exist; there is a statistically significant linear correlation between the residual strain-specific catalase activity and the strain-specific mean and maximum life spans (Mackay and Bewley 1989). Interestingly, the loss of catalase activity has no effect on SOD activity, but it does lead to a correlated acceleration in the appearance of biomarkers that are characteristic of aging and senescence (Bewley and Mackay 1989). Such null mutants presumably have life span patterns of catalase and peroxides that differ considerably from those of the controls. Such findings lend support to the idea that loss-of-function mutants in key antioxidant defense genes represent one mode by which genes control aging and longevity. In both these cases, then, the abolishment of a key antioxidant enzyme is correlated with an extraordinary shortening of the life span.

Finally, a consideration of all the data in several different species shows that there is growing evidence for a role of oxidative damage in the aging process, and that the antioxidant defense system plays an important role in combating this oxidative stress and modulating aging.

Energy, stress, and long life: A clue?   Our long-lived strains of *Drosophila* show a selection-associated fixation of certain alleles of particular metabolic enzymes, and these alleles are much less common in our normal-lived control strains. On the face of it, this evidence suggests the existence of a relationship between energy metabolism and antioxidant enzymes. This fixation likely is related to the fact that high levels of antioxidant enzyme activity make large demands on the body's NADPH resources (Feuers et al. 1995), an observation that makes plausible the idea that the alleles selected for in our long-lived strains are alleles that are perhaps more efficient in replenishing NADPH levels. Interestingly, De Oliveira and her colleagues (Da Cunha et al. 1995) have shown a similar pattern of allelic fixation in their *Drosophila* strain, which was selected for both development time and long life, and their strain is also more resistant to paraquat toxicity than are the controls, which do not display the allelic fixation. Using sister strains to ours, Luckinbill and colleagues (1989) showed a somewhat different pattern of allelic fixation, but one that led these investigators to suggest that energy metabolism was being affected (Riha and Luckinbill 1996). And the long-lived O strains of Rose (1984) were shown to have a different pattern of energy metabolism than their controls: The O strains seem to sequester calories as fat early in life, thus enabling them to survive the subsequent stresses of life (Service 1988).

Is this focus on energy metabolism a coincidence or a clue? The latter, I think. The associations we have described between energy metabolism and longevity are varied, but they are consistent with the idea that metabolic changes that enhance NADPH levels may be a necessary precondition for the effective operation of both enzymatic and nonenzymatic antioxidant defense systems, and that the elevated activity of such defenses is what results in lower levels of oxidative damage and a consequent extended longevity. In the absence of adequate levels of cofactors, these defense systems are rendered functionally inactive. Such a hypothesis might account for at least one way in which metabolism and oxidative stress processes might be integrated. The work done on *C. elegans* has shown that the *clock* and *daf* genes appear to be intimately involved in modulating metabolic processes. Future work will doubtless uncover other interesting connections between metabolism and aging.

Parsons (1995, 1996) has suggested that selection for resistance to oxidative stress is the main factor regulating longevity. Furthermore, it is plausible to assume that high stress resistance in general is linked to the efficient use of one's metabolic resources. Given the progressively accumulating energy costs during aging (see Chapter 13), one might then predict that animals that are stress resistant are better able to deal effectively with these high energy costs, and thus stress-resistant animals should live longer than non-stress-resistant animals, in part because they can deal better with the stresses of life and in part because they have a "better metabolism." This line of reasoning might reveal a deep biological similarity between these otherwise disparate strain phenotypes. A consideration of aging in human fibroblast cells has led to a similar point of view (Toussaint et al. 1995). If proven by future work, this perspective might well provide us with interesting insights of a more fundamental nature. In the meantime, you may want to consider how this suggested relationship between energy and oxidative stress would fit into the evolutionary scheme of things, as exemplified by the disposable-soma model discussed in Chapter 4 or by the MARS model discussed in Chapter 13.

Protein Synthesis

It is not surprising that the effect of aging on protein synthesis has been studied extensively. Proteins account for much of the structural, functional, and catalytic components of the cell. The ability to synthesize proteins to replace those lost to normal turnover or to various sorts of damage is crucial to the cell's ability to maintain and repair itself. Inhibitory or deleterious changes in the genetic and/or cellular apparatus that controls protein synthesis might significantly alter the cell's homeostatic ability and could constitute one of the mechanisms of the aging process. Several theories of aging have made specific predictions regarding alterations in protein synthesis during aging. The error catastrophe theory, for example, predicted that, as a result of stochastic damages, aging should be accompanied by a decrease in the fidelity with which the proteins are synthesized (see Chapter 9). As we have seen, this prediction was not upheld by the data. Its much more sophisticated successor, the MARS, or network, model (see Chapter 13), predicted that high oxygen free-radical levels should bring about increasing levels of protein errors (due to oxidative damage), which, if they affect the synthetic machinery, lead to a system collapse at high error rates. This is what happens in the computer simulation of the MARS model; it remains to be seen if it happens *in vivo*. Other theories, most of which view aging as a systemic process, suggest that it is the level of synthesis, and not its translational fidelity, that is primarily affected by the aging process; these are the concepts we will now explore.

A large body of literature empirically describes age-related changes in protein synthesis in a variety of experimental organisms and systems (see Makrides 1983; Finch 1990; van Remmen et al. 1995). Despite the inevitable existence of inconsistencies among some of these reports, there seems to be general agreement that, overall, the rate of total protein synthesis declines by about 40 to 70 percent with age in mammals; while even greater decreases (about 60 to 90 percent) have been observed in insects and other organisms. Figure 10.3 compares age-related changes in total protein synthesis by various different tissues in two different strains of rats. Each of these different tissues undergoes a similar decline in protein synthesis, and the patterns of decline are not dissimilar in the two strains. There are two other points of interest to note in this figure. First, the decline is seen even in mitochondria, which have their own genome and their own protein synthesis machinery. Second, the apparent terminal increase in the

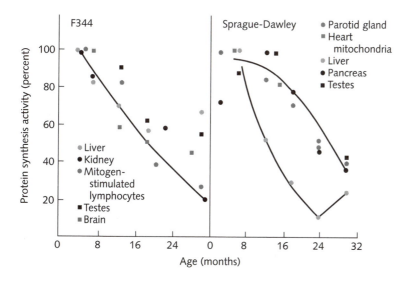

Figure 10.3 The effects of age on the protein synthesis activity of various tissues of Fischer 344 (F344) and Sprague-Dawley rats. The data are expressed as a percentage of the age at which protein synthesis activity was highest, and have been taken from the literature. (From Richardson and Birchenall-Sparks 1983. © Alan R. Liss.)

protein synthesis capabilities of the aged liver is the exception that tests the rule. The data obtained from several laboratories suggest that this increase may be attributed to an increase in the synthesis of one specific protein (albumin) and not to an overall increase in all liver proteins. Thus the general decline does not rigidly apply to every protein in the cell, and we might well expect there to be some proteins in addition to albumin that go against the general pattern. With this one exception, the age-related decline in protein synthesis seen in these two rat strains is also seen in numerous tissues in humans, as well as in a variety of *Drosophila*, rat, and mouse strains (van Remmen et al. 1995). It appears to be a widespread phenomenon that is closely associated with the aging process.

Nearly all the proteins of a cell are broken down and synthesized anew many times during its life span. The few proteins that do not undergo this process, such as the dentine of the tooth or the crystallin of the lens, are either extracellular or so rare as to call attention to themselves (see Chapter 3). It is believed that this continuous degradation process allows the cell not only to repair and replace damaged components, but also to exert control over transient metabolic processes by first inducing the necessary enzymes and then degrading them when their task is finished.

We have seen that protein synthesis declines with age. Although there often is an age-related decrease in "cell solids" with age (see Figure 5.2) when expressed on a whole-body basis, there also seems to be little or no change in the overall protein content of a given cell or tissue with age. The most obvious manner in which these two facts can be reconciled with the reality of degradation is to postulate that the rate of protein degradation decreases with age and that the half-life of the resident proteins consequently increases. Ward (1988b) did a carefully controlled study to measure the effect of age on protein degradation in the rat. The results show that the rate of protein degradation decreases continuously between 6 and 24 months of age (Figure 10.4). In addition, Ward (1988a) showed that the age-related decline in protein degradation is strongly correlated to the age-related decrease in protein synthesis.

In studies of various tissues (heart, skeletal muscle, liver) of rodents, as well as in whole-body studies of rodents, humans, and nematodes, protein degradation does appear to slow down (see van Remmen 1995 for review). Our knowledge of the mechanisms involved in protein degradation is complicated by the fact that the rate of degradation is relatively specific for a particular protein and varies considerably from protein to protein (Medvedev 1981a), as well as from tissue to tissue (van Remmen et al. 1995), and the factors controlling such specificity are still not well known. However they are brought about, such changes might be responsible for the appearance of altered proteins (see Chapters 4 and 9) and/or the persistence of damaged components (see Chapter 5) in the tissues of older organisms. Such abnormal proteins are degraded, but at a much slower rate in old animals relative to young ones. Lavie and colleagues (1982) measured this process and detected an increase from 30 minutes in 6-month-old mice to 150 minutes in 24-month-old mice. Oxidized proteins are also degraded less rapidly with age (Starke-Reed and Oliver 1989), and this slowing of degradation is correlated with a decline in protease activity. Richardson and Cheung (1982) sug-

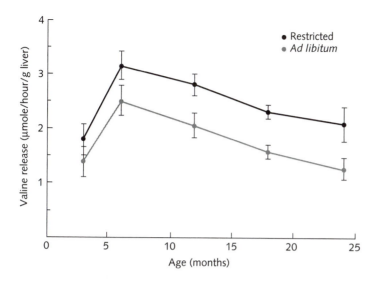

Figure 10.4 The effect of age on protein degradation in the rat liver. The age-related changes in the rate of protein degradation by perfused liver are shown in rats fed either *ad libitum* or on a calorie-restricted diet. Even though the same process takes place in both animals, the old, restricted animals have a level of degradation that is approximately equivalent to that of young, fully fed animals. (From Ven Rennen 1995.)

gested that the decreased ability of older organisms to alter their metabolic processes in response to environmental change is due to this inability to rapidly degrade unnecessary enzymes and/or signal proteins.

The molecular basis of protein synthesis has been the subject of numerous investigations during the past several decades, and its component steps have been identified and characterized. Many of these steps have been examined in an effort to gain an insight into the mechanisms responsible for the age-related decline in protein synthesis. There are at least two broad possibilities.

One concept rests on the accepted idea that protein synthesis is a process that requires significant amounts of metabolic energy. As postulated in the "oxygen radical–mitochondrial injury" theory discussed earlier in this chapter, the general decline in protein synthesis may be due to the preceding decline in ATP synthesis by the damaged mitochondria—a decline that would be expected to have systemic and widespread effects. If this is the case, then it should be possible to demonstrate that the ATP supply—an extrinsic factor—is the limiting factor in protein synthesis.

The second concept rests on the idea that the age-related decline in protein synthesis is due to intrinsic changes in the synthetic machinery itself. Protein synthesis may be divided into four principal steps: (1) the aminoacylation of tRNA, (2) the initiation of the peptide chain, (3) the elongation of the peptide chain, and (4) the termination and release of the completed peptide chain. Each of these steps is a highly specific process that normally takes place at a very rapid rate. (For example, more than 1 million peptide bonds are made every second in an average mammalian cell!) Aging appears to have no effect on the first step, aminoacylation (Richardson and Semsei 1987). The rapid pace of this process is facilitated by the fact that the last three steps take place on the ribosomes, highly organized structures composed of particular RNAs and at least 50 specific types of proteins and recent reviews suggest the ribosomes and the mRNA transcripts have evolved so as to maximize the efficiency of these synthetic regions (Danchin and Héneut 1997).

Ribosomes have been studied to see whether alterations in their structure are responsible for the declining rate of protein synthesis. Aged *Drosophila*, rats, and fungi all exhibit a decreased number of active ribosomes and an increased number of inactive ribosomes when compared to their appropriate controls (Baker et al. 1979; Richardson and Birchenall-Sparks 1983). There is no obvious alteration in the protein or RNA structural components of the ribosomes. Furthermore, active ribosomes obtained from young and aged donors functioned with equivalent fidelity when tested in a cell-free system. For these and other similar reasons, it was concluded that the intrinsic defect is not in the ribosomes themselves, but rather in a subsequent stage of protein synthesis. One of the factors regulating the initiation step appears to decrease. Changes in the level of protein synthesis closely correlate with changes in the level of eukaryotic initiation factor 2 (eIF-2), and this correlation might play an important role in the age-related decline of ribosome aggregation to mRNA. Unfortunately, there is no information on the activity of eIF-2 in rodents older than 10 months, so no firm conclusions can be drawn (van Remmen et al. 1995).

The elongation stage is the point at which other experiments seem to have localized an apparent intrinsic defect. This process was studied extensively by Webster (1988) in *Drosophila*, using a cell-free system to better control the many variables involved. The data obtained from this system demonstrated an age-related decline in protein synthesis of about 70 percent—a decline that we should note begins rather early in adult life (Figure 10.5). This decrease was found to be paralleled by a concomitant failure of the elongation step but not of the initiation or termination steps.

The elongation step is known to be regulated by a complex of specific proteins, called elongation factors, that bind to the ribosome and are responsible for guiding the incoming tRNA molecules to the correct location so that their amino acid can bind to (and elongate) the growing peptide chain. Investigating this decline, Webster and Webster (1984) found that the decreased protein synthesis activity in *Drosophila* appears to be due to a disappearance of one of these factors, elongation factor 1 (EF-1). Synthesis of the other proteins in the organism declined only after the initial decline of EF-1 activity. Furthermore, the disappearance of the EF-1 protein was shown to be due to the absence of the mRNA that normally codes for that particular protein, while the declining synthesis of the other proteins in the organism took place even though there was no observable decrease in their mRNAs.

This last point was indirectly supported by the results of Courtright, Sonstein, and Kumaran (1985), who detected significant decreases in the synthesis of yolk proteins in old females but could find no change in their mRNA levels. These results led Webster (1988) to suggest that the age-related decline of protein synthesis in *Drosophila* is the result of a systemic control of gene expression. The simplest mechanism would involve the switching off of the *EF-1* gene(s) early in adult life followed by a rapid decrease in the concentration of the EF-1 mRNA, an event that would occur as a result of the normal degradation

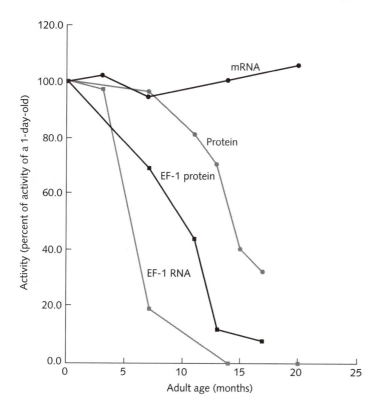

Figure 10.5 The role of posttranscriptional mechanisms in bringing about the postulated onset of senescence and aging in *Drosophila*, as shown by the *in vitro* analysis of the EF-1 alpha system performed by Webster and Webster (1983, 1984). Note the chronological sequence of events beginning with the qualitative disappearance of EF-1 alpha mRNA and culminating in the quantitative shutdown of protein synthesis in general. Also note that there appears to be no effect on the transcriptional activity of the other genes assayed. (Redrawn from Webster and Webster 1983 and 1984.)

processes. Consequently, the existing EF-1 proteins would likewise decrease in number, again via normal protein degradation processes, and their total synthetic activity would decrease. As a result, the synthesis of all proteins would begin to decrease markedly as the elongation step became the rate-limiting step in the process of protein synthesis. This general decrease would be observable only after the initial decline in EF-1 activity. There would be no effect on the transcriptional activity of the other genes, and consequently there would be no decrease in their mRNA concentrations. In effect, then, the synthesis of all body proteins would be equally reduced by means of translational control exerted at the elongation step, but the immediate genetic control would be the transcriptional control of the *EF-1* gene alone.

Analogous experiments done on rodents indicate that the old rats have much lower EF-1 activity than do the young rats (Moldave et al. 1979). One might be tempted to spin a tale based on this observation. However, the situation in the nematode cautions against blindly extrapolating from a limited data base. In this organism, the elongation factors appear to have no defect. Instead the ribosomes obtained from older animals appear to be incapable of binding the EF-1 complex (Egilmez and Rothstein 1985). Their protein synthesis declines because the same process as in *Drosophila* is inhibited, but apparently via a different molecular mechanism.

This caution has not been heeded. Shepherd and colleagues (1989) did a transgenic experiment in which *EF-1*–transformed flies were shown to have a significantly increased life span. This effect was attributed to the *presumed* 50 percent increase in expression of the EF-1 protein. However, it was later determined that the transgenic lines did not express more EF-1 mRNA or protein than did the control lines (Shikama, Ackermann, and Brack 1994). Although the transgenic flies did live longer, it was obvious that this longer life span was not the result of increased EF-1 expression. Stearns and Kaiser (1993) and Kaiser and colleagues (1997) suggested that the size of the insert, the genetic background of the host, and the effects of the transgene's position in the host genome were probably responsible for the observed extended longevity. Finally, it was shown that our long-lived (L) strains of *Drosophila* have no increased expression of EF-1 mRNA relative to their controls (Dudas and Arking 1994), thus indicating that the EF-1 mechanism is also not operative in nontransformed strains.

All in all, this is a good example of a beautiful hypothesis killed by an ugly fact. It is also an example of the need for confirmatory experiments and for the cultivation of a politely skeptical attitude on the part of all. Transgene experiments will require measurement of the gene product in question in every line produced, and at various appropriate ages as well. The question of genetic background is more difficult to solve unless one constructs animals that are isogenic for all chromosomes. Tower (1996) offers a better suggestion: Construct inducible expression systems so that the effect of having a transgene expressed or not expressed can be analyzed in identical genetic backgrounds.

In summary, the data clearly indicate that the levels of protein synthesis and protein degradation decrease with aging. It is not known whether the changes play a causal role in the aging process or whether they are simply secondary consequences of aging, or perhaps a mixture of both.

Caloric Restriction and Gene Activity

We have already reviewed the evidence demonstrating that caloric restriction is a highly effective method, particularly in mammals, of slowing the rate of aging and increasing longevity (see Chapter 7). Because of the relative ease with which this intervention may be applied to well-defined animals, caloric restriction has also emerged as an effective tool for studying how alterations in aging affect biological processes. One of the more interesting insights to come out of this work is the idea that caloric restriction alters the patterns of gene activity even as it extends the life span, thus encouraging the idea that a straightforward causal relationship exists between these two events.

The first report that caloric restriction altered gene expression was that of Richardson and his collaborators (1987), who showed that the protein levels, mRNA levels, and nuclear transcription rate of a specific protein in rats are significantly enhanced in restricted animals relative to the age-matched *ad libitum*–fed controls. Since protein synthesis and gene expression often decrease with age, the finding that caloric restriction might reverse this process was of special interest. However, as more data has accumulated, it has become clear that the effects of caloric restriction vary significantly from transcript to transcript, increasing some but having no effect on others (van Remmen et al. 1995; Papaconstantinou et al.

1996). For example, the levels of many mRNA transcripts that normally decrease with age are increased by caloric restriction (for example, alpha$_{2u}$-globulin, catalase, Cu–Zn superoxide dismutase, androgen receptor, hsp70), but the same intervention has no effect on the levels of other mRNA transcripts (for example, albumin, c-myc, c-jun, Sp1, glutathione peroxidase).

In an effort to account for this diversity of effect, Heydari and Richardson (1992) proposed that a two-step mechanism separates the cause of caloric restriction from its effects on gene activity. They suggested that the animals first undergo major hormonal changes after being placed on a restricted diet. (Data exist to support this statement, as we will see in Chapter 12.) These endocrine alterations then induce changes in the levels and/or activities of various transcription factors, and these changes are what bring about the observed changes in gene expression. It is well known that noxious stimuli, or stresses, applied to eukaryotic organisms or cells will induce the expression of natural genetic defense mechanisms consisting of several functionally related genes (see Papaconstantinou et al. 1996), and these systems are considered to serve as models of how gene expression is normally regulated (see Figure 10.6) on page 440.

These gene families are known to be regulated by a small number of *trans*-acting transcription factors. The expression of many of these genes is altered normally with age, suggesting that there are age-related changes in the activity of these transcription factors. The effect of caloric restriction then would be to reverse this age effect on the transcription factor activity. Heydari and colleagues (1993) demonstrated this to be true by showing that the liver cells of aged, restricted rats show an increased transcription of the *hsp70* gene that is correlated with the lack of decline in the activity of its transcription factor (HSF) within the nuclei of the liver cells, relative to nonrestricted rats. This finding suggests that caloric restriction delays or even prevents the normal age-related decline in the activity of this and other genes.

However, caloric restriction does more than just stimulate gene transcription. It also stimulates protein synthesis in most tissues of the rat, for example, as well as stimulating protein degradation (van Remmen et al. 1995). The net effect of stimulating both protein synthesis and degradation is to increase the rate of protein turnover. As already mentioned, this increased turnover rate may enable the restricted animal to reduce the levels of abnormal proteins and their subsequent effects. This change, and the others already discussed, are likely to be beneficial to the organism and lead to extended longevity. The promise that caloric restriction will enable us to identify key processes involved in aging is being fulfilled.

Earlier we discussed the possibility that alterations in energy metabolism underlie an organism's ability to resist stress and live long. Certainly caloric restriction results in a reorganization of the organism's metabolism such that it lowers the steady-state levels of oxidative stress and damage, retards the appearance of age-associated changes, and extends the maximum life span (Sohal and Weindruch 1996). We should keep in mind the possibility that the deep biological similarity between starved mice and selected flies involves similar metabolic alterations. However, as Martin, Austad, and Johnson (1996) have cogently pointed out, it is unlikely that mice and worms and flies and people each use the same mechanisms of resistance to oxidative stress. There must be important differences among these different species; oxidative stress may be a common operative mechanism of aging and senescence, but it must not be the only one. If this is true, we will need to understand the details of these metabolic changes much better than we do now, and especially how the caloric alteration brings about changes in protective enzyme activities. It may someday be possible to enjoy such protection without having to restrict one's diet.

Gene activity is believed to be manipulated by diet in many other organisms. For example, in some species, such as bees or termites, the reproductively active female may live for many years while the nonreproductive worker female lives less than 1 year. The only difference between these genetically identical types of females is their developmental history: Only the developing queens are fed special food ("royal jelly"). As discussed in Chapter 3, this dietary manipulation indirectly brings about the activation of a different hormonal regime and in this manner results in the induction of different patterns of gene activity in the two organisms—one pattern leading to sterility and short life, the other to fertility and long life.

Although the details vary widely, the concepts obtained from studies of both vertebrates and invertebrates are similar: Specific changes in the diet can induce specific changes in patterns of gene activity, which can then be translated into significant changes in life span.

Other Possible Genetic Mechanisms

Telomeres and the loss of genetic information   Other genetic processes have been put forth as potential mechanisms through which the genes might initiate and regulate the aging process. One such group of theories suggests that aging is due to the selective loss of particular kinds of genomic information. Strehler (1986) proposed that aging is due to a loss of the DNA regions coding for ribosomal components. Such a process clearly affects the synthetic and repair capabilities of the cell, although this particular suggestion is probably not correct. Excision and selective destruction of genes have already been observed in the fungus *Podospora* (see Chapter 6). In yeasts, null alleles of the *EST1* gene result in the gradual loss of chromosomal telomeric sequences (the peculiar sequences located at the chromosome tips in most but not all species). This loss leads to a progressive decrease in chromosome stability and eventually to the onset of senescence and cell death (Lundblad and Szostak 1989). On the other hand, telomeres do not shorten during the senescence of *Podospora* (Schwartz and Osiewacz 1996).

Telomere shortening has attracted a great deal of attention recently, particularly as it affects humans. Telomeres are composed of highly repeated DNA sequences combined with particular proteins, and they are found at the ends of chromosomes. We discuss them in more detail in Chapter 11, in the context of cellular aging processes. For the moment, we want to address the question of whether the normal process of telomere shortening could inactivate genes located near the ends of the chromosomes in organisms other than yeasts. If so, this might provide a mechanism for the progressive loss of genetic information with age. In a study of this question, a marker gene was transfected into a human cell line and integrated itself near the telomere of chromosome 13 (Sprung,

Sabatier, and Murname 1996). Measurements of the marker gene activity were obtained from subclones of the cell line with different telomere lengths. No alteration in marker gene expression was seen, thereby suggesting that proximity of a gene to a telomere need not result in a loss or repression of genetic information in human cells.

Thus, telomere-induced loss of genetic information occurs in yeasts and perhaps in other organisms, but it clearly is not a universal mechanism. And the hypothesis does not speak to the aging processes that take place in nondividing cells such as neurons and skeletal muscle, nor does it adequately address aging at the organismic level (see Chapter 12). The telomere hypothesis does not seem to be an adequate explanation for all aging, although telomeres seem to play a role in cellular replicative senescence and in cancers. We will discuss telomeres again in Chapter 11 from the perspective of cellular mechanisms of aging.

Signal transduction and the attenuation of information transmission Another group of genetic theories suggests that aging involves alterations in the functioning of the signal transduction pathways that regulate so much of cellular functioning. Whatever the nature of the genetic mechanisms regulating aging and longevity, they do not operate in isolation from the environment; longevity is environmentally modulated. Parsons (1978) and others have suggested that environmental stress in *Drosophila* might well alter the patterns of gene expression in such a manner as to retard aging and increase longevity. This suggestion is similar to the explanation given earlier for the mechanism by which dietary restriction achieves its effects and to the model that we have developed to depict the operation of the extended-longevity phenotype. This apparent unity of mechanisms suggests that such interactions between genes and environment are of general importance in regulating the individual's aging and longevity. Such interactions promise to be very complex.

One general example of the role of signaling mechanisms in aging might be the balance maintained by a tissue between the proliferation or the apoptotic death of its component cells. As discussed in Chapter 11, the balance between these two opposed processes appears to be maintained by means of tissuewide signaling mechanisms (Raff 1992).

Another example of the complicated manner in which these intrinsic and extrinsic factors interact to bring about alterations in gene activity can be found in signal transduction mechanisms. The essential point is that external signals impinge on the cell, are transduced into an appropriate intracellular signal, and in that form act to turn genes on and off. The cicuitry of this mechanism raises the possibility that age-related changes in either the reception of the signal or the transmission of the signal could lead to changes in gene expression. A thorough examination of the topic is beyond the scope of this text. Nonetheless, a well-studied example is briefly described in Figure 10.6 (Papaconstantinou et al. 1996). This diagram depicts the specific manner in which the NFκB transcription factor is acted on by internal and external factors, but it may also be viewed as a representative model of how signal transduction pathways integrate the signals from several different levels to activate stress-response genes. Alterations in any of the

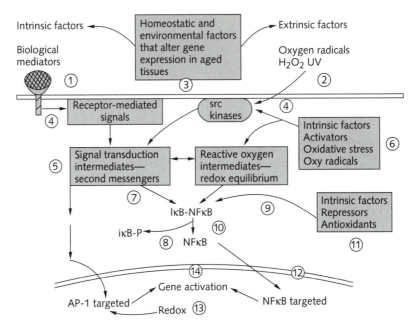

Figure 10.6   A model outlining the general interactions of the signal trans-duction–redox pathways that regulate the *trans*-acting factors of the stress-response genes. Turning on a particular stress-response gene (step 14) is but the end result of a complex cascade of interacting events. This diagram shows how the NFkB transcription factor can be recruited via pathway inter-mediates common to both intrinsic and extrinsic factors. Any age-associated effect of this cascade of events from external signals to gene activation will affect the expression and regulation of the stress response. (From Papaconstantinou et al. 1996.)

components of this complicated pathway could alter the sensitivity of the cell to these external signals or perhaps change the efficiency with which the signal is transmitted through the pathway. Any such change could decrease the organ-ism's ability to respond to stress. And it would do this, not through a direct effect on the particular stress-response gene being studied or on the transcription factor that turns it on and off, but indirectly via an effect on the pathway by which the external signals are sent to the nuclear genome.

Some data support this suggestion. For example, even low levels of H_2O_2 will, when applied to cells, cause the binding of heat shock factors to DNA (Becker et al. 1990) and will induce the expression of several genes known to be important in protection against oxidative stress (Crawford et al. 1996). Arlan Richardson and his colleagues have demonstrated that the age-related and caloric restriction-induced changes seen in the *hsp70* gene are brought about at the level of tran-scription (Heydari et al. 1993). The pathway developed by Papaconstantinou and his colleagues (1996) and outlined in Figure 10.6 provides a known mechanism for the regulated translation of environmental signals into new patterns of gene activity. We have pointed out elsewhere that aging-related changes involve alterations (often decreases) in the levels of various proteins, hormones, and other substances. Such normal age-related changes elsewhere in the body might attenuate the signal transduction process by which this single transcription factor is activated, and with its attenuation the gene expression levels of all the genes normally under the transcriptional control of this single factor are also attenuated.

Gene activity patterns and aging   It is an obvious observation that aging is something that happens at the end of life. But this does not mean that aging has no antecedents early in life. Ample data suggest that the rate of aging and the longevity of the adult can be influenced by events that take place during prenatal or juvenile stages. One identifying characteristic of developing systems is their characteristic tissue- and time-specific patterns of gene expression. Indeed, modern developmental genetics seeks to understand the processes by which an egg changes itself into an adult in terms of describing the ever-shifting mosaic of the interacting patterns of gene activity that modulate the appearance of specific structures in specific locations at specific times (Lawrence 1992; Gilbert 1997).

Aging was once considered by many to be based on the eroding away some of the animal's synthetic capabilities, and hence genetically uninteresting. Much of the genetic evidence presented in this text implies that there should be distinct patterns of gene activity in adults, reminiscent perhaps of the situation that prevails during development. Recent evidence presented by Helfand and his collaborators explicitly supports this implication. Using *Drosophila*, these investigators examined enhancer trap mutants, which secrete into the cell a stainable marker substance whenever their gene is active. They were able to visualize these gene activity patterns in the antennae of the fly during its adult life span (Helfand et al. 1995). The results showed that only 20 percent of the 49 genes examined are constitutive, while 80 percent show a changing expression. Of these, 55 percent increase their activities from an initially low level, and 25 percent decrease from an initially high level. When using mutants and/or temperature conditions that alter the absolute life span, these researchers found that the activity of many genes remained appropriately scaled to the altered longevity. In other words, these patterns of gene activity are linked to the animals' physiological age. John Tower has independently obtained data permitting the same interpretation (Tower 1996). Presumably, the *clock* mutants of *C. elegans* (discussed earlier), which apparently slow down all aspects of the animal's physiology, might offer some insight into the nature of the mechanism that coordinates gene expression patterns and regulates physiological age.

The activity patterns of some genes appear to be linked to chronological age (that is, they are time dependent) and not to physiological age (Rogina and Helfand 1996). It will be of interest to determine if such genes are themselves regulated directly by the biological clock mechanism known to be operative in the fly.

The importance of these studies is that they make clear that the aging adult is not a genetically uninteresting set of constitutively active or inactive genes, but is rather a continuation of the shifting mosaic of gene activities found in earlier stages. No evidence supports the view that these changing gene expression patterns reflect a senescence program of some sort. But the data do suggest that the genes active in the adult stage are presumably interacting with one another and with their environment; thus, the evidence reinforces our conviction that the regulation of gene expression plays a central role in the maturation and aging of the adult.

Does alteration of the patterns of gene activity lead to an altered life span?. Leffelaar and Grigliatti (1984) described a single-gene mutation in *Drosophila* that significantly shortens the life span by accelerating the aging process. They observed that the behavioral biomarkers used to determine the animals' functional age were accelerated so that they appeared at "younger" chronological ages. The shortened life span was brought about by an acceleration of aging, beginning at the earliest adult stage. Analogous strains (the SAM strains) have been found in the mouse (Takada et al. 1981). Although their utility as a model of aging has been questioned (Harrison 1994; see Chapter 6), the two experiments together are consistent with the idea that the rate of aging can be accelerated (as here) or slowed (as in the antioxidant experiments discussed earlier).

It is important to decide whether changes in gene expression are causally related to changes in longevity. These are difficult determinations to make. We have obtained what we regard as strong evidence supporting such a causal relationship. We know that selection for increased longevity in our flies was accompanied by a specific and coordinate up-regulation of antioxidant gene expression (see Figure 6.17). When we took these long-lived strains and reverse-selected them for shortened longevity, the antioxidant gene expression levels returned to values identical with those of the normal-lived control strains (see Figure 10.7). The large change in life spans is accompanied by large changes in antioxidant gene expression patterns; non-antioxidant enzyme activities showed only a small change. This experiment provides evidence supporting the existence of a causal link between gene activity and life span.

In several species it is possible to isolate mutants and/or strains that have either an accelerated or an extended aging process. One interpretation of these findings is that at least two genetic systems are intimately involved in regulating the normal aging process in these organisms. Both systems produce normal but temporally altered patterns of aging, and may be viewed as acting as positive and negative regulators of aging and longevity under normal circumstances. As we learn more about the different ways in which the organism can respond genetically to the various stresses it faces, and as we identify other and different genes that are necessary to an effective response, the systems we are trying to describe will become more difficult to describe in words alone. Complexity increases rapidly as the number of individual genes increases, and the intuitive understanding of feedback effects will be more difficult. At some time, we may well have to adopt a circuit simulation of genetic networks (McAdams and Shapiro 1995), in which the genetic circuitry is analyzed with the tools and symbols of electrical engineering. Treating the genome as an evolving, integrated, sequential logic circuit may help us to understand it better. The first steps in this process are computer simulations based on an interacting network of equations describing the observed kinetic changes in a few important metabolic processes (Chapter 13).

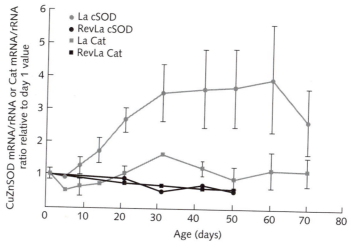

Figure 10.7 The CuZn superoxide dismutase (CuZnSOD) and catalase (Cat) mRNA prevalence levels were measured in the reverse-selected (Rev-La) strain and compared to normal-lived (R) and long-lived (La) controls. The figure shows the data for the Rev-La and La strains; the R strain data is omitted for clarity, but it ranges from 0.9 to 1.2 for both genes for the measured life span, such that it approximately overlaps the La data. Forward selection (i.e., from R to La) resulted in an increase in mean life span from ca. 48 days to ca. 75 days; this is accompanied by a significant increase in CuZnSOD mRNA levels. Reverse selection (i.e., from La to Rev-La) resulted in a decrease in mean life span to ca. 53 days. This is accompanied by a significant decrease in CuZnSOD mRNA levels. (From Arking et al.1998.)

• Summary

The systemic theories of aging range from those that view aging as the consequence of the coordinated effect of thousands of different genes to those that view aging as being under the control of one specific gene (or a comparably small number of specific genes). Despite the vast differences in the mechanisms proposed by each theory, they are all fundamentally rooted in a genetic, or systemic, approach to the analysis of aging. They are not purely deterministic, since all of them allow some extent of environmental modulation of aging and longevity.

What is perhaps most interesting about these several different theories is that the more successful of them (that is, the more predictive) seem to be based on experimental data pointing to the involvement of the antioxidant defense enzymes in the aging process. Thus some of the several theories may have more in common than initially meets the eye. Manipulation of the antioxidant defenses may well be of prime importance to the aging process, but one may be able to affect these enzymes by any one of a variety of approaches—either indirectly via dietary restriction or environmental modulation or directly via a genetic procedure. This suggests that there may be more than one mechanism acting to regulate these genes.

An early (or delayed) decrease in general protein synthesis would have the effect of decreasing the animal's antioxidant defense system at an early (or delayed) time and thus bring about the onset of senescence at an early (or delayed) time. The mitochondrial-damage theories suggest that both the ability to repair damage and the ability to deflect it may be of some importance. The discussion of protein degradation and turnover suggests a deeper mechanism than those discussed so far: namely, that the fundamental process of aging may be related to the cell's ability to repair, maintain, and replace itself. Any genomically based process that contributes to this homeostatic ability—be it an enhanced antioxidant defense or a temporally lengthened period of maximum gene activity or a delay in the slowing of the protein degradative processes or a delay in the free radical–induced damage to repair processes—will then be viewed as a genetically based, systemic mechanism of aging.

The same phenotype may be brought about by any one of several different genetic mechanisms. But the heterogeneity may be deceiving. At a deeper level, each of these several processes may be exerting its effects because it is affecting the time of occurrence of certain events crucial to the aging process. This effect may well involve an altered control of metabolism. In that sense, then, aging may turn out to be a genetically driven, environmentally modulated, event-dependent process composed of similar common changes at a deep level, but characterized by unique strain-specific changes at a superficial level.

Aging as an Intracellular Process

The Basic Assumptions Underlying Such Theories

Implicit in an intracellular theory of aging is the idea that the aging processes are autonomous within the cell. We age because our cells age. Some theories suggest that all cells contain this "aging clock" and are equally affected; others require that the "clock" be active only in certain defined subsets of cells, and the organism senesces as a pleiotropic consequence of the functional failure of these cells. Both concepts are plausible; the difficulty lies in obtaining the data necessary to test either one.

Adequate tests of these theories depend on the use of techniques that allow characterization of certain types of cells and assaying of their autonomy and fate under defined experimental conditions, with the eventual goal of describing the mechanisms responsible for the physiological decrements that are characteristic of the aging cell. There are several different but equally useful procedures whereby these goals may be met. A defined population of cells may be removed from the body and grown *in vitro*, where it may be isolated from the influences of other cells and tissues. Alternatively, one might examine aging cells *in situ* to characterize and manipulate the age-related changes that take place within them. Or one might combine these two approaches by allowing cells to age *in situ*, removing them from the organism at specified times, and assaying them *in vitro*. We will discuss examples of each of these approaches.

Aging in Dividing Cells: Cellular Life Spans and Organismic Longevity

Historical Background

From the point of view of gerontology, the history of cell culture may be divided into two phases. The first phase began in 1910 with the pioneering work of Ross

Harrison, who was the first to demonstrate not only that vertebrate tissue can be kept alive outside the body but also that the cells will continue growing and differentiating when bathed with body fluids *in vitro*. An early idea, popularized by the writings of August Weismann (see Figure 4.1), was that aging and death are the price of cellular differentiation. In other words, the organism is mortal, but if its component cells could be freed from the constraints of the body and from the need to differentiate into specialized parts, then they might be able to live forever. The rapid advance in *in vitro* culture techniques brought about by Harrison's discovery soon made it possible to test this proposition directly.

Carrel (1912) and Ebeling (1913) reported that they were able to keep fibroblast cells obtained from chicken embryonic heart tissue alive and in a state of continuous proliferation for at least 34 years by culturing them in laboratory glassware on plasma clots for support and nutrition. Since the maximum life span of the chicken is about 30 years, this seemed to be a good operational demonstration of cellular immortality. Further support for the concept of cellular immortality appeared to come from the discovery of several different cell lines, given identifying names such as L cells (Earle 1943) or HeLa cells (Gey, Coffman, and Kubicel 1952), that could be grown continuously in culture without showing any decline in proliferative vigor. Only later was it realized that these cell lines are derived from transformed (i.e., cancerous) cells, and thus the lessons drawn from them are not directly applicable to theories of normal cellular aging.

The second phase of cytogerontology may be conveniently dated from the now classic paper of Hayflick and Moorhead (1961) showing that cultured human fibroblast cells divide a finite number of times and then stop dividing. This key observation led both to new studies and to new interpretations of the older reports. For example, Hayflick (1982) has pointed out that not only had no one confirmed Carrel's and Ebeling's original observation of immortal cells, but the procedures used by Carrel for the preparation of his chick embryo extract probably permitted the contribution of new and viable cells to the chick heart strain at each feeding. And this suspicion was borne out by the fact that when Carrel's experiments were repeated using more modern and more stringent procedures, it was not possible to keep the chick cultures alive for more than 44 months (Gey et al. 1974). Accordingly, Carrel's culture was not composed of 34-year-old cells and their descendants but was instead a 34-year continuous culture in which fresh embryonic cells were added every week or so. These new insights, encouraged by the Hayflick and Moorhead report, logically led to the concept that the visible and functional manifestations of aging in organisms may very well have an intracellular basis. This is the concept that we will explore now in some depth.

The Cell Cycle

Our cells reproduce by mitosis, and the presence (or absence) of this event is what organizes the manner in which we view the cell. The cell cycle is defined as the interval between the completion of mitosis in the parent cell and the onset of mitosis in one or both daughter cells (Figure 11.1). The average length of the cell cycle and of its component phases varies widely from cell type to cell type and can be altered by a wide array of various factors. Baserga (1985) and Wigg (1995) provide good reviews of the topic.

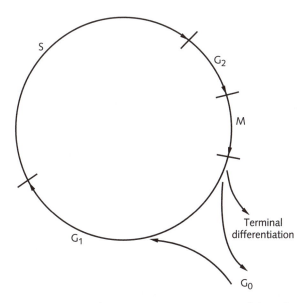

Figure 11.1   A diagrammatic representation of the cell cycle. After mitosis (M), the cell enters the first gap period (G_1), during which it prepares itself for genome replication. This replication takes place during the synthesis (S) period. The cell then enters a second gap period (G_2) preparatory to mitosis. Cells can leave the cycle via two mechanisms. Cells that are temporarily arrested in their growth (by removal of exogenous growth factors from the medium, for example) are termed quiescent cells, since they are capable of reentering the cycle if provided the proper conditions. Such cells are considered to be in the G_0 state. Terminally differentiated cells cannot be recalled into the cell cycle and will eventually die.

There are two types of nondividing cells. Cultured cells can be kept quiescent and viable in the G_0 state for long periods of time if a factor that is required for cell division is simply removed from the medium. *In vivo*, adult liver cells are metabolically very active but mitotically almost totally inactive. Yet, if part of the liver is surgically removed, these quiescent cells will leave the G_0 state and enter S phase after a lag of about only 18 hours or so. The cells are thus capable of reproducing if they receive the appropriate signal. The terminally differentiated cells are quite different from all other cells. They have ceased dividing and cannot be recalled into the cell cycle. Many of our tissues are composed of such terminally differentiated cells. Their life span is quite variable, ranging from 1 or 2 weeks for keratinocytes and intestinal epithelial cells, to 3 months for red blood cells, to a lifetime for most neurons.

Although all normal cells have a finite life span, they also have the capability, under extraordinary circumstances, of surviving substantially longer than they normally do. For example, transplantation experiments have shown that the cells of mouse skin (Krohn 1966) and of mouse mammary tissue (Daniel 1977) can survive *in vivo* for periods of time far exceeding the maximum life span of the original donor. The mouse mammary tissue has been kept alive longer than 6 years when transplanted to new hosts at yearly intervals. The tissue has a much shorter life span, about 2 years, when it is transplanted at quarterly intervals. In both cases, the growth tends to slow down as the number of transplant generations increases. Thus the number of transplant generations is a better indication of cellular aging *in vivo* than is the mere passage of time, and there appears to be a 15 percent loss of proliferative ability per transplant generation regardless of the time interval (Daniel 1977).

However, this loss of growth potential does not seem to be closely tied to a corresponding loss of the cell's physiological competence, for even very old and non-proliferating mammary gland cells will produce abundant milk if maintained in lactating hosts. Thus, although the loss of proliferative ability is one useful sign of cellular aging, it is probably not correct to equate it with a deteriorative event. The cell seems to be constructed such that a common precondition to its becoming functionally and structurally specialized is that it must first leave the cell cycle (see Figure 11.1; also seee Walsh and Perlman 1997). Differentiated tissues that are characterized by continuous cell replacement often rely on stem cells as the progenitor of the new cells. We will explore this topic in greater detail in the next section.

The only way a cell can stay in the cell cycle indefinitely is to be transformed. Human fibroblast cells are quite resistant (but not totally so) to both spontaneous and chemical or virus-induced transformation; rodent cells can be spontaneously or chemically transformed with relative ease. Regardless of their origin, transformed cells exhibit loss or inactivation of the control mechanisms that regulate cell movement and cell division. Such cells show no loss of their proliferative ability with each successive passage through the cell cycle. Of course, they usually have also lost the ability to form a normal differentiated cell type. Many transformed cells have the ability to induce tumors in appropriate host animals. Thus the acquisition of an indefinite growth potential is the first of several steps necessary to transform a normal cell into a neoplastic cell (see Baserga 1985 for an extended discussion of this point).

When normal cells are assayed *in situ* in normal host animals under normal conditions, many cell types exhibit changes analogous to those seen *in vitro*. In general, these changes include the following observations: (1) The length of the cell cycle increases with age, particularly in the G_1 and S phases, (2) the proportion of cells within a tissue that are able to divide decreases with age, and (3) there is much more heterogeneity in the transit time among cell populations taken from old animals than from young animals (Lesher, Fry, and Kohn 1961). It is reasonable to wonder if the decrements associated with aging and observed in most tissues have anything to do with this decreased proliferative ability of its component cells, as observed both *in vivo* and *in vitro*. This question has been addressed in several recent reviews (Cristofalo and Pignolo 1995; Campisi 1996; see also the more than two dozen articles dealing with various aspects of this topic in the January/April 1996 special issue of *Experimental Gerontology*).

Cellular Aging *In Vitro*

The typical history of a cell culture is shown in Figure 11.2. After the initial explantation of the cells from their *in vivo* donor to the *in vitro* environment of the

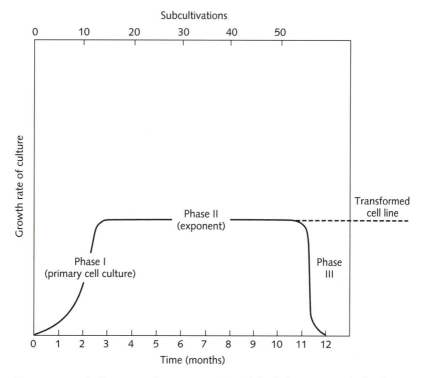

Figure 11.2 A diagrammatic representation of the behavior typical of cells in culture. During Phase I (the primary culture), the cells initially grow slowly, but the growth rate soon increases. This phase ends with the formation of the first confluent sheet. Phase II is characterized by rapid and luxuriant growth. Normal cells in this phase are termed "cell strains." The genome may be altered at any time during this phase such that the cell will be transformed and converted into a "cell line" that has a potentially infinite life span. Normal cells, on the other hand, enter Phase III after a characteristic number of population doublings, their growth rate decreases, and the strains can no longer be maintained by normal culturing techniques.

laboratory, there is a variable period of time (Phase I) during which the cells grow and divide rather slowly. One objective and convenient method of measuring the rate of cell division is to determine the amount of time it takes for the cell population to double in number. If the petri dish is initially half-filled with cells, then one population doubling (PD) occurs when the petri dish is completely filled with cells. The population doubles when every cell present in the beginning of the period divides once, when half of the cells divide twice consecutively, and so on. In Phase I, the first several PDs may take several weeks. This phase probably reflects the time needed for the cells to adapt to the somewhat different environment of test tube and culture flask.

Phase I is followed by a period (Phase II) characterized by a very rapid rate of cell proliferation, which maintains high numbers of cells in the culture. The PD time is relatively constant, usually measured in days. The cultures are usually quite healthy. This plateau period is followed by a time of declining proliferative capacity (Phase III), in which the amount of time required for the population to double appears to increase exponentially. Presumably, this phase is established as more and more cells become committed to terminal differentiation and slip out of the cell cycle.

Concomitant with the increasing number of nonproliferating cells are the passage-dependent changes displayed by a large number of other metabolic and morphological parameters (see Hayflick 1977 for a complete listing). The most consistent structural alterations noted in late-passage cells include the following (Norwood and Smith 1985): (1) an increase in the number of secondary lysosomes, (2) irregularly lobed nuclei, (3) abnormal mitochondria, (4) an increase in cell size, and (5) a decrease in the amount of free polysomes and rough endoplasmic reticulum (both of which are involved in protein synthesis). The cells' metabolism changes as well. Generally speaking, late-passage cells exhibit an increase in their cellular macromolecular content (except DNA) and a decrease in their macromolecular synthetic rate, while senescent cells show an uncoupling of DNA synthesis and a general dysregulation of the cells' coordinated processes (Cristofalo and Pignolo 1995).

In addition to these alterations, several different cell surface alterations are quite important, since the ability of the cell to respond appropriately to external signals depends on their being correctly transduced and modulated in or on the cell membrane. Changes in different types of cell surface receptors are known to take place (Norwood and Smith 1985). One potentially important cell surface change involves a particular membrane-associated glycoprotein called fibronectin. This protein is an essential part of the extracellular matrix to which normal cells *in vivo* and *in vitro* bind and which they use to guide their migration. Developmental studies have shown that extracellular matrix proteins such as fibronectin are capable of inducing specific patterns of gene activity in the cells that are attached to them and that these induced alterations in gene activity patterns are crucial to normal embryonic development. We have known for some time that the amount of fibronectin decreases with age; now we know that the nondividing senescent cells synthesize and express a variant form of fibronectin that is not found in nondividing quiescent (G_0) cells (Porter and Smith 1988). Perhaps the variant fibronectin is associated with the specific inhibition of DNA replication that characterizes these late-passage and senescent cells (Warner and Wang 1989).

In recent years, much attention has been paid to the differences in gene expression observed between proliferative and senescent cells. These differences involve large numbers of genes, some of which appear to play important regulatory roles. For example, when compared to proliferative cells, senescent human fibroblasts are known to have at least 21 different genes repressed, at least 13 other genes overexpressed, and at least 6 genes that show specific posttranslational modifications in their products (Campisi et al. 1996). Certain of these changes in gene expression are important and relevant to both cellular and organismic physiology. Dermal cells, for example, switch from matrix-producing to matrix-degrading when they become replicatively senescent; it is reasonable to wonder whether this change plays a role in the normal aging-related changes observed in our skin (although it must be kept in mind that substantive numbers of proliferative cells can be recovered even from old tissues and that senescent cells may constitute a small minority of the cells in old skin (Campisi et al. 1996).

These genetic differences between proliferative and senescent cells involve more than just the activation or inactivation of particular genes. The transition from one stage to the other also involves posttranslational modification of existing gene products in the cell. Some of these posttranslational changes are quite important in determining whether the cell will divide—a decision that has implications for both cancer and aging. For example, the retinoblastoma protein (RB) is a tumor suppressor, and its presence in the nonphosphorylated form causes the cell to arrest in the G_1 phase of the cell cycle (see Figure 11.1). If the RB protein is posttranslationally phosphorylated, it loses this inhibitory activity and the cell will proceed through the cell cycle. Eugenia Wang has shown that the RB is phosphorylated by a protein kinase termed p45, but that the p45 may be sequestered by a second protein termed statin, or p57. This removal of the p45 protein thereby prevents it from activating the RB protein and relieving the G_1 arrest (Jazwinski, Howard, and Nayak 1995). In effect, these posttranslational changes constitute an elaborate subcellular on–off switch that can be operated by specific molecules sensitive to particular details of cell physiology.

Senescent cells are now known to produce higher amounts of a stainable form of beta-galactosidase, and this difference can be used to identify senescent cells (Dimri et al. 1995). This staining technique has shown that only the skin of older people can contain cells with such high levels of beta-galactosidase, although even in these individuals most skin cells do not fall into this category. Nonetheless, the presence of this enzyme is the first evidence showing accumulation of senescent cells *in vivo*, and its existence confirmed the indirect evidence that such cells accumulate with age *in vivo* and *in vitro*. Thus senescent and proliferative cells are different from one another at several different levels of organization, and one might expect these differences to involve more than just the ability to divide, a point we will return to shortly.

Eventually the culture is lost when the proportion of proliferating cells in the population declines to the point at which less than one PD occurs per culture period. From this point on, there will be relatively fewer dividing cells than at the same point in the previous generation, so the population inevitably will show a decrease in growth rate. Hayflick and others (see below) have shown that such limitations on the cellular life span, however regulated, are intrinsic to the cells and do not appear to reflect other variables, such as the amount of time spent in culture, the nutritional state of the medium, and so forth. This is an important point that is essential to any cell-based systemic theory.

Certain cell cultures are immortal; they never enter Phase III but appear to be permanently locked into Phase II (see Figure 11.2). These transformed cells will continue to proliferate as long as the appropriate nutrients and other factors are supplied to them. In addition, many such immortal cell lines are composed of cells that have an abnormal chromosome constitution. Such mutants or variants probably have suffered some damage to the genetic mechanisms that regulate cell division, and they may be regarded as precancerous, as described earlier.

That there might be a direct connection between cellular and organismic aging was first suggested by Hayflick's report in 1965 that fibroblasts derived from human embryos underwent about 48 PDs *in vitro* (with a range of 35 to 63) while fibroblasts derived from human adults underwent only about 20 PDs (with a range of 14 to 29). Note that the ranges for the PD of fetal and adult tissues do not overlap, despite the obvious large variance. In addition, there is no tight correlation between donor age and PD number: The cells from an 87-year-old yielded 29 PDs, while those from a 26-year-old yielded 20 PDs. A more extensive cross-sectional analysis shows a decrease in the mean number of PDs with increasing age (Figure 11.3). On closer inspection, however, this decrease seems to be driven almost entirely by the apparently real difference in PDs between the very young (individuals 10 years old and younger) and the very old (individuals 70 years and older). There is no significant correlation between donor age and PDs for individuals between the ages of 11 and 69 years.

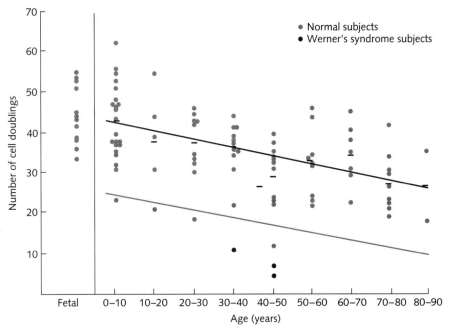

Figure 11.3   The cumulative number of cell doublings achieved by human skin fibroblast cultures plotted as a function of the age of the donor. The calculated linear regression line (black line) for the control group is drawn between the first and ninth decades and has a regression coefficient of −0.20 ± 0.005 standard deviation cell doublings per year, with a correlation coefficient of −0.50. The shaded line is the lower 95 percent confidence limit for the regression line. Note that cells from people with Werner's syndrome undergo significantly fewer PDs than do age-matched controls. (From Martin, Sprague, and Epstein 1970.)

Although there is a clear difference in the proliferative ability of cells derived from very old or very young donors, there does not appear to be a clear difference in the proliferative ability of cells derived from individuals of intermediate ages. This does not mean that there is no relationship between cellular aging and organismic longevity; on the contrary, it means simply that such a relationship may exist, but that if it does, it is neither linear nor very tight. Hayflick and Moorhead (1961) originally interpreted their findings as indicating that the limited proliferative ability of somatic cells is programmed and can be viewed as a repeatable cellular expression of senescence. This interpretation is commonly known as the "Hayflick hypothesis." Despite the temptation to do so, this hypothesis does not require us to extrapolate beyond the data and suggest that senescence of the organism is caused by the loss of its cells' proliferative ability. Whatever the nature of the intrinsic events that bring about the normal aging of the individual, they probably have only an indirect relationship to the events that take place at the cellular level. If long-lived somatic cells undergo changes that alter both their ability to undergo mitosis and their ability to consistently maintain their normal level of function *in situ*, then one could imagine how such a loose linkage could be empirically observed.

Data similar to the results reported by Hayflick and his colleagues, all showing that cells obtained from adult donors are reproducibly different from cells obtained from very young and/or embryonic donors, have been reported by several other investigators using a variety of other human tissues, including T lymphocytes, glial cells, keratinocytes, vascular smooth-muscle cells, lens cells, and endothelial cells (see Cristofalo and Pignolo 1995 for references). It is now a generally accepted observation. The term "Hayflick limit" refers to the repeatable number of population doublings that different cell types can typically achieve under standard culture conditions. Its widespread use reflects the widespread acceptance of the original observations and, to a lesser extent, of the Hayflick hypothesis.

That the replicative life spans are genetically determined was suggested by a study in which skin fibroblasts from three pairs of monozygotic twins showed no significant difference within each twin pair, but did show such differences between pairs (Ryan et al. 1981). In addition, the observation that fibroblasts obtained from patients suffering from Werner's syndrome or from progeria (see Chapter 6) both display a shortened replicative life span and a variable but poor growth capacity also suggests the existence of a genetically modulated relationship between organismic aging and cell proliferation ability. Whether embryonic stem cells, which have been determined but have not yet differentiated, are immortal is not known.

Perhaps the most interesting data are the interspecific comparisons of PD number and species-specific maximum life span (Table 11.1). These data are open to all the criticisms voiced by Promislow (1993); nonetheless they are interesting and illustrate some possible connections. The two variables—PD number and maximum life span—have an imperfect but clear relationship: Compared to long-lived species, short-lived species tend to lose their replicative ability after fewer PDs. The nature of the linkage between the two variables is far from being under-

Table 11.1	The Relationship between Species-Specific Cell Doublings and Species-Specific Maximum Life Span	
Species	*Number of PDs*	*Maximum life span (years)*
Mouse	14–28	3.5
Mink	30–34	10
Chicken	15–35	30
Cow	40–60	30
Man	40–60	115
Tortoise		
Young donor	112–130	175
Old donor	90–102	

Source: From data summarized in Hayflick 1977.

stood, but it could be due to the involvement of overlapping or interacting genes in both processes.

One assumption implicit in the Hayflick hypothesis is that a cell strain with a high number of PDs is composed of moribund cells; that is, the Phase III cells are mostly senescent and/or abnormal and/or dying cells. This is a crucial assumption and one that should be carefully examined. Two main points contradict this assumption. First, any two individual cells, including sister cells, isolated from the same generation of the same cell strain can show a very large variation in their ability to undergo future PDs, the number ranging from 0 to 33 (Smith and Whitney 1980). This variability suggests that in normal cultures a large fraction of the cells in every generation are characterized by a very low proliferation potential. Such cells will be present in the population in lower numbers than rapidly proliferating cells; thus they have a lower probability of surviving through the change of culture dishes associated with the beginning of each new cell generation. Nondividing cells appear to be recruited anew in each cell generation, possibly in a stochastic manner, as earlier suggested by Holliday and colleagues (1977). As a result, the cells that make up a cell strain are not in lockstep with each other, as is implied by the early data, and thus there can be no rigid or precise intracellular counting mechanism used by all the cells to determine their age synchronously.

The second point is that all of the data presented here that were used to support the concept of autonomous cell aging can be equally well used to support the opposing idea: that the departure of cells from the mitotic cycle may be a sign not of aging but of differentiation (Bell et al. 1978). Cell growth and cell differentiation have long been considered mutually exclusive or alternative possibilities for cells. In fact, differentiation leads in many cases to cells that cannot divide, such as our nerve cells or our enucleated red blood corpuscles. Bayreuther and colleagues (1988, 1992a,b, 1993) have shown that the nondividing fibroblasts are not moribund but will, if allowed to live *in vitro* for a long period of time, eventually differentiate into various sorts of normal-looking connective-tissue cells. It is instructive to consider these experiments in some detail.

Human skin fibroblasts were cultured and underwent about 53 PDs in about 300 days, at which time they had exhausted their growth potential. These results are consistent with the data obtained from many laboratories in the past 3 decades. By appropriate culture techniques, however, these nonmitotic cells were kept alive for about another 300 days, during which time the cells completed their differentiation. Bayreuther reported that these differentiated cells eventually either died via apoptosis (which we discuss later in the chapter) or were transformed. During this long period of time in culture, the cells do not stay the same but rather progress through a seven-stage sequence of cell differentiation (Table 11.2). The various stages are distinguished from one another by whether they are mitotic or postmitotic, and by their morphology and their biochemical activities, including that of having different patterns of gene activity. By these criteria, cell Types I through III are considered to be mitotic cells that differ in their shape and their mitotic potential, while cell Types IV through VI are postmitotic and differ in their size. Cell Type VII represents the final stage of cell differentiation and comprises the cells that are degenerating via apoptosis or have been transformed and are now immortalized. Note how the dominant cell type shifts over time, from a preponderance of Type II in the PD 17 culture to a preponderance of Type VI in the PM 40 culture. The cells in the culture at the end of the year are very different from the cells that were used to start the culture.

These mitotic and morphological changes are accompanied by striking quantitative changes in the cell's synthetic abilities (see Table 11.2). The PM 40 cells'

Table 11.2 Progressive Differentiation of HH8 Fibroblasts and Alterations in their Mitotic and Synthetic Capabilities

Mitotic?	Culture[a]	Percent distribution of cell types[b]							Macromolecular synthetic activity relative to PD 17 values		
		I	II	III	IV	V	VI	VIII	RNA	Protein	Collagen
Yes	PD 17	18	70	10	1	0.5	0.5	0	1.00	1.00	1.00
Yes	PD 30	3	78	16	2	0.5	0.5	0	1.33	5.6	1.4
Yes	PD 55	0	1	79	14	3	3	0	3.36	7.9	4.3
No	PM 1	0	0	30	18	40	12	0	6.51	9.5	5.7
No	PM 3	0	0	3	31	43	23	0	9.93	11.2	6.2
No	PM 7	0	0	0	16	32	51	1	11.5	12.6	6.3
No	PM 11	0	0	0	4	5	87	4	9.5	12.4	9.6
No	PM 24	0	0	0	0	2	89	9	10.8	12.9	9.7
No	PM 40	0	0	0	0	0	88	12	11.6	11.8	10.2

Source: Data from Table 1 of Bayreuther 1992.
[a]PD, population doubling generation number; PM, postmitotic weeks in culture.
[b]Cell types I through VII are described in the text.

ability to synthesize DNA has disappeared, but their ability to synthesize other macomolecules has increased greatly. In addition to these quantitative changes, each cell type is qualitatively distinguished by its own particular polypeptide pattern, indicating the synthesis of cell type–specific proteins. The quantitative and qualitative measures both suggest that reproducible changes in gene expression patterns are taking place. Certain proto-oncogenes (c-*fos* and c-*jun*) are down-regulated in the postmitotic cells, leading to speculation as to their role in inhibiting DNA synthesis and blocking the cells from entering mitosis (Brenneisen, Gogol, and Bayreuther 1994).

Finally, cells identified as being in particular stages of differentiation are found *in vivo* at particular and different locations in the skin; the mitotic Types I through III are stratified in the reticular layer; the postmitotic Types IV and V are localized in the papillary layer and Type VI under the basal lamina (Bayreuther et al. 1992). Thus the starting population of the fibroblasts usually used in these cultures is in a predifferentiated state and consists of different types of cells destined to form heterogeneous tissues within one particular organ. In addition to this spatial heterogeneity, the distribution of these six cell types in humans depends on age (Table 11.3). Note that, as might be predicted from the data in Figure 11.3, the younger the individual the greater the proportion of mitotic fibroblast cell types that are found in primary cultures of the skin. This description of progressive cell differentiation suggests that the growth curve of Figure 11.2 is too simple, since it reflects only the changes in growth rate and not the changes in the cells themselves. Presumably cell Types I through III would occupy the Phase I and part of the Phase II portions of that curve, while cell Types IV through VI would occupy the rest of the Phase II portion. Cell Type VII would probably occupy the Phase III section of the curve.

Late-passage, nondividng fibroblasts appear to be able to survive a very long time in culture and show signs of differentiation *in vitro*. There is still some controversy over the complexities of the differentiated cells observed by different lab-

Table 11.3   **The Age-Dependent Distribution of Fibroblast Cell Types in the Skin of Human Donors**

Age (years)	*Percent distribution of cell types*							
	MF I	MF II	MF III	Sum of MF	PMF IV	PMF V	PMF VI	Sum of PMF
10	15	59	13	87	3	1	9	13
30	7	54	12	73	11	3	13	27
50	0	38	30	68	6	7	19	32
70	0	6	39	45	14	5	36	55
90	0	2	12	14	21	8	57	86

Source: Data from Table 1 of Bayreuther et al. 1992.
Note: MF I, MF II, MF III: mitotic fibroblast stages I, II, and III; PMF IV, PMF V, PMF VI: postmitotic fibroblast stages IV, V, and VI.

oratories in their cultures, and over the eventual fate of these cells. Not every lab has duplicated Bayreuther's observations in detail. Nonetheless, there appears to be agreement on the two main points: that the postreplicative cells are stable and can survive for a long time, and that they resemble terminally differentiated cells (Campisi 1996). Thus these results suggest that what is encoded in the cell's genome is not an aging clock per se, but rather a mechanism that enables cells to slip out of an active mitotic mode into a terminal predifferentiation mode.

The probable existence of such a mechanism was supported by the findings of Lumpkin and collaborators (1986), who isolated poly-A+ RNA from senescent human diploid fibroblasts and injected it into cells that were capable of proliferating. These mRNAs significantly inhibited the host cells from entering mitosis, relative to controls. The inhibitory ability could be abolished if the mRNA fraction was treated with RNase before being injected. Finally, the authors noted that the inhibitory signal is not present in "young," or proliferation-competent, cells . The clear implication of these data is that the inhibition of cell proliferation is an active process that requires the transcription of some gene(s), and that the presence of the corresponding mRNA in the cell is necessary if the cell is to be inhibited from entering mitosis again.

There is at least one gene that is overexpressed in late-passage or quiescent cells and whose product acts to inhibit DNA synthesis. This gene, *SDI-1*, is induced by the p53 protein and has been identified as an inhibitor of multiple complexes of cyclin G1 and cyclin-dependent kinases (Smith 1992). The gene thus inhibits important regulatory complexes that govern cell division. Other factors are likely involved, given that at least four different complementation groups (groups of genes) control the senescent phenotype (Pereira-Smith and Smith 1983; Warner and Wang 1989). Recall that an independent investigation by Eugenia Wang found that the p57 inhibition of the RB protein also inhibits cell division. Therefore, both molecular and genetic investigations suggest the existence of multiple control pathways regulating cell division and the quiescent/senescent phenotype.

This analysis of somatic-cell genetics is based on the result of many cell fusion experiments showing that replicative senescence is dominant to replicative immortality (see Smith and Pereira-Smith 1996 or Campisi 1996 for references). The approach taken by Pereira-Smith and Smith (1983) assumed that the control of cell proliferation is genetic and that nonsenescing cell lines that complement each other (that is, that generate senescing hybrids) would prove to have mutations in different genes. On the other hand, if the two cells had lesions in the same gene, complementation would not be possible and their hybrid cell would display an immortal phenotype.

To test these hypotheses, the investigators fused different immortal cell lines and determined which cell pairs formed immortal hybrids. These studies identifed four complementation groups, suggesting that there are at least four genes or gene pathways controlling cell proliferative senescence. In some cases, it was possible to assign specific chromosomes to specific complementation groups, such as chromosome 4 to complementation group B (Ning et al. 1991). No immortal cell lines can be assigned to more than one complementation group, which means that a small number of highly specific genes are involved in promoting cell senescence (Pereira-Smith and Ning 1992). Finally, cells of diverse tissue origins may belong to the same complementation group, thus suggesting that the genes controlling replicative senescence do not act in a tissue-specific manner. Finally, one of these genes has been identified. The complementation group B gene on chromosome 4, mentioned above, has been tentatively identified as coding for a transcription factor (Ehrenstein 1998). The gene, now called *MORF4*, is up-regulated in senescent and quiescent cells, but down-regulated in actively dividing cells. Once its target genes are identified, then we will have a much better idea of the mechanisms underlying the genetic control of cell proliferation.

The large amount of information obtained by many laboratories in the past few years has led to an increased understanding of the mechanisms probably underlying replicative senescence in human fibroblasts. One possible mechanism suggesting the way in which the alteration of key growth regulators acts to bring about replicative senescence is shown in Figure 11.4. The first portion of the figure indicates some of the growth regulatory genes normally expressed in dividing or quiescent cells. The lower portion indicates genes that cannot be induced in senescent cells. A feedback control loop may be operative here, in that one function of the late genes is to down-regulate the p21 protein. This protein is an inhibitor of the various *CDK* genes whose activity is essential for cell division. This down-regulation of the inhibitor can take place in quiescent but not in senescent

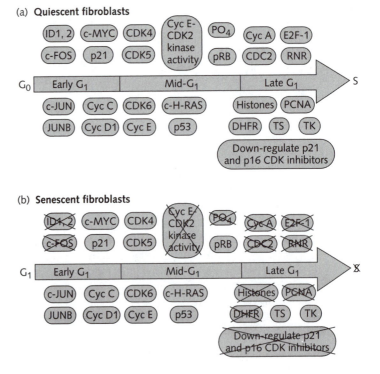

Figure 11.4 A comparison of mitogen induction on the expression of cell cycle regulatory genes in quiescent early-passage and senescent normal human diploid fibroblasts. The genes crossed out cannot be induced in senescent cells. CDK, cyclin-dependent kinase; Cyc, cyclin; DHFR, dihydrofolate reductase; PCNA, proliferating cell nuclear antigen; PO₄-pRB, phosphorylated form of retinoblastoma susceptibility gene product; RNR, ribonucleotide reductase; TK, thymidine kinase; TS thymidylate synthetase. (From Campisi 1996.)

cells. The inhibition enables the cell to divide and may account for its permanent state of replicative senescence. Transformation is the only process known that enables the cell to escape this inhibition. Not shown in the figure are the other multiple and parallel control paths, a few of which were discussed earlier.

There is a paradox here. The inhibition of cell proliferation is controlled by an active and positive genetic process, implying that the regulation has a function and that the function is adaptive. But we have already reviewed the evidence suggesting that aging is not adaptive. If our reasoning in the latter case was correct, the inhibition of cell proliferation should not be viewed as an aging phenotype. Yet proliferation-incompetent cells are much more prevalent in older organisms, so this inhibition seems to be part of the aging phenotype. One solution to the paradox was provided by Dykhuisen (1974) and Holliday (1990), who suggested that the limit to cell growth is a barrier against uncontrolled proliferation of potential or real tumor cells. Another solution is the suggestion that the loss of proliferation potential of somatic cells is simply another manifestation of the disposable-soma theory (Kirkwood 1987), which we discussed in Chapter 4.

Given these facts, we would expect very few cells from an embryonic donor to undergo replicative senescence, since most of them would be in the predifferentiation state. But with each cell divison, there is a finite chance that a given cell will be recruited into the nondividing or predifferentiation population and have its gene activity patterns altered, signal transduction patterns changed, DNA synthesis–inhibiting proteins synthesized, and future cell divisions inhibited. With time, one would expect more and more cells to cease dividing and to begin differentiating. Growth would thus be more often associated with cells from young donors. Such an explanation could indirectly account for the difference in the remaining PDs observed between cells from embryonic and adult donors (see Table 11.1) and may also account for the difference in the ease with which endothelial cells from adult donors of different ages are able to establish primary cultures—that is, enter Phase I (Ogborn and Martin 1985).

Taken together, these various findings suggest that it is unlikely that the ultimate life span of the individual organism is the simple result of a failure in the proliferative capacity of its component cells. However, changes in the regulation of the cell cycle may well be representative of the mechanisms that regulate other important physiological processes that play an important role in organismic senescence. The so-called Hayflick limit is the result of an intrinsic process that blocks indefinite cell division, but the relationship of this barrier to the normal aging process at the organismic level is not clear. It is a common clinical observation that the wounds of the elderly heal more slowly, so it is tempting, although somewhat premature, to suggest that this lower rate of healing has its biological basis in the described behavior of the fibroblast. Other cell types, such as the T lymphocyte (Perillo et al. 1989; Efros 1996), are also known to exhibit a characteristically limited *in vitro* life span, and these changes may be similarly related to the systematic decrements in function involving those cell types.

Finally, human diploid cells are more susceptible to oxidative stress at late passage than at early passage, apparently because of decreased glutathione concentration and catalase activity (Yuan, Kaneko, and Matsuo 1996)—a finding with certain parallels to the situation in aging organisms (see Chapters 6 and 9). In this sense, replicative senescence in cells *in vitro* is a highly accessible model, the study of which will enable us to better understand the changes with age of our own cells *in vivo*. Certainly cancer and atherosclerosis are the two most prevalent serious age-associated pathologies, and the successful treatment of at least the former will depend in part on the knowledge of cell division regulation that we will harvest from our studies on replicative senescence (Hartwell and Kastan 1994). The work initiated by Hayflick and Moorhead (1961) has enhanced our appreciation of the importance of basic cellular mechanisms in the aging process and has focused our attention on understanding how these mechanisms enhance our longevity at both the cellular and the organismic levels.

Telomeres and Cellular Aging

Regardless of the nature of the relationship between organismic aging and the Hayflick limit, the question remains as to how the cell counts off each cell division. How does it remember the number of its past mitotic events, and how does this memory act to eventually impede the cell from transiting the cell cycle again? We discussed telomeres briefly in Chapter 10, but now is the opportune time to discuss them again in some detail, since they have been proposed as being intimately involved in reckoning the number of cell divisions.

Barbara McClintock (1941) and H. J. Muller (1938) were the first to recognize, some 60 years ago, that chromosome ends are different from the rest of the chromosome. Once the structure of DNA was deduced and the enzymatic basis of its replication worked out, it became apparent first to Olovnikov (1971, 1996) that the replication mechanism was incomplete. Because of the synthetic characteristics of conventional DNA polymerases, which can replicate DNA only in the 5'-to-3' direction and cannot initiate synthesis of a DNA chain without the assistance of a primer template, the ends of the chromosome cannot be replicated completely. One DNA strand of a linear chromosome will be replicated to the very end, but the other strand will have a short 8- to 12-base gap at the 5' end. In principle, each chromosome in a cell that divides repeatedly will shorten progressively from both ends until an essential sequence becomes eliminated or inactivated (Olovnikov 1973). The loss of these presumably vital gene functions was assumed to initiate the aging process. The scenario is logical. The problem is determining whether it actually occurs in an aging animal.

Telomeres are the structures that cap the ends of chromosomes. They are now known to consist of short terminal DNA repeats (Figure 11.5a). They serve the triple functions of protecting the chromosome against damage, maintaining the normal length of each chromosome, and possibly maintaining nuclear organization via their association with the nuclear membrane and other cell structures. Telomeric DNA sequences of a variety of species were only recently obtained, and they show surprising patterns of similarities and differences among species. For example, TTAGGG/CCCTAA is the sequence of all telomeric DNA in all vertebrates, as well as some protozoans and fungi, but other fungi and other invertebrates have very different sequences, and *Drosophila* has no such sequence and uses an entirely different telomeric mechanism (Mason and Biessmann 1995; Zakian 1995). The telomeric DNA sequences are replicated not by the nor-

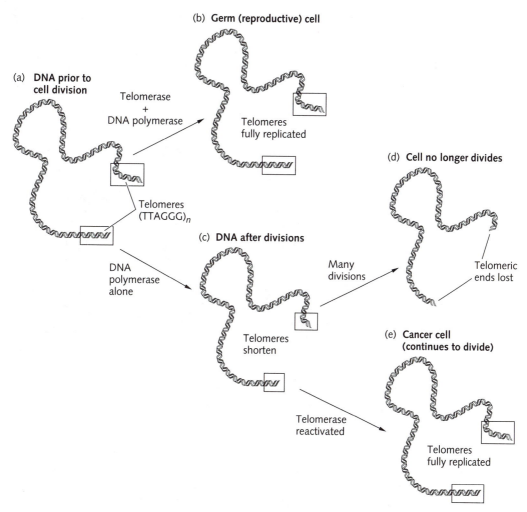

Figure 11.5 A diagrammatic outline of the status of the telomeric ends of chromosomes during cell division in normal and cancerous cells. (a) The full telomeric DNA sequence in a chromosome prior to cell division. (b) The chromosomes of germ cells that will reproduce to create the next generation contain both DNA polymerase and telomerase. In these cells, replicated chromosomes maintain their full telomeric length. (c) In the presence of DNA polymerase but the absence of telomerase, the telomeric ends shorten with each replication. (d) Once a cell "runs out" of telomeres, it no longer enters mitosis and cell division stops. (e) Should the telomerase become active again, the cell can continue to divide indefinitely, as cancer cells do.

mal DNA polymerase alone, but by DNA polymerase along with an unusual enzyme called telomerase, which contains short RNA sequences complementary to the DNA repeats. As long as telomerase is active, the short underreplicated gaps in the DNA are filled in by hexameric repeats of 5'-TTAGGG-3' DNA coded for by the RNA portion of the enzyme, so the chromosome will not shorten. But if the enzyme is inactivated, each chromosome will lose some telomeric DNA at every round of replication (Figure 11.5c,d).

The telomere hypothesis of cell aging postulates that potentially immortal cells (for example, germ cells and cancer cells) maintain their telomerase activity and can divide indefinitely, since their chromosomes will not shorten (Figure 11.5b,e). Cells with a limited replicative life span, on the other hand, should have no telomerase activity, so the progressive shortening of the telomeres during cell division may serve as a mitotic clock for replicative senescence. It was hoped that the hypothesis would explain the mechanism underlying the Hayflick limit.

Harley, Futcher, and Greider (1990) demonstrated that telomeres progressively shorten during replicative growth of human cells in culture, the mean telomere length decreasing by about 50 base pairs per doubling. Replicative capacity appeared to be proportional to mean telomere length (Allsopp and Harley 1995). When human fibroblasts are subjected to high oxygen partial pressure, the resulting oxidative stress irreversibly blocks proliferation. Under these conditions, the rate of telomere shortening increases fivefold, and the cells cease proliferating when the telomere length reaches about 4 kilobases (von Zglinicki et al. 1995). This last observation strongly implies that a critical telomere length provides the signal for cell cycle exit in replicative senescence. Differentiation of cells in culture is accompanied by loss of telomerase activity and shortening of the telomeres (Sharma et al. 1995; Kruk et al. 1996). Finally, it was known from the work of Peirera-Smith and her colleagues that hybrids between immortal cells (with telomerase activity) and normal cells (without such activity) have a limited life span (and lack telomerase). When an immortal cell was artificially stimulated to produce longer telomeres than normal, and then fused with a normal cell, the life span of the resulting hybrid was longer than expected (Wright et al. 1996). This observation also suggested that proliferative capacity is determined by telomere length.

The phenomenon is not limited to cells *in vitro*; the mean telomere length decreases by about 15 base pairs per year in cells of primary cultures obtained from donors of different ages (Harley, Futcher, and Greider 1990). In immortal tumor cells, however, a stabilization of the telomeres was shown to be correlated with the appearance in those cells of telomerase activity. However, not all immortal cells express telomerase (Bryan et al. 1995), nor is telomerase activity found only in immortal cells (Broccoli, Young, and deLange 1995). Many somatic cells (for example, skin, hair, intestinal, and blood cells) normally proliferate extensively, and these cells also express high levels of telomerase, if only during their periods of rapid division(Ramirez et al. 1997). High telomerase activity is also found in germ line cells, which also show no shortening of the chromosome ends.

Together these data provide the conceptual basis of the telomere hypothesis of aging and immortality. According to this hypothesis, germ line cells maintain the length of their chromosomes by maintaining their telomerase activity (Figure 11.5b). Sometime during embryogenesis (after 16 to 20 weeks in humans), telomerase becomes repressed, and, in somatic cells, the telomeres shorten until the cells reach a critical point (the Hayflick limit), where they stop dividing for reasons already explained (11.5c,d). Transformation enables cells to bypass the

Hayflick limit by reactivating their telomerase and maintaining their chromosomal integrity (11.5e). There may also exist a telomerase-independent mechanism that enables some immortal cells to maintain their telomere length.

Persuasive data showing that telomere shortening is in fact the molecular clock that triggers senescence was obtained by transforming either normal diploid human retinal epithelium cells or foreskin fibroblast cells with vectors containing the human telomerase reverse transcriptase (hTRT) subunit (Bodnar et al. 1998). Some of the clones they obtained expressed significantly elevated levels of telomerase activity, which was shown to be due to the transfected hTRT cDNA and not to their endogenous gene. These hTRT$^+$ cells showed increased telomere size, while hTRT$^-$ control cells displayed the telomere shortening characteristic of ordinary cell cultures, as described above. This observation demonstrates that the transfected telomerase is functionally active at the chromosome level. The most interesting observations stem from the comparisons of cellular life spans in these genetically engineered cells: the non-telomerase-expressing hTRT$^-$ cells stopped dividing at a number of cell population doublings characteristic of the cell type, while the telomerase-expressing hTRT$^+$ cells continued to divide for at least 40 doublings beyond the mean values of controls (Figure 11.6). The results of this gain-of-function experiment show that expression of exogenous

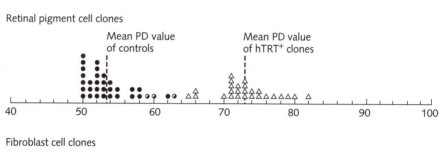

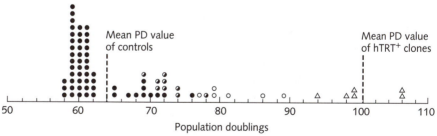

Figure 11.6 The effect of telomerase expression on the life spans of two cell types. In both cases, clones with hTRT$^-$ inserts (controls) are represented by circles and clones with hTRT$^+$ inserts (exogenous telomerase expression) are indicated by triangles. Cell life spans are represented as population doubling (PD) values for each clone—the number of times the clone's population doubles before the cells stop dividing. In both cell types, the clones expressing exogenous telomerase have mean PD values significantly higher (at least 20–40 doublings) than do the control clones. Note that almost all the control clones are senescent (filled symbols) or nearing senescence (half-filled symbols), while there are no senescent hTRT$^+$ clones (open symbols). (After Bodnar et al. 1998.)

telomerase can significantly increase the replicative life span of at least these two human cell types by acting so as to maintain the youthful length of their telomeres. The cell indeed seems to carry a "clock" at the end of its chromosomes.

However, some organisms (for example, *Drosophila, Podospora, Saccharomyces*) do not exhibit telomere shortening even though they are known to age. These exceptions demonstrate that the proposed hypothesis is not universal, at least in detail. In addition, the hypothesis says nothing about the aging of nondividing cells such as neurons and muscle. Thus the hypothesis cannot explain the aging processes in all the cells of any single organism. In addition, adult mice seem to have a tissue-specific regulation of telomere length, and not an age-dependent regulation (Prowse and Greider 1995)—an observation that complicates the extrapolation of the telomere hypothesis from the cell level to the organism level. In fact, a reasonably conservative interpretation of the data is that some type of mechanistic connection exists between telomere length and proliferative ability for the cells of many but not all organisms, but that identifying the role of telomeres does not make the connection between cell proliferation and organismal aging any clearer. But it does give us a potentially powerful tool for future manipulations.

What does seem to be clear, however, is the strong separation between normal and transformed, or immortalized, cells. Telomeres are lengthened or stabilized in almost every type of immortal or cancer cell line examined, via either the reactivation of telomerase or another novel mechanism (Bryan et al. 1995). This observation has opened up what appears to be a very fruitful line of inquiry for cancer therapies and aging interventions based on genetic engineering methods (Kim et al. 1994; Fossel 1998).

• *Aging in Nondividing Cells*

The senescent changes observed in Phase III fibroblasts are paralleled by similar morphological changes observed in nonproliferating differentiated cells found in older individuals. These changes in subcellular morphology, such as those affecting the size and number of the mitochondria, appear to be modulated by the organism's physiological and nutritional state and may be related to the alterations in cellular physiology known to take place in cells of the elderly. Should such changes result in the eventual death of some of the differentiated cells, then the same sort of mechanism that inhibits cell division in the Phase III fibroblasts is likely also responsible for preventing the surviving cells from replacing the lost cells. The result might thus be the observed decrease in the number of cells found in some tissues and organs of the elderly (see Figure 5.1). Such a process of physiological impairment of the cell followed by cell death and compounded by nonreplacement could, if allowed to continue, eventually result in the physiological failure of the tissue or organ involved. Undoubtedly, we need to examine the cell biology of the normal differentiated and nondividing cell both *in vivo* and *in vitro* in order to better understand the age-dependent changes that take place at the cellular level. In the sections that follow we will examine several such systems of aging in nondividing cells.

Lipofuscin and the Waste Accumulation Theory

In its simplest form, the waste product theory of aging proposes that cellular aging is caused by the accumulation of intracellular waste products that cannot be destroyed or eliminated except through the process of cell division. It is well established that postmitotic cells, such as neurons and cardiac-muscle cells, accumulate deposits of irregularly shaped, lipid-rich, yellowish brown cytoplasmic pigment granules during the aging process. Such lipofuscin granules were first observed in 1842, and the possibility of a relationship between aging and lipofuscin accumulation was discussed as long ago as 1886. Numerous studies have been carried out since then in an effort to understand the mechanisms responsible for the formation of lipofuscin and to clarify its role in the aging process.

The varied forms of pigment granules that are encompassed by the term "lipofuscin" likely are a diverse and heterogeneous group of molecules that may have little in common with one another save the fact that they all wound up in the same granule. We now know that there are at least two types of lipofuscin—one that is observed in normal aging and vitamin E deficiency states and one that is observed only in certain pathological or inherited metabolic disorders (Armstrong 1984). The latter type, the so-called ceroid lipopigments, differs in appearance and ultrastructure from the normal lipofuscins and will not be further considered here.

Lipofuscin is now generally believed to arise as a result of free radical–induced auto-oxidation of the molecular components of the cell, particularly the membranous structures that contain unsaturated lipids (see Chapter 9) . The evidence for this conclusion is persuasive but not yet definitive. Some studies have shown that lipofuscin contains chemical components similar to those generated by *in vitro* auto-oxidation of subcellular structures. Studies such as the one involving the low-activity and high-activity flies that we discussed in Chapter 9 were thought to have manipulated the *in vivo* auto-oxidation rate and to have affected the rate of lipofuscin accumulation.

In another study, crayfish were raised at five different temperatures ranging from 13 to 33°C, and their lipofuscin content was measured at different ages throughout life (Sheehy, Greenwood, and Fielder 1995). At any given age, the animals raised at the higher temperatures appeared to age more rapidly and had higher lipofuscin levels than did the animals raised at lower temperatures, suggesting a proportionality among temperature, rate of living, and free-radical production. But no evidence was put forth that lipofuscin was itself harmful or served in any way other than as an index of the organism's past metabolic history.

The auto-oxidation rate has also been manipulated through diet. Vitamin E is one of the better-known naturally occurring antioxidants (see Chapter 9). Animals deficient in vitamin E have elevated levels of lipid auto-oxidation products in their tissues, and such animals appear to have a higher rate of lipofuscin accumulation in their tissues (Nandy 1984). Taken all together, this evidence leads to the conclusion that the lipofuscin arises via the auto-oxidation of subcellular lipid components.

Does this age pigment have any deleterious effect itself? Lipofuscin appears to be chemically quite unreactive and thus probably doesn't interfere at the chemical level with the proper functioning of the cell. However, mechanical obstruction and/or interference with other cellular processes is certainly a possibility (Hirsch, Coomes, and Witten 1989). Nonetheless, in some regions of the brain the cells from birth onward are normally packed with lipofuscin (for example, the inferior olive) or with other sorts of pigment granules (for example, melanin granules in the substantia nigra), and there appears to be no obvious decrement in their functional ability.

Other studies also suggest but do not prove that it is not the presence of large amounts of lipofuscin itself that impairs cell function (Katz et al. 1984). The accumulation of lipofuscin in human glial cells in culture has been quantitatively measured, and the resulting data have served as the basis for mathematical analysis of the relationship between the amount of lipofuscin accumulation and the rate of cell division (Hirsch, Coomes, and Witten 1989). This analysis suggests that cellular reproduction is very sensitive to waste content: Relatively small amounts of lipofuscin are associated with a 50 percent reduction in cell division rate. Nondividing cells can survive much higher waste levels, but one cannot conclude from that observation that those cells are not also being adversely affected in some vital function. In fact, it has been demonstrated that cultured cells inhibited from dividing will accumulate lipofuscin at an accelerated rate (Nandy and Schneider 1976). Since the lipofuscin is thought to form as a result of free radical–induced lipid peroxidation, it seems reasonable to suggest that at least some of the nondividing cells are being adversely affected as a consequence of the cessation of mitosis and their consequent inability to get rid of their metabolic wastes.

Even though lipofuscin itself may not be fully responsible for the physiological deficits associated with aging, the particular molecular events underlying lipofuscin accumulation may be the primary events in senescence. Accordingly, one would expect to find an inverse relationship between the *in vivo* auto-oxidation rate and the species' maximum life span. Such information is difficult to obtain. However, *in vitro* measurements have shown that there is a very good relationship between the rate of auto-oxidation and the species-specific maximum life span (Figure 11.7). This relationship suggests that the level of free radical–induced auto-oxidation is the important factor in determining cell senescence. According to this point of view, the lipofuscin granules serve simply as visible biomarkers of free radical–induced cellular damage. The age pigments arise when the cells' antioxidant defense systems begin to decline and can no longer cope with the flux of free radicals. This conclusion not only points to the free-radical theory of aging (see Chapter 9) but also suggests that our understanding of the aging process in nondividing differentiated cells depends on our being able to characterize the mechanisms that control the antioxidant defense systems. The discussion in Chapter 10 strongly suggested that a large part of the answer lies in the regulatory genes that eventually control the activity levels of the various antioxidant defense system enzymes and metabolites.

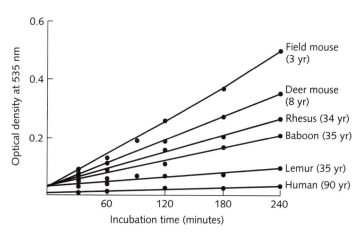

Figure 11.7 Auto-oxidation of whole-brain homogenates in air from different mammalian species as a function of life span potential. The auto-oxidation process produces a complex array of free radicals, aldehydes, and peroxides. Note that the shortest-lived animals produce the greatest amount of auto-oxidation products. There appears to be an inverse relationship between life span and auto-oxidation ability. (From Cutler 1983a. © Alan R. Liss.)

The Death of Terminally Differentiated Cells

Cell Death As a Stochastic Process: The Red Blood Cell Model

Most differentiated cells survive uneventfully for a long time. But some, such as keratinocytes, plasma cells, and erythrocytes, have a limited life span *in situ*. They senesce and die. In many cases, such cells are destroyed or phagocytized by other cells in the body that are specialized for that gruesome but necessary function. What markers distinguish a dying cell from a healthy cell, and what do they have to do with the aging process?

The fact that cells communicate with one another via their cell membranes suggests that a senescent cell has undergone important alterations at this structural level for it to be recognized as a target for phagocytosis. Moreover, the macrophage cells of the immune system are known to phagocytize the old, but not the young, red blood cells (RBCs) in humans and other mammals (Figure 11.8). (Note that here the terms "old" and "young" refer not to the age of the blood donor but to the length of time since the particular RBCs were terminally differentiated, and that the maximum life span of an RBC is about 90 days.) Investigations into the molecular changes occurring during aging revealed that a terminal-differentiation antigen, the so-called senescent-cell antigen, appears on the surface of cells as they age (see Kay 1985 and Kay, Wyant, and Goodman 1994 for review). The presence of this senescent-cell antigen was initially revealed by the fact that certain types of immunoglobulin G (IgG) autoantibodies bind in high amounts to the membranes of senescent human RBCs, but only in very low amounts to the membranes of young human RBCs. Middle-aged RBCs bind the IgG molecules at an intermediate level. Macrophages appear to recognize and target for destruction only those RBCs that have high numbers of IgG molecules on their membranes. These data suggested that the senescent-cell antigen appears gradually and that its gradual appearance leads to the increasing binding levels of IgG. The molecular aging of the RBC membrane is a cumulative process.

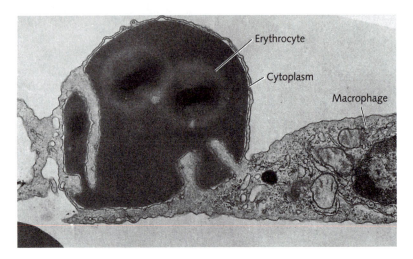

Figure 11.8   Phagocytosis of a red blood cell by a mouse macrophage. Note the thin rim of cytoplasm that completely envelops the engulfed erythrocyte. (From de Duve 1984. © The de Duve Trust.)

The real question is the identity not of the IgG molecule, but of the senescent-cell antigen to which it binds. What is this molecule? Does it have any function in the nonsenescent cell? And by what process does it gradually appear in the membrane? Finally, does this antigen have any general applicability to the problem of aging and senescence?

Since mature human RBCs have a very limited ability to synthesize new proteins, the senescent-cell antigen must have arisen as a result of the modification of a preexisting protein. Immunological investigations by Kay (1985) revealed that this antigen appears to be one of the breakdown products of a normal membrane protein that was given the trivial name "band 3 protein," otherwise known as the "anion exchanger" family of proteins. At least four isoforms have been identified, and they have been found in all membranes examined (Kay et al. 1995). Their presence in the aging RBC makes them a convenient model, but the processes involved may be of more general import. This transmembrane protein has a complex structure, is present in large amounts in the plasma membranes of normal RBCs and appears to be responsible for a multitude of important functions such as anion exchange and glucose transport, serving as the binding site for hemoglobin, as well as for various enzymes involved in glucose metabolism. It also appears to be the protein that links the internal surface of the cell membrane with the internal filamentous cytoskeleton. This is obviously an important molecule—one that is probably vital to the continued physiological functioning of the RBC. As the RBC ages, all of these normal functions decrease, while the number of IgG molecules bound to the surface of the cell membrane increases. The IgG molecules are binding to a particular segment of the band 3 protein that has been snipped off and translocated so that it now lies on the external surface of the membrane and can serve as a recognition and/or binding site for the autoanti-bodies. This altered molecule is termed the senescent-cell antigen and appears to arise in part as the result of oxidative damage (Kay, Wyant, and Goodman 1994).

Mutations affecting the band 3 protein also affect aging of the cells *in situ*. One mutant exhibits accelerated aging, another exhibits decelerated aging, and a third is associated with neurological defects (Kay, Wyant, and Goodman 1994). In fact, brain cells from people with Alzheimer's disease undergo posttranslational alterations in their band 3 proteins similar to those seen in the anion transport regions of the band 3 protein of aging RBCs (Kay and Goodman 1997). Evidence shows that the band 3 protein is conserved across all vertebrates, suggesting that it has an important function (Kay et al. 1995).

Molecules other than the band 3 protein may also be involved in this process (Aminoff 1988). If we assume that the RBC membrane is similar to that of the other cell types in mammals—and there is every reason to believe so—then it seems reasonable to conclude that the mechanism of membrane aging and breakdown is an important molecular process intimately involved in the regula-tion of the life span of some specialized somatic cells.

Cell Death As a Controllable Process: Programmed Cell Death

Organisms appear to lose cells as they age (see Figure 5.1). Some cells are killed by external injuries or trauma via necrotic cell death. Necrosis generally results from cell injury and is characterized by swelling of organelles, clumping of chromatin, and increased permeability of membranes. DNA breaks down randomly. The entire process is believed to be a chaotic breakdown of numerous cellular systems.

But some cells kill themselves deliberately, using a mechanism encoded in their own genome. Different cell types from different organisms, dying as the result of a variety of chronic (as opposed to traumatic) causes, nonetheless undergo a strikingly similar series of cytological and biochemical alterations that are now generally referred to by the name of "physiological (programmed) cell death" or "apoptosis" ("apoptosis" is the more common term). Apoptosis often represents terminal differentiation and is the evolved mechanism by which multi-cellular organisms rid themselves of unneeded or dangerous cells. This topic has been reviewed by Lockshin and Zakeri-Milovanovic (1984), Kerr and colleagues (1987), White and collaborators (1994), Zakeki and Lockshin 1994, Driscoll (1995), Steller (1995), and Vaux and Strasser (1996), and the following discus-sion is based largely on these sources.

The evidence suggests that all cells of multicellular organisms carry within themselves the information and the mechanisms necessary to bring about their own destruction, but that this terminal pathway can be invoked only by specific developmental and physiological signals. Such signals may be either autonomous or nonautonomous. The process is characterized by shrinkage and fragmentation of cytoplasm and compaction of chromatin accompanied by nonrandom DNA cleavage into 180–base pair fragments. Apoptosis is both a common and an evo-lutionarily conserved process, and is under strict genetic control because its inap-propriate occurrence could be detrimental for the organism. Nonetheless, a variety of different signals that may originate from either inside or outside the cell can influence the cell's decision between life and death. This multiplicity of signals suggests that the genetic control mechanisms are complex.

Examples of apoptosis during embryonic life include the loss of excess interdigital tissues, the death of unneeded neurons, the destruction of the "wrong" set of sexual primordia, and so forth. The process occurs during metamorphosis of all animals, as witnessed by the tadpole's resorption of its tail en route to becoming an adult frog. The continuous elimination of cells has been observed in a variety of adult tissues—both in slowly proliferating tissues such as liver epithelium, adrenal cortex, and prostate gland, and in rapidly proliferating tissues such as the intestinal epithelium. The cell death within the adrenal cortex has been quantitatively estimated to be just sufficient to balance the cell gain by mitosis. Programmed cell death occurs in endocrine-dependent tissues upon hormone withdrawal (for example, the human premenstrual endometrium) or, in some cases, upon hormone addition (for example, the tadpole tail, the insect intersegmental muscle, Müllerian ducts). Other signals involve the lack of particular growth factors.

Despite the heterogeneity of the signals, they all seem to focus in on one target—namely, the gene that will activate the apoptotic program. This target seems to be a gene called *reaper*, which responds to a wide variety of known death-inducing signals. Its response is to inactivate the gene that normally represses the apoptotic mechanism. The gene itself is not part of the cell death process. The process has been best studied in the nematode, so we will describe the events in that organism. The general regulator of apoptosis in *C. elegans* is encoded by the *ced-9* gene ("*ced*" stands for *c*ell *d*eath abnormal genes). When active, this gene acts to repress the system in cells that are not destined to die. Once the *ced-9* gene has been repressed by the appropriate signal, the *ced-3* and *ced-4* genes are activated and synthesize their products. The former gene encodes a cysteine protease, but its normal substrate(s) is unknown, so its function is still speculative. The latter gene product appears to contain calcium-binding motifs and thus might be involved in activating calcium-dependent enzyme activities. These two genes seem to be both necessary and sufficient to bring about the death of the cell. Removal of the corpse by phagocytosis requires the services of at least seven other *ced* genes.

What is the relationship of apoptosis to aging? There is no obvious direct relationship. Normal nematodes usually lose 131 specific cells to apoptosis during normal development. Animals carrying gain-of-function mutations of *ced*-9 develop and live normally, despite the presence of the extra cells. Loss-of-function *ced-9* mutations, however, are lethal and cause many extra cell deaths in embryos. The conclusion that aging and cell death proceed independently of each other is supported by the observation that loss-of-function *ced-3* and/or *ced-4* mutants appear to be normal and have normal life spans. But this does not preclude an important indirect relationship. The mammalian *Bcl-2* gene is homologous to the worm's *ced-9* gene. *Bcl-2* was first identified because its elevated expression in a mouse mutant prolonged the life span of B cells and thereby caused lymphomas. The inappropriate inhibition of cell death shortened organismic longevity. However, mice without a functional *Bcl-2* gene died as embryos, exhibiting massive cell death in their neural and hematopoietic systems, and thus showing that the inappropriate stimulation of cell death also shortens organismic longevity (Motoyama et al. 1995). The process must be precisely controlled.

These observations raise the possibility that one major function of apoptosis is to serve as a precisely targeted defense mechanism against dysfunctional and/or potentially immortal cells. This supposition is supported by the observation that some of the genes involved in proliferation control (such as the c-*myc* and c-*fos* oncogenes, or the *p53* tumor suppressor gene) have been shown to be actively involved in regulating apoptosis as well. Given that senescent cells often exhibit an inappropriate regulation of cell activities, the possibility also exists that inappropriate age-related implementation of apoptosis could result in the death of essential cells and thereby contribute to senescent decline.

Table 11.4 lists some diseases known to be associated with the abnormal induction or inhibition of apoptotic cell death. To the extent that these diseases arise as a result of the age-related breakdown of the cell's programmed cell death mechanisms, these diseases highlight a common age-related failure mode of somatic cells. These associations may not be entirely hypothetical. Vito, Lacana, and D'Adamio (1996) have reported that one of the mouse genes linked to the regulation of apoptosis is the homologue to the human familial Alzheimer's disease gene located on chromosome 1 (see Chapter 5). This finding raises the possibility of a real linkage between Alzheimer's and this cell-level process.

Warner, Fernandes, and Wang (1995) have presented a model in which they attempt to link together the roles of apoptosis, caloric restriction, and oxidative damage into a unifying hypothesis to explain the retardation of aging by caloric restriction. Given the assumption that the somatic cell's ability to undergo apoptosis decreases as the cell approaches its Hayflick limit, the proportion of oxidatively damaged cells in a given tissue will increase with increasing age. However,

Table 11.4 **Diseases Associated with the Abnormal Induction or Inhibition of Cell Death**

Cancer	AIDS
Follicular lymphomas	Neurodegenerative disorders
Carcinomas with *p53* mutations	Alzheimer's disease
Hormone-dependent tumors	Parkinson's disease
Breast cancer	Amyotrophic lateral sclerosis
Prostate cancer	Retinitis pigmentosa
Ovarian cancer	Cerebellar degeneration
Autoimmune disorders	Myelodysplastic syndromes
Systemic lupus	Aplastic anemia
Immune-mediated glomerulonephritis	Ischemic injury
Viral infections	Myocardial infarction
Herpesvirus	Stroke
Poxvirus	Reperfusion injury
Adenoviruses	Toxin-induced liver disease
	Alcohol

Source: After Thompson 1995.

some data suggest that caloric restriction up-regulates the incidence of apoptosis. Therefore caloric restriction not only would reduce the incidence of oxidative damage suffered by the cells according to its ability to up-regulate antioxidant defenses and attenuate the formation of reactive oxygen species (see Chapters 7 and 10), but also would improve the tissue's ability to get rid of defective cells. The result would be a longer period during which tissues were maintained and a slowing of the aging process. This model may be viewed as an independent elaboration of the de Grey model discussed in Chapter 10.

Some evidence suggests that individual cells cultured alone have a short survival time. Cells cultured *in vitro* with others of their kind do much better. Raff (1992) has raised the suggestion that there are important social controls on cell survival. Just as a cell seems to need to receive secreted signals from other cells in order for it to proliferate (Edgar and Lehner 1996), so too it seems to need to receive signals (either positive or negative) from other cells if it is not to activate its apoptosis program and kill itself. This observation suggests that we could view our cells as integral members of a population that are continuously being questioned as to the appropriateness of their continuing to live in that population. Cells that do not receive the signals kill themselves.

One conceptual advantage of such a mechanism is that it is a simple way to eliminate cells that are in the wrong place. In addition, competition among the cells for limiting amounts of such secreted signals could result in the continuous survey of the population by its members and provide a mechanism allowing for the control of cell numbers in particular tissues and organs, as well as the automatic elimination of abnormal cells and/or adjustment of normal cells to the changing internal environment of the organism (Ruhe, Curry, and McDonald 1997). Either alternative would provide a mechanistic cell-level explanation of homeostasis. Widespread failure of the signaling process might lead to a loss of tissue function and the decline of reserve capacity that is typical of many aging organs (Shock 1983). Alternatively, as Raff (1992) points out, cells that can acquire the ability to grow without relying on extracellular signals will give rise to tumors and the age-related pathologies associated with unrestrained growth.

The importance of this process to normal aging is that it provides us with a controllable process that is clearly of some importance in regulating cell numbers. Apoptosis and mitosis are controlled by complex gene-based signaling systems. These systems can interact at the population and cell levels to bring about the net gain or the net loss of cells in the particular tissue. Organ- and organism-level physiological decrements can presumably begin to be observed either when the loss of cells begins to impinge on the tissue's reserve capacity (Shock 1983) or when mutated cells begin to produce for themselves the signals that allow them to proliferate and to escape the bonds that restrain their normal neighbors and thus give rise to the cancers so prevalent in late life.

Summary

We are more than just the sum of our cells, but we cannot exist without them. Our cells have and will undergo complex transformations during our passage from the embryo we were to the aging adult we may become. We have touched on a few of the transitions that appear to have something to do with the aging process. The available evidence indicates that cells cultured *in vitro* under standard conditions undergo a more or less characteristic number of population doublings. At the intraspecific level, this number seems to vary as a function of donor age; at the interspecific level, it seems to vary as a function of the species' maximum life span.

The Hayflick hypothesis suggests that the limited proliferative ability of somatic cells is programmed and can be viewed as a repeatable cellular expression of senescence. Current data suggest that when the telomeres reach a critical length, the cell is triggered to exit the replicative mode. It will be most interesting to determine the relationships between the genes controlling cell proliferation and the telomeres. Despite the temptation to do so, the Hayflick hypothesis does not require us to extrapolate beyond the data and suggest that senescence of the organism is caused by the loss of its cells' proliferative ability. If long-lived somatic cells undergo changes that alter both their ability to undergo mitosis and their ability to consistently maintain their normal level of function *in situ*, then one could imagine how such a loose linkage could be empirically observed. The loss of proliferative ability with successive passes through the cell cycle is now a generally accepted observation. Its relationship to aging is indirect, however. What seems to be built into the cells is not a rigid internal clock that relentlessly ticks off our days, but a mechanism that enables cells to slip out of an active mitotic mode into a terminal predifferentiation mode.

Both the proliferation of new cells and the death of old cells are under multiple paths of strict genetic control. Apoptosis is an intrinsic program for killing the host cell. Both processes appear to depend on the continuous receipt of appropriate signals from neighboring cells, thus providing a possible set of mechanisms that can monitor the number and type of cells in the tissue.

For tissues that continuously produce new cells, there must be a mechanism for getting rid of the old cells. Erythrocytes use the band 3 protein as a membrane marker that can identify old red blood cells via their increased binding of immunoglobulin G molecules, and thereby stimulate their phagocytosis by macrophages.

As the differentiated cell functions within the mature organism, it suffers from the damage caused by stochastic processes such as free radical–induced auto-oxidation, as well as other sorts of destructive processes. Both mitotic and postmitotic cells are affected. For a period of time, the cell's antioxidant and other defense systems are more than adequate to the task of keeping such deleterious processes under control. At some point, for reasons that are only now becoming apparent, the defense systems falter and the damage level increases. The waste products of such stochastic damage, such as the lipofuscin granules, begin to accumulate at an increasing rate. For some period of time thereafter, the cell's normal repair processes may still be sufficient to replace the damaged intracellular structures and to keep the cell functioning within normal levels. Eventually, however, the damage level in some important component of the cell increases to the point at which the cell's physiological functioning is severely impaired. The cell is senescent. In some cases, the senescent cell may tag itself with the senescent-cell antigen(s) and be disposed of by the macrophages. In other cases, the senescent cell may simply respond to internal or external signals and initiate the process of programmed cell death, which will remove it as a functioning member of the tissue of which it is a part.

The network of intercommunicating cells sustains cumulative damage as here and there individual cells become too disabled to function properly and imperceptibly blink out. In the absence of mitotically active stem cells, they cannot be replaced. The loss of sufficient cells will, over time, eventually affect the functioning of the tissue or organ, presumably by adversely restricting the reserve capacity, and thus begin to affect the homeostatic balance of the body when the individual is subjected to the stresses of daily living. Failure to undergo apoptosis, on the other hand, may well cause inappropriate survival of abnormal cells, which, once they can overcome the checkpoints regulating their cell cycle, may well become immortal and begin to proliferate. This inappropriate cell multiplication will harm the normal functioning of the tissue and thus adversely affect the homeostatic balance of the body.

Aging as a Breakdown of Intercellular Regulatory Processes

● *Basic Assumptions Underlying Such Theories*

All multicellular organisms face the problem of coordinating the activities of their different specialized cells and tissues. The problem becomes more pressing as the number and types of cells increase. The homeostatic mechanisms of the vertebrate body are controlled mostly via the neuro-endocrine-immune system. The harmonious control of the body's many functions depends on the efficacy with which this coordinating and integrating system uses its feedback loops and antagonistic processes to regulate these activities. On the basis of his long experience with the Baltimore Longitudinal Study on Aging, Nathan Shock (1983, p. 137) suggested that the "impaired effectiveness of these coordinating mechanisms may be the primary factor involved in aging." Such coordinating mechanisms, or pacemaker tissues and organs, are not the only mechanism of aging that affects us. For example, the changes in our connective tissues may owe more to extracellular cross-linking processes than to a failure in a central coordinating center. However, it is reasonable to consider the proper functioning of these integrative mechanisms as constituting an extraordinarily important factor in organismic aging.

The importance of regulatory and homeostatic processes to the normal functioning of the adult was widely recognized some time ago, and their importance to the aging process has been reinforced by data collected in various long-term longitudinal studies. These integrative mechanisms can be affected by both internal and external sources of stress (Costa, McCrae, and Arenberg 1983; Rowe and Kahn 1987; House, Landis, and Umberson 1988). These external sources (for example, social processes) most likely exert their effects indirectly on the neuro-endocrine-immune system and in this manner modulate the body's homeostatic and regulatory mechanisms. We already know the detailed circuitry of the physiological mechanisms underlying the role of social interactions in bringing about the stress-induced death of the marsupial mouse and the Pacific salmon, both of which are good examples of organisms that senesce rapidly (see Chapter 4). The study of regulatory systems capable of integrating social and physical effects into well-known biological mechanisms may prove to be a fruitful path to an enhanced understanding of how genetic and environmental factors interact in the normal aging process.

In this chapter, we will examine several theories that attempt to relate the known roles of the neuroendocrine and the immune systems in the aging process of vertebrates. The underlying assumption of such theories is that homeostatic failure of the organism plays a key role in the onset of senescence and death, and that this failure may be traced to a more or less well-defined group of particular cells that have specific integrative functions. We will focus on only these two systems, simply because the wealth of information implicating them in the aging process makes them good examples of what appear to be mostly nonautonomous failures of control.

• *Neuroendocrine Theories of Aging*

Our development into mature adults depends on the proper functioning of our neuroendocrine system. It would be unusual if the integrative systems that played such a large role in our preadult development did not play a role in our later adult development.

In Chapter 4 we briefly described examples of species that die shortly after reproduction as a result of rapid senescent changes brought about by neuroendocrine mechanisms. But these senescent changes are not inevitable. Castrated salmon can continue living and growing for at least twice their normal life span. If *Antechinus* (the marsupial mouse) is castrated or socially isolated before mating, its life span is 2 to 3 years, as might be expected for rodents of its size. The normally rapid senescence of the marsupial mouse is not built into every one of its cells; rather it is a direct consequence of alterations taking place in the neuroendocrine system.

Although many might not consider the alterations that take place in these rapidly senescing organisms to be directly translatable to the changes that take place in organisms that senesce gradually, their importance lies in the fact that they illustrate the vast differences in life span that can be brought about by changes in regulatory systems. The proponents of this view strongly suggest that neural and endocrine changes can act as the pacemakers that will bring about senescent changes in many other cell types and that organismic aging depends on the activities of only a small proportion of the individual's cells. There is a huge literature on the neuroendocrine alterations that take place with aging, and the recent emphasis on trying to understand neurodegenerative diseases has stimulated even more interest in this area. It is impossible to adequately cover the entire field, and we will make no attempt to do so. We will focus instead on a few topics that illustrate if and how the loss of integrative ability might be associated with the course of senescence. Excellent reviews of the topic have been presented by Finch (1987), Finch and Landfield (1985), Merry and Holehan (1994a), Nelson (1995), Mobbs (1996), and Johnson and Finch (1996); this discussion draws mostly from those sources.

Mobbs (1996) has pointed out that the neuroendocrine system operates in two different integrative domains, the homeostatic and the homeodynamic. The main function of the homeostatic domain is to determine and regulate average physiological set points (for example, glucose levels), which are functions of the sensitivity of the neural components to hormonal signals. The main function of the homeodynamic domain is to regulate the temporal organization of physiological systems, largely by modulating the rhythms or pulses in these systems. This latter function is mediated mostly via the hypothalamus, the neurons of which are sensitive to circulating hormone levels. Thus alterations in either the number or the sensitivity of various neuroendocrine receptors could in principle give rise to the homeostatic or homeodynamic changes that are commonly associated with senescence.

An interesting phenomenon that appears to be of general importance is that the peripheral levels of target hormones (for example, estrogens) decrease with age, but the basal levels of the stimulating hormones (for example, luteinizing hormone) remain constant or increase (Mobbs 1996). One way to interpret these results is that the peripheral hormone levels fall as a result of glandular impairments, while the constant level of stimulating hormones implies that the older animal has an impaired sensitivity to negative feedback. Given this situation, the decrease in neuroendocrine receptors during aging may be viewed as a systemic adjustment to this increased sensitivity, and not as an indication of a decreased sensitivity of the organism toward the particular hormone. Our analysis will focus on the role of the neuroendocrine system in reproductive aging and in the response to stress.

Reproductive Senescence

Female reproductive aging has long been used as a model for studying neuroendocrine senescence because it includes an early, obvious, and nonlethal failure of an important physiological system. Its cyclic nature provides a sensitive assay of functional status. This system also offers the experimental advantage that it can be easily manipulated by means of surgical and/or hormonal treatments without major effects on other physiological systems. In humans, the median age at menopause is about 50 years and appears to be remarkably similar across various racial and ethnic groups (Merry and Holehan 1994a). Regardless of the age of entry into menopause, the menopausal transition takes about 6 years. The few populations that have a lower median age of onset suffer the confounding effects of poor nutrition, health, and/or socioeconomic situations.

As described in Chapter 5, the depletion of ovarian follicles in females of many species seems to be the primary endocrine-linked age-related change and might well be the primary cause of various senescence-related syndromes. This process results in the simultaneous decrease of the plasma estradiol, increase of the basal luteinizing hormone (LH) to castrate levels, and impairment of the surge LH levels. Cells and tissues that depend on ovarian steroids such as estradiol and progesterone flourish at puberty and wither at menopause, for their function is tied to the hormonal ebb and flow. The fact that estrogen replacement therapy can reverse these tissue hypoplasias shows that there is no problem with the estrogen receptor in the tissues and that these senescent changes may be due mostly to the lack of sufficient hormonal stimulation.

These and other observations led Finch and his colleagues to develop and test the hypothesis that the ovarian secretions have a cumulative effect on the pituitary and hypothalamus, which, when they pass a certain threshold, initiate senescent changes in these key regulatory components. They were testing, in other words, the concept that aging is driven by certain key physiological events and is not propelled by the mere passage of time. Of necessity, such experimental studies are carried out in laboratory animals, mostly mice and rats.

When young ovaries are transplanted into old postreproductive mice, the grafts fail to reinitiate the normal level of estrous cycles per month (Figure 12.1; Finch et al. 1984). The fact that the young grafted ovaries had sufficient follicles and were capable of normal functioning if transplanted into young mice suggested that in the older mice there is a problem with the neuroendocrine cells of the pituitary and hypothalamus. However, when young ovaries were transplanted into old animals that had been ovariectomized when young and allowed to age without their ovaries, these animals were found to have the ability to reinitiate regular estrous cycles (data not shown). Taken together, these two results suggested that the ovary normally has an adverse and irreversible influence on the hypothalamus and pituitary.

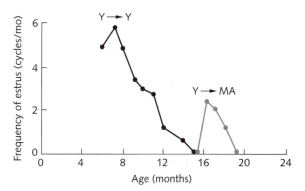

Figure 12.1 The effect of age on the ability of an ovary transplanted from a young donor to maintain estrous cycles. The questions asked in this experiment were whether the loss of ovarian function was due to systemic (presumably hypothalamic) damage to the host, and whether the systemic damage was cumulative over all cycles. When a young donor ovary was transplanted into a young (<15 months old) host female (Y → Y), the transplanted ovary functioned normally. If loss of function is due to host damage, later transplantation of a young ovary to a middle-aged (15–24 months old) cycling mouse (Y → MA) yields few if any additional cycles. Thus a young ovary that can function admirably in young hosts cannot reactivate reproductive cycles in 16-month-old hosts. (From Finch et al. 1984.)

This conclusion was supported by another series of experiments, in which reciprocal ovarian grafts were made between young and middle-aged mice (Figure 12.2; Mobbs and Finch 1992). If the middle-aged mice retained their own functioning ovaries until the young ovary was transplanted, their ability to maintain "young" estrous cycling was impaired (second bar in Figure 12.2). If the middle-aged mice were ovariectomized when young and then not further exposed to ovarian hormones until the time of the ovarian transplant, they were capable of maintaining "young" cycling (third bar in Figure 12.2). But if the middle-aged mice that were ovariectomized when young had also been given daily doses of estradiol since that time, their ability to maintain "young" estrous cycling was also impaired (fourth bar in Figure 12.2). Finally, when intact young mice were given daily doses of estradiol, their ability to maintain cycling was severely impaired (fifth bar in Figure 12.2). These results lead to the conclusion that reproductive senescence is the consequence of cumulative exposure to ovarian hormones and/or estradiol, in agreement with the data of Figure 12.1. However, when ovaries from middle-aged intact mice were transplanted into young

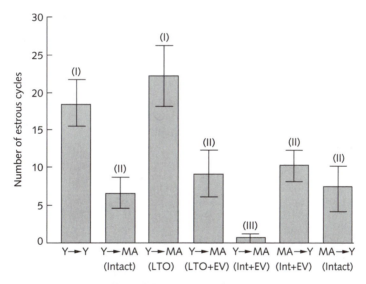

Figure 12.2 The effect of the presence of ovaries and/or a single injection of estradiol valerate (EV) on the the ability of mice to support young ovarian grafts. Words in parentheses indicate the state of middle-aged (MA) mice. Young (6-month-old) mice (Y) were either ovariectomized (LTO) or left intact, then given either 10 µg/g body weight of EV in oil or just oil. Six months later, ovaries from intact mice were grafted into young ovariectomized mice (MA → Y), and all middle-aged mice were given young ovarian grafts beneath the kidney capsule (Y → MA). As controls, young ovariectomized mice were given young ovarian grafts (Y → Y). A bar represents the mean number of estrous cycles (± the standard error of the mean) that occurred after the ovarian graft in each group of 6 to 8 mice each. Groups with the same Roman numerals (I, II, or III) differed ($p < 0.05$) by ANOVA followed by Newman-Keul's test. (From Mobbs and Finch.)

ovariectomized animals, the grafts displayed an impaired ability to maintain estrous cycling (sixth and seventh bars in Figure 12.2). This result shows that the aging ovary itself has autonomous defects that are not present in young ovaries. Taken together, all the data suggested that reproductive senescence arises from both ovarian and neuroendocrine impairments, and that the neuroendocrine impairments are at least partly the result of the cumulative exposure to estradiol.

Other data suggest that the ovary-induced neuroendocrine damage is done mostly during the period when the estrous cycles are becoming prolonged and irregular. In support of this assumption, Finch (1987) showed that many of the age-related changes that take place spontaneously in old rodents can be induced in young animals given sustained high levels of estradiol for several months. When 5-month-old mice were ovariectomized, kept on high levels of estradiol for 3 months, and then given an ovarian graft, they responded with estrous cycles characteristic of old animals. In contrast, the controls, which were also ovariectomized but were not medicated with estradiol during the 3 months before they received an ovarian graft, responded with estrous cycles characteristic of young animals. This experiment not only proved the role of estradiol, but also allowed Finch and his colleagues to quantify the relationship between the total amount of hormone exposure and the rate of aging of the reproductive system. Mice of the strain they used underwent a maximum of about 50 estrous cycles before they became nonreproductive—a state that is by definition the end point of aging in this system. Various calculations suggested that 5,000 units of hormone—the amount of hormone needed to induce 50 estrous cycles—constitute the lifetime exposure of certain mice to estradiol, and that irreversible damage to the hypothalamus and pituitary would follow once that exposure level was attained. In other words, the main aging event in this system was the organism's attainment of a cumulative lifetime threshold level of 5,000 units, the consequence of which was irreversible damage to the cells of the hypothalamus and pituitary.

The mechanisms that cause the damage are not yet known, but there are several plausible possibilities, including the hormonal regulation of gene activity patterns. If this hypothesis is correct, it should be possible to induce the same sorts of irreversible effects of aging by treating an animal with 100 units of hormone for 50 days, or with 20 units of hormone for 250 days, or with most other feasible combinations. The hypothesis suggests that aging, in this system at least, is the result of a quantitative dose–response situation, and that one should be able to dissociate aging from the mere passage of time (Figure 12.3). This hypothesis strongly supports and is consistent with the idea that aging is an event-dependent process, a conclusion remarkably similar to those independently derived from studies on other systems (see Chapter 10). In fact, these analyses have begun the process of converting time from an independent variable to a dependent variable in the analysis of aging! The eventual confirmation of this hypothesis should bring us a giant step forward in our ability to experimentally manipulate the aging process.

There is no indication of an age-related decrease in male reproductive capacity similar to that described here for females (see Chapter 5). This fact might suggest that the utility of female reproductive senescence as a model of aging is quite

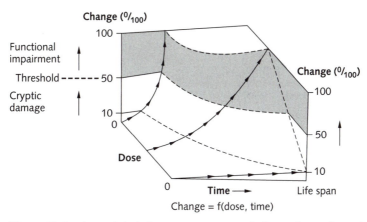

Figure 12.3   Age-related phenomena, represented on a three-dimensional experience surface whose axes represent time, dose, and change. This example is drawn from the effects of age and estradiol treatment on the reproductive ability of female mice; estradiol is known to be a cause of age-related change in the ovary-dependent neuroendocrine syndrome described in the text. Time is measured in months; dose is the total cumulative amount of estradiol administered to the mice; and change is the measured impairment in reproductive ability for each treatment. In many cases, the change may be cryptic (without overt functional consequences) until a threshold is reached (shaded background). Three trajectories at different doses are shown. (From Finch 1988.)

limited since it doesn't apply to half the members of the same species. On the other hand, the study of female reproductive mechanisms has allowed us to uncover detailed interactions between the hypothalamus–pituitary axis and the target organ that are similar to those operating in other processes regulated by the neuroendocrine system, such as are described in the section on stress responses later in this chapter.

It has recently been demonstrated that human females who undergo an early natural menopause (at an age less than 44 years) have a significantly higher probability of dying early than do women who report a natural menopause at ages 50 to 54 years (Snowden et al. 1989). No evidence suggested that this excess mortality is due to estrogen depletion, particularly since the slope of the Gompertz plot for women before and after 50 years of age, the median age of menopause, did not change. Another factor seems to be involved. This result suggests that ovarian aging in humans, although perhaps a very useful model, does not play a major role in limiting the maximum human life span. Each system likely has its own set of crucial events that must occur if aging is to proceed, of which the female reproductive system is merely the most accessible to experimental analysis. If so, it is unlikely that a single pacemaker determines the complete pattern of physiological senescence in an organism. Reproductive senescence may imply organismic senescence in some species but not in others; the explanation for the difference probably resides in the details of their respective life history strategies.

Gene Expression and Neuroendocrine Control

Much of the other evidence we have discussed in other chapters has pointed toward the important role of the genes in controlling and regulating the aging process. The same is true of the neuroendocrine theories. Because of the important role that the hypothalamus–pituitary axis and the limbic system play in the physiological regulation of bodily activities, any changes in gene expression in these brain regions will be of great interest, since they will likely either be due to changes in peripheral hormone levels or be the cause of changes in the trophic hormone levels. Johnson and Finch (1996) have reviewed the recent literature regarding mRNA levels of various genes examined in mature versus old adult brains. Of the 37 different genes studied, 20 show decreases, 14 show no change or have contradictory results in different studies, and only 3 show consistent increases.

These results are difficult to interpret, given our rudimentary knowledge of the structural changes that occur in the aging brain and given the diverse nature of the genes studied and their involvement in different sorts of cellular functions. The effects of the changes in gene expression may well have extensive ramifications, more so than their small numbers might imply. Mice transgenic for the bovine growth hormone gene produce large amounts of the hormone, are physically very large, have high corticosterone levels, neural damage, and a short life span (Miller, Batke, and O'Callaghan 1995). In aging Sprague-Dawley rats, the changes in growth hormone and other pituitary hormones are thought to be responsible for the age-related changes in antioxidant enzymes observed in some (but not all) tissues (Bolzan et al. 1995).

These findings illustrate the complex manner in which the product of one gene, such as growth hormone, interacts with and affects the cell and tissue interactions in a variety of other systems. In this context, we cannot overlook the important data demonstrating that exercise can up-regulate the mRNA levels of particular neurotrophic growth factors (Cotman and Neeper 1996). One of these, nerve growth factor (NGF), has been shown to be capable of activating the transcription factor NFkB in rat Schwann cells (Carter et al. 1996). NFkB is a potent regulator of gene expression. These intriguing findings suggest that the aging brain has a high level of molecular plasticity, such that physical activity can activate gene expression under certain circumstances. Even though it forces us to be realistic, this observation complicates our analysis of the changes we observe because we can no longer assume that the animal is static and unchanging. Taken all together, the data do suggest that a full understanding of neuroendocrine integration mechanisms and aging must encompass tissue- and stage-specific gene expression patterns and the processes that modulate them.

Not every change in gene expression will involve quantitative alterations in mRNA levels. A fascinating example is the homozygous mutant Brattleboro rat, whose genetically based diabetes insipidus is due to a frameshift mutation in its vasopressin gene. As the animal ages, the expression of the wild-type vasopressin molecule gradually increases during the first 79 weeks of life, even though the animal is a homozygous mutant! This paradoxical situation appears to be due to frameshift deletions at two hot spots in the gene that generate the wild-type sequence downstream of the mutation (Evans et al. 1994). Even more interesting is the observation that infusion of the animal with wild-type vasopressin during a 40-week period reduced the incidence of the deletions.

These data suggest that the neuroendocrine gene sequence can change qualitatively with age, and that the frequency of these somatic mutations can be modulated by a chronic exposure to particular target hormones (Mobbs 1996). The mutation frequency of this gene is much higher than normal, raising the question as to what mechanisms might account for this enhanced somatic instability of the gene. Inevitably, one wonders whether other genes undergo a similar process of age-related somatic mutation or whether this is an isolated but intriguing example. There is more than a passing resemblance between the Brattleboro rat and the directed mutations observed in bacteria raised under stress conditions (Travisano and Lenski 1996). We know that oxidatively driven age-related somatic mutations take place in the mitochondria; the example of the Brattleboro rat means that at least two processes are known to generate age-related somatic mutations. The problem, however, is to demonstrate that such mutations are directed, and not random in their appearance and expression.

Ovarian steroids such as estradiol and progesterone are known to be potent regulators of gene activity in a variety of systems. The estrogen-dependent onset and termination of reproduction in female mammals is just one example of such a system. There are others. Most of these other hormonally induced systems were chosen for investigation by molecular biologists and developmental geneticists because of their important role during early development. Yet, as Finch (1987) has observed, a subset of such genes with variable expression should also undergo detectable changes during senescence as a result of the withdrawal of the particular hormone or other regulatory molecule controlling that gene. A detailed analysis of this subset of genes should reveal the nature of the other events and control points important to the aging process. After certain events have been identified as being crucial to the aging process, an explanation of why there is so much variability in the aging process is still needed. The existence of subtle differences in the regulatory portions of the gene, the portions that respond to regulatory molecules such as hormones, appears to account for most of the variable responses noted in different systems. A fair amount of the genetic polymorphism characteristic of the human species probably resides in this regulatory gene heterogeneity.

Putting all of this evidence together, Finch (1987, p. 291) proposed that the expression of any gene with variable expression is itself "influenced by regulatory factors that are produced by other genes. . . . Thus, searching for the primary genetic determinants of senescence clearly involves analysis of pleiotropic cascades and interactions between many gene loci . . . [and] to trace cascading interactions of genes and physiological regulatory factors back into earlier stages of life." According to this point of view, the long-term regulatory effects of the neuroendocrine system on the aging process are mediated through the system's ability to regulate patterns of gene activity by changing the titers of various hormones. Moreover, the regulatory circuits are not likely to be very simple, but are probably composed of cascading and interlocking networks of genes. This concept, it should be noted, is very similar to Walford's (1987) idea of "hierarchial homeostasis" and to Wilkins's (1986) suggestion of "interacting regulatory networks." We will return to a consideration of these ideas in Chapter 13.

One example of these interacting networks involves the signal transduction mechanism (an example of which is shown in Figure 10.7), which plays a vital role in the functioning of the neuroendocrine system. The estrogen receptor must be phosphorylated before it becomes active, and this activation is mediated by growth factors (such as epidermal or insulin growth factors) acting through a protein kinase–Ras–Raf–MAP kinase signal transduction cascade (Kato et al. 1995). Manipulating receptor activity is one method of regulating specific endocrine activities, in a manner accessible to a wide variety of potential signal molecules.

Stress Responses

The organism's ability to respond to stress represents a major portion of its ability to adapt to environmental changes. Even though a large variety of diverse stimuli can initiate a stress response, the salient fact is that all these stimuli induce a complex but stereotypic response. The animal's response takes place on both the neuroendocrine and the molecular levels. Each level depends on accurate detection of feedback signals for its effective functioning. The hypothalamic–pituitary–adrenal (HPA) axis is the system responsible for the neuroendocrine response to stress, via the adrenocortical secretion of glucocorticoids. These steroids mobilize energy from storage sites, increase cardiovascular tone, and suppress various other functions that are not required during an emergency—the well-known "fight or flight" response (Carter and Wade 1996).

On the other hand, the same adaptive features of acute glucocorticoid action can give rise to various pathologies when prolonged stress results in a chronic excess of glucocorticoid levels. Since aging is often thought to involve a loss of the ability to retain homeostatic balance in the face of stress, an investigation of the effects of age on the HPA axis might shed some light on whether the degenerative aspects of stress and aging each act to accelerate the other. The answer to the question is species-specific: In rats, the endocrine dysfunctions noted in the HPA axis may lead to functional abnormalities in the animal; in humans the HPA abnormalities are much more subtle and lead to an increased vulnerability but not necessarily an abnormality (Sapolsky 1990). These findings illustrate the need for caution in extrapolating findings from one species to another.

The aging rat has the ability to start a normal stress reaction to any of various standard experimental stresses, but it is impaired in its ability to terminate the secretion of glucocorticoids. The hippocampal region of the brain is known to be rich in glucocorticoid receptors and is thought to be responsible for mediating the negative feedback portion of the HPA axis. During aging, there is a preferential loss of mRNA for the Type II glucocorticoid receptor in the rat hippocampus, with little loss observed elsewhere in the brain (van Eekelen et al. 1991). One experiment demonstrated that the cumulative exposure to stress-induced glucocorticoid secretion destroyed specific hippocampal neurons, particularly in older animals

(Landfield 1980; but see Wickelgren 1996 for arguments against hippocampal cell death). The observation that glucocorticoids killed hippocampal neurons led to the idea that this neuronal loss desensitizes the HPA axis to glucocorticoid feedback regulation, producing further glucocorticoid secretion, which leads to further neuronal death, and so on (Sapolsky et al. 1986).

This self-amplifying destructive feedback cycle appears to underlie the dramatic senescence of male marsupial mice, which die after a brief and very aggressive mating period (see Chapter 4). In this organism, *Antechinus*, the negative feedback system fails at the neuronal level and the glucocorticoid concentration increases unchecked. The hormonal hypersecretion induces a fatal array of symptoms reminiscent of Cushing's disease in humans, except that the reproductive ability of *Antechinus* is unimpaired. A similar situation is observed in the Pacific salmon (see Chapter 4). However, this catastrophic feedback cycle may not be operative in every rat (see the section "Other Hormonal Phenomena," later in this chapter) and is certainly not present in humans (Mobbs 1996). In people, both the hormone levels and the stress response show no significant alterations through age 80 years. After that age, some evidence suggests that humans show an increased glucocorticoid level and an impaired feedback process, although much milder than the situation in the aged rat (Sapolsky 1990). However, no evidence shows that the same mechanisms are involved. In fact, the chronic use of glucocorticoids in current medical practice means that millions of patients have been treated with large doses over long periods with no reported adverse effects indicative of hippocampal damage (Goya, Rivero, and Pascual-Leone 1995).

Finally, it should be mentioned that the two different levels of the stress response are not totally independent of each other. The molecular response to stress, consisting of heat shock protein gene expression in various tissues of the animal, is modulated by the neuroendocrine system, thus providing a link between these two levels of the stress response (Udelsman et al. 1993). Transplantation experiments have shown that young tissues put into an aged host have an "old" stress response, while old tissues put into a young host have a more nearly normal stress response (Udelsman et al. 1995), thus demonstrating that the changes in the stress response with age are the result of prior changes in the neuroendocrine system itself.

Factors Modifying an Individual's Neuroendocrine Status and Rate of Aging

The damages seen in the neuroendocrine system of older animals are not inevitable. The aging of the adult can be modified by several factors, including its developmental experience. Handling young rodents is known to induce persistent changes in the HPA axis such that old handled rats do not have as severe a hippocampal neuron loss or learning impairments as do the nonhandled controls (Sapolsky 1990; Meany et al. 1995). In one study, the treated rat pups were handled for only 15 minutes a day during the first 3 weeks of life. After that, the handled and nonhandled animals were raised under similar conditions until maturity. When tested with various stressors, the handled adults secreted glucocorticoids at levels lower than those of nonhandled animals and were more effective in rapidly shutting down the stress response once the stressors were removed. But the differences didn't stop there. Even in the absence of stress, the aged, non-handled animals had a basal level of glucocorticoids that was much higher than that of their handled sibs. This higher hormone level was estimated to be the functional equivalent of undergoing 12 hours of mild stress every night (Meany et al. 1995). Now, if hippocampal neurons can be killed by prolonged exposure to glucocorticoids, and if the nonhandled animals have higher cumulative exposure to these hormones than do handled animals, one would predict that the former animals should have higher levels of hippocampal degeneration than the latter.

Meany and colleagues (1995) have reported that the aged (24 months old), nonhandled animals have a loss of hippocampal neurons that is 40 percent higher than that of the aged, handled animals. These neuron losses have functional consequences. Aged, nonhandled rats do much poorer in tests of spatial memory than do aged, handled rats, and such cognitively impaired adults exhibit elevated basal and stress levels of glucocorticoids, as well as show a significantly greater loss of glucocorticoid receptors in the hippocampus (Meany et al. 1995). Just as exercise alters gene expression in the rat brain, so the organism's developmental experience modulates its hormonal response to stress. It will be instructive to determine the effects of these treatments on longevity and morbidity.

Caloric restriction is the most effective intervention known to extend the life span of mammals by slowing the rate of aging (see Chapter 7). The basal metabolic rate is not changed, but the decreased intake of energy per animal somehow retards the aging process. Gaining an understanding of the mechanisms underlying this process has been a major focus of recent research. The two general hypotheses put forth by Masoro (1995b) both involve the neuroendocrine system.

One hypothesis is that the reduction in energy intake changes the characteristics of carbohydrate fuel use such that plasma glucose and insulin levels are significantly lower in the restricted animals than in the *ad libitum*–fed controls (Figure 12.4a), even though the daily rate of carbohydrate fuel utilization per kilogram of lean body mass is similar in both. The efficiency with which glucose and insulin exert their effects must be increased in the restricted animals. In any event, hyperglycemia and hyperinsulinemia are damaging to cells. If the normal levels of each substance also cause a lower but significant level of damage, the lower life span concentrations brought on by caloric restriction should cause even less damage and hence slow the rate of aging in such animals.

The second hypothesis suggests that caloric restriction enables the animal to resist stress better. The pattern of corticosterone secretion is markedly different in restricted animals (Figure 12.4b). It has been suggested that such patterns represent optimally protective levels of glucocorticoids. Note that these two hypotheses are not mutually exclusive. A reasonable hypothesis is that caloric restriction exerts its effects via the neuroendocrine system. Certainly such a mechanism might be able eventually to explain the pleiotropic and integrated effects that caloric restriction has on the entire organism. It will be most useful to identify the operative mechanisms.

What about humans? The data are of necessity more sparse and more indirect than the rat data. In general, increased HPA activity is not normally associ-

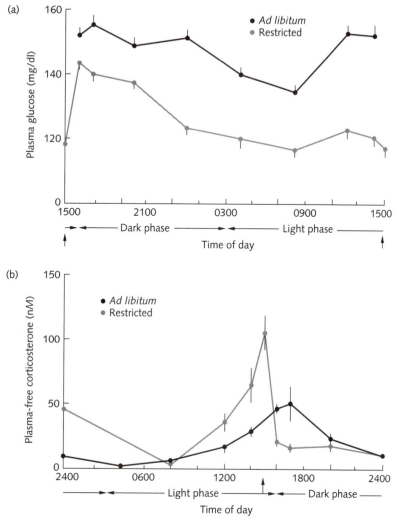

Figure 12.4 Diurnal patterns of glucose and corticosterone concentrations in the plasma. (a) Daily variation in plasma glucose concentration in male F344 rats in the age range of 9 to 13 months. The restricted rats were fed 60 percent of the *ad libitum* intake starting at 6 weeks of age. Short vertical arrows refer to the time at which the restricted rats received their daily food allotment. (From Masoro et al. 1992.) (b) Free corticosterone concentrations in plasma in 15- to 19-month-old male F344 rats treated as described for (a). Similar results were obtained in all age ranges. (From Sabatino et al. 1991.)

ated with aging in humans. But increased glucocorticoid levels are associated with certain age-related neuropathologies such as Alzheimer's disease or Cushing's disease. In the latter pathology, increased glucocorticoid levels were shown to be associated with impaired cognitive function. Among normal aged

(70-year-old) humans, patients that were apparently normal but had elevated cortisol levels performed worse on some learning tests than did patients with low cortisol levels (Meany et al. 1995). Studies on people with Cushing's syndrome also lead to the same conclusion. The existing data on humans thus are generally consistent with the rat data, but less extreme in their expression.

Much of what is termed "successful aging" may depend on our intrauterine and developmental history, our educational levels, our diet, and our physical activity. There are undoubtedly other variables operating as well. The plasticity of the brain should not be underestimated (or overestimated) and should enter into all calculations involving child rearing, education, and the like. For example, if rat pups age more successfully as a result of a total of only 5.25 hours of handling during their lifetime, what implications does this observation have for the role of social phenomena in modulating organismic patterns of aging in humans? Babies raised in orphanages where their physical needs are met but their emotional and/or social needs are neglected often show an abnormal developmental pattern termed "failure to thrive."

Warning us that this rhetorical question should not lead us to make too simplistic or sweeping an interpretation is the observation that early adoption of rat pups by a new mother leads to a lower level of stress-induced corticosterone secretion, while late adoption leads to prolonged stress-induced secretion of corticosterone (Barbazanges et al. 1996). The mechanistic interpretation of these phenomena may yield interesting insights into the antecedents of individual patterns of aging, but care must be taken that plausible but unverified explanations ("just-so stories") are not used in place of evidence.

Other Hormonal Phenomena

Ovarian steroids are not the only hormones that exhibit major decreases with age. The hormone dehydroepiandrosterone (DHEA) is produced by the adrenal gland and (in the sulfate form) is the most abundant steroid in the blood of humans. It is the only adrenal steroid that shows a strong age-dependent alteration in its concentration, suggesting that it is regulated by a mechanism other than that known to regulate glucocorticosteroids. In humans, it increases at puberty, reaches a peak level in the late teens or early twenties, and then steadily decreases such that older adults show a 90 percent decrease relative to the peak values (Orentreich et al. 1984). Free-living baboons show a similar pattern, providing the possibility of a primate model to eventually test the role of DHEA in aging (Sapolsky et al. 1993). Some rodent strains do not have detectable levels of DHEA. Thus, the observation that short-lived mutant mice suffering from obesity, diabetes, and tumors showed improvement in these conditions, as well as an extended life span following treatment with DHEA (Coleman, Schwizer, and Letier 1984), is difficult to interpret—especially in view of the report that lifetime feeding of DHEA to a healthy low-tumor strain of mouse (C57BL/6J) altered neither median nor maximum life span, nor affected the rate of aging (Orentreich et al. 1994), although it has been reported to improve immune function (Miller 1996). Not much can be said about the role of this hormone in aging, since it still has no known biological function, although it has been suggested that it may act as a prohormone and undergo intracellular conversion to a variety of active androgens or estrogens (Orentreich et al. 1994).

Given the important role that the endocrine glands play in regulating our neuroendocrine responses, one might initially conclude that the loss of function of any single gland has deleterious effects on the organism's physiological status. However, it has been reported that the removal of the anterior pituitary (hypophysectomy) appears to maintain good health status in rodents at ages when their controls appear senescent. Table 12.1 summarizes the reported effects of this treatment (Finch 1990). This alteration in hormonal stimulation appears to result not in an increase in either mean or maximum life span, but rather in a delayed onset of senescence in the treated animals. Presumably these beneficial effects arise from the lack of chronic hormonal stimulation of the tissues and the consequent alterations in gene expression in the various target tissues. In this context, this represents an interesting but puzzling model, the details of which still need to be worked out. It is also one that is not likely to see wide commercial application.

Finally, it should be noted that age-related changes have been described in neural structures other than those few described here. If we regard the essence of ourselves as being our mind and memories, then what we have learned suggests that the physical substrate that constitutes us is constantly changing us even as we change it. Some of these changes must adversely affect the integrative activities of our body and set in motion a chain of events that eventually culminates in our inability to surmount some challenge that we once could easily have overcome.

Table 12.1 Hypophysectomy and the Retardation of Senescence

Trait	Improved by hypophysectomy	Worsened by hypophysectomy
Collagen	Tail-tendon tensile strength	
Immune	Thymus weight; delayed hypersensitivity graft refection; in vivo phagocytosis; primary immune response	Primary immune response
Kidney disease	Proteinuria; thickened basement membrane	
Metabolism	Responsiveness of O_2 consumption to thyroxine; O_2 consumption in vivo; liver RNA synthesis	
Neuropathy	Hindlimb paralysis via spinal neuron degeneration	
Vascular	β-adrenergic mediated relaxation of smooth muscle; aortic thickness	
Tumors	Reduced incidence in endocrine glands and other organs	
Wounds	Healing improved	

Source: From Table 10.9 of Finch 1990; data from various sources.

• Immunological Theories of Aging

In Chapter 5 we described some of the known age-related changes that take place in the human immune system. Excellent reviews of the topic have recently been published (Miller 1995, 1996). Longitudinal studies of the age-related changes that take place in laboratory primates such as the macaque monkey are now under way and suggest that the numbers and types of lymphocytes change with age (Bowden et al. 1994). The conventional belief is that these known decreases in the quantity and quality of the immune response are due in part, directly or indirectly, to the early involution and senescence of the thymus. The thymus seems to be involved in regulating the quantitative extent of an immune response. The thymus also appears to determine quite early in life the qualitative array of immunological responses by the T cells that any single individual can mount. After the involution of the thymus, an age-related change affects the extent to which the immune cells can proliferate in response to an appropriate stimulus: The spleen or lymph node or blood cells of older animals respond to a lesser extent than those of younger animals.

This decreased vigor of the immune response seems to be due to a dramatic age-related shift in the proportion of naive and memory T cells (Miller 1995). T lymphocytes that leave the thymus and reach the peripheral immune system have not yet been immunologically triggered by a specific antigen, so they are referred to as "naive." Once the cell has been triggered and proliferated, some of the progeny cells return to the resting state and are termed "memory" cells. Such memory cells enable the organism to mount a rapid secondary response if the same antigen is encountered later. However, the involution of the thymus puts a cap on the number of naive cells in the immune system, and the continual activation of new memory cells implies that the proportion of naive cells must decline—which it does.

This shift in T cell types is thought to account for some of the age-related decline in immune function. This cannot be the only explanation, for it is also known that there is an age-related decrease in the ability of activated T cells to secrete and respond to lymphokines (such as interleukin-2, IL-2, which is required for growth of both T cells and B cells), and that this decrease is accompanied by an increased ability to produce interleukin-4 (IL-4) (Miller 1995). The data suggest that the T cells are functionally subdivided into several different types with different synthetic capabilities. Thus, the age-related decline in T cell responsiveness is due not to a progressive change affecting every cell but rather to a change in the proportion of cells that can respond versus the proportion that fail to respond at all. The suggestion has been made that the immune system should be viewed as a mosaic of responsive and hyporesponsive cells in which the latter become more frequent with age (Miller 1995).

Although multiple factors may be involved in immunosenescence, much attention has been paid to the progressive age-dependent involution of the thymus. This focus is based in part on the fact that the thymic involution precedes or accompanies the usual age-related functional changes seen in the immune system and thus might logically play an important role in bringing about immunosenescent changes. Structural changes in the mouse thymus begin quite early. Subtle signs of atrophy of the lobules and involution of the organ can be seen in the 6-month-old animal, as can a slight reduction in the staining of cortical thymocytes (Takeoka et al. 1996). Substantive changes begin later, however. The cortex and medulla of the thymus in the 12-month-old mouse have separated from each other and contain larger numbers of atrophying cells and other signs of structural degeneration (Takeoka et al. 1996).

The cortical cells seem to be primarily affected at first; the cells of the medulla appear normal until the later stages of involution (Nabarra and Andrianarison 1996). Macrophage numbers increase and increasingly show signs of phagocytic activity (see Chapter 11). By 18 to 20 months, the organ architecture has disappeared and the number of lymphocytes has decreased drastically. By 25 months and later, the terminally involuted thymus is much reduced in weight, has lost the cortical–medulla separation as well as the presence of multiple differentiated cells, and is composed mostly of adipose cells and connective tissue. The maintenance of immune function until relatively late in life suggests that the small number of thymic cells remaining in the old organ are immunocompetent (Nabarra and Andrianarison 1996). Nabarra and Andrianarison conclude, from the correlation of thymic involution with age-related immune dysfunction, that the thymus should be regarded as the aging "clock" or pacemaker of the immune system. They also suggest that the involution of the thymus is not intrinsic but is linked to an extrinsic cause, probably in the neuroendocrine system. This suggestion has been made by many other authors and is still being vigorously debated. We will explore it in some detail here.

Interestingly, the age-related degenerative changes that take place in the normal mouse thymus are not identical to those seen in animals suffering from autoimmune disease, suggesting that the loss of function in these two syndromes arises from different causes and that autoimmune models are not completely equivalent to the situation in normally aging animals. The normal structural changes observed during thymic involution are accompanied or even preceded by changes in the functional capacity of the thymus. The mouse thymus shows a sharp drop in its ability to promote T cell differentiation within the first month of life but remains steady thereafter (Utsuyama et al. 1991). Removing the thymus from adult mice has a less obvious effect on cell-mediated immunity, possibly because of the continuing existence of spleen and lymph node lymphocytes. The exact role of the thymus in mediating adult immune function still needs to be worked out. Nonetheless, the composition of the T cell subpopulations induced by transplanted thymus does change with age, reflecting the changing capacities of the gland to support and sustain the peripheral immune system, and this change probably has functional significance.

Another system in which to explore the role of the thymus in immunosenescence would be one in which the thymus either does not develop or does not degenerate. The Buffalo/Mna rat presents one such "natural" experiment in which the thymus does not involute but continues to grow with age, so it presents a much more useful model with which to explore the role of the thymus in aging.

The animal does not live forever, but instead dies at about 20 months as a result of thoracic compression resulting from the thymic overgrowth. The important point is that the animal's immune functions are well maintained in middle and old age. Interestingly, hypophysectomy performed on 8- to 9-month-old mice also gave rise to animals with larger thymuses and higher ratios of cortex–medulla areas than the age-matched controls, illustrating the close connection between the neuroendocrine and immune systems (Harrison, Archer, and Astle 1982).

Another "natural" experiment that addresses the question of thymic function involves the use of the nude mouse, a genetic mutant that has no thymus. Such mice have very low or no T cell functions and are very susceptible to infections. The thymic remnants in the head and neck region can give rise to a small number of functional T cells (Ikehara et al. 1987). Implantation of a thymus restores T cell function, at least in part (Furukawa et al. 1988). Nude mice have impaired neuroendocrine functions, again suggesting that the two systems are intimately intertwined (Daneva et al. 1995).

The B lymphocytes responsible for humoral immunity have been thought to be independent of the thymus. Yet one report correlates the age of thymic involution in mice with the age at which certain genes (for example, *Rag-1*) required for B lymphocyte formation are maximally active in the bone marrow (Ben-Yehuda et al. 1994). This correlation, and the demonstration that a diffusible factor obtained from T cell cultures can induce *Rag-1* activity in B cell precursors, suggests that thymic involution may affect both T and B cell functions. If so, then senescence of both major components of the immune system may originate in the loss of thymic function. However, debate on this point continues, and there is still no generally accepted unambiguous and definitive explanation for the dramatic functional changes seen in aging rodents and humans (Miller 1995). Thymic involution is presumed to play a critical role in the age-related loss of function, but the crucial details still elude us.

Despite this deep gap in our knowledge, a partial restoration of specific immune functions has been achieved by three different types of interventions. The first intervention—micronutrient supplementation—is low-tech but potentially very useful. Mocchegiani and colleagues (1995) have shown that oral zinc supplementation in old mice for a 1-month period reverses the age-related decline in zinc plasma levels. This treatment also leads to a recovery of thymic functions, a partial regrowth of the organ, and a partial restoration of peripheral immune efficiency. Zinc is known to be a required cofactor for thymulin, a well-known thymic peptide that is important for the maintenance of cell-mediated immunity. The low thymulin activity characteristic of older animals, and the age-related loss of immune functions, may be due, in part at least, to remediable deficiencies of zinc and perhaps other micronutrients (Fabris and Mocchegiani 1996).

The second intervention is caloric restriction. With a 60 percent caloric restriction, the thymus is initially much smaller than in the *ad libitum*–fed group, but it nonetheless has a larger proportion of active thymocytes by 6 months of age. Caloric restriction started at later ages also results in an apparent reversal and/or sparing effect on thymic size and function. The underlying mechanism is still unknown, although it is presumed to involve the neuroendocrine system, as discussed earlier.

The third intervention involves the use of synthetic oligopeptide analogues of thymic proteins (Miller 1995). Administration of these compounds to older mice led to a large and significant increase in the production of interleukin-2 (IL-2). IL-2 is produced primarily by helper T cells, regulates the growth and function of a variety of cells involved in both cellular and humoral immunity, and normally shows an age-related decline in its transcription (Pahlavani and Richardson 1996). Thus, restoring its higher levels of expression should lead to a generalized reversal of age-related losses. Other thymic peptides (see Miller 1995) demonstrate equally interesting effects.

Taken all together, these three interventions suggest that the age-related losses in immune function are reversible, at least in part. The same data can be interpreted as suggesting that the neuroendocrine mechanisms are involved in bringing about—or modulating—these age-related losses in immune function. This is a potentially important topic, which we will explore in the next section. A fuller understanding of the mechanisms involved in the maintenance of thymic and lymphocyte functioning would offer a promising base for the development of more effective interventions.

• *Integrative Aspects of the Neuro-Endocrine-Immune System*

We pointed out in Chapter 5 and elsewhere that the nervous, endocrine, and immune systems are integrated in a single neuro-endocrine-immune system in the sense that each of them affects the proper functioning of the others. Consider, for example, the differences in the functioning of the male and female immune systems as a result of their different hormonal milieus. The basic observation is that women usually mount a more vigorous immune response than men, yet women show a higher incidence of autoimmune disease than men. In addition, women suppress any immune response against their fetus but generate substantial postpartum antibody levels while they are nursing the baby. Recent research suggests that the answers to these and other puzzling questions involve the hormonal differences between the sexes.

A variety of studies have shown that estrogens and/or estradiol have a stimulatory effect on the levels of hormones such as prolactins and growth hormones, which then increase the production of T and B cells. Progesterone and testosterone, on the other hand, are reported to have a suppressive effect on the immune system. The net effect of these relationships in the context of the female rat estrous cycle is that estradiol secretion peaks before ovulation (see Chapter 5) and increases the immune response of the uterus, cleaning it of bacteria and preparing it for implantation. In the rat's cervix and vagina, however, the same estradiol induces a tissue-specific suppression of the immune response, presumably so that the sperm will not be attacked. After ovulation, when estradiol decreases and progesterone increases, the female's immune response is partly suppressed, presumably so that it does not attack the fetus. The drop in progesterone and the increase in prolactin and/or estradiol after birth stimulate the immune system and end its temporary suppression. The female's cyclic hormonal levels are reflected in her cyclic immune functions. Postmenopausal women are no longer cyclic, and their overall immune system responses are low and constant, much like an ordinary man's immune response.

More evidence of the intimate interactions between the neuroendocrine and immune systems is the simultaneous appearance in cells of components of both systems or, more convincingly, the demonstration that the secretory product of one system will significantly affect the functional status of the other system. The following several examples support the view that the three systems are integrated into one:

1. The Schwann cells of the peripheral nerves synthesize progesterone, which promotes myelin formation during nerve regeneration (Koenig et al. 1995).

2. Functionally impaired neurons, but not normal active neurons, express major histocompatibility complex Class I genes and thereby make themselves available for immunosurveillance by cytotoxic T cells (Neumann et al. 1995).

3. Bone resorption by osteoclasts is activated by various cytokines (IL-1, IL-6, tumor necrosis factor, and so on) secreted by thymic stromal cells and by peripheral blood monocytes. These activation processes are inhibited by estradiol acting directly on these cells (Horowitz 1993).

4. The saliva contains different antibodies, predominantly IgA and IgM. The levels of IgM are significantly affected by the light–dark cycle: The peak values in individuals overwintering in Antarctica are temporally correlated with the absence of daylight (Gleeson, Cripps, and Clancy 1995). It seems reasonable to assume that neuroendocrine factors involving the pineal gland and melatonin secretion are involved in this light–dark modulation of an individual's humorally mediated immune function.

5. Both single and extended periods of exercise have been shown to significantly alter T cell–mediated immune function (Mazzeo 1994; Nash 1994) such that the incidence and severity of infection is reduced. Again, the neuroendocrine system provides the most likely mechanisms through which physical exertion can affect immune function.

6. Patients suffering from hyperthyroidism do not show the age-related decline in thymulin levels found in normal individuals, while patients suffering from hypothyroidism have levels of thymulin that are significantly lower at all ages than in the normal controls (Fabris, Mocchegiani, and Provinciali 1995).

7. Cytokine treatments decrease the levels of thyroid hormone in rats and humans, while treatment of old mice and humans with thyroid hormone or thyroid-stimulating hormone gives rise to increased thymulin production, lymphocyte proliferation, and T cell–mediated immune function (Fabris, Mocchegiani, and Provinciali 1995).

8. Treatment of old mice with thymosin (TF-5) yields an increase in the release of adrenocorticotropic hormone (ACTH) and glucocorticoids, while treatment of old mice with growth hormone yields increased levels of IL-2 relative to controls.

Other examples are available in the literature, but these will suffice to illustrate that the two systems are probably functionally integrated. The findings need confirmation and elaboration, yet they appear persuasive. If confirmed, they imply that the age-related immune dysfunction is not intrinsic to the immune cells but arises as a result of age-related defects in other neuroendocrine functions. The reciprocal may also be true. If so—and the reader should be cautioned against undue optimism—the potential for effective intervention in the aging process may be greater than was previously suspected. Psychological factors have also been suggested as impinging on the modulation of these functions (Tricerei et al. 1995).

The complex interactions of the neuro-endocrine-immune system are also well illustrated by the role of the major histocompatibility genes in the aging process. The topic has been reviewed by Lerner and Finch (1991), Yunis and Salazar (1993), and Crew (1993), and this discussion draws heavily from those sources. Our knowledge of the histocompatibility genes originated in the genetics of transplantation. If skin from an inbred strain of mice is grafted to another individual of the same strain, it is accepted and will grow normally. But if it is grafted to an individual of a different inbred strain, the graft is eventually rejected. To find out which genes were involved in this tissue recognition and rejection process, the genetic differences between the strains were gradually minimized by inbreeding until one particular region of the mouse chromosome 17 could be identified as causing the rejection. Because of its role in tissue recognition and rejection, this region was named the major histocompatiblity complex (MHC), or H-2 region. A homologous region in humans is located on the short arm of chromosome 6 and is termed human leukocyte system A (HLA). All vertebrates that have been examined contain such a gene cluster.

The MHC complex in mice and the HLA complex consist of highly polymorphic series of a dozen or more loci, comprising at least 1 million base pairs, which code for proteins found in the blood serum as well as on cell membranes. The genes involved encode membrane glycoproteins and have been sorted into two classes. The class I genes code for antigens that are expressed ubiquitously throughout the body and are the main basis for graft rejection. The class II antigens occur mostly on cells derived from bone marrow, including B and T cells, macrophages, and other antigen-presenting cells. Thus, the MHC genes are intimately involved in immunological identity.

In humans, there are 30 to 60 alleles of each class I gene and slightly fewer of each class II gene. These polymorphisms are widespread in all human populations, such that any one allele rarely exceeds a gene frequency of 10 percent. In addition, the complex contains genes coding for several serum complement factors (class III genes) and a number of genes with no obvious role in immune function.

The complex affects reproduction. In mice, specific MHC genes and alleles are associated with mate selection, patterns of estrous cycles, fertility, fecundity, rate of embryonic development, and reproductive aging and senescence. For example, a comparison of three different H-2 haplotypes tested on a B10 genetic background shows that the H-2^r haplotype differs from the other two haplotypes in number of litters, number of pups per female, and age at last litter (Table 12.2). Since that data also shows a remarkable concordance between

Table 12.2   **Effect of MHC Genes on Reproduction and Longevity**

	Maximum life span (weeks)		Fecundity			
Haplotype	Male	Female	Number of litters	Age at last letter (wks)	Number of pups per female	Number of pups per letter
H-2^k	149 ± 1.1	161 ± 2.1	7.5 ± 0.5	44.4 ± 2.1	43 ± 3	5.8 ± 0.3
H-2^b	155 ± 0.4	148 ± 1.2	5.4 ± 0.5	37.1 ± 2.4	34 ± 3	6.4 ± 0.3
H-2^r	170 ± 0.8	165 ± 1.0	7.8 ± 0.5	45.3 ± 2.3	50 ± 3	6.7 ± 0.3

Source: Data taken from Table 1 of Crew 1993.
Note: Life spans of all three strains are significantly different (p < 0.02). The H-2^r haplotype is signficantly different from the others in number of litters, age at last litter, and number of pups per female.

age at last litter and maximum life span, we must conclude that the MHC genes are exerting some kind of controlling influence on both reproduction and longevity.

Another interesting aspect of the MHC and HLA complexes is the association of certain MHC or HLA genotypes with certain traits, some of which have a direct connection with immunological function but many of which have only an indirect connection, or none. By doing blood and tissue typing, one can determine an individual's HLA or MHC genotype. When this is combined with a retrospective medical history, one can begin to make statistical associations between particular HLA genotypes and diseases. When an HLA factor occurs with high frequency in patients with a specific disease but with low frequency in the general population, then one can deduce a statistical—and possibly even a causal—relationship between the two. Ryder et al. (1981) have shown that such associations exist between certain HLA genotypes and certain diseases, many of which are not obviously immunological in origin.

For example, an individual carrying the HLA-B27 genotype is 87.4 times more likely to develop ankylosing spondylytis (a degenerative bone disease) than is an individual who does not carry this genotype. The percentage of women with the HLA-B8 genotype declines with increasing age, an indication that such individuals may have a shortened life expectancy. An examination of centenarians and normal-lived controls revealed that three particular HLA alleles (DR7, DR11, and DR13) were significantly overrepresented in the long-lived groups. (Ivanova et al. 1998). Interestingly, two of these allele-specific effects appear to be gender-specific, with DR7 mostly affecting men and DR11 mostly affecting women. It appears to be advantageous to be heterozygous: there is a decreasing proportion with age of HLA-homozygous individuals. The mechanisms underlying these associations are far from clear, but they suggest that the MHC/HLA gene complexes may exert an effect on longevity because their effects are not limited to the immune system but are more widespread and affect basic body processes.

• *Summary*

We have examined the evidence relating the integrative and pacemaker role of the immune system and the neuroendocrine system in the aging process. The underlying assumption of such theories is that homeostatic failure of the the organism plays a key role in the onset of senescence and death, and that this failure may be traced to one or the other or both of these two systems.

Neuroendocrine theories are based in large part on detailed investigations into the age-related decrements of neuroendocrine-controlled processes. Female reproductive aging in rodents is well understood and experimentally accessible, so it has been intensively investigated. It is understood well enough that aging in this system can be viewed in terms of, and described as the result of, an event-dependent process (hormonal damage to neuroendocrine structures) rather than a time-dependent one. The organism's ability to resist stress depends on the normal functioning of the HPA axis; upsets in this system are reflected on anatomical (neuronal death) and functional (cognitive impairment) examination. There is an interesting and complicated interplay between the organism's experiential history and its patterns of neuroendocrine expression and gene expression.

The immunological theory rests on three key findings: (1) that there is a quantitative and qualitative decline in the ability of the immune system to produce antibodies; (2) that there are age-related changes in the ability to induce particular subsets of T cells and to produce different types of cell-mediated responses; and (3) that there is at least correlative evidence linking these alterations to the involution of the thymus. Finally, certain of the immune functions are neuroendocrine dependent, or can at least be modulated via the hypothalamic–pituitary axis, thus tying together the two systems. Taken together, these findings indicate decrements in function, which likely lead to an increased probability of infection and death.

We already practice effective anti-aging interventions on some functions governed by the neuroendocrine system: Estrogen replacement therapy extends normal function, delays morbidity, and lowers premature mortality for a significant subset of the population. Other potential hormonal interventions are under investigation, most notably those involving the stimulation of growth hormone secretion. Such interventions probably will be as successful as the estrogen replacement intervention. Pharmaceutical interventions are not our only recourse. Caloric restriction, micronutrient supplementation, and exercise all have reversing effects on the "normal" age-related declines in various neuroendocrine immune functions. The fact that certain of these integrative functions can be reversed by both high-tech and low-tech interventions should stimulate the development of more effective and specific inteventions.

The fact that the MHC/HLA genes have major effects on the organism's behaviors, reproductive history, immunological status, and longevity simply reinforces the view that the neural, endocrine, and immune systems are an integrated intercellular regulatory system intimately involved in aging and senescence.

Part IV

Conclusions and Prospects

13

Is There a Common Mechanism of Aging?

We have reached the end of our review of the biological facts and theories underlying the aging process. What can we say in the way of a conclusion? One thing that our tour of the field should have made obvious is that we know a great deal about the biological changes that accompany aging, but that we still do not know what mechanisms are involved in regulating the aging process. This is not the same as saying that we have no good ideas as to the causal mechanisms involved. The material covered in the last part of the book has clearly implicated the involvement of certain genes, certain types of damage-causing processes, and certain types of repair or synthetic processes as being central to the aging process. Not only has the large number of plausible mechanisms been reduced over the years to a probable few, but the nature of the research questions now being posed has been honed so that they can address very specific problems. A variety of good experimental animal models are available to us, each with characteristic strengths and weaknesses. There is every reason to believe that the current progress being made in deciphering these processes can be maintained and even increased in the future.

We have seen that several of the theories are supported by what appears to be good data. Some of the postulated mechanisms might well dovetail one another; others seem to be quite incompatible. This disparity is less of a problem than it might appear at first. There is no real reason to expect there to be only one biological mechanism responsible for aging in all of the different species and kingdoms of living organisms. The differences in life history strategies alone impose very real reproductive and physiological divergences even on the few species used in research on aging. In primates, life span seems to be correlated with brain size; in birds and bats, life span seems to be correlated with the requirements of flight (see Figure 4.12). These different statistical associations imply that the same outcome (an increased life span and/or a decreased rate of aging) is governed by multiple and varied inputs. Hayflick (1987) suggested that mechanisms of aging have not been selected for directly per se, but that natural selection has acted to develop "longevity assurance" mechanisms that can guarantee vigor in animals until the time of sexual maturation and reproduction. In that context, it is easy to imagine that there might be a wide variety of mechanisms that could be altered to maintain the optimum functioning of an organism for a limited period of time, and this diversity may be reflected in the disagreements we have noted between sets of experimental data obtained from different species.

On the other hand, there may well be multiple causes of aging, multiple processes that might impinge on cellular efficiency and survival. Some of these may use very diverse and independently originated mechanisms. The plant and animal kingdoms may represent an excellent example of how senescent processes have arisen independently and been put to very different uses, each in keeping with its kingdom's particular life history strategies. On a smaller scale, perhaps the excision of mitochondrial genes as seen in *Podospora* represents a peculiar mechanism of aging found only in a small number of species within the fungi, and which on the surface at least appears to be very different from the antioxidant defense mechanism adopted by other fungi, such as *Neurospora*. And on an even smaller scale, two different long-lived strains of *Drosophila*, each created by use of a similar selection scheme on different wild stocks, may well use different mechanisms to produce identical phenotypes.

Despite the existence of diversity, one lesson that biology suggests is that there are fundamental structural, functional, and biochemical similarities of cells and tissues. Among animals, at least, it seems reasonable to suggest that the diversity of aging processes is more apparent than real. The two different strains of *Drosophila*, for example, may share a deep biological unity in that they each may have altered their energy metabolism to better enable them to withstand physiological stresses, and their apparent differences are quite secondary, simply reflecting the manner in which each strain has organized the details of their metabolic changes. It is quite possible that the different mechanisms of aging operate in a variety of disparate ways to produce distinctive types of cellular damage, the end results of which, however, will be similar in any animal cell. It is a reasonable and interesting exercise, although an admittedly speculative one, to search for such common themes, as we will do now.

• Aging and the Maintenance of Function

Our cells and tissues are thermodynamically unstable structures. Their highly ordered molecular structures are under continual attack by stochastic degradative events and processes. Even a cursory study of cell biology lets us see that the typical animal cell is a very highly integrated construct of exceedingly complex and intricate structures. Anatomy, however, can barely begin to suggest functions and mechanisms. By using the techniques of molecular biology to delve deep into the cell, we continue to find layer upon layer of intricate molecular regulatory processes, all of which appear to be important for the continued smooth and homeostatic operation of the cell.

Such processes are both the strength and the weakness of a cell. They allow for an impressive degree of subtlety in responding to a large variety of physiological changes. However, any structure becomes more susceptible to being disrupted by stochastic damage as the number of potential targets—the regulatory processes and/or molecules—increases. As with any complex structure, the cell not only requires a continuous and stable supply of nutrients and raw materials in order to maintain itself; it must also be able to combat the stochastic degradative processes that threaten the integrity of its regulatory mechanisms. If our cells were not able to detect, repair, and replace their damaged structural and functional components, they would probably have a limited life span. Consider, for example, our red blood cells. As highly specialized and enucleated cells, they have no repair capabilities to speak of. Consequently, they die within about 90 days as a result of irreparable damage to important membrane components.

We have examined numerous postulated stochastic mechanisms of aging. Our discussion of the evidence has suggested that the free-radical or oxidative-damage theory might be not only plausible but even probable. The oxygen-induced free radicals are produced as an inevitable consequence of aerobic respiration. The mere act of breathing oxygen to produce the energy needed to take another breath also produces the free radicals that threaten to impair your ability to take that breath. These highly active chemical species cause substantial amounts of oxidative damage to the subcellular components. The cell can maintain itself in the face of these insults only by focusing substantial amounts of energy on antioxidant defenses and on repair processes.

Much of the genetic evidence that we reviewed also points toward the involvement of free radicals in the aging process, and the evidence that seems to point in another direction (such as the alteration of gene activity patterns by caloric restriction) may in fact be pointing toward the necessity of maintaining active genetically based defense or repair processes in order to delay the onset of senescent damage. The large body of evidence dealing with *in vitro* cell studies can also be interpreted as suggesting that the efficiency of the repair and replacement mechanisms is adversely affected in differentiated cells, perhaps because they are linked to the processes of cell division, which seems to be inhibited in such cells.

Finally, in large multicellular animals such as ourselves, some of the more important aspects of senescence likely do not involve primarily changes in autonomous and general cell functions per se, but rather the intercellular processes that regulate our complex physiology and provide us with our intercellular homeostatic mechanisms. Certainly both the immunological and the neuroendocrine theories of aging rest, at bottom, on concepts of gene action in one cell affecting the outcome of processes in another cell. The only effective technique we have at present of extending mammalian life spans is caloric restriction, and this intervention appears to exert its effects on gene activity via the neuroendocrine system. The study of reproductive aging in mammalian females has shown that aging may best be viewed as a genetically based, event-driven process in which the fundamental events occur on one physiological level (the hypothalamus) but are translated by the target cells into an alteration of gene activity patterns.

The genetic activity patterns implicated by these several different theories may be related to the repair activities of the affected cells. The term "repair" should be defined to include more than just the concept of DNA repair; it should be broadened to refer to the maintenance of all cellular activities. In fact, the most fundamental aging process that we can yet identify may well be the decrease in the organism's ability to maintain its functional integrity.

● *Two Types of Integrative Models: Qualitative and Quantitative Approaches*

The central role of repair is the essence of the disposable-soma theory of aging. Interestingly, two different investigators have independently made this concept the centerpiece of their respective integrative theories of aging. We will now explore two such models, as developed by Lamb (1977) and by Kowald and Kirkwood (1994, 1996). The first of these is a verbal, or qualitative, approach to organismic aging; the second is a mathematical, or quantitative, simulation of the repair and damage events central to aging and senescence at the cellular level.

Lamb (1977), following a review of the literature, developed her seven-step model as a chain of events that might lead in many cases to senescence and death, as follows:

First, stochastic damage is normally caused by a wide variety of diverse mechanisms and can affect any component of the cell from the DNA level to the cell membrane. Similar types of damage may arise from different types of mechanisms. A large part of our discussion of theories of aging was devoted to a recital of the many mechanisms that are known to cause significant and diverse damage to the cell. The fact that damage is caused may be more important than the mechanism by which it is produced. Perhaps all the damage-causing mechanisms we have discussed play a role in the aging process; if so, that might explain why there are plausible data for all of the mechanisms but no overwhelming proof in favor of any single one.

Second, the cell usually has several different types of repair processes that are normally operating at levels sufficient to cope with the stochastic damage and thereby maintain the structural and functional integrity of the cell. The cell has a reserve capacity sufficient that the fact that the repair processes are not perfectly efficient raises no operational problems, even though recurring cycles of repair will make the cell less efficient than it would have been in the absence of damage.

Third, for reasons that are still imperfectly understood, these repair processes become less efficient with age. This situation may arise as a result of event-driven alterations in gene transcription and translation, or of decreased energy production, or of a shift in the cellular economy to maintain the specialized functions of the cell at the expense of the repair processes, or of another plausible process. In any event, the mechanism(s) responsible for this temporal decrease in repair efficiency are likely to be the key step(s) in the aging process.

Fourth, the combination of a more or less constant rate of damage coupled with a declining efficiency of repair processes ensures that the number of structural abnormalities will increase with time. The rate of increase will depend on the kinetic details involved, but it will increase. The persisting damage will affect both structural and regulatory components.

Fifth, as a result of unrepaired damage to its homeostatic regulatory mechanisms, the cell will no longer be able to perform the same functions and maintain the same homeostatic balance with the same efficiency as it has in the past. Early signs of this decreased cellular efficiency may be noted in an increased variance of certain functions, in an altered response time between functional periods, in a decrease in the rate of synthesis of important components, or in a decrease in the functional output of the cell.

Sixth, the decreased cellular efficiency leads to a decreased functional capacity of tissues, organs, and organ systems. This would be especially evident if the cell were a key member of a homeostatic regulatory network, for its decreased efficiency would then cascade to all the cells that it controlled, even if those latter cells were themselves not affected by autonomous cell damage.

Seventh, the ability of the organism to cope with the changing environmental demands becomes progressively diminished. The probability of dying increases to a near certainty.

It is likely that any one of these processes can be significantly altered by environmental interventions. The work done with *Drosophila* and discussed in Chapter 10 is an excellent example of how the genotype and the environment interact to produce a characteristic life span. In fact, ignorance of the operative environmental modulations is likely what has made many studies on aging so fraught with difficulties of interpretation.

A good start toward a quantitative systems approach has been presented by Kowald and Kirkwood (1994, 1996). They developed the idea that aging and longevity may be understood as the outcome of a network of maintenance processes that control the capability of the system to preserve homeostasis. What is important about their analysis is that it is a quantitative model. It has been said that the beginning of true understanding lies in being able to measure what you are talking about, and a numerical analysis does permit one to make specific predictions and thus continually refine the accuracy of one's thoughts. Kowald and Kirkwood (1994) considered that the free-radical theory and the protein error theory were each important but incomplete descriptions of the aging processes within a cell—incomplete because each could well interact with one another at particular points and provide sources of damage and/or protection not specifically predicted by either theory alone. As one example of such interaction, Kowald and Kirkwood suggested that free radicals could damage enzymes and thereby provide another source of abnormal protein not specifically foreseen by the original theory. To the extent that such abnormal proteins included abnormal antioxidant enzymes, the level of protection against free radicals would be reduced because of this protein error, another source of damage not specifically foreseen by the original theory.

Other sorts of interactions may well be imagined. Kowald and Kirkwood (1994, 1996) first considered that a simplified system comprising these two theories of aging could be composed of free radicals, antioxidant enzymes, antioxidant scavengers, and the ribosomes, synthetases, and/or mRNAs involved in protein synthesis. Figure 13.1 illustrates the reactions and interactions of their

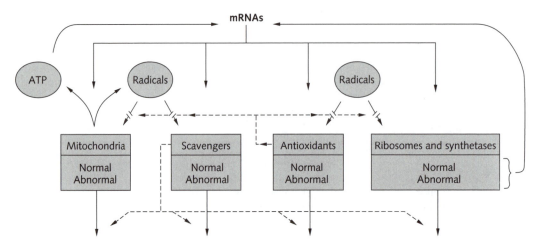

Figure 13.1   The reaction scheme of the MARS (*m*itochondria, *a*berrant proteins, *r*adicals, and *s*cavengers) network model of aging. For clarity the reactions of ribosomes and amino-acyl transfer synthetases, as well as the two different types of proteolytic enzymes, are presented in one functional compartment each. Radicals can damage all components and are removed by antioxidants; this is indicated by the interrupted reaction path for the radicals. (From Kowald and Kirkwood 1996.)

MARS (*m*itochondria, *a*berrant proteins, *r*adicals, and *s*cavengers) model. In this model, the free-radical production rate is the key variable and depends on the kinetics of their production in the free-radical source (mitochondria) and their destruction in their sink (superoxide dismutase and other antioxidants). The production of free radicals thus depends on the level of energy provided by the mitochondria, and on the synthesis, turnover, and degradation of the mitochondria themselves. The model also takes into account the diffusion of free radicals out from the mitochondria into the cytoplasm and the damaging effects such radicals might have on different classes of cytoplasmic components.

After making several literature-based assumptions regarding the concentrations, reactions, synthesis, turnover, and energy consumption of each of the several components, Kowald and Kirkwood derived a series of 15 differential equations to describe the interactions of the system components. Subsequent computer simulations yielded some interesting results. High levels of free radicals, insufficient levels of free-radical protection, and high levels of protein error each lead to an integrated breakdown of homeostatic process and cell death (Figure 13.2). This particular simulation suggests that the main targets of free-radical damage in the "typical" cell are the mitochondria, damage to which results in decreased energy production, an increased damage rate to various cytosolic proteins, and a shift in the proportion of damaged or erroneous proteins present in the cell. The net result of these insults is the breakdown of cellular homeostasis, In effect, the stability of the cell is undermined by the instability of one of its major components (the mitochondria), which initiates an eventually

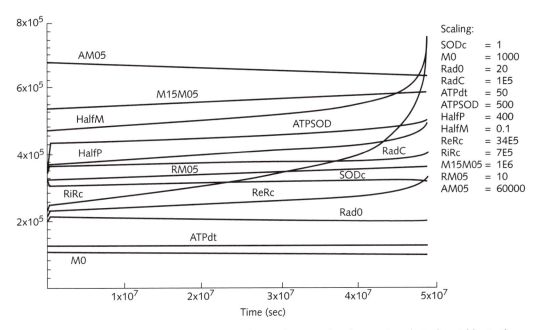

Figure 13.2 A computer simulation showing the changes in selected variables in the MARS model during the course of a cellular collapse caused by insufficient free-radical protection. The relative scaling of each of the 13 variables in this simulation is given in the figure; note that there may be as much as six orders of magnitude separating any two related variables. As time passes, the cell shows a decrease in the proportion of undamaged mitochondria (M0) coupled with an increase in the proportion of damaged mitochondria (M15M05). The free-radical production in intact mitochondria (Rad0) decreases as a result, while the radical concentration in the cytoplasm (RadC) slowly increases. This leads to an increase in the half-life of mitochondria (HalfM) and to the increase in radical production/mitochondria (RM05) and the decrease in ATP production/mitochondria (AM05). The increase in the ratio of erroneous (i.e., damaged) ribosomes to correct ribosomes (ReRc) is presumably related to the significant increase in the ratio of inactive to correct protein (RiRC) and to the increased half-life of proteins (HalfP), reflecting the difficulty in degrading aberrant proteins. The ATP consumed/protein molecule synthesized (ATPdt) slowly decreases as well, although more energy is expended on antioxidant protection (ATPSOD). There is only an initial and terminal decrease in the level of correct antioxidants (SODc). (From Kowald and Kirkwood 1996.)

disastrous positive feedback cycle of free-radical production and ensuing damage to mitochondria and proteins.

The model is obviously an incomplete description of the real cell, as its authors are the first to acknowledge. Yet the fact that the model yields a predicted life span that is approximately correct is reassuring, as is the fact that its predictions regarding changes in the mitochondrial and protein populations are entirely consistent with the empirical data described in the preceding chapters. The MARS model also provides us with a detailed look at the processes underlying the failure to repair, which we noted as being the critical step in Lamb's model, described above.

Given this simulation, is it possible to avoid cell death by devoting more energy to repair processes? Kowald and Kirkwood have done this simulation and find that a "virtual immortality" might be achieved if 55 percent of the total energy of the simulated cell were devoted to repair and/or prevention of free-radical and oxidative damage. Below that level of expenditure, the loss of cellular homeostasis was inevitable, although it could be significantly modulated by various treatments. For example, simulating the effects of dietary restriction by decreasing the rate of free-radical production led to a significant delay in the time at which cellular homeostasis was lost. The specific value of the number of calories needed for indefinite repair may not be as important as its general magnitude. It is so high that it becomes plausible that devoting so much energy to long life will preclude being able to participate in other energy-requiring activities, such as reproduction. Thus this computer simulation brings us back to the evolutionary precepts on which modern biogerontology is based.

The reader might wonder why these outcomes are so important when we already know these results to be empirically true. The point is that the fact that the computer simulation accurately reproduced the empirical results testifies to the accuracy of the equations and of the postulated interactions. The way is now clear to use the computer model to suggest to us relationships we did not know beforehand. One such relationship would be the observed low level of free-radical leakage observed in pigeon mitochondria relative to rat mitochondria. Herrero and Barga (1997) observed that unknown changes in complexes I and III of pigeon mitochondria are responsible for the low levels of peroxide production. Describing these changes in more detail should give us an opportunity to see the nature and variety of these evolutionary alterations. Just as interesting will be to plug the appropriate kinetic values for pigeons in the MARS simulation and determine whether the simulated pigeon cell yields a substantively different longevity and failure mode than does the simulated mammalian cell of Figure 13.2.

Inevitably, a network model is complex, even one that aspires to offering only a partial explanation of aging, so Kowald and Kirkwood rightfully regard their MARS model as but one step on the path to that goal. The value of the quantitative MARS model over the qualitative model of Lamb (1977) does not lie in its conceptual complexity, for they are both subtle and they both postulate the same sorts of events and interactions; rather the value is in the ability of the computer model to expose hidden causal links between diverse phenomena and thereby provide us with valuable information in the design of further studies. Note that the network model provides a detailed analysis of only the intracellular effects described in the first five steps of Lamb's model; the consequences of the aging of the cell on the functioning of the organism have not yet been described quantitatively. Of course, quantitative models can be developed only when the qualitative concepts on which they are based are known to be empirically sound. Lamb had to develop her model before Kowald and Kirkwood could develop theirs.

The events that take place inside the cell, which are represented by the processes summarized in Table 8.2 and in many of the figures of Chapters 9 through 12, will have different effects on the organism depending on the type of cell being affected by these processes. The failure of cells that themselves constitute an important part of the organism's integrative mechanism, such as the hypothalamus or pituitary, will have far different effects than will the failure of a skin stem cell, for example. The latter effect, serious though it may be, is delimited in time and space; it is a local effect. The failure of the hypothalamus or pituitary cells might have global effects on the organism. By adversely affecting important regulatory systems, the body's ability to shut down corticosteroid secretion or to respond effectively to insulin or estrogen levels in the blood will be impaired. As described in Chapter 12, the impairment of these processes will lead to further damage to these and other cells elsewhere in the body. Dysregulation of bodily functions will begin to occur, and the organism's homeostatic ability might be lessened. Such decreases will make the organism more susceptible to an environmental insult that would not have bothered it when its homeostatic and integrative mechanisms were fully functional.

A somewhat different approach to modeling the aging process is provided by Jazwinski's (1996) drawing together into one model all of the different metacellular relationships that are known to be important in the regulation of aging and senescence (Figure 13.3). Our look at the biology of aging has led us to examine in prior chapters each of these individual topics; Figure 13.3 explicitly pulls them together into an interesting viewpoint that is not at odds with the models described earlier. The life maintenance reserve is defined by Jazwinski (1996) as composing both the organism's metabolic capacity and its ability to respond to stress. Together, these are considered to be a genetically determined functional potential that allows the organism to survive at least until reproductive maturity. Metabolism results in the generation of pro-oxidants, which call forth the

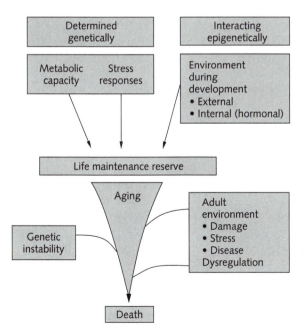

Figure 13.3 One view of the determinants of aging and longevity. Physiological relationships, not specific molecular mechanisms, are shown. Metabolic capacity, stress responses, and environment during development all contribute to the life maintenance reserve, where they interact. Genetic instability is genetically determined, results in genetic alterations, and is influenced by environmental factors. Aging plays itself out at all levels of biological organization; it is not possible to separate cellular changes from organismic aging. (From Jazwinski 1996.)

response to oxidative stress. The life maintenance reserve is diminished by mitochondrial damage, and its potential expression can be significantly modulated by internal and external environmental factors.

The postdevelopment environment exerts its effects through damage, stress, and disease. Epigenetic changes affecting the chromatin that occur during the lifetime of a somatic cell result in small changes in gene regulation that, if the cell enters a positive feedback cycle, can result in gene dysregulation. Together, the processes of gene dysregulation and environmental insults lead to increased stress responses. Such increased stress is deleterious in its own right and affects the organism's ability to respond effectively to acute stress. The model in Figure 13.3 postulates that the factors that affect aging are genetic, epigenetic, and environmental in origin, while the factors that limit longevity are metabolic capacity, efficiency of stress response, and gene dysregulation.

There is no contradiction among these several models, for each is attempting to describe the interactions of positive and negative forces interacting over several different levels of organization. Each one is accurate; taken all together, they afford us a good conceptual view of the aging process in all its complexity. The two-dimensional plane of the written page appears to reduce these schemes to a linear model, but this is almost certainly not the case. There are both empirical and theoretical reasons to support this belief. For example, we know that there are positive feedback effects from one stage to an earlier stage and that such effects can only accelerate the process. An example of feedback occurs when damage to certain key cells, such as those in the pituitary or the hypothalamus, has cascading deleterious effects on the undamaged cells regulated by these key cells, whose decreased feedback functioning might further decrease the physiological functioning of the neuroendocrine cells. We need to be able to view this process in four dimensions.

The theoretical arguments against considering aging to be adequately represented by a linear model stem from many sources, but we will limit our view to those deriving from two independent considerations of the nature of gene action. Two of the central paradigms of developmental and molecular genetics were once thought to be (1) that there are simple unidirectional hierarchies of gene control and (2) that each qualitatively different pattern of gene activity results in a novel and specific phenotype. From this point of view, each aspect of the aging process could logically be viewed as being under the control of different and specific genes; thus a large number of genes might be involved in the control of aging. However, the work of Cutler (1975) and of Sacher (1975) suggested that one could explain the evolution of aging on the assumption that only a relatively few genes are involved.

Their analyses were supported both by Martin's review (1978) of human genetic diseases, which led him to conclude that only a small percent of our total genes are likely to be strong determinants of senescence and by Crew's (1993) view that a "small" group of genes such as the major histocompatibility complex could adequately account for the known genetic differences in mammalian longevity. Thus there was for some time an implicit contradiction between genetic theory and gerontological conclusions, although Martin (1978) did point out that allelic variation at a very large number of genetic loci could modulate various specific aspects of the complex senescent phenotype.

Recent advances in the field of developmental genetics have led to the realization that neither one of the two extreme assumptions regarding the nature of gene control is strictly true. The same phenotype may be produced by more than one set of genes; the gene control circuits uncovered so far do not appear always to be simple or unidirectional; allelic variation can modulate the phenotype. These paradoxes have led Wilkins (1986) to suggest that the genetic control of development may reside not in the simple hierarchial circuits, but in interacting regulatory networks in which a particular phenotype would be produced by the combined effects of different batteries of genes controlled by multiple regulatory genes. This suggestion bears an uncanny resemblance to the suggestion (made independently by many authors) that the eventual explanation of development and of aging may not lie in the analysis of simple closed gene circuits, but that it should be sought in the interactions among components of the system. Furthermore, these concepts are essentially identical to Finch's (1987) idea that aging is under the control of interacting regulatory networks. What this does mean is that the key to understanding the genetics of aging probably lies in understanding the mechanisms of gene regulation.

Studies done in my laboratory have shown that, in *Drosophila* at least, the same long-lived phenotype may be brought about by different genetic mechanisms (Force et al. 1995; Arking et al. 1996), the regulation of which is likely to be rather complex. The convergence of ideas based on independent data sets suggests that we may be working toward a more realistic portrayal of how the genes work. The systems analysis approach independently advocated by each of these authors might well be able to better adjust our theoretical constructs of gene action with the multiple dimensions of the aging process as we have been able to briefly sketch it in these pages. The models of Lamb (1977) and of Kowald and Kirkwood (1994, 1996) represent the best attempts to date of constructing a systems analysis approach to the understanding of aging and senescence. They will likely be superseded in the near future by the even more realistic models now being derived from the study of mutant genes affecting aging (Jazwinksi 1996).

• *The Ultimate and Proximal Mechanisms of Aging*

The ultimate cause of aging derives from the evolutionary imperative to pass on copies of our genes to the next generation. Thus, our bodies have to be merely good enough to last until reproduction is completed. Postreproductive longevity, particularly past the age at which parental care is no longer required, is simply invisible to evolution, and its existence testifies only to the fact that a mechanism designed to last until a certain point inevitably has enough intrinsic reserve capacity to be able to stumble on awhile longer.

More than one way might have evolved that would have enabled our bodily mechanisms to continue for a significant portion of postreproductive life. We have discussed examples of both *damage prevention* strategies and *damage repair* strategies. Much empirical evidence implicates either or both in the aging processes of various species, and these particular strategies constitute the proximal mechanisms of aging. It is unlikely that any single species uses all of the known proximal mechanisms. Not all of them apply equally to humans, but they do illustrate the range of problems inherent in different sorts of biological design and the types of solutions evolved to address these design failures.

Elsewhere we have pointed out that the human population is very heterogeneous. All human populations show extensive phenotypic variability, a variability due as much to our polymorphic genetic background as it is to the variability of the environmental factors characteristic of our different habitats. This phenotypic diversity among different individuals must surely be reflected in many physiological parameters, not the least of which are those that are important to the aging process. We must keep in mind this phenotypic variation in age-related functions when translating to humans the results obtained from highly inbred and standardized animal strains.

Let's consider some of the implications of our findings. Recall the evolutionary data showing that energy considerations preclude both high levels of reproduction and high levels of repair. Does this mean that efforts to increase the maximum human life span are doomed? Or more modestly, does this mean that senescence at least cannot be delayed until later in life? The answer is no, at least not in principle. All that is required to overcome this hurdle is to develop means of maintaining the body's repair mechanisms for a longer period of time via exogenous behavioral, pharmacological, and/or biological interventions as discussed in Chapter 14. Human culture allows us to use external energy to assist our internal processes and thereby evade the claims of thermodynamics, for a little while longer anyway. The real question is, once having evaded those claims, what will we do with the extra time?

14

Aging-Related Research and Societal Goals

A reasonable appraisal of the past data and present theories should suggest to any skeptical but reasonable inquirer that aging is a modifiable biological process under combined genetic and environmental control and, as such, represents a legitimate and promising area of biological research. The old views, which held that aging was inevitable and/or was not worthy of serious interest, since it could be due to nothing more than the wear and tear of the body, are no longer tenable and are being discarded, as indeed they deserve to be.

Of course, the detrimental effects of the biological damage caused by aging can be ameliorated to some extent by various behavioral, social, and cultural practices. Social organisms may receive enough support from their group to enable them to survive past the time when they would otherwise have been able to survive on their own. And such supportive behavior may be selected for by either cultural or biological means. But such amelioration, even though it may be an intrinsic part of the species' life history strategy, does not defer senescence. In our own species, our intelligence has made it inevitable that this social support of aging individuals would become a societal goal and take the form of devising interventions designed to retard or reverse the aging processes.

● *Demographic Changes*

The extraordinary demographic changes that have already taken place in our society (see Figure 2.16) do not appear to have resulted from any alteration of basic aging processes. They are due almost entirely to a mix of alterations in cultural habits and biomedical practices. Torrey, Kinsella, and Taeuber (1987) have examined these changes and suggest that these transformations are not limited to developed societies such as the United States, but are global in their impact. Different societies are simply in different phases of this demographic transition.

The relative ratio of birth rates and death rates determines the age structure of a population. The advances in public health and biomedical interventions have greatly reduced premature mortality. The enhanced survival of such cohorts leads to a large increase in the number of people who reach reproductive age and reproduce. When this large cohort, upon reaching adulthood, undergoes a decline in fertility rates, as occurred in the United States and Europe, the proportion of older adult cohorts in the population increases relative to younger cohorts.

But this is not the only component responsible for the "aging" of the population. In most developed nations, increases in life expectancy at age 65 are now outpacing increases in life expectancy at birth, largely because of the reduction of heart disease and stroke among older individuals. Therefore, the already low mortality rates for older adults can only be expected to continue to decrease, and the proportion of elderly can be expected to increase. In addition, we may already be experiencing the beginnings of the stabilization of mortality among the very old, as would be predicted from the most recent animal studies (see Chapter 2).

Continuation of the recent increases in life expectancy is probably not a guaranteed phenomenon, but depends on the existence of health-promoting cultural and social factors. If these are not present, the life expectancy may actually decline. As of this writing, the mean life span of males in Russia is estimated to be about 59 years. The life expectancy was never as high there as in the West, but this estimate represents about a 5- to 10-year decrease in life span over a period of 2 decades or so. As pointed out in Chapter 5, the historical record shows that our societies took much longer than 2 decades to gain an additional decade of life. This is an extraordinary example of the dependency of a group's life span on the social practices of that group. The same situation appears also to have been the case for life expectancy at age 65 in Australia and in eastern Europe, and for an increase in infant mortality in the United States. For humans, longevity depends to a large extent on social support.

The decreases in fertility, driven by socioeconomic considerations, and the decreases in adult mortality, driven by cultural and biomedical considerations, interact to ensure that the proportion of elderly will continue to increase for some time. The significant growth of the elderly population has important implications for both private individuals and families, as well as for public-policy makers and planners. One of these implications will almost certainly be the desire to better understand the biological basis of aging so as to develop possible interventions. Such interventions will be needed not only to enhance the quality of life of the elderly, but also to contain the economic costs implicit in a future where senescent changes are dealt with only after the fact.

• *The Future of Human Mortality and Longevity*

Before the development of the biomedical and public health interventions that succeeded in reducing the premature deaths once characteristic of youth and middle age, most human populations had a survival curve resembling curve B in Figure 2.11. Since life expectancy is increasing rapidly in most countries, it seems reasonable to suppose that continuing the removal of premature deaths would eventually result in a human population having the shape of curve A in Figure 2.11. This "rectangularization of the curve," as it has been called, suggested to Fries and Crapo (1981) that we are heading for a society in which the maximum life span will be fixed as it is now at about 120 years, and the median life span will be fixed at about 100 years. They suggested that in such a rectangular society, most persons will live a vigorous and healthy life and succumb to relatively short-term illnesses in the compressed and final senescent period. Such a scenario has implications for the future health and social service obligations of our society, so the topic has been much debated.

There are perhaps two biological aspects of this debate that we can profitably address. One point is the question of whether the human life span is intrinsically fixed. Certainly the animal data we reviewed in earlier chapters strongly indicate that species-specific life spans can be significantly modified by means of appropriate interventions. Caloric restriction has proven to be extraordinarily effective in increasing the mean and maximum life spans of rodents. And we have seen that the force of mortality appears to level off and even decline with very advanced age. Some people have overoptimistically interpreted these data as suggesting that there are no inherent limits to the species-specific maximum life span. This is probably not correct. However, the laboratory studies have clearly demonstrated that the maximum life span is plastic and not fixed at the conventional limit.

Analysis of the U.S. mortality data suggests that life span limits are not yet observed in this population and further indicates that the maximum individual longevity potential is more than 130 years (Manton and Stallard 1996). Yet it seems intuitively obvious that there must be some sort of intrinsic biological limit to the life span, if only because of entropy. The integrative models presented in Chapter 13 may be viewed as a general statement of such biological limits. No similar formal life span manipulation experiments have been done on humans, for obvious reasons. Yet the absence of such data cannot be construed as evidence in favor of a fixed human life span, especially since the informal human data available are consistent with the conclusions drawn from animal studies. The maximum human life span is probably plastic within the limits implied by the animal experiments.

In addition, the concept of rectangularization has been criticized on demographic grounds by Myers and Manton (1984). As desirable as such a society might seem today, it is not the only choice in our future. Since the life span is not rigidly fixed, and since there appear to be no demographic data supporting the idea of mortality compression (Myers and Manton 1984; see also Figure 2.16), it is at least equally logical to suggest that an alternative survival curve that might also describe our future society might well still resemble the 1980 curve in Figure 2.16, but with the numerical values of the mean and maximum life spans significantly increased as a result of an extension of the curve to the right. Such a survival curve would suggest a rather different set of future societal health and social service obligations than would either our present situation or a society characterized by a more rectangular survival curve. The kind of future society we desire may well depend on our own decisions and actions, and that debate is beyond the scope of this book. But no biological data support the view that one or the other survival curve is an *inevitable* component of our future.

• *Anti-Aging Interventions*

The odds against our achieving a shift in the survival curve such as that described in the previous section in the near future are high. At the moment, caloric restriction is the only intervention known to be effective in laboratory mammals, and it might be effective in primates, including humans, as well. Someday we might be able to effectively exploit the currently promising insights into the genetic mechanisms regulating the aging processes that current research affords us. Even though it is unlikely, we might one day be able to develop a "magic molecule" that can ensure that our gene transcription and translation patterns remain intact to maintain our molecular repair activities at a high level for a long time. But such a breakthrough, even if possible, is most likely several decades away. Any near-term alterations in human survival and aging are limited by the knowledge and the interventions now at hand.

Caloric Restriction and Other Drastic Interventions

Malnutrition, in the form of overeating and the resulting problems associated with excess weight and poor choice of nutrients, is a major public health problem in developed countries such as the United States. This situation has persisted despite the best efforts of public agencies and private concerns to assist individuals in losing and maintaining weight. People in our society have great difficulty in eating less and losing weight, even when their reasons for doing so are immediate and pertinent to their everyday needs and wishes and even when these reasons are continually reinforced by the blandishments of the advertising industry and the nagging of physicians. This task is so difficult that many of us are willing to spend good money and precious time to join diet and health groups, to go to "fat farms," or to buy the newest diet book—all too often to no avail. And all this effort is being expended in the hope of attaining a "normal" weight.

It is probably unrealistic to expect many of our neighbors and friends to suddenly change their ways and uncharacteristically elect to initiate and follow the stringent permanent caloric reduction regimes dictated by the animal studies, even when these are logically presented and packaged into attractive menus (Walford 1986). This unhappy history suggests that people, for the most part, want to follow healthy regimes but will abandon them and put up with the unknown future consequences if the effort and willpower required by the regime yield no short-term success. This unmet need most likely creates a large market waiting to be satisfied by more palatable or less strict regimes. One example of a product designed to meet this need is synthetic foods, such as olestra, that have no caloric value but can still satisfy our taste for fats and other foods that carry a high health risk. If olestra succeeds in the marketplace, there will surely be increased incentives to develop other fake foods. The biotechnology industry is taking steps to create and market genetically engineered foods that have had their nutritional composition deliberately altered (*Genetic Engineering News*, December

1997). Dietary restriction can take many forms, and eating less need not be one of them!

Pharmacological Interventions

Although the bulk of research and development in the pharmacological industry is still geared toward the identification, synthesis, and production of agents targeted to treat specific age-associated diseases, the interest in natural and synthetic substances touted to affect the processes of aging is growing. The administration of L-dopa in the treatment of Parkinson's disease is a well-known example of the former interest, while the burgeoning market for health food "products," many of which are of dubious value, illustrates the latter. In the long term, however, what is more important in meeting unmet needs is the development and marketing of substances that can improve, maintain, or supplement normal host defense mechanisms. In this regard, antioxidant vitamins and free-radical scavengers are examples of presently available commercially marketed products that offer the potential for slowing the onset of some age-associated diseases and/or retarding normal physiological declines.

Mixed with these useful products in such a way that it is probably difficult for the consumer to distinguish between reality and hype are more dubious antioxidant interventions. Many health food stores carry expensive bottles of capsules containing superoxide dismutase. Purchasing these will probably have no effect beyond lightening your wallet and providing you with some very expensive amino acids following the digestion of the capsules in your intestinal tract. But future innovations might be more useful. One fanciful example of a possibly useful pharmacological intervention is the development of antioxidants targeted to travel to the inner mitochondrial membrane, where they can assist in reducing the oxidative stress within the organelle and possibly in reducing the levels of oxidative damage to mtDNA. The advances being made in deciphering the functional differences between bird and mammalian mitochondria suggest that this innovation should be shifted from the fanciful to the possible category.

Another example of such a potentially useful pharmacological intervention is a drug that can mimic the effects of caloric restriction, perhaps by acting to increase the efficiency with which insulin and glucose bring about their physiological effects in the body, and hence permit the pharmacological establishment of lower levels of these two potentially harmful substances. Such drugs are being tested now. Another pharmacological intervention being translated into reality is the development of drugs based on the operation of leptin and related proteins, which would have the effect of enabling us to lose weight and maintain a more optimal weight. This work is also underway. Translating dreams into reality will take a bit more work, but the success of the efforts is something more than just a pipe dream.

Whether these would be desirable products depends on other factors. We have written elsewhere in the book that one of the main drawbacks with current pharmacological approaches is that they might persuade people that they can pop a pill and thereby adopt a healthy lifestyle. Today that belief is not justified, so popping a pill is (mostly) detrimental to your health. But if and when such products as we have described become a reality, there might no longer be a contradiction between people's behavior and their desires. Popping pills might become beneficial to your health, much as taking (some) vitamin pills every morning is today regarded as being a reasonable and conservative approach to maintaining your health. Yet it must be admitted that even a valid pharmacological intervention will probably be more effective if it can exert its effects within the context of a healthy physiology rather than having to fight against a spectrum of unhealthy activities. Popping pills may become more effective in the future, but maintaining a healthy lifestyle will not go out of fashion and certainly represents the fundamental basis for our continuing health and longevity.

Biological Interventions

Biological interventions include therapies that are designed to retard, restore, or stabilize declining physiological functions with age. The most obvious example is the restoration of circulating levels of hormones necessary to an important function, such as is already done for diabetes or for postmenopausal women. But these clinical interventions have had little direct application to the problems of human aging. This situation is now changing. Consider the following facts, all derived from recent research. First, the pulsatile release of growth hormone is decreased in older individuals. Second, the administration of growth hormone has beneficial effects on older men such that it segmentally reverses the effects of aging. Third, the use of growth hormone releasing factor may eliminate many of the undesirable side effects associated with the experimental administration of growth hormone itself. These three findings combine to make it likely that growth hormone supplementation as a biological intervention into the aging process will become as common in the near future as estrogen replacement therapy is today (but see Wolfe 1998).

A second example of a probable biological intervention is the regulation of body weight by means of injections of the proteins involved in controlling body weight (the proteins made by the genes *obese*, *tubby*, *fat*, *diabetes*, and *agouti yellow*), their signaling molecules, or derivatives thereof. The benefits of weight control are well known, including the prevention of diabetes, hypertension, and other chronic diseases that both decrease the quality of life and shorten the life span. In recognition of the possible benefits, the Food and Drug Administration has recently relaxed its guidelines for obesity drug applications, and several such drugs are now under development. The history of drugs such as dexfenfluramine ("fen-fen") shows that drugs with a beneficial history (Davis and Faulds 1996) can have unsuspected and lethal side effects, especially if taken in combination with other drugs. Current guidelines for the use of obesity medications recommend that they be used only for medically significant obesity (Atkinson 1997). Perhaps a better understanding of the leptin system will allow the development of safer agents for the control of "ordinary" obesity.

A third type of useful biological intervention is the targeted application of various cell signaling molecules, which might allow for the modulation of specific functions in particular cells. Such modulations might be particularly useful in altering immunological functions, and this goal has been the target of much recent research involving cytokines and similar molecules.

As we have seen, molecular genetic knowledge and techniques have played a large role in our increased understanding of aging processes. Further research on the identification of the molecular genetic factors that are responsible for age-related decrements in humans is likely to identify appropriate candidates for alteration and/or enhancement with tomorrow's molecular therapies. But the promise is always greater than the reality, so such a discussion should await a time when the clinical application of such techniques is less speculative than it is today.

Lifestyle Interventions

In 1975, a person reaching the age of 85 had only a 1 in 1,500 chance of attaining the age of 101 and only a 1 in 10,000 chance of reaching the age of 110 (Leaf 1984). These odds seem to be changing. For the past 3 decades, increases in overall life expectancy are reflected in decreased mortality rates among middle-aged and older individuals (Kannisto et al. 1994). These decreases can be attributed in large measure to alterations in lifestyle (exercise, diet, weight control, and stopping smoking), as well as to significant advances in clinical medicine, particularly in the treatment of chronic conditions.

Education is another important lifestyle intervention. Timiras (1995) has reviewed the epidemiological data showing that life expectancy, particularly active life expectancy, varies directly with the amount of schooling or educational level. The prevalence and incidence of dementia also seems to be reduced as a function of increased education. Some of this educational effect is undoubtedly the result of a better socioeconomic status, with all that that implies. But some of it is due to the interaction of environmental and biological factors in significantly modulating the organism's life span potential. For example, the number of dendrites in a portion of Wernicke's area of the brain (concerned with comprehension of visual and auditory information) varies as a function of educational level (Jacobs, Schall, and Scheibel 1993). This effect may well be the result of direct action by hormones on the dendrites and indirectly via the hormones' stimulation of neurotrophic growth factors (Timiras 1995). There are known mechanisms by which hormones and growth factors affect neural growth and/or induce neural cell death, and the educational effect is presumed to be mediated via such mechanisms. In this connection, we must not forget that activities such as exercise are also known to stimulate the increase in these growth factors (Cotman and Neeper 1996), so the Greeks' dicta of "a sound mind in a sound body" may have a firm biological basis after all.

Because the incidence of a wide spectrum of disorders increases with age, factors that act to delay the onset of morbidity should improve general health across the spectrum and thereby increase the life span itself. As we might have expected, few people have adopted a strict dietary regime akin to that of the laboratory mice. But, it must be admitted, elderly people are doing something different. Today's elderly are, by and large, much healthier than were past cohorts, at least as judged by their ability to carry on the tasks associated with independent living (see Chapter 6). The National Long Term Care Survey, a federal study that regularly surveys about 20,000 people 65 years and older, finds that every year there is a smaller percentage of elderly who are unable to take care of themselves. The annual decline in disability is small but continuous, and there is a possibility that the statistically significant mean rate of decline of 0.3 percent per year may even be increasing (Manton, Corder, and Stallard 1997). Certainly, the current emphasis of the culture on health-promoting activities such as not smoking, engaging in daily moderate exercise, and eating a more healthful (albeit not calorically restricted) diet must be responsible for this delay in the appearance of morbidity and the consequent decrease in the force of mortality for this elderly cohort.

Recall the data of Figure 7.11, which showed that tobacco use, poor diet, and inadequate exercise were contributory causes in about 70 percent of the deaths in the United States in 1990. The adoption of healthy activities such as those we have mentioned likely has a greater statistical impact on the population's life expectancy than do the current pharmacological interventions. However, should the development of new pharmacological interventions such as anti-obesity drugs prove more successful than at present, the combination of healthy living and targeted drug interventions may prove to be more effective, perhaps even synergistic, than we might reasonably expect. Magic pills do not yet exist and probably never will. Effective, albeit imperfect, drugs probably will.

One thing that may have happened is that biomarkers, imperfect though they may be as both a retrospective and prospective indicator of age-related changes, have become informally and gradually more widespread. Many of them have been incorporated into our ongoing physical or self-examinations. Their progressive refinement coupled with their intelligent use might make it possible for more and more of us to monitor our body's operation more closely. Acting on this knowledge has probably allowed us to postpone or reduce the rate of decrease in physiological efficiency in one or more of our own systems. Exercise and weight reduction have been demonstrated to prevent or even correct various metabolic disturbances and chronic conditions, as well as reduce the probability of some death-precipitating acute event such as a heart attack.

Sarcopenia, or age-related muscle loss, has been associated with a range of chronic disorders. The demonstration that sarcopenia can be retarded and even reversed by exercise in elderly men and women appears to represent a feasible lifestyle in\[rvervention for many people. When "little old ladies" start lifting weights and boast that they can outpress their granddaughters, as some former students have told me, then I believe that a behavioral sea change is under way. In our youth, many of us have probably taken better care of our cars than we have of our bodies. Coming of age in this society at this time gives us the incentive to take equal care of both. This may appear to be a very modest goal, but the morbidity and mortality statistics suggest that its achievement yields significant benefits. The prevention of system failure and the maintenance of the body's repair abilities will allow many more of us to look forward to and enjoy a healthy old age increasingly free of the specter of the debilitating diseases of senescence. And this can be done quite apart from any effect it might have on the statistical extension of the maximum human life span.

Social Effects of Successful Aging

Our future likely will catch us unawares. In March 1995, *Science* magazine asked 60 prominent scientists what they saw in the future for science. All sorts of interesting scenarios ranging from physics to economics were set forth—some plausible, some fanciful, all imaginative. But not one of these scientists speculated about the effect of our increasing knowledge of aging processes on our future. It is as plausible as any other scenario in their predictions that the maintenance of functional status and the postponement of mortality that individuals in developed societies are currently experiencing will have a wide-ranging effect on the way in which we live our lives and organize our societies. It appears as if we will not recognize it until it has taken place.

Such a long-term trend has important implications for the society as a whole. In recent years, various popular magazines have carried lengthy articles discussing the social and economic effects that the aging of the "baby boomer" generation will have on this country's economy and society. The predictions, on the economic front at least, have been uniformly pessimistic, given the high cost of medical and long-term care over the greater number of years the elderly will likely live. Peter Peterson in *The Atlantic Monthly* (May 1996) and Matthew Miller in *The New Republic* (15 April 1996) are but two of the many commentators who point out that it will be financially impossible to continue the current Social Security and Medicare arrangements without change for the next 50 or 60 years and at the same time adequately fund the educational needs of the younger generations and the capital accumulation needs of the adult generations. The monetary shortfall has the potential to lead to a generational "war"—a situation to be avoided at all costs, since no one would really win such a competition.

The improving health of the current elderly population suggests that the future may not hold quite the economic drain that these writers have projected. It has been estimated, for example, that the decreasing disability rates between 1982 and 1994 have saved Medicare more than $200 billion so far, and such "savings" appear likely to continue for as long as the elderly continue to maintain and improve their physical health and independence. But such bookkeeping manipulations do not address the central issue, which is whether spending a large amount of public monies on the elderly is a desirable societal goal. This issue is being debated in the context of our current public philosophy, which values private or market solutions over public initiatives, and thus the range of possibilities available to us is perceived as limited.

What should our societal goals be? The best way to define these is not to convene a conference, but to examine the data to determine what we are doing now. Let's look at the numbers. One interesting data set consists of the dependency numbers, in which people under the age of 15 or over the age of 65 are considered to be dependent on the financial and social efforts of the 16-to-64 age group. This simple assignment overlooks the different contributions and needs of young and old, but gives us a clear idea of the problem.

The data of Table 14.1 show that historically a large majority of the population has been dependent on the efforts of the working 20 to 40 percent. In modern times, the dependency ratio peaked in 1960, will reach its nadir in 2010, and should return to historical levels during the remaining half of the twenty-first century. The dependency ratio today is about the same as it was in 1940, which many self-appointed commentators on the topic refer to as "the good old days." So it is not the dependency ratio itself that is so upsetting. The fact that about 38

Table 14.1 **Young, Elderly, and Total Support Ratios: Age Groups Needing Support, 1900–2050**

Year	Elderly	Young	Total
1900	7.4	76.3	83.7
1920	8.0	67.7	75.7
1940	10.9	51.9	62.8
1960	16.8	65.1	82.0
1980	18.6	45.8	64.4
1990	20.6	41.9	62.5
2000	21.1	40.7	61.8
2010	21.9	36.2	58.1
2020	28.7	36.9	65.6
2030	37.0	37.8	74.8
2040	37.9	36.7	74.6
2050	38.0	36.6	74.6

Source: U.S. Senate Committee on Aging, 1987–1988, p.22.

percent of the population must support about 62 percent of the population is as true today as it was more than a half-century ago. Most members of the support-requiring group are still young people. What is different is that the mix of people requiring support has shifted from a 5:1 ratio of young to old in 1940 to a 2:1 ratio today, and is predicted to reach a 1:1 ratio by the year 2030.

What purportedly makes the present and future situations qualitatively different from the past is the fact that the life span has increased dramatically, so individuals may need more expensive support for a longer period of time. Nothing is said in this media-led debate about the increasing time and expense that educating the young now entails. Nor is too much made of the "excess" health care costs that other potentially high-risk groups may cost society. The obese, for example, have higher morbidity levels and account for about 7 percent of all health care expenditures (Seidel 1995; Gorsky et al. 1996; Wolf and Colditz 1996). Yet it is not proposed to withdraw or reduce public support for their health care. The old are peeled off from the young and left to stand on their own. There may be political reasons for doing this, but are there logical reasons?

The tenor of the current debate gives one the impression that we face a dismal future. Actually, the future is nowhere near that bleak. First, a recent review of the social security systems in a number of countries suggests that the problems faced by the U.S. Social Security system are really quite manageable compared to those in Japan and elsewhere (Crown 1998). The same review points out that people decide whether to retire or continue working based on all sorts of different and conflicting reasons that have to do with their health, financial status, and family concerns, as well as pension plan requirements, the presence or absence of labor shortages in their field and resulting corporate early retirement or extended work incentives, and government policies (Crown 1998). Trying to understand our future based on the assumption that people respond to only one signal (e.g., social security policies) is simplistic and will likely give rise to unrealistic and perhaps overly pessimistic scenarios.

The net result of this overly pessimistic perception is that we view the results of the unparalleled success of the past half-century's biomedical research efforts as a problem rather than as a societal achievement of which to be proud. What we are facing is a new challenge born out of that success. No society has ever figured out what to do with people who are dependent and experienced at the same time. No other society has ever been fortunate enough to have this problem to face, so we have no precedent. But we should not let political players and "media" commentators, neither of whom are known for foresight, define the unprecedented successes of our society as a dire problem. The fact that much of the public is no longer willing to approve local school bond issues suggests that the reluctance to pay the necessary costs for young and old alike may have its roots in emotions and motives not simply related to the costs of medical treatment. The current ideology favoring market solutions to private problems may underlie this apparent reluctance. Regardless of its origins, the perception exists that the increased longevity we have strived for has become an unforeseen problem. Let's examine this perception for possible solutions.

There are two issues here. One is the question of increasing health care costs for the elderly. The other is the issue of how to adjust our society to minimize the costs and maximize the contributions from all members of the society. Let's first address the question of health care costs for the elderly. Some older empirical data do show that hospital charges increase as a function of age, being some 6 percent higher in patients older than 85 years (see, for example, Rosenthal and Landefeld 1993). However, a more recent large-scale study covering all 60-year-old and older patients in Massachusetts (Perls and Wood 1996) showed that hospitalization costs peaked in the 70- to 79-year-old group and significantly decreased thereafter (Table 14.2). In fact, an inspection of these data suggests that the highest costs were incurred by members of the population who were younger than 79 years old and died in the hospital. These individuals constituted about 3.1 percent of the population, but utilized about 7 percent of the total hospital costs incurred by the approximately 680,000 discharges for this population. In contrast, the people who were 90 years or older and died in the hospital constituted about 0.6 percent of the population and accounted for about 0.6 percent of the total hospital costs. As opposed to rhetoric, these data suggest that the health care funding crisis cannot be laid at the feet of the elderly. Even the elderly who were not in good health (and who died in the hospital) used only their proportional share of the health care dollar. The disproportionate share was taken not by the elderly but by the people in their sixties and seventies—the late middle-aged and early old. Since the current median life span for the population is now in the mid- to late seventies, depending on gender and socioeconomic status, it appears as if the people who were not in particularly good health and died before or around the median life span can be viewed as "causing" the funding crisis. Failure to live long is both expensive and unpatriotic.

The contributory causes of death listed in Figure 7.11 may be the proximal causes of their extensive and expensive hospital stays. To be sure, better health

| *Table 14.2* | **Costs of Acute Hospital Care as a Function of Age** | | | | |

Estimated total costs and length of stay by age group in nonteaching versus teaching hospitals

Age group (years)	Nonteaching hospitals		Teaching hospitals		Number of discharges (N)
	Mean total cost ($)	Mean length of stay (days)	Mean total cost ($)	Mean length of stay (days)	
60–69	6,030	7.0	10,524	7.8	210,270
70–79	6,406	8.3	11,524	9.2	256,781
80–89	6,177	9.4	9,499	9.5	171,725
90–99	5,616	9.5	7,338	9.0	39,170
>100	5,330	9.8	6,198	8.3	1,008
					678,954 Total *N*

Average estimated total and ancillary costs per discharge by age group and survivor status at discharge

Age group (years)	Descendants			Survivors		
	Total costs ($)	Ancillary costs ($)[a]	n	Total costs ($)	Ancillary costs ($)[a]	n
60–69	16,886	9,463	7,387	6,981	3,705	201,939
70–79	14,917	8,059	13,467	7,163	3,470	241,820
80–89	10,557	4,654	12,887	6,492	2,622	157,481
90–99	6,977	2,737	4,050	5,784	2,044	34,866
>100	6,523	1,660	145	5,313	2,499	857

Source: Data from Perls and Wood 1996.
[a]Charges other than those for the hospital room, such as use of the operating room, radiology, and the like.

habits and preventive regimes might alleviate this situation in future cohorts. But the data of Table 14.2 do not support the notion that the societal success in extending the mean life span is responsible for the funding crisis. They might support the idea that obesity, smoking, lack of exercise, and poor health habits generally are very expensive vices but ones in which our society has encouraged our indulgence. Now we must pick up the tab, and many commentators are looking for someone to blame. Perhaps we should look in the mirror.

Let's address the second issue we raised earlier. If we discard the elderly and their experience, we raise the possibility of an intergenerational warfare for a too-small pot of money. Both the young and the elderly require support for their particular needs. Since the elderly are conscientious voters, the young either cannot or will not vote, and the middle-aged are likely to be split on the issues, the young likely will lose in the short run. In addition, once the middle-aged accept that they too will grow old someday, they may likely vote their future interests over those of their children. But this would be a Pyrrhic victory in that diversion of funds away from the educational needs of the young would eventually wound the elderly. As Peter Peterson, a retired CEO, wrote in the May 1996 issue of the *Atlantic Monthly,*

If we are going to rely on just 1.6 to 2.0 workers to support every retiree, as the Social Security Administration forecasts suggest, then we should want today's children to become the best educated, most skilled, and most productive citizens imaginable. How does that square with our current rush to cut discretionary spending and defund social programs, from Head Start to vocational schools, that have long provided education and training? How can we generate the funding and the political support to educate our young in today's overburdened economy? How can we make the twenty-first century the century for our children?"

And what will be our response as parents and grandparents to the words of Dietrich Bonhoeffer, who said "The ultimate test of a moral society is the kind of world it leaves to its children."

The needs of young and old are identical. Both groups need support and both need to contribute. And to meet those needs requires additional cash. Where will it come from? The current debate is constrained by by the current market ideology and by a particular view of the future. Most commentators suggest raising the retirement age, an idea that receives timid support among many politicians and is not liked by many prospective retirees, in part perhaps because it is viewed as shortening their retirement. And it would be self-defeating if the goal of increasing the active life expectancy of the elderly were attained at the expense of the young. The needs of the young for health and education cannot be compromised or their future as the first generation to be truly healthy and to exhibit large and signficant increases in the median life span will be compromised unnecessarily. Intergenerational warfare is not the answer.

Let's consider another possibility—one that like a Jules Verne story is fanciful but not impossible. Suppose that the current trends discussed in this book continue such that we continue to prevent or at least postpone deaths due to cancer, cardiovascular problems, and other age-related diseases. During the past decade, mortality among people over 80 years of age has decreased at the rate of 2 percent per year in most developed countries (Kannisto et al. 1994). This change alone would increase life expectancy by about 2 years per decade for the elderly. Let's also assume that these future elderly will be healthier than today's elderly, in part because more of them are adopting a health-promoting diet and exercise regime and in part because they are better educated as youths and they are increasingly involved in continuing adult education (and perhaps alleviating to some extent the disproportionately expensive hospital costs discussed earlier). This, too, is just a continuation of current trends. Finally, let's assume that some anti-aging interventions now being used for research purposes—for example, GHRH (growth hormone–releasing hormone) supplementation (see Chapter 7)—become validated and move into more general use.

It seems reasonable to assume, on the basis of the current data, that such segmental interventions will slow down or even reverse the rate of age-related loss of function. Each of these factors will likely lead to an increase in both total and active life expectancy. If their effects are additive, then it is not unreasonable to suggest that in the future they might add as much as 20 years to the mean or median life span. This estimate is based on the fact that caloric restriction in the rat is known to decrease the slope of the Gompertz curve (and hence increase the mortality rate doubling time) by 45 percent. If we make the conservative assumption that all of these interventions taken together would have only half this effect, we arrive at an estimated increase in the median life span of these fortunate humans of about 20 years (Finch and Pike 1995), to a new median age of about 95 to 100 years. This may sound fanciful and unreal, but you should remember that the current decline in old mortality and the increase of life expectancy by 2 years per decade will, by itself, ensure that 10 years will be added to the life expectancy of the elderly by the year 2040, and the full 20 years by the end of the twenty-first century. We are talking about the probable life expectancies of the children being born today. These estimates may or may not come true, but they cannot be regarded as figments of an overheated imagination.

Presently, people work no more than 45 years, from the ages of 20 to 65, and they must use their earnings from these years to fund a retirement of about 5 to 20 years. Most of their heavy medical expenses take place in the last year or two of life (see Table 14.2). Their funding is inadequate to the combined tasks, and this constitutes the origin of the current problem. In our imagined future, people might be able to work for up to 60 years, from the ages of 20 to 70 or 80, at two or more careers. This might be only a part-time job in the last years of work; such "bridge jobs" are fairly common today (Quinn and Kozy 1996). Those earnings would fund a (longer) retirement, of about 20 years. Perhaps the extra time will be spent in a different career, where the pay is lower, the demands lighter, and payoff comes in emotional satisfaction. Child care is one such obvious secondary career choice; mentoring teens and young adults is another; advising new businesses is yet another. Regardless of how the gift of extra time is spent, the extra 15 years or so of compounding interest on all or part of an individual's prospective retirement funds would likely generate enough additional funds to fully fund the longer retirement and supply the capital accumulation necessary for society's other needs, such as education of the young.

Of course, not every working person would welcome such a future. People laboring at physically difficult, stressful, or repetitive jobs might look forward to the end of work, as might individuals who wish to pursue their interests in such things as travel or their hobbies. But our society is transiting from a manufacturing to a service economy. Fewer people are engaged in hard manual labor, and most of the financial rewards of the past 2 decades have gone to highly paid service professionals. And they are one of the groups that has taken an active interest in their health and responded positively to the advice of the health professions. As long as such people are healthy and view their work as an interesting, enjoyable, and profitable challenge, then some substantial portion of these individuals are likely to continue working and to postpone their complete retirement. This trend could be encouraged if public laws and private pension policies were changed in order to permit people to enter a second career while still receiving a portion of their Social Security and pension funds without penalty; the combination of an acceptable income, continued involvement in the workplace, and more time for other interests might prove to be a very attractive package. And their pension funds that are not being spent in support of this second career would be quietly compounding and generating the funds necessary for their full-time retirement. Not everybody has to exercise this option for the Social Security problem to be radically altered. It is too soon and the information is too fragmentary to compute how many people must delay retirement for how long to bring the program into balance, but it is time to point out that the current definition of the problem is likely to be radically altered by the current trends in biogerontology.

Is there any independent evidence to support this contention? There is no solid data yet, but the harbingers are all about us. Married women in their sixties are increasingly choosing to continue working. Some do this because of the economic considerations of getting a bigger pension later, but some have reasons such as the need to be involved and stay connected. Today almost one half of all married women aged 55–64 are still in the work force, up from about one third in 1980. And they are not retiring when their husbands do. In a survey of 813 married women with retired husbands, 45 percent still worked, most of them full-time and at serious jobs (*The New York Times*, December 14, 1997).

So what is going on? Will men in the future imitate their wives? I look around and note that increasing numbers of professors are choosing not to retire but to continue an active scholarly life as long as they can keep up the pace. There is no reason why academics should differ in this regard from other well-educated service professionals. In the same edition of *The New York Times* cited above, Betty Friedan said:

> The idea of retiring at 65 is obsolete; it is based on an outdated life expectancy. Should we have two or three careers? Once liberated from the need to prove yourself and be promoted, the second career can be chosen with different considerations. We are on the verge of having to do a lot of new thinking for a society in which the working years last until age 80. . . . The mix at work will be different. There will be periods for study, for job training, for sabbaticals, for time out for children and adventure. Work will become more flexible as it sinks in that people will spend many more years at work.

Exactly right! The social implications of the new gerontology will shift our future from something we once thought we knew to something that is different, something a bit blurry because it is still in the process of being formed. And once again it appears as if some women will show all of us the way into this transformed future.

Much of the medical costs associated with aging occur in the last few years of life, and there is no reason why this should change. In fact, if the elderly stay healthy and independent longer, those costs might be reduced in the sense that costs of preventable chronic illnesses may be minimized or delayed (see Table 14.2 and the relevant discussion). In the past, people used to worry about being old in a young society; today some worry about being young in an old society. The way out is to help each other—to use the energy of the young and the experience of the old to improve our lives and our society.

If this sort of possible future strikes a responsive chord in enough people, it might constitute an acceptable societal goal. How we get there from here is a difficult problem, but it is not insoluble if we are willing to invest in the societal infrastructures of education and research necessary to make it happen. It will require some expenditure of public funds. George Soros (*Atlantic Monthly*, February 1997) is a successful world-class player in the marketplace, yet he points out that the private marketplace, although powerful, is a limited tool. Its vision does not effectively extend to all societal needs. It can follow but it cannot lead. Intelligently focused public funds and policies can increase the return of private funds that follows their lead. To focus the debate on only the issue of near-term health care and/or social security costs is to ignore all the other real problems and opportunities facing our society today. This narrow focus will likely lead to narrow answers, which may not serve us well as a societal goal capable of generating a broad consensus.

To define the successes of the past half-century of biomedical and social advances as a problem, as is now the current craze, is extraordinarily short-sighted. It causes us to overlook the possibility that one consequence of our present biogerontological studies might be the gift of an additional 20 years of life. When it comes about, that gift will transform society largely for the better. It will offer us the potential to live our lives fully. We should plan for it.

If we are to take responsibility for our own lives, then we must also have the knowledge with which to judge our progress and make the adjustments we deem necessary. A better understanding of the biology of aging has been the goal of our quest through all these chapters. Our understanding is as imperfect as are the data. Yet we have seen that the aging process can be defined, described, measured, and modified. We can detect fundamental similarities in the biological processes involved in aging. We can begin to view aging as the playing out of a fundamental biological process susceptible to intervention. This knowledge should allow us now to view aging in a somewhat different light than we did when we first opened this book. And perhaps we have now reached the final destination in our journey through the fact and theory of the biology of aging—to return to where we started and see it with a new vision.

Literature Cited

Abbot, M. H., E. A. Murphy, D. R. Bolling and H. Abbey. 1974. The familial component in longevity. A study of offspring of nonagenarians. II. Preliminary analysis of the completed study. Johns Hopkins Med. J. 134: 1–16.

Abdenur, J. E., W. T. Brown, S. Friedman, M. Smith and F. Lifshitz. 1997. Response to nutritional and growth hormone treatment in progeria. Metabolism: Clin. Exp. 46: 851–856.

Abraham, C. R., D. J. Selkoe and H. Potter. 1988. Immunochemical identification of the serine protein inhibitor alpha 1-antichymotrypsin in the brain amyloid deposits of Alzheimer's disease. Cell 52: 487–501.

Agarwal, S. and R. S. Sohal. 1995. Differential oxidative damage to mitochondrial proteins during aging. Mech. Ageing Devel. 85: 55–63.

Agarwal, S. and R. S. Sohal. 1996. Relationship between susceptibility to protein oxidation, aging and maximum life span potential of different species. Exp. Gerontol. 31: 365–372.

Akiyama, S., T. Katagiri, M. Namiki, N. Yamaji, N. Yamamoto, K. Miyama, H. Shibuya, N. Ueno, J. M. Wozney and T. Suda. 1997. Constitutively active BMP type I receptors transduce BMP-2 signals without the ligand in C2C12 myoblasts. Exp. Cell Res. 235: 362–369.

Alberts, B., D. Bray, J. Lewis, M. Raff, K. Roberts and J. D. Watson. 1983. *Molecular Biology of the Cell*. Garland, New York.

Alberts, M. S. and M. A. Naeser. 1982. CT scan measurements as biological markers of aging. Pp. 188–201 in M. E. Reff and E. L. Schneider (eds.), *Biological Markers of Aging*. NIH Publ. No. 82–2221, Washington, DC.

Allsopp, R. C. and C. B. Harley. 1995. Evidence for a critical telomere length in senescent human fibroblasts. Exp. Cell Res. 219: 130–136.

Allsopp, R. C., H. Vaziri, C. Patterson, S. Goldstein, E. V. Younglai, A. B. Futcher, C. W. Greider and C. B. Harley. 1992. Telomere length predicts replicative capacity of human fibroblasts. Proc. Nat. Acad. Sci. USA 89: 10114–10118.

Alpha-Tocopherol, Beta Carotene Cancer Prevention Study Group. 1994. The effect of vitamin E and beta carotene on the incidence of lung cancer and other cancers in male smokers. New England J. Med. 330: 1029–1035.

Ames, B. 1988. Endogenous genetic damage as related to cancer and aging. Talk presented at 41st Annual Meeting of the Gerontological Society of America, 19 November 1988.

Ames, B. N. 1994. The assay of endogenous oxidative DNA damage as related to aging. Pp. 397–405 in A. K. Balin (ed.), *Practical Handbook of Human Biologic Age Determination*. CRC Press, Boca Raton, FL

Ames, B. N., M. K. Shigenaga and T. M. Hagen. 1993. Oxidants, antioxidants and the degenerative diseases of aging. Proc. Natl. Acad. Sci. USA 90: 7915–7922.

Aminoff, D. 1988. The role of sialoglycoconjugates in the aging and sequestration of red cells from circulation. Blood Cells 14: 229–247.

Anderton, B. H. 1987. Progress in molecular pathology. Nature 325: 658–659.

Andres, R. 1984. Mortality and obesity: The rationale for age-specific height-weight tables. Pp. 759–766 in R. A. Andres, E. L. Bierman and W. R. Hazzard (eds.), *Principles of Geriatric Medicine*. McGraw-Hill, New York.

Araki, T., H. Kato, Y. Kanai and K. Kogure. 1993. Selective changes of neurotransmitter receptors in middle-aged gerbil brain. Neurochem. Int. 23: 541–548.

Archer, J. R. and D. E. Harrison. 1996. L-deprenyl treatment in aged mice slightly increases life spans, and greatly reduces fecundity by aged males. J. Gerontol.: Biol. Sci. 51A: B448–B453.

Arking, R. 1987a. Genetic and environmental determinants of longevity in *Drosophila*. Pp. 1–22 in A. D. Woodhead and K. H. Thompson (eds.), *Evolution of Longevity in Animals: A Comparative Approach*. Plenum, New York.

Arking, R. 1987b. Successful selection for increased longevity in *Drosophila*: Analysis of the survival data and presentation of a hypothesis on the genetic regulation of longevity. Exp. Gerontol. 22: 199–220.

Arking, R. 1988. Genetic analyses of aging processes in *Drosophila*. Exp. Aging Res. 14: 125–135.

Arking, R. and S. P. Dudas. 1989. A review of genetic investigations into aging processes of *Drosophila*. J. Am. Geriatr. Soc. 37: 757–773.

Arking, R. and R. A. Wells. 1990. Genetic alteration of normal aging processes is responsible for extended longevity in Drosophila. Devel. Genet. 11: 141–148.

Arking, R., S. Buck, R. A. Wells and R. Pretzlaff. 1988. Metabolic rates in genetically based long lived strains of *Drosophila*. Exp. Gerontol. 23: 59–76.

Arking, R., S. Buck, A. Berrios, S. Dwyer and G. T. Baker III. 1991. Elevated paraquat resistance can be used as a bioassay for longevity in a genetically based long-lived strain of *Drosophila*. Devel. Genet. 12: 362–370.

Arking, R., A. G. Force, S. P. Dudas, S. Buck and G. T. Baker III. 1996. Factors contributing to the plasticity of the extended longevity phenotype of *Drosophila*. Exp. Gerontol. 31: 623–643.

Arking, R., V. Burde, K. Graves, S. Buck, R. Hari, S. Soliman, A. Saraiya, K. Sathrasala, N. Wehr and R. Levine. 1997. Extended longevity is due to altered antioxidant gene expression. Gerontologist 37: 323 (abstract).

Armstrong, D. 1984. Free radical involvement in the formation of lipopigments. Pp. 129–141 in D. Armstrong, R. S. Sohal, R. G. Cutler and T. F. Slater (eds.), *Free Radicals in Molecular Biology, Aging and Disease*. Raven Press, New York.

Arnheim, N. and G. Cortopassi. 1992. Deleterious mitochondrial DNA mutations accumulate in aging human tissues. Mutation Res. 275: 157–167.

Atchley, W., S. Xu and C. Vogl. 1994. Developmental quantitative genetic models of evolutionary change. Devel. Genet. 15: 92–103.

Atkinson, J., I. Lartaud and C. Capdeville-Atkinson. 1992. Debit sanguin cerebral: Evolution de la regulation avec l'age. Presse Medicale 21: 1227–1230.

Atkinson, R. L. 1997. Use of drugs in the treatment of obesity. Annu. Rev. Nutrition 17: 383–403.

Aufderheide, K. J. 1987. Clonal aging in *Paramecium aurelia*. II. Evidence of functional changes in the macronucleus with age. Mech. Ageing Devel. 37: 265–279.

Austad, S. N. 1989. Life extension by dietary restriction in the bowl and doily spider, *Frontinella pyramitela*. Exp. Gerontol. 24: 83–92.

Austad, S. N. 1993. Retarded senescence in insular populations of Virginia opossums (*Didelphis virginiana*). J. Zool. 229: 695–708.

Austad, S. N. and K. E. Fischer. 1991. Mammalian aging, metabolism and ecology: Evidence from the bats and marsupials. J. Gerontol.: Biol. Sci. 46: B47–B53.

Avise, J. C. 1993. The evolutionary biology of aging, sexual reproduction and DNA repair. Evolution 47: 1293–1301.

Baker, G. T. III and R. Sprott. 1988. Biomarkers of aging. Exp. Gerontol. 23: 223–239.

Baker, G. T. III, R. E. Zschunve and E. M. Podgorski, Jr. 1979. Alteration in thermal stability of ribosomes from *Drosophila melanogaster* with age. Experientia 35: 1053–1054.

Baker, G. T., M. Jacobson and G. Mokrynski. 1985. Aging in *Drosophila*. Pp. 511–578 in V. Cristofalo (ed.), *Cell Biology Handbook in Aging*. CRC Press, Boca Raton, FL.

Balazs, E. A. 1977. Intercellular matrix of connective tissue. Pp. 227–240 in C. E. Finch and L. Hayflick (eds.), *Handbook of the Biology of Aging*. Van Nostrand Reinhold, New York.

Balin, A. K. 1983. Testing the free radical theory of aging. Pp. 137–182 in R. C. Adelman and G. S. Roth (eds.), *Testing the Theories of Aging*. CRC Press, Boca Raton, FL.

Balin, A. K. (ed.). 1994a. *Practical Handbook of Human Biologic Age Determination*. CRC Press, Boca Raton, FL.

Balin, A. K. 1994b. Skin changes as a reflection of biologic age. Pp. 343–373 in A. K. Balin (ed.), *Practical Handbook of Human Biologic Age Determination*. CRC Press, Boca Raton, FL.

Bank, L. and L. F. Jarvik. 1979. A longitudinal study of aging human twins. Pp. 303–333 in E. L. Schneider (ed.), *The Genetics of Aging*. Plenum, New York.

Barbazanges, A., M. Vallee, W. Mayo, J. Day, H. Simon, M. LeMoal and S. Maccari. 1996. Early and later adoptions have different long-term effects on male rat offspring. J. Neurosci. 16: 7783–7790.

Barinaga, M. 1995. Obese protein slims mice. Science 269: 475–476.

Barja, G., S. Cadenas, C. Rojas, R. Perez-Campo and M. Lopez-Torres. 1994. Low mitochondrial free radical production per unit O_2 consumption can explain the simultaneous presence of high longevity and high aerobic metabolic rate in birds. Free Radical Res. 21: 317–328.

Barker, D. J. P. 1995. Intrauterine programming of adult disease. Mol. Medicine Today 1: 418–423.

Baron, J. C. and G. Marchal. 1992. Viellissement cerebral et cardiovasculaire et metabolisme energetique cerebral: Etudes chez l'homme par la tomographie a positons. Presse Medicale 21: 1231–1237.

Barrett, J. et al. 1986. *Biology*. Prentice-Hall, Englewood Cliffs, NJ.

Barrows, C. H. and G. C. Kokkonen. 1982. Dietary restriction and life extension—biological mechanisms. Pp. 219–243 in G. Moment (ed.), *Nutritional Approaches to Aging Research*. CRC Press, Boca Raton, FL.

Baserga, R. 1985. *The Biology of Cell Reproduction*. Harvard University Press, Cambridge, MA.

Bates, S. R. and E. C. Gangloff (eds.). 1986. *Atherogenesis and Aging*. Springer-Verlag, New York.

Bayreuther, K. and J. Gogol. 1993. Terminal differentiation, aging, apoptosis, or transformation of the WI-38 fibroblasts in the fibroblast stem cell system in vitro. Pp. 264–271 in A. Bernd, J. Bereiter-Hahn, F. H Hevert and H. Holzmann (eds.), *Cell and Tissue Culture Models in Dermatological Research*. Springer-Verlag, Berlin.

Bayreuther, K., H. P. Rodemann, R. Hommel, K. Dittman, M. Albiez and P. I. Francz. 1988. Human skin fibroblasts in vitro differentiate along a terminal cell lineage. Proc. Natl. Acad. Sci. USA 85: 5112–5116.

Bayreuther, K., P. I. Francz, J. Gogol and K. Kontermann. 1992a. Terminal differentiation, aging, apoptosis and spontaneous transformation in fibroblast stem cell systems in vivo and in vitro. Ann. N.Y. Acad. Sci. 663: 167–179.

Bayreuther, K., P. I. Francz and H. P. Rodemann. 1992b. Fibroblasts in normal and pathological terminal differentiation, aging, apoptosis and transformation. Arch. Gerontol. Geriatr., Suppl. 3: 47–74.

Beaverton, R. J. H. 1987. Longevity in fish: Some ecological and evolutionary considerations. Pp. 161–186 in A. D. Woodhead and K. H. Thompson (eds.), *Evolution of Longevity in Animals: A Comparative Approach*. Plenum, New York.

Becker, J., V. Metzger, A.-M. Courgeon and M. Best-Belpomme. 1990. Hydrogen peroxide activates immediate binding of a *Drosophila* factor to DNA heat-shock regulatory element in vivo and in vitro. Eur. J. Biochem. 189: 553–558.

Beizer, J. L. and M. L. Timiras. 1994. Pharmacology and drug management in the elderly. Pp. 279–284 in P. S. Timiras (ed.), *Physiological Basis of Aging and Geriatrics*, 2nd edition. CRC Press, Boca Raton, FL.

Bell, A. G. 1918. *The Duration of Life and Conditions Associated with Longevity. A Study of the Hyde Genealogy*. Genealogical Record Office, Washington, DC.

Bell, E., L. F. Mareck, D. S. Levinstone, C. Merrioll, S. Sher, I. T. Yong and M. Eden. 1978. Loss of division potential in vitro: Aging or differentiation. Science 202: 1158–1162.

Bell, G. 1985. Evolutionary and nonevolutionary theories of senescence. Am. Nat. 124: 600–603.

Bell, G. 1988. Uniformity and diversity in the evolution of sex. Pp. 126–138 in R. E. Michod and B. R. Levin (eds.), *The Evolution of Sex*. Sinauer Associates, Sunderland, MA.

Bellamy, D. 1988. Degenerative diseases of ageing as problems of natural selection: A commentary upon the concept of Ònormal ageing.Ó Gerontology 34: 315–326.

Benne, R. and H. F. Tabak. 1986. Senescence comes of age. Trends Genet. 2: 147–148.

Ben-Yehuda, A., P. Szabo, R. Dyall and M. E. Weksler. 1994. Bone marrow declines as a site of B-cell precursor differentiation with age: Relationship to thymus involution. Proc. Natl. Acad. Sci. USA 91: 11988–11992.

Benzi, G., F. Marzatico, O. Pastoris and R. F. Villa. 1989. Relationship between aging, drug treatment and the cerebral enzymatic antioxidant system. Exp. Gerontol. 24: 137–148.

Berlett, B. S. and E. R. Stadtman. 1997. Protein oxidation in aging, disease, and oxidative stress. J. Biol. Chem. 272: 20313–20316.

Bernet, J. 1992. In *Podospora anserina*, protoplasmic incompatibility genes are involved in cell death control via multiple gene interactions. Heredity 68: 79–87.

Bernier, L. and E. Wang. 1996. A prospective view on phosphatases and replicative senescence. Exp. Gerontol. 31: 13–19.

Bernstein, C. and H. Bernstein. 1991. *Aging, Sex and DNA Repair*. Academic Press, San Diego.

Bewley, G. and C. C. Laurie-Ahlberg. 1984. Genetic variation affecting the expression of catalase in *Drosophila melanogaster*: Correlations with rates of enzyme synthesis and degradation. Genetics 106: 435–448.

Bewley, G. C. and W. J. Mackay. 1989. Development of a genetic model for acatalasemia: Testing the oxygen free radical theory of aging. Pp. 359–378 in D. E. Harrison (ed.), *Genetic Effects of Aging*, vol. II. Growth Publishing, Bar Harbor, ME.

Bidder, G. P 1925. The mortality of plaice. Nature 115: 495–496.

Bidder, G. P. 1932. Senescence. Brit. Med. J. 115: 5831.

Bjπrksten, J. 1968. The cross linkage theory of aging. J. Am. Geriatr. Soc. 16: 408–427.

Bjπrksten, J. and W. J. Champion. 1942. Mechanical influence upon tanning. J. Am. Chem. Soc. 64: 868–869.

Black, I. B., J. E. Adler, C. F. Dreyfuss, W. F. Friedman, E. F. LaGamma and A. H. Roach. 1987. Biochemistry of information storage in the nervous system. Science 236: 1263–1268.

Blackett, A. D. and D. A. Hall. 1981a. The effect of vitamin E on mouse fitness and survival. Gerontology 27: 133–139.

Blackett, A. D. and D. A. Hall. 1981b. Tissue vitamin E levels and lipofuscin accumulation with age in the mouse. J. Gerontol. 36: 529–533.

Block, G. 1991. Vitamin C and cancer prevention: The epidemiologic evidence. Am. J. Clin. Nutr. 53(Suppl. 1): 270S–282S.

Bloom, F. E., A. Lazerson and L. Hofstadter. 1985. *Brain, Mind and Behavior*. Freeman, New York.

Bloom, W. and D. W. Fawcett. 1968. *A Textbook of Histology*, 9th edition. Saunders, Philadelphia.

Bodnar, A. G., M. Ouellette, M. Frolkis, S. E. Holt, C. P. Chiu, G. B. Morin, C. B. Harley, J. W. Shay, S. Lichteiner and W. E. Wright. 1998. Extension of life-span by introduction of telomerase into normal human cells. Science 279: 349–352.

Bohr, V. A. and R. M. Anson. 1995. DNA damage, mutation and fine structure DNA repair in aging. Mutation Res. 338: 25–34.

Bolzan A. D., O. A. Brown, R. G. Goya and M. S. Bianchi. 1995. Hormonal modulation of antioxidant enzyme activities in young and old rats. Exp. Gerontol. 30: 169–175.

Borkan, G. A. and A. H. Norris. 1980. Assessment of biological age using a profile of physical parameters. J. Gerontol. 35: 177–184.

Bouliere, F. and S. Parot. 1962. Le veillissement de deux populations blanches vivant dans des conditions ecologiques tres differentes, stude comparative. Rev. France Etudes Clin. Bio. 7: 629–635.

Bowden, D. M. 1990. Primate aging research in the USA and the challenge of measuring the rate of aging in long-lived species. Jikken Dobutsu 39: 183–184.

Bowden, D. M., R. Short, D. D. Williams and E. A. Clark. 1994. Immunologic markers in a longitudinal study of aging in pigtailed macaques (*Macaca nemestrina*). J. Gerontol.: Biol. Sci. 49: B93–B103.

Brandfonbrener, M., M. Landowne and N. W. Shock. 1955. Changes in cardiac output with age. Circulation 12: 557–566.

Brant, L. J., J. L. Fozard and E. J. Metter. 1994. Age differences in biological markers of mortality. Pp. 458–470 in A. K. Balin (ed.), *Practical Handbook of Human Biologic Age Determination*. CRC Press, Boca Raton, FL.

Bremner, W. J., M. V. Vitiello and P. N. Prinz. 1983. Loss of circadian rhythmicity in blood testosterone levels with aging in normal men. J. Clin. Endocrinol. Metab. 56: 1278–1281.

Bremner, W. J., A. M. Matsumoto, R. A. Steiner, D. K. Clifton and D. M. Dursa. 1986. Neuroendocrine correlates of aging in the male. Pp. 47–57 in L. Mastroianni, Jr. and C. A. Paulsen (eds.), *Aging, Reproduction and the Climacteric*. Plenum, New York.

Brenneisen, P., J. Gogol and K. Bayreuther. 1994. DNA synthesis and fos and jun protein expression in mitotic and post mitotic WIO38 fibroblasts in vitro. Exp. Cell Res. 211: 219–230.

Brenner, D. A., M. O'Hara, P. Angel, M. Chojkrer and M. Karin. 1989. Prolonged activation of *jun* and collagenase genes by tumour necrosis factor. Nature 337: 661–663.

Brenner, S. 1974. The genetics of *Caenorhabditis elegans*. Genetics 77: 87–94.

Broccoli, D., J. W. Young and T. deLange. 1995. Telomerase activity in normal and malignant hematopoietic cells. Proc. Natl. Acad. Sci. USA 92: 9082–9086.

Brody, H. and N. Vijayashankar. 1977. Anatomical changes in the nervous system. Pp. 241–261 in C. E. Finch and E. L. Schneider (eds.), *Handbook of the Biology of Aging*. Van Nostrand Reinhold, New York.

Brody, J. A. and T. P. Miles. 1990. Mortality postponed and the unmasking of age-dependent non-fatal conditions. Aging 2: 283–289.

Brooks, A., G. J. Lithgow and T. J. Johnson. 1994. Mortality rates in a genetically heterogeneous population of *Caenorhabditis elegans*. Science 263: 668–671.

Brown, G. W. and M. M. Flood. 1947. Tumbler mortality. J. Am. Statist. Assn. 42: 562–574.

Brown, M. 1987. Changes in fibre size, not number, in ageing skeletal muscle. Age and Ageing 16: 244–248.

Brown, M. S. and J. L. Goldstein. 1996. Heart attacks: Gone with the century? Science 272: 629 (editorial).

Brown, W. T. 1985. Genetics of human aging. Pp. 105–114 in M. Rothstein (ed.). *Review of Biological Research in Aging*, vol. 2. Alan R. Liss, New York.

Brown, W. T. 1992. Progeria: A human-disease model of accelerated aging. Am. J. Clin. Nutr. 55(Suppl. 6): 1222S–1224S.

Brown-Sequard, C. E. 1889. Des effects produits chez l'homme par des injections sous-cutanees d'un liquide retire des testicules frais de cobayes et de chiens. Comptes Rend. Soc. Biol. 41: 415–422.

Browner, W. S., J. Westenhouse and J. A. Tice. 1991. What if Americans ate less fat? A quantitative estimate of the effect on mortality. JAMA 265: 3285–3291.

Browning, R. 1864. Rabbbi Ben Ezra. P. 306 in T. R. Cole and M. G. Winkler (eds.), *The Oxford Book of Aging: Reflections on the Journey of Life*. Oxford University Press, Oxford, 1994.

Brunk, C. F. 1986. Genome reorganization in *Tetrahymena*. Int. Rev. Cytol. 99: 49–83.

Bryan, T. M., A. Englezou, J. Gupta, S. Bacchetti and R. R. Reddel. 1995. Telomere elongation in immortal human cells without detectable telomerase activity. EMBO J. 14: 4240–4248.

Bucala, R., R. Model and A. Cerami. 1984. Modification of DNA by reducing sugars: A possible mechanism for nucleic acid aging and age-related dysfunctions in gene expression. Proc. Natl. Acad. Sci. USA 81: 105–109.

Buck, S., M. Nicholson, S. P. Dudas, G. T. Baker III and R. Arking. 1993a. Larval regulation of adult longevity in a genetically selected long lived strain of *Drosophila melanogaster*. Heredity 71: 23–32.

Buck, S., R. A. Wells, S. P. Dudas, G. T. Baker III and R. Arking. 1993b. Chromosomal localization and regulation of the longevity determinant genes in a selected strain of *Drosophila melanogaster*. Heredity 71: 11–22.

Buffon, G. L. Leclerc, comte de. 1749–1804. Histoire naturelle, générale et particuliΣre. 44 vols. Imprimerie Royale, Paris.

Bulfield, G. 1988. Genetics of atherosclerosis and plasma lipoproteins in mice. Trends Genet. 4: 3–4.

Bulpitt, C. J. 1995. Assessing biological age: Practicality? Gerontology 41: 315–321.

Buskirk, E. R. 1985. Health maintenance and longevity: Exercise. Pp. 894–931 in C. E. Finch and E. L. Schneider (eds.), *Handbook of the Biology of Aging*, 2nd edition. Van Nostrand Reinhold, New York.

Butler, R. 1995. Human aging study. Pp. 481–482 in G. L. Maddox (ed.-in-chief), *The Encyclopedia of Aging*, 2nd edition. Springer, New York.

Butlin, R. K. and H. I. Griffiths. 1993. Ageing without sex. Nature 364: 680.

Butterfield, D. A., B. J. Howard, S. Yatin, K. L. Allen and J. M. Carney. 1997. Free radical oxidation of brain proteins in accelerated senescence and its modulation by *N*-tert-butyl-alpha-phenylnitrone. Proc. Natl. Acad. Sci. USA 94: 674–678.

Calleja, M., P. Pena, C. Ugalde, C. Ferreiro, R. Marco and R. Garesse. 1993. Mitochondrial DNA remains intact during *Drosophila* aging, but the levels of mitochondrial transcripts are significantly reduced. J. Biol. Chem. 268: 18891–18897.

Campbell, S. D., A. J. Hilliker and J. P. Phillips. 1986. Cytogenetic analysis of the cSOD microregion in *Drosophila melanogaster*. Genetics 112: 205–215.

Campfield, L. A., F. J. Smith, Y. Glusez, R. Devos and P. Burn. 1995. Recombinant mouse OB protein: Evidence for a peripheral signal linking adiposity and central neural networks. Science 269: 546–548.

Campisi, J. 1996. Replicative senescence: An old lives' tale? Cell 84: 497–500.

Cantin, M. and J. Genest. 1986. The heart as an endocrine organ. Sci. Am. 254(2): 76–81.

Caplan, A. I., M. Y. Fiszman and H. M. Eppenberger. 1983. Molecular and cell isoforms during development. Science 221: 921–927.

Carey, J. R., P. Liedo, D. Orozco and J. W. Vaupel. 1992. Slowing of mortality rates at older ages in large medfly cohorts. Science 258: 457–461.

Carlson, A. 1987. Brain neurotransmitters in aging and dementia: Similar changes across diagnostic dementia groups. Gerontology 33: 159–167.

Carrel, A. 1912. On the permanent life of tissues outside the organism. J. Exp. Med. 15: 516–528.

Carter, B. D., C. Kaltschmidt, B. Kaltschmidt, N. Offenhauser, R. Bohm-Matthaei, P. A. Baeuerle and Y.-A. Barde. 1996. Selective activation of NF-kB by nerve growth factor through the neurotrophin receptor p75. Science 272: 542–545.

Casper, R. C. 1995. Nutrition and its relationship to aging. Exp. Gerontol. 30: 299–314.

Cefalu, W. T., A. D. Bell-Farrow, Z. Q. Wang, W. E. Sonntag, M. X. Fu, J. W. Baynes and S. R. Thorpe. 1995. Caloric restriction decreases age-dependent accumulation of the glycoxidation products, N epsilon-(carboxymethyl)lysine and pentosidine, in rat skin collagen. J. Gerontol.: Biol. Sci. 50A: B337–B341.

Cerami, A. 1985. Glucose as a mediator of aging. J. Am. Geriatr. Soc. 33: 626–634.

Cerami, A., H. Vlassara and M. Brownlee. 1987. Glucose and aging. Sci. Am. 256(5): 90–97.

Chang-Claude, J., R. Frentzel-Beyme and U. Eilber. Mortality pattern of German vegetarians after 11 years of follow-up. Epidemiology 3: 395–401.

Charlesworth, B. 1994a. Evolution in Age-Structured Populations, 2nd edition. Cambridge University Press, Cambridge.

Charlesworth, B. 1994b. Evolutionary mechanisms of senescence. Pp. 13–21 in M. R. Rose and C. E. Finch (eds.), *Genetics and Evolution of Aging*. Kluwer, Dordrecht, The Netherlands.

Cheal, M. L. 1986. The gerbil, a unique model for research on aging. Exp. Aging Res. 12: 3–21.

Chen, J. B., J. Sun and S. M. Jazwinski. 1990. Prolongation of the yeast life span by the *v-Ha-RAS* oncogene. Mol. Microbiol. 4: 2081–2086.

Chen, M., J. B. Halter and D. Porte, Jr. 1987. The role of dietary carbohydrate in the decreased glucose tolerance of the elderly. J. Am. Geriatr. Soc. 35: 417–424.

Chippindale, A. K., A. M. Leroi, S. B. Kim and M. R. Rose. 1993. Phenotypic plasticity and selection in *Drosophila* life-history evolution. I. Nutrition and the cost of reproduction. J. Evol. Biol. 6: 171–193.

Chou, M. W., R. A. Pegram, P. Gao, S. R. Hansard, J. G. Shaddock and D. A. Casciano. 1991. The effects of dietary restriction and aging on in vivo and in vitro binding of aflatoxin B1 to cellular DNA. Biomed. Environmental Sci. 4: 134–143.

Christenson, B. A. and N. E. Johnson. 1995. Educational inequality in adult mortality: An assessment with death certificate data from Michigan. Demography 32: 215–229.

Clark, A. G. 1994. Mutation-selection balance and the evolution of senescence. Pp. 22–28 in M. R. Rose and C. E. Finch (eds.), *Genetics and Evolution of Aging*. Kluwer, Dordrecht, The Netherlands.

Clark, A. M., H. A. Bertrand and R. E. Smith. 1963. Lifespan differences between haploid and diploid males of *Habrobracon serinopae* after exposure as adults to X-rays. Am. Nat. 97: 203–208.

Clark, D. H. 1975. *Exercise Physiology*. Prentice-Hall, Englewood Cliffs, NJ.

Clark, M. A. and A. S. Weiss. 1993. Elevated levels of glycoprotein gp200 in progeria fibroblasts. Mol. Cell. Biochem. 120: 51–60.

Clarke, J. M. and J. Maynard Smith. 1955. The genetics and cytology of *Drosophila subobscura*. XI. Hybrid vigor and longevity. J. Genet. 53: 172–180.

Clarkson, T. B., M. R. Adams, K. W. Weingard, L. C. Miller and S. Hendrick. 1987. Effect of age on atherosclerosis progression in non-human primates. Pp. 57–71 in S. R. Bates and E. C. Gangloff (eds.), *Atherogenesis and Aging*. Springer-Verlag, New York.

Cohen, B. H. 1964. Family patterns of mortality and life span. Quart. Rev. Biol. 39: 130–181.

Cohen, M., L. Cheng and H. N. Bhagavan. 1994. Vitamin C and the elderly—an update. Pp. 203–262 in R. Watson (ed.), *Handbook of Nutrition in the Aged*, 2nd edition. CRC Press, Boca Raton, FL.

Cohn, L., A. G. Feller, M. W. Draper, I. W. Rudman and D. Rudman. 1993. Carpal tunnel syndrome and gynecomastia during growth hormone treatment of elderly men with low circulating IGF-1 concentrations. Clin. Endocrinol. (Oxford) 39: 417–429.

Coleman, D. L., K. W. Schwizer and E. Letier. 1984. Effect of genetic background on the therapeutic effects of dehydroepiandrosterone (DHEA) in diabetes-obesity mutants used in aged mice. Diabetes 33: 26–32.

Coleman, R., M. Silbermann, D. Gershon and A. Z. Reznick. 1987a. Effect of long term stress on the ultrastructure of the aging mouse heart. Gerontology 33: 19–33.

Coleman, R., M. Silbermann, D. Gershon and A. Z. Reznick. 1987b. Giant mitochondria in the myocardium of aging and endurance-trained mice. Gerontology 33: 34–39.

Colige, A., B. Nusgens and C. M. Lapiere. 1991a. Altered response of progeria fibroblasts to epidermal growth factor. J. Cell Sci. 100: 649–655.

Colige, A., J. C. Roujeau, F. De la Rocque, B. Nusgens and C. M. Lapiere. 1991b. Abnormal gene expression in skin fibroblasts from a Hutchinson-Gilford patient. Lab. Invest. 64: 799–806.

Comfort, A. 1956. *The Biology of Senescence*. Holt, Rinehart and Winston, New York.

Comfort, A. 1960. Discussion session. I. Definition and universality of aging. Pp. 3–13 in B. L. Strehler (ed.), *The Biology of Aging*. AIBS, Washington, DC.

Comfort, A. 1964. *Ageing: The Biology of Senescence*, 2nd edition. Holt, Rinehart and Winston, New York.

Comfort, A. 1979. *The Biology of Senescence*, 3rd edition. Elsevier, New York.

Cooper, E. L. (ed.). 1984. *Stress, Immunity, and Aging*. Marcel Dekker, New York.

Corpas, E., S. M. Harman, M. A. Pineyro, R. Roberson and M. R. Blackman. 1992. Growth hormone (GH)-releasing hormone (1–29) twice daily reverses the decreased GH and insulin like growth factor-I levels in old men. J. Clin. Endocrinol. Metab. 75: 530–535.

Corral-Debrinski, M., T. Horton, M. T. Lott, J. M. Shoffner, M. F. Beal and D. C. Wallace. 1992. Mitochondrial DNA deletions in human brain: Regional variability and increase with advanced age. Nature Genet. 2: 324–329.

Cortopassi, G. A. and E. Wang. 1996. There is substantial agreement among interspecies estimates of DNA repair activity. Mech. Ageing Devel. 91: 211–218.

Corwin, J., M. Loury and A. N. Gilbert. 1997. Workplace, age, and sex as mediators of olfactory function: Data from the National Geographic Smell Survey. J. Gerontol.: Psychol. Sci. 50B: P179–P186.

Costa, P. T. and R. R. McCrae. 1980. Functional age: A conceptual and empirical critique. Pp. 23–49 in S. G. Haynes and M. Feinleib (eds.), *Proceedings of the Second Conference on the Epidemiology of Aging*. NIH Publ. No. 80-969, Washington, DC.

Costa, P. T. and R. R. McCrae. 1984. Concepts of functional or biological age: A critical review. Pp. 30–37 in R. Andres, E. L. Bierman and W. R. Hazzard (eds.), *Principles of Geriatric Medicine*. McGraw-Hill, New York.

Costa, P. T. and R. R. McCrae. 1995. Design and analysis of aging studies. Pp. 25–36 in E. J. Masoro (ed.), *Handbook of Physiology. Section 11: Aging*. Oxford University Press, New York.

Costa, P. T., R. R. McCrae and D. Arenberg. 1983. Recent longitudinal research on personality and aging. Pp. 222–265 in K. W. Schaie (ed.), *Longitudinal Studies of Adult Psychological Development*. Guilford, New York.

Cotman, C. W. and V. K. Holets. 1985. Structural changes at synapses with age: Plasticity and regeneratrion. Pp. 617–644 in C. E. Finch and E. L. Schneider (eds.), *Handbook of the Biology of Aging*, 2nd edition. Van Nostrand Reinhold, New York.

Cotman, C. W. and S. Neeper. 1996. Activity-dependent plasticity and the aging brain. Pp. 284–299 in E. L. Schneider and J. W. Rowe (eds.), *Handbook of the Biology of Aging*, 4th edition. Academic Press, San Diego.

Cotman, C. W., R. E. Brinton, A. Galaburda, B. McEwen and D. M. Schneider. 1987. *The Neuro-Immune-Endocrine Connection*. Raven Press, New York.

Courtright, J. B., J. Sonstein and A. K. Kumaran. 1985. Age specific regulation of gene expression in *Drosophila*. Pp. 209–222 in R. S. Sohal, L. S. Birnbaum and R. G. Cutler (eds.), *Molecular Biology of Aging: Gene Stability and Gene Expression*. Raven Press, New York.

Crawford, D. R., G. P. Schools, S. L. Salmon and K. J. A. Davies. 1996. Hydrogen peroxide induces the expression of adapt15, a novel RNA associated with polysomes in hamster HA-1 cells. Arch. Biochem. Biophys. 325: 256–264.

Crew, M. D. 1993. Genes of the major histocompatibility complex and the evolutionary genetics of lifespan. Genetica 91: 225–238.

Cristofalo, V. J. and R. J. Pignolo. 1995. Cell culture as a model. Pp. 58–82 in E. J. Masoro (ed.), *Handbook of Physiology. Section 11: Aging*. Oxford University Press, New York.

Crown, W. H. 1998. Social Security and employment policy. Gerontologist 38: 132–135.

Curtis, H. J. 1963. Biological mechanisms underlying the aging process. Science 141: 686–694.

Curtis, H. J. and K. Miller. 1971. Chromosome aberrations in liver cells of guinea pigs. J. Gerontol. 26: 292–293.

Curtsinger, J. W. 1995a. A book review of *Evolution in Age-Structured Populations*, 2nd edition, by Brian Charlesworth. Exp. Gerontol. 30: 663–665.

Curtsinger, J. W. 1995b. Density and age-specific mortality. Genetica 96: 179–182.

Curtsinger, J. W. 1995c. Density, mortality and the narrow view. Genetica 96: 187–189.

Curtsinger, J. W. 1996. The old fly: Genetics of aging in *Drosophila*. Talk presented at the Gerontology Society of America meeting, November 1996.

Curtsinger, J. W., H. H. Fukui, D. R. Townsend and J. W. Vaupel. 1992. Demography of genotypes: Failure of the limited life-span paradigm in *Drosophila melanogaster*. Science 258: 461–463.

Curtsinger, J. W., H. H. Fukui, A. Khazaeli, A. Kirscher, S. D. Pletcher, D. E. L. Promislow and M. Tatar. 1995. Genetic variation and aging. Annu. Rev. Genet. 29: 553–575

Cutler, R. G. 1975. Evolution of human longevity and the genetic complexity governing aging rate. Proc. Natl. Acad. Sci. USA 72: 4664–4668.

Cutler, R. G. 1982. Longevity is determined by specific genes: Testing the hypothesis. Pp. 25–114 in R. C. Adelman and G. S. Roth (eds.), *Testing the Theories of Aging*. CRC Press, Boca Raton, FL.

Cutler, R. G. 1983a. Species probes, longevity and aging. Pp. 69–144 in W. Regelson and F. M. Sinex (eds.), *Intervention in the Aging Process, Part B. Basic Research and Preclinical Screening*. Alan R. Liss, New York.

Cutler, R. G. 1983b. Superoxide dismutase, longevity and specific metabolic rate: A reply. Gerontology 29: 113–120.

Cutler, R. G. 1984. Antioxidants, aging and longevity. Pp. 371–428 in W. A. Pryor (ed.), *Free Radicals in Biology*, vol. VI. Academic Press, New York.

Cutler, R. G. 1985. Dysdifferentiative hypothesis of aging: A review. Pp. 307–340 in R. S. Sohal, L. S. Birnbaum and R. G. Cutler (eds.), *Molecular Biology of Aging: Gene Stability and Gene Expression*. Raven Press, New York.

da Cunha, G. L., I. B. da Cruz, P. Fiorino and A. K. de Oliveira. 1995. Paraquat resistance and starvation conditions in the selection of longevity extremes in *Drosophila melanogaster* populations previously selected for long and short developmental period. Devel. Genet. 17: 352–361.

Danchin, A. and A. HΣnaut. 1997. The map of the cell is in the chromosome. Curr. Opinion Genet. Devel. 7: 852–854.

Daneva, T., E. Spinedi, R. Hadid and R. C. Gaillard. 1995. Impaired hypothalamo-pituitary-adrenal axis function in Swiss nude athymic mice. Neuroendocrinology 62: 79–86.

Daniel, C. W. 1977. Cell longevity in vivo. Pp. 122–158 in C. E. Finch and L. Hayflick (eds.), *Handbook of the Biology of Aging*. Van Nostrand Reinhold, New York.

David, J., J. Van Herrewege and P. Fouiller. 1971. Quantitative underfeeding of *Drosophila*: Effects on adult longevity and fecundity. Exp. Gerontol. 6: 249–257.

Davis, R. and D. Faulds. 1996. Dexfenfluramine: An updated review of its therapeutic use in the management of obesity. Drugs 52: 696–724.

Davis, R. E., S. Miller, C. Herrnstadt, S. S. Ghosh, E. Fahy, L. A. Shinobu, D. Galasko, L. J. Thal, M. F. Beal, N. Howell and W. D. Parker, Jr. 1997. Mutations in mitochondrial cytochrome c oxidase genes segregate with late-onset

Alzheimer disease. Proc. Nat. Acad. Sci. USA 94: 4526–4531.

Davison, A. N. 1987. Pathophysiology of aging brain. Gerontology 33: 129–135.

Dean, W. 1988. *Biological Aging Measurements: Clinical Applications.* Center for Bio-Gerontology, Los Angeles.

de Duve, C. 1984. *A Guided Tour of the Living Cell*, vol. 1. Scientific American Library, New York.

Deevey, E. S., Jr. 1947. Life tables for natural populations of animals. Quart. Rev. Biol. 22: 283–314.

De Flora, S., A. Izzotti, K. Randerath, E. Randerath, H. Bartsch, J. Nair, R. Balansky, F. van Schooten, P. Degan, G. Fronza, D. Walsh and J. Lewtas. 1996. DNA adducts and chronic degenerative disease: Pathogenic relevance and implications in preventive medicine. Mutation Res. 366: 197–238.

DeFronzo, R. A., J. A. Tobin and R. Andres. 1979. Glucose clamp technique: A method for quantifying insulin in secretion and resistance. Am. J. Physiol. Endocrinol. 237(E6): E214–E223.

de Grey, A. D. N. J. 1997. A proposed refinement of the mitochondrial free radical theory of aging. BioEssays 19: 161–166.

de Grey, A. D. N. J. 1998. A mechanism proposed to explain the rise in oxidative stress during aging. J. Anti-Aging Med. 1: 53–66.

Demple, B. and L. Harrison. 1994. Repair of oxidative damage to DNA: Enzymology and biology. Annu. Rev. Biochem. 63: 915–948.

Dewji, N. N. and S. J. Singer. 1996. Genetic clues to Alzheimer's disease. Science 271: 159–160.

Dimri, G. P., X. Lee, G. Basile, M. Acosta, G. Scott, C. Roskelley, E. E. Medrano, I. Linskens, I. Rubeli, O. Pereira-Smith, M. Peacocke and J. Campisi. 1995. A biomarker that identifies senescent human cells in culture and in aging skin in vivo. Proc. Natl. Acad. Sci. USA 92: 9363–9367.

D'Mello, N. P., A. M. Childress, D. S. Franklin, S. P. Kale, C. Pinswadi and S. M. Jazwinski. 1994. Cloning and characterization of *LAG1*, a longevity assurance gene in yeast. J. Biol. Chem. 269: 15451–15459.

Docherty, J. R. 1996. Effects of aging on prejunctional control of neurotransmission in the rat. Ann. N.Y. Acad. Sci. 786: 264–273.

Donis-Keller, H. et al. 1987. A genetic linkage map of the human genome. Cell 51: 319–337.

Dorman, J. B., B. Albinder, T. Shoyer and C. Kenyon. 1995. The *age-1* and *daf-2* genes function in a common pathway to control the lifespan of *Caenorhabditis elegans*. Genetics 141: 1399–1406.

Doty, R. L., P. Shaman, S. C. Applebaum, R. Giberson, L. Sikosorski and L. Rosenberg. 1984. Smell identification ability: Changes with age. Science 226: 1441–1443.

Doyle, F. H. 1969. Radiological measurements of skin thickness and bone mineral. Sci. Basis Med. Annu. Rev. 8: 133–145.

Draye, X. and F. A. Lints. 1995. Geographic variations of life history strategies in *Drosophila melanogaster*. II. Analysis of laboratory-adapted populations. Exp. Gerontol. 30: 517–532.

Driscoll, M. 1995. Genes controlling programmed cell death: Relation to mechanisms of cell senescence and aging? Pp. 45–60 in K. Esser and G. M. Martin (eds.), *Molecular Aspects of Aging.* Wiley, Chichester, England.

Drori, D. and Y. Folman. 1986. Interactive environmental and genetic effects on longevity in the male rat. Litter size, exercise, castration and electronic shock. Exp. Aging Res. 12: 59–64.

Duara, R., E. D. London and S. I. Rapoport. 1985. Changes in structure and energy metabolism of the aging brain. Pp. 595–616 in C. E. Finch and E. L. Schneider (eds.), *Handbook of the Biology of Aging*, 2nd edition. Van Nostrand Reinhold, New York.

Dudas, S. P. and R. Arking. 1994. The expression of the *EF1* genes of *Drosophila* is not associated with the extended longevity phenotype in a selected long lived strain. Exp. Gerontol. 29: 645–657.

Dudas, S. P. and R. Arking. 1995. A coordinate up-regulation of the antioxidant gene activities is associated with the delayed onset of senescence in a long lived strain of *Drosophila*. J. Gerontol.: Biol. Sci. 50A: B117–B127.

Duffy, P. H., R. J. Feuers, J. A. Leakey, A. Turturro and R. W. Hart. 1989. Effect of chronic calories restriction on physiological variables related to energy metabolism in the male Fischer 344 rat. Mech. Ageing Devel. 48: 117–133.

Duhon, S. A. and T. E. Johnson. 1993. Detection of new long-lived mutants in *Caenorhabditis elegans*. Gerontologist 33: 96 (abstract).

Dusenbery, R. L. and P. D. Smith. 1996. Cellular responses to DNA damage in *Drosophila melanogaster*. Mutation Res. 364: 133–145.

Dworkin, L. D., T. H. Hostetter, H. G. Rennke and B. M. Brenner. 1984. Hemodynamic basis for glomerular injury in rats with desoxycorticosterone-salt hypertension. J. Clin. Invest. 73: 1448–1461.

Dykes, C. W. 1996. Genes, disease and medicine. Brit. J. Clin. Pharmacol. 42: 683–695.

Dykhuisen, D. 1974. The evolution of cell senescence, atherosclerosis and benign tumours. Exp. Cell Res. 144: 455–562.

Eakin, T. and M. Witten. 1995a. A gerontological distance metric for analysis of survival dynamics. Mech. Ageing Devel. 78: 85–101.

Eakin, T. and M. Witten. 1995b. How square is the survival curve of a given species. Exp. Gerontol. 30: 33–64.

Eakin, T., R. Shouman, Y-L. Qi, G. Liu and M. Witten. 1995. Estimating survival model parameters in gerontological aging studies: Methodological problems and insights. J. Gerontol.: Biol. Sci. 50A: B166–B176.

Earle, W. R. 1943. Production of malignancy in vitro. IV. The mouse fibroblast cultures and changes seen in living cells. J. Natl. Cancer Inst. 4: 165–212.

Ebbesen, P. 1973. Papilloma induction in different aged skin grafts to young recipients. Nature 241: 280–281.

Ebbesen, P. 1974. Aging increases susceptibility of mouse skin to PMBA carcinogenesis independent of general immune status. Science 183: 217–218.

Ebeling, A. H. 1913. The permanent life of connective tissue outside of the organism. J. Exp. Med. 17: 273–285.

Eberling, J. L., T. E. Nordahl, N. Kusubov, B. R. Reed, T. F. Budinger and W. J. Jagust. 1995. Reduced temporal lobe glucose metabolism in aging. J. Neuroimaging 5: 178–182.

Ebert, R. H., V. A. Cherkasova, R. A. Dennis, J. H. Wu and S. Ruggles. 1993. Longevity determining genes in *Caenorhabditis elegans*: Chromosomal mapping of multiple noninteractive loci. Genetics 135: 1003–1010.

Economos, A. C. and F. A. Lints. 1984. Growth rate and life span in *Drosophila*. I. Methods and mechanisms of growth rate. Mech. Ageing Devel. 27: 1–13.

Edelman, G. M. 1988. *Topobiology: An Introduction to Molecular Embryology*. Basic Books, New York.

Edelson, R. L. and E. M. Fink. 1985. The immunologic function of skin. Sci. Am. 252(6): 46–53.

Edgar, B. A. and C. F. Lehner. 1996. Developmental control of cell cycle regulators: A fly's perspective. Science 274: 1646–1652.

Edington, D. W., A. C. Cosmos and W. B. McCafferty. 1972. Exercise and longevity: Evidence for a threshold age. J. Gerontol. 27: 341–343.

Effros, R. B. 1996. Insights on immunological aging derived from the T lymphocyte cellular senescence model. Exp. Gerontol. 31: 21–27.

Egilmez, N. K. and M. Jazwinski. 1989. Specific alterations in transcript prevalence during the yeast life span. J. Biol. Chem. 264: 14312–14317.

Egilmez, N. K. and M. Rothstein. 1985. The effect of aging on cell-free protein synthesis in the free-living nematode *Trubatrix aceti*. Biochim. Biophys. Acta 840: 355–363.

Egilmez, N. K., J. B. Chen and S. M. Jazwinski. 1989. Specific alterations in transcript prevalence during the yeast life span. J. Biol. Chem. 264: 14312–14317.

Ehrenstein, D. 1998. Immortality gene discovered. Science 279: 177.

Eiseley, L. 1977. Somewhere beyond the pawnshops. Pp. 73–74 in *Another Kind of Autumn*. Scribner, New York.

Engelberg, D., C. Klein, H. Martinetto, K. Struhl and M. Karin. 1994. The UV response involving the Ras signaling pathway and AP-1 transcription factors is conserved between yeast and mammals. Cell 77: 381–390.

Esposito, D., G. Fassina, P. Szabo, P. DeAngelis, L. Rodgers, M. Weksler and M. Siniscalco. 1989. Chromosomes of older humans are more prone to aminopterine-induced breakage. Proc. Natl. Acad. Sci. USA 86: 1302–1306.

Esposito, J. L. 1987. *The Obsolete Self: Philosophical Dimensions of Aging*. University of California Press, Berkeley.

Esser, K. 1985. Genetic control of aging: The mobile intron model. Pp. 3–20 in M. Bergener et al. (eds.), *Thresholds in Aging*. Academic Press, London.

Esser, K. and W. Keller. 1976. Genes inhibiting senescence in the ascomycete *Podospora anserina*. Mol. General Genet. 144: 107–110.

Evans, D. 1995. Human studies. Pp. 83–92 in E. J. Masoro (ed.). *Handbook of Physiology. Section 11: Aging*. Oxford University Press, New York.

Evans, D. A. 1996. Descriptive epidemiology of Alzheimer's disease. Pp. 51–60 in Z. S. Katchaturian and T. Radebaugh (eds.), *Alzheimer's Disease: Cause(s), Diagnosis, Treatment, and Care*. CRC Press, Boca Raton, FL.

Evans, D. A., A. A. van der Kleij, M. A. Sonnermans, J. P Burbach and F. W. van Leeuwen. 1994. Frameshift mutations at two hotspots in vasopressin transcripts in post-mitotic neurons. Proc. Nat. Acad. Sci. USA 91: 6059–6063.

Evans, W. F. 1983. *Anatomy and Physiology*, 3rd edition. Prentice-Hall, Englewood Cliffs, NJ.

Evans, W. J. 1995. Effects of exercise on body composition and functional capacity of the elderly. J. Gerontol.: Biol. Sci. 50A(special issue): B147–B150.

Everitt, A. V., C. D. Shorey and M. A. Ficarra. 1985. Skeletal muscle aging in the hind limb of the old male Wistar rat: Inhibitory effect of hypophysectomy and food restriction. Arch. Gerontol. Geriatr. 4: 101–115.

Ewbank, J. J., T. M. Barnes, B. Lakowski, M. Lussier, H. Bussey and S. Hekimi. 1997. Structural and functional conservation of the *Caenorhabditis elegans* timing gene *clk-1*. Science 275: 980–983.

Exton-Smith, A. N. 1985. Mineral metabolism. Pp. 511–539 in C. E. Finch and E. L. Schneider (eds.), *Handbook of the Biology of Aging*, 2nd edition. Van Nostrand Reinhold, New York.

Ezzell, C. 1995. Fat times for obesity research: Tons of new information but how does it all fit together? J. NIH Res. 7: 40–43.

Fabian, T. J. and T. E. Johnson. 1995. Identification of genes that are differentially expressed during aging in *Caenorhabditis elegans*. J. Gerontol.: Biol. Sci. 50A: B245–B253.

Fabris, N. and E. Mocchegiani. 1985. Endocrine control of thymic serum factor production in young-adult and old mice. Cellular Immunol. 91: 325.

Fabris, N. and E. Mocchegiani. 1996. Zinc, human diseases and aging. Aging 7: 77–93.

Fabris, N., E. Mocchegiani and M. Provinciali. 1995. Pituitary-thyroid axis and immune system: A reciprocal neuroendocrine-immune interaction. Hormone Res. 43: 29–38.

Farrell, P. M. and J. G. Bieri. 1975. Megavitamin supplementation in man. Am. J. Clin. Nutr. 28: 1381–1386.

Feldman, M. L. 1976. Aging changes in the morphology of cortical dedrites. Pp. 211–246 in R. D. Terry and S. T. Gershon (eds.), *Neurobiology of Aging*. Raven Press, New York.

Fernandes, G. and J. T. Venkatraman. 1994. Effect of food restriction on immunoregulation and aging. Pp. 331–348 in R. Watson (ed.), *Handbook of Nutrition in the Aged*, 2nd edition. CRC Press, Boca Raton, FL.

Feuers, R. J., D. A. Casciano, J. G. Shaddock, J. A. Leakey, P. H. Duffy, R. W. Hart, J. D. Hunter and L. E. Schering. 1991. Modification in regulation of intermediary metabolism by caloric restriction in rodents. Pp. 198–206 in L. Fishbein (ed.), *Biological Effects of Dietary Restriction*. Springer-Verlag, New York.

Feuers, R. J., P. H. Duffy, F. Chen, V. Desai, E. Oriaku, J. G. Shaddock, J. W. Pipkin, R. Weindruch and R. W. Hart. 1995. Intermediary metabolism and antioxidant systems. Pp. 180–195 in R. W. Hart, D. A. Neumann and R. T. Robertson (eds.), *Dietary Restriction: Implications for the Design and Interpretation of Toxicity and Carcinogencity Studies*. ILSI Press, Washington, DC.

Fiatarone, M. A., E. F. O'Neill, N. Doyle, K. M. Clements, S. B. Roberts, J. J. Kehayias, L. A. Lipsitz and W. J. Evans. 1993. The Boston FICSIT study: The effects of resistance training and nutritional supplementation on physical frailty in the oldest old. J. Am. Geriatr. Soc. 41: 333–337.

Finch, C. E. 1987. Neural and endocrine determinants of senescence: Investigation of causality and reversibility by laboratory and clinical interventions. Pp. 261–308 in H. R. Warner, R. N. Butler, R. L. Sprott and E. L. Schneider (eds.), *Modern Biological Theories of Aging* (Aging, vol. 31). Raven Press, New York.

Finch, C. E. 1988. Neural and endocrine approaches to the resolution of time as a dependent variable in the aging processes of mammals. Gerontologist 28: 29–42.

Finch, C. E. 1990. *Longevity, Senescence, and the Genome.* University of Chicago Press, Chicago.

Finch, C. E. and R. G. Gosden. 1986. Animal models for the human menopause. Pp. 3–34 in L. Mastroianni, Jr. and C. A. Paulsen (eds.), *Aging, Reproduction and the Climacteric.* Plenum, New York.

Finch, C. E. and P. W. Landfield. 1985. Neuroendocrine and autonomic function in aging mammals. Pp. 567–594 in C. E. Finch and E. L. Schneider (eds.), *Handbook of the Biology of Aging*, 2nd edition. Van Nostrand Reinhold, New York.

Finch, C. E. and M. C. Pike. 1995. Maximum life span predictions from the Gompertz mortality model. J. Gerontol.: Biol. Sci. 51A: B183–B194.

Finch, C. E. and R. Tanzi. 1997. Genetics of aging. Science 278: 407–411.

Finch, C. E., L. S. Felicio, C. V. Mobbs and J. F. Nelson. 1984. Ovarian and steroidal influences on neuroendocrine aging processes in female rodents. Endocrine Rev. 5: 467–497.

Finch, C. E., M. C. Pike and M. Witten. 1990. Slow mortality rate accelerations during aging in some animals approximate that of humans. Science 249: 902–905.

Fink, L. and F. S. Collins. 1997. The Human Genome Project: View from the National Institutes of Health. J. Am. Med. Womens Assn. 52: 4–7, 15.

Finkel, D., N. L. Pedersen, M. McGue and G. E. McClearn. 1995. Heritability of cognitive abilities in adult twins: Comparison of Minnesota and Swedish data. Behavior Genet. 25: 421–431.

Fisher, R. A. 1930. *The Genetical Theory of Natural Selection.* Clarendon, Oxford.

Fleming, J. E., G. Spicer, R. C. Garrison and M. R. Rose. 1993. Two-dimensional protein electrophoretic analysis of postponed aging in *Drosophila.* Genetica 91: 183–193.

Force, A. G., T. Staples, S. Soliman and R. Arking. 1995. A comparative biochemical and stress analysis of genetically selected *Drosophila* strains with different longevities. Devel. Genet. 17: 340–351.

Fossel, M. 1998. Implications of recent work in telomeres and cell senescence. J. Anti-Aging Med. 1: 39–43.

Frank, L. 1985. Oxygen toxicity in eukaryotes. Pp. 1–44 in L. W. Oberly (ed.), *Superoxide Dismutase*, vol. III. CRC Press, Boca Raton, FL.

Freeman, G. and J. W. Lundelius. 1992. Evolutionary implications of the mode of D quadrant specification in coelomates with spiral cleavage. J. Evol. Biol. 5: 205–247.

Friedman, D. B. and T. E. Johnson. 1988a. A mutation in the *age-1* gene in *Caenorhabditis elegans* lengthens life and reduces hermaphrodite fertility. Genetics 118: 75–86.

Friedman, D. B. and T. E. Johnson. 1988b. Three mutants that extend both mean and maximum life span of the nematode, *Caenorhabditis elegans*, define the *age-1* gene. J. Gerontol.: Biol. Sci. 43: B102–B109.

Fries, J. F. 1980. Aging, natural death, and the compression of mortality. New England J. Med. 303: 130–135.

Fries, J. F. and L. F. Crapo. 1981. *Vitality and Aging: Implications of the Rectangular Curve.* Freeman, San Francisco.

Frolkis, V. V. 1982. *Aging and Life-Prolonging Processes.* Translated from the Russian by Nicholas Bobrov. Springer-Verlag, Vienna.

Fryer, J. H. 1962. Studies of body composition on men aged 60 and over. Pp. 59–78 in N. W. Shock (ed.), *Biological Aspects of Aging.* Columbia University Press, New York.

Frymoyer, J. W. 1986. Musculoskeletal disabilities. Pp. 273–300 in S. J. Brody and G. E. Ruff (eds.), *Aging and Rehabilitation: Advances in the State of the Art.* Springer, New York.

Fujibayashi, Y., A. Waki, K. Wada, M. Ueno, Y. Magata, Y. Yonekura, J. Konishi, T. Takeda and A. Yokoyama. 1994. Differential aging pattern of cerebral accumulation of radiolabeled glucose and amino acid in the senescence accelerated mouse (SAM), a new model for the study of memory impairment. Biol. Pharmacol. Bull. 17: 102–105.

Fukui, H. H., L. Xiu and J. W. Curtsinger. 1993. Slowing of age-specific mortality rates in *Drosophila melanogaster.* Exp. Gerontol. 28: 585–599.

Fulop, T., Jr. and I. Seres. 1994. Age-related changes in signal transduction: Implications for neuronal transmission and potential for drug intervention. Drugs and Aging 5: 366–390.

Furukawa, F., S. Ikehara, R. A. Good, T. Nakamura, S. Inoue, H. Tanaka, S. Imamura and Y. Hamashinma. 1988. Immunological status of nude mice engrafted with allogeneic or syngeneic thymuses. Thymus 12: 11–26.

Furukawa, T. 1994. Assessment of the adequacy of the multiregression method to estimate biological age. Pp. 471–484 in A. K. Balin (ed.), *Practical Handbook of Human Biologic Age Determination.* CRC Press, Boca Raton, FL.

Gadaleta, M. N., G. Rainaldi, A. M. Lezza, F. Milella, F. Fracasso and P. Cantore. 1992. Mitochondrial DNA copy number and mitochondrial DNA deletion in adult and senescent rats. Mutation Res. 275: 181–193.

Gafni, A. and L. Cook. 1988. Protection of rat muscle phosphoglycerate kinase from aging by specific methylation. Gerontologist 28: 229A (abstract).

Gaillard, J-M., D. Allaine, D. Pontier, N. G. Yoccoz and D. E. L. Promislow. 1994. Senescence in natural populations of mammals: A reanalysis. Evolution 48: 509–516.

Gambert, S. R. and D. A. Kassur. 1994. Protein calorie malnutrition in the elderly. Pp. 295–302 in R. Watson (ed.), *Handbook of Nutrition in the Aged*, 2nd edition. CRC Press, Boca Raton, FL.

Ganetzky, B. and J. R. Flanagan. 1978. On the relationship between senescence and age-related changes in two wild-type strains of *Drosophila melanogaster.* Exp. Gerontol. 13: 189–196.

Garen, S. 1975. Bone loss and aging. Pp. 39–58 in R. Goldman (ed.), *The Physiology and Pathology of Human Aging.* Academic Press, New York.

Gavrilov, L. and N. Gavrilova. 1991. *The Biology of Life Span: A Quantitative Approach.* V. P. Skulacher (ed.). Revised and updated English edition, translated from the Russian by John and Liliya Payne. Harwood Academic Publishers, Chur, Switzerland.

Gavrilov, L. and N. Gavrilova. 1997. Parental age at conception and offspring longevity. Rev. Clin. Geron. 7: 5–12.

Gearing, M., S. S. Mirra, J. C. Hedreen, S. M. Sumi, L. A. Hansen and A. Heyman. 1995. The Consortium to Establish a Registry for Alzheimer's Disease (CERAD). Part X. Neuropathology confirmation of the clinical diagnosis of Alzheimer's disease. Neurology 45: 461–466.

Gee, E. M. and J. E. Veevers. 1984. Accelerating sex differentials in mortality: An analysis of contributing factors. Social Biol. 30: 75–85.

Gekakis, N., L. Saez, A. M. Delayaye-Brown, M. P. Myers, A. Sehgal, M. W. Young and C. J. Weitz. 1995. Isolation of timeless by PER protein interaction: Defective interaction between timeless protein and long-period mutant PER^L. Science 270: 811–815.

Gelman, R., A. Watson, R. Bronson and E. Yunis. 1988. Murine chromosomal regions correlated with longevity. Genetics 118: 693–704.

Gensler, H. L. and H. Bernstein. 1981. DNA damage as the primary cause of aging. Quart. Rev. Biol. 56: 279–303.

Gershon, D. 1979. Current status of age altered enzymes: Alternative mechanisms. Mech. Ageing Devel. 9: 189–196.

Gershon, H. and D. Gershon. 1970. Detection of inactive enzyme molecules in ageing organisms. Nature 227: 1214–1217.

Gey, G. O., W. D. Coffman and M. Kubicel. 1952. Tissue culture studies of the proliferative capacity of the cervical carcinoma and normal epithelium. Cancer Res. 12: 264–265.

Gey, G. O., M. Svotelis, M. Foard and F. B. Bang. 1974. Long-term growth of chicken fibroblasts on a collagen substrate. Exp. Cell Res. 84: 63–71.

Ghirardi, O., R. Coxxolino, D. Guaraldi and A. Giuliani. 1995. Within- and between-strain variability in longevity of inbred and outbred rats under the same environmental conditions. Exp. Gerontol. 30: 485–494.

Gilbert, S. F. 1997. *Developmental Biology,* 5th edition. Sinauer Associates, Sunderland, MA.

Giro, M. and J. M. Davidson. 1993. Familial co-segregation of the elastin phenotype in skin fibroblasts from Hutchinson-Gilford progeria. Mech. Ageing Devel. 70: 163–176.

Giubilei, F., R. D'Antona, R. Antonini, G. L. Lenzi, G. Ricci and C. Fieschi. 1990. Serum lipoprotein pattern variations in dementia and ischemic stroke. Acta. Neurol. Scand. 81: 84–86.

Gleeson, M., A. W. Cripps and R. L. Clancy. 1995. Modifiers of the human mucosal immune system. Immunol. Cell Biol. 73: 397–404.

Go, C. G., J. E. Brustrom, M. F. Lynch and C. M. Aldwin. 1995. Ethnic trends in survival curves and mortality. Gerontologist 35: 318–326.

Goldberg, P. B. 1978. Cardiac fuction of Fischer 344 rats in relation to age. Pp. 87–100 in G. Kaldor and W. J. D. Battista (eds.), *Aging in Muscle.* Raven Press, New York.

Goldman, J. E., N. Y. Calingasan and G. E. Gibson. 1994. Aging and the brain. Curr. Opinion Neurol. 7: 287–293.

Goldstein, A. L., G. G. Thurman, T. L. K. Low, G. E. Trivers and J. L. Rossie. 1979. Thymosin: The endocrine thymus and its role in the aging process. Pp. 51–60 in A. Cherkin, C. E. Finch, N. Kharasch, T. Makinodan, F. L. Scott and B. L. Strehler (eds.), *Physiology and Cell Biology of Aging* (Aging, vol. 8). Raven Press, New York.

Goldstein, S. 1971. The role of DNA repair in aging of cultured fibroblasts from xeroderma pigmentosum and normals. Proc. Soc. Exp. Med. 137: 730–734.

Gompertz, B. 1825. On the nature of the function expressive of the law of human mortality and on a new mode of determining the value of life contingencies. Philos. Trans. Royal Soc. London 115: 513–585.

Goodrick, C. L. 1975. Life-span and the inheritance of longevity of inbred mice. J. Gerontol. 30: 257–263.

Goodrick, C. L. 1980. Effects of long-term voluntary wheel exercise on male and female Wistar rats. 1. Longevity, body weight and metabolic rate. Gerontology 26: 22–23.

Gorsky, R. D., E. Pamuk, D. F. Williamson, P. A. Shaffer and J. P. Koplan. 1996. The 25 year health care costs of women who remain overweight after 40 years of age. Am. J. Preventive Med. 12: 388–394.

Gould, S. J. 1981. *The Mismeasure of Man.* Norton, New York.

Goya, L., F. Rivero and A. M. Pascual-Leone. 1995. Stress, glucocorticoids and aging. Pp. 249–266 in P. S. Timiras, W. D. Quay and A. Vernadakis (eds.), *Hormones and Aging.* CRC Press, Boca Raton, FL.

Grady, C. L. 1996. Age-related changes in cortical blood flow activation during perception and memory. Ann. N.Y. Acad. Sci. 777: 14–21.

Grady, C. L., J. M. Maisog, B. Horwitz, L. G. Ungerleider, M. J. Mentis, J. A. Salerno, P. Pietrini, E. Wagner and J. V. Haxby. 1994. Age-related changes in cortical blood flow activation during visual processing of faces and location. J. Neurosci. 14: 1450–1462.

Graf, J-D. and F. J. Ayala, 1986. Genetic variation for superoxide dismutase level in *Drosophila melanogaster.* Biochem. Genet. 24: 153–168.

Graham, C. F. and P. F. Wareing. 1984. *Developmental Control in Animals and Plants,* 2nd edition. Blackwell, Oxford.

Graves, J. L., Jr. and L. D. Mueller. 1995. Population density effects on longevity revisited. Genetica 96: 183–186.

Graves, J. L., E. C. Toolson, C. Jeung, L. N. Vu and M. R. Rose. 1992. Dessication, flight, glycogen, and postponed senescence in *Drosophila melanogaster.* Physiol. Zool. 65: 268–286.

Greenblatt, D. J., M. D. Allen and R. I. Shader. 1977. Toxicity of high-dose fluorazepam in the elderly. Clin. Pharmacol. Ther. 21: 355–361.

Gregerman, R. I. 1967. The age-related alteration of thyroid function and thyroid hormone metabolism. Pp. 161–173 in L. Girtman (ed.), *Endocrines and Aging.* Charles C. Thomas, Springfield, IL.

Grell, K. G. 1973. *Protozoology*. Springer-Verlag, New York.

Griffiths, A. J. F. 1992. Fungal senescence. Annu. Rev. Genet. 26: 351–372.

Guiamet, J. J., E. Pichesky and L. D. Nooden. 1995. Senescence-inhibiting effects of the stay-green gene *cytG* in soybean. Plant Physiol. 108: 121 (abstract).

Guralnik, J. M. and G. A. Kaplan. 1989. Predictors of healthy aging: Prospective evidence from the Alameda County study. Am. J. Public Health 79: 703–708.

Guralnik, J. M. and E. M. Simonsick. 1993. Physical disability in older Americans. J. Gerontol. 48: 3–10.

Gutmann, E. and V. Hanzlikova. 1972. *Age Changes in the Neuromuscular System*. Scientechnia, Bristol, England.

Guyton, A. C. 1966. *Textbook of Medical Physiology*, 3rd edition. Saunders, Philadelphia.

Hadorn, E. 1978. Transdetermination. Pp. 556–617 in M. Ashburner and T. R. F. Wright (eds.), *The Genetics and Biology of Drosophila*, vol. 2C. Academic Press, London.

Hagen, G. and G. Kochert. 1980. Protein syntheis in a new system for the study of senescence. Exp. Cell Res. 127: 451–457.

Hakim, A. A., H. Petrovich, C. M. Burchfiel, G. W. Ross, B. L. Rodriguez, L. R. White, K. Yano, J. D. Curb and R. D. Abbott. 1998. Effects of walking on mortality among nonsmoking retired men. New England J. Med. 338: 94–99.

Halaas, J. L., K. S. Gajiwala, M. Maffei, S. L. Cohen, B. T. Chait, D. Rabinowitz, R. L. Lallone, S. K. Burney and J. M. Friedman. 1995. Weight reducing effects of the plasma protein encoded by the obese gene. Science 269: 543–546.

Haldane, J. B. S. 1927. A mathematical theory of natural and artificial selection, part IV. Proc. Cambridge Philos. Soc. 23: 607–615.

Hall, G. S. 1922. *Senescence: The Last Half of Life*. Appleton, London.

Halliwell, B. and J. M. C. Gutteridge. 1989. *Free Radicals in Biology and Medicine*, 2nd edition. Clarendon Press, Oxford.

Halter, J. B. 1995. Carbohydrate metabolism. Pp. 119–146 in E. J. Masoro (ed.), *Handbook of Physiology: Section 11: Aging*. Oxford University Press, New York.

Ham, R. G. and M. J. Veomett. 1980. *Mechanisms of Development*. C. V. Mosby, St. Louis.

Hamilton, J. B. and G. E. Mestler. 1969. A comparison of eunuchs with intact men and women in a mentally retarded population. J. Gerontol. 24: 395–411.

Hanawalt, P. C. 1987. On the role of DNA damage and repair processes in aging: Evidence for and against. Pp. 183–198 in H. R. Warner, R. N. Butler, R. L. Sprott and E. L. Schneider (eds.), *Modern Biological Theories of Aging* (Aging, vol. 31). Raven Press, New York.

Hangartner, J. R. M., N. J. Marley, A. Whitehead, A. C. Thomas and M. I. Davies. 1985. The assessment of cardiac hypertrophy at autopsy. Histopathology 9: 1295–1306.

Hardt, H. and M. Rothstein. 1985. Altered phosphoglycerate kinase from old rat muscle shows no change in primary structure. Biochim. Biophys. Acta 831: 13–21.

Hari, R. V. Burde and R. Arking. 1998. Immunological confirmation of elevated levels of CuZn superoxide dismutase protein in an artificially selected long-lived strain of *Drosophila melanogaster*. Exp. Gerontol. 33: 227–238.

Harley, C. A., A. B. Futcher and C. W. Greider. 1990. Telomeres shorted during ageing of human fibroblasts. Nature 345: 458–460.

Harley, C. A., H. Vaziri, C. M. Counter and R. C. Allsopp. 1992. The telomere hypothesis of cellular aging. Exp. Gerontol. 27: 375–382.

Harman, D. 1956. Aging: A theory based on free radical and radiation chemistry. J. Gerontol. 11: 298–300.

Harris, R. E. and R. P. Forsythe. 1973. Personality and emotional stress in essential hypertension in man. Pp. 125–132 in G. Onesta, K. E. Kim and J. H. Meyer (eds.), *Hypertension: Mechanisms and Management*. Grune and Stratton, New York.

Harris, S. B., R. Weindruch, G. S. Smith, M. R. Mickey and R. L. Walford. 1990. Dietary restriction alone and in combination with oral ethoxyquin/2-mercaptoethylamine in mice. J. Gerontol.: Biol. Sci. 45: B141–B147.

Harrison, D. 1982. Must we grow old? Biol. Digest 8: 11–25.

Harrison, D. 1985. Cell and tissue transplantation: A means of studying the aging process. Pp. 322–356 in C. E. Finch and E. L. Schneider (eds.), *Handbook of the Biology of Aging*, 2nd edition. Van Nostrand Reinhold, New York.

Harrison, D. E. 1994. Potential misinterpretations using models of accelerated aging. J. Gerontol.: Biol. Sci. 49: B245.

Harrison, D. E. and J. R. Archer. 1987. Genetic differences in effects of food restriction on aging in mice. J. Nutr. 117: 376–382.

Harrison, D. E. and T. Roderick. 1997. Selection for maximum longevity in mice. Exp. Gerontol. 32: 65–78.

Harrison, D. E., Jr., J. R. Archer, G. A. Sacher and F. M. Boyce III. 1978. Tail collagen aging in mice of thirteen different genotypes and two species: Relationship to biological age. Exp. Gerontol. 13: 63–73.

Harrison, D. E., J. R. Archer and C. M. Astle. 1982. The effect of hypophysectomy on thymic aging in mice. J. Immunol. 136: 2673.

Harrison, D. E., J. R. Archer and C. M. Astle. 1984. Effects of food restriction on aging: Segregation of food intake and adiposity. Proc. Natl. Acad. Sci. USA 81: 1835–1838.

Harrison, R. G. 1910. The outgrowth of the nerve fiber as a mode of protoplasmic movement. J. Exp. Zool. 9: 787–848.

Hart, R. and R. B. Setlow. 1974. Correlation between deoxyribonucleic acid excision-repair and life-span in a number of mammalian species. Proc. Nat. Acad. Sci. USA 71: 2169–2173.

Hart, R. W. and A. Turturro. 1983. Theories of aging. Pp. 5–18 in M. Rothstein (ed.), *Review of Biological Research in Aging*, vol. 1. Alan R. Liss, New York.

Hart, R. W., D. A. Neumann and R. T. Robertson (eds.). 1995. *Dietary Restriction: Implications for the Design and Interpretation of Toxicity and Carcinogenicity Studies*. ILSI Press, Washington, DC.

Hartman, P. E. and R. W. Morgan. 1985. Mutagen-induced focal lesions as key factors in aging: A review. Pp. 93–136 in R. S. Sohal, L. S. Birnbaum and R. G. Cutler (eds.), *Molecular Biology of Aging: Gene Stability and Gene Expression*. Raven Press, New York.

Hartman, P., E. Childress and T. Beyer. 1995. Nematode development is inhibited by methyl viologen and high oxygen concentrations at a rate inversely proportional to life span. J. Gerontol.: Biol. Sci. 50A: B322–B326.

Hartung, G. H., E. J. Farge and R. E. Mitchell. 1981. Effects of marathon running, jogging and diet on coronary risk factors in middle-aged men. Preventive Med. 10: 316–323.

Hartwell, L. H. and M. B. Kastan. 1994. Cell cycle control and cancer. Science 266: 1821–1828.

Harvell, C. D. and R. K. Grossberg. 1988. The timing of sexual maturity in clonal animals. Ecology 69: 1855–1864.

Hass, B. S. et al. 1996. Dietary restriction in humans: Report on the Little Rock Conference on the value, feasibility and parameters of a proposed study. Mech. Ageing Devel. 91: 79–94.

Hausman, P. B. and M. E. Weksler. 1985. Changes in the immune response with age. Pp. 414–432 in C. E. Finch and E. L. Schneider (eds.), *Handbook of the Biology of Aging*, 2nd edition. Van Nostrand Reinhold, New York.

Hayflick, L. 1965. The limited *in vitro* lifetime of human diploid cell strains. Exp. Cell Res. 37: 614–636.

Hayflick, L. 1977. The cellular basis for biological aging. Pp. 159–188 in C. E. Finch and L. Hayflick (eds.), *Handbook of the Biology of Aging*. Van Nostrand Reinhold, New York.

Hayflick, L. 1982. Biological aspects of human aging. Brit. J. Hospital Med. 27: 366.

Hayflick, L. 1985. Theories of biological aging. Exp. Gerontol. 20: 145–159.

Hayflick, L. 1987. Origins of longevity. Pp. 21–31 in H. R. Warner, R. N. Butler, R. L. Sprott and E. L. Schneider (eds.), *Modern Biological Theories of Aging* (Aging, vol. 31). Raven Press, New York.

Hayflick, L. and P. S. Moorhead. 1961. The limited in vitro lifetime of human diploid cell strains. Exp. Cell Res. 25: 585–621.

Hazzard, D. G. and J. Soban. 1988. Studies of aging using genetically defined rodents: A bibliography. Exp. Aging Res. 14: 59–81.

Hazzard, W. R. 1986a. Aging, lipoprotein metabolism and atherosclerosis: A clinical conundrum. Pp. 75–103 in S. R. Bates and E. C. Gangloff (eds.), *Atherogenesis and Aging*. Springer-Verlag, New York.

Hazzard, W. R. 1986b. Biological basis of the sex differential in longevity. J. Am. Geriatr. Soc. 34: 455–471.

Heikkinen, E., H. Suominen, P. Era and A-L. Lyyra. 1994. Variations in aging parameters, their sources and possibilities of predicting physiological age. Pp. 71–92 in A. K. Balin (ed.), *Practical Handbook of Human Biologic Age Determination*. CRC Press, Boca Raton, FL.

Hekimi, S., P. Boutis and B. Lakowski. 1995. Viable maternal-effect mutations that affect the development of the nematode *Caenorhabditis elegans*. Genetics 141: 1351–1364.

Helfand, S. L., K. J. Blake, B. Rogina, M. D. Stracks, A. Centurion and B. Naprta. 1995. Temporal patterns of gene expression in the antenna of the adult *Drosophila melanogaster*. Genetics 140: 549–555.

Hermanns, J. and H. D. Osiewacz. 1995. Evidence for a life span prolonging effect of a linear plasmid in a longevity mutant of *Podospora anserina*. Mol. General Genet. 243: 297–305.

Herrero, A. and G. Barja. 1997a. ADP-regulation of mitochondrial free radical production is different with complex I- or complex II-linked substrates: Implications for the exercise paradox and brain hypermetabolism. J. Bioenergetics Biomembranes 29: 241–249.

Herrero, A. and G. Barja. 1997b. Sites and mechanisms responsible for the low rate of free radical production of heart mitochondria in the long-lived pigeon. Mech. Ageing Devel. 92: 95–111.

Hershcopf, R. J., D. Elahi, R. Andres, H. L. Baldwin, G. S. Raizes, D. D. Schocken and N. W. Shock. 1982. Longitudinal changes in serum cholesterol in man: An epidemiologic search for etiology. J. Chronic Diseases 35: 101–114.

Heydari, A. R. and A. Richardson. 1992. Does gene expression play any role in the mechanism of the antiaging effect of dietary restriction? Ann. N.Y. Acad. Sci. 663: 384–395.

Heydari, A. R., B. Wu, R. Takahashi, R. Strong and A. Richardson. 1993. Expression of heat shock protein 70 is altered by age and diet at the level of transcription. Mol. Cellular Biol. 13: 2909–2918.

Higami, Y., B. P. Yu, I. Shimokawa, E. J. Masoro and T. Ikeda. 1994. Duration of dietary restriction: An important determinant for the incidence and age of onset of leukemia in male F344 rats. J. Gerontol.: Biol. Sci. 49: B239–B244.

Higami, Y., B. P. Yu, I. Shimokawa, H. Bertrand, G. B. Hubbard and E. J. Masoro. 1995. Anti-tumor action of dietary restriction is lesion dependent in male Fischer 344 rats. J. Gerontol.: Biol. Sci. 50A: B72–B77.

Himes, C. L. 1994. Age patterns of mortality and cause-of-death structures in Sweden, Japan and the United States. Demography 31: 633–650.

Hirano, T., R. Yamaguchi, S. Asami, N. Iwamoto and H. Kasai. 1996. 8-hydroxyguanine levels in nuclear DNA and its repair in rat organs associated with age. J. Gerontol.: Biol. Sci. 51A: B303–B307.

Hirsch, H. R., J. A. Coomes and M. Witten. 1989. The waste-product theory of aging: transformation to unlimited growth in cell cultures. Exp. Gerontol. 24: 97–112.

Hochschild, R. 1989. Improving the precision of biological age determinations. II. Automatic human tests, age norms and variability. Exp. Gerontol. 24: 301–316.

Hochschild, R. 1994. Validating biomarkers of aging—mathematical approaches and results of a 2462 person study. Pp. 93–144 in A. K. Balin (ed.), *Practical Handbook of Human Biologic Age Determination*. CRC Press, Boca Raton, FL.

Hodgkin, J. 1989. Early worms. Genetics 121: 1–3.

Hoff, S. F., S. W. Scheff, L. S. Bernardo and C. W. Cotman. 1982. Lesion induced synaptogenesis in the dendate gyrus of aged rats. I. Loss and reacquisition of normal synaptic density. J. Comp. Neurol. 205: 246–252.

Hoffmann, A. and P. Parsons. 1989. Selection for increased desiccation resistance in *Drosophila melanogaster*. Additive genetic control and correlated responses for other stresses. Genetics 122: 837–845.

Hofman, M. A. 1983. Energy metabolism, brain size and longevity in mammals. Quart. Rev. Biol. 58: 495–512.

Holden, C. 1987a. The genetics of personality. Science 237: 598–601.

Holden, C. 1987b. Why do women live longer than men? Science 238: 158–160.

Holliday, R. 1984. The unsolved problem of cellular ageing. Monogr. Devel. Biol. 17: 60–77.

Holliday, R. 1989. Food, reproduction and longevity: Is the extended longevity of calorie-restricted animals an evolutionary adaptation. BioEssays 10: 125–127.

Holliday, R. 1990. The limited proliferation of cultured human diploid cells: Regulation or senescence? J. Gerontol.: Biol. Sci. 45: B36–B41.

Holliday, R. 1994. Longevity and fecundity in eutherian mammals. Pp. 217–225 in M. R. Rose and C. E. Finch (eds.), *Genetics and Evolution of Aging*. Kluwer, Dordrecht, The Netherlands.

Holliday, R. 1995. *Understanding Ageing*. Cambridge University Press, Cambridge.

Holliday, R. 1996a. The evolution of human longevity. Perspect. Biol. Med. 40: 100–107.

Holliday, R. 1996b. The urgency of research on ageing. BioEssays 18: 89–90.

Holliday, R. and T. B. L. Kirkwood. 1981. Predictions of the somatic mutation and mortalization theories of cellular ageing are contrary to experimental observations. J. Theoret. Biol. 93: 627–642.

Holliday, R., L. I. Huschtscha, G. M. Tarrant and T. B. L. Kirkwood. 1977. Testing the commitment theory of cellular aging. Science 198: 366–372.

Holloszy, J. O. 1993. Exercise increases average longevity of female rats despite increased food intake and no growth retardation. J. Gerontol.: Biol. Sci. 48: B97–B100.

Holloszy, J. O. and W. M. Kohrt. 1995. Exercise. Pp. 633–666 in E. J. Masoro (ed.), *Handbook of Physiology. Section 11: Aging*. Oxford University Press, New York.

Holmes, D. J. and S. N. Austad. 1995a. Birds as animal models for the comparative biology of aging: A prospectus. J. Geontol.: Biol. Sci. 50A: B59–B66.

Holmes, D. J. and S. N. Austad. 1995b. The evolution of avian senescence patterns: Implications for understanding primary aging processes. Am. Zool. 35: 307–317.

Holmes, G. E. and N. R. Holmes. 1986. Accumulation of DNA changes in aging *Paramecium tetraurelia*. Mol. General Genet. 204: 108–114.

Hopkin, K. 1995. Chromosome 21 genes in Down syndrome and development. J. NIH Res. 7: 29–30.

Horowitz, M. C. 1993. Cytokines and estrogen in bone: Anti-osteoporotic effects. Science 260: 626–627.

Horton, D. L. 1967. The effect of age on hair growth in the CBA mouse: Observations on transplanted skin. J. Gerontol. 22: 43–46.

Horvath, S. M. 1981. Aging and adaption to stressors. Pp. 437–451 in S. M. Horvath and M. K. Yousef (eds.), *Environmental Physiology: Aging, Heat and Altitide*. Elsevier/North Holland, New York.

House, J. S., K. R. Landis and U. Umberson. 1988. Social relationships and health. Science 241: 540–545.

Hovemann, B., S. Richter, U. Walldorf and C. Cziepluch. 1988. Two genes encode related cytoplasmic elongation factors (EF-1 alpha) in *Drosophila melanogaster* with

continuous and stage specific expression. Nucleic Acids Res. 16: 3175–3194.

Hsiao, K., P. Chapman, S. Nilsen, C. Eckman, Y. Harigaya, S. Younkin, F. Yang and G. Cole. 1996. Correlative memory deficits, Abeta elevation, and amyloid plaques in transgenic mice. Science 274: 99–102.

Hughes, A. L. and M. K. Hughes. 1995. Small genomes for better flyers. Nature 377: 391.

Hutchinson, E. W. and M. R. Rose. 1991. Quantitative genetics of postponed aging in *Drosophila melanogaster*. I. Analysis of outbred populations. Genetics 127: 719–727.

Hutchinson, E. W., A. J. Shaw and M. R. Rose. 1991. Quantitative genetics of postponed aging in *Drosophila melanogaster*. II. Analysis of selected lines. Genetics 127: 729–737.

Ikari, H., L. Zhang, J. M. Chernak, A. Mastrangeli, S. Kato, H. Kuo, R. G. Crystal, D. K. Ingram and G. S. Roth. 1995. Adenovirus-mediated gene transfer of dopamine D2 receptor cDNA into rat striatum. Mol. Brain Res. 34: 315–320.

Ikehara, S., J. Shimiu, R. Yasumizu, T. Nakamura, M. Inaba, S. Inoue, N. Oyaizu, K. Sugiura, M. M. Oo, Y. Hamashima and R. Good. 1987. Thymic rudiments are responsible for induction of functional T cells in *nu/nu* mice. Thymus 10: 193–205.

Ingram, D. K. and M. A. Reynolds. 1987. The relationship of body weight to longevity within laboratory rodent species. Pp. 247–282 in A. D. Woodhead and K. H. Thompson (eds.), *Evolution of Longevity in Animals: A Comparative Approach*. Plenum, New York.

Ingram, D. K., R. Weindruch, L. E. Spangler, J. R. Freeman and R. L. Walford. 1987. Dietary restriction benefits learning and motor performance of aged mice. J. Gerontol. 42: 78–81.

Ingram, D. K., R. G. Cutler, R. Weindruch, D. M. Renquist, J. J. Knapka, M. April, C. T. Belcher, M. A. Clark, C. D. Hatcherson, B. M. Marriott and G. S. Roth. 1990. Dietary restriction and aging: The initiation of a primate study. J. Gerontol.: Biol. Sci. 45: B148–B163.

Ingram, D. K., S. Stoll and G. T. Baker III. 1995. Is attempting to assess biological age worth the effort? Gerontologist 35: 707–710 (book review).

Inokuchi, S., H. Ishikawa, S. Iwamoto and T. Kimura. 1975. Age related changes in the histological composition of the rectus abdominis muscle of the adult human. Human Biol. 47: 231–249.

Iovino, M., P. Monteleone and L. Steardo. 1989. Repetitive growth hormone releasing hormone administration restores the attenuated growth hormone (GH) response to GH-releasing hormone testing in normal aging. J. Clin. Endocrinol. Metab. 69: 910–913.

Ivanova, R. N. Henon, V. Lepage, D. Charron, E. Vincent and F. Schachter. 1998. HLA-DR alleles display sex-dependent effects on survival and discriminate between individual and familial longevity. Human Mol. Genet. 7: 187–194.

Iwasaki, K., C. A. Gleiser, E. J. Masoro, A. McMahan, E. J. Seo and B. P. Yu. 1988. The influence of dietary protein source on longevity and age related disease processes of Fischer rats. J. Gerontol.: Biol. Sci. 43: B5–B12.

Iwase, M., M. Wada, N. Shinohara, H. Yoshizumi, M. Yoshinari and M. Fujishima. 1995. Effect of maternal diabetes on longevity in offspring of spontaneously hypertensive rats. Gerontology 41: 181–186.

Jacob, F. 1982. *The Possible and the Actual.* Pantheon, New York.

Jacobs, B., M. Schall and A. B. Scheibel. 1993. A quantitative dendritic analysis of Wernicke's in humans. II. Gender, hemispheric and environmental factors. J. Comp. Neurol. 327: 97–111.

Jacobs, P. A. and W. M. Court-Brown. 1966. Age and chromosomes. Nature 212: 823.

Jalavisto, E. 1951. Inheritance of longevity according to Finnish and Swedish genealogies. Ann. Med. Internae. Fenniae 40: 263–274.

Jarvik, L. F. 1979. Genetic aspects of aging. Pp. 86–109 in I. Rossman (ed.), *Clinical Geriatrics*, 2nd edition. Lippincott, Philadelphia.

Jarvik, L. F. 1988. Aging of the brain: How can we prevent it. Gerontologist 28: 739–747.

Jazwinski, S. M. 1993. The genetics of aging in the yeast *Saccharomyces cerevisiae*. Genetica 91: 35–51.

Jazwinski, S. M. 1996. Longevity, genes and aging. Science 273: 55–59.

Jazwinski, S. M., N. K. Egilmez and J. B. Chen. 1989. Replication control and cellular life span. Exp. Gerontol. 24: 423–436.

Jazwinski, S. M., B. H. Howard and R. K. Nayak. 1995. Cell cycle progression, aging and cell death. J. Gerontol.: Biol. Sci. 50A: B1–B8.

Jernigan, T. L., L. M. Zatz, I. Feinberg and G. Fein. 1980. The measurement of cerebral atrophy in the aged by computed tomography. Pp. 86–96 in L. Poon (ed.), *Aging in the 1980's*. APA Press, Washington, DC.

Johnson, S. A. and C. E. Finch. 1996. Changes in gene expression during brain aging: A survey. Pp. 300–327 in E. L. Schneider and J. W. Rowe (eds.), *Handbook of the Biology of Aging*, 4th edition. Academic Press, San Diego.

Johnson, T. E. 1987. Aging can be genetically dissected into component processes using long lived lines of *Caenorhabditis elegans*. Proc. Natl. Acad. Sci USA 84: 3777–3781.

Johnson, T. E. 1988. Genetic specification of lifespan: Process, problems and potentials. J. Gerontol.: Biol. Sci. 43: B87–B92.

Johnson, T. E. and W. G. Wood. 1982. Genetic analysis of life span in *Caenorhabditis elegans*. Proc. Natl. Acad. Sci. USA 79: 6603–6607.

Johnson, T. E., P. M. Tedesco and G. J. Lithgow. 1993. Comparing mutants, selective breeding and transgenics in the dissection of aging processes of *Caenorhabditis elegans*. Genetica 91: 65–78.

Jones, H. B. 1959. The relation of human health to age, place, and time. Pp. 336–363 in J. E. Birron (ed.), *Handbook of Aging and the Individual*. University of Chicago Press, Chicago.

Jost, B. C. and G. T. Grossberg. 1995. The natural history of Alzheimer's Disease: A Brain Bank study. J. Am. Geriatr. Soc. 43: 1248–1255.

Julius, M. and C. M. Lang. 1988. Blood glutathione levels reflect subjective and objective health status in Southfield elderly. Gerontologist 28: 228A (abstract).

Kadenbach, B., C. Munscher, V. Frank, J. Muller-Hocker and J. Naplwotzki. 1995. Human aging is associated with stochastic somatic mutations of mitochondrial DNA. Mutation Res. 338: 161–172.

Kaiser, M., M. Gasser, R. Ackermann and S. C. Stearns. 1997. P-element inserts in transgenic flies: A cautionary tale. Heredity 78: 1–11.

Kakkar, R., J. S. Bains and S. P. Sharma. 1996. Effect of vitamin E on life span, malondialdehyde content and antioxidant enzymes in aging *Zaprionus paravittiger*. Gerontology 42: 312–321.

Kale, S. P. and S. M. Jazwinski. 1996. Differential response to UV stress and DNA damage during the yeast replicative life span. Devel. Genet. 18: 154–160.

Kallman, F. J. 1957. Twin data on the genetics of aging. Pp. 131–143 in G. E. Wolstenholme and C. M. O'Connor (eds.), *Methodology of the Study of Aging*. Little Brown, Boston.

Kamboh, M. I. 1995. Apolipoprotein E polymorphism and susceptibility to Alzheimer's disease. Human Biol. 67: 195–215.

Kannel, W. B. and H. Hubert. 1982. Vital capacity as a biomarker of aging. Pp. 145–160 in M. E. Reff and E. L. Schneider (eds.), *Biological Markers of Aging*. NIH Publ. No. 82-2221, Washington, DC.

Kannisto, V., J. Lauritsen, A. R. Thatcher and J. W. Vaupel. 1994. Reductions in mortality at advanced ages: Several decades of evidence from 27 countries. Pop. Devel. Rev. 4: 793–810.

Kappus, H. 1985. Lipid peroxidation. Pp. 152–195 in H. Sies (ed.), *Oxidative Stress*. Academic Press, New York.

Katchaturian, Z. S. and T. S. Radebaugh. 1996a. *Alzheimer's Disease: Cause(s), Diagnosis, Treatment, and Care*. CRC Press, Boca Raton, FL.

Katchaturian, Z. S. and T. S. Radebaugh. 1996b. A synthesis of critical topics in Alzheimer's disease. Pp. 3–14 in Z. S. Katchaturian and T. S. Radebaugh (eds.), *Alzheimer's Disease: Cause(s), Diagnosis, Treatment, and Care*. CRC Press, Boca Raton, FL.

Kato, H., M. Harada, K. Tsuchiya and K. Miriwaki. 1980. Absence of correlation between DNA repair in ultraviolet irradiated mammalian cells and life span of the donor species. Jap. J. Genet. 55: 99–108.

Kato, S., H. Endoh, Y. Masuhiro, T. Kitamoto, S. Uchiyama, H. Sasaki, S. Masushige, Y. Gotoh, E. Nishida, H. Kawashima, D. Metzger and P. Chambon. 1995. Activation of the estrogen receptor through phosphorylation by mitogen-activated protein kinase. Science 270: 1491–1494.

Kator, K., V. Cristofalo, R. Charpentier and R. G. Cutler. 1985. Dysdifferentiative nature of aging: Passage number dependency of globin gene expression in normal human diploid cells grown in tissue culture. Gerontology 31: 355–361.

Katz, M. L., W. G. Robison, R. K. Herrmann, A. B. Groone and J. G. Bieri. 1984. Lipofucsin accumulation resulting from senescence and vitamin E deficiency: Special properties and tissue distribution. Mech. Ageing Devel. 25: 149–159.

Kay, M. M. B. 1985. Aging of cell membrane molecules leads to appearance of an aging antigen and removal of senescent cells. Gerontology 31: 215–235.

Kay, M. M. and J. Goodman. 1997. Brain and erythrocyte anion transporter protein, band 3, as a marker for Alzheimer's disease: Structural changes detected by electron microscopy, phosphorylation, and antibodies. Gerontology 43: 44–66.

Kay, M. M., T. Wyant and J. Goodman. 1994. Autoantibodies to band 3 during aging and disease and aging interventions. Ann. N.Y. Acad. Sci. 719: 419–447.

Kay, M. M., C. Cover, S. F. Schluter, R. M. Bernstein and J. J. Marchalonis. 1995. Band 3, the anion transporter, is conserved during evolution: Implications for aging and vertebrate evolution. Cellular Mol. Biol. 41: 833–842.

Kay, S. A. and A. J. Millar. 1995. New models in vogue for circadian clocks. Cell 83: 361–364.

Kemnitz, J. W., R. Weindruch, E. B. Roecker, K. Crawford, P. L. Kaufmann and W. B. Ershler. 1993. Dietary restriciton of adult male rhesus monkeys: Findings from the first year of study. J. Gerontol.: Biol. Sci. 48: B17–B26.

Kennedy, B. K., N. R. Austriaco, Jr., J. Zhang and L. Guarente. 1995. Mutation in the silencing gene *SIR4* can delay aging in *S. cerevisiae*. Cell 80: 485–496.

Kenyon, C., J. Chang, E. Gensch, A. Rudner and R. Tabtiang. 1993. A *C. elegans* mutant that lives twice as long as wild type. Nature 366: 461–464.

Kerr, J. F. R., J. Searle, B. V. Harman and C. J. Bishop. 1987. Apoptosis. Pp. 93–128 in C. S. Potten (ed.), *Perspectives on Mammalian Cell Death*. Oxford University Press, Oxford.

Kerwin, J. M., C. M. Morris, M. Johnson, R. H. Perry and E. K. Perry. 1993. Hippocampal p75 nerve growth factor receptor immunoreactivity in development, normal aging and senescence. Acta Anatomica 147: 216–222.

Kevles, D. J. and L. Hood. 1992. *The Code of Codes: Scientific and Social Issues in the Human Genome Project*. Harvard University Press, Cambridge, MA.

Kibler, K. H. and H. D. Johnson. 1961. Metabolic rate and aging in rats during exposure to cold. J. Gerontol. 16: 13–19.

Kim, N. W., M. Platyszek, K. R. Prowse, C. B. Harley, M. D. West, P. L. C. Ho, G. M. Coviello, W. E. Wright, S. L. Weinrich and J. W. Shay. 1994. Specific association of human telomerase activity with immortal cells and cancer. Science 266: 2011–2015.

Kirby, G. C. 1974. Greying with age: A coat-color variant in wild Australian populations of mice. J. Heredity 65: 126–128.

Kirk, D. L. 1988. The ontogeny and phylogeny of cellular differentiation in *Volvox*. Trends Genet. 4: 32–36.

Kirk, M. M., A. Ransick, S. E. McCrae and D. L. Kirk. 1993. The relationship between cell size and cell fate in *Volvox carteri*. J. Cell Biol. 123: 191–208.

Kirkwood, T. B. L. 1985. Comparative and evolutionary aspects of longevity. Pp. 27–44 in C. E. Finch and E. L. Schneider (eds.), *Handbook of the Biology of Aging*, 2nd edition. Van Nostrand Reinhold, New York.

Kirkwood, T. B. L. 1987. Immortality of the germ-line versus disposability of the soma. Pp. 209–218 in A. D. Woodhead and K. H. Thompson (eds.), *Evolution of Longevity in Animals: A Comparative Approach*. Plenum, New York.

Kitado, H., K. Higuchi and T. Takeda. 1994a. Molecular genetic characterization of the senescence-accelerated mouse (SAM) strains. J. Gerontol.: Biol. Sci. 49: B247–B254.

Kitado, H., K. Higuchi and T. Takeda. 1994b. Response to guest editorial. J. Gerontol.: Biol. Sci. 49: B245–B246.

Klebba-Goodman, A. A. 1986. Osteoporosis. Unpublished essay, Wayne State University, Detroit, MI.

Kligman, A. M., G. L. Grove and A. K. Balin. 1985. Aging of human skin. Pp. 820–841 in C. E. Finch and E. L. Schneider (eds.), *Handbook of the Biology of Aging*, 2nd edition. Van Nostrand Reinhold, New York.

Klocke, R. A. 1977. Influence of aging on the lung. Pp. 432–444 in C. E. Finch and L. Hayflick (eds.), *Handbook of the Biology of Aging*. Van Nostrand Reinhold, New York.

Koenig, H. L., M. Schumacker, B. Ferzaz, A. N. D. Thi, A. Ressouches, R. Guennoun, I. Jung-Testas, R. Robel, Y. Akwa and E-E. Baulieu. 1995. Progesterone synthesis and myelin formation by Schwann cells. Science 268: 1500–1503.

Kohn, R. R. 1977. Heart and cardiovascular system. Pp. 281–317 in C. E. Finch and L. Hayflick (eds.), *Handbook of the Biology of Aging*. Van Nostrand Reinhold, New York.

Kohn, R. R. 1978. *Principles of Mammalian Aging*, 2nd edition. Prentice-Hall, Englewood Cliffs, NJ.

Korenman, S. 1982. Introduction. Pp. 1–8 in L. V. Avidi and S. G. Korenman (eds.), *Endocrine Aspects of Aging*. Elsevier, New York.

Kormondy, E. J. 1969. *Concepts of Ecology*. Prentice-Hall, Englewood Cliffs, NJ.

Kowald, A. and T. B. Kirkwood. 1994. Towards a network theory of ageing: A model combining the free radical theory and the protein error theory. J. Theoret. Biol. 168: 75–94.

Kowald, A. and T. B. Kirkwood. 1996. A network theory of ageing: The interactions of defective mitochondria, aberrant proteins, free radicals and scavengers in the ageing process. Mutation Res. 316: 209–236.

Kreil, G. 1994. Conversion of L- to D-amino acid: A post-translational reaction. Science 266: 996–997.

Kristal, B. S. and B. P. Yu. 1992. An emerging hypothesis: Synergistic induction of aging by free radicals and Millard reactions. J. Gerontol.: Biol. Sci. 47: B107–B114.

Krohn, P. L. 1966. Transplantation and aging. Pp. 125–138 in P. L. Krohn (ed.), *Topics of the Biology of Aging*. Wiley, New York.

Kruk, P. A., A. S. Balajee, K. S. Rao and V. A. Bohr. 1996. Telomere reduction and telomerase inactivation during neuronal cell differentiation. BBRC 224: 487–492.

Kuck, U., H. D. Osiewacz, U. Schmidt, B. Kappelhoff, E. Schulte, U. Stahl and K. Esser. The onset of senescence is affected by DNA rearrangements of a discontinuous mitochondrial gene in *Podospora anserina*. Curr. Genet. 9: 373–382.

Lack D. 1943. The age of some more British birds. Brit. Birds 36: 193–197.

Lakatta, E. G. 1985. Heart and circulation. Pp. 377–413 in C. E. Finch and E. L. Schneider (eds.), *Handbook of the Bi-*

ology of Aging, 2nd edition. Van Nostrand Reinhold, New York.

Lakowski, B. and S. Hekimi. 1996. Determination of life-span in *Caenorhabditis elegans* by four clock genes. Science 272: 1010–1013.

La Marche, V. C. 1969. Environment in relation to age of bristlecone pines. Ecology 50: 53–59.

Lamb, M. J. 1977. *Biology of Ageing*. Halsted (Wiley), New York.

Lamb, M. J. 1978. Ageing. Pp. 43–104 in M. Ashburner and T. R. F. Wright (eds.), *The Genetics and Biology of Drosophila*, vol. 2c. Academic Press, London.

Landfield, P. W., S. K. Sundberg, M. Smith, J. C. Eldridge and M. Morris. 1980. Mammalian aging: Theoretical implications of changes in brain and endocrine systems during mid and late life. Peptides 1(suppl. 1): 185–196.

Lane, M. A., D. J. Baer, E. M. Tilmont, W. V. Rumpler, D. K. Ingram, G. S. Roth and R. G. Cutler. 1995. Energy balance in Rhesus monkeys (*Macaca mulatta*) subjected to long-term dietary restriction. J. Gerontol.: Biol. Sci. 50A: B295–B302.

Lansing, A. I. 1947. A transmissible, cumulative and reversible factor in aging. J. Gerontol. 2: 228–239.

Lansing, A. I. 1954. A nongenic factor in the longevity of rotifers. Ann. N.Y. Acad. Sci. 57: 455–464.

Larsen, P., P. S. Albert and D. L. Riddle. 1995. Genes that regulate both development and longevity in *Caenorhabditis elegans*. Genetics 139: 1567–1583.

Lavie, L., A. Reznick and D. Gershon. 1982. Decreased protein and puromycinil-peptide degradation in livers of senescent mice. Biochem. J. 202: 47–51.

Lawrence, P. A. 1992. *The Making of a Fly: The Genetics of Animal Design*. Blackwell, Oxford.

Leaf, A. 1984. Long-lived populations (extreme old age). Pp. 82–86 in R. Andres, E. L. Bierman and W. R. Hazzard (eds.), *Principles of Geriatric Medicine*. McGraw-Hill, New York.

Leakey, J. A., H. C. Cunny, J. Bazare, Jr., P. J. Webb, J. C. Lipscomb, W. Slikker, Jr., R. J. Feuers, P. H. Duffy and R. W. Hart. 1989. Effects of aging and caloric restriction on hepatic drug metabolizing enzymes in the Fischer 344 rat. II: Effects on conjugating enzymes. Mech. Ageing Devel. 48: 157–166.

Lebo, C. P. and R. C. Reddell. 1972. The prebycusis component in occupational hearing loss. Laryngoscope 82: 1399–1409.

Lee, D. W. and B. P. Yu. 1990. Modulation of free radicals and superoxide dismutases by age and dietary restriction. Aging 2: 357–362.

Leeson, C. F. and T. S. Leeson. 1967. *Histology*. Saunders, Philadelphia.

Leeson, C. F. and T. S. Leeson. 1970. *Histology*, 2nd edition. Saunders, Philadelphia.

Leffelaar, D. and T. A. Grigliatti. 1984. A mutation in *Drosophila* that appears to accelerate aging. Devel. Genet. 4: 199–210.

Lerner, S. P. and C. E. Finch. 1991. The major histocompatibility complex and reproductive functions. Endocrine Rev. 12: 78–90.

Lesher, S., R. J. M. Fry and H. I. Kohn. 1961. Age and the generation time of the mouse duodenal epithelial cells. Exp. Cell Res. 24: 334–343.

Lewin, R. 1988. Disappointing brain graft results. Science 240: 1407.

Lewis, V. M., J. J. Twoney, P. Beatmar, G. Goldstein and R. A. Good. 1978. Age, thymic involution and circulating thymic hormone activity. J. Clin. Endocrinol. Metab. 47: 145–150.

Lichtig, C., J. Levy, D. Gershon and A. Z. Reznick. 1987. Effect of aging and exercise on the kidney. Gerontology 33: 40–48.

Lifton, R. P. 1996. Molecular genetics of human blood pressure variation. Science 272: 676–680.

Lindeman, R. D., J. D. Tobin and N. W. Shock. 1985. Longitudinal studies on the rate of decline in renal function with age. J. Am. Geriatr. Soc. 33: 278–285.

Linton, M. F., J. B. Atkinson and S. Fazio. 1995. Prevention of atherosclerosis in apolipoprotein E-deficient mice by bone marrow transplantation. Science 267: 1034–1038.

Lints, F. A. 1978. *Genetics and Aging* (Interdisciplinary Topics in Gerontology, vol. 14). S. Karger, Basel, Switzerland.

Lints, F. A. 1988. Parental age effects. Pp. 176–185 in F. A. Lints and M. H. Soliman (eds.), Drosophila *as a Model Organism for Ageing Studies*. Blackie, Glasgow.

Lints, F. A. 1989. The rate of living theory revisited. Exp. Gerontol. 35: 36–57.

Lints, F. A. and C. V. Lints. 1971. Influence of preimaginal environment on fecundity and ageing in *Drosophila melanogaster* hybrids. II. Developmental speed and life span. Exp. Gerontol. 6: 427–445.

Lints, F. A. and M. H. Soliman (eds.). 1988. Drosophila *as a Model Organism for Ageing Studies*. Blackie, Glasgow, Scotland.

Lipman, J. M., A. Turturro and R. W. Hart. 1989. The influence of dietary restriction on DNA repair in rodents: A preliminary study. Mech. Ageing Devel. 48: 135–143.

Lippman, R. D. 1983. Lipid peroxidation and metabolism in aging. Pp. 315–342 in M. Rothstein (ed.), *Review of Biological Research in Aging*, vol. 1. Alan R. Liss, New York.

Lissner, L., P. M. Odell, R. B. D'Agostino, J. Stokes III, B. E. Kreger, A. J. Belanger and K. D. Brownell. 1991. New England J. Med. 324: 1839–1844.

Lockshin, R. A. and Z. Zakeri-Milovanovic. 1984. Nucleic acids in cell death. Pp. 243–268 in I. Davies and D. C. Siegel (eds.), *Cell Ageing and Cell Death*, I. Cambridge University Press, Cambridge.

Loeb, J. and J. H. Northrop. 1917. On the influence of food and temperatures on the duration of life. J. Biol. Chem. 32: 103–121.

Loomis, W. F. and P. W. Sternberg. 1995. Genetic networks. Science 269: 649.

Luckinbill, L. S., R. Arking, M. J. Clare, W. C. Cirocco and S. A. Buck. 1984. Selection for delayed senescence in *Drosophila melanogaster*. Evolution 38: 996–1003.

Luckinbill, L. S., M. J. Clare, W. L. Krell, W. C. Cirocco and P. Richards. 1987. Estimating the number of genetic elements that defer senescence in *Drosophila*. Evol. Ecol. 1: 37–46.

Luckinbill, L. S., J. L. Graves, A. H. Reed and S. Koetsawang. 1988. Localizing genes that defer senescence in *Drosophila melanogaster*. Heredity 60: 367–374.

Luckinbill, L. S., T. A. Grudzien, S. Rhine and G. Weisman. 1989. The genetic basis of adaptation to selection for longevity in *Drosophila melanogaster*. Evol. Ecol. 3: 31–39.

Luhtala, T. A., E. B. Roecker, T. Pugh, R. J. Feuers and R. Weindruch. 1994. Dietary restriction attenuates age-related increases in rat skeletal muscle antioxidant activities. J. Gerontol.: Biol. Sci. 49: B231–B238.

Lumpkin, C. K., J. K. McClung, O. M. Pereira-Smith and J. R. Smith. 1986. Existence of high abundance antiproliferative mRNAs in senescent human diploid fibroblasts. Science 232: 393–395.

Lundblad, V. and J. W. Szostak. 1989. A mutant with a defect in telomere elongation leads to senescence in yeast. Cell 57: 633–643.

MacArthur, R. H. and E. O. Wilson. 1967. *The Theory of Island Biogeography*. Princeton University Press, Princeton, NJ.

Mackay, W. J. and G. C. Bewley. 1989. The genetics of catalase in *Drosophila melanogaster*: Isolation and characterization of acatalasemic mutants. Genetics 122: 643–652.

Maeda, H., C. A. Gleiser, E. J. Masoro, I. Murata, C. A. McMahan and B. P. Yu. 1985. Nutritional influences on aging of Fischer 344 rats: II. Pathology. J. Gerontol. 40: 671–688.

Makrides, S. C. 1983. Protein synthesis and degradation. Biol. Rev. 58: 344–422.

Manson, J. E., W. C. Willet, M. J. Stampfer, G. A. Colditz, D. J. Hunter, S. E. Hakinson, C. H. Hennekens and F. E. Speizer. 1995. Body weight and mortality among women. New England J. Med. 333: 677–685.

Manton, K. G. and E. Stallard. 1996. Longevity in the United States: Age and sex-specific evidence on life span limits from mortality patterns 1960–1990. J. Gerontol.: Biol. Sci. 51A: B362–B375.

Manton, K. G. and J. W. Vaupel. 1995. Survival after the age of 80 in the United States, Sweden, France, England, and Japan. New England J. Med. 333: 1232–1235.

Manton, K. G., E. Stallard, M. A. Woodbury and J. E. Dowd. 1994. Time varying covariates in models of human mortality and aging: Multidimensional generalizations of the Gompertz. J. Gerontol.: Biol. Sci. 49: B169–B190.

Manton, K. G., E. Stallard and L. Corder. 1995a. Changes in morbidity and chronic disability in the U.S. elderly population: Evidence from the 1982, 1984, and 1989 National Long Term Care Surveys. J. Gerontol.: Psychol. Sci. 50B: S194–S204.

Manton, K. G., M. A. Woodbury and E. Stallard. 1995b. Sex differences in human mortality and aging at late ages: The effect of mortality selection and state dynamics. Gerontologist 35: 597–608.

Manton, K. G., L. Corder and E. Stallard. 1997. Chronic disability trends in elderly United States populations: 1982–1994. Proc. Natl. Acad. Sci. USA 94: 2593–2598.

Martin, G. M. 1978. Genetic syndromes in man with potential relevance to the pathobiology of aging. Pp. 5–39 in D. Bergsma and D. E. Harrison (eds.), *Genetic Effects on Aging*. Alan R. Liss, New York.

Martin, G. M. 1992. Clonal attenuation and cell senescence: The next 30 years. Exp. Gerontol. 27: 455–459.

Martin, G. M. and M. S. Turker. 1988. Model systems for the genetic analysis of mechanisms of aging. J. Gerontol.: Biol. Sci. 43: B33–B39.

Martin, G. M., S. M. Gartler, C. J. Epstein and A. G. Motulsky. 1965. Diminished lifespan of cultured cells in Werner's syndrome. Fed. Proc. 24: 678.

Martin, G. M., C. A. Sprague and C. J. Epstein. 1970. Replicative life-span of cultivated human cells: Effects of donor's age, tissue and genotype. Lab. Invest. 23: 867–892.

Martin, G., M. Fry and L. A. Loeb. 1985. Somatic mutation and aging in mammalian cells. Pp. 7–21 in R. S. Sohal, L. S. Birnbaum and R. G. Cutler (eds.), *Molecular Biology of Aging: Gene Stability and Gene Expression*. Raven Press, New York.

Martin, G. M., M. Bergener, C. R. Harrington, J. W. Heinecke, H. Hoehm, R. A. Miller, R. Stocker and C. M. Wischik. 1995. Group report: Do *common* underlying mechanisms of aging contribute to the pathogenesis of major geriatric disorders? (Dahlem Workshop report). Pp. 281–292 in K. Esser and G. M. Martin (eds.), *Molecular Aspects of Aging*. Wiley, Chichester, England.

Martin, G. M., S. N. Austad and T. E. Johnson. 1996. Genetic analysis of ageing: Role of oxidative damage and environmental stresses. Nature Genet. 13: 25–34.

Martinez, D. E. and J. S. Leviton. 1992. Asexual metazoans undergo senescence. Proc. Natl. Acad. Sci. USA 89: 9921–9923.

Mason, J. and H. Biessmann. 1995. The unusual telomeres of *Drosophila*. Trends Genet. 11: 58–63.

Masoro, E. J. 1985. Metabolism. Pp. 540–563 in C. E. Finch and E. L. Schneider (eds.), *Handbook of the Biology of Aging*, 2nd edition. Van Nostrand Reinhold, New York.

Masoro, E. J. 1988a. Food restriction in rodents: An evaluation of its role in the study of aging. J. Gerontol.: Biol. Sci. 43: B59–B64.

Masoro, E. J. 1988b. Physiological system markers of aging. Exp. Gerontol. 23: 391–394.

Masoro, E. J. 1992a. Aging and proliferative homeostasis: Modulation by food restriction in rodents. Lab. Animal Sci. 42: 132–137.

Masoro, E. J. 1992b. Potential role of the modulation of fuel use in the antiaging action of dietary restriction. Ann. N.Y. Acad. Sci. 663: 403–411.

Masoro, E. J. 1995a. Aging: Current concepts. Pp. 3–21 in E. J. Masoro (ed.), *Handbook of Physiology. Section 11: Aging*. Oxford University Press, New York.

Masoro, E. J. 1995b. Dietary restriction. Exp. Gerontol. 30: 291–298.

Masoro, E. J. and S. N. Austad. 1996. The evolution of the antiaging action of dietary restriction: A hypothesis. J. Gerontol.: Biol. Sci. 51A: B387–B391.

Masoro, E. J., M. S. Katz and C. A. McMahan. 1989. Evidence for the glycation hypothesis of aging from the food-restricted rodent model. J. Gerontol.: Biol. Sci. 44: B20–B22.

Masters, P. 1982. Amino acid racemization in structural proteins. Pp. 120–137 in M. E. Reff and E. L. Schneider (eds.), *Biological Markers of Aging*. NIH Publ. No. 82-2221, Washington, DC.

Masters, W. H. and V. E. Johnson. 1966. *Human Sexual Response*. Little, Brown, Boston.

Matrovic, V., K. Kostial, I. Simorivoc, R. Buzina, A. Brodarec and B. E. Nordin. 1979. Bone status and fracture rates in two regions of Yugoslavia. Am. J. Clin. Nutr. 35: 540–549.

Mayer, P. J. 1991. Inheritance of longevity evinces no secular trend among members of six New England families born 1650–1874. Am. J. Human Biol. 3: 49–58.

Maynard Smith, J. 1962. Review lectures on senescence. I. The causes of ageing. Proc. Roy. Soc. London, Series B 157: 115–127.

Maynard Smith, J. 1988. The evolution of recombination. Pp. 106–125 in R. E. Michod and B. R. Levin (eds.), *The Evolution of Sex*. Sinauer Associates, Sunderland, MA.

Mayne, R. 1984. The different types of collagen and collagenous peptides. Pp. 33–42 in R. L. Trelstad (ed.), *The Role of Extracellular Matrix in Development*. Alan R. Liss, New York.

Mayr, E. 1961. Cause and effect in biology. Science 134: 1501–1506.

Mazzeo, R. S. 1994. The influence of exercise and aging on immune function. Med. Sci. Sports Exercise 26: 586–592.

McAdams, H. H. and L. Shapiro. 1995. Circuit simulation of genetic networks. Science 269: 650–656.

McCarter, R. 1978. Effects of age on contraction of mammalian skeletal muscle. Pp. 1–21 in G. Kaldor and W. J. DiBattista (eds.), *Aging in Muscle*. Raven Press, New York.

McCarter, R., W. Mejia, H. P. Bertrand and B. P. Yu. 1996. Anti-aging effect of mild calorie restriction (CR) in combination with low level voluntary wheel running. Gerontologist 36: 165 (abstract).

McCay, C. M. and M. F. Crowell. 1934. Prolonging the life span. Sci. Monthly 39: 405–414.

McCay, C., M. Crowell and L. Maynard. 1935. The effect of retarded growth upon the length of life and upon ultimate size. J. Nutr. 10: 63–79.

McClearn, G. E. 1997. Biomarkers of age and aging. Exp. Gerontol. 32: 87–94.

McClintock, B. 1941. The stability of broken ends of chromosomes in *Zea mays*. Genetics 41: 234–282.

McGandy, R. B., C. H. Barrows, Jr., A. Spania, A. Meredith, J. L. Stone and A. H. Norris. 1966. Nutrient intake and energy expenditure in men of different ages. J. Gerontol. 21: 581–587.

McGue, M., J. W. Vaupel, N. Holm and B. Harvald. 1993. Longevity is moderately heritable in a sample of Danish twins born 1871–1880. J. Gerontol.: Biol. Sci. 48: B237–B244.

McKusick, V. A. and F. H. Ruddle. 1978. The status of the gene map of the human chromosomes. Science 196: 390–405.

McLachlan, M. S. F. 1978. The ageing kidney. Lancet (London) 2(8081): 143–145.

McMichael, A. J. Vegetarians and longevity: Imagining a wider reference population (editorial). Epidemiology 3: 389–391.

Meany, M. J., D. O'Donnell, W. Rowe, B. Tannenbaum, A. Steverman, M. Walker, N. P. V. Nair and S. Lupien. 1995. Individual differences in hypothalamic-pituitary-adrenal activity in later life and hippocampal aging. J. Gerontol. 30: 229–251.

Medawar, P. B. 1946. Old age and natural death. Mod. Quart. 1: 30–56.

Medawar, P. B. 1952. *An Unsolved Problem of Biology*. H. K. Lewis, London.

Medvedev, Z. A. 1981. On the immortality of the germ line: Genetic and biochemical mechanisms. A review. Mech. Ageing Devel. 17: 331–359.

Medvedev, Z. A. 1986. Age structure of Soviet populations in the Caucasus: Facts and myths. Pp. 181–200 in A. H. Bittles and K. J. Collins (eds.), *The Biology of Human Ageing*. Cambridge University Press, Cambridge.

Melov, S., G. J. Lithgow, D. R. Fischer, P. M. Tedesco and T. E. Johnson. 1995. Increased frequency of deletions in the mitochondrial genome with age of *Caenorhabditis elegans*. Nucleic Acids Res. 23: 1419–1425.

Melov, S., J. A. Schneider, B. J. Day, D. Hinerfeld, P. Coskun, S. S. Mirra, J. D. Crapo and D. C. Wallace. 1998. A novel neurological phenotype in mice lacking mitochondrial manganese superoxide dismutase. Nature Genet. 18: 159–163.

Menzies, R. A. and P. H. Gold. 1972. The apparent turnover of mitochondria, ribosomes and sRNA of the brain in young adult and aged rats. J. Neurochem. 19: 1671–1683.

Merry, B. J. and A. M. Holehan. 1994a. Aging of the female reproductive system: The menopause. Pp. 147–170 in P. S. Timiras (ed.), *Physiological Basis of Aging and Geriatrics*, 2nd edition. CRC Press, Boca Raton, FL.

Merry, B. J. and A. M. Holehan. 1994b. Effects of diet on aging. Pp. 171–178 in P. S. Timiras (ed.), *Physiological Basis of Aging and Geriatrics*, 2nd edition. CRC Press, Boca Raton, FL.

Meyer, J. S., S. Takashima, Y. Terayama, K. Obara, K. Muramatsu and S. Weathers. 1994. CT changes associated with normal aging of the human brain. J. Neurol. Sci. 123: 200–208.

Miall, W. E. and H. G. Lovell. 1967. Relation between change of blood pressure and age. Brit. Med. J. 2: 660–664.

Miller, A. R. 1988. A set of test life tables for theoretical gerontology. J. Gerontol.: Biol. Sci. 43: B43–B49.

Miller, D. B., A. Batke and J. P. O'Callaghan. 1995. Increased glial fibrillary acidic protein (GFAP) levels in the brains of transgenic mice expressing the bovine growth hormone (bGH) gene. Exp. Gerontol. 30: 383–400.

Miller, R. A. 1995. Immune system. Pp. 555–590 in E. J. Masoro (ed.), *Handbook of Physiology. Section 11: Aging*. Oxford University Press, New York.

Miller, R. A. 1996. Aging and the immune response. Pp. 355–392 in E. L. Schneider and J. W. Rowe (eds.), *Handbook of the Biology of Aging*, 4th edition. Academic Press, San Diego.

Miller, R. M., F. Bookstein, J. van der Meulen, S. Engle, J. Kim, L. Mullins and J. Faulkner. 1997. Candidate biomarkers of aging: Age-sensitive indices of immune and muscle function covary in genetically heterogenous mice. J. Gerontol.: Biol. Sci. 52A: B39–B47.

Millis, A. J., M. Hoyle, H. M. McCue and H. Martini. 1992. Differential expression of metalloproteinase and tissue inhibitor of metalloproteinase genes in aged human fibroblasts. Exp. Cell Res. 201: 373–379.

Minaker, K. L., G. S. Meneilly and J. W. Rowe. 1985. Endocrine systems. Pp. 433–456 in C. E. Finch and E. L. Schneider (eds.), *Handbook of the Biology of Aging*, 2nd edition. Van Nostrand Reinhold, New York.

Miquel, J. and J. E. Fleming. 1984. A two step hypothesis on the mechanism of in vitro cell aging: Cell differentiation followed by intrinsic mitochondrial mutagenesis. Exp. Gerontol. 19: 31–36.

Mishkin, M. and T. Appenzeller. 1987. The anatomy of memory. Sci. Am. 256(6): 80–89.

Miskin, R. and T. Masos. 1997. Transgenic mice overexpressing urokinase-type plasminogen activator in the brain exhibit reduced food consumption, body weight and size and increased longevity. J. Gerontol.: Biol. Sci. 52A: B118–B124.

Mitchell-Olds, T. 1995. The molecular basis of quantitative genetic variation in natural populations. Trends Ecol. Evol. 10: 324–328.

Miyashita, M., S. Haga and T. Mozota. 1978. Training and detraining effects on aerobic power in middle-aged and older men. J. Sports Med. 18: 131–137.

Miyata, M. and J. D. Smith. 1996. Apolipoprotein E allele-specific antioxidant activity and effects on cytotoxicity by oxidative insults and beta-amyloid peptides. Nature Genet. 14: 55–61.

Mlekusch, W., H. Tillian, M. Lamprecht, H. Trutnovsky, R . Horejsi and G. Reibnegger. 1996. The effect of reduced physical activity on longevity of mice. Mech. Ageing Devel. 88: 159–168.

Mobbs, C. V. 1996. Neuroendocrinology of aging. Pp. 234–283 in E. L. Schneider and J. W. Rowe (eds.), *Handbook of the Biology of Aging*, 4th edition. Academic Press, San Diego.

Mocchegiani, E., L. Santarelli, M. Muzzoli and N. Fabris. 1995. Reversibility of the thymic involution and of age-related peripheral immune dysfunctions by zinc supplementation in old mice. Int. J. Immunopharmacol. 17: 703–718.

Moeller, J. R., T. Ishikawa, V. Dhawan, P. Spetsieris, F. Mandel, G. E. Alexander, C. Grady, P. Pietrini and D. Eidelberg. 1996. The metabolic topography of normal aging. J. Cerebral Blood Flow and Metabolism 16: 385–398.

Mohs, M. E. 1994a. Adult protein-calorie malnutrition among special populations and developing countries. Pp. 11–36 in R. R. Watson (ed.), *Handbook of Nutrition in the Aged*, 2nd edition. CRC Press, Boca Raton, FL.

Mohs, M. E. 1994b. Assessment of nutritional status in the aged. Pp. 145–164 in R. R. Watson (ed.), *Handbook of Nutrition in the Aged*, 2nd edition. CRC Press, Boca Raton, FL.

Moldave, K., J. Harris, W. Sabo and I. Sadnik. 1979. Protein synthesis and aging: Studies with cell-free mammalian systems. Fed. Proc. 38: 1979–1983.

Moment, G. 1982. Theories of aging: An overview. Pp. 2–23 in R. C. Adelman and G. S. Roth (eds.), *Testing the Theories of Aging*. CRC Press, Boca Raton, FL.

Moore, C. J. and A. G. Schwartz. 1978. Inverse correlation between species life span and capacity of cultured fibroblasts to convert benzo[a]pyrene to water-soluble metabolities. Exp. Cell Res. 116: 359–364.

Moore, W. R., M. E. Anderson, A. Meister, K. Murata and A. Kimura. 1989. Increased capacity of glutathione synthesis enhances resistance to radiation in *Escherichia coli*: A possible model for mammalian cell protection. Proc. Natl. Acad. Sci. USA 86: 1461–1464.

Mori, H., J. Kendo and Y. Ihara. 1987. Ubiquitin in a component of paired helical filaments in Alzheimer's disease. Science 235: 1641–1644.

Morris, J. Z., H. A. Tissenbaum and G. Ruvkum. 1996. A phosphatidylinositol-3-OH kinase family member regulating longevity and diapause in *Caenorhabditis elegans*. Nature 382: 536–539.

Morse, H. C., R. A. Yetter, J. H. Stimpfling, O. M. Pitts, T. N. Fredrickson and J. W. Hartley. 1980. Greying with age in mice: Relation to expression of murine leukemia viruses. Cell 41: 439–448.

Motoyama, H., F. Wang, K. A. Roth, H. Sawa, K. Nakayama, K. Nakayama, I. Negishi, S. Senju, Q. Zhang, S. Fujii and D. Y. Loh. 1995. Massive cell death of immature hematopoietic cells and neurons in Bcl-x-deficient mice. Science 267: 1506–1510.

Moyer, J. H., M. J. Lee-Tischler, H-Y. Kwon, J. J. Schrick, E. D. Avner, W. E. Sweeney, V. L. Godfrey, N. L. A. Cacheiro, J. E. Wilkinson and R. P. Woychik. 1994. Candidate gene associated with a mutation casing recessive polycystic kidney disease in mice. Science 264: 1329–1333.

Muggleton-Harris, A. L. 1979. Reassembly of cellular components for the study of aging and finite lifespan. Int. Rev. Cytol. 9(suppl.): 279–301.

Muller, H. J. 1938. The remaking of chromosomes. Collect. Net 13: 1181–1198.

Muller, H. J. 1964. The relation of recombination to mutational advance. Mutation Res. 1: 2–9.

Munkres, K. D. 1985. The role of genes, antioxidants and antioxygenic enzymes in the aging of *Neurospora*: A review. Pp. 237–248 in L. W. Oberly (ed.), *Superoxide Dismutases, vol. III. Pathological States*. CRC Press, Boca Raton, FL.

Munkres, K. D. 1990. Genetic coregulation of longevity and anti oxienzymes in *Neurospora crassa*. Free Radical Biol. Med. 8: 355–361.

Munkres, K. D. 1992. Selection and analysis of superoxide dismutase mutants of *Neurospora*. Free Radical Biol. Med. 13: 305–318.

Munkres, K. D. and C. Furtek. 1984. Linkage of conidial longevity determinant genes in *Neurospora crassa*. Mech. Ageing Devel. 25: 63–77.

Munkres, K. D., R. S. Rana and E. Goldstein. 1984. Genetically determined conidial longevity is positively correlated with superoxide dismutase, catalase, glutathionine peroxidase, cytochrome c peroxidase and ascorbate free radical reductase activities in *Neurosopora crassa*. Mech. Ageing Devel. 24: 83–100.

Munnell, J. F. and R. Getty. 1968. Rate of accumulation of cardiac lipofuscin in the aging canine. J. Gerontol. 23: 154–158.

Munscher, C., J. Muller-Hocher and J. Naplwotzki. 1993. Human aging is associated with various point mutations in tRNA genes of mitochondrial DNA. Biol. Chem. Hoppe Seyler 374: 1099–1104.

Murphy, E. A. 1978. Genetics of longevity in man. Pp. 261–302 in E. L. Schneider (ed.), *The Genetics of Aging*. Plenum, New York.

Murphy, W. J., S. K. Durum and D. L. Longo. 1993. Differentiation effects of growth hormone and prolactin on murine T cell development and function. J. Exp. Med. 178: 231.

Murray, V. and R. Holliday. 1981. Increased error frequency of DNA polymerases from senescent human fibroblasts. J. Mol. Biol. 146: 55–76.

Myers, G. C. and K. G. Manton. 1984. Compression of mortality: Myth or reality? Gerontologist 24: 346–353.

Nabarra, B. and I. Andrianarison. 1996. Ultrastructural study of thymic microenvironment involution in aging mice. Exp. Gerontol. 31: 489–506.

Nakamura, E. 1994. Statistical approach for the assessment of biological age. Pp. 439–456 in A. K. Balin (ed.), *Practical Handbook of Human Biologic Age Determination*. CRC Press, Boca Raton, FL.

Nakamura, E., K. Miyao and T. Ozeki. 1988. Assessment of biological age by principal component analysis. Mech. Ageing Devel. 46: 1–18.

Nakamura, K., P. H. Duffy, M. H. Lu, A. Turturro and R. W. Hart. 1989. The effect of dietary restriction on MYC protooncogene expression in mice: A preliminary study. Mech. Ageing Devel. 199–205.

Nandy, K. 1984. Effects of antioxidant on neuronal lipofuscin pigment. Pp. 223–233 in D. Armstrong, R. S. Sohal, R. G. Cutler and T. F. Slater (eds.), *Free Radiation in Molecular Biology, Aging and Disease*. Raven Press, New York.

Nandy, K. and H. Schneider. 1976. Lipofuscin pigment formation in neuroblastoma cells in culture. Pp. 245–264 in R. D. Terry and S. Gershon (eds.), *Neurobiology of Aging*. Raven Press, New York.

Nash, M. S. 1994. Exercise and immunology. Med. Sci. Sports Exercise 26: 125–127.

National Research Council. 1981. *Mammalian Models for Research on Aging*. National Academy Press, Washington, DC.

Nelson, J. F. 1995. The potential role of selected endocrine systems in aging processes. Pp. 377–394 in E. J. Masoro (ed.), *Handbook of Physiology: Section 11: Aging*. Oxford University Press, New York.

Nesse, R. M. and G. C. Williams. 1994. *Why We Get Sick: The New Science of Darwinian Medicine*. Vintage Books, New York.

Neumann, H., A. Calalie, D. E. Jenne and H. Wekerle. 1995. Induction of MHC Class 1 genes in neurons. Science 269: 549–552.

Newton, J. R. and R. Yernas. 1986. Changes in the contractile properties of the human first dorsal interosseous muscle with age. Gerontology 32: 98–104.

Niedermuller, H. 1985. DNA repair during aging. Pp. 173–194 in R. S. Sohal, L. S. Birnbaum and R. G. Cutler (eds.), *Molecular Biology of Aging: Gene Stability and Gene Expression*. Raven Press, New York.

Nieschlag, E. and E. Michael. 1986. Reproductive functions in grandfathers. Pp. 59–71 in L. Mastroianni, Jr. and C. A. Paulsen (eds.), *Aging, Reproduction and the Climacteric*. Plenum, New York.

Nigg, E. A. 1995. Cyclin-dependent protein kinases: Key regulators of the eucaryotic cell cycle. BioEssays 17: 471–480.

Nikitin, A. G. and R. C. Woodruff. 1995. Somatic movement of the mariner transposable element and lifespan of *Drosophila* species. Mutation Res. 338: 43–49.

Ning, Y. and O. M. Pereira-Smith. 1991. Molecular genetic approaches to the study of cellular senescence. Mutation Res. 256: 303–310.

Nooden, L. D. 1988a. Postlude and prospects. Pp. 499–517 in L. D. Nooden and A. C. Leopold (eds.), *Senescence and Aging in Plants*. Academic Press, San Diego.

Nooden, L. D. 1988b. Whole plant senescence. Pp. 392–441 in L. D. Nooden and A. C. Leopold (eds.). 1988. *Senescence and Aging in Plants*. Academic Press, San Diego.

Nooden, L. D. and J. J. Guiamet. 1996. Genetic control of senescence and aging in plants. Pp. 94–120 in E. L. Schneider and J. W. Rowe (eds.), *Handbook of the Biology of Aging*, 4th edition. Academic Press, San Diego.

Nooden, L. D. and A. C. Leopold (eds.). 1988. *Senescence and Aging in Plants*. Academic Press, San Diego.

Nooden, L. D. and D. S. Letham. 1993. Cytokinin metabolism and signalling in the soybean plant. Australian J. Plant Physiol. 20: 639–653.

Nooden, L. D. and J. E. Thompson. 1985. Aging and senescence in plants. Pp. 105–127 in C. E. Finch and E. L. Schneider (eds.), *Handbook of the Biology of Aging*, 2nd edition. Van Nostrand Reinhold, New York.

Nooden, L. D., M. J. Schneider, J. Hifllsberg and S. Levy. 1995. Induction of senescence in *Arabidopsis* by long days and light dosage. Plant Physiol. 108: 61 (abstract).

Norris, A. H. and N. W. Shock. 1974. Exercise in the adult years. Pp. 346–365 in W. R. Johnson and E. R. Buskirk (eds.), *Science and Medicine of Exercise and Sport*. Harper and Row, New York.

Norton, H. T. J. 1928. Natural selection and Mendelian variation. Proc. London Math. Soc. 28: 1–45.

Norwood, T. H. and J. R. Smith. 1985. The cultured fibroblast-like cell as a model for the study of aging. Pp. 291–321 in C. E. Finch and E. L. Schneider (eds.), *Handbook of the Biology of Aging*, 2nd edition. Van Nostrand Reinhold, New York.

Nussbaum, T. J., L. D. Mueller and M. R. Rose 1996. Evolutionary patterns among measures of aging. Exp. Gerontol. 31: 507–516.

Ogborn, C. E. and G. M. Martin. 1985. Age-related declines in the replicative potentials of aortic cells from rhesus monkeys: Evidence from primary cloning and organoid culture techniques. Pp. 101–106 in R. Davis (ed.), *Behavior and Pathology of Aging in Rhesus Monkeys*. Alan R. Liss, New York.

Ohtani, S., S. Kato and H. Sugeno. 1996. Changes in D-aspartic acid in human deciduous teeth with age from 1–20 years. Growth Devel. Aging 60: 1–6.

Olovnikov, A. M. 1971. Principles of marginotomy in template synthesis of polynucleotides. Doklady Adad. Nauk SSSR 201: 1496–1499.

Olovnikov, A. M. 1973. A theory of marginotomy: The incomplete copying of template margin in enzymic synthesis of polynucleotides and biological significance of the phenomenon. J. Theoret. Biol. 41: 181–190.

Olovnikov, A. M. 1996. Telomeres, telomerase and aging: Origin of the theory. Exp. Gerontol. 31: 443–448.

Olshansky, S. J., B. A. Carnes and C. Cassel. 1990. In search of Methuselah: Estimating the upper limits to human longevity. Science 250: 634–640.

Olson, M. V. 1995. A time to sequence. Science 270: 394–396.

Ono, T. and R. G. Cutler. 1978. Age-dependent relaxation of gene repression: Increase of endogenous murine leukemia virus-related and globin-related RNA in brain and liver of mice. Proc. Natl. Acad. Sci. USA 75: 4431–4435.

Ono, T. and S. Okada. 1978. Does the capacity to rejoin radiation-induced DNA breaks decline in senescent mice? Int. J. Radiation Biol. 33: 403–407.

Ono, T., S. Okada and T. Sugahara. 1976. Comparative studies of DNA size in various tissues of mice during the aging process. Exp. Gerontol. 11: 127–132.

Orentreich, D. S. and N. Orentreich. 1994. Hair changes with aging as a parameter to utilize in the estimation of human biological age. Pp. 375–390 in A. K. Balin (ed.), *Practical Handbook of Human Biologic Age Determination*. CRC Press, Boca Raton, FL.

Orentreich, N., J. L. Brind, R. L. Rizer and J. H. Vogelman. 1984. Age changes and sex differences in serum dehydroepiandrosterone sulfate concentrations throughout childhood. J. Clin. Endocrinol. Metab. 59: 551–555.

Orentreich, N., J. A. Zimmerman and J. R. Matias. 1994. Dehydroepiandrosterone: Marker or modifier of aging. Pp. 391–396 in A. K. Balin (ed.), *Practical Handbook of Human Biologic Age Determination*. CRC Press, Boca Raton, FL.

Orgel, L. E. 1963. The maintenance of the accuracy of protein synthesis and its relevance to aging. Proc. Natl. Acad. Sci. USA 49: 517–521.

Orive, M. E. 1995. Senescence in organisms with clonal reproduction and complex life histories. Am. Nat. 145: 90–108.

Ornish, D. 1993. Regression of coronary artery disease by a multifactorial approach: The Lifestyle Heart Trial. Pp. 319–329 in P. C. Weber and A. Leaf (eds.), *Atherosclerosis Reviews*, vol. 25. Raven Press, New York.

Orr, W. C. and R. C. Sohal. 1992. The effects of catalase gene overexpression on life span and resistance to oxidative stress in transgenic *Drosophila melanogaster*. Arch. Biochem. Biophys. 297: 35–41.

Orr, W. C. and R. C. Sohal. 1993. Effects of Cu/Zn superoxide dismutase overexpression on life span and resistance to oxidative stress in transgenic *Drosophila melanogaster*. Arch. Biochem. Biophys. 301: 34–40.

Orr, W. C. and R. C. Sohal. 1994. Extension of life-span by overexpression of superoxide dismutase and catalase in *Drosophila melanogaster*. Science 263: 1128–1130.

Osborne, T. B., L. B. Mendel and E. L. Ferry. 1917. The effect of retardation of growth upon the breeding period and duration of life of rats. Science (NY) 45: 294–295.

Osiewacz, H. D. 1995. Aging and genetic instabilities. Pp. 29–44 in K. Esser and G. M. Martin (eds.), *Molecular Aspects of Aging*. Wiley, Chichester, England.

Ostfeld, A., C. M. Smith and B. A. Stotsky. 1977. The systemic use of procaine in the treatment of the elderly: A review. J. Am. Geriatr. Soc. 25: 1–9.

Otero, P., M. Viana, E. Herrera and B. Bonet. 1997. Antioxidant and prooxidant effects of ascorbic acid, dehydroascorbic acid, and flavonoids on LDL submitted to different degrees of oxidation. Free Radical Res. 27: 619–626.

Pahlavani, M. A. and A. Richardson. 1996. The effect of age on the expression of interleukin-2. Mech. Ageing Devel. 89: 125–154.

Painter, R. S., J. M. Clarkson and B. R. Young. 1973. Ultraviolet-induced repair replication in aging diploid human cells (WI-38). Radiation Res. 56: 560–564.

Palmore, E. B. 1982. Predictors of the longevity difference: A 25 year follow-up. Gerontologist 22: 513–518.

Papaconstantinou, J., P. D. Reisner, L. Liu and D. T. Kuninger. 1996. Mechanisms of altered gene expression with aging. Pp. 150–183 in E. L. Schneider and J. W. Rowe (eds.), Handbook of the Biology of Aging, 4th edition. Academic Press, San Diego.

Park, J-W., C-H. Choi, M-S. Kim and M-H. Chung. 1996. Oxidative status in senescence-accelerated mice. J. Gerontol.: Biol. Sci. 51A: B337–B345.

Parsons, P. A. 1978. The genetics of aging in optimal and stressful environments. Exp. Gerontol. 13: 357–363.

Parsons, P. A. 1995. Inherited stress resistance and longevity: A stress theory of aging. Heredity 75: 216–221.

Parsons, P. A. 1996. The limit to human longevity: An approach through a stress theory of ageing. Mech. Ageing Devel. 87: 211–218.

Partridge, L. and N. H. Barton. 1993. Optimality, mutation and the evolution of ageing. Nature 362: 305–311.

Partridge, L. and K. Fowler. 1992. Direct and correlated responses to selection on age at reproduction in *Drosophila melanogaster*. Evolution 46: 76–91.

Paterson, A. H., E. S. Lander, J. D. Hewitt, S. Peterson, S. E. Lincoln and S. D. Tanksley. 1988. Resolution of quantitative traits into Mendelian factors by using a complete linkage map of restriction fragment length polymorphisms. Nature 335: 721–726.

Pearl, R. 1922. A comparison of the laws of mortality in *Drosophila* and in man. Am. Nat. 61: 398–405.

Pearl, R. 1928. *The Rate of Living*. University of London Press, London.

Pearl, R. and J. R. Miner. 1935. Experimental studies on the duration of life. XIV. The comparative mortality of certain lower organisms. Quart. Rev. Biol. 10: 60–79.

Pedigo, N. W., Jr. 1994. Neurotransmitter receptor plasticity in aging. Life Sciences 55: 1985–1991.

Pelleymounter, M. A., M. J. Cullen, M. B. Baker, R. Hecht, D. Winters, T. Boone and F. Collins. 1995. Effects of the obese gene product on body weight regulation in ob/ob mice. Science 269: 540–543.

Pereira-Smith, O. M. and Y. Ning. 1992. Molecular genetic studies of cellular senescence. Exp. Gerontol. 27: 519–522.

Pereira-Smith, O. M. and J. R. Smith. 1983. Evidence for the recessive nature of cellular immortality. Science 221: 964–966.

Perillo, N. L., R. L. Walford, M. A. Newman and R. B. Effros. 1989. Human T lymphocytes possess a limited in vitro life span. Exp. Gerontol. 24: 177–187.

Perls, T. T. and E. R. Wood. 1996. Acute care costs of the oldest old: They cost less, their care intensity is less and they go to nonteaching hospitals. Arch. Internal Med. 156: 754–760.

Petkov, V. D., V. V. Petkov and S. L. Stancheva. 1988. Age-related changes in brain neurotransmission. Gerontology 34: 14–21.

Phair, J. P. 1983. Host defense in the aged. Pp. 1–12 in R. A. Gleckman and N. M. Gantz (eds.), *Infections in the Elderly*. Little Brown, Boston.

Phelan, J. 1992. Genetic variability and aging models. Exp. Gerontol. 27: 147–159.

Phillips, J. P. and A. J. Hilliker. 1990. Genetic analysis of oxygen defense mechanisms in *Drosophila melanogaster*. Adv. Genet. 28: 43–71.

Pierpaoli, W. and W. Regelson. 1994. Pineal control of aging: Effect of melatonin and pineal grafting in aging mice. Proc. Natl. Acad. Sci. USA 91: 787–791.

Pierpaoli, W. and W. Regelson. 1995. *The Melatonin Miracle*. Simon and Schuster, New York.

Pitskhelauri, G. Z. 1982. *The Longliving of Soviet Georgia* (trans. and ed. by G. Lesneff-Caravaglia). Human Sciences Press, New York.

Plomin, R., N. L. Pedersen, P. Lichtenstein and G. E. McClearn. 1994. Variability and stability in cognitive abilities are largely genetic later in life. Behavior Genet. 24: 207–215.

Pohley, H. J. 1987. A formal mortality analysis for populations of unicellular organisms (*Saccharomyces cerevisiae*). Mech. Ageing Devel. 38: 231–243.

Poirier, J. et al. 1995. Apolipoprotein E4 allele as a predictor of cholinergic deficits and treatment outcome in Alzheimer disease. Proc. Natl. Acad. Sci. USA 92: 12260–12264.

Polson, C. D. A. and G. C. Webster. 1982. Age-related DNA fragmentation in two varieties of *Drosophila melanogaster*, *Phaseolus* (cotyledons) and three tissues of the mouse. Exp. Gerontol. 17: 11–17.

Popp, R. A., E. G. Bailiff, G. P. Hirsch and R. A. Conrad. 1976. Errors in human hemoglobin as a function of age. Interdiscipl. Topics Gerontol. 9: 209–218.

Porter, M. B. and J. R. Smith. 1988. Generation of monoclonal antibodies reacting specifically with senescent cells. Gerontologist 28: 230A (abstract).

Poulsen, H. E., S. Loft and K. Vistisen. 1996. Extreme exercise and oxidative DNA modification. J. Sports Sci. 14: 343–346.

Promislow, D. E. L. 1991. Senescence in natural populations of mammals: A comparative study. Evolution 45: 1869–1887.

Promislow, D. E. L. 1993. Minireview: On size and survival: Progress and pitfalls in the allometry of life span. J. Gerontol.: Biol. Sci. 48: B115–B123.

Promislow, D. E. L. and M. Tatar. 1994. Comparative approaches to the study of senescence: Bridging genetics and phylogentics. Pp. 45–53 in M. R. Rose and C. E. Finch (eds.), *Genetics and Evolution of Aging*. Kluwer, Dordrecht, The Netherlands.

Prothero, J. and K. D. Jurgens. 1987. Scaling of maximal lifespan in mammals: A review. Pp. 44–74 in A. D. Woodhead and K. H. Thompson (eds.), *Evolution of Longevity in Animals: A Comparative Approach*. Plenum, New York.

Prowse, K. R. and C. W. Greider. 1995. Developmental and tissue-specific regulation of mouse telomerase and telomere length. Proc. Natl. Acad. Sci. USA 92: 4818–4822.

Pryde, F. E., H. C. Gorham and E. J. Lowis. 1997. Chromosome ends: All the same under their caps. Curr. Opinion Genet. Devel. 7: 822–828.

Ptashne, M. 1988. How eucaryotic transcriptional activators work. Nature 335: 683–689.

Quinn, J. F. and M. Kozy. 1996. The role of bridge jobs in the retirement transition: Gender, race and ethnicity. Gerontologist 36: 363–372.

Raff, M. C. 1992. Social controls on cell survival and cell death. Nature 356: 397–400.

Ramirez, R. D., W. E. Wright, J. W. Shay and R. S. Taylor. 1997. Telomerase activity concentrates in the mitotically active segments of human hair follicles. J. Invest. Dermatol. 108: 113–117.

Raven, P. H. and G. B. Johnson. 1985. *Biology*. Times Mirror/Mosby, St. Louis.

Rebar, R. W. and T. B. Spitzer. 1987. The physiology and measurement of hot flashes. Am. J. Obstetr. Gynecol. 156: 1284–1288.

Reff, M. E. and E. L. Schneider (eds.). 1982. *Biological Markers of Aging*. NIH Publ. No. 82-2221, Washington, DC.

Reiter, R. J. 1995. The pineal gland and melatonin in relation to aging: A summary of the theories and of the data. Exp. Gerontol. 30: 199–212.

Reppert, S. M. and D. R. Weaver. 1995. Melatonin madness. Cell 83: 1059–1062.

Reveillaud, I., A. Niedzwiecki, K. G. Bensch and J. E. Fleming. 1991. Expression of bovine superoxide dismutase in *Drosophila melanogaster* augments resistance to oxidative stress. Mol. Cellular Biol. 11: 632–640.

Reveillaud, I., J. Phillips, B. Duyf, A. Hilliker, A. Kongpachith and J. E. Fleming. 1994. Phenotypic rescue by a bovine transgene in a Cu/Zn superoxide dismutase-null mutant of *Drosophila melanogaster*. Mol. Cellular Biol. 14: 1302–1307.

Richardson, A. and M. C. Birchenall-Sparks. 1983. Age-related changes in protein synthesis. Pp. 255–274 in M. Rothstein (ed.), *Review of Biological Research in Aging*, vol. 1. Alan R. Liss, New York.

Richardson, A. and H. T. Cheung. 1982. The relationship between age-related changes in gene expression, protein turnover and the responsiveness of an organism to stimuli. Life Sci. 31: 605–613.

Richardson, A. and M. A. Pahlavani. 1994. Thoughts on the evolutionary basis of dietary restriction. Pp. 226–231 in M. R. Rose and C. E. Finch (eds.), *Genetics and Evolution of Aging*. Kluwer, Dordrecht, The Netherlands.

Richardson, A. and I. Semsei. 1987. Effect of ageing on translation and transcription. Pp. 467–483 in M. Rothstein (ed.), *Review of Biological Research on Aging*. Alan R. Liss, New York

Richardson, A., M. S. Roberts and M. S. Rutherford. 1985. Aging and gene expression. Pp. 395–419 in M. Rothstein (ed.), *Review of Biological Research in Aging*, vol. 2. Alan R. Liss, New York.

Richardson, A., J. A. Butler, M. S. Rutherford, I. Semsei, M. Z. Gu, G. Fernandes and W. H. Chiang. 1987. Effect of age and dietary restriction on the expression of alpha 2μ-globulin. J. Biol. Chem. 262: 12821–12825.

Riddle, D. L., M. M. Swanson and P. S. Albert. 1981. Interacting genes in nematode dauer larva formation. Nature 290: 268–271.

Ridley, R. M. and H. F. Baker. 1993. Behavioral effects of cholinergic grafts. Ann. N.Y. Acad. Sci. 695: 274–277.

Riggs, B. L. and L. J. Melton. 1986. Involutional osteoporosis. New England J. Med. 314: 1676–1686.

Riha, V. F. and L. S. Luckinbill. 1996. Selection for longevity favors stringent metabolic control in *Drosophila melanogaster*. J. Gerontol.: Biol. Sci. 51A: B284–B294.

Rimm, E. B., M. J. Stampfer, A. Ascherio, E. Giovannucci, G. A. Colditz and W. C. Willet. 1993. Vitamin E consumption and the risk of coronary heart disease in men. New England J. Med. 328: 1450–1456.

Rinkevitch, B., R. J. Lauzon, B. W. M. Brown and I. L. Weissman. 1992. Evidence for a programmed life span in a colonial protochordate. Proc. Natl. Acad. Sci. USA 89: 3546–3550.

Robert, A. M., M. Schaeverbeke, J. Schaeverbeke and L. Robert. 1997. Viellissement et circulation cerebrale: Role de la matrice extracellulaire des microvaisseaux du cerveau. Comptes Rendus des Seances de la Societe de Biologie et de Ses Filiales 191: 253–260.

Robert, C., B. Lesty and A. M. Robert. 1988. Ageing of the skin: Study of elastic fiber network modifications by computerized image analysis. Gerontology 34: 291–296.

Roberts, L. 1988. Questions raised about anti-wrinkle cream. Science 239: 564.

Robertson, M. 1987. Molecular genetics of the mind. Nature 325: 755.

Robinson, T. F., S. M. Factor and E. H. Sonnenblick. 1986. The heart as a suction pump. Sci. Am. 254(6): 84–91.

Rodeheffer, R. J., G. Gerstenblith, L. C. Becker, J. L. Fleg, M. L. Weisfeldt and E. G. Lakatta. 1984. Exercise cardiac output is maintained with advancing age in healthy human subjects: Cardiac dilation and increased stroke volume compensate for a diminished heart rate. Circulation 69: 203–213.

Rodin, J. 1986. Aging and health: Effects of the sense of control. Science 233: 1271–1276.

Rogers, J. and F. E. Bloom. 1985. Neurotransmitter metabolism and function in the aging central nervous system. Pp. 645–691 in C. E. Finch and E. L. Schneider (eds.), *Handbook of the Biology of Aging*, 2nd edition. Van Nostrand Reinhold, New York.

Rogina, B. and S. L. Helfand. 1996. Timing of expression of a gene in the adult *Drosophila* is regulated by mechanisms independent of termperature and metabolic rate. Genetics 143: 1643–1651.

Roitberg, B. D., J. Sircom, C. A. Roitberg, J. J. M. van Alphen and M. Mangel. 1993. Life expectancy and reproduction. Nature 364: 108.

Rose, M. R. 1984. Laboratory evolution of postponed senescence in *Drosophila melanogaster*. Evolution 38: 1004–1010.

Rose, M. R. 1991. *Evolutionary Biology of Aging*. Oxford University Press, New York.

Rose, M. R. 1996. Genetic analysis of mechanisms of aging. Curr. Opinion Genet. Devel. 6: 366–370.

Rose, M. R. and B. Charlesworth. 1981. Genetics of life history in *Drosophila melanogaster*. II. Exploratory selection experiments. Genetics 97: 187–196.

Rose, M. R., L. N. Vu, S. U. Park and J. L. Graves, Jr. 1992. Selection on stress resistance increases longevity in *Drosophila melanogaster*. Exp. Gerontol. 27: 241–250.

Rosenberg, M. B., T. Friedmann, R. C. Robertson, M. Tuszynski, J. A. Wolff, X. O. Breakefield and F. H. Gage. 1988. Grafting genetically modified cells to the damaged brain: Restorative effects of NGF expression. Science 242: 1575–1577.

Rosenblum, J. S., N. B. Gilula and R. A. Lerner. 1996. On signal sequence polymorphisms and diseases of distribution. Proc. Nat. Acad. Sci. USA 93: 4471–4473.

Rosenthal, G. E. and C. S. Landefeld. 1993. Do older Medicare pateints cost hospitals more? Evidence from an academic medical center. Arch. Internal Med. 153: 89–96.

Rossle, R. and F. Roulet. 1932. *Zahl und Mass in Pathologie*. Springer-Verlag, Berlin.

Rossman, I. 1977. Anatomic and body composition changes with aging. Pp. 189–221 in C. E. Finch and L. Hayflick (eds.), *Handbook of the Biology of Aging*. Van Nostrand Reinhold, New York.

Rossman, I. 1979. *Clinical Geriatrics*, 2nd edition. Lippincott, Philadelphia.

Roth, G. S. and J. A. Joseph. 1994. Cellular and molecular mechanisms of impaired dopaminergic function during aging. Ann. N.Y. Acad. Sci. 719: 129–135.

Rothstein, M. 1982. *Biochemical Approaches to Aging*. Academic Press, New York.

Rothstein, M. 1983. Detection of altered proteins. Pp. 1–8 in R. C. Adelman and G. S. Roth (eds.), *Altered Proteins and Aging*, CRC Press, Boca Raton, FL.

Rothstein, M. 1987. Evidence for and against the error catastrophe hypothesis. Pp. 139–154 in H. R. Warner, R. N. Butler, R. L. Sprott and E. L. Schneider (eds.), *Modern Biological Theories of Aging* (Aging, vol. 31). Raven Press, New York.

Rowe, J. W. and R. L. Kahn. 1987. Human aging: Usual and successful. Science 237: 143–149.

Rowe, J. W. and R. L. Kahn. 1997. Successful aging. Gerontologist 37: 433–440.

Rowe, J. W. and K. L. Minaker. 1985. Geriatric medicine. Pp. 932–959 in C. E. Finch and E. L. Schneider (eds.), *Handbook of the Biology of Aging*, 2nd edition. Van Nostrand Reinhold, New York.

Rowe, J. W., R. Andres, J. D. Tobin, A. H. Norris and N. W. Shock. 1976. The effect of age on creatinine clearance in men: A cross-sectional and longitudinal study. J. Gerontol. 31: 155–163.

Rowley, M. J., H. Buchanan and I. R. Mackay. 1968. Reciprocal change with age in antibody to extrinsic and intrinsic allergens. Lancet (London) 2: 24–26.

Roy, A. K. and B. Chatterjee. 1984. Hormonal regulation of hepatic gene expression during aging. Pp. 143–166 in

A. K. Roy and B. Chatterjee (eds.), *Molecular Basis of Aging*. Academic Press, Orlando, FL.

Rubner, M. 1908. *Das Problem der Levensdauer und seine Beziehungen zum Wachstom und Ernahrung* Oldenbourg, Munich.

Rudman, D, A. G. Feller, H. S. Nagraj, G. A. Gergans, P. Y. Lalitha, A. F. Goldberg, R. A. Sclenker, L. Cohn, L. W. Rudman and D. E. Mattson. 1990. Effects of human growth homone in men over 60 years old. New England J. Med. 323: 1–6.

Rudman, D. and K. Shetty. 1994. Unanswered questions concerning the treatment of hyposomatorpism and hypogonadism in elderly men. J. Am. Geriatr. Soc. 42: 522–527.

Ruhe, R. C. and R. B. McDonald. 1994. Aging, insulin secretion and cellular senescence. Pp. 93–110 in R. Watson (ed.), *Handbook of Nutrition in the Aged*, 2nd edition. CRC Press, Boca Raton, FL.

Ruhe, R. C., D. L. Curry and R. B. McDonald. 1997. Altered cellular heterogeneity as a possible mechanism for the maintenance of organ function in senescent animals. J. Gerontol.: Biol. Sci. 52A: B53–B58.

Russell, R. L. and L. A. Jacobson. 1985. Some aspects of aging can be studied easily in nematodes. Pp. 128–145 in C. E. Finch and E. L. Schneider (eds.), *Handbook of the Biology of Aging*, 2nd edition. Van Nostrand Reinhold, New York.

Rustagi, J. S. 1985. *Introduction to Statistical Methods. Vol. II. Application to the Life Sciences.* Rowman and Allanheld, Torowa, NJ.

Ryan, J. M., D. G. Ostrow, X. O. Breakefield, E. S. Gershon and L. Upchurch. 1981. A comparison of the proliferative and replication lifespan kinetics of cell cultures derived from monozygotic twins. In Vitro Cellular Devel. Biol. 17: 20–27.

Sacher, G. A. 1959. Relation of lifespan to brain weight and body weight in mammals. Pp. 115–133 in G. E. W. Wolstenholme and M. O'Conner (eds.), *The Life Span of Animals* (CIBA Foundation Colloquium on Aging, vol. 5). Churchill, London.

Sacher, G. A. 1975. Maturation and longevity in relation to cranial capacity in hominid evolution. Pp. 417–430 in R. Tuttle (ed.), *Antecedents of Man and After. Primates: Functional Morphology and Evolution*, vol. 1. Mouton, The Hague.

Sacher, G. A. 1977. Life table modification and life prolongation. Pp. 582–638 in C. E. Finch and L. Hayflick (eds.), *Handbook of the Biology of Aging*. Van Nostrand Reinhold, New York.

Sacher, G. A. and R. W. Hart. 1978. Longevity, aging, and comparative cellular and molecular bioloby of the house mouse, *Mus musculus*, and the white-footed mouse, *Peromyscus leucopus*. Pp. 71–96 in D. Bergsma and D. E. Harrison (eds.), *Genetic Effects on Aging*. Alan R. Liss, New York.

Saksela, E. and P. S. Moorhead. 1963. Aneuploidy in the degenerative phase of serial cultivation of human cell strains. Proc. Natl. Acad. Sci. USA 50: 390–395.

Salk, D., K. An, H. Hoehn and G. M. Martin. 1981. Cytogenetics of Werner's syndrome cultured skin fibroblasts:

Variegated translocation mosaicism. Cytogenet. Cell Genet. 30: 92–107.

Samiy, A. H. 1983. Renal disease in the elderly. Med. Clinics North America 3: 463–480.

Sandbrink, R., C. L. Masters and K. Beyreuther. 1996. APP gene family: Alternative splicing generates functionally related isoforms. Ann. N. Y. Acad. Sci. 777: 281–287.

Sapolsky, R. M. 1990. The adrenocortical axis. Pp. 330–348 in E. L. Schneider and J. W. Rowe (eds.), *Handbook of the Biology of Aging*, 3rd edition. Academic Press, San Diego.

Sapolsky, R. M., L. C. Krey and B. S. McEwen. 1986. The neuroendocrinology of stress and aging: The glucocorticoid cascade hypothesis. Endocrine Rev. 7: 284–301.

Sapolsky, R. M., J. H. Vogelman, N. Orentreich and J. Altmann. 1993. Senescent decline in serum dehydroepiandrosterone sulfate concentrations in a population of wild baboons. J. Gerontol.: Biol. Sci. 48: B196–B200.

Schacter, F., L. Faure-Delanef, F. Geunot, H. Rouger, P. Froguel, L Leseuer-Ginot and D. Cohen. 1994. Genetic associations with human longevity at the APOE and ACE loci. Nature Genet. 6: 29–34.

Scheibel, A. B. 1978. Structural aspects of the aging brain: Spine systems and the dendritic arbor. Pp. 353–373 in R. Katzman, R. D. Terry and K. L. Bick (eds.), *Alzheimer's Disease: Senile Dementia and Related Disorders* (Aging, vol. 1). Raven Press, New York.

Scheiner, S. M. 1993. Genetics and evolution of phenotypic plasticity. Annu. Rev. Ecol. Syst. 24: 35–68.

Schellenberg, G. D. 1995. Genetic dissection of Alzheimer disease, a heterogeneous disorder. Proc. Natl. Acad. Sci. USA 92: 8852–8859.

Schlenker, E. D. 1984. *Nutrition in Aging*. Times Mirror/ Mosby, St. Louis.

Schnebel, E. M. and J. Grossfield. 1988. Antagonistic pleiotropy: An interspecific *Drosophila* comparison. Evolution 42: 306–311.

Schneider, E. L. 1985. Cytogenetics of aging. Pp. 357–376 in C. E. Finch and E. L. Schneider (eds.), *Handbook of the Biology of Aging*, 2nd edition. Van Nostrand Reinhold, New York.

Schneider, E. L. and J. A. Brody. 1983. Aging, natural death and the compression of mortality: Another view. New England J. Med. 309: 854–856.

Schwartz, R. S. 1995. Trophic factor supplementation: Effect on the age-associated changes in body composition. J. Gerontol.: Biol. Sci. 50A(special issue): 151–156.

Schwartz, T. and H. D. Osiewacz. 1996. Telomere length does not change during senescence of the ascomycete *Podospora anserina*. Mutation Res. 316: 193–199.

Schwetz, B. A. 1995. Reproductive effects associated with dietary restriction. Pp 341–350 in R. W. Hart, D. A. Neumann and R. T. Robertson (eds.), *Dietary Restriction: Implications for the Design and Interpretation of Toxicity and Carcinogenicity Studies*. ILSI Press, Washington, DC.

Sehgal, A., A. Rothenfluh-Hilfiker, M. Hunter-Ensor, Y. Chen, M. P. Myers and M. W. Young. 1995. Rhythmic expression of timeless: A basis for promoting circadian cycles in period gene autoregulation. Science 270: 808–811.

Seidel, J. C. 1995. The impact of obesity on health status: Some implications for health care costs. Int. J. Obesity & Related Metabolic Disorders 19(Suppl. 6): S13–S16.

Selkoe, D. J. 1997. Alzheimer's disease: Genotypes, phenotypes and treatments. Science 275: 630–631.

Sell, D. R. and V. M. Monnier. 1995. Long lived proteins: Extracellular matrix (collagens, elastins, proteoglycans) and lens crystallins. Pp. 235–308 in E. J. Masoro (ed.), *Handbook of Physiology. Section 11: Aging*. Oxford University Press, New York.

Sen, S., G. Talukder and A. Sharma. 1987. Age-related alterations in human chromosome composition and DNA content in vitro during senescence. Biol. Rev. 62: 25–44.

Service, P. M., E. W. Hutchinson and M. R. Rose. 1988. Multiple genetic mechanisms for the evolution of senescence in *Drosophila melanogaster*. Evolution 42: 708–716.

Shakespeare, W. 1600. As you like it: Act 2, Scene 7. P. 701 in S. Wells and G. Taylor (eds.), *The Complete Oxford Shakespeare*. Oxford University Press, Oxford. 1987.

Sharma, H. K. and M. Rothstein. 1980. Altered enolase in aged *Turbatrix aceti* results from conformational changes in the enzyme. Proc. Natl. Acad. Sci. USA 77: 5865–5868.

Sharma, H. W., J. A. Sololoski, J. R. Perez, J. Y. Maltese, A. C. Sartorelli, C. A. Stein, G. Nichols, Z. Khaled, N. T. Telang and R. Narayanan. 1995. Differentiation of immortal cells inhibits telomerase activity. Proc. Natl. Acad. Sci. USA 92: 12343–12346.

Sharma, S. P., M. Sharma and R. Kakkar. 1995. Methionine-induced alterations in the life span, antioxidant enzymes and peroxide levels in aging *Zaprionus paravittiger* (Diptera). Gerontology 41: 86–93.

Sheehy, M. R. J., J. G. Greenwood and D. R. Fielder. 1995. Lipofuscin as a record of Òrate of livingÓ in an aquatic poikilotherm. J. Gerontol.: Biol. Sci. 50A: B322–B326.

Shephard, R. A. 1982. *Physiology and Bioichemistry of Exercise*. Praeger, New York.

Shepherd, J. C. W., U. Walldorf, P. Hug and W. J. Gehring. 1989. Fruit flies with additional expression of the elongation factor EF-1α live longer. Proc. Nat. Acad. Sci. USA 86: 7520–7521.

Shikama, N., R. Ackermann and C. Brack. 1994. Protein synthesis elongation factor EF-1 alpha expression and longevity in *Drosophila melanogaster*. Proc. Natl. Acad. Sci. USA 91: 4199–4203.

Shimokawa, I., B. P. Yu, Y. Higami, T. Ikeda and E. J. Masoro. 1993. Dietary restriction retards onset but not progression of leukemia in male F344 rats. J. Gerontol.: Biol. Sci. 48: B68–B73.

Shock, N. W. 1972. Energy metabolism, caloric intake, and physical activity of the aging. Pp. 12–23 in L. A. Carlson (ed.), *Nutrition in Old Age*. Almqvist and Wiksell, Uppsala, Sweden.

Shock, N. W. 1977. System regulation. Pp. 639–665 in C. E. Finch and E. L. Schneider (eds.), *Handbook of the Biology of Aging*. Van Nostrand Reinhold, New York.

Shock, N. W. 1981. Indices of functional age. Pp. 270–286 in D. Danon, N. W. Shock and M. Marois (eds.), *Aging: A Challenge to Science and Society. Vol. 1: Biology*. Oxford University Press, New York.

Shock, N. W. 1983. Aging of physiological systems. J. Chronic Diseases 36: 137–142.

Shock, N. W. 1985. Longitudinal studies of aging in humans. Pp. 721–743 in C. E. Finch and E. L. Schneider (eds.), *Handbook of the Biology of Aging*, 2nd edition. Van Nostrand Reinhold, New York.

Shock, N. W., R. Andres, A. H. Norris and J. D. Tobin. 1979. Patterns of longitudinal changes in renal function. Pp. 525–527 in H. Orimo, K. Shimada and D. Maede (eds.), *Recent Advances in Gerontology. XI International Congress of Gerontology*. Excerpta Medica, Amsterdam.

Shock, N. W., R. C. Greulich, P. T. Costa, Jr., R. Andres, E. G. Lakatta, D. Arenberg and J. D. Tobin. 1984. *Normal Human Aging: The Baltimore Longitudinal Study of Aging*. NIH Publ. No. 84-2450, Washington, DC.

Shook, D. R., A. Brooks and T. E. Johnson. 1996. Mapping quantitative trait loci affecting life history traits in the nematode *Caenorhabditis elegans*. Genetics 142: 801–817.

Short, R. A., D. D. Williams and D. M. Bowden. 1987. Cross-sectional evaluation of potential biological markers of aging in pigtailed macaques: Effects of age, sex and diet. J. Gerontol. 42: 644–654.

Short, R. A., D. D. Williams and D. M. Bowden. 1994. Modeling biological aging in a nonhuman primate. Pp. 409–418 in A. K. Balin (ed.), *Practical Handbook of Human Biologic Age Determination*. CRC Press, Boca Raton, FL.

Short, R. A., D. D. Williams and D. M. Bowden. 1997. Circulating antioxidants as determinants of the rate of biological aging in pigtailed macaques (*Macaca nemestrina*). J. Gerontol.: Biol. Sci. 52A: B26–B38.

Shoulson, I. 1992. Antioxidative therapeutic strategies for Parkinson's disease. Ann. N.Y. Acad. Sci. 648: 37–41.

Shouman, R. and T. M. Witten. 1995. Survival estimates and sample size: What can we conclude? J. Gerontol.: Biol. Sci. 50A: B177–B185.

Shrimpton, A. E. and A. Robertson. 1988. The isolation of polygenic factors controlling bristle score in *Drosophila melanogaster*. II. Distribution of third chromosome bristle effects within chromosome sections. Genetics 118: 445–459.

Silverman, H. G. and R. S. Mazzeo. 1996. Hormonal responses to maximal and submaximal exercise in trained and untrained men of various ages. J. Gerontol.: Biol. Sci. 51A: B30–B37.

Sinclair, D. A. and L. Guarente. 1997. Extrachromosomal rDNA circles: A cause of aging in yeast. Cell 91: 1033–1042.

Singh, J. and A. K. Singh. 1979. Age-related changes in human thymus. Clin. Exp. Immunol. 37: 507–511.

Slade, N. A. 1995. Failure to detect senescence in persistence of some grasslands rodents. Ecology 76: 863–870.

Slonaker, J. R. 1912. The normal activity of the albino rat from birth to natural death, its rate of growth and duration of life. J. Anim. Behav. 2: 20–42.

Smeal, T., J. Claus, B. Kennedy, F. Cole and L. Guarente. 1996. Loss of transcriptional silencing causes sterility in old mother cells of *S. cerevisiae*. Cell 84: 633–642.

Smith, D. E. W. and H. R. Warner. 1989. Does genotypic sex have a direct effect on longevity? Exp. Gerontol. 24: 277–288.

Smith, D. W. E. 1993. *Human Longevity*. Oxford University Press, New York.

Smith, J. R. 1992. Inhibitors of DNA synthesis derived from senescent human diploit fibroblasts. Exp. Gerontol. 27: 409–412.

Smith, J. R. and O. M. Pereira-Smith. 1996. Replicative senescence: Implications for in vivo aging and tumor suppression. Science 273: 63–67.

Smith, J. R. and R. G. Whitney. 1980. Intraclonal variation in proliferative potential of human diploid fibroblasts: Stochastic mechanism for cellular aging. Science 207: 82–84.

Smith, J. R., A. L. Spiering and O. Pereira-Smith. 1987. Is cellular senescence genetically programmed? Pp. 283–294 in A. D. Woodhead and K. H. Thompson (eds.), *Evolution of Longevity in Animals: A Comparative Approach*. Plenum, New York.

Smith, K. D. 1987. Paper presented to the 1987 National Institutes of Health Conference on Gender and Longevity.

Smith-Sonneborn, J. 1979. DNA repair and longevity assurance in *Paramecium tetraurelia*. Science 203: 1115–1117.

Smith-Sonneborn, J. 1985. Aging in unicellular organisms. Pp. 79–104 in C. E. Finch and E. L. Schneider (eds.), *Handbook of the Biology of Aging*, 2nd edition. Van Nostrand Reinhold, New York.

Smith-Sonneborn, J. 1990. Aging in protozoa. Pp. 24–44 in E. L. Schneider and J. W. Rowe (eds.), *Handbook of the Biology of Aging*, 3rd edition. Academic Press, San Diego.

Snowden, D. A. 1997. Aging and Alzheimer's Disease: Lessons from the nun study. Gerontologist 37: 150–156.

Snowden, D. A., R. L. Dane, L. Beeson, G. L. Burke, M. Sprafka, J. Bitter, H. Iso, D. R. Jacobs and R. L. Phillips. 1989. Is early natural menopause a biologic marker of health and aging? Am. J. Public Health 79: 709–714.

Sohal, R. S. 1983. Aging in insects. Pp. 595–632 in G. Kerkut and L. Gilbert (eds.), *Comprehensive Insect Physiology, Biochemistry and Pharmacology*. Pergamon, Oxford.

Sohal, R. S. 1986. The rate of living theory: A contemporary interpretation. Pp. 23–44 in K. G. Collatz and R. S. Sohal (eds.), *Insect Aging: Strategies and Mechanisms*. Springer-Verlag, Berlin.

Sohal, R. S. and H. Donato. 1978. Effects of experimentally altered life span on the accumulation of fluorescent age pigment in the housefly, *Musca domestica*. Exp. Gerontol. 13: 335–341.

Sohal, R. S. and R. Weindruch. 1996. Oxidative stress, caloric restriction, and aging. Science 273: 59–63.

Sohal, R. S., K. J. Farmer, R. G. Allen and N. R. Cohen. 1983. Effects of age on oxygen consumption, superoxide dismutase, catalase, glutathione, inorganic peroxides and chloroform-soluble antioxidants in the adult male housefly, *Musca domestica*. Mech. Ageing Devel. 24: 185–195.

Sohal, R. S., P. L. Toy and R. G. Allen. 1986. Relationship between life expectancy, endogenous antioxidants and products of oxygen free radical reactions in the housefly, *Musca domestica*. Mech. Ageing Devel. 36: 71–77.

Sohal, R. S., S. Agarwal and B. H. Sohal. 1995. Oxidative stress and aging in the Mongolian gerbil (*Meriones unguiculatus*). Mech. Ageing Devel. 81: 15–25.

Sorlie, P., E. Rogot, R. Anderson, N. J. Johnson and E. Backlund. 1992. Black-white mortality differences by family income. Lancet (London) 340: 346–350.

Spence, A. P. 1988. *Biology of Human Aging*. Prentice-Hall, Englewood Cliffs, NJ.

Spence, J. C. 1921. Some observations on sugar tolerance with special reference to variations found at different ages. Quart. J. Med. 4: 314–326.

Spinage, C. A. 1972. African ungulate life tables. Ecology 53: 645–652.

Sprott, R. 1991. Development of animal models of aging at the National Institute of Aging. Neurobiology of Aging 12: 635–638.

Sprott, R. 1997. Mouse and rat genotype choices. Exp. Gerontol. 32: 79–86.

Sprung, C. N., L. Sabatier and J. P. Murname. 1996. Effect of telomere length on telomeric gene expression. Nucleic Acids Res. 24: 4336–4340.

Srivastava, V. K., S. Miller, M. D. Schroeder, R. W. Hart and D. Busbee. 1993. Age-related changes in expression and activity of DNA polymerase alpha: Some effects of dietary restriction. Mutation Res. 295: 265–280.

St. George Hyslop, P. H. et al. 1987. The genetic defect causing familial Alzheimer's disease maps on chromosome 21. Science 235: 885–890.

Stahelin, H. B., M. Eichholzer, F. Gey and G. Brubacher. 1989. Antioxidant vitamins and mortality in the elderly: Results of the prospective Basle study. P. 201 in *Proceedings of the XIV International Congress of Gerontology* (abstract).

Stampfer, M. J., C. H. Hennekens, J. E. Manson, G. A. Colditz, B. Rosner and W. C. Willett. 1993. Vitamin E consumption and the risk of coronary disease in women. New England J. Med. 328: 1444–1449.

Starke-Reed, P. and C. N. Oliver. 1989. Protein oxidation and proteolysis during aging and oxidative stress. Arch. Biochem. Biophys. 275: 559–567.

Stary, H. 1986. Evolution and progression of atherosclerosis in the coronary arteries of children and adults. Pp. 20–36 in S. R. Bates and E. C. Gangloff (eds.), *Atherogenesis and Aging*. Springer-Verlag, New York.

Staveley, B. E., J. P. Philips and A. J. Hilliker. 1990. Phenotypic consequences of copper-zinc superoxide dismutase over-expression in *Drosophila melanogaster*. Genome 33: 867–872.

Stearns, S. C. and M. Kaiser. 1993. The effects of enhanced expression of EF-1 alpha on life span in *Drosophila melanogaster*. IV. A summary of three experiments. Genetica 91: 167–182.

Steller, H. 1995. Mechanisms and genes of cellular suicide. Science 267: 1445–1449.

Sternberg, H. 1994. Aging of the immune system. Pp. 75–88 in P. S. Timiras (ed.), *Physiological Basis of Aging and Geriatrics*, 2nd edition, CRC Press, Boca Raton, FL.

Stevens, J. J. Cai, E. R. Pamuk, D. F. Williamson, M. J. Thun and J. L. Wood. 1998. The effect of age on the association between body-mass index and mortality. New England J. Med. 338: 1–7.

Strehler, B. 1982. *Time, Cells and Aging*. Academic Press, New York.

Strehler, B. 1986. Genetic instability as the primary cause of human aging. Exp. Gerontol. 21: 283–319.

Strother, S. 1988. The role of free radicals in leaf senescence. Gerontology 34: 151–156.

Stuchlikova, E., M. Juricova-Herakiva and Z. Deyl. 1975. New aspects of the dietary effect of life prolongation in rodents. What is the role of density in aging? Exp. Gerontol. 10: 141–144.

Sugawa, M., H. Coper, G. Schulze, I. Yamashina, F. Krause and N. A. Dencher. 1996. Impaired plasticity of neurons in aging: Biochemical, biophysical, and behavioral studies. Ann. N.Y. Acad. Sci. 786: 274–282.

Sugita, K., N. Suzuki, K. Fujii and H. Nimi. 1995. Reduction of unscheduled DNA synthesis and plasminogen activator activity in Hutchinson-Gilford fibroblasts during passaging in vitro: Partial correction by interferon-beta. Mutation Res. 316: 133–138.

Sun, J., S. P. Kale, A. M. Childress, C. Pinswadi and S. M. Jazwinski. 1994. Divergent roles of RAS1 and RAS2 in yeast longevity. J. Biol. Chem. 269: 18638–18645.

Svanborg, A. and L. Selker. 1993. Postponement of aging-related disability. World Health Forum 14: 150–157.

Sweeney, K. J. and A. S. Weiss. 1992. Hyaluronic acid in progeria and the aged phenotype? Gerontology 38: 139–152.

Szakmary, A., S-M. Huang, D. T. Chang, P. A. Beachy and M. Sander. 1996. Overexpression of a *Rrp1* transgene reduces the somatic mutation and recombination frequency induced by oxidative DNA damage in *Drosophila melanogaster*. Proc. Natl. Acad. Sci. USA 93: 1607–1612.

Szilard, L. 1959. On the nature of the aging process. Proc. Natl. Acad. Sci. USA 45: 30–45.

Takata, H., M. Suzuki, T. Ishii, S. Sekiguchi and H. Iri. 1987. Influence of major histocompatibility complex region genes on human longevity among Okinawan-Japanese centenarians and nonagenarians. Lancet (London) 2(8563): 824–826.

Takeda, T., M. Hosokawa, S. Takeshita, M. Irino, K. Higuchi, T. Matsushita, Y. Tomita, K. Yasuhira, H. Hamamoto, K. Shimizu, M. Ishii and T. Yamamuro. 1981. A new murine model of accelerated senescence. Mech. Ageing Devel. 17: 183–194.

Takeoka, Y., S. Y. Chen, H. Yago, R. Boyd, S. Suehiro, L. D. Schultz, A. A. Ansari and M. E. Gershin. 1996. The murine thymic microenvironment changes with age. Int. Arch. Allergy Immunol. 111: 5–12.

Talbert, G. B. 1977. Aging of the reproductive system. Pp. 318–356 in C. E. Finch and L. Hayflick (eds.), *Handbook of the Biology of Aging*. Van Nostrand Reinhold, New York.

Tanner, J. M. 1955. *Growth at Adolescence*. Blackwell, Oxford.

Tanzi, R. E., J. F. Gusella, P. C. Watkins, G. A. Bruns, P. St. George-Hyslop, M. L. Van Keuren, D. Patterson, S. Pagan, D. M. Kurnit and R. L. Neve. 1987. Amyloid beta protein gene: cDNA, mRNA distribution and genetic linkage near the Alzheimer's locus. Science 235: 880–884.

Tappel, A. L., B. Fletcher and D. Deamer. 1973. Effect of antioxidants and nutrients on lipid peroxidation fluorescent products and ageing parameters in the mouse. J. Gerontol. 28: 415–424.

Thomas, D. 1953. Do not go gentle into that good night. P. 262 in T. R. Cole and M. G. Winkler (eds.), *The Oxford Book of Aging: Reflections on the Journey of Life*. Oxford University Press, Oxford, 1994.

Thomas, J. and D. Nyberg. 1988. Vitamin E supplementation and intense selection increase clonal life span *Paramecium tetraurelia*. Exp. Gerontol. 23: 501–512.

Thompson, C. R. 1995. Apoptosis in the pathogenesis and treatment of disease. Science 267: 1456–1462.

Thompson, J. N. 1975. Quantitative variation and gene number. Nature 258: 665–668.

Tice, R. R. and R. B. Setlow. 1985. DNA repair and replication in aging organisms and cells. Pp. 173–224 in C. E. Finch and E. L. Schneider (eds.), *Handbook of the Biology of Aging*, 2nd edition. Van Nostrand Reinhold, New York.

Timiras, P. S. 1994. Aging of the adrenals and pituitary. Pp. 133–146 in P. S. Timiras (ed.), *Physiological Basis of Aging and Geriatrics*, 2nd edition. CRC Press, Boca Raton, FL.

Timiras, P. S. 1995. Education, homeostasis and longevity. Exp. Gerontol. 30: 189–198.

Tobin, J. D. 1981. Physiological indices of aging. Pp. 286–294 in D. Danon, N. W. Shock and M. Marois (eds.), *Aging: A Challenge to Science and Society. Vol. 1: Biology*. Oxford University Press, New York.

Tonna, E. A. 1977. Aging of skeletal-dental systems and supporting tissues. Pp. 470–495 in C. E. Finch and L. Hayflick (eds.), *Handbook of the Biology of Aging*. Van Nostrand Reinhold, New York.

Torrey, B. B., K. Kinsella and C. M. Taeuber. 1987. *An Aging World* (International Population Reports Series P-95, no. 78). U.S. Government Printing Office, Washington, DC.

Toussaint, O., C. Michiels, M. Raes and J. Remacle. 1995. Cellular aging and the importance of energetic factors. Exp. Gerontol. 30: 1–22.

Tower, J. 1996. Aging mechanisms in fruit flies. BioEssays 18: 799–807.

Tower, J., J. Wheeler, R. Kurapati and E. Bieske. 1993. Novel promoter elements direct aging-specific transcriptional regulation of heat shock and other genes. P. 310 in *Proceedings of the 34th Drosophila Research Conference* (abstract).

Travisano, M. and R. E. Lenski. 1996. Long-term experimental evolution in *Escherichia coli*. IV. Targets of selection and the specificity of adaptation. Genetics 143: 15–26.

Tricerei, A., A. R. Errani, M. Vangeli, L. Guidi, I. Pavse, L. Antico and C. Bartoloni. 1995. Neuorimmunomodulation and psychoneuroendocrinology: Recent findings in adults and aged. Panminerva Medica 37: 77–83.

Trout, D. L. 1991. Vitamin C and cardiovascular risk factors. Am. J. Clin. Nutr. 53(Suppl. 1): 322S–325S.

Tucker, M. J. 1979. The effect of long-term food restriction on tumours in rodents. Int. J. Cancer. 23: 803–807.

Tyler, R. H., H. Brar, M. Singh, A. Latorre, J. L. Graves, L. D. Mueller, M. R. Rose and F. J. Ayala. 1993. The effect of superoxide dismutase alleles on aging in *Drosophila*. Genetica 91: 143–149.

Tzarkoff, S. P. and A. H. Norris. 1978. Longitudinal changes in basal metabolism in man. J. Appl. Physiol. 45: 536–539.

Udelsman, R., M. J. Blake, C. A. Stagg, D. G. Li, D. J. Putney and N. Holbrook. 1993. Vascular heat shock protein expression in response to stress: Endocrine and autonomic regulation of the age-dependent response. J. Clin. Invest. 91: 465–473.

Udelsman, R., D. G. Li, C. A. Stagg and N. K. Holbrook. 1995. Aortic crosstransplantation between young and old rats: Effect upon the heat shock protein 70 stress response. J. Gerontol.: Biol. Sci. 50A: B187–B192.

U.S. Senate Committee on Aging. 1987–1998. Aging America: Trends and Projections.

Utsuyama, M., M. Kasai, C. Kurashima and K. Hirokawa. 1991. Age influence on the thymic capacity to promote differentiation of T cells: Induction of different composition of T cell subsets by aging thymus. Mech. Ageing Devel. 58: 267–277.

Uvnas-Moberg, K. 1989. The gastrointestinal tract in growth and reproduction. Sci. Am. 261(1): 78–83.

van Bockxmeer, F. M. 1994. *ApoE* and *ACE* genes: impact on human longevity. Nature Genet. 6: 4–5.

van Eekelen, J. A., N. Y. Rots, W. Sutanto, M. S. Oitzl and E. R. de Kloet. 1991. Brain corticosteroid receptor gene expression and neuroendocrine dynamics during aging. J. Steroid Biochem. Mol. Biol. 40: 679–683.

Van Rommen, H., W. F. Ward, R. V. Sabin and A. Richardson. 1995. Gene expression and protein degredation. Pp. 171–238 in E. J. Masoro (ed.), *Handbook of Physiology. Section 11: Aging*. Oxford University Press, New York.

Vaughn, D. W. 1977. Age-related deteriorations of pyramidal cell basal dendrites in rat auditory cortex. J. Comp. Neurol. 171: 501–516.

Vaux, D. L. and A. Strasser. 1996. The molecular biology of apoptosis. Proc. Natl. Acad. Sci. USA 93: 2239–2244.

VERIS. 1991. *Safety of Oral Vitamin E*. Vitamin E Research and Information Service, LaGrange, IL.

VERIS. 1996. *The Role of Antioxidants in Prevention of Coronary Heart Disease*. Vitamin E Research and Information Service, LaGrange, IL.

Vesselinovitch, D. 1986. Age-related changes in selected animal species. Pp. 154–175 in S. R. Bates and E. C. Gangloff (eds.), *Atherogenesis and Aging*. Springer-Verlag, New York.

Vestal, R. E. 1978. Drug use in the elderly: A review of problems and special considerations. Drugs 16: 358–382.

Vestal, R. E. and G. W. Dawson. 1985. Pharmacology and aging. Pp. 744–819 in C. E. Finch and E. L. Schneider (eds.), *Handbook of the Biology of Aging*. Van Nostrand Reinhold, New York.

Via, S., R. Gomulkiewicz, G. De Jong, S. M. Scheiner, C. D. Schlichting and P. H. Van Tienderen. 1995. Adaptive phenotypic plasticity: Consensus and controversy. Trends Ecol. Evol. 10: 212–217.

Viidik, A., H. M. Nielsen and M. Skalicky. 1996. Influence of physical exercise on aging rats. II. Life-long exercise delays aging of tail tendon collagen. Mech. Ageing Devel. 88: 139–148.

Vijg, J., A. G. Vitterlinden, E. Mullaart, P. A. M. Lohman and D. L. Knook. 1985. Processing of DNA damage during aging: Induction of genetic alterations. Pp. 155–172 in R. S. Sohal, L. S. Birnbaum and R. G. Cutler (eds.), *Molecular Biology of Aging: Gene Stability and Gene Expression*. Raven Press, New York.

Vito, P., E. Lacana and L. D'Adamio. 1996. Interfering with apoptosis: Ca^{2+}-binding protein ALG-2 and Alzheimer's disease gene *ALG-3*. Science 271: 521–525.

Vlassara, H., M. Brownlee, K. R. Manogue, C. A. Dinarello and A. Pasagian. 1988. Cachectin/TNF and IL-1 induced by glucose-modified proteins: Role in normal tissue remodeling. Science 240: 1546–1548.

von Zglinicki, T., G. Saretzki, W. Docke and C. Lotze. 1995. Mild hyperoxia shortens telomeres and inhibits proliferation of fibroblasts: A model for senescence? Exp. Cell Res. 220: 186–193.

Waldron, I. 1987. Causes of the sex difference in longevity. J. Am. Geriatr. Soc. 35: 365–366 (letter to the editor).

Walford, R. H. 1983. Supergenes: Histocompatibility; Immunologic and other parameters in aging. Pp. 53–68 in W. Regelson and F. M. Sinex (eds.), *Intervention in the Aging process, Part B: Basic Research and Preclinical Screening*. Alan R. Liss, New York.

Walford, R. L. 1986. *The 120 Year Diet: How to Double Your Vital Years*. Pocket Books, New York.

Walford, R. L., S. B. Harris and M. W. Gunion. 1992. The calorically rstricted low-fat nutriet-dense diet in Biosphere 2 significantly lowers blood glucose, total leukocyte count, cholesterol and blood pressure in humans. Proc. Natl. Acad. Sci. USA 89: 11533–11537.

Wallace, D. C. 1992. Mitochondrial genetics: A paradigm for aging and degenerative disease? Science 256: 628–632.

Wallace, D. C. 1995. Mitochondrial DNA mutations in human disease and aging. Pp. 163–178 in K. Esser and G. M. Martin (eds.), *Molecular Aspects of Aging*. Wiley, Chichester, England.

Wallace, D. C., V. A. Bohr, G. Cortopassi, B. Kadenbach, S. Linn, A. W. Linnane, C. Richter and J. W. Shay. 1995. Group report: The role of bioenergetics and mitochondrial DNA mutations in aging and age-related diseases. Pp. 199–226 in K. Esser and G. M. Martin (eds.), *Molecular Aspects of Aging*. Wiley, Chichester, England.

Walsh, K. and H. Perlman. 1997. Cell cycle exit upon myogenic differentiation. Curr. Opinion Genet. Devel. 7: 597–602.

Wang, S. M., C. Nishigori, T. Yagi and H. Takebe. 1991. Reduced DNA repair in progeria cells and effects of gamma-ray irradiation on UV-induced unscheduled DNA synthesis in normal and progeria cells. Mutation Res. 256: 59–66.

Ward, W. F. 1988a. Enhancement by food restriction of liver protein synthesis in the aging Fischer 344 rat. J. Gerontol.: Biol. Sci. 43: B50–B53.

Ward, W. F. 1988b. Food restriction enhancement of the proteolytic capacity of aging rat liver. J. Gerontol.: Biol. Sci. 43: B121–B124.

Warner, H. R. and E. Wang. 1989. Control of cell proliferation in senescent cells—a synopsis. J. Gerontol.: Biol. Sci. 44: B23–B25 (meeting report).

Warner, H. R., G. Fernandes and E. Wang. 1995. A unifying hypothesis to explain the retardation of aging and tumorigenesis by caloric restriction. J. Gerontol.: Biol. Sci. 50A: B107–B109.

Watkinson, A. R. and J. White. 1985. Some life-history consequences of modular construction in plants. Philos. Trans. Royal Soc. London, Series B 313: 31–51.

Weaver, J. K. and J. Chalmers. 1966. Cancellous bone: Its strength and changes with aging and an evaluation of some methods for measuring its mineral content. I. Age changes in cancellous bone. J. Bone Joint Surgery 48A: 289–308.

Webster, C., L. Silberstein, A. P. Hays and H. M. Blair. 1988. Fast muscle fibers are preferentially affected in Duchenne muscular dystrophy. Cell 52: 503–513.

Webster, G. C. 1988. Protein synthesis. Pp. 119–130 in F. A. Lints and M. H. Soliman (eds.), Drosophila *as a Model Organism for Ageing Studies*. Blackie, Glasgow.

Webster, G. C. and S. L. Webster. 1979. Decreased protein synthesis by microsomes from aging *Drosophila melanogaster*. Exp. Gerontol. 14: 343–348.

Webster, G. C. and S. L. Webster. 1983. Decline in synthesis of elongation factor one (EF-1) precedes the decreased synthesis of total protein in aging *Drosophila melanogaster*. Mech. Ageing Devel. 22: 121–128.

Webster, G. C. and S. L. Webster. 1984. Specific disappearance of translatable messenger RNA for elongation factor one in aging *Drosophila melanogaster*. Mech. Ageing Devel. 24: 335–342.

Weidemann, A., G. Konig, D. Bunke, P. Fischer, J. M. Salbaum, C. L. Masters and K. Bayreuther. 1989. Identification, biogenesis and localization of precursors of Alzheimer's disease A4 amyloid protein. Cell 57: 115–126.

Weindruch, R. 1995a. Animal models. Pp. 37–52 in E. J. Masoro (ed.), *Handbook of Physiology. Section 11: Aging*. Oxford University Press, New York.

Weindruch, R. 1995b. Diet restriction. Pp. 276–279 in G. Maddox (ed.-in-chief), *The Encyclopedia of Aging*, 2nd edition. Springer, New York.

Weindruch, R. 1995c. Interventions based on the possibility that oxidative stress contributes to sarcopenia. J. Gerontol.: Biol. Sci. 50A(special issue): 157–161.

Weindruch, R. and R. L. Walford. 1982. Dietary restriction in mice beginning at 1 year of age: Effect on life-span and spontaneous cancer incidence. Science 215: 1415–1418.

Weindruch, R. and R. L. Walford. 1988. *The Retardation of Aging and Disease by Dietary Restriction*. Charles Thomas, Springfield, IL.

Weindruch, R., R. L. Walford, S. Fligiel and D. Guthrie. 1986. The retardation of aging in mice by dietary restriction: Longevity, cancer, immunity and lifetime energy intake. J. Nutr. 116: 641–654.

Weirach-Schwaiger, H., H. G. Weirich, B. Gruber, M. Schweiger and M. Hirsch-Kauffmann. 1994. Correlation between senescence and DNA repair in cells from young and old individuals and in premature aging syndromes. Mutation Res. 316: 37–48.

Weismann, A. 1891a. The continuity of the germ plasm as the foundation of a theory of heredity (1885). Pp. 163–256 in E. B. Poulton, S. Schonland and A. E. Shipley (eds.), *Essays upon Heredity and Kindred Biological Problems*, 2nd edition, vol. 1. Clarendon Press, Oxford. Reprint: Baker Science, Oceanside, NY.

Weismann, A. 1891b. The duration of life (a paper presented in 1881). Pp. 1–66 in E. B. Poulton, S. Schonland and A. E. Shipley (eds.), *Essays upon Heredity and Kin-dred Biological Problems*, 2nd edition, vol. 1. Clarendon Press, Oxford. Reprint: Baker Science, Oceanside, NY.

Weismann, A. 1891c. Life and death (a paper presented in 1883). Pp. 111–157 in E. B. Poulton, S. Schonland and A. E. Shipley (eds.), *Essays upon Heredity and Kindred Biological Problems*. Clarendon Press, Oxford. Reprint: Baker Science, Oceanside, NY.

Westing, A. H. 1964. The longevity and aging of trees. Gerontologist 4: 10–15.

Wheeler, K. T. and J. T. Lett. 1974. On the possibility that DNA repair is related to age in non-dividing cells. Proc. Natl. Acad. Sci. USA 71: 1862–1865.

Whitbourne, S. K. 1985. *The Aging Body: Physiological Changes and Psychological Consequences*. Springer-Verlag, New York.

White, K., M. E. Grether, J. M. Abrams, L. Young, K. Farrell and H. Steller. 1994. Genetic control of programmed cell death in *Drosophila*. Science 264: 677–683.

Whitehead, I. and T. A. Grigliatti. 1993. A correlation between DNA repair capacity and longevity in adult *Drosophila melanogaster*. J. Gerontol.: Biol. Sci. 48: B124–B132.

Whitfield, K. E. 1994. The use of quantitative genetic methodology to gain insights into the origins of individual differences in later life. Exp. Aging Res. 20: 135–143 (letter to the editor).

Whitman, C. O. 1894. Evolution and epigenesis. Biol. Lect. (Woods Hole) 3: 205–224.

Wickelgren, I. 1996. Is hippocampal cell death a myth? Science 271: 1229–1230.

Wilkins, A. S. 1986. *Genetic Analysis of Animal Development*. Wiley-Interscience, New York.

Willett, W. C. 1994. Diet and health: What should we eat? Science 264: 532–537.

Williams, G. C. 1957. Pleiotropy, natural selection and the evolution of senescence. Evolution 11: 398–411.

Williams, J. R. 1983. Alteration in DNA/chromatin structure during aging. Pp. 145–153 in W. Regelson and F. M. Sinex (eds.), *Intervention in the Aging Process. Part B. Basic Research and Preclinical Screening*. Alan R. Liss, New York.

Wilson, A. C. 1991. From molecular evolution to body and brain evolution. Pp. 331–340 in *Perspectives on Cellular Regulation: From Bacteria to Cancer* (MBL Lectures in Biology, vol. 11). Wiley, New York.

Wilson, D. 1994. The analysis of survival (mortality) data: Fitting Gompertz, Weibull and logistic functions. Mech. Ageing Devel. 74: 15–33.

Wilson, D. L. 1988. Aging hypotheses, aging markers and the concept of biological age. Exp. Gerontol. 23: 435–438.

Winston, M. L. 1987. *The Biology of the Honey Bee*. Harvard University Press, Cambridge, MA

Wise, P. M. 1986. Changes in the central nervous system and neuroendocrine control of reproduction in males and females. Pp. 81–96 in L. Mastroianni, Jr. and C. A. Paulsen (eds.), *Aging, Reproduction and the Climacteric*. Plenum, New York.

Wissler, R. W. and D. Vesselinovitch. 1986. The pathogenesis of atherosclerosis: Myths and established facts about its relationship to aging. Pp. 7–19 in S. R. Bates and E. C.

Gangloff (eds.), *Atherogenesis and Aging.* Springer-Verlag, New York.

Witten, M. 1984. A return to time, cells, systems and aging. II. Relational and reliability theoretic aspects of senescence in mammalian systems. Mech. Ageing Devel. 27: 323–340.

Witten, M. 1987. Information content of biological survival curves arising in aging experiments: Some further thoughts. Pp. 295–318 in A. Woodhead and K. H. Thompson (eds.), *Evolution of Aging Processes in Animals.* Plenum, New York.

Witten, M. 1988. A return to time, cells, systems and aging: V. Further thoughts on Gompertzian survival dynamics— the geriatric years. Mech. Ageing Devel. 46: 175–200.

Witten, M. 1989. Re-examining the Gompertzian model of aging. Institute for Mathematics and Its Applications, University of Minnesota Reprint Series no. 483.

Witten, M. 1992. The Frankenstein project: Building a man in the machine and the arrival of the computional physician. Int. J. Supercomputer Applic. 6: 245–319.

Witten, M. 1994. Can stochasticity explain variation in clonal population survival curves. Mech. Ageing Devel. 73: 33–64.

Wolf, A. M. and G. A. Colditz. 1996. Social and economic effects of body weight in the United States. Am. J. Clin. Nutr. 63(Suppl. 3): 466S–469S.

Wolfe, J. 1998. Growth hormone: A physiological fountain of youth? J. Anti-Aging Med. 1: 9–26.

Wong, A., P. Boutis and S. Hekimi. 1995. Mutations in the *clk-1* gene of *Caenorhabditis elegans* affect developmental and behavioral timing. Genetics 139: 1247–1259.

Wood, S. M. and R. R. Watson. 1994. Antioxidants and cancer in the aged. Pp. 281–294 in R. Watson (ed.), *Handbook of Nutrition in the Aged,* 2nd edition. CRC Press, Boca Raton, FL.

Woodruff, R. C. and A. G. Nikitin. 1995. P DNA element movement in somatic cells reduces lifespan in *Drosophila melanogaster*: Evidence in support of the somatic mutation theory of aging. Mutation Res. 338: 35–42.

Wozney, J. M., V. Rosen, A. J. Celeste, L. M. Mitsock, M. J. Shitters, R. W. Kriz, R. M. Hewick and E. A. Wang. 1988. Novel regulators of bone formation: Molecular clones and activities. Science 242: 1528–1534.

Wright, R. M. and D. J. Cummings. 1983. Integration of mitochondrial gene sequences within the nuclear genome during senescence in a fungus. Nature 302: 86–88.

Wright, W. E., D. Brasiskyte, M. A. Piatyszek and J. W. Shay. 1996. Experimental elongation of telomeres extends the lifespan of immortal ↔ normal cell hybrids. EMBO J. 15: 1734–1741.

Wurtman, R. J. 1985. Alzheimer's disease. Sci. Am. 252(1): 62–74.

Yakes, F. M. and B. Van Houten. 1997. Mitochondrial DNA damage is more extensive and persists longer than nuclear DNA damage in human cells followng oxidative stress. Proc. Natl. Acad. Sci. USA 94: 514–519.

Yan, S. D., X. Chen, J. Fu, M. Chen, H. Zhu, A. Roher, T. Slattery, L. Shao, M. Nagashima, J. Morser, A. Migheli,

P. Nawroth, D. Stern and A. M. Schmidt. 1996. RAGE and amyloid-β peptide neurotoxcicity in Alzheimer's disease. Nature 382: 685–691.

Yashin, A. I. and I. A. Iachine. 1995a. Genetic analysis of durations: Correlated frailty model applied to survival of Danish twins. Genet. Epidemiol. 12: 529–538.

Yashin, A. I. and I. A. Iachine. 1995b. How long can humans live?: Lower bound for biological limit of human longevity calculated from Danish twin data using correlated frailty model. Mech. Ageing Devel. 80: 147–169.

Yu, B. P. 1995. Putative interventions. Pp. 613–633 in E. J. Masoro (ed.), *Handbook of Physiology. Section 11: Aging.* Oxford University Press, New York.

Yu, B. P., E. J. Masoro and C. A. McMahan. 1985. Nutritional influences on aging of Fischer 344 rats. I. Physical, metabolic and longevity characteristics. J. Gerontol. 40: 657–670.

Yu, C. E., J. Oshima, Y. H. Fu, E. M. Wijsman, F. Hisama, R. Alisch, S. Matthews, J. Nakura, T. Miki, S. Ouais, G. M. Martin and G. D. Schellenberg. 1996a. Positional cloning of the Werner's syndrome gene. Science 272: 258–262.

Yu, C. E., J. Oshima, F. M. Hisama, S. Matthews, B. J. Trask and G. D. Schellenberg. 1996b. A YAC, P1, and cosmid contig and 17 new polymorphic markers for the Werner syndrome region at 8p12–p21. Genomics 35: 431–440.

Yu, C. E., J. Oshima, E. M. Wijsman, J. Nakura, T. Miki, C. Piussan, S. Matthews, Y. H. Fu, J. Mulligan, G. M. Martin, J. Mulligan and G. D. Schellenberg. 1997. Mutations in the consensus helicase domains of the Werner syndrome gene. Am. J. Human Genet. 60: 330–341.

Yuan, H., T. Kaneko and M. Matsuo. 1996. Increased susceptibility of late passage human diploid fibroblasts to oxidative stress. Exp. Gerontol. 31: 465–474.

Yuan, I. C. 1932. The influence of heredity upon the duration of life in man based on a Chinese genealogy from 1365 to 1914. Human Biol. 4: 41–68.

Yuh, K. C. M. and A. Gafni. 1987. Reversal of age-related effects in rat muscle phosphoglycerate kinase. Proc. Natl. Acad. Sci. USA 84: 7458–7462.

Yunis, E. J. and M. Salazar. 1993. Genetics of life span in mice. Genetica 91: 211–223.

Zakeri, Z. and R. A. Lockshin. 1994. Physiological cell death during development and its relationship to aging. Ann. N.Y. Acad. Sci. 719: 212–229.

Zakian, V. A. 1995. Telomeres: Beginning to understand the end. Science 270: 1601–1607.

Zaug, A. J. and T. R. Cech. 1986. The Tetrahymena intervening sequence ribonucleic acid enzyme is a phosphotransferase and an acid phosphatase. Biochemistry 25: 4478–4482.

Zhang, C., A. Baumer, R. J. Maxwell, A. W. Linnane and P. Nagley. 1992. Multiple mitochondrial DNA deletions in an elderly human individual. FEBS Lett. 297: 34–38.

Zwaan, B., R. Bijlsma and R. Hoekstra. 1995. Direct selection on lifespan in *Drosophila melanogaster*. Evolution 49: 649–659.

Index

About the Book

Editor: Andrew D. Sinauer
Project Editor: Carol J. Wigg
Copy Editor: Stephanie Hiebert
Index: Space Coast Indexers
Production Manager: Christopher Small
Art and Book Production: Michele Ruschhaupt
Book Design: Jean Hammond
Book Manufacturer: Courier Companies, Inc.
Cover Manufacturer: Henry N. Sawyer Company, Inc.